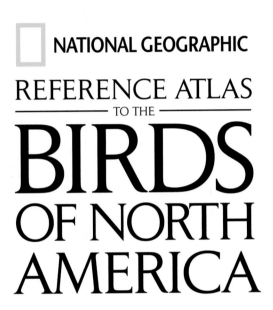

NATIONAL GEOGRAPHIC

REFERENCE ATLAS
TO THE
BIRDS
OF NORTH
AMERICA

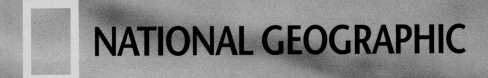

NATIONAL GEOGRAPHIC

REFERENCE ATLAS
—— TO THE ——

BIRDS
OF NORTH
AMERICA

NATIONAL GEOGRAPHIC
WASHINGTON, D.C.

CONTENTS

CONTENTS

CONTENTS

BIRDING LORE

Little more than two generations ago, following in the tradition of John James Audubon, professional ornithologists went into the field and shot birds on the wing, for they were of the passionate opinion that positive identification could only be made by studying the dead bird in hand.

In the early 1900s a boy consumed with his own passion in the field study of birds, dodged through Central Park with his binoculars, defying the admonitions of his parents and enduring the hostility of the locals. Ludlow Griscom later recounted these early birding adventures: "I started learning local birds back in 1898. In New York City...an interest in birds was not respectable. It just wasn't done. You could hunt and shoot birds, but you couldn't ogle birds with a glass. Many is the time a derisive and unfriendly crowd has run me out of Central Park!"

At about the same time, Frank Chapman, an officer of the National Audubon Society, created the Christmas Bird Count as an alternative to the annual Christmas Side Hunt, an event in which communities vied to shoot the most birds. A great feast followed, but only if the number of dead birds warranted it.

Young Griscom participated in the CBCs and, demonstrating his extraordinary field identification prowess with binoculars alone, began attracting the attention of many influential ornithologists. By the 1930s the trend was moving away from shooting birds and people were beginning to take pride in their ability to identify birds still on the wing. Ludlow Griscom is credited with leading the way from "shotgun ornithology" to today's methods of going afield to identify and study live birds with binoculars and spotting scopes.

The birding community today is large, counted in the millions, and more knowledgeable and skilled than ever before. We understand that what we do is of consequence, that we participate in the vital cause to save wild birds and their essential habitat. We follow our passion with great spirit as we go afield lured by the promise of each season, by the exciting chance of observing a bird for the first time, by the warm hope of seeing a familiar friend once again. As our talent for identifying birds increases, we begin to feel the need to know more: To learn about their behavior, when and where they breed, how they embrace the challenges of survival, and where they go during the winter. The answers seem to lead to more questions.

It has been a special experience for me to work with our staff and contributors, today's trend setters, birders, and field ornithologists, whose combined knowledge and devotion to their work has resulted in more than an invaluable reference book. Here they answer many of our questions, but more important they tell a tale of adventure and science and knowledge, a tale of joy that reflects their talents, their skills, their passion for these special creatures with whom we share our fragile earth. Here is the continuing story of the fascinating lives of birds.

Mel Baughman

(Left) American Kestrel

HOW TO USE THIS BOOK

For any bird-watcher—novice or pro—there is nothing like hearing a vibrant call or gazing at a graceful arc of wing or witnessing a mother feeding its young. And there is nothing like putting your finger on the name of that calling bird or identifying its flight pattern or understanding the ingenuity of a mother facing her young's hungry chirps.

The *National Geographic Reference Atlas to the Birds of North America* opens the door to this knowledge. As companion to the *National Geographic Field Guide to the Birds of North America,* the *Reference Atlas* offers the same high-quality information, images, and easy-to-use format. And it invites the reader to the next level of birding. The *Field Guide* is for seeing, identifying, and prompting that most important question: Why? *The Reference Atlas* is for answering that question clearly and concisely—and more.

It is for giving every birder the read of a lifetime. Put it on your bedside table, and enjoy it as you would a novel. Keep it on hand on your library desk or near the front door, or in the back seat of your car. When you return from the field burning with questions about the avian groups you have observed, you will want to pore over the *Reference Atlas,* to look more deeply into the lives and habits of the birds you've identified with your *Field Guide.*

And you may find that it is like a work of art. The more you visit it, the more you will discover within. While this comprehensive reference presents vital statistics in charts, maps, sidebars, and cross-referencing, it also features compelling essays and insightful, lively discussions of all bird families in North America.

The depth and breadth of information it offers is supplemented by more than 170 color photographs of birds in their natural habitat, and some 400 original paintings of poses, structures, and behaviors, not to mention the more than 700 maps that show ranges and migrations.

The book is clearly organized, cleanly designed, and easy to use. It is divided into three distinct parts: the Introduction, the Body, and the Appendix.

The Introduction by John Fitzpatrick, Director of the Cornell Laboratory of Ornithology, sets the stage. Fitzpatrick, one of North America's premier ornithologists, introduces readers to the fascinating development of the adaptable bird from the feathered *Archaeopteryx* some 180 million years ago to present day. Readers discover the evolution of bird structure, movement, and behavior. Fitzpatrick's words are accompanied by carefully rendered artwork—a roadmap to the basic stucture of birds, from beak to wing bar. Other art pieces in the Introduction display important comparisons for identifying birds, such as feather makeup; varied wingspread, shape, and span; and head shapes.

Now launch into the Body. This is the part—with its statistics, anecdotes, and myriad facts—that you will interpret and re-interpret as you become more familiar with bird species.

The Body comprises 42 chapters, organized by family group, following the sequence established by the American Ornithologists' Union (AOU) *Check-list of North American Birds.* The check-list arranges species according to their natural and evolutionary links. Within the 42 groups you will find 78 individual families. Within these families you will find over 800 species that regularly breed across the United States and Canada.

Each chapter opens with a stunning full-color photograph of a member of the family group, accompanied by an anecdotal essay by an expert—either an ornithologist or longstanding birder or journalist.

Then each family is documented in a discrete 2-8-page entry, depending on the number of species in it. Each entry begins with a small color portrait of the most conspicuous bird in that family in its natural habitat. This is accompanied by its range map and a concise paragraph about its characteristics and "rank" in the larger family. The entry then goes on to address the main features that identify the family itself: Classification, Structure, Plumage, Feeding, Vocalization, Breeding Behavior, Breeding Range, and Migration and Winter Range. Two additional sections are Observing—with tips for astute bird-watching—and Status and Conservation

A vital part of the family entry is a box that lists all species in the family. It is concise: For each species you will find the bird's common name, its scientific name in Latin, its body length from beak to tail, and a short description for quick identification in the field. A range map for each species is in the Appendix.

Some of the entries have sidebars that reveal unique behaviors, recent finds, or perhaps comparisons of body parts—all for deeper appreciation of the complexity and wonder of varied species. Each entry ends with a cross-referencing block to access related birds.

On the final two pages of each chapter is the coup de grace: A Specialty Map—unique to this book. Custom designed by National Geogrpahic cartographers, each map reveals information appropriate to that family: either its migration routes, historical ranges, or summer and winter breeding ranges.

The Appendix reinforces the book's wealth of information. First, it carries a full set of Range Maps for each species. In addition, there are Special Feature Maps including Important Bird Areas and American Christmas Count, all compiled by experts.

Readers will find a Glossary with up-to-date entries from experts at the Cornell Laboratory of Ornithology. A complete Index is accompanied by boxes for maintaining a life list.

Finally, what reference book is complete without a comprehensive Bibliography—with entries from guide books to encyclopedias and other references on the market. You will want this Bibliography. For once you take flight, you will want to keep going–and reading.

(Above) **Wood Ducks**

Family Portrait

Opening each of 42 chapters is the full-color photograph of one bird in the family group.

CARDINALS, GROSBEAKS, BUNTINGS

CARDINALS, GROSBEAKS, BUNTINGS

Chapter Tag

For quick access, the family group name appears on a reference bar on each right hand page of the chapter.

Expert's Essay

A fact-filled, anedotal essay by an ornithologist or other birding expert opens the chapter.

Characteristic Species

Each individual family section begins with the portrait of a characteristic species and a sketch of its role in the family. and the.

CARDINALS

Range Map

Beside the sketch is the range map for the characteristic species. Maps for other species in the family are in the Appendix.

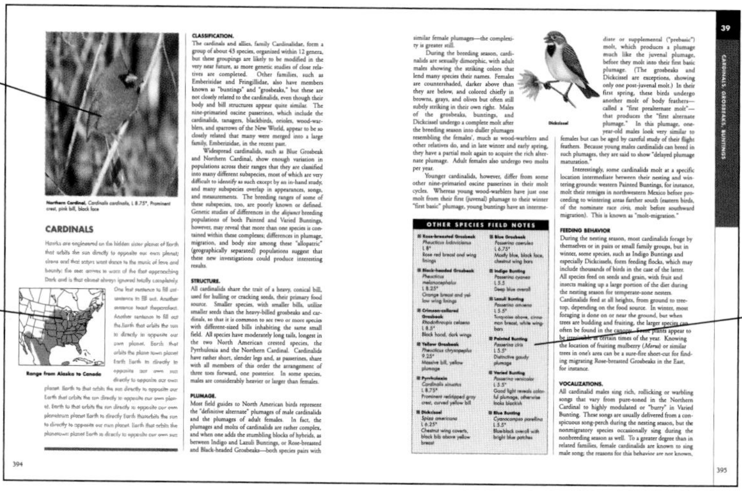

Other Species

Other species in the family are listed in a block with basic field notes including size and markings for quick identification.

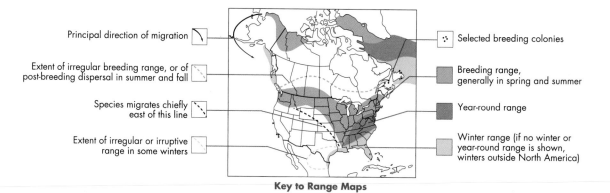

Principal direction of migration

Extent of irregular breeding range, or of post-breeding dispersal in summer and fall

Species migrates chiefly east of this line

Extent of irregular or irruptive range in some winters

Selected breeding colonies

Breeding range, generally in spring and summer

Year-round range

Winter range (if no winter or year-round range is shown, winters outside North America)

Key to Range Maps

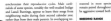

Vital Statistics

Each family entry comprises 11 sections, including Classification, Structure, Plumage, Feeding Behavior, Vocalization, and Observation Tips.

Sidebar

For large families with much information a sidebar reveals unique behavior and sturctures.

Chapter Tag

As on the chapter's opening page, the family group name appears again on this reference bar —for quick access.

Cross Reference

Ending each family entry is a list of other families or single species with related information.

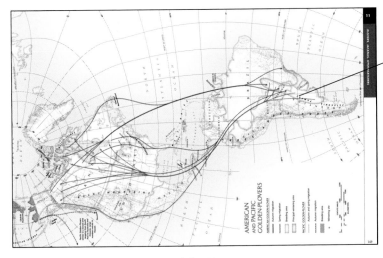

Sample Map

This migration map shows the routes for two representative birds of the plover family. The migration route from North America to South America is unique to this family. The names of the birds are highlighted in the key at the bottom left of the map.

Specialty Maps

Ending each family chapter is a Specialty Map that shows important migration or range information about that family. The map above is the migration map for American and Pacific Golden Plovers.

For families that do not migrate, maps at the end of the chapter show other vital information. This could be: 1) Winter and summer breeding ranges. 2) Historic ranges (how a bird population may have declined, or multiplied and spread out of its original area.) 3) Where species wander when environmental pressures come to bear. 4) The spread of non-native species introduced to North America.

Each map is unique, researched and compiled by ornithologist/cartographer Paul Lehman with the National Geographic Book Division Cartographic team. Several different projections were used in generating these maps. After an ornithologist identified the species to be mapped within each family, a projection was chosen to best characterize the ranges of those birds.

Due to the great variation in the distance some birds travel and the large areas they occupy from season to season, no one map design would properly represent all families. Data for each featured bird was plotted on the projection offering the best scale and area coverage possible.

THE ADAPTABLE BIRD

Nothing in nature captures our fancy or arouses our curiosity more than birds. They live from the windswept high Arctic to the world's driest deserts, and everywhere in between. Christopher Columbus studied them far out at sea, as beacons of hope foretelling approach to a new continent. Some hunt in the darkest of nights, navigating by listening for their own echoes. Others hunt from high in the sky using eyesight far keener than our own. Some raise just a single chick every two to three years, others can hatch a flock of their own several times a year. They may eat other animals (tiny to large), vegetables (seeds and fruits to leaves and buds), and even minerals (clay to sheep bones). They flap, soar, stoop, glide, swim, dive, walk, hop, and run like the wind. They can dance with choreography that baffles us, sing with melodies that haunt us, display with decorations that enchant us, and feign injury so convincingly as to fool us. Some mate for life and live in extended families, others mate for an instant and never see their offspring. Some never leave the local woodlot all their lives, others know the planet as a north-south stage to move across twice a year.

John W. Fitzpatrick

Despite their bewildering diversity and the astonishing variety of places they can live, all birds have features in common that make them unique among animals. They are vertebrates, with highly specialized skeletons. All maintain a body temperature (104°F to 105°F) that is far higher than our own (98.6°F), and they do this with the help of a spectacular adaptation (the feather) found in no other animal group past or present. Every bird has wings (specialized forelimbs with fused hand bones), although the wings of some have evolved downward in size and are too tiny for flight. All birds have beaks, and all birds lay eggs. Internally, all birds possess a remarkable system of one-way airflow through their lungs, permitting much more efficient capture of oxygen than our cumbersome "in, then-back-out" breathing pattern permits.

Whether we're beginning bird-watchers or seasoned experts, and whether we watch as an occasional hobby or a lifetime profession, we can experience two remarkable sensations every time we see or hear a bird. For their beautiful colors, ability to fly, wonderful sounds, and active habits, birds bring us pure enjoyment. In addition, for their capacity to live as seemingly delicate creatures in harsh and ever-changing environments, and for their striking variety of form and function, birds never stop teaching us new things regardless of how much we already know. This beautiful and fact-filled book expresses both of these gifts, introducing us to the lives of birds and the amazing array of ways in which they share the planet with us.

FEATHERED REPTILES

Scientists have no doubt that birds began as an

early evolutionary "experiment" by a single species of reptile. This experiment occurred about 200 million years ago, on the vast land mass of Gondwanaland before it split apart to become today's separate continents (the oldest fossil birds are being discovered in modern-day Europe and Asia). Remarkably, the oldest known fossil bird (called *Archaeopteryx*, meaning "ancient wing") lived 180 million years ago, yet it already was highly advanced as a bird. Most important, it had fully formed feathers covering its body, wings, and tail, and its wing feathers already were shaped to withstand the forces of flight. One of the most famous "missing link" fossil discoveries in history, *Archaeopteryx* also displays many features that clearly demonstrate its reptilian ancestry. It had a long, bony tail, peg-like teeth in its bony jaws (no modern bird has real teeth), well-developed fingers having sharp claws, and many features of its skeleton that closely resembled those of small, ground-living reptiles. In fact, some of the earliest dinosaurs were so close in structure to *Archaeopteryx* that many authorities today believe birds originated as a species of dinosaur. This idea is still being debated vigorously, but if true it means that birds actually represent the only group of dinosaurs that survived the great extinction 65 million years ago.

All authorities do agree that the reptile from which birds arose was a primitive "Archosaur," the lineage that clearly did give rise to the dinosaurs *and* to the crocodiles and alligators. This relationship brings to light the amazing fact that although they look superficially like big, leathery lizards, today's crocodiles and alligators are actually much more closely related to birds than to lizards.

WHAT'S INSIDE?

Birds are filled with unique anatomical features, most of them associated with flight. Their skeleton is highly unusual, as many of the bones of more typical vertebrates have been modified, fused together, or decreased in size. Instead of having individual digits, the hand has most bones fused together to form a stiff, pointed "manus" to which the primary flight feathers are attached. The bony, reptilian tail has shrunk into a short series of tiny bones, and the final one (called "pygostyle") bears the tail feathers, surrounded by muscles that control them. The two bones that represent collarbones in mammals and reptiles are fused into a V-shaped "furcula" (the wishbone in a turkey), which

(Above) Anhinga

acts as a timing spring during flight. The furcula rests directly in front of a peculiar, keel-shaped "sternum," or breastbone, which provides attachment surfaces for the extraordinary breast muscles required for flight. (The sternum is tiny in species that have lost the power of flight, such as ostriches and kiwis.)

Watch any long-legged bird walk (such as a heron, stork, or shorebird) and one is struck by the impression that its "knee" bends in the wrong direction, opposite to our own. This is because the visible joint in a bird's leg is actually its ankle. The long bone below that joint is not a true leg-bone at all, but a unique fusion of foot bones, called a "tarsometatarsus." The true knee (at the fat end of a chicken's drumstick) actually bends exactly as ours does, but is usually hidden under skin and feathers of the belly.

One of the most peculiar features of an adult bird's skeleton is that most bones are filled with tiny air pockets, so that a cross section of the bone resembles Swiss cheese. This adaptation allows bones to remain structurally rigid, yet extremely lightweight—crucial for reducing overall body weight in a flying bird.

The muscular system of birds is similar to that of other vertebrates, with one enormous exception. Birds power their flight with a remarkable pair of muscles on each side of the sternum. The huge "pectoral" muscle attaches broadly to the sternum

Lark Sparrow

supercilium
postocular stripe
ear patch (auricular)
moustachial stripe
submoustachial stripe

median crown stripe
lateral crown stripe
supraloral area
lores
malar stripe

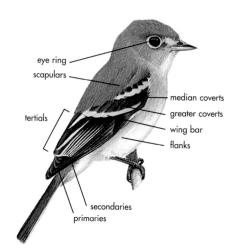

Least Flycatcher

eye ring
scapulars
tertials

median coverts
greater coverts
wing bar
flanks

secondaries
primaries

and to the underside of the upper arm bone ("humerus"), providing the strong down-stroke in a bird's wing flap. This muscle overlays a second, somewhat smaller muscle ("supracoracoideus") that is *also* attached to the sternum. This muscle supplies the powerful, upward return-stroke for each flap of the wing. How can both of these muscles have opposite purposes, yet attach to the same side of the sternum (together forming the huge, white breast meat of a chicken)? The trick is that the front end of the supracoracoideus forms a strong tendon that loops over the front of the sternum and another bone (coracoid), and attaches to the *top* of the humerus, thus pulling the arm upward when the muscle contracts along the sternum.

A very unusual feature of bird muscles explains the difference between white meat and dark meat in game birds (such as chicken, turkey, or pheasant). Muscles of most flying birds are filled with myoglobin, a red-pigmented protein that stores oxygen in the tissue and permits muscles to perform for extended periods of time (such as an overnight migration). However, myoglobin and its delivery system are expensive to maintain, and many kinds of birds do not fly very often (because they mainly walk on the ground), nor do they have to fly very far (just far enough to escape a predator). These ground-dwelling birds maintain only a small amount of myoglobin in their large breast and wing muscles. The oxygen supply in these white muscles is sufficient for a sudden burst of flight but quickly runs low, and the muscles fatigue as the bird glides to safety. This means that flushing a game bird repeatedly makes it lose its ability to fly for many minutes until its breast muscles recover.

FEATHERS AND FLIGHT

All birds possess feathers, perhaps the most versatile adaptation among all vertebrates. Originally a modified scale of an early reptile (probably to aid in maintaining body temperature), the true feather set into motion a truly remarkable 200-million-year evolutionary story that is still unfolding. Feathers begin as a living structure at the surface of the skin, and as they grow the dying outermost cells produce an extremely durable protein called "keratin," the same class of proteins that forms reptilian scales and mammalian hair and claws (including our fingernails). Each complete feather consists of a hollow, central shaft supporting a variable number of smaller shafts ("barbs"). In most feathers the barbs also support even tinier structures ("barbules") that hook against one another along a plane, thus locking into a strong, fabric-like layer on each side of the shaft. This layer is highly durable, yet filled with air and flexible enough to bend somewhat as air currents press against it. There is no other structure

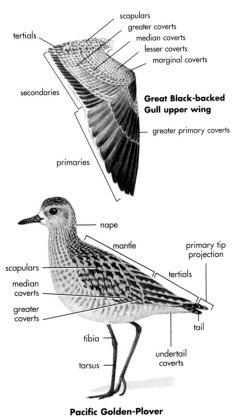

Great Black-backed Gull upper wing

scapulars
greater coverts
median coverts
lesser coverts
marginal coverts

tertials

secondaries

greater primary coverts

primaries

nape

mantle

scapulars

median coverts

greater coverts

primary tip projection

tertials

tail

tibia

tarsus

undertail coverts

Pacific Golden-Plover

like it in the entire natural world.

The most amazing feature of the feather is that with only minor modifications, it can perform a huge variety of functions. Birds' bodies are covered by thousands of soft, pliable contour feathers that protect the skin and supply a layer of insulation. Individual birds can manipulate the amount of insulation supplied by their own feathers, moment to moment, simply by changing the angle at which each feather leaves the skin. They do this using small muscles attached to the base of each feather. This behavior accomplishes the same thing as our adding or subtracting layers of clothing on cold or warm days, and it explains why woodpeckers, chickadees, jays, and cardinals can look almost twice their normal size on icy cold winter mornings. Except in a few groups of diving birds (such as penguins), contour feathers are not distributed evenly across the entire skin surface, but grow out of dense "feather tracts" running from the head to tail along the lower and upper flanks. Birds spend considerable time each day preening these tracts with their bills to remove parasites, discard loose bits of skin, and smooth the feathers so they lie evenly across the entire body.

Wing and tail feathers are longer and far stiffer than contour feathers. Their exact shapes vary enormously with the ecology and flight behavior of the different bird groups. The largest flight feathers supply the major surface area of the extended wing, and are divided into "primaries" and "secondaries." Most birds have nine or ten primaries, the long outermost flight feathers that attach to the hand bones and provide the bulk of the wing length and power in each wingbeat. At least ten additional secondaries are connected at regular intervals along the entire length of the larger forearm bone (the ulna). The larger birds have additional inner secondaries, sometimes called "tertials," that provide additional wing surface in flight and also can become quite ornamental (especially in the ducks).

The wings of birds are spectacularly adaptable to different ways of life, and by noting the shape of the wing we can quickly appreciate how each different bird uses the air. Wing shape adaptations are accomplished through differences both in the length of the arm bones and in the length and breadth of flight feathers.

The longest-winged birds (such as albatrosses and frigatebirds) live in windy, oceanic environments where they can glide for hours on end without a single flap. The long, broad wings of hawks, eagles, and vultures provide a huge surface area for soaring on updrafts produced by the daily heating of air over land. Long, pointed wings of falcons supply enormous power for chasing prey through the open air. These predators can fly so fast that they kill their fleeing prey simply by impact. Sandpipers and plovers also have very long, pointed wings (explaining why a Killdeer overhead can often look like a falcon) as an adaptation for powerful flight during their extended migrations across continents and oceans.

In contrast, birds such as chickadees that make brief flights within vegetation and do not migrate long distances have short, rounded wings. The most rounded wings of all belong to game birds such as quail and grouse, whose flight feathers are also sharply curved downward ("cambered"). This wing shape delivers extra lift at very slow speeds, just as aircraft pilots achieve by lowering the rear wing flaps on take-off or landing. Such wings permit the explosive take-off that surprises us when we flush a game bird from its hiding place.

While insulation and flight are their two most important functions, feathers provide many other crucial services across the world of birds. Because they can be supplied with pigment or modified to refract light in various ways, feathers supply almost unlimited opportunity for variation in color and pattern, hence they are a principal means of both communication (such as sex- and species-identification marks among ducks and warblers) and protection (such as the camouflaged, dead-leaf pattern of ground-nesting birds like woodcocks and nightjars).

The peacock's tail, the cardinal's crest, and the quail's topknot are just a few of the bewildering array of ornaments used by birds to display their individual quality to one another. Feathers along the lower back of herons break easily into a chalky powder ("powder down") that is used for waterproofing and protection against parasites. Barbless feathers around the mouth ("rictal bristles") protect many birds' eyes from damage while foraging for food. Ptarmigan living through the snowy northern winters of Canada and Europe molt into pure white plumage, and even grow feathery "snowshoes" for half the year. The distinctive facial-disk feathering of most owls helps gather and focus sound into the ear openings located at each side of the head just behind the eyes.

Although they are amazingly durable, feathers do wear out over time. For this reason, birds must replace every feather on their body about once each year in a vital process called "molt." The molt usually is timed to occur just after some major activity such as breeding or migrating, because it requires considerable energy and can place the molting bird at some increased risk. Most birds molt their wing and tail feathers sequentially over a period of many weeks, so that only a few replacement feathers are being grown at any one time. Both wings molt simultaneously, which explains why soaring hawks and vultures often appear to have symmetric gaps in their flight feathers. Ducks and loons undergo an unusual, simultaneous wing molt in which all the flight feathers are dropped at once, leaving the birds flightless during this post-breeding period. These species usually are hard to find in mid-summer, as they remain hidden deep in the vegetation while growing back a new set of wing feathers.

IDENTIFYING A BIRD BY ITS PARTS

In identifying birds it is helpful to focus on parts of the bird where the most distinctive differences in color or shape occur. The main regions are head and neck, back and rump, breast and belly, wings, tail, beak, and legs (including feet). Knowing just a little about how these regions vary can quickly make an expert of us in identifying almost every bird we encounter.

The head and neck are important for communication among birds themselves, so this region is filled with information we can use to identify different species. Features of special importance are: crown (what color? Is it striped or solid? Is there a crest?), forehead and lores (any distinctive color marks?), eye and superciliary (Is an eye ring or eyebrow present?), auriculars (any distinctive patch on the cheek?), nape (same color as crown?), malar region (Is one or more "whisker" mark present?), chin (Is there a contrasting chin patch?), and throat (same color as breast?).

The back and rump are often colored differently from the rest of the bird, and usually are darker than the underparts. Besides its overall color, the key feature of the back is whether it is striped, solid, barred, or scaly. Many species of warbler and finch have distinctively colored rump patches that con-

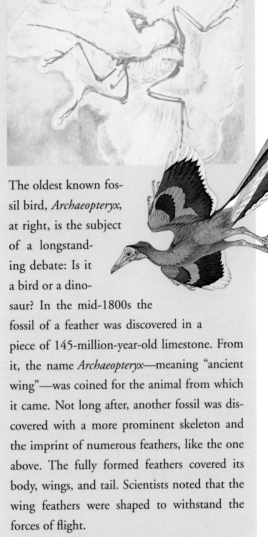

ARCHAEOPTERYX

The oldest known fossil bird, *Archaeopteryx*, at right, is the subject of a longstanding debate: Is it a bird or a dinosaur? In the mid-1800s the fossil of a feather was discovered in a piece of 145-million-year-old limestone. From it, the name *Archaeopteryx*—meaning "ancient wing"—was coined for the animal from which it came. Not long after, another fossil was discovered with a more prominent skeleton and the imprint of numerous feathers, like the one above. The fully formed feathers covered its body, wings, and tail. Scientists noted that the wing feathers were shaped to withstand the forces of flight.

Still, *Archaeopteryx* displays many features that demonstrate a reptilian ancestry, including long, bony tail, peg-like teeth, sharp-clawed fingers. In fact, a later fossil of *Archaeopteryx* that had no feathers was misidentified as the dinosuar *Compsognathus*.

In the late 20th century, further comparison between bone structures of dinosaurs and birds has led some experts to think that certain small dinosaurs might be the ancestors of birds.

trast with the back, and in a variety of birds (e.g., some woodpeckers, hawks, shorebirds) the rump is a conspicuous patch of pure white.

The breast and belly often are key to separating similar species from one another. What is the overall color, and does it change from breast to belly? Does the breast show a bib (Northern Flicker), spots (Wood Thrush), bars (Barred Owl), or streaks (Cape May Warbler)? Are the streaks dark and heavy (Song Sparrow) or pale and thin (Lincoln's Sparrow)? If streaks are present, do they extend more down the sides than they do at the center of the breast? Many sparrows have a central spot in the breast (like the "stickpin" of an American Tree Sparrow). Do the flanks show a distinctly different color from the center (as in Eastern and Spotted towhees)?

The wings of many birds show contrasting patches of white or color against a dark background. Located along the base of the folded wing, the "scapulars" usually are the same color as the back or wing, but occasionally stand out in stark contrast (as in the white scapulars of the Bobolink). "Wing bars" are pale tips to several rows of feathers near the base of the folded wing, called "secondary coverts." Separating different species of warblers and vireos usually starts by asking "wing bars or no wing bars?" Light-dark patterns in the wings of flying birds can be diagnostic, as in the white bar midway out the primaries of the Common Nighthawk, or the all black flight feathers of the otherwise white Wood Stork.

Quick impression of tail-length can be one of the most useful ways to identify a bird, because although fundamentally similar in structure (12 to 24 feathers attached to the pygostyle), tails vary greatly in shape, size, and function. Soaring hawks (the common Red-tailed Hawk) have broad, rather short tails, while those of fast-flying hawks (Peregrine Falcon) are long and slender. The tail length of most perching birds is shorter than the body, making it easy to pick out certain species (Common Grackle, Scissor-tailed Flycatcher) with oversized tails. Patches of white or color on the tail (American Redstart) or contrasting white outer tail feathers (Dark-eyed Junco) can be conspicuous clues for identification. Finally, with only a little experience, one can use the bird's *behavior* with its tail as an important diagnostic. If a drab green flycatcher repeatedly pumps its tail up and down, chances are it's an Eastern Phoebe. If a distant falcon on a utility pole is doing the same thing, it is an American Kestrel. A warbler foraging actively near the ground and pumping its tail is probably a Palm Warbler. A small brown bird holding its tail cocked upward is almost certainly a wren.

BEAKS AND FEET

The beak, legs, and feet of a bird are filled with information about its behavior, as these are the body parts that allow birds to fill a wider range of ecological niches than in any other group of vertebrates. In fact, one of the most enjoyable exercises while watching any bird is to focus on how it uses its beak and its feet together. Amazingly, these two "opposite ends" are almost always mechanically interrelated to accomplish the job of gathering nutrients in a particular kind of place. The beak tells us *what* a bird eats and *how* it captures its food, while the legs and feet tell us much about *where* these essential tasks take place.

All bird beaks (also called "bills") consist of an upper and a lower "mandible," each being a covering of dead, hardened skin surrounding bone. The legs and feet may be feathered or exposed, and always consist of tough skin surrounding bones and tendons, with a claw at the end of each toe. Most birds have four toes, but a few have dropped to three, and one (the Ostrich) has just two external toes, only one of which is functional. A consummate runner, the Ostrich has virtually converged on the same toe structure as the horse!

Waterfowl (ducks, geese, and swans) clearly display the close relationship between beak and feet. These birds make their living by feeding on small aquatic animals and plants, so their webbed feet placed far back on the body allow easy swimming along the water's surface in search of the right places to feed (but make for awkward waddling while on land). Ducks that feed in very shallow water strain out tiny invertebrates by sifting water or mud through their broad, flattened bill that is equipped with comb-like structures. Ducks that dive to feed in deeper water (such as the mergansers) have saw-tooth edges to their mandibles, permitting them to hold fast to crawfish, snails, and fish.

Hawks, eagles, falcons, and owls are "raptorial" birds, meaning that they eat other animals (the smallest hawks and owls also eat many large insects). The feet of raptors are specialized "talons" with each toe bearing a razor-sharp claw, providing the chief means of capturing and killing live prey. Their sharply hooked beak allows them to tear the prey apart. The Snail Kite uses an extreme version of this raptorial beak to extract giant apple snails from their shells in the marshes of the American tropics. The worldwide group of birds called shrikes are actually songbirds that have evolved the same hooked beak and predatory habits as the hawks.

The variety of bill and leg lengths in sandpipers and plovers allow this group to exploit hundreds of different kinds of wet places (beaches, mudflats, sandbars, river margins, tidal flats, rocky coastlines) where invertebrates live. Stilts, godwits, and yellowlegs forage in deep water on long legs, probing to varying depths with their long bills. Shorter-legged sandpipers forage along the water's edge, or wet mud, probing with shorter bills.

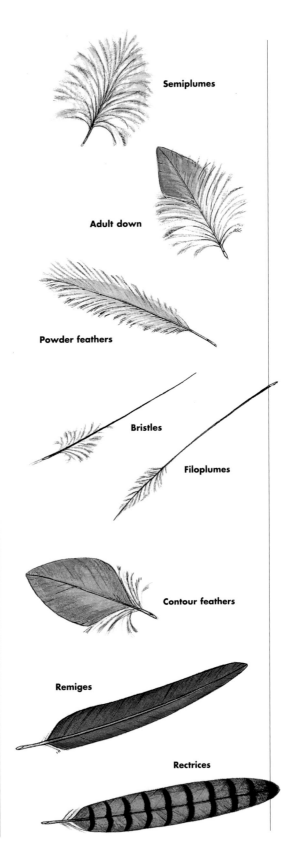

Semiplumes

Adult down

Powder feathers

Bristles

Filoplumes

Contour feathers

Remiges

Rectrices

Mallard
wings propel from rest to full flight without running start

Peregrine Falcon
pointed, swept-back wings for speed

Cooper's Hawk
wide wings maneuver through brush

Black-browed Albatross
soars on high-aspect-ratio wings

Snow Bunting
wide wings for propelling and soaring

Larger wading birds such as herons and storks can venture into even deeper water, where the heron uses its dagger-sharp bill to spear fish and the stork feeds by probing in the ooze and literally feeling its prey with sensitive nerves near the bill tip. Cranes forage like herons, but do so in very tall grass rather than deep water. Flamingos—among the world's most absurd-looking birds—wade with enormously long legs into muddy waters, lower their heads upside-down to the water line, and vigorously pump invertebrate-laden muck through the filters inside their bizarre, flat-topped beaks.

Woodpeckers exploit the insects living in dead and dying wood of the world's forests by clinging to tree trunks using feet in which the outer, front toe has evolved to point backward. The powerful beak of a woodpecker hides an elastic, extendible tongue that can probe deep inside cracks and bore-holes to impale insects with its barbed tip.

The array of bill specializations is almost endless, as every bird we see captures its food slightly differently from every other—and there is a lot of food out there to capture. The Black Skimmer drags a razor-thin lower mandible (much longer than the upper) along the water's surface, snapping the bill shut each time it touches a fish. The Brown Pelican's lower mandible balloons into a huge fish-sack as the bird plunges into the water following a long dive. Chuck-will's Widows (the largest nightjar in the Americas) dart up to open their tiny beak into an enormous, gaping white mouth to snatch large insects and small birds from the evening sky.

Toucans use their oversized bill both to snatch fruit from overhanging branches and to snatch baby birds from deep inside hanging bird nests. Hummingbirds probe into flowers using a needle-like beak and a tiny, deeply forked tongue to lap nectar (the hundreds of species of hummingbirds in South America include "sword-bills" and "sickle-bills," each species adapted to its own type and size of flower).

ORGANIZING THE AVIAN ARRAY

About 900 of the world's 9,500 species of birds have been recorded from North America north of the Mexican border, and over 700 of these regularly breed in the United States or Canada. An official list is kept up to date by the Committee on Classification and Nomenclature, in the scientific society called the American Ornithologists' Union (AOU). Periodically, this committee publishes the *Check-list of North American Birds* to serve as the scholarly reference for all field guides, technical papers, popular books, and public policies dealing with birds of this continent. This Checklist presents both the official names of our birds and the recommended sequence by which the species are presented in any list or book.

The names of birds, both scientific and common (or "vernacular"), are filled with interesting stories and history. Most were described and officially named during the 1800s, as great explorers such as Wilson, Audubon, and Lewis and Clark traversed the landscape to make the first systematic collections. A few species, however, escaped detection until quite recently. The latest and most remarkable of the recent discoveries was the Gunnison Sage Grouse of western Colorado, found to be fully distinct from the Greater Sage Grouse only at the very end of the 20th century.

New discoveries are constantly being made regarding how closely our various bird species are related to one another. Over the past 50 years, many species names have changed in the field guides, only to change back again as new information emerged. The Baltimore Oriole, for example, was long treated by the AOU as the same species as the Bullock's Oriole, because these two forms of the "Northern Oriole" were found to hybridize in the Great Plains. Scientists now recognize that this hybrid zone is stable, perhaps even acting as a barrier between the two species. Therefore, the AOU and all modern field guides again recognize Baltimore and Bullock's Orioles as two distinct species. With DNA sequencing now a relatively easy tool for investigating evolutionary history, the possibilities for exciting new discoveries—and, yes, even more bird names—continue to grow.

How we group and sequence birds in a Checklist (or an Atlas) reflects scientists' best guesses about which birds are most closely related to one another. Within the single class (Aves), the easiest grouping to accomplish is the order. There are 20 orders of birds regularly living in North America, and most of these groups are intuitively comfortable to us: loons; grebes; shearwaters and petrels; pelicans and boobies; herons and storks; ducks, geese, and swans; hawks and falcons; grouse and quail; rails and cranes; shorebirds, terns, gulls, and alcids; doves; parrots; cuckoos; owls; nightjars; swifts and hummingbirds; trogons; kingfishers; woodpeckers; and perching birds.

Within each order, birds belonging to the same "family" are grouped together. Families divide the larger orders, and most of these also are easy to picture intuitively. For example, the diverse order Charadriiformes contains the plovers (Charadriidae), oystercatchers (Haematopodidae), sandpipers (Scolopacidae), gulls and terns (Laridae), and alcids (Alcidae). The huge order Passerifomes, or perching birds, contains about half the world's bird species. Families in this order include crows and jays (Corvidae), swallows (Hiruninidae), nuthatches (Sittidae), wrens (Troglodytidae), waxwings (Bombycillidae), sparrows and towhees (Emberizidae), and many others.

Within families, species belonging to the same "genus" are always listed together. A genus (plural: genera) is a group of species believed to share a relatively recent common ancestor. Some examples of common genera are dabbling ducks (*Anas*), falcons (*Falco*), woodland woodpeckers (*Picoides*), crows (*Corvus*), a large group of wood warblers (*Dendroica*), towhees (*Pipilo*), and buntings (*Passerina*).

The traditional sequence for the orders of birds begins with those once believed to be evolutionarily most "primitive." The sequence proceeds through many orders containing large, ground- and water-dwelling birds, and ends with those considered most "advanced" (the rapidly evolving perching birds).

Today, ideas about the ages and relationships among avian orders are being completely scrambled as a result of significant, often surprising new insights about ancient evolutionary history provided by DNA sequencing. Our sequence of orders and families remains the same as the traditional one, however, while we watch and wait for more convincing ones to emerge.

HAVING FUN WITH BIRDS

Whether we want to study them, or just enjoy them, birds supply us endless fascination any time we stop and simply *watch* them. At the bird feeder, at the city park, in the grocery store parking lot, at the beach, or in the woods, these creatures share the planet with us and do so largely in disregard of our watching them.

Pausing to watch birds use their adaptations of flight and foraging behavior is one of the most satisfying ways we can connect personally with how the natural world works. The more we watch, the more we want to know. The exciting book you are holding right now opens a universe of recent discoveries about where birds occur, how they use their resources, and how they treat the world as a single planet.

Times have never been more thrilling in the world of bird study, and anyone who wants to do

so can have an influence on what we are learning today. There is still much more to understand, even about the birds in our own back yards. Are their numbers declining? Are they adapting to human modified habitats? As the planet warms, are birds changing where they spend the winter? Are they arriving earlier each spring? What habitats do our most endangered species depend upon? Do birds we think of as a single species sing the same song across their whole range?

Opportunities abound for citizens to take part in new, large-scale studies of birds, their use of habitats, and their relationships with humans. The growth of "citizen science" as a legitimate scientific process has been fostered mainly by thousands of ordinary people contributing bird observations into shared databases. Two examples are the Christmas Bird Count and Project FeederWatch. In fact, most of the maps that are depicted in this book were created in large part by reports from common citizens. How will these maps change through time? You can put your observations to use in bird study and bird conservation by taking part in the growing movement of citizen science (see http://birds.cornell.edu and http://birdsource.org).

Most of all, you should feel excited by having this book in your hands. It is a masterful compilation of a remarkable global spectacle, the living and always moving universe of birds around the world. We are lucky, indeed, to live on a planet and in a time, when we can enjoy birds in every habitat we visit, and can learn from them so richly. Let us all hope that humans continue to cherish and guard this privilege.

Have fun watching birds, for they will repay you for every moment you spend with them.

(Overleaf) Great Blue Heron

Blue Grosbeak
heavy beak for cracking seeds

Red Crossbill
beak for extracting seeds from
pine cones

American Oystercatcher
beak for opening crustaceans

Mallard
beak for feeding on aquatic
vegetation

Northern Parula
beak for gleaning insects

Common Loon
beak for catching fish underwater

American White Pelican
beak with pouch for catching fish

Peregrine Falcon
beak for ripping flesh off prey

American Avocet
recurved bill for catching small
crustaceans

Roseate Spoonbill
beak for sweeping underwater

LOONS, GREBES

Believed to be members of two of the oldest lineages of birds, there is something seemingly primordial about loons and grebes, whether they are wailing plaintively, swimming peacefully, or submerging without a ripple into the glassine waters of a lake. Indeed, primordial they are: The earliest ancestors of loons and grebes first appeared in the late Cretaceous period, some 70 million to 80 million years ago, whereas modern species date back some 20 million to 30 million years. Loons tend to be larger and heavier than grebes—only the Clark's and Western Grebes rival loons in size. Both groups possess thick, waterproof plumage that keeps them dry and warm, yet plumage differences set them apart, giving loons a sleeker, harder appearance than grebes, which look fluffier overall and often sport a crest.

Having adapted to an aquatic life in the freshwater lakes and ponds where they breed, and in coastal seas where many winter, both families are superb swimmers and divers. Only penguins and some of the alcids are known to dive deeper and stay submerged longer.

Several shared adaptations allow for their prowess in the water. Diving is partially facilitated by their dense bones that yield a specific gravity closer to that of water combined with the ability to reduce their heart rate and regulate oxygen use in other organs. A high myoglobin content in their muscles further helps them store relatively larger amounts of oxygen for use under water; and the ability to expel air from their bodies and feathers helps regulate buoyancy.

In addition, the legs of both loons and grebes are positioned far back on the body, which is a major, positive adaptation for swimming and diving. This foot and leg placement helps streamline the body and gives both groups of birds maximum leverage for power and steering as they swim and dive. Although an advantage in the water, the rear-set legs and feet prove awkward on land, making loons, and to a lesser extent, grebes, virtually incapable of walking on solid ground. This awkwardness on land makes it hard for the birds to take flight. Most loons and grebes seem to exert a great effort, furiously flapping their wings while paddling and skittering across the surface of the water, to achieve liftoff.

Once in the air, loons and grebes extend their necks and hold their heads lower than their backs, yielding a "humpbacked" appearance. Their feet extend far behind their bodies in flight and are used to help steer. Loons hold their feet together sole to sole. Grebes are rather weak fliers, rarely taking to the air except for migration, whereas loons are strong fliers often reaching speeds in excess of 60 miles per hour. Both species prefer to dive or swim, not fly, to escape danger.

With so many similarities in dietary and habitat requirements, it is little wonder that loons and grebes are fierce competitors. They often call loudly, rearing up out of the water, noisily flapping their wings, and rushing at suspected intruders where their territories overlap.

Given their shared characteristics, loons and grebes were once thought to be closely related, but recent studies seem to indicate that they are not, and they are grouped into separate families. However, clear relationships of loons and grebes to other avian families are uncertain.

Philip Brandt George

(Left) Common Loon

Red-throated Loon: *Gavia stellata*, L 25",
bill appears upturned, gray head, brick red throat patch

LOONS

The smallest of the five loons found in North America, the Red-throated Loon (above) is most frequently seen during the winter months along the Atlantic and the Pacific coasts of Canada and the United States. Unlike other loons, it droops its neck noticeably, and while swimming, it holds its small, delicate bill in a slightly upturned position. In alternate plumage on its breeding grounds, which range from Alaska and northern Canada to the north coast of Greenland, the Red-throated Loon is readily identifiable by

Range of Red-throated Loon

its gray head and neck and diagnostic brick red throat patch. In its basic, or winter plumage, however, the throat patch disappears. In all plumages the Red-throated Loon has dark brown upperparts, but lacks the bold white spots displayed by the the four other loon species. The Red-throated Loon feeds mainly by diving for fish, mostly herring and cod in saltwater, and salmonids in freshwater, but is also known to eat mussels, shrimp, other crustaceans, and aquatic insects. The population of Red-throated Loons is stable, but vulnerable to loss of nesting habitat and pollution in the coastal waters of its wintering grounds. A powerful flyer, the Red-throated Loon is the only loon capable of leaping directly into flight from either land or water.

CLASSIFICATION

The order Gaviiformes contains a single family, Gaviidae, with a single genus, *Gavia,* suggesting that all loons are closely related. Arctic and Pacific Loons are so similar that some scholars consider them to be a single species. That pair and one other—the Common and the Yellow-billed Loons—are considered by many to constitute two superspecies. Given each pair's similarities in appearance, breeding, and foraging behavior, were they not isolated geographically, they would probably interbreed and, eventually become a single species.

STRUCTURE

The Gaviidae are well suited for diving. Eye adaptations that increase light-gathering ability provide good vision under water. Their more solid, less hollow bones increase their specific gravity and protect against heavy water pressure as they dive. Diving loons commonly stay submerged up to three minutes and reach depths of 250 feet. Webbed feet, set far back on their body, provide strong paddling power, and laterally flattened tarsi, coupled with small tails, reduce drag as they move through water. The aft positioning and leg muscles set into the body mass aid in streamlining and provide more efficient thrust when swimming and diving, but also make it nearly impossible for loons to walk on land. Front-weighted as they are, they have difficulty standing upright and must push themselves, breast sliding on the ground, with their powerful hind legs. The name loon is thought to derive from Scottish or Scandinavian words meaning, "lame" or "clumsy."

PLUMAGE

Male and female loons of each species are similar in appearance. They are stunning in their breeding plumage of grays and patterned, contrasting blacks and whites. Only the Red-throated Loon, as its name suggests, has a red patch. In nonbreeding plumage all loons appear rather plain with counter-shaded browns and grays on the back and lighter tones on the throat, breast, and belly. Their body feathers often appear chiseled or tightly compacted, while those of the head and neck seem sleeker and softer. A simultaneous fall molt of all flight feathers renders loons flightless for several weeks. Recently hatched loon chicks are covered in a thick, monotone insulating down, and juveniles usually resemble nonbreeding adults.

FEEDING BEHAVIOR

Loons feed on fish, mollusks, crustaceans, insects, marine worms, frogs, and occasionally plant matter. They scout for prey by scanning the surrounding surface or by poking their head underwater. Most of their food is found underwater, and once prey is spotted, they dive in pursuit and strike out with their sinuous neck to make the capture. They consume all but the largest prey underwater. Fish are usually swallowed headfirst. Loons ingest grit and pebbles into their gizzards to aid in the grinding of fish bones and crustacean shells. Red-throated Loons are unique in that they regularly forage away from their nesting sites, flying to larger lakes to feed and catch fish to take to their young.

VOCALIZATION

Though usually silent on their wintering grounds, Loons can be noisy in spring and summer. Their yodeling, wailing, hooting, and tremolo calls, especially by the Common and Yellow-billed Loons, have been likened to the demented laughter of demons or the lonely cries of banshees, leading to the expression, "crazy as a loon," yet to some listeners they represent the quintessential "call of the wild." Red-throated Loon pairs are the only ones to perform territorial songs in duet.

BREEDING BEHAVIOR

Loon pairs are at least seasonally monogamous, although many stay together for more than one season, even for life. Loons reach sexual maturity and first breed when two or three years old. Courtship displays vary from species to species, but most indulge in swimming,

Pacific Loon

diving, and synchronous head dipping. These movements are often accompanied by loud calls.

Loons mate on land, often using the same spot again and again, causing a depression in the soil, sometimes called a "false nest." Given their awkwardness on land, loons prefer to nest where they can easily escape predators by slipping into, or skittering over, the water. Both sexes build the nest, usually on the shoreline or at the edge of islands. A sitting loon pulls vegetation from the surrounding area to form a hollow mound around its body. Both groups produce only one brood a year, but a second may be attempted if the first fails early in the breeding season. Loon clutches average two eggs. Hatching is asynchronous. Both sexes incubate and feed

the precocial young. Newly hatched loons require 24 to 48 hours of parental care before venturing into the water. They may ride on the parents' back for protection from predators and to keep warm and dry until they get their full, waterproof plumage.

BREEDING RANGE

The Common Loon nests across lower Canada and the extreme reaches of the northern tier of the United States; most other loons favor the lakes and ponds of the high Arctic of Canada and Alaska.

MIGRATION

Following a fall molt, all loons abandon the northern lakes as the weather gets colder, and most birds head for warmer waters. They fly alone or in flocks in diurnal migration.

WINTER RANGE

All loons leave their inland, freshwater breeding areas to winter on the coasts of the Pacific and Atlantic, where they often form large rafts off shore or in sheltered bays. Nonbreeding juveniles may spend their entire first year or two on the wintering range.

OBSERVING LOONS

In breeding plumage, the Red-throated Loon is easily identified by its red throat. Bill color is the surest field mark for separating Common from Yellow-billed Loons. To distinguish between Arctic and Pacific Loons is difficult in the field—subtle differences in the amount of white they show are the main clues. Nonbreeding loons present even greater challenges by minor variations in color, bill, and head shapes.

STATUS AND CONSERVATION

Loons are not endangered, but they are subject to a variety of threats. Ingested chemicals such as lead from gun pellets and fishing sinkers, PCBs, mercury, and pesticides can kill or render the birds incapable of producing viable eggs. Human incursions have produced changes in water levels and the acidity and salinity of freshwater habitats, causing the disappearance of key plant and prey populations. Discarded fishing line and fishing nets often ensnare loons, leading to strangulation or drowning.

OTHER SPECIES FIELD NOTES

■ **Pacific Loon**
Gavia pacifica
L 26"
Dark flanks, no white, extends upward on rump

■ **Arctic Loon**
Gavia arctica
L 28"
Extensive white on flanks

■ **Common Loon**
Gavia immer
L 32"
Large, thick bill with curved culmen

■ **Yellow-billed Loon**
Gavia adamsii
L 34"
Yellow bill with straight culmen

See also

Auks, Murres, Puffins, page 177
Diving ducks, page 100

Pied-billed Grebe: *Podilymbus podiceps*, L 13.5", black ring around bill of breeding adult

GREBES

The only grebe found in all of the lower 48 states and southern Canada, the Pied-billed Grebe (above) breeds in freshwater lakes, marshes, and ponds throughout the United States and southern Canada, then moves south to winter in both fresh- and saltwater environments. In alternate, or breeding plumage, the overall brownish gray Pied-billed Grebe displays a black chin and a bold, black ring around its light, ivory-colored bill. The bill-ring disappears with the return of its basic plumage in the winter and the chin turns white. A rather unsociable bird, the Pied-billed Grebe is usually seen alone on small lakes and ponds. It dives to feed

Range of Pied-billed Grebe

on aquatic insects, fish, and crustaceans, and, like all grebes, it consumes feathers, which it also feeds to its young. It constructs a nest of matted vegetation near shore, or floating and anchored to growing plants. The nest is usually sited so that it can be approached underwater. Though common, the Pied-billed Grebe is very wary, and often slowly sinks into the water to elude intruders leaving only its head and bill visible above the surface.

CLASSIFICATION

Grebes—sole members of the family Podicipedidae—are found everywhere on the globe except in Antarctica. Only four of the family's six genera are found in North America. Clark's and Western Grebes of the genus *Aechmophorus* were once thought to be color morphs of the same species, but genetic studies, differing vocalizations, and the fact that they rarely interbreed where their ranges overlap, indicate that each probably deserves its present separate status. Of the other three grebe genera *Tachybaptus*, a primarily Old World genus often called "dabchicks," is represented in North America only by the Least Grebe. Following the apparent extinction of the Atitlán Grebe of the western highlands of Guatemala, the Pied-billed is probably the only living member of the genus *Podilymbus* on Earth. Of nine *Podiceps* species worldwide, only the Red-necked, Eared, and Horned Grebes appear in North America. The family ranges in size from the Least Grebe at 9.75 inches to the Clark's and Western Grebes at 25 inches.

STRUCTURE

Grebes, like loons, have evolved into quintessential divers—the larger grebes routinely dive to near 90 feet and remain underwater for up to 40 seconds. More solid bones—displaying less pneumaticization than most bird skeletons—and the ability to compress their feathers to expel air contribute to a reduction in specific gravity, allowing for deep dives. Their specialized structure also lets them submerge slowly, submarine-like, either completely or partially, leaving only their head and eyes above the surface. When diving, a reduction in the heart rate, decrease in oxygen use by several organs, and high myoglobin content in the muscles that allows for the storing of oxygen, all permit longer and deeper dives. A high concentration of rods in the eyes, which gather more light, allows grebes to see well underwater in the search for prey. As they dive, their wings are held close to their sides and are used only to aid with rapid turns or to give a quick burst in speed.

The family name Podicipedidae derives from the Latin terms *podex* and *pes*, meaning "rump" and "foot," respectively, indicating that, as with loons, grebe feet and legs are located far astern on the body. This rearward location of the strong legs and feet serves to increase power and steering leverage as they swim and dive. The position of the legs, along with lobed toes—like those of phalaropes and coots—which collapse as the foot moves forward in the water but expand on the backstroke, laterally flattened tarsi, and virtual lack of a tail, increases streamlining, allowing grebes to slip and glide easily through their watery domain.

Although the position of the legs is a useful adaptation on water, it somewhat limits their ability to walk or run on land. With their bulky body and relatively small wings the birds must build up speed to take flight. Too awkward on land, the birds need a lengthy watery runway along which they can paddle and skitter to achieve takeoff. When threatened, given their problems in getting airborne, grebes usually dive rather than fly to escape danger.

During migration, especially on misty evenings or at night, grebes have been known to mistake the wet, reflective surfaces of highways or parking lots for a body of water, with disastrous consequences. Even if they survive the landing on the hard pavement with its potential for broken wings or legs, the birds are unable to get airborne again unless knowledgeable humans intervene, transporting them to a nearby lake or pond so they can resume their migratory flight.

PLUMAGE

Throughout the year, some grebes change their appearance a great deal; others remain unchanged. As the rather drably attired Pied-billed and Least Grebes switch from breeding to nonbreeding plumage, only minor changes occur in bill and facial coloring. The same is true for Clark's and Western Grebes. Their contrasting, nonpatterned, black-and-white coloring varies only slightly throughout the year. Some grebes, however, present a more colorful appearance in the spring and summer, molting to duller tones for winter.

Breeding Horned and Eared Grebes have golden tufts and sprays that extend from behind the eye, rearward across the face and head. (The name grebe is thought to derive from the Breton term *krib,* meaning "crest.") Like the Red-necked Grebe, Horned and Eared Grebes sport rusty red or chestnut coloring on

Eared Grebe

the breast, flanks, and neck. At any time of year it is almost impossible to distinguish between male and female grebes in the field. During the fall molts, grebes, like loons and most ducks, lose all of their flight feathers at one time, leaving them grounded for several weeks.

Most grebe chicks sport heavy black striping, eventually molting to resemble their parents, although some juveniles may retain a vestige of their natal stripes on their faces. Over all, Grebes have feathers that appear less dense and more "hairy" than those of loons, and the soft, thick, lustrous feathers of some species were much in demand by the millinery trade during the late 19th and early 20th centuries. After hearing reports that some 20 to 30 camps in southern Oregon were solely dedicated to killing and skinning of grebes for their feathers, Pres. Theodore Roosevelt established Malheur Lake and Klamath Lake as bird sanctuaries.

FEEDING BEHAVIOR

Most grebes eat fish as the staple of their diet, but they also feed on other aquatic creatures such as worms, insects, frogs, mollusks, and other crustaceans, as well as some plant matter. The larger grebes, especially the Western and Clark's, concentrate on fish when available, whereas the smaller grebes consume larger proportions of the smaller creatures.

Grebes will take insects and some vegetable matter from the surface, but most of their foraging is done with only the head submerged in an attempt to espy game below. Diving in pursuit, they grasp fish in the bill, rotate it to a headfirst position, and eat it whole while still under water. Occasionally some grebe species will spear their prey, and larger fish may be brought to the surface before being consumed. Grebes are unique among birds in that adults pluck feathers from their own body and eat them or feed them to the young, perhaps to provide some protection to the stomach from hard, sharp fish bones or animal shells.

VOCALIZATION

Although grebes can be noisy on their breeding grounds most are generally "speechless" on their wintering grounds. During courtship, territorial defense, and in everyday intraspecies communications, grebes utter a wide variety of clucks, clicks, and squeaks, as well as whinnies, and whistles that can sound a bit eerie at times. Only the Red-necked Grebe is regularly heard to produce drawn-out wails, shorter tremolos, and a chattering trill.

OTHER SPECIES FIELD NOTES

 Horned Grebe
Podiceps auritus
L 13.5"
Golden "horns" in breeding adult

 Eared Grebe
Podiceps nigricollis
L 12.5"
Golden "ears" fan out behind eyes in breeding adult

 Least Grebe
Tachybaptus dominicus
L 9.75"
Small with golden yellow eyes

 Red-necked Grebe
Podiceps grisegena
L 20"
Heavy, tapered, yellowish bill, whitish throat and cheeks

 Clark's Grebe
Aechmophorus clarkii
L 25"
Orange bill, black cap above eye

 Western Grebe
Aechmophorus occidentalis
L 25"
Long, thin neck, black cap extends below eye

BREEDING BEHAVIOR

Grebes tend to be seasonally monogamous and, depending on the species, first breed when they are one or two years old. Their pair formation and mating displays are often far more complex than those of loons. The male and female frequently swim together, nodding and turning their heads from side to side. They dive in unison to retrieve plants from the bottom, resurface and, facing one another, repeatedly bow and posture with their offerings. Many have a rushing display in which both raise themselves to a vertical stance and then flap their wings while pattering and splashing across the lake. In the most spectacular versions of these performances, Clark's and Western Grebes rise up, coil their necks, extend their wings rearward, and race across the water—truly a wonder to behold.

Grebes such as the Pied-billed and Least which breed in dense, marshy areas may rely more on vocalizations than on physical displays for intraspecies communications. As part of the mating ritual, male and female grebes create nests by building up mounds in shallow water and copulate on the finished nest.

The nests are usually anchored to emergent vegetation at the water's edge or even in shallow open water, affording easy access for the birds but thwarting many land-based predators. Given their semifloating nature, these nests are also partially protected from small fluctuations in the water level.

Most species lay between three and four eggs; a few others such as the Horned and Pied-billed Grebes produce on average five to seven eggs. Grebes are among the few birds that cover their nests when leaving them. The covering vegetation helps camouflage the nest from predators and may generate enough heat to aid incubation. Both sexes incubate for 20 to 30 days, and both feed and care for their precocial young. Hatchlings leave the nest quickly and can swim and dive almost immediately.

BREEDING RANGE

Most grebes spend their summers in southern and western Canada and southward across the border as far as the central part of the United States. Only the Pied-billed and Horned Grebes nest as far north as the 60th parallel. The Pied-billed Grebes nest throughout most of Canada and the United States, south through Mexico, Central America, and a large part of South America. Least Grebes share those breeding grounds from extreme southern Texas southward to Tierra del Fuego, Argentina. The Red-necked and Horned Grebes nest primarily in the northwestern reaches of Canada, whereas Clark's, Western, and Eared Grebes concentrate in the northwestern quadrant of the United States. All breed in or around fresh water, most preferring larger lakes and ponds, but the Pied-billed and Least Grebes may nest in marshy ponds and sloughs, and even ditches.

MIGRATION

With the exception of the Least Grebe, which is a permanent resident throughout its southern breeding range, grebes are all at least partially migratory. Some populations of southern Pied-billed, Western, and Clark's Grebes are joined by migrating populations which have abandoned their colder northern breeding grounds for the winter. Overland migrations take place

WESTERN GREBE

Most famous for their elaborate and energetic courtship sprints across the water's surface, these striking black-and-white grebes are similar to Clark's Grebe, formerly considered to be one species. The Western Grebe is identified by its long, thin yellow-green bill and black cap that covers the forehead and crown and extends down the sides of its face to include its bright red eyes. In winter plumage, the Western Grebe acquires a whitish lore area similar to the Clark's Grebe, but the bill color will help in identifying this spectacular bird. Western Grebes are a social species throughout the year, nesting in spring in colonies among the reeds along the margins of large, inland bodies of water, and wintering in large flocks, especially along coastal bays and marshes and inland freshwater lakes. The Western Grebe feeds almost exclusively on fish by diving from the surface and pursuing prey by swimming, propelled mainly by its feet. Clark's and Western are the only grebes equipped with heron-like necks providing them a quick, snake-like strike with their long, sharp bills.

largely at night as they move to coastal winter grounds, but once the coast is reached, some species follow along the coast, swimming or flying farther south during the day. Migration patterns vary and some species, such as Clark's and Western, apparently prefer to move in flocks, whereas others such as the Horned Grebe usually go it alone. Yet, it is possible to see migrating flocks or lone birds of virtually any species.

WINTER RANGE

Most grebes move from their freshwater inland lake, marsh, and pond breeding grounds to saline coastal waters with some species—Horned, Pied-billed, and Red-necked—going to both Atlantic or Pacific shores. Instead of heading for the coast, some populations of Eared Grebes fly to the inland waters of extreme southern California, Arizona, New Mexico, and Texas, or along the western part of the Gulf Coast.

Northern breeding populations of Pied-billed Grebes often move to overlap with other populations which remain on the western and southern breeding grounds. Nonbreeding juveniles may spend their first couple of years entirely on the wintering range.

OBSERVING GREBES

It is easy enough to distinguish between grebe species, when they are sporting their breeding plumage. Winter plumage, with its drabber counter-shaded tones and a lack of reds, yellows, and the unique head patterns of summer, creates a challenge at times. Birders may confuse wintering Horned, Eared, and Red-necked Grebes, as well as their cousins the Clark's and Western Grebes. Only careful attention to size, bill shape and color, head shape, and eye color will cinch the identification. Most birds are viewed singly, in pairs, or as small family groups on their freshwater breeding grounds, or in large rafts in coastal waters in winter. It is a delight to watch them dive briskly without causing a ripple, or submerge slowly, disappearing from view for a protracted time, then popping up far away—an ability that has earned them the names "hell-diver" and "water witch."

STATUS AND CONSERVATION

Although none of the grebe species is officially designated as endangered, the birds face a variety of threats, most of which are related to industrial, sporting, and recreational activities. Pollutants like PCBs, mercury, and pesticides present a serious problem when waterfowl either directly ingest the poisons or consume quantities of already poisoned aquatic prey. Some of

these chemicals sicken the birds directly and may lead to weakened eggshells, causing shell breakage and general nesting failure. Changes in the acidity, alkalinity, and salinity of freshwater habitats can cause the disappearance of key plants and a collapse in prey populations. Such alterations may come as the result of acid rain, especially in the lakes and ponds of the northeastern United States, or from agriculture, flood prevention methods, or other projects that alter water levels.

Lead poisoning caused by scooping up lead gun-pellets and fishing sinkers with other food from the lake bottom can lead directly to death.

Grebes, loons, and other waterfowl often drown or otherwise perish after becoming entangled in fishing nets or discarded fishing line. Some populations have been threatened by the introduction of large, predatory game fish that may kill chicks and compete with the birds for other prey. High wakes from personal watercraft, speedboats, and water skiers can swamp and destroy the low nests of these birds at the water's edge. Often well-meaning, curious humans, hoping for a better look, approach the nesting area too closely, disrupting the birds' foraging and breeding activities. Nests are sometimes abandoned owing to human encroachment, and the time and energy the birds spend escaping would be better spent foraging and nesting.

Red-necked Grebe

Fortunately, numerous private and governmental groups have instituted a wide variety of measures that have reduced the impact of some of these dangers. In many places, lead shot and sinkers are forbidden. No-wake and limited-access zones have been established on many lakes to protect known nesting sites. The reduction of hours for the use of high-powered water vehicles has partially reduced noise levels and helped create a more bird-friendly atmosphere. The installation of floating platforms that rise and lower with changing water levels has provided safer, more inviting nesting sites. These and similar measures go a long way toward protecting the habitats these birds prefer—especially on many of the smaller freshwater lakes across the eastern parts of lower Canada and the northern United States—providing a brighter future for the birds themselves.

See also

Diving ducks, page 100
Herons and Egrets, page 71

◀ WESTERN GREBE

BREEDING AND WINTER RANGES

— Autumn and Spring migr

☐ Principal breeding range

☐ Permanent resident rang

☐ Principal wintering range

Not all populations of Western Grebes migrate south for the winter. Many northern birds move west and north to the Pacific coast along southern Alaska and British Columbia.

STATUTE MILES
0   500
0   500
KILOMETERS

PACIFIC LOC

AUTUMN AND SPRING MIGRAT

Principal migratory route   —

Rare but regular migration   - - -
route (autumn only)

Breeding range   ☐

Winter range   ☐

*Pacific Loons winter from the co
southern Alaska to northwest Me
with very large concentrations a
the Baja Peninsula. During the s
migration many thousands can be
moving north along the Pacific
Some loons can be seen as far e
the Great Plains while migrating
route taken by populations bree
along the eastern Hudson Ba
southeastern Baffin Island is un
Also unknown, is the path travel
those birds wintering in the nor
Gulf of California. A few birds are
east to the Atlantic coast each*

STATUTE N
0   - - -
0
KILOME

ARCTIC
OCEAN

QUEEN ELIZABETH
ISLANDS

PARRY ISLANDS

Banks
Island

Victoria
Island

Baffin Island

CHUKCHI SEA

BERING Str.

BEAUFORT SEA

ARCTIC CIRCLE

U.S.
CANADA

Gulf of Alaska

Great
Bear Lake

C A N A D A

Great
Slave Lake

HUDSON
BAY

Lake
Athabasca

Reindeer
Lake

R O C K Y   M O U N T A I N S

G R E A T   P L A I N S

L. Superior

Lake
Huron

L. Michigan

L. Ontario

L. Erie

U N I T E D   S T A T E S

A P P A L A C H I A N   M O U N T A I N S

ATLANTIC
OCEAN

O C E A N

Baja California

Gulf of California

TROPIC OF CANCER

M E X I C O

GULF OF
MEXICO

TROPIC OF CANCER

BAHAMAS

W E S T   I N D I E S

C U B A

G R E A T E R   A N T I L L E S

HAITI

DOMINICAN
REPUBLIC

P.R. U.S.

JAMAICA

C A R I B B E A N   S E A

LESSER ANTILLES

Yucatán
Pen.

BELIZE

GUATEMALA

HONDURAS

EL SALVADOR

NICARAGUA

COSTA RICA

PANAMA

COLOMBIA

VENEZUELA

110°
100°
Longitude West 90° of Greenwich
80°
70°

ALBATROSSES, SHEARWATERS, STORM-PETRELS

Jonathan Alderfer

The open ocean is the greatest wilderness left on our planet, and the birds of this group—the order Procellariiformes—are its avian citizens. Many species are prodigious wanderers with extraordinary powers of flight; some species number in the millions, while others are critically endangered; and some such as the majestic albatrosses have taken on mystical importance for the likes of sailors and poets—and birders, too.

The order Procellariiformes is divided into four families made up of about 120 species worldwide. Three families and 41 species can be found in North American waters: They are albatrosses (family Diomedeidae, 7 species), petrels and shearwaters (family Procellariidae, 24 species), and storm-petrels (family Hydrobatidae, 9 species). They share many aspects of body structure and lifestyle, forming a well-defined group of seabirds not closely related to any other. There is debate over their nearest relatives: Penguins, loons, and frigatebirds have all been proposed.

As a group, they are popularly known as "tubenoses" for their unique, tubed nostrils, located on the top or sides of their bill. Other characteristics of the order include hooked bills made up of separate bill plates, webbed feet, waterproof plumage, large olfactory glands, the ability to excrete excess salt, and highly developed powers of flight, especially in the albatrosses. Most species have rather drab, monochromatic plumage, which complicates identification. They are extremely variable in size—the Wandering Albatross has the largest wingspan of any living bird (up to 12 feet), whereas the diminutive Least Storm-Petrel is about the size of a House Sparrow.

All are essentially oceanic in lifestyle, coming on land only to breed and raise young. Many species take years to reach sexual maturity and are continuously at sea during that time. Only six species breed in North America: Northern Fulmar; Manx Shearwater; and Leach's, Fork-tailed, Black, and Ashy Storm-Petrels. The other 35 species in our waters are a far-flung group, nesting on remote islands scattered across the globe, mainly in the Southern Hemisphere. A few of these distant-nesting species, such as the Sooty Shearwater, can be common in North American waters, and their annual migrations are well known. Others are extremely rare, or at least rarely observed, frequenting far-offshore waters where birders seldom venture.

Just as the oceans are a frontier, so is the study of pelagic seabirds. Ornithologists Robert Cushman Murphy and Alexander Wetmore were seabird pioneers working in the early 20th century. An important milestone for ocean-going birders came in 1983 with the publication of *Seabirds, an Identification Guide* by Peter Harrison. Active seabirders realize how much more remains to be discovered. The status and distribution of many species is still poorly known, especially when they are away from their breeding islands, and the identification of some species still confounds us. "Dark" storm-petrels and *Pterodroma* petrels are challenging to identify. Trying to separate some common species, such as Sooty and Short-tailed Shearwaters, can be fiendishly difficult. A few species, such as Galápagos and Hawaiian Petrels, are on the North American list as a group because *nobody* can tell them apart at sea—yet.

(Left) **Northern Fulmar**

Laysan Albatross: *Phoebastria immutabilis,* L 32" W 79", white flash in primaries, white underwing

ALBATROSSES

The Laysan Albatross (above) is the most common albatross of the North Pacific. This great ocean bird spends most of its life at sea, and ranges far offshore along our western coast. The Laysan is readily distinguished by its large size, blackish brown back and upperwings with a white flash in the primaries, and contrasting white head and underparts. An epic flight of a foraging female Laysan, lasting 29 days and covering over 7,500 miles was documented by satellite tracking. They forage at sea,

Range of Laysan Albatross

often feeding while swimming at night when squid rise to the surface. Though long-lived, up to 50 years or more in the wild, Laysans do not begin to breed before seven to nine years of age, and fledge only one chick per nesting season. The majority breed in the Hawaiian Islands, though since the mid-1980s some have begun nesting on Isla Guadalupe and Isla Clarion off the west coast of Mexico, thus extending their range by several hundreds of miles. The population is slowly expanding, but still vulnerable to human activities. Many are regularly drowned on the hooks of the international long-line fishing fleet, and observers report adults regurgitating disposable lighters and other human trash the parents have mistaken for food items while foraging to feed their young.

CLASSIFICATION

The albatrosses—family Diomedeidae—form a distinct taxonomic group of 14 species worldwide. Seven species have occurred in North American waters, although only two—Black-footed and Laysan of the Pacific Ocean—are commonly seen. Albatrosses breed on isolated oceanic islands, and numerous subspecies have evolved. Some of these subspecies may be valid, and an alternative taxonomy recognizes 24 species.

STRUCTURE

All albatrosses are large birds—Wandering Albatrosses are huge (11-to 12-foot wingspan, 18 to 25 pounds), Laysan Albatrosses are one of the smaller species (6.5 foot wingspan, 5 to 7 pounds). They have stout bodies, large heads, long hooked bills, webbed feet, and short tails. Their nostril openings form short tubes on either side of the bill, unlike the other tubenoses whose nostril tubes are fused at the top of the bill. The most exceptional aspects of their structure are their extremely long and narrow (high aspect ratio) wings, which have co-evolved with their distinctive flight style. They stay aloft by dynamic soaring—the almost effortless style of flight that takes advantage of reliable ocean winds and the gradient of slower wind speed near the surface vs. higher wind speed above it. The resulting "roller coaster" flight is often enhanced by slope soaring—gaining lift from air deflected upward from a wave—and ground effect dynamics—taking advantage of reduced drag by flying close to the water's surface. By instinctively balancing these aerodynamic principles, a heavy albatross with its high aspect wings is able to fly almost effortlessly, cruising hundreds of miles in a single day. On the rare occasions when there are no winds or waves to assist them, albatrosses are becalmed and must wait for conditions to improve to become airborne.

PLUMAGE

Albatross plumages are monochromatic combinations of whites, blacks, and grays. Most species are white below, and the primary and secondary wing feathers are always blackish—the dark pigment (melanin) greatly improves a feather's resistance to wear from abrasion or sunlight. Many species go through a series of immature plumages that lighten as adulthood approaches, although this is not true of Black-footed and Laysan Albatrosses.

FEEDING BEHAVIOR

Squid is the staple food of many albatrosses; other foods include fish, fish eggs, galley refuse, and offal. Albatrosses feed after alighting on the water, where they pick at surface items or dip for them underwater (complete submersion is rare). Because squid often migrate vertically to the ocean surface at night, some albatrosses are nocturnal feeders. All tubenoses have a developed sense of smell that helps them locate potential food sources.

VOCALIZATION

At sea, albatrosses are generally silent, except when squabbling over food with other birds. At breeding colonies, pairs engage in elaborate courtship displays that are accompanied by an amazing repertoire of grunts, groans, and whinnies, besides nonvocal sounds made by clacking or snapping their bill.

Black-footed Albatross

BREEDING BEHAVIOR

Albatrosses are monogamous, maintaining pair bonds for life. They are long lived, with records of birds living over 60 years. Most do not even attempt to breed before 8 to 12 years, although they may return to their natal islands before then to begin establishing a pair bond. Pair bonds may take several years and are formed through highly ritualized dancing, posturing, and vocalizations. Once established, the pair bond remains intact until one of the partners dies or disappears.

Nests are simple scrapes on the ground or are situated on raised platforms built of mud and plant material. The female lays a single, large egg, and both partners share the long incubation period (50 to 85 days). The time from hatching to fledging varies between species, but can be exceptionally long—up to 300 days in the largest species. As a consequence, some species can only breed every other year.

BREEDING RANGE

Albatross diversity is greatest in the southern oceans, particularly on the sub-Antarctic islands between the latitudes of 40° S and 55° S—the so-called Roaring Forties and Furious Fifties. Only three species breed in the North Pacific: the Laysan Albatross (Leeward Islands of Hawaii, Midway, and Laysan; a few on islands west of Mexico); the Black-footed Albatross (Leeward Islands of Hawaii; a few on islands south of Japan); and the Short-tailed Albatross (Torishima, a volcanic island south of Japan).

OTHER SPECIES FIELD NOTES

■ **Shy Albatross**
Thalassarche cauta
L 37" W 87-101"
Bill yellowish gray with yellow tip

■ **Black-footed Albatross**
Phoebastria nigripes
L 32" W 80"
Mostly dark in all plumages

■ **Yellow-nosed Albatross**
Thalassarche chlororhynchos
L 32" W 80"
Blackish bill with yellow ridge and red tip

■ **Black-browed Albatross**
Thalassarche melanophris
L 35" W 88"
Bill bright orange with reddish tip

MIGRATION AND WINTER RANGE

The three Northern Hemisphere albatrosses range widely across the North Pacific—actual migration routes are not well known. After leaving their breeding islands (June to July), all three species tend to disperse to the north, as far as the Gulf of Alaska and the Bering Sea. Black-footed and Laysan Albatrosses occur along the West Coast, most abundantly north from Monterey Bay, California. Laysans favor deeper water and are much scarcer. The Short-tailed Albatross is a rare bird, with an estimated world population of 1,400 birds—but the population is growing, and West Coast records have been increasing. Wandering Albatross has occurred once in North America (photographed standing on a coastal promontory in Sonoma County, California). Shy Albatross has been seen less than ten times off the West Coast, although most records have been within the last five years. Light-mantled Albatross has been seen once off California, but its origin has been questioned. In the Atlantic Ocean, two Southern Hemisphere albatrosses have occurred in North American waters—Black-browed (about 20 records) and Yellow-nosed Albatross (about 30 records).

OBSERVING ALBATROSSES

With rare exceptions, to see an albatross you must go to sea, preferably on an organized pelagic trip to areas of known occurrence. This means trying for Black-footed or Laysan Albatrosses along the West Coast, from central California to Alaska. Check the Internet for upcoming boat trips and past trip reports. Seeing an albatross, other than Black-footed or Laysan, depends mostly on luck, although the more time you spend offshore the better your chances are. The same holds true for encountering any albatrosses off the East Coast.

STATUS AND CONSERVATION

Albatross populations have fluctuated over the last 200 years, primarily due to human exploitation. Millions of North Pacific albatrosses were slaughtered on their breeding islands for the Japanese feather trade in the late 1800s and early 1900s. The Short-tailed Albatross was nearly harvested to extinction. It survived as a species only because an unknown number of immature birds were safely at sea when the last adults on Torishima were killed in the late 1930s.

See also

Magnificent Frigatebird, page 52

Sooty Shearwater: *Puffinus griseus*, L 18" W 40", dark overall with whitish underwing coverts

PETRELS AND SHEARWATERS

Common in the Atlantic and especially abundant in the Pacific Ocean, the Sooty Shearwater (above) glides closely over the surface propelled by fast, intermittent wingbeats. Identified by its overall dark or sooty plumage and whitish wing linings, especially the primary underwing coverts, this true seabird is often seen from shore in spring and summer along our West Coast. At

Range of Sooty Shearwater

sea, the Sooty gathers in large flocks of hundreds, even thousands of birds, and either plunge dives or dives from the surface and propels itself underwater with its wings in pursuit of small fish and squid. Attracted to long-line trawlers, it is vulnerable to being hooked and drowned as it attempts to snatch the bait from the rapidly descending fishing line. It breeds from September to May in burrows, some up to ten feet long, or rock crevices on the sea islands of southern South America, New Zealand, and Australia. The young are fed by both parents, mainly at night, for about three months, then abandoned. Hunger drives the chick to leave the nest and fly off into the night in search of food and to begin its life at sea.

CLASSIFICATION

The petrels and shearwaters—family Procellariidae—are a varied group of tubenose seabirds occurring in all the oceans of the world. They are particularly well represented in the Southern Hemisphere, where they probably originated about 50 million years ago. Traditional taxonomy splits the family into 71 species and 12 genera. Four natural groupings are: fulmar petrels—seven species, one in North America; gadfly petrels—34 species, 10 in North America; shearwaters—23 species, 13 in North America; and prions—seven species, none in North America. Subspecies variation is most pronounced in the shearwaters, and ornithologists continue to debate whether or not some subspecies merit full species status.

STRUCTURE

The petrels and shearwaters are marine birds highly adapted to a pelagic lifestyle. Males and females are virtually identical, although males are larger in most species. They have a compact build, long narrow wings, and their powers of flight are highly developed. In high winds, most species are capable of dynamic soaring (see Albatrosses pp. 40-41), rocketing across the ocean in typical, roller coaster style. This towering flight becomes more exaggerated as wind speed increases. In light winds, normal flight requires frequent intervals of flapping, interspersed with stiff-winged glides.

All petrels and shearwaters have hooked bills made up of horny plates. Bills vary—short and stout in fulmars and petrels, and relatively long and slender in the shearwaters. In all members of this family, the two tubed nostrils are joined at the top of the bill. These tubed nostrils and large olfactory bulbs in the brain contribute to a developed sense of smell (unusual in birds)—a useful adaptation to locating food on a featureless ocean or a nesting burrow in the dark of night.

The tubenoses are able to drink seawater. They have evolved specialized salt glands located in the forehead that filter excess salt from the blood. This excess salt is excreted as a concentrated liquid that either drips from the bill or is forcibly sprayed from the nostrils.

The feet are webbed and used for swimming and diving; they also assist in running takeoffs during periods of light wind. On land, most shearwaters and petrels are incapable of normal walking because their legs are set so far back on the body.

PLUMAGE

Plumage coloration is a combination of monochromatic colors—whites, blacks, and grays ranging from bluish to brownish. Some species are entirely dark or pale, but the great majority is countershaded—dark above and pale below. Countershading renders a bird less visible to prey (looking up) and predators (looking down). Many petrels and a few shearwaters exhibit a prominent, dark M-pattern on the upperparts, extending from wing tip to wing tip. Since darker feathers are more resistant to wear, this pattern might have evolved to protect the most exposed coverts and the important flight feathers. Juvenile birds can sometimes be distinguished from adults by their uniformly fresh plumage, which often features crisply outlined, contrasting feather edges. The feathers of all tubenoses exhibit a strong musty smell that lingers even on long-dead museum specimens.

The plumage of some species is polymorphic—that is, it varies between individuals of the *same* species. Color morphs of the same species can look completely different from each other, although the birds are structurally identical. Northern Fulmars come in a bewildering array of plumage with many intermediate birds that are difficult to characterize. Other polymorphic species show a more consistent variation and fall neatly into categories such as light, dark, or intermediate. The percentage of birds of a particular morph can vary between different populations, and some morphs are

Greater Shearwater

very rare. Different color morphs can and do interbreed—their offspring are not necessarily intermediate morphs.

FEEDING BEHAVIOR

Petrels and shearwaters feed on a variety of marine prey. Important food items include squid, fish, pelagic crustaceans, floating carrion, and ship refuse. Many species feed at night, when some prey animals move closer to the ocean surface.

Feeding techniques vary—food may be picked from the surface or pursued underwater in shallow dives. Some species execute short, aerial plunge dives, while others dive from the surface using their webbed feet and partially opened wings for propulsion. Feeding flocks may form to exploit temporarily abundant food sources, such as schooling baitfish. Flocking activity often attracts more distant seabirds, and the resulting aggregations may contain a variety of species—offering excellent birding possibilities. For this reason, many pelagic birding trips try to maintain a flock of birds (even gulls) in the wake of the boat by chumming continuously.

OTHER SPECIES FIELD NOTES

Northern Fulmar
Fulmarus glacialis
L 19" W 42"
Flash on inner primaries

Black-capped Petrel
Pterodroma hasitata
L 16" W 37"
Dark cap, white collar, white uppertail coverts

Fea's Petrel
Pterodroma feae
L 14" W 34"
Brownish gray above with dark M-pattern

Bermuda Petrel E
Pterodroma cahow
L 15" W 35"
Black cap, dark gray neck

Herald Petrel
Pterodroma arminjoniana
L 15.5" W 37.5"
White flash on underwing

Hawaiian Petrel (Endangered)
Pterodroma sandwichensis
L 17" W 39"
Mostly black crown, partial collar, white forehead

Murphy's Petrel
Pterodroma ultima
L 16" W 38"
White chin around bill

Mottled Petrel
Pterodroma inexpectata
L 14" W 32"
Dark belly patch, black bar on white underwings

Cook's Petrel
Pterodroma cookii
L 10" W 26"
Dark M on upperwings

Stejneger's Petrel
Pterodroma longirostris
L 10" W 26"
Dark half hood, white forehead

Buller's Shearwater
Puffinus bulleri
L 16" W 40"
Dark M-pattern on upperwings

Streaked Shearwater
Calonectris leucomelas
L 19" W 48"
Pale fringes give upperparts a scaly look

Pink-footed Shearwater
Puffinus creatopus
L 19" W 43"
Pink bill and feet

Black-vented Shearwater
Puffinus opisthomelas
L 14" W 34"
Brown above, white below, dark undertail coverts

Wedge-tailed Shearwater
Puffinus pacificus
L 18" W 40"
Long, pointed tail

Flesh-footed Shearwater
Puffinus carneipes
L 17" W 41"
Pink bill and feet

Bulwer's Petrel
Bulweria bulwerii
L 10" W 26"
Small size, sooty brown overall, long tail

Short-tailed Shearwater
Puffinus tenuirostris
L 17" W 39"
Pale underwing panels

Cory's Shearwater
Calonectris diomedea
L 18" W 46"
Dark above merges to white below, yellowish bill

Greater Shearwater
Puffinus gravis
L 18" W 44"
Brown cap, white cheeks, U-shape band on rump

Manx Shearwater
Puffinus puffinus
L 13.5" W33"
Black above, white below, white undertail coverts

Little Shearwater
Puffinus assimilis
L 11" W 25"
Small size, dark wings with pale bar

Audubon's Shearwater
Puffinus lherminieri
L 12" W 27"
Dark brown above, white below, dark undertail coverts

VOCALIZATION

Petrels and shearwaters are quiet at sea, although they make a variety of croaks and grunts during squabbles over food. On their breeding grounds, most species have a rich repertoire of calls—wails, howls, cackles, screams, moans, cries, and coos. These weirdly beautiful sounds are heard at night, especially during the first hours after dark and before first light.

BREEDING BEHAVIOR

Petrels and shearwaters are monogamous and mate for life. If a partner dies or fails to return, a new partnership is formed. Most species have a long period of immaturity, and the age of first breeding varies from three to 12 years.

Most tubenoses are gregarious birds and colonial nesters. Many dig burrows for their nests, others nest in rock piles, and a few nest directly on the ground or on cliff ledges. The same pair often uses the identical nest site year after year. Since they are vulnerable to aerial predators (particularly skuas, gulls, and raptors) at their nest sites, most species will only enter them or leave them at night.

After courtship and nestbuilding, they copulate, which is followed by a period of foraging at sea—the "honeymoon" exodus—during which the single, large egg develops in the female. Both sexes must feed heavily to gain the necessary body mass needed for them to survive the long periods of fasting that accompany incubation and brooding.

After the chick hatches and no longer requires brooding, both parents will leave to feed. Chick development is slow, and unfledged birds may be at the nest site for months. The adults convert prey into a concentrated, oily liquid stored in the stomach, which they later regurgitate directly into the fledgling's mouth. As they grow, young tubenoses develop deposits of fat that serve to tide them over those times when the parents are away or food becomes scarce. A well fed, unfledged chick can weigh substantially more than an adult bird.

BREEDING RANGE

Petrels and shearwaters favor remote, oceanic islands for breeding. Species diversity is greatest in the southern oceans, and the majority of the world's species nest there. Only two species—Northern Fulmar and Manx Shearwater—have bred in North America. The Northern Fulmar is a widespread species with large colonies in the North Pacific and North Atlantic. The Manx Shearwater is a rare breeder in North America—most breed on islands off Scotland, Ireland, and Wales.

Pink-footed Shearwater

The first North American nest was found in 1973 on Penikese Island, Massachusetts, a single nesting attempt that has not reoccurred. In 1977, a small colony was discovered on Middle Lawn Island off Newfoundland—the only known colony in North America. A handful of other petrels and shearwaters breed in the Northern Hemisphere, but not in North America. The Bermuda Petrel, which visits the Gulf Stream off Cape Hatteras, is recovering from near extinction (see sidebar opposite).

In the Southern Hemisphere, petrels and shearwaters have colonized many remote islands. Some species are common migrants to North American waters, but have restricted breeding ranges. For example, although Greater Shearwaters are common summer visitors to the North Atlantic, nearly the entire world population (10 to 15 million birds) breeds on two tiny islets in the Tristan da Cunha group and on Gough Island, in the southern Atlantic.

MIGRATION

Many petrels and shearwaters undertake immense migrations after the breeding season, traveling thousands of miles as they follow traditional sea routes. Migrations have evolved for numerous reasons: Seasonal changes may make a particular breeding location inhospitable, abundant colonial species may need to disperse so as not to overburden the prey base, or food may be only seasonal.

Although some species seem to disperse randomly from their breeding locales, most species migrate along routes that take them to specific places at specific times of year. These routes and timings may vary among different populations of the same species.

A number of common species that breed on islands off Australia and New Zealand (Sooty and Short-tailed Shearwaters) make enormous figure-eight migrations that take them well into the North Pacific and close to North America. The majority of their journey (the upper loop of the figure eight) is a clockwise circumnavigation of the Central and North Pacific, taking advantage of the prevailing winds. North-bound birds enter Asian waters, pass through waters off Japan, continue north, and then east into the rich waters of the Bering Sea and the Gulf of Alaska (where they linger), and eventually turn south into waters off the western United States. The lower loop of the figure-eight pattern is much smaller (see migration maps pp. 48-49). These extremely long migrations are impressive feats of navigation and timing that bring the birds back to their remote breeding islands, ready for the next breeding season.

Astronomical, magnetic, and olfactory cues are important components of a successful migration. Lost birds can even reorient themselves. In a famous experiment, a nesting Manx Shearwater from the Skokholm Islands off Wales was transported to Boston by airplane. After its release, it returned home—3,200 miles across the Atlantic—in a little over 12 days.

WINTER RANGE

For long-distance migrants, much of the winter season may be spent in migration, with stops of varying length at favorable feeding locations. Shorter distance migrants travel to discrete wintering locations for several months. A few species, especially tropical ones, simply disperse short distances from their breeding islands.

Traditional winter grounds are in areas that support an abundance of prey species—regions of oceanic upwelling, fish spawning grounds, and current interfaces. Because of the reversal of seasons in the Southern Hemisphere, post-breeding migrants from that part of the world winter in North American waters during our summer. This includes such common species as Sooty and Greater Shearwaters.

OBSERVING PETRELS AND SHEARWATERS

With few exceptions, you must go to sea to observe these species. Some species can occasionally be seen from headlands with a good telescope and onshore winds. Along the West Coast, large flocks of migrating Sooty Shearwaters pass close to shore. On rare occasions, tubenoses are driven onshore by hurricanes and end up on inland bodies of water—an exciting event that is sure to be reported on local birding hotlines.

Identification at sea can be challenging. On distant birds, concentrate on plumage patterns—the distribution of dark and light feathers—and flight style. On closer birds, bill structure and color can be good identification clues. Feather wear and the quality of the light can greatly affect the perception of the color and tone of a bird's plumage. Worn plumage and strong sunlight can add a warm brown cast to the plumage. The same bird in fresh plumage or when seen in overcast conditions, can appear much grayer. A bright background can make a bird appear distinctly darker, than when seen against dark seas or clouds.

The amount of flapping and the quickness of the wingbeats vary from species to species and can be helpful in making identifications. Pink-footed and Black-vented Shearwaters have similar plumage patterns, and their size differences may be obscured by distance, but they have utterly different flight styles. The heavier Pink-foot's flight style is lumbering, whereas the Black-vented's is flickering, with shorter intervals of flapping and gliding. This difference is discernable at great distances, although in high winds it is less apparent.

BERMUDA PETREL

For almost 300 years no one had seen a living Bermuda Petrel (*Pterodroma cahow*). Early 17th-century settlers described the birds as "fabulously abundant," but the petrels quickly succumbed to hunting and the depredations of introduced pigs and rats. In 1906 a live *cahow* was captured, and over the next few decades two more specimens were obtained.

In 1951 Robert Cushman Murphy, Louis Mowbray, and 16-year-old David Wingate discovered an active nest on a Bermuda islet. That year, 17 nesting pairs were located. The young Wingate went on to study ornithology and, as Bermuda's Chief Conservation Officer, made saving the *cahow* his life's work. The petrels have slowly increased—surveys found 63 breeding pairs and 32 fledglings in 2001. Today North American birders may experience rare sightings of Bermuda Petrels in Gulf Stream waters off North Carolina.

STATUS AND CONSERVATION

Petrels and shearwaters include some of the most populous bird species and some of the most endangered. Traditionally these species have been most vulnerable when breeding. On the breeding islands, introduced predators (especially rats, feral pigs, and cats), human harvesting (for food, feathers, and other byproducts), and loss of habitat have decimated some species. Seabird deaths from fishing by long-lining and gill nets number in the millions annually. Changes in equipment and technique could lessen this problem, but the fishing industry has been slow to make them.

See also

Tropicbirds, page 54
Gannets, Boobies, page 56
Skuas, Jaegers, page 164

Wilson's Storm-Petrel: *Oceanites oceanicus*, L 7.25", W 16", bold, white U-shape rump, long legs

STORM-PETRELS

Probably the most common seabird off the U.S. Atlantic coast, the Wilson's Storm-Petrel (above) is distinguished by its bold white, U-shape rump band that extends onto its undertail coverts, conspicuous even on a sitting bird. Wings are short and rounded, and its long legs trail behind the tip of its tail in flight. The Wilson's feeds by skimming with fluttery wingbeats while pattering the surface with its yellow webbed feet, picking food items with its bill. It feeds on small fish, shrimp, and squids, and will readily scavenge offal and carrion. It breeds November to May in burrows or crevices on islands in the Antarctic region of South America, then moves north into the Atlantic and Indian Oceans during spring and summer. Its population, though large and stable, is vulnerable to any degradation of its ocean wilderness environment. Contrary to its small size and delicate aspect, it is a tough little seabird that flourishes in the hard world of the open ocean, flying through raging storms by finding shelter in the troughs between huge waves.

Range of Wilson's Storm-Petrel

CLASSIFICATION

The storm-petrels (family Hydrobatidae) form a distinct taxonomic group of small tubenose seabirds that occur in all the oceans of the world. Taxonomy splits the family into 20 species in seven genera. Two natural groupings have been described. (1) Subfamily Oceanitinae—Southern Hemisphere breeders of a diverse group of nine species in five genera. These species have long legs, square-tipped tails, and shorter, rounded wings; represented in North America by Wilson's and White-faced Storm-Petrels. (2) Subfamily Hydrobatinae—Northern Hemisphere breeders that form a closely related group of 11 species in two genera. These species have shorter legs, forked tails, and longer, more pointed wings; represented in North America by eight species.

STRUCTURE

Storm-petrels are small marine birds. Males and females are indistinguishable. Compared to the petrels and shearwaters, their wings are shorter and broader, adapting them for a more powered flight. The larger surface area of their wings accounts for their buoyant flight, and they do not rely on strong winds for lift. All species tend to fly close to the water.

Southern Hemisphere species have shorter wings that are adapted to the windier conditions there. They often dangle their long legs and patter their feet on the surface, sometimes pushing off wave crests or dragging their feet as they are held aloft by an oncoming wind. Northern Hemisphere species exhibit a more active, erratic flight style with more flapping and hovering. Their long, forked tails add to their maneuverability. As in the other tubenoses, storm-petrels have hooked bills made up of horny plates. The two, tubed nostrils are joined at the top of the bill and contribute to their developed sense of smell. Their long legs and webbed feet are weakly built, not suitable for normal walking.

PLUMAGE

Plumage coloration is a combination of whites, blacks, and grays ranging from bluish to brownish. Most North American species are dark bodied (except Fork-tailed and White-faced) with a pale carpal bar of variable intensity on the upper wing. The rump—the upper tail coverts—varies in color from uniformly blackish, to gray, and white. The distribution of the white in the "white-rumped" species—Wilson's, European, Leach's, Band-rumped, and Wedge-rumped—are important identification clues. Leach's Storm-Petrel is unique in that the rump color of Pacific birds varies from light to dark. Birds seen off California can be either type.

FEEDING BEHAVIOR

Storm-petrels feed mainly on planktonic crustaceans, squid, and small fish. Prey is captured on the wing while the bird hovers and snatches the prey with its hooked bill. Foraging flight varies between species and reflects differences in wing and leg lengths: Northern Hemisphere Leach's hovers with deep wingbeats, while Southern Hemisphere Wilson's frequently foot-patters on the surface and hovers with wings held in a V. Experts think that the foot-pattering may attract prey or scare it, making it more visible. Storm-petrels

Fork-tailed Storm-Petrel

are fond of fatty substances. Pelagic boat operators sometimes try to lure them with a slick of fish oil. Many species feed actively at night, so it is not unusual to see flocks roosting on the water during daylight hours.

VOCALIZATIONS

Storm-petrels are generally silent at sea. At breeding colonies at night they make a variety of squeaks, peeps, moans, purrs, and harsh grating notes.

BREEDING BEHAVIOR

Storm-petrels are monogamous breeders, but it is unknown whether they maintain life-long pair bonds. Most species have a relatively long immaturity and do not attempt breeding before age four or five.

They are underground nesters in self-dug burrows or rocky crevices. Most species nest colonially, sometimes in dense colonies, visiting only at night to reduce the risk of predation. Courtship includes pursuit flights accompanied by frequent vocalizing—all in total darkness. The white rump of some species may help the birds to see one another. Large colonies seethe with nocturnal activity, only to look deserted by day, when birds are underground or at sea. After copulation, the female goes to sea to feed. Both sexes share incubation, averaging several days in turn, until the egg hatches some 40 to 60 days later. Young birds fledge at seven to eleven weeks.

BREEDING RANGE

Storm-petrels favor offshore islands for nesting and nearshore stacks and promontories if they offer some protection from predators. Four species breed in North America: Fork-tailed Storm-Petrels breed along remote coasts and on islands in the North Pacific, particularly the Aleutian Islands; Leach's Storm-Petrels breed on islands in both the Pacific and Atlantic Oceans, and "dark-rumped" Leach's nest on islands off Baja California; Ashy Storm-Petrels' small world population—about 5,200 birds—is restricted to California; Black Storm-Petrels nest on islands off both coasts of Baja California, with a small colony near Santa Barbara Island, California.

MIGRATION AND WINTER RANGE

Most storm-petrels undertake regular, post-breeding migrations. Some species (Ashy and Fork-tailed Storm-Petrels), disperse into nearby waters or move farther offshore. Other species undertake longer migrations south. Black and Least Storm-Petrels migrate to Pacific waters off Central and South America. The incredible migration of the diminutive Wilson's Storm-Petrel takes it from its sub-Antarctic breeding islands to the North Atlantic. It can be abundant at the Grand Banks during the North American summer.

OBSERVING STORM-PETRELS

When identifying storm-petrels, concentrate on rump pattern (especially distribution of any white feathering), leg length, tail shape (forked or square cut), relative size, and flight style.

STATUS AND CONSERVATION

None of the species that breed in North America is endangered.

OTHER SPECIES FIELD NOTES

■ **Band-rumped Storm-Petrel**
Oceanodroma castro
L 9" W 17"
Square to slightly notched tail with white rump band

■ **Leach's Storm-Petrel**
Oceanodroma leucorhoa
L 8" W 18"
Notched tail with divided white rump band

■ **White-faced Storm-Petrel**
Pelagodroma marina
L 7.5" W 17"
White underparts, wing linings and face, long legs

■ **Black Storm-Petrel**
Oceanodroma melania
L 9" W 19"
Blackish brown overall, forked tail, deep wingbeats

■ **Ashy Storm-Petrel**
Oceanodroma homochroa
L 8" W 17"
Gray-brown overall, pale mottling on underwing coverts

■ **Least Storm-Petrel**
Oceanodroma microsoma
L 5.75" W 15"
Tiny size, blackish brown overall, short tail

■ **Fork-tailed Storm-Petrel**
Oceanodroma furcata
L 8.5" W 18"
Blue-gray above, pearl gray below

■ **Wedge-rumped Storm-Petrel**
Oceanodroma tethys
L 6.5" W 13.25"
Bold, white triangular patch on tail

See also

Phalaropes, page 158

SHEARWATERS AND PETRELS

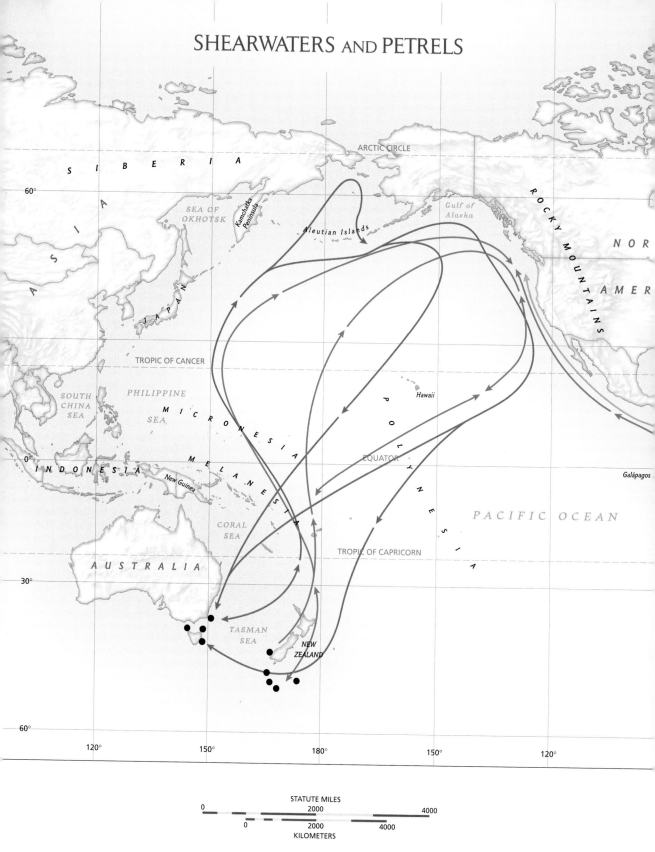

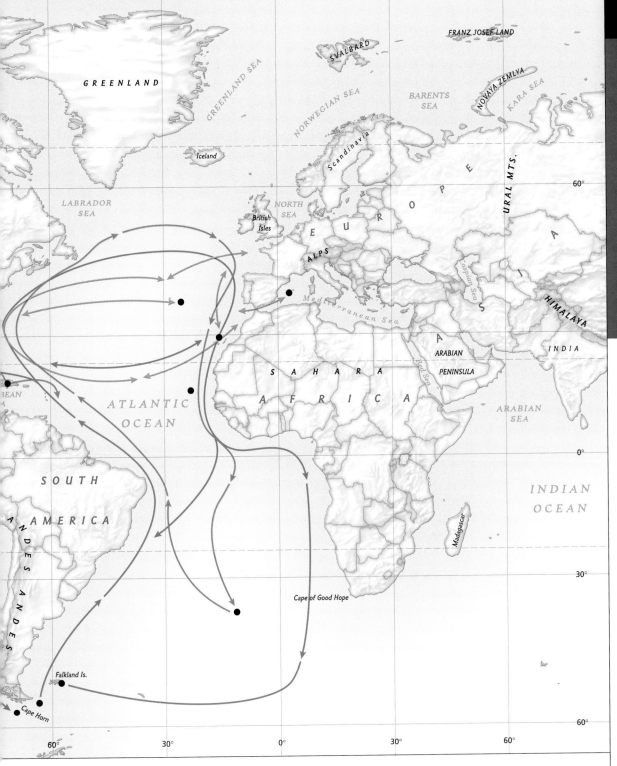

GREENLAND

GREENLAND SEA

SVALBARD

FRANZ JOSEF LAND

NOVAYA ZEMLYA

KARA SEA

BARENTS SEA

NORWEGIAN SEA

Iceland

LABRADOR SEA

NORTH SEA

British Isles

SCANDINAVIA

E U R O P E

URAL MTS.

60°

A S I A

ALPS

Caspian Sea

HIMALAYA

Mediterranean Sea

SAHARA

AFRICA

Red Sea

ARABIAN PENINSULA

INDIA

ARABIAN SEA

ATLANTIC OCEAN

0°

SOUTH

AMERICA

A N D E S

INDIAN OCEAN

Madagascar

30°

Cape of Good Hope

Falkland Is.

Cape Horn

60°

60°   30°   0°   30°   60°

MIGRATION OF SELECTED SHEARWATERS AND PETRELS

Greater Shearwater	Sooty Shearwater	● Nesting area
Cory's Shearwater	Pink-footed Shearwater	
Short-tailed Shearwater	Black-capped Petrel	

FRIGATEBIRDS, TROPICBIRDS, BOOBIES

Jonathan Alderfer

The favored haunts of tropicbirds, boobies, and frigatebirds are warm waters and subtropical coastlines. Only the Northern Gannet, one of the boobies, inhabits more northerly ocean climes. These three families—along with the three families in the next chapter (pelicans, cormorants, and darters)—make up the ancient order of fish-eating waterbirds, known as the Pelecaniformes. The fossil record of the Pelecaniformes goes back 50 million years.

The tropicbirds (family Phaethontidae) are particularly charismatic seabirds with long central tail streamers, colorful bills, and mostly white plumage. At a distance tropicbirds somewhat resemble large terns, but are easily recognizable close-up. They are high-energy fliers with deep, rowing wingbeats, with a knack for appearing—somewhat magically—directly overhead. When at rest on the water, they float buoyantly with their tail streamers cocked up at a jaunty angle. Look for these special birds on pelagic boat trips exploring waters off southern California or in the Gulf Stream. They are visitors to North America, breeding farther to the south. All three species of tropicbird have been recorded in North America, but the Red-tailed is extremely rare.

Four species of booby and one gannet (family *Sulidae*) have occurred in North American waters, although only two species—Masked Booby and Northern Gannet—are known to breed here. The name booby (derived from the Spanish *bobo*, for "fool") refers to their lack of fear of humans and the ease with which early sailors caught them. They are all superb fishers capable of turning their bodies into missiles to be sent plunge diving into the sea in pursuit of prey. All sulids have large, fully webbed feet, which in some species are brightly colored and serve as important visual elements during courtship, such as the aptly named Red-footed and Blue-footed Boobies.

Frigatebirds (family Fregatidae) are the greatest aerialists of the bird world. With the lowest ratio of body weight to wing area of all birds, they can soar effortlessly, high above the ocean—appearing to hang motionless for hours on end—buoyed by the slightest winds. When actively feeding, their long, forked tails allow them great maneuverability. Their favorite food is flying fish, which they snatch from the surface with their long, hooked bills—never getting wet in the process. Frigatebirds shun contact with the water because their plumage is not waterproof, and their tiny feet are only partially webbed. They are also well known for stealing food from other seabirds, notably boobies and terns. This is accomplished by an acrobatic aerial pursuit that may include the frigatebird biting and tugging at the victim's plumage. Few of these targeted birds escape without dropping or regurgitating some morsel, which is caught in mid-air by the masterful frigatebird.

Of the world's five species of frigatebirds, only the Magnificent visits North America on a regular basis, and breeds in southern Florida on the Dry Tortugas. Caribbean breeders wander to the Gulf Coast states, and birds breeding on Mexico's west coast are casual along the southern California coast and the Salton Sea. The Great and Lesser Frigatebirds that have reached North America are extreme rarities.

(Left) Brown Booby

Magnificent Frigatebird: *Fregata magnificens*, L 40",
W 90", long, forked tail, long wings

FRIGATEBIRDS

Of the family Frigatidae, the Magnificent Frigatebird
(above) is unmistakable when seen soaring over the Florida
and Gulf coasts with its deeply forked tail and long, pointed wings. The only seabird family that displays sexual
dimorphism, the female is about 20 percent heavier than
the male and has a bright white chest patch. The all-black

Range of Magnificent Frigatebird

male sports an orange gular
sac that turns bright red and
is inflated to balloon-size
during the mating season.
Their feathers do not repel
water, so they must feed by
deftly picking fish and squid
from the surface. They never
swim, and their legs are so
short they are poor walkers,
but they are magnificent flyers, capable of soaring on
the lightest breeze for hours, and agile enough to force
other birds to disgorge food, which the frigatebird often
catches in midair. The female constructs a twig nest and lays
a single egg. At about three months the male abandons the
family and often goes off to breed with another female,
while the mother continues to care for the young bird for up
to a full year. Unique among seabirds, the males breed
annually, and the females breed in alternate years.

CLASSIFICATION

The frigatebirds (family Fregatidae) are a family of five
species of marine birds with a pantropical distribution.
Of the three species that occur in North America, only
the Magnificent Frigatebird is regularly observed; the
other two are extremely rare. All frigatebird species are
closely related and placed in a single genus. Similarities
in plumage make them hard to identify.

STRUCTURE

Frigatebirds are superbly adapted to an aerial existence.
They have the largest wing surface—relative to body
weight—of all living birds. Their wings are long, and the
bones are hollow and lightweight. The body is relatively
small, as are the legs and feet. The Magnificent
Frigatebird is a very large bird with a seven-foot
wingspan and a five-inch bill, yet weighs only three
pounds. As a result, frigatebirds can soar effortlessly on
light tropical winds. During the day, they often take
advantage of rising air currents or upper-level trade
winds, appearing to hang motionless high in the sky.

Frigatebirds have long, deeply forked tails, giving
them great maneuverability in flight—useful when chasing another bird in an attempt to steal a meal. In direct
flight, the tail may be held closed into a single point, but
it is often spread for added lift while soaring.

Their bills are long, with a prominent hook at the
tip for grasping prey. Beneath the bill, males have a large
area of bare skin—the gular pouch. They hugely inflate
this intensely red pouch, as part of the breeding display;
when deflated it is nearly invisible.

Although they are marine birds, frigatebirds shun
contact with water—never swimming or resting on the
ocean. Their plumage is not waterproof. Their tiny feet
are fully webbed, but the webs are reduced. Barely able
to walk, they perch and nest in trees and bushes.

PLUMAGE

Males and females have different plumages, which is
unusual in seabirds. The predominant color is glossy
black in adult males, with additional areas of white on
the breast and belly in females. Juvenile plumage is
duller and browner above, with extensive white on the
head and underparts. The progression of immature
plumages is complex—subadult males look different
from subadult females and both take three or more years
to reach adult plumage.

A diagonal bar of lighter feathers is often a feature
of the upper wing. This bar—the ulnar (or alar) bar—is
formed by secondary coverts overlaying the ulna bone.

FEEDING BEHAVIOR

Fish and squid are the birds' primary food. They snatch
food from the surface by lowering their head and dip
with the long, hooked bill. Flying fish are an important

component of their diet, and they may catch them airborne as the fish take flight. Frigates readily consume floating refuse from ships and pick up hatchling sea turtles or stranded fish on beaches, occasionally eggs and nestlings from seabird colonies, or even their own.

Their penchant for food piracy is well known, but that is not a major source of food. A former name is Man-o'-War Bird. They pursue boobies, terns, and other seabirds in flight, and may grab them until they drop or regurgitate some morsel. The frigatebird—usually a female—then swoops down and deftly catches the item before it hits the water. These twisting, turning chases are tour de force displays of flying skill—almost always ending in favor of the frigatebird.

VOCALIZATION
Frigatebirds vocalize only when they are at their breeding colonies, making harsh, chattering calls.

BREEDING BEHAVIOR
Frigatebirds are highly gregarious birds, and their breeding colonies may reach several thousand pairs or more. Colonies are usually located on predator-free islands and may be shared with other species, particularly boobies.

Courtship is a ritualized and drawn-out affair. Although frigatebirds are monogamous, they establish new pair bonds each breeding season. The ritual begins with small groups of males gathering in the top of the nesting trees or bushes. The male display begins with the inflation of its crimson-colored gular pouch. Then, with bill pointing skyward and wings spread open and inverted, he displays the pouch to females passing overhead.

Frigatebird

After a female chooses a male, pairing ceremonies over the course of a few days cement the relationship. Following copulation, the male forages for nesting material, which he presents to the female for nest construction. She lays a single egg, and both parents share in its incubation. The chick hatches 40 to 55 days later.

Chicks grow slowly, and fledging takes place about five to seven months after hatching. By this time the male may have deserted the colony, but the female continues caring for the dependent and full-grown juvenile. This period of post-fledgling care is the longest of any seabird, and may continue for up to 18 months. During this time juveniles make short forays in the vicinity of the colony, but are dependent on the parent for food. Therefore, females can only breed every other year. Even with such extended care, juvenile mortality is high, averaging 75 percent. Only 5 percent of all chicks reach breeding age.

BREEDING RANGE
The five frigatebird species occupy tropical seas around the globe, but they do not overlap extensively. Only the Magnificent Frigatebird nests in North America. Approximately 200 pairs breed in South Florida on the Dry Tortugas. An estimated 8,000 pairs breed throughout the Caribbean and off western Mexico.

MIGRATION AND WINTER RANGE
Many frigatebirds stay within their breeding range. Others, particularly juveniles and post-breeding males, disperse over vast ocean areas. On the East Coast, a few birds may follow the Gulf Stream to North Carolina. On the West Coast, small numbers visit California.

The Great Frigatebird has occurred twice off central California, where more records might be expected. An unprecedented specimen was recorded in Oklahoma. The single record of Lesser Frigatebird is of a bird photographed at Deer Isle, Maine—the nearest breeding colony is off the coast of Brazil.

OBSERVING FRIGATEBIRDS
Magnificent Frigatebirds are not difficult to observe along the Florida coast or in the northern Gulf of Mexico—peak numbers occur in the summer months. Working out the sex and age of birds is challenging. Because it is so complicated, the standard field guides give just the basics—see an article by Steve Howell in the December 1994 issue of *Birding* magazine for details.

Out-of-range and, especially, out-of-season frigatebirds should always be well documented—there is the remote chance of a species other than the Magnificent. Take careful notes on the distribution of any pale or white plumage and bare parts colors, if they are visible.

STATUS AND CONSERVATION
In the Caribbean, numerous Magnificent Frigatebird colonies have been lost in recent times, and the population continues to decrease. Threats to colonies come from tourist disturbance, coastal development, hunting, and introduced predators. The expanded protection of Caribbean colonies is an important conservation goal. Large, but not well-protected, colonies of Magnificents still exist off western Mexico. Low reproduction success and a lengthy period of immaturity make recovery of degraded colonies tenuous.

See also

White-tailed Tropicbird: *Phaethon lepturus*, L 30", W 37", orange bill, black stripe on upper wings

TROPICBIRDS

The smallest and most common of the family Phaethontidae is the White-tailed Tropicbird (above), a rare and beautiful species. Fortunate are the few who see it as it suddenly appears from the ether like a spirit. With some luck it is possible to encounter this elegant flyer on the Dry Tortugas and in the Gulf Stream off the coast of North Carolina, especially in the summer. This stunning species has the distinctive, long streaming, white central tail feathers; the plumage is all white, sometimes lightly tinged with pink. The White-tailed Tropicbird has an orange bill, a black eye-patch, and diagnostic diagonal black bars on the upper wings. As a true sea bird, it spends most of its time far offshore, preferring warmer tropical waters where it feeds by plunge diving mainly for flying fish and squid. The White-tailed Tropicbirds we see in the Atlantic and Gulf of Mexico breed in Bermuda, throughout the Bahamas, and the Greater and Lesser Antilles, nesting in crevices away from predators. They raise one young per season, then leave the nesting grounds to disperse throughout the pantropic marine environment, returning again to a solitary life at sea.

Range of White-tailed Tropicbird

CLASSIFICATION

The tropicbirds (family Phaethontidae) compose a small and highly distinctive family of marine birds. Tropicbirds differ from the other Pelecaniformes in a number of features: They lack a gular pouch, they have external nostril slits and small legs and feet, and the young hatch with down—enough to warrant their own suborder. Three, closely related species—Red-billed, Red-tailed, and White-tailed—make up the entire family. All have been recorded in North American waters.

STRUCTURE

Tropicbirds are medium-size seabirds—similar to a small gull. All adults have elongated tail streamers, which effectively double their length, and have earned them the nickname Longtail. The tail streamers, composed of the two central tail feathers, are narrow and flexible. They play an important visual role in courtship flights—and also enthrall birders.

Tropicbirds have stout, sharply pointed bills with lightly serrated cutting edges. Bill color varies from red to orange and yellow in the various species and age groups; juvenile bills are duller or grayer. All tropicbirds have disproportionately small legs and feet. The resultant lowering of body mass may be an evolutionary adaptation that favors their ability to hover. In fact, tropicbirds are approaching "walklessness"—highly unusual in birds. Though all four toes are webbed (totipalmate), tropicbirds are rather poor swimmers.

The wings are relatively long and slender, similar to a tern, but tropicbird flight is much more direct and energetic, with rapid, powerful wingbeats—recalling a falcon. Tropicbirds are capable of hovering, often doing so during courtship, nest prospecting, and before plunge diving. The front of the body is protected by air sacs that cushion the impact of plunge diving.

PLUMAGE

Tropicbird plumage is primarily white with limited black patterning that varies between different species and age groups. Juveniles are more heavily marked and lack the elongated tail streamers—these develop over the first two years of life. The white body plumage has a satiny patina, sometimes exhibiting a rosy tint, thought to derive from the oil produced for waterproofing the plumage.

The tail streamers vary between the three species: White-tailed—white (sometimes pink or apricot), relatively long, and wide; Red-billed—white and thin; and Red-tailed—red, thin and spiky, and difficult to see against a background of blue sky or water.

FEEDING BEHAVIOR

Tropicbirds feed on squid, flying fish, and other marine organisms captured by plunge diving. When they spot prey, they briefly hover before the dive. The birds may submerge completely, but do not pursue prey underwater for more than a short distance. Foraging flight is generally 40 to 100 feet above the water, but solitary tropicbirds are often seen flying much higher. This behavior may allow them to see distant schooling fish or other seabird activity worth investigating.

VOCALIZATION

At sea, tropicbirds are usually silent. Around the breeding islands and especially during courtship flights, tropicbirds make a variety of shrill cries or whistles.

BREEDING BEHAVIOR

Tropicbirds breed on islands, atolls, and near shore cliffs. In prime habitat they are gregarious and form moderate-size colonies; at other locations they are solitary nesters. White-tailed and Red-billed Tropicbirds prefer to nest in burrows or hidden in rocky crevices. Red-taileds nest on the surface, in areas with some overhanging vegetation. They may clear a simple scrape of debris, but construct no nest.

Aerial courtship is a highly evolved behavior in tropicbirds. All three species engage in elaborate, synchronized flights, accompanied by loud vocalizing. Tropicbirds are monogamous—pairs stay partnered for years—and birds may live 20 years or more.

Red-billed Tropicbird

The female lays a single egg, and both parents share in the incubation and chick-rearing duties. Chicks hatch in a downy plumage and fledge in 70 to 90 days. When they leave the nest, they are completely independent. After one to three years at sea, they will return close to their birthplace as breeding adults.

BREEDING RANGE

Tropicbirds inhabit tropical and subtropical oceans around the world. They do not breed in North America. In the Atlantic, the closest breeders to North America are White-taileds and Red-billeds nesting on various Carib-

bean islands; White-taileds also nest on Bermuda. In the Pacific, Red-billed Tropicbirds breed off western Mexico and probably account for most California records; the closest Red-tailed and White-tailed Tropicbirds breed in central tropical Pacific locations, such as Hawaii.

MIGRATION AND WINTER RANGE

After breeding, adults become highly pelagic, some wander far from their nesting areas, while others disperse to nearby waters, following reliable food sources.

In the Atlantic, small numbers of White-tailed Tropicbirds visit the islands of the Dry Tortugas, the Gulf of Mexico, and the Gulf Stream, but are rarely seen north of Cape Hatteras. The Red-billed Tropicbirds are scarce in the western Atlantic, and most records come from the Gulf Stream off Cape Hatteras. In the Pacific, tropicbirds rarely occur north of central California. The Red-billeds are the most common. Multiple sightings are recorded in most years. The Red-tailed Tropicbirds are rare (fewer than 20 California records), but they may be more common far offshore. There is only one California record of the White-tailed Tropicbird: In 1964, an adult male was observed as it engaged in courtship flight with remote-controlled model airplanes.

OBSERVING TROPICBIRDS

To see tropicbirds in North America you must get on a boat. A distant bird can resemble a large tern. Sometimes an inquisitive bird will appear—seemingly out of nowhere—directly above the boat. Tropicbirds regularly sit on the water with their tails held high, so any distant white bird is worth investigating.

If you have sighted a bird, look at the pattern of black on the upper wings. Bill color is unreliable for identification and adults may lack tail streamers due to molt or breakage. Juveniles always lack tail streamers and are more difficult to identify. Concentrate on the barring on the upperparts, in addition to the wing pattern.

STATUS AND CONSERVATION

Although they are rare in North America, tropicbirds are not threatened worldwide. Substantial populations are scattered over a vast ocean area.

OTHER SPECIES FIELD NOTES

■ **Red-billed Tropicbird**
Phaethon aethereus
L 40" W44"
Red bill, black primaries, barring on back and wings

■ **Red-tailed Tropicbird**
Phaethon rubricauda
L 37" W 44"
Red bill, red tail streamer, mostly white plumage

See also

Terns, page 170

Northern Gannet: *Morus bassanus*, L 37" W 72", large size, white plumage with black wingtips, pointed tail

GANNETS AND BOOBIES

With its six-foot wingspan, the Northern Gannet (above) is one of the largest seabirds of the Atlantic. Common offshore, the birds can often be viewed from the beach with the aid of binoculars or a spotting scope during winter migration. The gannets also regularly come near shore when following schools of fish offering astonishing close-up views. These stark white birds with black-tipped wings are famous for their plunge diving. Both beak and tail are sharply pointed, giving the bird a spear-like silhouette, especially with wings folded as it slices into the water from 100 feet or more above the surface. Gannets feed mainly on schooling baitfish such as herring and menhaden and may occasionally feed on squid. About 90 percent of the Northern Gannet population breeds on Bonaventure Island, Quebec.

Range of Northern Gannet

CLASSIFICATION

The boobies and gannets (family Sulidae, often called sulids) form a distinct group of ten species worldwide—five have occurred in North America. Seven species of booby inhabit tropical and subtropical oceans, and three species of gannets live in temperate waters—one in the Northern Hemisphere. Boobies and gannets are so closely related that they are placed in the same genus by most taxonomists. Three booby species—Masked, Red-footed, and Brown—are widespread and have been subdivided into numerous subspecies. Recently, one subspecies of Masked Booby has been elevated to full species status—the Nazca Booby.

STRUCTURE

Being closely related, all boobies and gannets share many structural features. They are medium-to-large seabirds with long, conical bills, cylindrical bodies, and wedge-shape tails. The overall effect is of a spear-shape body, highly evolved for plunge diving after fish. The eyes—pale in many species—face forward, which gives sulids excellent binocular vision for tracking underwater prey. The external nostrils are closed and the front of the body is protected by subcutaneous air sacs that cushion the impact of plunge diving.

Strong legs and large, fully webbed feet make sulids excellent swimmers and allow them to perch on pilings, buoys, and ship rigging. In some species, the feet are prominently colored and play an important role in courtship display. The facial skin and bill may also develop more intense breeding colors.

The wings are long, narrow, and pointed—well adapted for cruising flight under windy conditions—and the long, graduated tail adds maneuverability. Flapping and gliding tend to be interspersed, although the Northern Gannet may utilize dynamic soaring.

PLUMAGE

Plumage colors are subdued, but light and dark patterns are often striking and important for identification. Males and females are similar in plumage details, although females are larger in most species. Most adult sulids are white below—decreasing their visibility to underwater prey—with dark flight feathers. The Red-footed Booby occurs in numerous color morphs, one of which is completely brown. Juvenile and subadult birds are generally darker than adults and may take three to six years to develop full adult plumage.

FEEDING BEHAVIOR

All sulids are obligate plunge divers, feeding chiefly on schooling fish, squid, and flying fish. This method of feeding is utilized by other Pelecaniformes, but reaches its zenith with the sulids. Flocks of birds may gather over large schools of fish, and descend on them like guided missiles from heights of well over a hundred feet. During the descent, the wings are folded back along the body, completing the transformation into a spear-like missile. The water is struck at high speed and birds are capable of reaching prey many feet underwater. Where flying fish occur, Red-footed Boobies are adept at swooping down and snatching them out of the air.

VOCALIZATION

Sulids are quiet at sea, although they may vocalize during food squabbles. During courtship, they are quite vocal. Typically, male boobies produce a thin whistle; females make loud honking or braying sounds.

BREEDING BEHAVIOR

Sulids breed on islands and near shore cliffs. Some species, especially gannets, form large, densely populated colonies. Nests are simple scrapes on the ground augmented with guano or a few sticks. The Red-footed Booby nests in bushes or trees, and constructs a flimsy stick nest.

Birds may remain partnered from year to year, reestablishing their bonds with elaborate rituals that include stylized postures, movements, and vocalizations.

Blue-footed Booby

Most species lay a single egg. Brown and Masked Boobies lay two eggs, but they rarely raise more than one chick. The second egg is "insurance" against the loss of the first chick—the second chick usually perishes as a result of siblicide or starvation.

The boobies place their large, webbed feet over the thick-shelled egg to incubate it. The egg hatches in 42 to 47 days. The chick grows slowly and fledges between 90 to 120 days after hatching. In most species, the chick is dependent on its parents up to two months after fledging, while it gains the skills needed to fish.

BREEDING RANGE

Two sulid species breed in North America: Northern Gannet and Masked Booby. A cold water species, the Northern Gannet breeds abundantly on a few Canadian Maritime Islands. In 1984, small numbers of the pantropical Masked Booby started to breed on the Dry Tortugas, Florida. Red-footed and Brown Boobies are also pantropical species; their closest colonies are in the Caribbean and off western Mexico. The Blue-footed Booby is restricted to the eastern tropical Pacific, with nearby colonies in the Sea of Cortez, Mexico.

MIGRATION AND WINTER RANGE

Boobies are not true migratory birds. After breeding many stay in the vicinity of their colonies, while others disperse out to sea. Conversely, the Northern Gannet is highly migratory, moving south out of the North Atlantic in late fall. Most North American birds winter off the eastern seaboard, although a few continue south into the Gulf of Mexico and the northern Caribbean. The adults migrate north in spring, returning to the North Atlantic for another breeding season. Subadults stay at sea for the first three years and do not attempt to breed before seven or eight years of age.

OBSERVING SULIDS

Northern Gannets are easy to observe from shore along the eastern seaboard. Peak numbers occur in winter. The boobies require more effort. Masked, Brown, and Red-footed Bobbies can be difficult to find, most reliably on the Dry Tortugas. Wanderers are occasionally found in the northern Gulf of Mexico or may follow the Gulf Stream north.

On the West Coast, Masked, Brown, and Red-footed are all considered rare in California waters. The Salton Sea is the most reliable place to see Blue-footed Boobies. In late summer, post-breeding adults and juveniles sometimes wander up from Mexico's Sea of Cortez—a trip of more than one hundred miles across the desert. During "invasion" years, dozens of Blue-foots and the occasional Brown Booby have occurred.

STATUS AND CONSERVATION

Northern Gannets are abundant in the North Atlantic and are maintaining their population. The various booby species have suffered declines at some breeding locations. Introduced predators—rats, cats, pigs—on the breeding islands have wiped out some colonies.

OTHER SPECIES FIELD NOTES

■ **Red-footed Booby**
Sula sula
L 28" W 60"
All adults show coral red feet, plumage variable

■ **Brown Booby**
Sula leucogaster
L 30" W 57"
Dark brown head and neck, white belly and underwing coverts

■ **Blue-footed Booby**
Sula nebouxii
L 32" W62"
Blue feet, bluish gray bill, streaked head

■ **Masked Booby**
Sula dactylatra
L 32" W 62"
Black facial skin, black trailing edge to wings

See also

Albatrosses, page 40
Brown Pelican, page 62

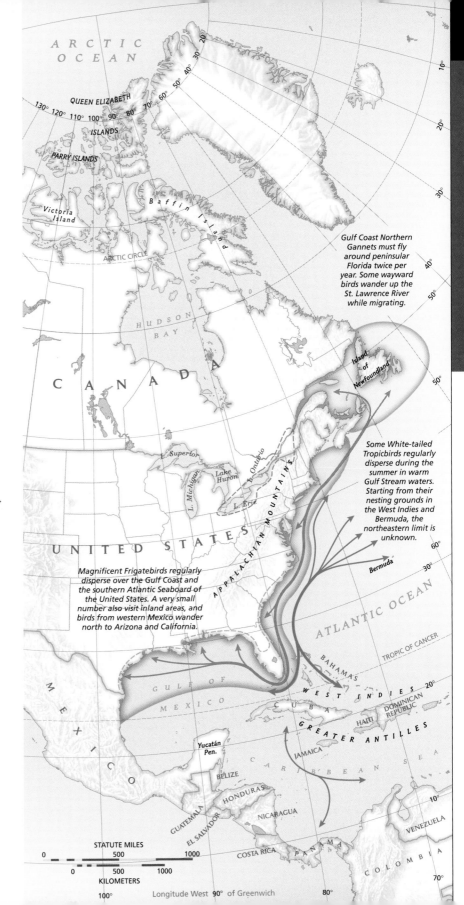

JE-FOOTED
○ BROWN
OBIES

FOOTED BOOBY

– Vagrant wandering

 ̄N BOOBY

- Vagrant wandering

▢ Year-round range

SPECIES

▢ Year-round range

*past, small numbers of Blue-
 ̄ and Brown Boobies wandered in
̄e summer and early autumn to
ˉton Sea and lower Colorado River.
̄he early 1980's, this has become
̄re for unknown reasons. At the
̄ime, more Brown Boobies have
̄ecorded wandering along the
̄Coast. Some of these vagrants
̄ave originated in Hawaii.*

MAGNIFICENT ▶
FRIGATEBIRD,
NORTHERN
GANNET AND
WHITE-TAILED
TROPICBIRD

MAGNIFICENT FRIGATEBIRD

Dispersal range ------

NORTHERN GANNET

Autumn and
spring migration ▬▬▬

Late fall and winter ------
wandering range

Breeding range ▢

Winter range ▢

WHITE-TAILED TROPICBIRD

Dispersal route ▬▬▬

*Gulf Coast Northern
Gannets must fly
around peninsular
Florida twice per
year. Some wayward
birds wander up the
St. Lawrence River
while migrating.*

*Some White-tailed
Tropicbirds regularly
disperse during the
summer in warm
Gulf Stream waters.
Starting from their
nesting grounds in
the West Indies and
Bermuda, the
northeastern limit is
unknown.*

*Magnificent Frigatebirds regularly
disperse over the Gulf Coast and
the southern Atlantic Seaboard of
the United States. A very small
number also visit inland areas, and
birds from western Mexico wander
north to Arizona and California.*

STATUTE MILES

0   500   1000

0   500   1000

KILOMETERS

Longitude West **90°** of Greenwich

PELICANS, CORMORANTS, DARTERS

Distributed world-wide and common in both fresh- and saltwater habitats, these three family groups exploit almost any situation that will yield up a fish dinner. They make up the ancient order of waterbirds, known as the Pelecaniformes, along with the three families in the previous chapter (frigatebirds, tropicbirds, and boobies).

The pelicans (family Pelecanidae) with their large, pouched bills and gregarious habits are well known to the general public. Two species—American White and Brown—inhabit North America. The American White Pelican breeds at freshwater locales, while the Brown is strictly a marine species. American White Pelicans can weigh over 20 pounds, and are among the heaviest birds to fly. Once aloft, they are excellent fliers, and a high-flying flock of migrating birds paints an artful, black-and-white arrangement against the sky.

The Brown Pelican has long served as a bell-weather species for the health of our environment. In 1903, when Teddy Roosevelt established the first National Wildlife Refuge—Pelican Island NWR in Florida—it was to protect Brown Pelicans from plume hunters. By the 1960s, the species was under threat again. This time the culprit was DDT, concentrated in fish the pelicans ate, causing thinner eggshells that were easily crushed by incubating birds. With the ban on DDT and the added protection of the Endangered Species Act of 1973, Brown Pelicans have made a substantial recovery.

The cormorants (family Phalacrocoracidae) are the most numerous family in the Pelecaniformes—39 species worldwide and 6 species in North America.

Jonathan Alderfer

The North American species are similar in appearance: black plumage in adults with paler underparts in young birds, which can give rise to some difficulty in their identification. Close examination of facial coloration and ornamental feathering is important; bill structure and body size are also helpful clues. One species—the Double-crested Cormorant—vastly outnumbers all other North American cormorants, and its population continues to grow. It frequents both marine and freshwater habitats and is one of the few native species that is legally "controlled" (killed) to protect fishing and fish-farming interests. Many conservation groups oppose this policy. In Asia and other parts of the world, cormorants have even served as man's fishing partner: tethered birds, fitted with neck rings to prevent them from swallowing large fish are released by the fisherman to capture fish underwater. The practice has largely died out.

The darters (family Anhingidae) are a family of only two species worldwide, represented in the Americas by the Anhinga. This denizen of southern swamps pursues fish underwater, impaling them on its spear-like bill. The reptilian-looking Anhinga frequently swims with only its sinuous neck and slender head above water, earning itself the popular, southern name of "snakebird." The plumage of the Anhinga, even more than cormorants, is not waterproof—the reduced buoyancy improves underwater performance—and the birds spend long periods drying their spread wings and warming themselves in the sun. They are excellent fliers, with a habit of soaring high on afternoon thermals, sometimes in large groups.

(Left) American White Pelican

Brown Pelican, *Pelecanus occidentalis*, L 48" W 84", white head and neck washed with yellow, grayish brown body

PELICANS

The smallest of the world's pelicans, the endangered Brown Pelican (above) was almost extirpated from North America between the early 1950s and 1970s by the widespread use of DDT. Colonies along the Gulf and Pacific Coasts were so devastated that the species completely disappeared from Louisiana, the Pelican State. In 1972 the use of DDT was outlawed in the United States and Canada and the population began to rebound immediately. Today we can readily see Brown Pelicans soaring in long, staggered lines, inches above the surf, alternately flapping, and gliding in unison. These plunge divers are the only dark-plumaged and exclusively marine pelicans.

Range of Brown Pelican

CLASSIFICATION

The pelicans—family Pelecanidae—are a small, distinctive family with a worldwide distribution. All seven species of pelicans are closely related and placed in the same genus (*Pelecanus*). Two species occur in North America—American White Pelican and Brown Pelican. This ancient family of waterbirds has not changed much over the last 40 million years—the 11 known fossil species are classified in the same genus as modern-day pelicans.

STRUCTURE

Pelicans are huge birds with distinctive features. Most notable is the long, hook-tipped bill with a large, fleshy pouch attached to the lower mandible. This flexible pouch is used underwater, where it balloons open to corral fish. During the onset of breeding, the color of the adult's pouch and other skin areas become more vivid. Eye color also varies according to the season—pale in spring and dark the rest of the year. In late winter, the American White Pelican grows a unique, horny knob on the upper mandible that is shed after egg-laying.

American White Pelicans can weigh over 20 pounds and Brown Pelicans—the smallest pelican species—average half that. To get their bulky bodies airborne, pelicans need lengthy, running starts. To stay aloft, they have long, broad wings that generate substantial lift. American White Pelicans have wingspans up to nine feet, and the long inner wing has over 30 secondaries. Their bones are hollow and very light, a quality that adds to their buoyancy when swimming. Once airborne, pelicans are graceful fliers, able to soar at great altitudes or to cruise low over the water. Typical flight involves a few flaps followed by a long glide. Flocks of pelicans travel in V-formation or long lines, their wingbeats synchronized with the leader.

PLUMAGE

Adult males and females have identical plumage; males are larger in overall size. American White Pelicans are predominantly white with black primaries and secondaries—a pattern shared by all the world's pelican species, except the Brown Pelican. Adult Brown Pelicans are dark bodied with seasonably variable neck and head feathers. In addition, juvenile Brown Pelicans differ from adults—they have white bellies and brown heads. Juveniles molt into a series of subadult plumages before reaching full-adult plumage in their fourth or fifth year.

FEEDING BEHAVIOR

The two North American pelican species have different feeding techniques, although both use their large pouches to catch fish. American White Pelicans capture fish by dipping the open bill and pouch into the water while swimming. Although they sometimes feed alone, they are most successful when hunting in a group. The formation of cooperative hunting groups is unusual among birds, and American White Pelicans employ a remarkable range of strategies. Often, ten or more birds will swim in an open crescent, driving fish toward shallow water, where they can be scooped up with ease. The pelicans sometimes jab their bill into the water or open and close their wings to help herd the fish. Variations include driving fish with their bill held underwater and beating the water with their wings. Another strategy involves forming two parallel lines that swim toward each other, concentrating fish between them.

Brown Pelicans are plunge divers. They locate their prey from the air and execute high-altitude attacks, with the wings folded back along the body just before impact. As they hit the water, the pouch balloons open, capturing any small fish in its path. After surfacing, the pouch is drained of water, and the prey swallowed with a backward toss of the head. Brown Pelicans sometimes gather in large groups over ephemeral schools of fish. A feeding frenzy may involve dozens of pelicans and other seabirds drawn to the activity. Gulls often attempt to rob pelicans of their catch.

VOCALIZATION
At their breeding colonies, pelicans make a variety of grunts, groans, hisses, and belching sounds. Otherwise, they are almost always silent.

BREEDING BEHAVIOR
Breeding pelicans gather together in large colonies. They are monogamous breeders, but new pairs are formed each year. Courtship displays include various ritual postures and movements.

American White Pelicans nest on the ground and build up a substantial nest mound that elevates the eggs. Brown Pelicans on the West Coast utilize a simple scrape on the ground, but some East and Gulf Coast birds build stick nests in trees or bushes. Nest material is gathered (or stolen from a neighbor) by the male, and presented to the female for construction.

Clutches consist of two or three eggs (rarely six) that are incubated on top of the parent's webbed feet. The eggs hatch in the order laid. When food is scarce the larger, first-hatched chick may push the smaller chicks out of the nest. In ground-nesting colonies, unfledged chicks gather in crèches for protection against predators and to help thermoregulate—keep cool during the day

and warm at night. Young birds fledge 70 to 85 days after hatching. First-year mortality is high and only a small percentage reach breeding age, three to five years later. Thereafter, pelicans have a long life expectancy—20 years is not uncommon.

BREEDING RANGE
Pelicans need breeding sites that provide access to large quantities of fish. Predator-free islands, remote marshes, and inaccessible sea cliffs are suitable. White Pelicans breed in the interior West of the United States and Canada. They favor large lakes with low-lying, unobstructed islands for nesting and will fly many miles to reach productive fishing areas. Brown Pelicans are marine birds that breed along the Gulf and East Coasts, north to Maryland, and on the West Coast north to central California on coastal islands.

MIGRATION AND WINTER RANGE
American White Pelicans are highly migratory, moving south in fall to spend winter at coastal estuaries and sheltered bays as far south as Mexico. The Salton Sea in California supports a large winter population.

Some Brown Pelicans are sedentary in the vicinity of their breeding colonies. Others undertake extensive post-breeding dispersals, particularly southern birds moving north. Thousands of birds which originate in Mexico move up the West Coast during summer and fall; most return south by late November. On the East Coast, birds wander north to New England every summer. During winter these northern wanderers retreat to the vicinity of their colonies or move farther south.

OBSERVING PELICANS
In the proper habitat and at the right time of year pelican species are easy to identify. Their varied feeding techniques present opportunites for prolonged observation. Separating the various age classes of Brown Pelican deserves more study and is not well presented in the standard field guides. Out-of-range American White Pelicans must be identified with care—distant birds can resemble Wood Storks or Snow Geese—and they must be separated from other "white pelicans," escaped species from different parts of the world.

STATUS AND CONSERVATION
At present both North American pelicans are maintaining healthy populations.

OTHER SPECIES FIELD NOTES

■ **American White Pelican**
Pelecanus erythrorhynchos
L 62" W 108"
White with black primaries and outer secondaries

See also

Gannets, Boobies, page 56
Frigatebirds, Tropicbirds, Boobies, page 51

Anhinga, *Anhinga anhinga,* L 35" W 45", white spots and streaks on wings and upper back, long tail

DARTERS

A truly aquatic bird, the Anhinga (above) swims with its body submerged and only its neck and slim head visible above the surface. The largely black male and the female with its buff-colored neck and breast are often seen perched with their silver-streaked wings fanned out to dry in the sun. Their feathers absorb water, causing the birds to loose body heat, so they must spend time drying their feathers and absorbing the sun's heat to maintain normal body temperature. This dependence on the sun's essential warmth limits their range to the subtropical regions of our southern coasts. The Anhinga's bones are especially dense, enhancing their ability to attain neutral buoyancy that facilitates their submerged stalking-hunting style. Both mandibles are edged with fine, backward-pointing serrations that aid in securing speared fish. These short-legged, clumsy walkers are superb flyers, often soaring at high altitudes with their long neck and tail held out straight, and their flat, perpendicular wings forming a distinctive cross.

Range of Anhinga

CLASSIFICATION

The darters—family Anhingidae—are represented in the Americas by a single species, known simply as the Anhinga (from an Amazonian tribal language). Worldwide, the family includes one other species, the darter, which is widely distributed in Africa, Asia, and Australia and classified as three separate species by some authorities.

STRUCTURE

The Anhinga is a distinctive waterbird that resembles an elongated cormorant, to which it is closely related. Like cormorants, they have large, fully webbed feet set far back on the body and strong legs, adapted to propelling them underwater. The head is small and supports a stiletto-like bill. The bill, in combination with a long, sinuous neck, is capable of lightning-fast jabs used to spear fish underwater (hence the name darter). The accuracy and speed of the strike is increased by a hinge mechanism between the eighth and ninth vertebrae—similar to one in herons and egrets. Located under the bill is a small gular pouch, which expands to allow the Anhinga to swallow larger prey. The color of the pouch and the bare skin around the face varies seasonally. Most of the year, these skin areas are a dull pink or yellow, but prior to courtship the gular pouch turns jet black and the facial skin turns bright emerald or turquoise. Males have carmine red eyes; the eyes of females and immatures are less vivid.

Their wings are long and broad. Anhingas are excellent fliers, and they alternate gliding with flapping. For unknown reasons, they engage in long periods of soaring, often in flocks, and by utilizing thermals (rising columns of warmer air), Anhingas can reach considerable height. The far-off birds resemble tiny crosses—the lengthwise head and tail are balanced by the crosswise wings.

PLUMAGE

Males and females differ in plumage coloration, which is unusual in the Pelecaniformes. The body plumage of the male is a uniform, glossy black. On the female, the head, neck, and breast are a pale tan, with a chestnut border to the lower breast. Both sexes have scapulars and upperwing coverts with silvery white markings. The long, black tail with a pale tip is reminiscent of a turkey's tail—earning it the name "water turkey" in the rural South. In early spring, there is a partial molt; males develop a shaggy crest and mane, and both sexes grow brownish tan filoplumes (decorative, hair-like feathers) on the sides of the face and neck. Young birds of both sexes resemble the adult female, but their plumage is duller and the silvery white markings are less striking. Anhingas acquire full-adult plumage in two or three years.

FEEDING BEHAVIOR

The solitary Anhinga hunts for fish in the shallow waters of southern swamps, bayous, lakes, and slow-moving rivers. The body plumage is not waterproof, and this allows the birds to control their buoyancy. They are often seen swimming with just the head and neck above water. The uncanny resemblance to a swimming serpent has earned them another popular name, "snakebird." The stealthy Anhinga is able to submerge with barely a ripple and searches underwater with its neck coiled back, ready to impale its next victim. The bill is held slightly open, resulting in two puncture wounds, and the skewered fish is carried to the surface. Smaller fish are shaken off the bill, and then tossed in the air or dropped in the water, to allow the food to be swallowed headfirst. Larger fish may be carried to shore and further subdued. After a successful feeding, the Anhinga will clamber up a waterside log to dry its thoroughly soaked plumage. The Anhinga uses the same spread-wing posture of cormorants when drying its plumage, but, in addition, this behavior helps to warm the bird. Because the Anhinga has a low metabolic rate and is easily chilled, it may spend up to a third of its waking hours sunning—much longer than a cormorant.

VOCALIZATION

Anhingas sometimes make clicking or chattering noises while perched or in flight. In the vicinity of their nest, they make a variety of low rattles, grunts, and groans; chicks are noisy when begging for food.

BREEDING BEHAVIOR

Anhingas do not form large breeding colonies among themselves, but often associate with other nesting, colonial waterbirds, such as herons, egrets, and ibises. Anhingas are monogamous breeders, and the same birds may remain paired for years. Pair bonds are strengthened through an elaborate set of courtship rituals. These displays include neck stretching at various angles, twig offering, tail posturing, and wing waving—in which the wings are alternately raised and lowered, displaying their white markings, while the stretched-out neck is kept low and horizontal.

The bulky nest is located in a tree that overhangs the water, typically situated low enough to be reached by climbing—Anhingas have strong claws and climb well. The male gathers (or steals) nesting material and presents it to the female for actual nest construction. The final touch is a lining of green twigs and leaves. An established breeding pair will often reuse the same nest year after year, and some birds refurbish an existing heron or egret nest.

The clutch of two to six eggs (often four) is laid at one-to-three day intervals, and incubation lasts 25 to 30 days. The eggs hatch in the order in which they were laid—the firstborn chick is larger and more dominant. Within two weeks, the flightless birds are actively clambering around the nest site, and even enter the water if threatened. They return to the nest by climbing with the help of their well-developed claws. By six weeks of age the fully feathered juveniles are active and ready to fly. The young birds will reach adulthood and breeding age in two to four years.

BREEDING RANGE

The Anhinga has a wide distribution in Central and South America. Anhingas are restricted by climate and habitat requirements—warm and humid with abundant water. They prefer still or slow-moving freshwater, but will utilize mangrove swamps, coastal estuaries, and brackish water. Their North American range extends from the states bordering the Gulf of Mexico, north into Arkansas and along the East Coast to North Carolina.

MIGRATION AND WINTER RANGE

In the United States, the northernmost breeders migrate south by early October to escape cooler temperatures. Their northerly nest sites are reoccupied in the next spring (March to April). The birds breeding farther south are less migratory; however, banding recoveries indicate that some of these birds disperse into Mexico.

OBSERVING DARTERS

In the proper habitat, Anhingas are not difficult to find. Wary birds may not allow close observation; perched birds will often drop into the water when disturbed. In protected parklands, such as Everglades National Park, Anhingas have become accustomed to people and are more approachable. Any out-of-range Anhinga should be checked carefully—escaped zoo or aviary specimens of the Darter (an African subspecies) have been seen in California.

STATUS AND CONSERVATION

Anhingas appear to be maintaining healthy populations in the United States. The draining of swamps, timber harvesting, and coastal development have lead to local declines.

Anhinga

See also

Magnificent Frigatebird, page 52
Skuas, Jaegers, page 164

Double-crested Cormorant: *Phalacrocorax auritus*, L 32"
W 52", yellow-orange throat pouch

CORMORANTS

Because it is able to adapt to almost any aquatic environment, fresh- or saltwater, the Double-crested Cormorant (above) has the greatest range and is the most numerous cormorant of the six species that inhabit North America. Entirely dark brown to black in its plumage, with a greenish, oily sheen to new feathers, this cormorant is most often seen perched with its wings spread to dry. The birds swim low in the water, often sticking their head below the surface in search of prey. Their feathers absorb water, aiding in the birds' ability to forage underwater. When prey is spotted, the cormorant dives and, using its totipalmate (webbed between all four toes) feet, swims in pursuit, seldom using its wings to aid in propulsion. Named for the feather tufts that form behind the eyes of breeding adults, these "crests," can be difficult to see.

Range of Double-crested Cormorant

CLASSIFICATION

The cormorants (family Phalacrocoracidae) are the largest family—39 species worldwide—in the order of pelicaniform birds. Six closely related species occur in North America, all in the genus *Phalacrocorax*. Double-crested and Great Cormorants are widespread and have been divided into numerous subspecies.

STRUCTURE

Cormorants are medium to large waterbirds with elongated bodies, long necks, and large, fully webbed feet, set far back on the body—adaptations to the underwater pursuit of fish. They dive from the surface and use their powerful legs and feet—not their wings—to propel themselves underwater. They can dive to substantial depths: the Pelagic Cormorant has reached 180 feet. The slender bill is hooked at the tip (to grasp fish), with a gular pouch situated below. This expandable pouch allows a bird to swallow larger prey and helps dissipate extra heat when the bird pants, by fluttering the loose skin. The gular pouch and bare facial skin develop intense colors—reds, blues, oranges, or yellows—prior to breeding. Eye color also varies by season, turning emerald green, turquoise, or cobalt blue in spring and losing intensity after breeding.

Compared to many seabirds, their wings are short, broad, and rounded, and tails are long and stiff, to assist in steering underwater. The heavy body and short wings make getting airborne difficult, and takeoffs require long, running starts, during which both feet push off the water surface in unison. Once aloft, cormorants fly well, with powerful, regular wingbeats. Flocks fly low over the water in long lines or V-formations; migrating birds fly at greater heights and sometimes soar. On land, cormorants stand and perch in a confident, upright posture. They perch on rocks, buoys, docks, dead trees, and cables or ropes, where they spend time preening and drying their plumage.

PLUMAGE

A close look at the conspicuous black plumage of adult cormorants reveals that the black is often accented with a beautiful metallic gloss—green, purple, bronze, or blue—that shimmers and changes with the light. Many species acquire small, but distinctive, crests in the spring and grow filoplumes on various parts of the body. Filoplumes are decorative feathers that in cormorants are white and hairlike. They are lost or wear away after courtship. Three species—Great, Pelagic, and Red-faced—also have prominent white flank patches in spring and early summer. Adult males and females have identical plumages, although males are larger on average. Young birds are brownish, often with pale underparts that darken with age. Full-adult plumage is acquired in two to four years.

FEEDING BEHAVIOR

Many cormorant species target slow-moving, bottom-dwelling fish, while others pursue mid-level schooling fish underwater. Sometimes food includes squid, mollusks, and crustaceans, or inland waters frogs, tadpoles, and various reptiles. Cormorant plumage is dense and wettable, which reduces buoyancy and improves underwater performance. During a dive, the webbed feet provide excellent propulsion, and the snaky neck and body react quickly to a fleeing fish's movements. After returning to the surface, they reposition the catch so that it can be swallowed headfirst. Later they regurgitate the bones and scales in the form of a pellet. Cormorants dry their plumage, standing on docks or pilings with their wings held open in the typical spread-wing drying position.

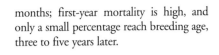

Brandt's Cormorant

VOCALIZATION

Cormorants are normally quiet, restricting their vocalizations to the breeding sites, with a limited repertoire of hisses, grunts, groans, and other throaty sounds.

BREEDING BEHAVIOR

Cormorants often nest in the company of other colonial waterbirds. They are monogamous breeders, but new pairs are formed each year. The marine species—Brandt's, Great, Red-faced, and Pelagic—breed on islands, rocky outcrops, and cliff ledges. Their nests are simple scrapes on the ground, embellished with some vegetation or debris. The Neotropics favor freshwater and brackish areas, and Double-cresteds breed in both inland and coastal locations. Inland, most Neotropic and Double-crested Cormorants build stick nests in trees.

Clutches of two to four eggs (rarely seven) are incubated on top of the parent's webbed feet. The eggs hatch in the order they were laid. The last chicks to hatch rarely survive, unless food is abundant. Chicks fledge at two

months; first-year mortality is high, and only a small percentage reach breeding age, three to five years later.

BREEDING RANGE

Several species breed from California to the Bering Sea. Where multiple cormorant species breed, studies have shown that each species exploits a different feeding niche. Greats nest in the Canadian Maritimes and Newfoundland; Neotropics nest along the Texas to Louisiana coast; and Double-cresteds nest from Florida to Canada. The abundant Double-crested also breeds across the interior of the United States and Canada.

MIGRATION AND WINTER RANGE

Most cormorant species do not undertake long migrations. Northern populations of Pelagic Cormorant move south out of the Bering Sea, but breeders farther south disperse only short distances. Great Cormorants in the North Atlantic migrate south from their northernmost colonies, but birds breeding farther south either winter nearby if conditions allow or undertake long migrations to winter along the eastern seaboard.

Most of the inland population of Double-cresteds is highly migratory—spring and fall flights of small flocks are conspicuous as they follow large river systems and lakeshores. Many birds spend the winter as far south as Mexico and the Caribbean. The Florida population is sedentary or disperses only short distances. East and West Coast populations migrate south in fall or disperse according to weather or food conditions.

OBSERVING CORMORANTS

In most of North America, the Double-crested Cormorant is the de facto cormorant. At some time of year, its range overlaps that of every other cormorant species. When identifying a cormorant, consider this species first and check the field marks. Distant swimming cormorants can be confused with loons. Note the longer neck, different bill shape, and more submerged body.

STATUS AND CONSERVATION

Worldwide, many species of cormorants are in decline. By comparison, North American species are maintaining healthy numbers and the Double-crested is increasing.

OTHER SPECIES FIELD NOTES

■ **Neotropic Cormorant**
Phalacrocorax brasilianus
L 26" W 40"
Long tail, white-bordered throat pouch

■ **Great Cormorant**
Phalacrocorax carbo
L 36" W 63"
Broadly white-bordered lemon yellow throat pouch

■ **Pelagic Cormorant**
Phalacrocorax pelagicus
L 26" W 39"
Small, glossy dark overall

■ **Red-faced Cormorant**
Phalacrocorax urile
L 31" W 46"
Red facial skin, yellow bill, bluish at base

■ **Brandt's Cormorant**
Phalacrocorax penicillatus
L 35" W 48"
Pale, buffy feathers border throat pouch

See also

Loons, Grebes, page 29
Magnificent Frigatebird, page 52
Anhinga, page 64

OWN PELICAN

BREEDING RANGE EXPANSION

— Historic extent of growth

Breeding range 1950

Breeding range expansion

*wing the banning of the pesticide
n 1971, the suppressed population
wn Pelicans rebounded quickly.
evitalized birds spread outward, re-
zing old territory, and establishing
g outposts in some new areas.*

TE MILES
500

500
METERS

GREAT▶ AND NEOTROPIC CORMORANTS

GREAT CORMORANT

ering and isolated records – –/ •

Combined range
ng, resident, and winter)

NEOTROPIC CORMORANT

Wandering range – – – – –

Isolated records – –/ •

Combined range
ng, resident, and winter)

*Over the last 25 years, Neotropic
Cormorant populations in the southern
Great Plains and the southwestern U.S.
have increased and spread northward.*

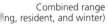

STATUTE MILES
0   500

0   500
KILOMETERS

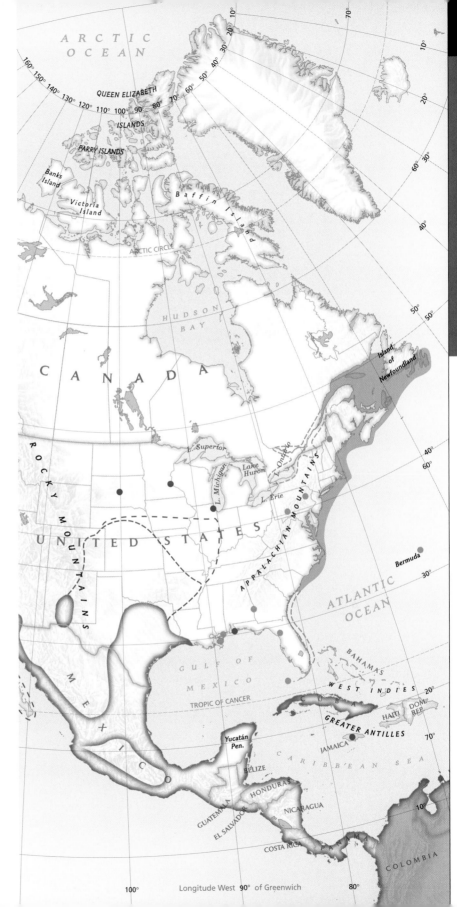

HERONS, EGRETS

Public dismay over the slaughter of Great and Snowy Egrets led to the first federal legislation to protect birds. Although the Lacey Act (1900) forbids the interstate traffic of any creature killed in violation of state laws, the act was principally designed to end the interstate trade in bird feathers, particularly the nuptial plumes of egrets. In 1886 these long, lacy, plumes commanded more dollars per ounce than gold. It wasn't until 1910, though, that laws were passed protecting these elegant birds from being hunted to extinction in North America.

As the 20th century progressed, the American public became increasingly aware of the value of wetlands, largely because of its growing appreciation for the birds that live there. No nestling is more awkward or gawky than a heron chick, yet no adult bird better embodies the beauty and magic of our national wetlands. Small fishes, amphibians, reptiles, worms, crabs, and other creepy-crawlies may compose the heart of any healthy swamp or marsh, but the herons and egrets that prey on these creatures compose its soul.

All 13 species of North America's herons and egrets have breast and rump patches (some species also have back and thigh patches) in which feather down disintegrates into a powder. The birds use this portable "dust bath" for preening with their long, comb-like middle toes. The dry powder down is essential in a family whose members spend much of their lives wading in water.

Another feature shared by these birds is a long, slender neck in which the esophagus and trachea cross over and lie behind the vertebrae. In providing the shortest possible distance for these organs between beak and body, this unique evolutionary trait enables herons to compress and coil their neck like snakes and strike at prey with lightning speed. It also protects the esophagus and trachea from injury, if the striking bird hits something other than its target.

George Reiger

This feeding strike enables herons and egrets to tap a spectrum of living prey. Although Great Blue Herons typically feed on fish and frogs, various observers have seen these birds consume small turtles, snakes, voles, baby muskrats, and even smaller wetland birds, such as Mallard ducklings and Black Rails. Great Blue Herons have even been known to visit backyard ponds to gulp down prize koi.

Any ardeid may become a nuisance at fish farms, but Black- and Yellow-Crowned Night-Herons have the worst reputations, because they visit in flocks capable of consuming thousands of dollars worth of fish or crayfish in a single evening. In Louisiana, night-herons are called *gros-bec,* French for "fat beak," and up until the 1990s, many crayfish farmers shot the birds, both to protect profits and to provide food for their workers. However, after U.S. Fish and Wildlife Service wardens began cracking down—especially when several well-known violators went to prison—signs appeared throughout the swamps, pleading: "No Shoot Gros-Bec!"

In spite of the numerous laws written over the years designed to preserve wetlands, in reality this legislation has only reduced the rate at which swamps and marshes are drained or filled. And since all herons and egrets depend on wetlands for their very existence, local populations continue to be diminished or even disappear.

(Left) Reddish Egret

Great Blue Heron: *Ardea herodias*, L 46", W 72", llarge, gray-blue overall, black stripe above eye

HERONS

Known to casual observers as "cranes," Great Blue Herons (above) are the most familiar of the family of herons and egrets, found across the North American continent in a variety of habitats. Great Blues are generalists when feeding, taking an astonishing range of prey, from fish, snakes and frogs, mice, and even small woodchucks, to large insects and a number of birds, including the rare Black Rail. The ability to forage flexibly, whether by day or night, means that Great Blue Herons are less tied to aquatic habitats than other species: They can also be found foraging in farm fields, meadows, and forest edges. Great Blues build large stick nests high in the trees, usually associated with other nesting pairs of Great Blues, in loose colonies called "heronries," which may be miles away from water.

Range of Great Blue Heron

CLASSIFICATION

Two bitterns, six herons, and four egrets regularly occur in North America. The Little Egret, similar to the Snowy Egret, is an Old World species and a casual visitor in spring and summer to the East Coast. Herons, egrets, and bitterns are all members of the Ardeidae family, and are included with other families of large wading birds, flamingos, storks, ibises, and spoonbills, in the order Ciconiiformes. The current trend is to divide the family into four subfamilies, Ardeinae, the typical herons; Nycticoracinae, the night-herons; Botaurinae, the bitterns; and Tigrisomatinae, the tiger-herons of Central and South America. DNA-DNA hybridization studies indicate that the tiger-herons may be the oldest family, from which the other three subfamilies originated. Controversy continues among the taxonomic community regarding the classification of the heron family. Museum specimens indicated that the Green Heron hybridized with the neotropical Striated Heron, and the two were lumped into the Green-backed Heron. In the 1990s the American Ornithologists' Union determined that this hybridization was too infrequent to sustain the lumping, and resplit the two into separate species, and the Green-backed Heron became the Green Heron once again. Color morphs also add complexity to the desired orderly classification of the herons. Formerly considered a separate species, scientists now generally agree that the Great White Heron of southern Florida is a color morph of the Great Blue Heron, but still the same species. Occasionally the Great White Heron breeds with a Great Blue, producing the Wurdemann's Heron—a Great Blue with an all-white head—but all three are considered the same species, *Ardea herodias*. As new technology is applied and new knowledge discovered, we can expect the classification of the heron family to continually be updated.

STRUCTURE

The heron family is comprised of the familiar "large wading birds" and most, such as the tall and elegant Great Blue Heron, are fitted with extremely long legs affording them the capability of foraging in the deeper water along the margins of lakes, ponds, marshes, and streams. These ardent fishers are often seen wading into water deep enough to lap against their bellies. Herons are strictly carnivorous, and most are equipped with long, sharp beaks—typified by the Great Blue, Little Blue, and the Tricolored Herons—used mainly for capturing small fish. The Yellow-crowned and Black-crowned Night-Herons have shorter, broader bills better adapted to their more specialized diets of insects, crabs, crayfish, and mussels. Herons' sixth cervical vertebra is adapted to permit them to draw their neck into the cocked S-position allowing for a lightning-fast, snake-like strike when foraging for fish and crustaceans. Herons characteristically draw their neck into this S-position in flight as well, unlike storks, ibises, and flamingos, which hold their long neck straight out, neatly counter-balancing their long legs. Males are larger than females, but in the field this difference is almost imperceptible.

Green Heron

PLUMAGE

Herons are sexually monomorphic, meaning the plumage of both sexes is alike. Unique among herons in displaying an age-related color morph, the immature Little Blue is all white and can be easily confused with the immature Snowy Egret, until it assumes its characteristic slate blue adult basic plumage after the first year. All herons are equipped with powder-down rump and breast patches. These feathers are designed to disintegrate into a fine talcum-like powder used to preen and condition contour and flight feathers. Their pectinate, or comb-like middle toes, aid in this crucial preening process. With the exception of the white morph of the Great Blue Heron, the plumage of this family is generally dark and highly variable. The most cryptic plumage is that of the solitary American Bittern, a marsh denizen, its alternately light and dark brown vertically streaked breast blends perfectly with its reedy environment. In flight its blackish brown primaries contrast sharply with its brown upperparts. The American Bittern is the only heron to display a black patch extending from below its eye down the side of its neck. Our smallest heron, the Least Bittern is boldly and beautifully patterned with a metallic greenish black crown, back, and tail, with chestnut wing tip and light, buff underparts. A rare, dark morph, Cory's Least Bittern, with all chestnut underparts and wings, is seldom seen. In alternate, or breeding plumage, the night-herons are an arresting sight. Both species develop long, whitish head plumes, but the soft, blue-gray body plumage with the yellow crown and white cheek patch of the Yellow-crowned Night-Heron is simply a stunning sight. The Green Heron spends most of the day in the shade so we seldom see the detail in its greenish black head and chestnut neck and belly. When threatened the Green Heron will raise its crest and elongate its neck, revealing the lovely streaked throat plumage. It really is prettier when it is mad. The Tricolored is the only heron to display countershading, or dark upperparts and light or white underparts. Both adults develop white head plumes during the breeding season. Our largest and most widespread heron, the adaptable Great Blue develops ornate head and neck plumes and extensive lacy plumes along its back during the breeding season. The plumage of this family ranges from the highly cryptic of the American Bittern to the garishly ornate of the Great Blue, from the dark, blackish green of the Green Heron to the all-white Great White Heron, manifestations of this successful family's ability to adapt to its varied environment.

FEEDING BEHAVIOR

Herons are carnivorous stalkers, and each species has evolved its own unique time of day, place, and method of foraging for its preferred prey. The family of herons will eat almost anything, from live fish to eggs and chicks of nesting birds to scavenging from dumpsters and landfills, and like most generalists, they flourish. The most common food item among members of this family is fish. Using their long, sharp bill, they have developed several uncommon ways of attracting and capturing fish. Certainly the most innovative fisher is the Green Heron, which uses bait, and more spectacularly, fashions "lures" by breaking off bits of twigs and tossing them into the water to attract minnows. This is one of the few instances of toolmaking in the bird world. We must admire this use of artificial bait, and like most fishermen, the Green Heron also shamelessly resorts to live bait to obtain a meal. They are known to use bread, popcorn, insects, and even dig up earthworms to use as bait. A more specialized feeder is the Yellow-crowned Night-Heron, which especially prefers

---

OTHER SPECIES FIELD NOTES

■ **American Bittern**
Botaurus lentiginosus
L 28" W 42"
Rich brown upperparts, dark flight feathers

■ **Least Bittern**
Ixobrychus exilis
L 13" W 17"
Dark back and crown, buffy inner-wing patches

■ **Yellow-crowned Night-Heron**
Nyctanassa violacea
L 24" W 42"
Buffy white crown, black face, white cheeks

■ **Black-crowned Night-Heron**
Nycticorax nycticorax
L 25" W 44"
Black crown and neck

■ **Green Heron**
Butorides virescens
L 18" W 26"
Greenish black crown, chestnut neck and sides

■ **Tricolored Heron**
Egretta tricolor
L 26" W 36"
Blue upperparts, white foreneck and belly

■ **Little Blue Heron**
Egretta caerulea
L 24" W 40"
Slate blue overall, gray bill with dark tip

crabs and other crustaceans. Both the Yellow-crowned and Black-crowned Night-Herons feed mainly at night, perhaps an adaptation allowing these birds to forage the same territory used by other waders, but at a different time. The night-herons are also known to forage during the day, especially when feeding nestlings. The Great Blue is the great generalist in terms of its diet, known to eat insects, frogs, crabs, shrimp, small birds, and nestlings, eggs, and even small mammals such as mice, which it often wets before swallowing. Mostly though, the Great Blue Heron uses its long, sharp bill to capture fish. Most herons will remove the sharper fins, or subdue a fish by beating it before swallowing it.

VOCALIZATION

Heron calls are not "musical" to human ears, but they do communicate in their own unique, guttural way. The most notable heron sound is the "booming call" of the American Bittern, heard in spring and early summer as it calls through the dense marsh reeds, a booming "oonk-a-lunk," or is it "pump-er-lunk?" The sound, though not translatable from the heron to the human vocabulary, has earned the American Bittern the sobriquet Thunder-pumper. This low-frequency sound better penetrates the dense vegetation in which the bittern lives, than would a more "normal" higher pitched call. The Least Bittern has been reported to make a dove-like cooing sound during the spring, but most of its calls are more heron-like "keks" and grunts. The Black-crowned Night-Heron can be heard late at night into early dawn making, usually, a single definitive "quwock" sound. The heron call we are most likely to hear is that of the Great Blue as it takes flight and emits an annoyed, deep, guttural squawk, the typical heron call.

BREEDING BEHAVIOR

Pair bonds among herons usually occur in early spring with the arrival of the females to the breeding grounds where the males have staked out their nuptial territories. The specialized feeding habits of the Yellow-crowned Night-Heron links the emergence of crabs in the spring to the beginning of pair bonding and nesting. Crabs emerge when the water temperature is right for them, so a colder spring will delay the nesting of the Yellow-crowned. Copulation occurs within two to three days of pairing and initiates nestbuilding, with the male usually supplying the nestbuilding materials and the female doing the actual nest construction. Most herons

lay three to five eggs and raise one brood per season. They will re-nest if the first clutch is lost. Herons tend to be seasonally monogamous, but extra-pair bonds do occur. Studies indicate that among Great Blue Herons, new mates are often chosen with each new season, but more field information is needed. The bitterns construct their nests on the ground or on floating mats among the dense, emergent marsh vegetation. Interestingly, Redhead Ducks, noted brood parasites, have been known to lay their eggs in American Bittern nests, but not regularly and usually without success. Most herons, however, are colonial nesters, nesting in trees preferably on islands or near water where food is readily available. And most herons are very elegantly attired for the breeding season, developing long, lacy neck, back, and head plumes, and the facial skin and bill taking on a bright, showy coloration.

Little Blue Heron

BREEDING RANGE

The American and Least Bitterns prefer freshwater wetlands offering thick, reedy vegetation in which to nest. The American Bittern breeds across northern North America, as far north as Great Slave Lake. The Least Bittern breeds in the United States east of the Mississippi. The Yellow-crowned Night-Heron breeds along the southeast coast and Gulf Coast where it can readily procure its preferred crabs. The much more adaptable and more general feeder, the Black-crowned Night-Heron breeds on every continent except Australia and Antarctica in any habitat suitable for fishing. The Tricolored and Little Blue Herons tend to be coastal fishers and breed along the coasts of the southeast U.S., Mexico, and Central America. The Green Heron breeds throughout the eastern U.S. and along the Pacific Northwest coast. The Great Blue Heron finds suitable breeding habitat throughout the U.S. and southern Canada.

MIGRATION

After fledging, herons tend to disperse into less densely populated territory, many moving north and west as does the Green Heron, and often merging with southward moving populations in the fall. Green Herons occasionally wander as far north as England in the summer and as far south as Central America and Puerto Rico in the fall. Bitterns and other herons will move south in the fall and early winter as ponds and marshes ice over, denying access to prey. It is believed they move only far enough south to enter sustainable feeding grounds, mixing with the nonmigratory herons of warmer climes. The Great Blue Heron tends to migrate in small groups both day and night, as far north in the summer as the Alaskan coast, and moving south in the winter to suitable feeding grounds. Amazingly, some Great Blues are recorded in Canada during Christmas Bird Counts each year. Herons are generally not long-distance migrants, and are sedentary where an accommodating environment will allow.

WINTER RANGE

To feed, herons need an ice-free environment and many spend the winter nearer the coastal wetlands, salt marshes, and mangrove swamps where the nearby ocean moderates the colder seasons. Bitterns, which normally prefer freshwater, will utilize brackish coastal marshes during the winter season. Generally, the winter range of herons closely coincides with their breeding range.

AMERICAN BITTERN

A solitary denizen of extensive freshwater ponds and marshes, the American Bittern stands as stationary as the tall shoreline grass, which its cryptic coloration emulates, ready to ambush any prey that comes into range of its lightning quick strike. Unlike most herons, the American Bittern seldom perches in trees. This species is very difficult to detect until it moves, or better yet, flies. Then it can be positively identified by the chocolate brown primaries contrasting with its overall light brown plumage. This secretive but relatively common heron is distributed throughout North America and Mexico. Loss and degradation of remote, pristine habitat is the greatest threat to the steadily declining population of the American Bittern.

OBSERVING HERONS

In almost any aquatic environment herons will be year-round residents. They are readily found foraging and fishing, usually singly, along any shoreline. Birders observing the intense aspect and beauty of these large birds always find the sight rewarding. During the spring breeding season, herons are at their finest, and it is the time birders are likely to watch their most interesting behavior as they court, defend their territory, and care for their young.

The Great Blue Heron is noted for its upright-and-spread-wing display, a threat to foraging-grounds intruders, be they other herons, gulls, or even people approaching too near. The Great Blue Heron spreads its wings, and draws its neck over its back holding the head and bill horizontally, then raises its head to near vertical. In the more aggressive forward-and-full-forward display, with plumes erect, the Great Blue Heron draws back its neck, pointing its bill at the opponent, and makes ready to strike. Actual attacks seldom occur, but some engagements between herons have been known to be fatal.

The secretive and cryptically colored American Bittern may be the most difficult heron to see as it stands motionless with its head and bill pointing almost straight up, stretching its streaked breast to align with the marsh grasses in which it is hiding. But in flight, the dark primaries, dangling legs, and brown upperparts make for a positive field identification. These are startlingly beautiful birds to observe and study.

STATUS AND CONSERVATION

Herons are at the top of the food chain and for that reason their presence is a good indicator of environmental quality. If the herons begin to disappear in a neighborhood or region, then the water in which they fish and the general environment are probably being degraded. Increasing habitat loss is the greatest threat to this family of birds.

Herons are known to take fishing lures, which often results in the hook securing a bird's bill shut and dooming the bird to starvation. Abandoned fishing line can also ensnare these fellow fishers and is a risk to individual herons and other birds. Currently, heron populations are stable and are endangered only as their habitat is diminishing.

See also

Snowy Egret: *Egretta thula,* L 24" W 41", black bill, yellow eyes, black legs, yellow feet

EGRETS

At the turn of the 19th century, large ladies' hats sporting breeding plumes, "aigrettes," of Snowy Egrets were much in vogue. As a consequence, their nesting areas along the coasts of the United States were wiped out by plume hunters supplying the millinery trade. In the nick of time, a grassroots campaign against this practice began, a campaign that evolved into the National Audubon Society. The

Range of Snowy Egret

Snowy Egret is one of the showier species in the Ardeidae family. Its white plumage is set off by a coal black bill and legs and saffron gold feet. In breeding displays, Snowy Egrets erect their aigrettes, flash the usually yellow skin at the bill's base to a deep vermilion, and make startling, guttural braying noises. The birds withdraw from their northern breeding areas and spend the winter in the subtropics and tropics where the local nesting populations are sedentary. Snowy Egrets can be active feeders, but they also forage in nearly motionless poses, stirring up the bottom with their bright yellow feet to flush prey.

CLASSIFICATION

Three of our North American egrets, the Reddish, the Little, and the Snowy, belong to the genus *Egretta.* The Cattle Egret belongs to the genus *Bubulcus,* and the Great Egret belongs to the Genus *Ardea* with the Great Blue Heron. That we consider egrets separately from herons is a matter of convenience, partly because of the common name, egret, and because they are all white, except for the Reddish Egret. The taxonomic designation of this family will continue to be updated as we learn more about the birds, but today all egrets belong to the family Ardeidae, and all egrets are herons.

STRUCTURE

Egrets are long-legged wading birds adapted to the shallow water environment in which they forage. The Cattle Egret has shorter legs and eats mainly insects disturbed by grazing cattle herds. Egrets have a long, sharply pointed bill used to capture fish and aquatic prey and long necks that they draw into their shoulders in flight. The Cattle Egret has a shorter neck that in its "hunched" posture causes the throat to look swollen. Its short bill is adapted to its ground-feeding style.

PLUMAGE

Early in the breeding season the dazzlingly white Snowy and Great Egrets grow long, showy feathers, or aigrettes, from their scapulars that were so prized by the millinery fashion industry in the late 1800s that these birds were hunted almost to extinction in North America. We think of egret plumage as being white, but the Reddish Egret comes in both a white and a dark morph, with a shaggy rufous head and neck, and blue-gray body plumage. It also develops the long, filamentous aigrettes during the breeding season. A few individual dark morphs show white on their wings and resemble molting immature Little Blue Herons. The Cattle Egret is typically all white, but during the breeding season it is adorned with orange-buff plumes on its crown, back, and throat.

FEEDING BEHAVIOR

The most spectacular feeder is the Reddish Egret as it careens and pirouettes through the shallows in its wing-flicking display, startling prey into the open. The Reddish also employs the canopy-feeding method whereby it runs with its wings flared, then stops and folds its wings forward over its head forming a "canopy." This casts a shadow upon the water that is believed to attract fish and make them more visible in the reduced glare of the bright sunlight. The Cattle Egret feeds mostly on land, eating insects flushed by grazing cattle. The Snowy Egret shuffles and shakes its bright yellow feet to flush prey and feeds on a variety of prey including fish, crabs, snails, shrimp, frogs, snakes, and lizards. The Great Egret feeds in both fresh- and saltwater habitats mainly on fish, but also eats frogs and snakes, birds and small mammals.

VOCALIZATION

Like most herons, egrets are mainly silent, especially when feeding. In the nesting colonies they are more vocal, emitting guttural squawks and croaks of recognition and when taking flight. The Cattle Egret call has been described as a two-note "rick-rack" sound given on the nesting grounds, but it, too, is mainly silent.

BREEDING BEHAVIOR

The Cattle Egret's courtship ritual is elaborate and begins with a group of males aggressively establishing territories within a nesting area. Females gather around a male as a group and within 24 hours they begin to alight beside and upon the male, biting his neck and back in order to calm and subdue him. He initially repulses the females, but within three to four days he allows one of the females to stay, and a pair bond is formed. They engage in mutual backbiting, stretching displays by the female, and twig shaking by the male. The male then leads the female to another site where nestbuilding begins. Snowy Egrets engage in a tumbling flight display during formation of the pair bond, in which one or both birds spiral into the air then tumble to earth and right themselves just before landing. Egrets are generally monogamous during the breeding season, but do not necessarily pair for life.

BREEDING RANGE

Egrets are colonial nesters, breeding in and near wetlands where forage is readily available. The Reddish Egret breeds strictly along the Florida and Gulf Coasts in the United States, and throughout the Bahamas and the Cuban coastline. The Cattle Egret continues to expand its range and now breeds throughout the U.S., but is still concentrated in the Southeast. The Great and Snowy Egrets breed locally across the U.S. and are concentrated in the Southeast.

OTHER SPECIES FIELD NOTES

■ **Reddish Egret**
Egretta rufescens
L 30" W 46"
Rufous head and neck, dark body, white morph, all white

■ **Cattle Egret**
Bubulcus ibis
L 20" W 36"
White with orange-buff wash on crown, back, and foreneck

■ **Little Egret**
Egretta garzetta
L 24" W 36"
Resembles Snowy Egret, but with grayish lores

■ **Great Egret**
Ardea alba
L 39" W 51"
White overall, yellow bill, black legs

Cattle Egret

MIGRATION

The Reddish Egret is only weakly migratory. In contrast, the Cattle Egret is strongly migratory, though distinguishing between its extraordinary and continuing range expansion and migration is difficult. Thought to have arrived in Surinam from Africa in the late 1870s, the Cattle Egret was nesting in South Florida by 1943. Today it is well established throughout North America and is distributed worldwide. Populations of the Great and Snowy Egrets breeding in the interior U.S. and northern coastal areas move south in the fall. Actual migratory routes are unclear.

WINTER RANGE

The Reddish Egret spends the winter in its breeding area. Cattle Egrets move to southern Florida, the mouth of the Mississippi, the Texas coast, and the Salton Sea. The Great and Snowy Egrets winter along the coast of Oregon and California, throughout Mexico and Central America, and south on the East Coast to the Carolinas.

OBSERVING EGRETS

You can see the Reddish Egret along the Gulf Coast and South Florida coast. The Cattle Egret can be seen across the country wherever cattle are grazing. The stark white Great and Snowy Egrets are wetland birds.

STATUS AND CONSERVATION

The Cattle Egret is in no danger. Since the outlawing of hunting and the ban on DDT, egrets have increased and stabilized their populations. Degradation of the coastal environment continues to threaten the Reddish Egret, and loss of wetlands will continue to have a negative impact upon the Great and Snowy Egrets.

See also

Anhinga, page 64
Cormorants, page 66
Greater Flamingo, page 84

CATTLE EGRET

RANGE EXPANSION IN NORTH AMERICA

● 1975   First reported or isolated incedence with date

▢ 1975   Area of breeding range expansion with date

Cattle Egrets probably arrived in the Ne
World from Africa by over-water dispers
The first recorded sightings were from
northeast South America, between 187
and 1912. By the late 1940's, it was
common in that area. Their range
continued to grow, with egrets sighted
the West Indies by the mid 1930's. By th
1950's they had spread throughout th
islands. Expansion has been largely by
leaps and bounds rather than a steady
increase. Since 1980, some populations
the Northeast and around the Great Lak
have declined and disappeared.

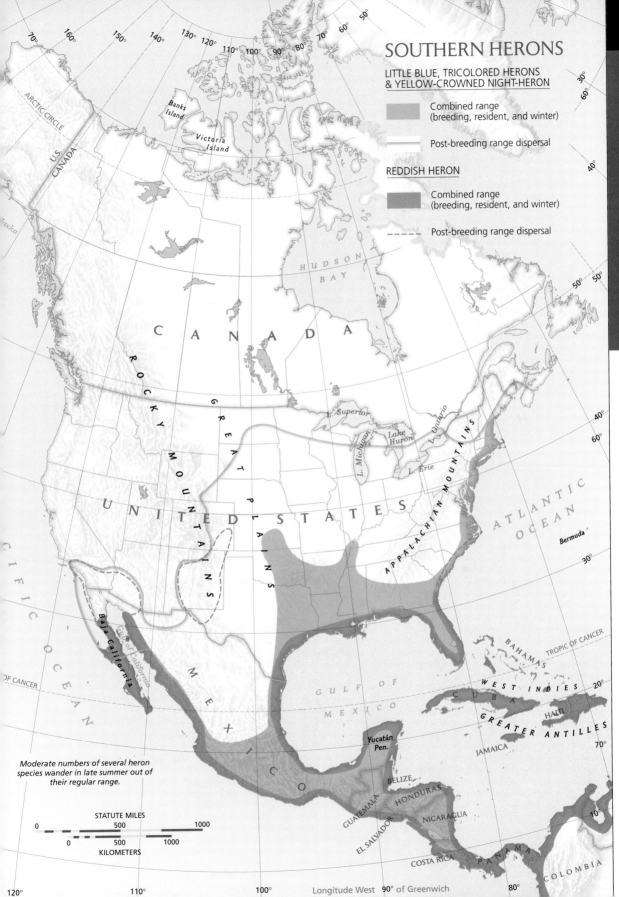

SOUTHERN HERONS

LITTLE BLUE, TRICOLORED HERONS & YELLOW-CROWNED NIGHT-HERON

Combined range
(breeding, resident, and winter)

Post-breeding range dispersal

REDDISH HERON

Combined range
(breeding, resident, and winter)

Post-breeding range dispersal

ARCTIC CIRCLE

Banks
Island

Victoria
Island

U.S.
CANADA

Alaska

C A N A D A

HUDSON
BAY

ROCKY MOUNTAINS

GREAT PLAINS

L. Superior

L. Michigan

Lake
Huron

L. Ontario

L. Erie

APPALACHIAN MOUNTAINS

ATLANTIC
OCEAN

Bermuda

UNITED STATES

PACIFIC OCEAN

OF CANCER

Baja California

Gulf of California

M E X I C O

GULF OF
MEXICO

TROPIC OF CANCER

BAHAMAS

WEST INDIES

CUBA

GREATER ANTILLES

HAITI

JAMAICA

Yucatán
Pen.

BELIZE

GUATEMALA

HONDURAS

EL SALVADOR

NICARAGUA

COSTA RICA

PANAMA

COLOMBIA

*Moderate numbers of several heron
species wander in late summer out of
their regular range.*

STATUTE MILES
0   500   1000

0   500   1000
KILOMETERS

120°   110°   100°   Longitude West 90° of Greenwich   80°

IBISES, STORKS, FLAMINGOS

Greater Flamingo, Wood Stork, Roseate Spoonbill, and ibises are among the largest wading birds in North America. They are long-legged birds with flexible necks that feed in salt- and fresh-water wetlands, marshes, coastal lagoons, mudflats, and croplands such as rice fields. Their distinctive feeding behavior includes probing or sieving water for food with their bill, often sensing prey by touch. The group feeds on a wide variety of fish and aquatic worms and mollusks, as well as seeds and insects.

These species are migratory and their movements depend on available food sources. In the winter, when fish and other prey are less plentiful, the birds congregate in southern states or migrate farther south. During the spring breeding season and early summer, all but the White-faced Ibis remain near the Gulf Coast or along the southern Atlantic states.

Long-legged waders travel great distances northward and are sighted throughout the Midwest and southern Canada. An exception with a small range are Greater Flamingos, found only in South Florida.

A distinctive behavior of many long-legged waders is communal roosting and nesting. Roseate Spoonbills, Wood Storks, and ibises, along with several heron and egret species, gather in dense colonies to build nests and raise chicks. They often choose small islands for their nesting colony to guard against predation. They build nests within a few feet of each other, and it's an extraordinary sight to witness the constant motion of a large colony at work, building nests and feeding their hatchlings.

The Greater Flamingo is among the largest of North American waders. Once numerous in Florida,

Jerry Uhlman

it is a tropical species that breeds in the Caribbean. Flamingos are bright reddish pink in color, and their feathers were highly prized in the late 1800s as ornaments for ladies hats. Plume hunters decimated the North American population, and the species is now sighted in the wild only in extreme southern Florida. Flamingos are popular zoo species, and it's often difficult to tell escapees from wild birds, but captive birds loose their vivid red tone and appear lighter than vagrant Flamingos.

The Wood Stork, slightly smaller than the flamingo, is endangered in the United States, but large numbers exist in the Caribbean and Mexico. The species is distinctive for its naked head, white wings with black-tipped primaries, and long bill that is decurved at the tip. The birds often use thermals to soar, flying with neck and legs extended. A close family member, the Jabiru, is a tropical stork of Central and South America that rarely visits southern Texas.

The Roseate Spoonbill and the White-faced, Glossy, and White Ibis species are closely related, although the spoonbill's color, head, and bill are unique features among the four species.

The White-faced Ibis is primarily a western species although all ibis species share a common range along the coastline of Texas and Louisiana.

The White Ibis is larger, has a red face, and feeds in small groups. When feeding, smaller waders such as herons and egrets often follow to catch prey that has been stirred up.

The distinctive Roseate Spoonbill, with a bare head that is grayish green, nests in dense rookeries with heron and ibis species.

(Left) Roseate Spoonbill

Wood Stork: *Mycteria americana*, L 40" W 61", black flight feathers and tail, white body; bald, blackish gray head

STORKS

The Wood Stork (above) is a denizen of southern river-bottom forests and swamps, particularly areas that are seasonally wet, trapping and concentrating fish into small ponds. The birds forage by opening their bill in the water waiting for fish to swim by, then snap it shut in less than a tenth of a second. They often move together in a line to herd and trap fish. Their manner of flight—rising on warm air columns in search of foraging habitat—is a behavior shared with vultures, which some believe are the stork's nearest relatives. On occasion, young storks will disperse far beyond the warm Gulf Coast states, seeking out habitat as far north as the Great Lakes.

Range of Wood Stork

CLASSIFICATION

Wood Storks belong to a two-member Ciconiidae family of North American birds that also includes an incidental visitor to the continent from South America, the Jabiru. Both Wood Storks and Jabirus are among the Ciconiiformes, an order of large wading birds that also includes vultures, which are not waders.

Worldwide, there are 17 species of the Ciconiidae family, and members of this order are generally long-necked and long-legged waders. They are adapted for wading in relatively shallow water to forage, and the toes of these birds are not webbed.

STRUCTURE

The Wood Stork is one of the largest wading species at 40 inches long, with a wingspan of 61 inches, slightly smaller than a flamingo. With vertical thermal air currents, storks can soar thousands of feet into the air and glide for miles with only occasional wing flapping.

Wood Stork physical features include an unusual naked blackish gray head, long dark legs, and a long bill that is decurved at the tip.

A close family member of the Wood Stork, the Jabiru is a tropical stork of Central and South America that occasionally visits in southern Texas. It is a large bird at 52 inches in length and a 90-inch wingspan. When a vagrant is spotted, the Jabiru is often with Wood Storks and appears much larger, with a distinctive long black upturned bill and black head.

PLUMAGE

Wood Storks are predominantly a grayish white color, with a white back, lower neck and breast, and white wings with black-tipped primaries.

FEEDING BEHAVIOR

Wood Storks feed by touch in salt- and freshwater marshy wetlands along the Gulf Coast and southern Atlantic. Birds generally submerge their head and grope for any prey within reach. This tactile, nonvisual method is an advantage when feeding in shallow, muddy, weed-choked ponds. When likely prey is encountered, their spring-like bill quickly snaps closed on it, and this action is considered to be one of the fastest reflexes in the animal world. While feeding as a group, birds often stand still and wait for prey to swim near, or walk together to stir up prey. Usual prey for storks includes wetland and rice-field inhabitants such fish, frogs, snakes, aquatic worms, crabs, and crayfish.

VOCALIZATION

Wood Stork vocalization is nearly lacking since the species has a weak, almost nonfunctional voice box. Instead, birds in flocks often exhibit tongue rattling and bill clacking as a form of communication.

BREEDING BEHAVIOR

Wood Storks are colonial birds that occupy trees in dense numbers. They build nests in cypress or mangrove trees, and their breeding cycle is dependent on a reliable food source. Storks seek nesting sites near pools with high fish concentrations, waiting to breed until the water source begins to dry so that fish are readily available to feed hatchlings. The Wood Stork does not breed until it is four years old.

The male and female build a platform of sticks and the female usually lays three to four dull white colored eggs that are incubated by both adults for 28 to 32 days. The eggs hatch in the same order they are laid, and the young are dependent on the parents for feeding and care until 55 to 60 days after hatching. Two chicks usually survive to fledge and are fed by their parents, who catch and partially digest fish, then regurgitate the mixture in the nest for the young.

A pair of wood storks needs roughly 400 pounds of fish during a breeding season to feed themselves and their young. Therefore, breeding is carefully synchronized with wetland cycles so food is most plentiful when the young are being raised. During other times of the year, when less food is required, storks fly greater distances to search for shallow feeding ponds, and young storks may head north to find more to eat.

BREEDING RANGE

In North America, Wood Storks nest from coastal South Carolina, Georgia, and Florida to Louisiana, and their breeding range extends into the Caribbean and Mexico. In the United States, the largest nesting colonies are in the Big Cypress region of Florida, particularly the National Audubon Society's Corkscrew Swamp Sanctuary. Other significant nesting colonies reside in central and northern Florida and the southern portion of coastal Georgia.

MIGRATION

Storks are generally migratory, and their winter range extends into South America to northern Argentina. After the breeding season in North America, some individuals travel great distances north and have been sighted in upper midwestern states.

WINTER RANGE

Most Wood Storks migrate south, but some remain all year in isolated coastal areas of the southeast United States, primarily along the coast of Florida.

OBSERVING STORKS

Observing Wood Storks is most easily done in the many wildlife refuges and state parks along the coast of Florida, Georgia, and South Carolina. When spotted, Wood Storks are easy to identify as large wading birds, readily distinguished by their dark featherless heads, thick bills, and white plumage trimmed with black.

STATUS AND CONSERVATION

At the turn of the century, there were more than 150,000 Wood Storks in Florida, whereas recent surveys counted only 7,000 to 10,000 storks in all of the United States. The species has been on the endangered list since 1984. Habitat loss and the destruction of nesting areas have been major causes for declining numbers of Wood Storks. While the species is in serious decline in North America, substantial numbers exist in the Caribbean and Mexico.

The U.S. Fish and Wildlife Service initiated a recovery plan for Wood Storks in 1986, and recent aerial surveys indicate that the number of nests in South Carolina, Georgia, and Florida has increased from 4,073 to 7,853.

The Jabiru stork, an occasional visitor to North America and once abundant in Latin America, has also declined in numbers throughout Central and South America because of habitat destruction and human interference. Cultivation and tree cutting have reduced the species' population in Central America to fewer than 250 individuals. Although greater numbers survive in the flood plains of Venezuela, Colombia, Brazil, and Argentina, the Jabiru storks face a threat in South America from hunters, particularly in Suriname and the Amazon Basin. Several Latin American countries have placed the Jabiru on the endangered list for protection.

Jabiru

See also

New World Vultures, page 108
Herons, Egrets, page 71

Greater Flamingo: *Phoenicopterus ruber,* L 46" W 60", pink legs, black flight feathers, tricolored bill

FLAMINGOS

The vivid colors, extremely long neck and legs, and truly unique bill define the exotic flamingo, and are adaptions for specialized foraging on algae, insects, crustaceans, and other invertebrates; their curved bills contain filters to strain mud for tiny prey. There are five species throughout the world, but only the North American Greater Flamingo (above) is found in Florida, where a few dozen live in Everglades National Park. Their numbers fluctuate, with some birds coming from Mexico's Yucatán Peninsula. Birders rarely encounter flamingos in the field away from

Range of Greater Flamingo

southernmost Florida, and most are escapees from captivity, with Chilean and Lesser Flamingos seen almost as often as Greater Flamingos of both races. Some ornithologists consider the North American Greater Flamingo separate from the Old World's Greater Flamingo, which has much less pink in the plumage. The intense pink adult plumage is constructed with pigment elements from prey; it takes a young flamingo several years to attain this color.

CLASSIFICATION

Greater Flamingos are in a separate taxonomic order from other wading birds, known as Phoenicopteriformes, in the Phoenicopteridae family, and there are six species worldwide, distributed mainly in tropical areas in the Southern Hemisphere.

Over the years, flamingos have been considered to be Ciconiiformes, grouped with heron, egret, ibis, and stork species since the species have similar body structure. Other characteristics, such as bill structure and webbed feet, have led some authorities to consider them closer to a classification with geese and ducks. Because flamingos have similar fossilized structural remains and behavioral traits as avocets and stilts, some ornithologists believe flamingos should be grouped with shorebirds as Charadriiformes in the Recurvirostridae family. Currently, there remains no definitive taxonomic classification for flamingos.

STRUCTURE

The Greater Flamingo is among the largest of North American waders, 46 inches in length with a wingspan of nearly five feet. Flamingos are social and gregarious birds that live and breed in very large colonies.

Flamingos have long legs and necks, pink feet and legs, a hooked, pink bill with a black tip. What appear to be knees on flamingos are actually ankles that bend backward when the birds recline to rest and preen.

In flight, the graceful birds form loose flocks and glide in long, single lines, or V-formation. Like other large wading birds, flamingos are capable of soaring long distances with the aid of thermals or wind currents.

PLUMAGE

Greater Flamingos' feathers are bright reddish pink with black primaries and secondaries, and both sexes have similar coloration and markings. Their feathers were highly prized in the late 1800s as ornaments for ladies hats, which decimated the North American population. The bird is now sighted in the wild only in extreme southern Florida.

It's often difficult to tell escapees from wild birds when sighted, but captive birds gradually lose their vivid red tone and appear much lighter than vagrant flamingos.

FEEDING BEHAVIOR

Most of the flamingo's day is spent feeding in shallow water. When feeding, the Greater Flamingo submerges its head upside down with its face pointed backward. It has a specially adapted bill with a comb-like structure, called a lamella, along the inner bill that strains water taken into the mouth.

The flamingo uses its thick tongue like a plunger to suck water into the mouth and force it back out through the comb-like lamella. The food caught by the lamella is pushed into the back of the mouth to be swallowed at the same time the next mouthful of water is drawn in. Their long legs and necks allow them to wade through deep water and mud in search of food.

Greater Flamingos feed on a variety of aquatic life, including blue-green and red algae, protozoa, aquatic plants, worms, larval and adult forms of small insects, small mollusks, crustaceans, and small fish.

The presence of fish in a potential habitat often determines whether or not flamingos will inhabit a particular body of water. Some species avoid lakes with fish that could compete for a common food source. Greater Flamingos, though, do not compete with fish populations since they generally rely on different sources of food that are plentiful, such as algae and aquatic creatures.

VOCALIZATION

Greater Flamingos have few vocalizations beyond a low-pitched squawk or grunt. They click their bills as a form of communication.

BREEDING BEHAVIOR

The Greater Flamingo seeks out a habitat with shallow, very salty or alkaline lagoons and lakes in which to feed and breed successfully. They often prefer estuarine lagoons that have rich mudflats, but also will nest and feed in mangrove swamps, tidal flats, and sandy islands in the intertidal zone where vegetation is scant.

Greater Flamingo

The Greater Flamingo nests in colonies that often contain thousands of birds. Flamingo pairs have a unique communal display that includes wing flapping, posturing, posing, and preening. In early spring a 12- to 20-inch mud nest is built in the water near the shore, usually on a mudflat, but sometimes in a less than ideal onshore or even rocky area. The nest is a rounded mound of mud from 5 to 18 inches high and very susceptible to a rising water level that may immerse or wash it away.

A nesting pair will produce one or two whitish eggs that are incubated by both parents for a period of 28 to 32 days. The hatchlings are fed a regurgitated liquid called crop milk. They begin to feed themselves in roughly a month, but parents continue to feed young birds for several weeks. Young chicks flock together with other juveniles in a group, called a creche, to feed and preen. After roughly ten weeks, young birds have lost their gray down and grown grayish brown feathers. Juveniles will have their adult plumage within three to four years of age and reach adult size within two years.

BREEDING RANGE

Once numerous in Florida, the Greater Flamingo is a tropical species that breeds closest to North America in the Caribbean Islands of the Bahamas and Cuba. These are very sociable birds and generally will not breed unless they can flock together in large numbers.

MIGRATION

The species is resident on a number of Caribbean Islands, Mexico's Yucatán Peninsula, in northern South America, and on the Galápagos Islands, where it migrates between breeding grounds in the warmer tropical portion of its range and its wintering grounds in Mexico, Central America, and South America.

WINTER RANGE

Greater Flamingos winter throughout the Caribbean islands and southward into Latin America, as far south as Ecuador and Brazil. Many flamingos remain on their territory year-round and only migrate with unseasonably cold temperature changes or because of drought conditions.

OBSERVING FLAMINGOS

This tropical species is incidental to North America and sighted only rarely. Because Greater Flamingos occupy such a small range in North America at the southern tip of Florida, observing the species can be quite difficult. Public access into the Everglades in southern Florida is limited, which further impedes observation of flamingos. Bird-watchers in search of this species usually turn to local birders or professional guides who are aware of sightings and can arrange special access to observe vagrant birds.

STATUS AND CONSERVATION

Early in the last century, flamingos were hunted for their colorful feathers and most of the birds on the North American continent were decimated. For the past several decades, hunting regulations have helped the Greater Flamingo species rebound to a relatively stable worldwide population of roughly 100,000. Hunting continues to jeopardize flamingo populations in the Southern Hemisphere.

See also

Pelicans, page 62
Wood Stork, Jabiru, page 82
Cranes, page 136

Glossy Ibis: *Plegadis falcinellus*, L 23" W 36", dark chestnut plumage glossed with green or purple

IBISES AND SPOONBILLS

A curious species not well known to most bird-watchers, the Glossy Ibis (above) inhabits the coast of the eastern United States, nesting as far north as southern New England. In the West, the Glossy is essentially "replaced" by the White-faced Ibis, with which it rarely hybridizes. The existence of these similar species is thought to have

Range of Glossy Ibis

arisen from of a "double colonization" event of the Americas by Glossy Ibis, originally an Old World species. The first colonization was prehistoric and gave rise to the White-faced Ibis, with its band of white around the eye and base of the bill, red eyes, and red "knees." The relatively recent colonization of the Glossy Ibis has not resulted in a new species distinct from the Old World Glossy, which has pale blue lines along the edge of the facial skin but no white feathering. Ibises of all species feed on mudflats, swamps, and wet farmland by probing with their long, curved bills, much like curlews. They feed by touch for varied invertebrate prey and take small fish if the opportunity arises.

CLASSIFICATION

There are more than 30 species of Roseate Spoonbill and ibis species worldwide, currently classified in the Threskiornithidae family with two separate subfamilies. Spoonbills are in the Plataleinae subfamily, whereas the ibises are in the Threskiornithinae subfamily. The classification and family names have been in dispute over the years, and remain unclear because the two subfamilies are closely related structurally.

The Threskiornithidae family is characterized by bills that are long and decurved, or grooved, and long necks that are held out straight forward during flight. The two subfamilies are distinct in bill shape and foraging habits. Spoonbills have spatula- or spoon-shape bills and forage by sweeping the bill side to side, grasping prey that the bill touches. Ibises have slender, downcurved bills and probe in muddy marshland soil for prey.

STRUCTURE

Glossy and White-faced Ibises are of nearly equal size, with a 23-inch length and a 36-inch wingspan, and the two species also have a similar appearance. The White Ibis species is somewhat larger at 25 inches in length with a wingspan of 38 inches. The three Ibis species have a long downcurved bill that is used to probe while feeding. The bills of the Glossy and White-faced Ibises are a pale greenish yellow in color whereas White Ibises have a bright reddish bill.

Very distinctive among the larger waders is the Roseate Spoonbill, 32 inches in length with a 50-inch wingspan. The most prominent physical features are the bird's gray crown and spoon-shape bill.

PLUMAGE

Glossy and White-faced Ibises both look dark from a distance, but have rich mocha brown necks and iridescent green or purplish patches on their wings and crowns. Both species are usually a rufous-brown during the summer and more gray or charcoal in winter.

The White Ibis has a reddish bill and legs; immature birds are mottled brown and white until attaining adult white plumage after the first fall. The species has black wingtips that can be easily seen in flight.

The Roseate Spoonbill's bare head is grayish green, and it it has reddish legs, pink wings, and red shoulders. The species is easily identified by its spoonshape bill, as well the colorful plumage.

FEEDING BEHAVIOR

The four Threskiornithidae family members are longlegged birds with flexible necks that feed in salt- and freshwater wetlands, marshes, coastal lagoons, and mudflats, and croplands such as rice fields. Their distinctive feeding behavior includes probing or sieving water for food with their bill, often sensing prey by touch. Ibises typically wade through shallow water, mudflats, or marshland and thrust their bills into the soil to probe for prey. In contrast, spoonbills slog through shallow water with a partially open bill, moving their head from side to side. When the spoon-shape tip of the bill encounters prey, the bill snaps shut and traps the object inside. The group feeds on a variety of fish and aquatic animals, including crabs, crayfish, snakes, snails, frogs, earthworms, and mol-

White Ibis

lusks. When other sources are scarce the species will turn to seeds and insects.

VOCALIZATION

The ibises and Roseate Spoonbills have similar vocalizations often described as a nasal croaking or grunting, repeated often when alarmed before taking flight and during breeding season at nesting colonies

BREEDING BEHAVIOR

Males of the four species claim and establish a nesting territory before females return to the nesting grounds. During courtship displays, a mating pair rubs heads together, offers grass or sticks to each other, and engages in mutual preening. Males gather nesting materials, while females arrange and build the nest in trees or bushes, often on islands that offer protection against predators.

A distinctive behavior of many long-legged waders is communal roosting and nesting. Roseate Spoonbills, Wood Storks, and ibises, along with several heron and egret species, gather in dense colonies to build nests and raise chicks. They construct nests within a few feet of each other, and it's an extraordinary sight to witness the constant motion of a large colony at work building nests and feeding their hatchlings.

The Glossy and White-faced Ibises have three or four greenish blue eggs and incubate them for 21 or 22 days. Young birds fledge at 28 to 30 days. White Ibises produce three to five greenish white eggs that are

incubated from 21 to 23 days. Roseate Spoonbills have one to five eggs, white in color with dark marks, and incubate them from 22 to 24 days. Both parents incubate the eggs. The four species have just one brood, and the young are highly dependent on the parents until they have fledged. Ibis species generally fledge within 28 to 35 days, but spoonbills take 35 to 42 days.

BREEDING RANGE

In spring the four breeding species can be found along the Gulf Coast and the southern Atlantic states. The Glossy Ibis's range extends to the upper Atlantic coast. White-faced Ibis, a western species, breeds throughout the lower Midwest, Gulf Coast, and westward toward the lakes and rivers near the Rocky Mountains.

MIGRATION

The four species are partial migrants and their movements depend on plentiful food and water. Following breeding season the four species often range substantial distances from their coastal habitats into the interior.

WINTER RANGE

In winter when fish and other prey are less plentiful, the species congregate in southern states. Mexico and the Caribbean are also winter destinations, with Glossy and White-faced Ibises migrating the greatest distances.

OBSERVING IBISES AND SPOONBILLS

Observing the four species in their habitat is not difficult since they are relatively large in size. Because waders forage through wetland habitats that make close observation impossible at times, a spotting scope is indispensable to see markings and plumage color.

STATUS AND CONSERVATION

The four long-legged wading species have robust populations in North America and are usually easy to locate on the customary ranges. This was not always the case. Besides plume hunters, the wide use of pesticides took a toll on these birds, making eggshells thin and vulnerable. DDT continues to be used in some countries in the Southern Hemisphere and this practice can adversely affect overwintering birds.

OTHER SPECIES FIELD NOTES

■ **White-faced Ibis**
Plegadis chihi
L 23" W 36"
Reddish legs, white border around red facial skin

■ **White Ibis**
Eudocimus albus
L 25" W 38"
White plumage, pink facial skin and bill

■ **Roseate Spoonbill**
Platalea ajaja
L 32" W 50"
Long, spatulate bill, pink body

See also

Limpkin, page 135

Avocets, Stilts, page 154

Long-billed Curlew, page 157

GLOSSY AND
WHITE-FACED IBISES

GLOSSY IBIS

- Combined range
- - - - Limit of dispersal
- • Vagrant record

WHITE-FACED IBIS

- Combined range
- Limit of dispersal
- • Vagrant record

Populations of both the Glossy and White-faced Ibises have increased in North America. The Glossy Ibis first appeared in the early 1800's, expanding its range into the 1980's. Beginning in the late 1970's, a decline was observed in some of the northeastern populations, while sightings far west of its core range have increased. White-faced Ibis numbers have grown substancially over the last 25 years, and it's range has spread north. As awareness of both species has increased, the number of vagrant sightings has grown.

STATUTE MILES

| 0 | 500 | 1000 |

| 0 | 500 | 1000 |

KILOMETERS

WOOD STORK

POST-BREEDING DISPERSAL

Resident range

- - - - Limits of regular
post-breeding dispersal

- - - - Former post-breeding dispersal

ARCTIC CIRCLE

U.S.
CANADA

Alaska

Banks
Island

Victoria
Island

HUDSON
BAY

C A N A D A

R
O
C
K
Y

M
O
U
N
T
A
I
N
S

G
R
E
A
T

P
L
A
I
N
S

U N I T E D   S T A T E S

L. Superior

L. Michigan

Lake
Huron

L.
Ontario

L. Erie

A
P
P
A
L
A
C
H
I
A
N

M
O
U
N
T
A
I
N
S

P
A
C
I
F
I
C

O
C
E
A
N

Baja California

Gulf of California

M
E
X
I
C
O

GULF   OF

M E X I C O

ATLANTIC

OCEAN

BAHAMAS

TROPIC OF CANCER

OF CANCER

W E S T   I N D I E S

C U B A

HAITI

G R E A T E R   A N T I L L E S

JAMAICA

Yucatán
Pen.

BELIZE

GUATEMALA

HONDURAS

EL SALVADOR

NICARAGUA

COSTA RICA

P A N A M A

COLOMBIA

*After nesting in Mexico, some
nomadic Wood Storks disperse
northward into the U.S. Gulf states
during the later half of summer. A
similar movement into southern
Arizona and southeastern California
has nearly ceased due to population
declines. Much less regular, Wood
Storks can disperse from South into
North Carolina. Very rarely do
individuals wander any farther
north along the East Coast.*

STATUTE MILES

0   500   1000

0   500   1000

KILOMETERS

SWANS, GEESE, DUCKS

Much of the appeal of Anatidae—swans, geese, ducks,
and whistling-ducks—lies in their
remarkable diversity. Sir Peter Scott,
who founded Britain's Wildfowl
Trust, once observed that his devotion to waterfowl
began by hunting them, grew by painting them, and
matured by studying them. And what a spectrum
there is to study. In North America, geese and swans
compose 11 species in four genera; dabbling
and diving ducks cover 39 species in 15 genera. They range in size from the majestic
Trumpeter Swan, with an 80-inch wingspan, to the rare and secretive Masked Duck, whose
wings span barely 17 inches. Waterfowl also flaunt
an amazing array of colors, from the snow white
plumage of the adult Tundra Swan, to the cobalt and
cinnamon hues of the drake Harlequin Duck, and
the intricate palette of the drake Wood Duck. Beginning birders often batten on waterfowl because
they are some of the most observable of all birds,
congregating around the continent, often in assemblages that hold several dozen species in view simultaneously. Only the shorebirds rival the waterfowl in
the size and diversity of their aggregations, but the
highly variable, brightly plumaged waterfowl are
acknowledged to be the more "birder friendly."

Variability is an important marker of adaptability, and most anatids have indeed shown remarkable
resilience in the face of vast continental changes and
occasional overharvesting by hunters. Some local
populations even exploit environmental alterations.
For example, each evening at the Bronx Zoo in New
York City and the National Zoo in Washington,
D.C., flocks of wild Mallards and American Black
Ducks fly into the waterfowl enclosures to feed on

George Reiger

pellets intended for the institutions'
pinioned birds. Unfortunately, nonmigratory populations of Canada
Geese have carried their adaptability
to an extreme and become nuisances
on golf courses, farms, and subdivisions all across the
country. Despite the overall resilience of Anatidae,
several sea duck species are in trouble, even though
their breeding and wintering habitats appear essentially unaltered over the past 150 years. Both
the Spectacled Eider and Steller's Eider are
classified as threatened under the U.S.
Endangered Species Act, whereas the Atlantic
race of the Harlequin Duck is designated as endangered by the Canadian government. The only North
American anatid to become extinct was also a sea
duck: the striking Labrador Duck.

The anatids are arguably the most valuable wild
avian family from an economic point of view. In
addition to the billions of dollars contributed annually to local economies and conservation organizations by amateur wildlife-watchers, American hunters have contributed millions of dollars directly to
conservation efforts in their pursuit of waterfowl,
and much of this money helps sustain other wetland
species. Revenues from the Migratory Bird Hunting
and Conservation Stamp in the United States have
been a principal source of funding for the national
wildlife refuge system. In its first 70 years, the Duck
Stamp has raised over $600 million. Excise taxes
paid on hunting equipment help preserve countless
nongame species. Organizations such Ducks Unlimited and nongovernmental state waterfowl associ-
ations have preserved, restored, or created hundreds
of thousands of wetland acres across the continent
with funds provided by their hunter members.

(Left) Wood Duck

Tundra Swan: *Cygnus columbianus*, L 52", black facial skin with small yellow spot

SWANS

Among the seven species of swans, the magnificent Tundra Swan (above) never fails to impress the first-time observer by virtue of its great size, slow and graceful habits, and stark white plumage. The swan's beautiful bugling call is often heard at night as family groups pass overhead. Several centuries ago, these giants were far more numerous than they are now, but hunting pressure, along with severe degradation of major wintering sites such as the Cheasapeake Bay, have reduced populations to mere shadows of past numbers. Tundra Swans nest along open tundra ponds in northern Canada and Alaska, and family groups migrate southward, both diurnally and nocturnally, along traditional routes to wintering grounds on the coasts of Washington, Oregon, and California, and also in Virginia and North Carolina. So conservative are these birds in their migratory movements that Tundra Swans are rarities across the interior of the continent and easternmost Canada and New England. In winter, they feed extensively on submerged aquatic vegetation.

Range of Tundra Swan

CLASSIFICATION

Swans and geese belong to the same subfamily, Anserinae. Unto themselves, swans compose the tribe Cygnini, of which there are only seven species worldwide. Two of them are native to North America: the rare Trumpeter Swan and the more wide-spread Tundra Swan, formerly known as the Whistling Swan and now considered conspecific with the Eurasian Bewick's Swan. The Mute Swan was first brought to this continent from Europe in the early 19th century. It has now established strongholds in several areas, most notoriously in the Chesapeake Bay region, where it has become a pest species. The Whooper Swan has bred occasionally in the Aleutian Islands but is otherwise a rare visitor to the New World.

STRUCTURE

All anatids have webbed feet to facilitate swimming, but swans and geese have relatively long legs to facilitate walking. Swans also have long necks that enable them to feed in shallow water without having to "tip" to reach bottom. One way to distinguish the swan species is in the way they hold their neck at rest. Those of Tundra Swans stick straight up from the breast; those of Trumpeter Swans kink back at the base; those of Mute Swans curve in an S-shape with the bill pointed down.

PLUMAGE

Unlike swans in the Southern Hemisphere, the adult plumage of all swan species north of the Equator is uniformly white, with a dark or bicolored bill and dark legs and feet. Juvenile plumages are gray. Such synonymity of color may suggest a common Arctic-breeding ancestor, but it complicates identification. Although the Trumpeter Swan is half again as large as the Tundra Swan, if there is no other background but sky, it is not easy to distinguish the two species. Bill shape and color are the best features on which to concentrate to identify swans but, even then, a stationary bird and a good pair of binoculars are needed.

FEEDING BEHAVIOR

Swans are ideally adapted for feeding on submerged aquatic vegetation in shallow water. But they can also walk and graze comfortably on wheat, rye, oats, and barley growing in winter fields. This latter habit—especially because swans do not merely crop grasses, but root out entire plants—has earned them the enmity of farmers in eastern North Carolina and Virginia and was a major justification for establishing a strictly regulated hunting season for this species in those two states. Meanwhile, the Mute Swan's appetite for the ecologically critical but depleted grass beds of the Chesapeake Bay has persuaded Maryland officials to pursue an eradication program for this exotic species.

VOCALIZATION

The Tundra Swan's call is often described as a yelp, whoop, or yodel—or, a high-pitched and oft repeated "woo-oh." The Trumpeter Swan's call is a sonorous single or double honk, whereas the Mute Swan is not as mute as its name implies, though most of its vocalizations are unattractive hisses, grunts, and snorts.

BREEDING BEHAVIOR

As with most species in which both sexes share the same color patterns, swans are generally monogamous. Hence, the most elaborate courtship displays of wing flapping, brief chase flights, and urgent, repeated calling are performed by young birds establishing pair bonds for the first time. As in our own species, the intensity of a given courtship seems to depend on the newness of the pair bond—or the time of day and weather. Although previously paired birds may spend less time on preliminaries, mated swans (or geese) continue to perform nuptial rituals during egg laying, incubation, and rearing of cygnets (or goslings).

Immature Tundra and Trumpeter Swans stay near their parents through the first winter and follow them north in the spring. Upon arrival on the nesting grounds, the young birds are either chased away by the adults or voluntarily move to communal feeding areas with other immatures. If a local food supply is good, breeding

Mute Swan

swans may not only tolerate the proximity of their previous offspring but that of other breeding adults as well. Such behavior can be most clearly seen among non-migratory Mute Swans. When they have a dependable food source, as they do in many urban parks, a breeding pair of Mute Swans can be surprisingly tolerant of other birds. When a pair must make it on their own on a small lake or pond, they are quick to drive off any potential competition, including their own young.

OTHER SPECIES FIELD NOTES

■ **Trumpeter Swan**
Cygnus buccinator
L 60"
Black facial skin forms
V-shape at forehead

■ **Whooper Swan**
Cygnus cygnus
L 60"
Large yellow patch on
lores and bill

■ **Mute Swan**
Cygnus olor
L 60"
Black knob at base
of orange bill

MIGRATION

The Tundra Swan is the greatest migrant among swans. It flies thousands of round-trip miles between breeding grounds on the coastal tundra of Alaska and Arctic Canada to wintering quarters along both coasts as far south as North Carolina in the East and the Mexican border in the interior West. The birds fly these great distances in surprisingly few days and often at extraordinary altitudes. Pilots have observed swans at nearly 27,000 feet. Trumpeter Swans breeding in interior Alaska winter in British Columbia and at times as far south as Washington State. Most Trumpeter populations—such as those in Yellowstone National Park, which offers open water year-round—are small and local. Trumpeter and Mute Swans may live their entire lives within a few miles of where they were hatched.

STATUS AND CONSERVATION

Swans of both indigenous species were seasonally abundant across North America well through the colonial period. On November 2, 1770, while leading a survey party down the Ohio River, George Washington recorded all the game he saw that day, including "a great many small grassy Ponds or Lakes which are full of Swans, Geese, and Ducks of different kinds." Over the next century, swan populations plummeted due to overshooting. Between 1853 and 1877, the Hudson Bay Company bought 17,671 swan skins for the ladies'- apparel trade, most from nesting Trumpeter Swans, an unsustainable harvest. The Tundra Swan's remote breeding grounds still protected the smaller bird. Later, after a network of rails was built to connect most major towns east of the Mississippi, the Tundra Swan joined its cousin's steep decline. When commercial gunning ended in the 1920s, only a handful of both species remained— about 450 Trumpeter Swans. Thanks to protection and the birds' inherent resilience, Trumpeter Swans now number more than 23,000, while approximately 200,000 Tundra Swans crisscross our North American skies. Reintroduced Trumpeter Swans to the Great Lakes region are flourishing.

See also

Pelicans, page 62
Geese, page 94
Ducks, page 96

Canada Goose: *Branta canadensis*, L 25-45", black head and neck with white chin strap.

GEESE

The Canada Goose (above) is one of the most variable species found across the New World Arctic and subarctic, where small forms are found mostly in western Canada and Alaska, larger forms in the eastern part. Some ornithologists are studying this species to learn whether different "taxa" (races, subspecies) might behave more like full species. In the lower 48 states many of the nesting Canada Geese are not native but from introductions of "Giant" Canada Geese, a subspecies that was threatened with extirpation from hunting and other pressures on the population. These birds have adapted so successfully to golf courses, farms, and other man-made habitats that they have become pests, chasing off nesting waterbirds and fouling lawns. The call of Canada Geese on migration is emblematic of the call of the wild to millions.

Range of Canada Goose

CLASSIFICATION

From a strict taxonomic standpoint, there are only six species of North American geese in three genera. When former subspecies are considered, the number jumps to at least 18 different subspecies, or forms, within the three genera. The Canada Goose includes an Aleutian, Cackling, Common, Dusky, Giant, Lesser, Richardson's, and Western forms. The Brant includes Black, Gray-bellied, and Atlantic or Pale-bellied forms, and there are several recent records of the Dark-bellied form from Eurasia. The three North American races of Greater White-fronted Geese are distinguished by their preference for breeding, or wintering habitat: Tundra, Taiga (Tule), and Greenland. The Snow Goose is divided into a western or Lesser form, an eastern or Greater form, and a completely different color morph, often called "Blue Goose." The diminutive, distinct Ross's Goose is like a miniature Snow Goose, and it, too, has a blue morph, which is quite rare. Considering the genetic vigor of the Anserinae, if Emperor Geese were more numerous, they would likely evolve another race or two of their own. When one adds such Old World strays as the Barnacle, Bean, and Pink-footed Goose to the equation, North American birders have got quite a selection of geese to identify. Although the Hawaiian Goose or Nene is not a North American species, it is native to the United States and merits mention.

STRUCTURE

Geese are well adapted for walking and exploiting the winter grainfields that have played a crucial role in the increase of some species that were once scarce.

PLUMAGE

As with swans, the plumage of male and female geese is the same—an indication that such birds form long-lasting pairbonds. The overall white of the Snow Goose and Ross's Goose hints at their evolution in the high Arctic, where white is a cryptic color for birds nesting in a snow-swathed environment; these species both have black primary feathers. Several large, unrelated, but otherwise all-white species (Snow Goose, White Ibis, American White Pelican, Wood Stork) have black wing primaries or wing tips; the dark pigmentation appears to strengthen this part of the wing, reducing wear caused by the elements.

FEEDING BEHAVIOR

Geese feed early and late in the day. During the hunting season, they also feed on moonlit nights. Midday finds field-feeders loafing on the same waters where they roost. Sea geese, such as Brant and Emperor Goose, feed according to the tide. They are active at low tide, rest at high tide. Even after some populations of Atlantic Brant learned to exploit winter grainfields, they have kept to a tidal schedule. Regardless of the time of day, the birds lift off fields as the tide in nearby bays begins to rise. The Brant then fly to open water and wait for the falling tide to trigger their appetites.

Barnacle Goose

VOCALIZATION

Almost everyone is familiar with variations on "honk" or "ong" made by Canada Geese, which also make a murmuring sound when feeding and a hissing sound when defending nests or young. Many people are now also familiar with the falsetto "yelps" of Snow Geese as their numbers have skyrocketed. Less familiar are the clanging cackles made by Greater White-fronted Geese or gabbling murmurs of a Brant flock overhead.

BREEDING BEHAVIOR AND RANGE

Geese nest in an extraordinary variety of habitats. Greater Snow Geese prefer to be in colonies along the coasts of Arctic islands, while isolated pairs of Nene are found thousands of feet above sea level. The different races of Canada Geese can be found nesting from lichen-bordered ponds on the tundra to urban lakes in Florida and southern California. Some Canada Geese like elevated sites, such as the tops of beaver houses, abandoned Red-tailed Hawk nests, and narrow ledges overlooking the Missouri River. Conservationists tap this impulse by providing Canada Geese with straw-filled tires on floating platforms or raised poles.

The usual number of eggs in a goose nest is half that in a duck's nest: five or six, versus 10 to 12. Yet because both parent geese guard their eggs and young and frequently drive off predators as large as themselves, gosling survival rates are generally higher than those of ducklings.

MIGRATION

The Emperor Goose remains in its Bering Sea range, wintering mainly in the Aleutians, and the rare visitors to the continental United States draw birders from hundreds of miles. Most other species move to the southern United States and Mexico after breeding. The situation with Canada Geese is more problematic as populations of resident Canada Geese continue to soar, making them a nuisance in communities all across the nation. Without many large predators nor the stress of migration, resident Canada Geese fledge larger broods which compete for food with wintering migratory birds and other species. Although the U.S. Fish and Wildlife Service has approved, where possible, hunting seasons for the residents, the reproduction rate of Canada Geese continues to outstrip hunting mortality.

STATUS AND CONSERVATION

Thanks to the inherent capacity of geese to rebound and the special interest of conservationists and sportsmen, every species that was sorely depleted by unregulated shooting a century ago has now fully recovered. Even the Nene, which once numbered only a handful of birds, can now be counted in the hundreds. As far as some populations of Canada and Snow Geese are concerned, the problem is not that there are too few—but too many. Lesser Snow Geese have become superabundant, thanks largely to their switch from a winter diet of cordgrass along the Gulf Coast to the tender young shoots and roots of domestic grains. Lesser Snow Goose numbers ballooned in the 1990s until about 5.8 million birds crowded the flyways. Huge flocks began to devastate their feeding and breeding grounds in the North as well as farm fields in the South. In 1999, the U.S. Fish and Wildlife Service began an effort to reduce the population by lengthening the hunting season and the plan seems to be working, since Lesser Snow Geese now number under three million.

OTHER SPECIES FIELD NOTES

■ **Greater White-fronted Goose**
Anser albifrons
L 28"
Distinctive white band at base of bill, barring on belly

■ **Bean Goose**
Anser fabalis
L 31"
Black bill with orange-yellow band

■ **Pink-footed Goose**
Anser brachyrhynchus
L 26"
Pink legs, dark base and tip to pinkish bill

■ **Snow Goose**
Chen caerulescens
L 26-33"
Large pinkish bill with "grinning patch," two color morphs

■ **Ross's Goose**
Chen rossii
L 23"
Stubby, triangular, pinkish red bill, rare blue morph

■ **Emperor Goose**
Chen canagica
L 26"
Head and back of neck white, chin and throat black

■ **Brant**
Branta bernicla
L 25"
Black head and neck with whitish patch on neck

■ **Barnacle Goose**
Branta leucopsis
L 27"
White face, black neck and breast

See also

Swans, page 92
Ducks, page 96

Mallard: *Anas platyrhynchos*, L 23", male glossy green head, yellow bill, female mottled brown

DABBLERS, WHISTLING-DUCKS

Perhaps no bird is as well known as the Mallard (above), a handsome species of dabbling duck that nests across the northern latitudes around the globe and one that has been domesticated. The proliferation of the species, however, has had serious side effects on other dabbling ducks of the

Range of Mallard

genus *Anas* such as Mottled Duck and American Black Duck, both of which occasionally hybridize with Mallards that were once in farmyards or bird collections. The "Mexican Duck" of Mexico now considered a subspecies *(diazi)* of Mallard, has lost genetic integrity due to the spread of northern Mallards. The Mexican Duck has little sexual dimorphism: The male lacks the green head and pale upperparts and appears similar to the female. It can be difficult to identify ducks that show features of several species; these birds often are hybrids or backcrosses, and they can produce viable young. Wild Mallards nest in the northern United States and Canada, migrating to the southern U.S. and Mexico for the winter.

CLASSIFICATION

Dabbling ducks and whistling-ducks are groups within the Anatidae. The generic name of the whistling-ducks—*Dendrocygna* (tree swan)—underscores the taxonomic fact that the Black-bellied and Fulvous Whistling-Ducks are more closely related to swans and geese than to ducks. This is apparent when they stretch out their neck and legs for landing, unlike other ducks. Once known as "tree-ducks," the former English common name for these birds indicated nicely their penchant for perching in trees. Sixteen dabbling ducks are classed in the genus *Anas,* whereas the unique Wood Duck is placed in *Aix* and Muscovy Duck in *Cairina.*

STRUCTURE

Whistling-ducks are strikingly alike in having long legs, long necks, and relatively large bills, all adaptations to their arboreal lifestyles. Overall, dabbling ducks are similar to one another in body shape, but they differ in the shape and fine details of the bill. Most duck species have comb-like lamellae along the edges of both mandibles for straining small food items from water. This feature reaches its highest development in the Northern Shoveler, whose bill is specially broadened to sift large quantities of watery mud to extract small invertebrates. The upper mandible of all waterfowl is hardened at the tip. This "nail" is especially effective for stripping grain from seed heads by field-feeding birds.

PLUMAGE

Birds in which both sexes share the same plumage patterns and colors form long-lasting and often lifelong pair bonds. The whistling-ducks, Mottled Duck, and a significant percentage of American Black Ducks fall into this category. Most dabbling ducks, though, show strong sexual dimorphism, with the male being more gaudily pigmented, the female typically clad in browns and grays, so as to be less conspicuous at the nest. Drake dabbling ducks' colors are often striking, especially in the Cinnamon Teal, Northern Shoveler, Wood Duck, American Wigeon, Green-winged Teal, and Mallard, but many species' colors are more subtle, though no less beautiful. After the breeding season, ducks molt into an eclipse (or basic) plumage, in which the males resemble the females. In most species (Blue-winged Teal is an exception), the birds molt rapidly back into their breeding (alternate) plumage, which is held through the winter into the spring.

FEEDING BEHAVIOR

Whistling-ducks and dabbling ducks are both omnivorous, and their diets change during the course of the year, depending on availability of certain foods and the particular needs for minerals and proteins during migration, breeding, and the molt. The most common way for dabbling ducks to feed is to pick insects from the water's surface or to tip in the shallows and pluck grasses and invertebrates from the bottom. Waste grain in agricultural areas currently constitutes an important food source for many species of dabbling duck. Each fall across rural North America, flocks of Mallards and Northern Pintails bustle over cut grain fields, quickly "mumbling" remnant corn from the cob. At times, dabbling ducks have become agricultural pests, in the opinion of farmers. Following World War II, for instance, large flocks of American Wigeon began feeding in the expanding lettuce fields of California's Central Valley. The birds were so abundant and persistent that the U.S. Fish and Wildlife Service provided area landowners with a legal exemption that would allow them to use food to attract the ducks to hunt-

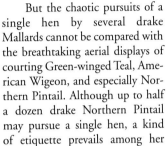

Green-winged Teal

ing blinds. Likewise, in the Deep South, rice farmers complain of the toll on their crops taken by Blue-winged Teal and other species.

BREEDING BEHAVIOR

The courtship rituals of sex-similar species are less spectacular than those of sexually dimorphic species, in which strikingly patterned drakes must compete annually for the acceptance of hens. A drake Mallard, for instance, courts a female by pumping his head to highlight its green iridescence. He also dips his bill and brings it up smartly so that bright sun turns the dripping water into liquid jewelry. If that fails to impress her, he plumps and rears up in the water to exaggerate his size and chestnut breast. Yet throughout all this, most hens appear quite nonchalant. The first sign that a drake has made a connection is when the female begins to duplicate his head pumping. As do most ducks, Mallards also court on the wing.

But the chaotic pursuits of a single hen by several drake Mallards cannot be compared with the breathtaking aerial displays of courting Green-winged Teal, American Wigeon, and especially Northern Pintail. Although up to half a dozen drake Northern Pintail may pursue a single hen, a kind of etiquette prevails among her suitors—a very different situation than with the every-drake-for-himself Mallards. The Northern Pintail hen sets the course and pace. She veers, swerves, even makes abrupt turns and climbs, often covering more than a mile of prairie in a few brief minutes. So long as the drake who first followed her can match her moves, the other males hang back. The hen may then reward the dominant drake's skill by allowing him to take her tail in his beak or to pass under her, so close that their

OTHER SPECIES FIELD NOTES			

Fulvous Whistling-Duck
Dendrocygna bicolor
L 20"
Dark bill and legs, tawny plumage, black wings

Black-bellied Whistling-Duck
Dendrocygna autumnalis
L 21"
Red bill and pinkish legs, white wing patch

Wood Duck
Aix sponsa
L 18.5"
Male glossy green head, red eye, female eye patch

Muscovy Duck
Cairina moschata
L 26-33"
Glossy black

Mottled Duck
Anas fulvigula
L 22"
Pale head and bluish speculum, sexes alike

American Black Duck
Anas rubripes
L 23"
Pale on face and foreneck, violet speculum

Spot-billed Duck
Anas poecilorhyncha
L 22"
Black bill with yellow tip

Gadwall
Anas strepera
L 20"
Male gray with black tail coverts, female mottled

Falcated Duck
Anas falcata
L 19"
Male sickle-shape (falcated) tertials

Green-winged Teal
Anas crecca
L 14.5"
Male dark green ear patch, female small bill, mottled brown

Baikal Teal
Anas formosa
L 17"
Male has long gray and rufous scapulars

American Wigeon
Anas americana
L 19"
Grayish head, warm breast, male has white forehead and cap

Eurasian Wigeon
Anas penelope
L 20"
Reddish brown head with creamy forehead and cap

Northern Pintail
Anas acuta
Male L 26" Female 20"
Male has chocolate head, white neck, long tail

White-cheeked Pintail
Anas bahamensis
L 17"
White cheeks and throat

Northern Shoveler
Anas clypeata
L 19"
Long, spatulate bill

Blue-winged Teal
Anas discors
L 15.5"
Male has violet-gray head, white facial crescent. Female has large bill, spotted undertail coverts

Garganey
Anas querquedula
L 15.5"
Bold white eye stripe, whitish edge to tertials

Cinnamon Teal
Anas cyanoptera
L 16"
Male is rich cinnamon, female is rich brown

wing tips touch and briefly clatter. If he fails to keep up, she signals another male to try. While such displays may enthrall us human observers, we should remember that they are an essential evolutionary challenge for the participants. Most dabbling ducks build nests on the ground close to wetland edges. Mallard hens prefer the natural cover of dense vegetation, whereas incubating Blue-winged Teal hens pull additional leaves over themselves to prevent avian predators from spotting them. Although the Wood Duck and Mandarin Duck are the dabblers best known for nesting in tree cavities and man-made boxes, both the Muscovy Duck and Black-bellied Whistling-Duck will often use such sites.

Many species of hens lay their eggs in the nests of other hens. So many eggs may ultimately be laid in so-called "dump nests" that they are abandoned: the first female may continue to try to brood all the eggs, including those of strangers, but once the egg count exceeds 30, her brooding instinct shuts down, and she goes elsewhere to start again. Wood Duck hens, however, have hatched up to eight eggs in a nest where as many as two dozen "cold eggs" remained.

BREEDING RANGE AND MIGRATION

Although the Black-bellied Whistling-Duck is most commonly seen in southern Texas, where birds are found perching on telephone poles along roadways, strays have turned up throughout the center of the continent and the East Coast as far north as southern Canada. Similarly, Fulvous Whistling-Ducks frequently pioneer up all four flyways, as far north as Nova Scotia and Alberta, and there are even records of West Indian Whistling-Duck and White-faced Whistling-Duck for North America, both tropical species that are kept in captivity, possibly the source of such records.

Also likely to be found in trees are the Wood Duck and the closely related, introduced Mandarin Duck of eastern Asia. Although there is a breeding population of Wood Ducks in the Pacific flyway, and some are found nesting in cottonwood boles on Canadian prairie waterways, their core nesting and wintering habitat has always been in the forested swamps of the Southeast. Also found in trees is the Muscovy Duck, genus *Cairina*, a unique species among North American ducks and currently found only along the Rio Grande in southernmost Texas.

Several species in the genus *Anas* have the greatest distribution of any ducks. The Northern Pintail is a Holarctic species breeding in the upper latitudes of North America and Eurasia and wintering south to Central America, Africa, and Southeast Asia. Such natural vagrancy in a species of waterfowl is extraordinary. Another great wanderer is the Northern Shoveler, which frequently winters almost as far south as the Equator. Of the four blue-winged ducks in the genus *Anas*—Northern Shoveler, Garganey, Blue-winged Teal, and Cinnamon Teal—only the latter species is not a notable migrant. The Garganey is a Eurasian species that occasionally turns up in North America. The Blue-winged Teal regularly migrates between breeding grounds as far north as Alaska to wintering grounds as far south as Colombia. By contrast, the Cinnamon Teal breeds primarily in the western United States and winters there. In South America, it's replaced by a look-alike subspecies that moves between the Pampas and breeding grounds farther south.

The Green-winged Teal is not closely related to the Blue-winged Teal. Although the North American race

BLACK-BELLIED WHISTLING-DUCK

These large, goose-like ducks were formerly known as Black-bellied Tree Ducks because of their preference for tree cavity nest sites. But this social and vocal bird also has a unique, musical whistling call that is often repeated assisting the birdwatcher in readily locating a noisy flock. The Black-bellied Whistling-Duck is unmistakable with it bright red bill and pink legs and feet; large chestnut breast, gray head with bold white eye ring, and a rich black belly. Whistling-Ducks have a noticably slower wingbeat than smaller ducks, and the feet extend beyond the tail in flight. In North America they breed mainly along the Texas Gulf Coast seeking out natural cavities or nest boxes located near shallow freshwater ponds and lakes. Decidedly nocturnal feeders, they often leave their roosts at sunset to feed until early morning especially on Bermuda grass, sorghum, and millet. A game bird, but the population is stable over its range.

(*carolinensis*) migrates sometimes great distances within the continent, it rarely strays beyond. There are hundreds of records of *carolinensis* from Europe, as there are hundreds of the Old World form from North America. Some scientists believe these forms to be separate species, based on DNA investigations. The Green-winged Teal migrates surprisingly late and winters surprisingly far north for such a small and cold-vulnerable duck.

The Gadwall is found throughout the world, but nowhere in abundance—except in western North America. In the 1920s, Gadwalls were released by hunters in Long Island, New York, and gradually spread throughout eastern North America.

The American Wigeon is not as cosmopolitan as others in this genus, probably because the closely related Eurasian Wigeon fills the same ecological niche. Stray American Wigeon regularly turn up in Europe, and stray Eurasian Wigeon show up in North America, especially along the Atlantic and Pacific coasts.

Because the Mallard can cope with man-made habitats, this species is now the most widespread duck

Gadwall

on Earth, found feeding in marinas from Norway to New Zealand, and breeding in backyards from Seattle to Singapore. Each spring, in Washington, D.C., Mallard broods in the Tidal Basin below the Jefferson Memorial provide photo-ops for the tourists. As a rule, captive- and urban-reared Mallards migrate little, whereas a growing percentage of wild Mallards appear to migrate less with each passing decade. So long as food and open water are available in the North, Mallards linger rather than run the autumn gauntlet.

The Mallard has two closely related cousins, one of which, the Mottled Duck, has solved the problem of finding safe winter quarters by living along the southern coastal plain and not migrating. Like resident Canada Geese, most Mottled Ducks are permanently pair bonded and lead narrowly prescribed lives bounded by secure feeding, roosting, and breeding wetlands rarely separated by more than a few miles. Most American Black Ducks migrate, but nonmigratory representatives such as those which once bred on marshy islands in the Chesapeake Bay are disappearing.

STATUS AND CONSERVATION

The 20th-century history of waterfowl is one of imperilment and slow but steady recovery. The ornithologist George Bird Grinnell expressed the belief in 1901 that Wood Ducks "are becoming very scarce and are likely to be exterminated before long." Thanks to protection and careful management, including the construction and

maintenance of tens of thousands of nesting boxes throughout its range, the Wood Duck is now once again a common sight for birders and hunters alike. The erection of nest boxes is also aiding the recovery of the little-known but fascinating Muscovy Duck, whose Spanish name, *pato real* (royal duck) harks back to the time when domesticated forms of this species were taken from Mexico by the Conquistadores and presented as proof of the New World's bounty to King Phillip II of Spain. Since England and Spain were adversaries at the time, the bird probably entered Britain through the Baltic, and the seemingly inapt name Muscovy was likely intended to honor the Muscovy Company, an English joint-stock trading group founded in 1553 to explore a possible northeast passage to Asia through Russia. Mottled domestic forms of the Muscovy Duck have been introduced in the United States, but the wild birds, found only in Central America north to southernmost Texas, are handsome glossy blackish green birds with large white wing patches. The species is considered vulnerable if not endangered in its range.

For all of the efforts of government agencies, conservation groups, and wildfowlers on their behalf, some problems persist for dabbling ducks. The most pervasive problem is the ongoing loss of optimum wetland habitat. Although a battery of laws in the U.S. insists that for every wetland acre lost, an acre of equal value must be restored, these laws are not always enforced, and the courts often find it difficult to determine just what an "acre of equal value" is. Another poorly known issue concerns the impact of predators on nesting birds. The Northern Pintail has declined dramatically over the past two decades, because of hunting regulations that were slow to take into account the species' rapid decline and the pintail's inclination to nest well out in fields where farm machinery destroys countless nests each spring. Recent research by the Delta Waterfowl Foundation in Manitoba has shown that populations of predators—especially raccoons and foxes—have grown manyfold in what was traditionally the best waterfowl production habitat in Canada. In past centuries, trapping kept a lid on the number of furbearing predators, but the fading fashion in fur coats means this form of broad-scale control is little practiced.

See also

Swans, page 92
Geese, page 94

Ring-necked Duck: *Aythya collaris*, L 17", peaked head, bold white ring near tip and base of bill

DIVING DUCKS

The Ring-necked Duck (above) is one of a larger group of diving ducks of the genus *Aythya* that is often called "bay duck," including Greater and Lesser Scaup, Tufted Duck, Redhead, and Canvasback. These birds share the attributes of a dark head and breast and lighter sides, but only the Ring-necked and Tufted Ducks show a dark back, and these two are often found on freshwater lakes and ponds rather than saltwater bay or ocean. The Ring-necked Duck has an unusually shaped head with a distinct peak, which makes identification easier. The same cannot be said of the fine magenta ring that separates the glossy purple head from the black breast in adult males: Exceptionally close views in good light are required to see this mark, and many birders use the name "Ring-billed Duck" in reference to the prominent white band around the bill of males and females. The ducks nest in Canada and eastern Alaska, on wooded ponds and swamps; like mergansers and Wood Ducks, they nest in tree cavities. In autumn, they migrate south.

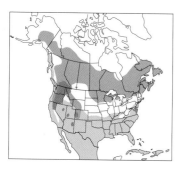

Range of Ring-necked Duck

CLASSIFICATION

The diving ducks of North America include 23 species in 11 genera. The largest group of these is the *Aythya*, or pochards, also known as "bay ducks" for their tendency to flock and forage in inshore waters: the Canvasback, Redhead, Greater and Lesser Scaup, Ring-necked Duck, and Tufted Duck, all in the tribe Aythyini. The "sea ducks," which can forage in open ocean, may be classified into three groups of three species each, all in tribe Mergini. The first are eiders of the genus *Somateria*: Common, King, and Spectacled Eiders. The second grouping includes scoters of the genus *Melanitta*: the Surf, Black, and White-winged Scoters. A third group of sea ducks, for convenience, might be the three disparate species in genera *Polysticta* (Steller's Eider), *Histrionicus* (Harlequin Duck), and *Clangula* (Long-tailed Duck), each unique in several respects. The three mergansers, in the genera *Lophodytes* (Hooded Merganser) and *Mergus* (Common and Red-breasted Mergansers), are also rather divergent, while their close relatives in *Bucephala* (Bufflehead, Barrow's, and Common Goldeneyes) have similar natural histories. The last and certainly most peculiar ducks in this category, both in tribe Oxyurini, are the "stiff-tails," the Masked Duck and the Ruddy Duck.

STRUCTURE

Diving ducks tend to have stout, sturdy bodies and short necks. Their legs are shorter than most dabblers', set far back on the body, and have a lobed hind toe. Pochards have bills like those of dabblers in shape, and this reflects the varied diet of an omnivore. Most of the sea ducks, along with Greater Scaup and mergansers specialize in foraging on ocean invertebrates, and their heavy bill, larger than that of most dabbling and bay ducks, are adaptations for their prey. The large bill of eiders and scoters can even crack open mollusks, which they pry off submerged rocks. The bill of mergansers does not resemble that of other ducks, being long and streamlined, with the lamellae bearing small, tooth-like points adapted for gripping fish, their chief prey.

PLUMAGE

Diving ducks in North America have a dazzling array of plumages, most easily told apart by narrowing a bird down to its genus or tribe, then searching for field marks specific to species. The pochards are rather similar to one another—dark-headed and pale-flanked in the drake. In Redhead and Canvasback, drakes have red heads that allow them to be distinguished by hue alone (the Canvasback's head is more maroon than red), as well as by shape (the Canvasback has a Roman or "patrician" profile), and an adult drake Canvasback's eyes are red, whereas an adult drake Redhead's are yellow. Some field characteristics are difficult to see: A mature male Ring-necked Duck shows a faint collar that gives this species its common name, but it is only visible at close range in good light. The dark peaked hind crown and bright white ring around the bill of the drake Ring-necked distinguish it from the similarly dark-backed male Tufted Duck, whose head sports a

Canvasback

tuft of feathers that falls to the neck, and a bill that is only faintly ringed. Female pochards, which are mostly brown, cause the greatest problems of identification, and the problem of telling species apart is even more challenging with the Greater Scaup and Lesser Scaup. The green highlights in the head of the mature male Greater Scaup and the purple highlights in the head of the mature male Lesser Scaup are not always apparent, even in good light. Years ago, sportsmen distinguished the two species by calling the Greater "Broadbill" and

the Lesser "Bluebill." Although the Greater Scaup's slate-colored bill is thicker and broader than the Lesser Scaup's, the Lesser's bill is not much bluer, if at all. Head shape is a much more reliable indicator for identification: The small corner on the hind-crown of the Lesser is distinctive on a resting bird.

Mature drake eiders in each of the three *Somateria* species are easily distinguished by their striking head patterns. Even hens can be told apart on the basis of relative size, bill structure; in the case of the Spectacled Eider, the hen sports a set of pale "goggles" resembling the drake's. As with eiders, adult drake scoters are readily distinguished by their strikingly patterned bill and head. Hens are more difficult and often confused with juveniles, not only of their own species, but of other scoters.

OTHER SPECIES FIELD NOTES

■ **Canvasback**
Aythya valisineria
L 21"
Forehead slopes to long, dark bill

■ **Common Pochard**
Aythya ferina
L 18"
Bill dark at base and tip, gray in center. Female gray on upperparts

■ **Redhead**
Aythya americana
L 19"
Round head, tricolored bill

■ **Tufted Duck**
Aythya fuligula
L 17"
Rounded head with distinct crest, smaller in female

■ **Greater Scaup**
Aythya marila
L 18"
Male has rounded head with green gloss. Female white patch at base of bill

■ **Lesser Scaup**
Aythya affinis
L 16.5 "
Peaked head, male's with purple gloss

■ **Common Eider**
Somateria mollissima
L 24"
Sloping forehead with feathering along sides of bill to nostrils

■ **King Eider**
Somateria spectabilis
L 22"
Male ornate with bulbous forehead. Female has rounded head

■ **Spectacled Eider**
Somateria fischeri
L 21"
Distinctive spectacled head

■ **Steller's Eider**
Polysticta stelleri
L 17"
Male has black eye patch and greenish head tufts. Female pale eye ring

■ **Black Scoter**
Melanitta nigra
L 19"
Male has orange knob at base of bill. Female has pale face and throat

■ **White-winged Scoter**
Melanitta fusca
L 21"
White wing patches

■ **Surf Scoter**
Melanitta perspicillata
L 20"
Male has colorful bill, white head patches

■ **Harlequin Duck**
Histrionicus histrionicus
L 16.5"
Male ornately patterned, female round head, distinct white facial spots

■ **Long-tailed Duck**
Clangula hyemalis
Male L 22" Female L 16"
Male has streamer tail, female dark cheek patch

■ **Barrow's Goldeneye**
Bucephala islandica
L 18"
Oval-shape head, steep forehead, stubby, triangular bill

■ **Common Goldeneye**
Bucephala clangula
L 18.5"
Male has round white spot on face. Female has dark bill with yellow tip

■ **Bufflehead**
Bucephala albeola
L 13.5"
Small duck with large, puffy head

■ **Common Merganser**
Mergus merganser
L 25"
Thin, orange bill, white breast and sides

■ **Red-breasted Merganser**
Mergus serrator
L 23"
Shaggy double crest, thin orange bill

■ **Hooded Merganser**
Lophodytes cucullatus
L 18"
Puffy, rounded crest, thin, dark bill

■ **Smew**
Mergellus albellus
L 16"
Male white with black markings. Female, chestnut head with white throat

■ **Ruddy Duck**
Oxyura jamaicensis
L 15"
Large head, broad bill, long tail often cocked up

■ **Masked Duck**
Nomonyx dominicus
L 13.5"
Male has black face, . female and winter male have dark stripes on face

The stunning drake Harlequin Duck lives up to both its common and scientific names, and the drake Long-tailed Duck's exceptionally long tail (up to six inches) accentuates his intricate black, brown, and white plumage. This species goes through the most complex molts of any waterfowl, with intermediate phases adding up to four distinct patterns. Since each bird seems to follow its own molt schedule, even drakes that are seen on the same day and in the same area may appear different. The cavity-nesting Common Goldeneye, Barrow's Goldeneye, and Bufflehead drakes are easily distinguished by the color patterns and the shape of their head, as are the three mergansers and two stiff-tailed ducks, though females and eclipse-plumaged males require considerably more study—fortunately, there are usually a few drakes around to provide a clue.

FEEDING BEHAVIOR

Diving ducks, as the moniker suggests, pursue prey and food sources by diving and swimming underwater, using their strong feet to propel them during foraging. Some species, such as mergansers, take mostly fish, and these birds often hunt cooperatively. Since a single bird attacking a school of fish has less of a chance than a number of birds attacking in a coordinated fashion, all three merganser species have been observed to dive and feed in "skirmish lines" that effectively block small streams or shallow bays. The smaller and more teal-like Hooded Merganser occasionally eats other food besides fish. On some wintering grounds, it even acquires a taste for shelled corn, enabling biologists to bait traps with the grain so they can catch and band the birds.

Canvasback, as is true of many pochards, is flexible in its foraging, taking aquatic vegetation, invertebrates, and fish. The Canvasback species name *(valisineria)* refers to wild celery, once a major component of the Canvasback's diet. Today native submerged aquatic vegetation is most everywhere fighting a losing battle against pollution, siltation, and exotic introductions such as *Hydrilla*. Wintering Canvasbacks along both coasts now feed mainly on invertebrates and fish. As a result, their flesh is indistinguishable from other birds in this genus, whose diets have always featured shellfish. The adaptability of diving ducks to changing prey resources is remarkable. In the Great Lakes, the accidental introduction of the non-native Zebra Mussel has become a source of food for countless diving ducks, whose migrational pathways have changed as a result of this new bounty. It remains to be seen whether these mussels' tendency to concentrate toxins will have a negative impact on diving duck populations.

VOCALIZATION

The various pochards are best known for the hens' low growls; on wintry days when the birds are flocked, the

RUDDY DUCK

One of two stiff-tailed ducks in the United States, the Ruddy Duck is often referred to informally as the "stiff-tail" in reference to the long tail feathers frequently cocked sharply up lending a rather jaunty, and even toy-like aspect to this charming duck. These rigid tail feathers are used as rudders for steering during foraging dives. Ruddys breed in the prairie pothole region of the upper Midwest and Canada and lay the largest egg in relation to their body size of all ducks. An average clutch of seven eggs is about equal to the female's mass. Ducklings are cared for by the female, but are very precocial, leaving the nest within 12 to 24 hours after hatching. They find their own food without assistance, and are diving for food by their second day. Ruddy Ducks may be the most aquatic of ducks and are considered to be the least mobile, tending to push themselves along the ground rather than walking upright. In the winter they are readily seen along both coasts and at large inland lakes. The Ruddy is considered a pest in Europe where it was introduced.

growls sound like the distant purring of many cats. Memorable, too, are the calls of flocking Black and Surf Scoters, whose gentle wails and cries sound like faint boats' bells and high foghorns. Eiders are less musical. Females cluck and croak; males make ghostly yodels. The Long-tailed Duck is the most vocal of sea ducks. From late winter through spring, females constantly grunt and quack; males softly howl, and their many common names reflect these almost human calls. Masked and Ruddy Ducks are mostly silent. But male courtship displays in both species are accompanied by eerie noises impossible to duplicate in print.

The most haunting sound made by any duck in this category is not vocal. It is the low, stirring whistling made in flight by the wings of adult male scoters and goldeneyes—especially the Common Goldeneye—a sound that gives the latter species its other common name: "Whistler." A prettier but less familiar sound is the in-flight cricket-like trill made by the wings of mature drake Hooded Mergansers.

BREEDING BEHAVIOR

Unlike waterfowl species with sexes in similar plumage, diving ducks tend to form new pair bonds each year. Most sea ducks begin to breed at two years of age, although they may participate in courtship displays in their first winter and spring. These displays can involve complex courtship flights, as in White-winged Scoters, which fly in group formations; or elaborate posturing and posing, as in Red-breasted Mergansers, Buffleheads, and the goldeneyes. Ruddy and Masked Duck drakes both erect their tails during the head-pumping, water-splashing displays; in other forms of behavior, these species are different. The Masked Duck is extremely secretive and often solitary, whereas Ruddy Ducks are sociable. When discussing the importance of breeding colors, the eyes are often overlooked. Yet the bright color of drake Canvasback, Redhead, and Hooded Merganser eyes offer females important clues regarding the health and suitability of males as potential mates. Mature drake Canvasbacks have brilliant ruby red eyes, mature drake Redheads and Hooded Mergansers have bright yellow eyes. Immature drakes and hens have dark eyes.

In territoriality, diving ducks differ in approach: eiders tend to form loose colonies of nests, Redheads' nests can be close together with little territoriality in evidence, but most species are solitary nesters, either in tree cavities (Hooded and Common Mergansers, Bufflehead, the goldeneyes) or on the ground. The Barrow's Goldeneye and Red-breasted Merganser have even appropriated abandoned seabird and animal burrows. Several pochard species accept platform nests erected for them in marshes. Most species lay 5 to 12 eggs, though nests with more eggs are frequently seen. Of the eight duck species known to practice parasitic egg-laying, five are divers: Redhead, Ruddy Duck, Hooded Merganser, Common Goldeneye, and Common Eider. The Redhead is the champion in this department: One nest contained 80 eggs. Not all such "egg dumping" is interspecific. A significant percentage of hen Redheads deposit their eggs in the nests of other species. Since Canvasbacks and Redheads share much of the same breeding range, and since they both make nests over water, either by building a dense mat of aquatic vegetation or by commandeering the floating feeding station of a muskrat, Canvasbacks bear the brunt of Redhead egg dumping. This activity may be an important reason why

Canvasbacks struggle to maintain a population of 500,000 birds, whereas Redheads have a 1990s average of 750,000. Hatching success is reduced in these dump nests, and predation can be higher, with complete losses common, so this strategy will likely continue to evolve over time.

MIGRATION

All diving ducks migrate away from nesting areas, though some are truly long-distance migrants; others travel only a few hundred miles. Much of what is known about waterfowl migration comes from careful studies in the field, including banding returns. Diving ducks can be difficult to capture for banding, although the species that accept nest boxes are readily banded. Hens of Hooded Mergansers occasionally use Wood Duck nesting boxes maintained by researchers, so that the migration paths of individual "Hairyheads," as they are called, can be recorded. Neither the Common Merganser nor Red-breasted Merganser use man-made nests, and since both species prefer open water on which to winter, these birds are rarely banded. What we know of their migration routes is based on field observation. A few tropical species, such as Masked Duck, make irregular movements based on availabile habitat rather than season.

Common Goldeneye

STATUS AND CONSERVATION

Conservation for diving ducks has focused on the pochards in the 20th century; studies and conservation programs for sea ducks, mergansers, and *Bucephala* have been more recent. These measures came too late for the handsome Labrador Duck, which has not been seen since 1878. The U.S. Fish and Wildlife Service classifies the Steller's and Spectacled Eiders as threatened under the Endangered Species Act; the Atlantic population of Harlequin Duck as endangered. Worldwide population of Steller's Eiders is an estimated 220,000, Spectacled Eiders 360,000, and Canvasbacks 360,000. Despite marginal numbers for Canvasbacks and Redheads, the Canadian and U.S. Fish and Wildlife Services try to keep the birds on the game list. Common Goldeneye and Greater and Lesser Scaup—known to have declining populations—continue to be hunted.

See also

Loons and Grebes, page 29
Plovers, Jacanas, Oystercatchers, page 141
Skuas, Gulls, Terns, page 163

ROSS'S GOOSE

BREEDING RANGE EXPANSION

Breeding range 1980

Breeding range 2003

WINTER RANGE EXPANSION

Winter range 1980

Winter range 2003

Individuals and small flocks now turn up regularly in much of the United States and Canada.

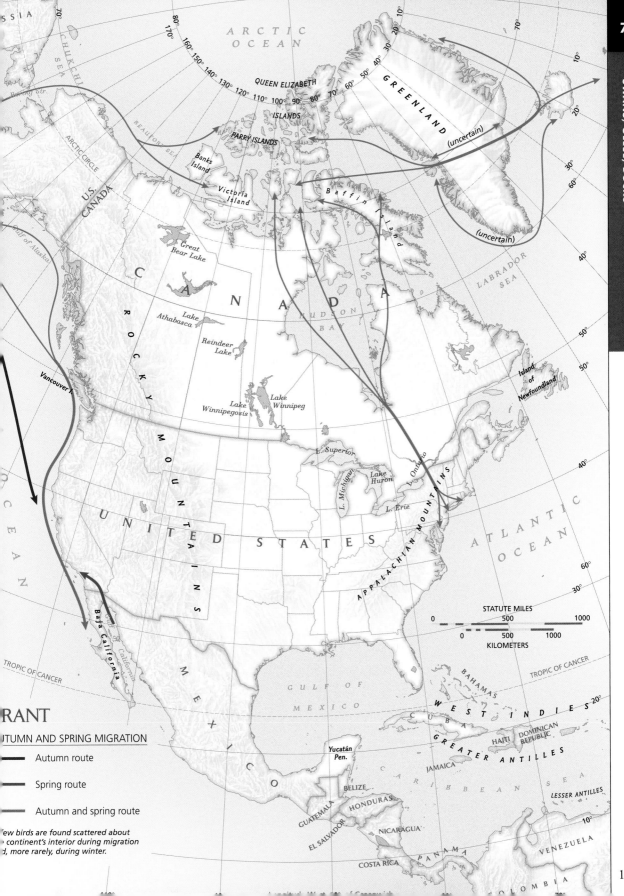

ARCTIC
OCEAN

QUEEN ELIZABETH
ISLANDS

G R E E N L A N D

(uncertain)

Banks
Island

PARRY ISLANDS

(uncertain)

Victoria
Island

Baffin Island

CHUKCHI
SEA

BEAUFORT SEA

ARCTIC CIRCLE

Gulf of Alaska

U.S.
CANADA

Great
Bear Lake

C A N A D A

LABRADOR
SEA

H U D S O N
B A Y

Lake
Athabasca

Reindeer
Lake

R O C K Y

Island
of
Newfoundland

Vancouver I.

Lake
Winnipegosis

Lake
Winnipeg

M O U N T A I N S

L. Superior

L. Michigan

Lake
Huron

L. Ontario

L. Erie

APPALACHIAN MOUNTAINS

ATLANTIC
OCEAN

U N I T E D   S T A T E S

Baja California

Gulf of California

TROPIC OF CANCER

TROPIC OF CANCER

STATUTE MILES

0   500   1000

0   500   1000
KILOMETERS

M E X I C O

GULF OF
MEXICO

BAHAMAS

W E S T   I N D I E S

C U B A

HAITI   DOMINICAN
REPUBLIC

G R E A T E R   A N T I L L E S

JAMAICA

Yucatán
Pen.

C A R I B B E A N   S E A

LESSER ANTILLES

BELIZE

GUATEMALA   HONDURAS

EL SALVADOR

NICARAGUA

COSTA RICA

P A N A M A

VENEZUELA

COLOMBIA

RANT

UTUMN AND SPRING MIGRATION

—— Autumn route

—— Spring route

—— Autumn and spring route

*ew birds are found scattered about
  continent's interior during migration
d, more rarely, during winter.*

105

VULTURES, EAGLES, HAWKS, FALCONS

Few groups of birds are as evocative as raptors, those great birds of prey that include such diverse species as eagles, hawks, and falcons. Whether we are watching a gathering of Bald Eagles feasting on salmon on a remote Alaskan river, thrilling to buteos belting down the ridge at Hawk Mountain on a brisk November day, delighting in an American Kestrel "mousing" over a grassy interstate median, or just enjoying a Red-tailed Hawk perched patiently on a suburban woodlot, raptors inspire in us a sense of beauty and wildness. Even if seen in a less-than-pristine setting, raptors summon for us a feeling that there are still wild places and that as long as there are predators and prey, there is still the chance for a healthy environment.

Clay Sutton

Raptors, predators at or near the top of the food chain, are often perceived as powerful, and rightly so. In their flight they achieve a grace and beauty of movement equaled perhaps only by seabirds. Few groups of birds have conquered the aerial realm as well as hawks. They soar regularly up to 2,500 feet on rising thermals, and ride updrafts off mountain ridges with supreme efficiency. The dives or "stoops" of Peregrine Falcons and Golden Eagles, at speeds of more than 125 miles an hour, are some of the most dramatic sights in the animal world.

Of the 313 currently recognized species of vultures, eagles, hawks, and falcons found worldwide, 34 are regularly seen in North America north of the Mexican border. Raptors are a diverse group in both size and plumage, as well as behavior and food preferences. All North American birds of prey are carnivorous and either tear apart their prey or, if it is small enough, such as a mouse, swallow it whole. The size and type of prey can vary widely. A Golden Eagle has been known to take prey as large as a coyote or pronghorn, but American Kestrels will feed on grasshoppers and Mississippi Kites mostly on dragonflies. Ospreys feed exclusively on fish, and Turkey Vultures on carrion which in itself can be as varied as a beached whale or a road-killed rabbit.

Size, shape, and behavior of raptors varies considerably. The California Condor, with a ten-foot wingspan and weighing 20 pounds, bears little resemblance to a Sharp-shinned Hawk, which may weigh as little as three ounces and have a 20-inch wingspan. The graceful and colorful Swallow-tailed Kite differs widely from the almost tailless-appearing and monochrome Black Vulture, and the sleek angular lines and rapid, direct flight pattern of a Merlin have little in common with the lazy circle of a wide-winged, Red-tailed Hawk.

Raptors can be found in virtually any habitat in North America. Northern Harriers nest north to the edge of the Arctic Ocean in Alaska, and Hook-billed Kites build their nests above the lazy meanders of the Rio Grande in Texas. Golden Eagles hunt the high dry deserts of the Southwest, and Northern Goshawks are a top predator in the vast northern forests.

A birder can spot raptors almost anytime and anywhere in North America, be it in the Bronx or the Florida Everglades, but most hawks are seen during migration. Although a few species, such as Crested Caracara and Black Vulture are largely resident, most species are migratory. Wherever they are seen, raptors provide the birder with a memorable experience.

(Left) Sharp-shinned Hawk

Turkey Vulture: *Cathartes aura*, L 27" W 69", red head, two-toned wings in flight

VULTURES

The most widespread vulture in the Americas, popularly known as "buzzard," the Turkey Vulture (above) plies the skies of the temperate through tropical habitats, where it is a familiar sight, even in some urban settings. Few observers of this species find it aesthetically appealing: Its naked, wrinkled, red head, disheveled-looking, dark

Range of Turkey Vulture

plumage, and its fondness for dead animals make it unpleasant to behold. In the air, however, the species is most graceful: Soaring on the uplifted dihedral of their great wings, Turkey Vultures tilt back and forth on warm air currents from mid-morning to late afternoon. The sight of hundreds gathered, circling high in the air (a "kettle" of vultures), is breathtaking. Unlike its relative the Black Vulture, the Turkey Vulture possesses a keen sense of smell that enables it to locate dead animals, even if the carrion is concealed in a forested setting.

CLASSIFICATION

The three vulture species in North America, Turkey Vulture, Black Vulture, and California Condor are in the family Cathartidae. They are generally considered among the raptors, yet recent DNA studies show New World vultures to be ancestrally more closely related to storks. Of interest is that Old World vultures are closely related to other hawks and eagles. The similar structure of Old World vultures and New World vultures is a wonderful example of form following function and of convergent evolution, wherein similar features have developed despite widely different origins.

STRUCTURE

Vultures are large, heavy-bodied birds, with long, broad wings designed for lengthy, effortless soaring on thermals and updrafts. Like other raptors, their long, slotted (narrow-tipped) primary feathers function as air foils, providing lift and control.

Vultures are excellent flyers. Turkey Vultures can tease lift from conditions under which no other raptor can soar. Black Vultures are steadier than the tippy Turkey Vulture and soar to great heights, looking like miniature sailplanes. The California Condor is one of the greatest flyers in the world of birds, able to cover hundreds of miles in a single day. They do this by converting altitude (gained while soaring) into distance, in long, efficient glides. Vultures all show bare, unfeathered heads that facilitate their scavenger lifestyle, allowing them to reach inside carcasses to feed without soiling their feathers. Being carrion feeders, the feet and talons are small and weak. Only the Black Vulture will occasionally feed on live prey and generally eats it alive rather than killing it first as hawks do.

PLUMAGE

The plumage of vultures is dark, with little difference between juveniles and adults. Black Vultures are truly black, with silvery patches at the wing tips. Turkey Vultures are dark brown below and paler above, with silvery flight feathers running the length of the wing (primaries and secondaries). The otherwise dark California Condor shows, as an adult, brilliant white underwing coverts below, and a brilliant orange head. Black Vultures have a bare black head, and Turkey Vultures have a black head, when juvenile, and a bright red head, when adult.

FEEDING BEHAVIOR

New World Vultures are scavengers, feeding on dead animals from the size of mice to deer and elk. Historically, California Condors were seen feeding on dead beached whales. Condors and Black Vultures search for food visually; Turkey Vultures are known to locate carcasses by smell. Vultures feed on site and regurgitate the food to the young. They will feed heavily when food is available and can go for many days without food if necessary. Turkey and particularly Black Vultures regularly feed at dumps and landfills. The increase in White-tailed Deer, their overabundance and resultant frequency of roadkills, is thought to be a major factor in the increasing numbers and range expansion of Turkey Vultures and Black Vultures in the Northeast.

VOCALIZATION

Vultures are generally silent except for hissing and grunting noises made at the nest or when approached by a predator. As a defense mechanism, they will regurgitate on a potential predator when threatened.

BREEDING BEHAVIOR

Compared to other raptors, vultures have restrained, yet definite courtship flights and territorial displays. They are solitary nesters in hollow logs, crevices, caves, mine shafts, and sometimes in hollow trees. Black Vultures commonly use abandoned buildings. They do not build nests. Both sexes incubate and carefully attend the young. Young follow the parents for months after fledging.

BREEDING RANGE

Vultures are found throughout the continental United States, and Turkey Vultures range into southern Canada. The Black

California Condor

Vulture is more southerly and eastern in distribution than the Turkey Vulture, but is rapidly expanding its range. The California Condor is currently found only in southern California and northern Arizona, where it has been reintroduced into its former range.

MIGRATION

The California Condor and Black Vulture are largely nonmigratory, but the Turkey Vulture is highly migratory, withdrawing from the northern portions of its range in winter. While some may go only short distances, others go a long way. Hundreds of thousands of Turkey Vultures are counted at hawk-watches in Veracruz, Mexico, and Panama each spring and fall.

OTHER SPECIES FIELD NOTES

- **Black Vulture**
  Coragyps atratus
  L 25" W 57"
  Large white patch at base of primaries

- **California Condor**
  Gymnogyps californianus
  L 47" W 108"
  Huge size, orange head, white wing linings

WINTER RANGE

With global warming and the increasing number of roadkilled deer available in the East, Turkey Vultures regularly winter farther north than formerly. Currently, many Turkey vultures winter as far north as southern New England. In much of the West, Turkey Vultures are absent in winter, withdrawing into Mexico and farther south during the cold months.

OBSERVING VULTURES

Rarely difficult to find, the familiar, tilting, rocking flight of Turkey Vultures is a common sight throughout North America, and the steady Black Vulture is ubiquitous in the Southeast and along the Gulf Coast.

The California Condor is a different story, and the words spoken by ornithologist Arthur Cleveland Bent in the 1930s still apply today. "To see one of these great birds in the solitude of its native haunts gives a thrill well worth the time and effort required. Few have enjoyed the experience, and many are not equal to the task."

Today California Condors can only be seen in the few areas where they have been reintroduced. They require a very specific search, but bird-finding guides and hotlines readily provide information on these rare viewing opportunities.

STATUS AND CONSERVATION

The Turkey and Black Vulture are abundant and expanding, even to the extent that their numbers are controlled, through depredation permits, in some agricultural areas in the East where they are alleged to kill just-born livestock. The dire plight of the California Condor has led to one of the greatest conservation struggles of our time. Once widespread from British Columbia to Baja California, by the early 1980s fewer than 20 condors remained in the wild. Since then, an intensive capture, captive breeding, and reintroduction program has brought them back from the brink, yet the California Condor is still one of the most severely endangered birds in America. Today condors are found only in southern California and in the Grand Canyon region of Arizona, where they still face many threats and require the strongest management and protection efforts possible.

See also

Wood Stork, page 82

Eagles, page 112

Crested Caracara, page 116

Osprey: *Pandion haliaetus*, L 22-25" W 58-72", dark brown above, white below, dark eye stripe

HAWKS AND EAGLES

The high, piping call of the Osprey (above) announces the arrival of spring for residents of the Atlantic coast, much as the piping of the Broad-winged Hawk heralds spring in the interior of the East. Both of these raptors return early from their wintering grounds in the subtropical and tropical regions of the Americas. The Osprey is the only exclusively fish-eating raptor in North America, catching fish on the wing by a swoop to the water's surface. During the 1950s and the early 1960s, this diet exposed Ospreys to high levels of DDT, which concentrated in the fish on which the birds fed and thus in the Ospreys' tissue. As with other predatory and piscivorous species such as Bald Eagle, Brown Pelican, and Peregrine Falcon, the Osprey's eggshells were weakened by the pollutant, becoming so thin they were crushed during incubation. The banning of DDT in 1972, in the United States and Canada, helped reverse the population decline and has set these species on the road to recovery through most of their former ranges.

Range of Osprey

CLASSIFICATION

Many birds prey on other animal species, be they insects or earthworms, but the words "birds of prey," or raptors, are popularly used to describe hawks, eagles, falcons, and their allies. About 313 species of raptors are currently recognized worldwide, including falcons, which are placed in their own family, the Falconidae. Hawks and eagles are in the family Accipitridae.

There are 24 species in the family Accipitridae, which regularly breed in North America, and several nonbreeders—vagrants from Europe and Asia that appear in Alaska from time to time, such as the White-tailed Eagle and Steller's Sea-Eagle, or wanderers from tropical Mexico such as Roadside Hawk, which rarely appears along the Rio Grande in Texas.

Despite remarkable diversity, all species are easily recognizable as raptors, yet birds of prey are generally divided into several distinct groupings. The buteos are perhaps the most widely recognized and most often sighted raptors. Buteos are large, wide-winged, short-tailed soaring hawks, often seen circling on thermals or riding mountain updrafts. Some are forest dwellers and others are found in open country. The Red-tailed Hawk, found from treelines in the Canadian Arctic south through Mexico, is the quintessential buteo, its robust shape found on trees, snags, crags, poles, and transmission towers in all regions and most habitat types.

The Broad-winged Hawk is also widespread, nesting throughout the vast eastern forests from the Southeast to southern Canada. The Broad-winged Hawk is "replaced" in the West by the Swainson's Hawk. The Swainson's is an open-country bird, breeding in grassland and prairie from Arizona to southern Alaska. The Rough-legged Hawk is a high Arctic breeder, and other buteos, such as the Gray, Black, and Zone-tailed Hawks are tropical species. In the United States, they are found only from Texas west through Arizona.

Accipiters can be small or large, but are characterized by relatively short, rounded wings and long, rudder-like tails which aid in their amazing maneuvers. Except during migration, accipiters are mostly forest birds, and are primarily bird-eating hawks, catching other birds in short dashing chases or ambushes. Of the three North American accipiters, the Sharp-shinned Hawk is the smallest, with a breeding distribution which is more northerly than that of the larger Cooper's Hawk. The large and powerful Northern Goshawk is a northern forest dweller and the least common of the accipiters.

Harriers are open-country birds, hunting low over tundra, marsh, meadow, and field. They have long thin wings and a very long tail. Only one harrier species is found in North America, the Northern Harrier, still commonly called the Marsh Hawk by many. It is most often recognized by its bright white rump, one of the most noticeable field marks of any hawk, yet when high overhead the hawk is probably most often misidentified by hawk-watchers, looking quite falcon-like in a glide and accipiter-like when soaring.

Eagles are heavy-bodied, large, robust birds of prey, with gigantic feet and talons. No single morphological feature makes an eagle an eagle. Eagles are simply very large hawks, and the use of the term is a matter of semantics. Several European eagles are smaller than our Red-tailed Hawk. Bald Eagles and Golden Eagles are not closely related, attested to by the fact that they are not listed together on the official American Ornithologists' Union checklist.

The kites are a diverse group of medium-size hawks in a variety of shapes, colors, and behavior. Two species feed on snails, but many feed mainly on insects. Kites lack the bony ridge over the eye exhibited by all other hawks, lending them a benign appearance. The large and striking Swallow-tailed Kite is one of the most graceful of all flying birds. Mississippi Kites are wonderful flyers,

White-tailed Kite

too, often remaining aloft for many hours, feeding on the wing. Mississippi Kites can appear falcon-like due to their long, pointed wings.

The Osprey is sometimes placed in its own family, Pandionidae. It feeds exclusively on fish, caught by plunging feet first into the water. The Osprey shares with the Peregrine the honor of being the most cosmopolitan of all raptors, found on all continents except Antarctica. There are four races of Osprey, but only a single species is recognized worldwide.

STRUCTURE

Up close, raptors are best characterized by their distinctive beaks and feet. A hawk's hooked upper bill and spoonlike lower bill let it easily pierce and dismember prey. Hawks have strong specialized feet and four sharp, pointed talons for catching, holding, and carrying prey. The Osprey has specialized barbs on its toes to help with holding slippery fish, and its outer toe is reversible, like

---

OTHER SPECIES FIELD NOTES

■ **Osprey**
Pandion haliaetus
L 22-25"W 58-72"
Brown above, dark eye-stripe

■ **Mississippi Kite**
Ictinia mississippiensis
L 14.5" W 35"
Gray plumage, pointed wings

■ **Swallow-tailed Kite**
Elanoides forficatus
L 23" W 48"
Deeply forked tail

■ **White-tailed Kite**
Elanus leucurus
L 16" W 42"
Black shoulders

■ **Snail Kite**
Rostrhamus sociabilis
L 17" W 46"
Reddish legs and facial skin, white tail coverts

■ **Hook-billed Kite**
Chondrohierax uncinatus
L 16" W33"
Heavy hooked bill

■ **Northern Harrier**
Circus cyaneus
L 17-23" W38-48"
White rump, low flight

■ **Golden Eagle**
Aquila chrysaetos
L 30-40" W 80-88"
Tawny head and neck

■ **White-tailed Eagle**
Haliaeetus albicilla
L 26-35" W 72-94"
Short white tail

■ **Steller's Sea-Eagle**
Haliaeetus pelagicus
L 33-41" W87-96"
White tail, huge bill

■ **Bald Eagle**
Haliaeetus leucocephalus
L 31-37" W 70-90"
White head and tail

■ **Sharp-shinned Hawk**
Accipiter striatus
L 10-14" W 20-28"
Small head, long tail

■ **Cooper's Hawk**
Accipiter cooperii
L 14-20" W 29-37"
Long rounded tail

■ **Northern Goshawk**
Accipiter gentilis
L 21-26" W 40-46"
Conspicuous eyebrow

■ **Common Black-Hawk**
Buteogallus anthracinus
L 21" W 50"
Blackish plumage, two-toned tail

■ **Harris's Hawk**
Parabuteo unicinctus
L 21" W 46"
Chestnut shoulders, leggings and wing linings

■ **Zone-tailed Hawk**
Buteo albonotatus
L 20" W 51"
Barred flight feathers

■ **Short-tailed Hawk**
Buteo brachyurus
L 15.5" W 35"
Dark secondaries

■ **Broad-winged Hawk**
Buteo platypterus
L 16" W 34"
Underwings white with dark borders

■ **Gray Hawk**
Asturina nitida
L 17" W 35"
Gray upperparts, gray barred underparts

■ **Red-shouldered Hawk**
Buteo lineatus
L 15-19" W37-42"
Reddish shoulders

■ **Red-tailed Hawk**
Buteo jamaicensis
L 22" W 50"
Reddish tail, dark bar on leading edge of underwing

■ **Swainson's Hawk**
Buteo swainsoni
L 21" W 52"
Long pointed wings

■ **Rough-legged Hawk**
Buteo lagopus
L 22" W 56"
Long white tail with dark bar, dark belly band

■ **Ferruginous Hawk**
Buteo regalis
L 23" W 53"
Rusty back, shoulders and leggings, extended gape

■ **White-tailed Hawk**
Buteo albicaudatus
L 23" W 50"
Long legs, white tail with single black band

an owl's, which aids them both in catching and carrying fish. Raptors have extraordinary vision to aid them in their predatory lifestyle. A hawk's vision is thought to be about eight times better than that of a human, a visual acuity gained from the density of sensory cells on the retina, and the large size of the eye itself. The eyes are forward directed, giving hawks a greater degree of binocular vision. While this eyesight does not allow the extreme depth perception owls have, it is better than most birds' vision. Hearing is well developed in some raptors, particularly harriers, whose owl-like facial disks reflect sound back toward their hidden ears. Accordingly, harriers use hearing when hunting to a greater degree than other hawks and are often crepuscular, hunting in the dim light of dawn and dusk.

PLUMAGE

Although many raptors exhibit muted plumage, studies in grays and browns, a few species are surprisingly striking. The bright plumage of the Harris's Hawk and the brick red-orange barring of an adult Red-shouldered Hawk are as dramatic and bright as that of any bird, except perhaps our most colorful songbirds.

A general pattern is seen in accipiters and buteos where juveniles are streaked and adults are barred below. All raptors show discernable juvenile and adult plumages. Many species of buteos show polymorphism, distinct dark and light-plumaged individuals that will occur in the same race, population, or even the same brood. These birds, for example Rough-legged Hawks, are commonly said to be either dark morph or light

COMPARING EAGLES

Bald Eagle

Golden Eagle

Although appearing similar in size and structure, the Bald Eagle and the Golden Eagle are not closely related. The Bald Eagle is placed in the genus *Haliaeetus*, the Sea Eagle group, and as this implies, it is almost always found near water— coasts, lakes, and rivers. Throughout its range the Bald Eagle feeds extensively on fish and often also on carrion, although it can be a highly efficient hunter if need be. The Golden Eagle in the genus *Aquila* has a more westerly distribution and is more commonly associated with mountains, tundra, and grasslands. The Golden Eagle is a true hunter, a skilled catcher of ground squirrels, jackrabbits, and waterfowl.

Both eagles are huge, with wingspans up to nearly seven feet in females, which are larger than males. This sexual size dimorphism is seen in all raptors. The Bald Eagle shows a larger head and heavier bill than the sleeker Golden Eagle and generally a shorter tail. In flight the white head and tail of an adult Bald Eagle are unmistakable, yet the golden hackles of a Golden Eagle can make the head appear very pale, almost white, in some individuals when in bright sunlight.

Both Bald Eagle and Golden Eagle take about four years to achieve their full adult plumage. To separate young

Balds and Goldens in the field, pay careful attention to the white in the wing. Balds show white at the base of the wing, on the underwing coverts, and often on the belly, too. Young Goldens usually show a distinct white patch on the outer wing, at the base of the primaries and a bold white tail with a black tip. A Golden's wings are more tapered than the plank-like wings of a Bald. Bald Eagles usually soar on flat wings, and Goldens show a comparative dihedral, wherein the wings are held above the body, creating a slight V when viewed head on. Despite this dihedral, Golden Eagles are rock-steady in flight, showing none of the rocking or tipping commonly seen in Turkey Vultures. Bald Eagles are just as steady. This characteristic is of great help when picking out eagles at a distance.

Spotting eagles is one of the true joys of raptorwatching. Even now that the Bald Eagle has made a remarkable recovery and comeback from the ravages of DDT and can again be seen in good numbers in its range, it is still a special day when you can say that you saw an eagle.

morph individuals, and the coloration is carried for life. For some hawks plumage can vary over the species' geographical range. A dark Harlans race Red-tailed Hawk found in western Canada looks unlike the pale Fuertes race found in the desert Southwest.

Snail Kite, Hook-billed Kite, and Northern Harrier are sexually dimorphic; for example, the gray back, white-bellied appearance of the adult male Northern Harrier is different from the warm brown streaking of the adult female. Young harriers show a bright, rusty, or cinnamon coloration unlike that of the adults.

Raptors molt their entire plumage once a year, usually in the spring. The timing can vary. Bald Eagles molt once a year, but the molt can be delayed or protracted due to weather and food availability. Birds of prey molt their flight feathers sequentially, the same primary on each wing, for example, so they remain "balanced" and fully flightworthy at all times.

FEEDING BEHAVIOR

Raptors show reversed sexual dimorphism, wherein the females are larger than the males. This has benefits for breeding, when the female does most of the brooding of eggs and young, as well as in food specialization. The differences allow the larger females to take larger prey than males, and the availability of a variety of prey in nesting season has benefits for nesting success. For example, the smaller, more lanky and agile male Northern

Cooper's Hawk

Harrier takes far more birds than the larger female, which usually takes mice and voles, and often selects a different habitat for hunting. As a result the male and female of a mated pair do not compete with each other while hunting.

All hawks catch live prey after giving chase, be it dropping on prey from a low perch or rocketing down from high above in a dramatic stoop. Many hawks will eat carrion when stressed for food or still learning to hunt. Accipiters primarily take birds they catch in ambush or in short and quick spirited chases. Male Sharp-shinned Hawks mostly catch sparrows or warblers, the larger females usually take the larger blackbirds and doves. Northern Goshawks and Cooper's Hawks often eat squirrels, and Northern Goshawks catch prey as large as Snowshoe Hare and grouse.

Buteos feed primarily on mammals—rabbits, squirrels, rats, mice, and voles. Some buteos such as Broad-winged and Red-shouldered Hawks feed from low perches and take many reptiles and amphibians, but the Red-tailed and Rough-legged Hawks hunt from high overhead. A Red-tailed Hawk will hover in place, searching for prey, or sometimes will "kite," hanging

motionless in the wind, in effect using an aerial perch to sight potential prey. The western Swainson's Hawk has a variety of hunting techniques, but is commonly seen on the ground in freshly plowed fields, searching for grubs and earthworms. The White-tailed Hawk of the Texas coast region routinely follows prairie brush fires, taking advantage of prey flushed by the fires. The Short-tailed Hawk of the Florida prairies is a true aerialist, a buteo which specializes in small birds, which it catches in dramatic stoops from high overhead.

Kite feeding behavior varies greatly. Hook-billed Kites scan for tree snails from a low perch and Snail Kites take aquatic Apple Snails directly out of the water. Mississippi and Swallow-tailed Kites are consummate aerialists, aloft for many hours at a time, deftly taking dragonflies in flight. The White-tailed Kite is an opportunist and a generalist. Every raptor is different.

VOCALIZATION

Raptor voices are variable. Some hawks such as Red-taileds and Red-shouldereds have loud, harsh calls, heard over vast distances. Northern Harriers have a thin, insistent whistle, as do some kites. Accipiters voice a chattering bark or cackling. Ospreys have a clear, resonant, repeated whistle, and the calls of eagles are surprisingly weak—a stuttering chirping. Voice is used for communication between a mated pair, as a challenge to other raptors, or if a predator strays too near the nest or perch. Calls are used for identification, but more important for birders, a raptor's call is an alert that a raptor is present.

BREEDING BEHAVIOR

Hawks and eagles have elaborate courtship displays, some of the most dramatic of all North American birds. Eagle and buteo display flights are prolonged and energetic. Red-taileds have a dramatic and lengthy roller-coaster display flight wherein the male swoops on closed wings and at the bottom of the dive skyrockets straight up again. Male Ospreys loudly call as they circle above with a prized fish, then hover, dive, and swoop back up. Bald Eagles will lock talons and cartwheel together through the sky. Northern Harriers may have the most elaborate courtship flight; males perform actual loops or somersaults in the air, displaying to a female below. All Accipitridae build their own nests, usually substantial stick nests placed in a tall tree. Golden Eagles will use tree nests, but primarily nest on ledges and cliffs in the West, and north of treeline in the Arctic. Snail Kites create basket-like nests in reeds and low shrubs. Ospreys take readily to both transmission line poles and man-made nest platforms. The Northern Harrier is the only obligate ground nester of the group, but Bald Eagles will use ground nest sites in the barren Aleutian Islands. Both male and female incubate and tend the young. Some species vigorously defend the nest and chicks, most notably the Northern Goshawk, a bird that has driven many an errant hiker from the forest if he has strayed too close to a nest.

The number of eggs will vary by species. The clutch size can depend on food availability. In years of food abundance, clutch size may be considerably larger. Young follow parents for some time, begging for food until they learn to hunt on their own. Mortality is high in young raptors—only about 10 percent survive to adulthood. Yet, their lifespan can be quite long; an adult Bald Eagle may live over 25 years in the wild.

BREEDING RANGE

Raptors are found in every habitat type in North America. Rough-legged Hawks breed on high Arctic tundra cliffs, whereas Common Black Hawks breed in riparian areas in the deserts of the Southwest. Some buteos such as Swainson's and Ferruginous Hawks breed in open country, but Broad-winged and Red-shouldered Hawks are forest dwellers. Harris's Hawks prefer dry, scrubby brushland. Red-tailed Hawks have adapted to almost all habitat types. All accipiters are normally forest birds in breeding season, but Cooper's Hawks are decidedly suburban in many regions, subsisting on starlings and pigeons in cities. Kites are southerners, mainly found below the Mason-Dixon Line, where temperatures support large insect and snail populations in breeding season. Some kites, such as the Mississippi Kite, are widespread; other tropical species only barely make it into the United States such as the Snail Kite in Florida and the Hook-billed Kite in south Texas.

Red-tailed Hawk

MIGRATION

The annual raptor migration creates one of the great spectacles in the animal world. All species migrate to some degree—Snail Kites are nomadic—and some are true long-distance migrants. They are diurnal migrants, and often flock during migration. Broad-winged and Swainson's Hawks are the most dramatic flocks or "kettles." Sometimes thousands or even tens of thousands can be seen on migration at places such as Hazel Bazemore Park in Corpus Christi, Texas, in both fall and spring. Over four million raptors are counted each fall at a geographic bottleneck, where mountains meet the sea, as in Veracruz, Mexico. Swainson's Hawks vie with Peregrine

Falcons for the long-distance award among Western Hemisphere hawks. A Swainson's—breeding in southern Alaska and wintering in Argentina—will travel over 18,000 miles round-trip each year. Raptors are long lived; if a Swainson's Hawk lives ten years, it will have migrated over 180,000 miles in its lifetime, and at about four months a year will have spent well over three years of its life in migration. The young migrate separately from their parents and generally migrate before the adults. In many temperate-region species, some adult birds are resident and never migrate, remaining on the breeding territory throughout the year.

WINTER RANGE

Species such as Osprey, Swallow-tailed Kite, Mississippi Kite, Swainson's Hawk, and Broad-winged Hawk mostly vacate the United States in winter. Broad-wingeds winter in South American cloud forests, Swainson's in the grasslands of Argentina's pampas region. Swallow-tailed and Mississippi Kites migrate to South America, and Ospreys commonly winter south through Brazil. Only the Florida Osprey population is resident year-round.

For most other raptor species, we mainly see birds withdraw from the northern part of their range, with southern populations augmented by "snowbirds." Of two Texas Red-tailed, for example, perched on adjacent roadside telephone poles, one might be a local resident, the other a wintering bird that will return to Manitoba to breed. On New Jersey's Delaware Bayshore, the 25 pairs of resident Bald Eagles are often supplemented by over 100 visitors from as far north as the Canadian Maritimes, particularly during the harshest winters, when northern snows push eagles south. Hawks select the same type of habitat they are known for in the breeding season. Rough-legged Hawks choose prairies, pasture land, marsh, and meadow, all open country which is similar to their Arctic tundra summer range.

OBSERVING HAWKS AND EAGLES

Watching hawks and eagles is easiest during migration and in winter. During migration, geography and topographical features concentrate raptors. Weather, snow and ice cover, and food availability concentrate birds. Winter gatherings of hawks are extraordinary in areas such as the Texas coast, southern Florida, and for one example, the Sulphur Springs Valley in southeastern Arizona, where they are concentrated by a mild climate, habitat preference, and an abundance of prey.

Most hawks are secretive on the breeding grounds, hard to find, and even harder to watch. They are highly sensitive to human disturbance. Use caution and good birding ethics around any raptor nest. Because hawks have large territories and soar high in the sky, observing raptors requires good binoculars—not high magnification, but of high optical quality. Hawk-watching challenges all but the best binoculars, and ID skills must be at a premium. Because height and distance of the hawk often preclude being able to see classic field marks, hawks are identified more often by behavior—general impression, shape, and size, the "GISS" or "jizz"—than perhaps any other group of birds.

To find hawks, scan edges—where field meets forest, or where wetlands intersect with woodlands. Hawks seek edges, due to the variety of prey and hunting opportunity, which these transition areas provide. Time of day will play a role. In early morning, most hawks are perched. Some secretive species may be deep in forests, but many buteos seek commanding perches or snags, transmission line poles, or fenceposts. Towers and billboards along interstate highways are commonly used as perches by Red-tailed Hawks. Check all such sites, both visually and with binoculars, to find hawks.

Later in the day many hawks are aloft. Winds are often stronger in midday, and this is also when thermals develop. Thermals are invisible rising bubbles of heated air, and soaring hawks actively seek them for the free ride to high altitude. Higher altitude gives hawks a greater view of their territory and of potential meals.

Hawks soar as high as 5,000 feet, and are often seen as mere specks against the blue. One hint is to actually scan puffy white clouds with your binoculars. You will often pick out high-flying hawks which are much too high to be seen with the naked eye.

STATUS AND CONSERVATION

Some of the most compelling conservation stories of our time involve raptors. Well into the late 20th century, hawks and eagles were severely persecuted by humans, and even today many are still shot as "chicken hawks" or because they are said to take livestock. DDT had a huge impact on some raptor species. Osprey and Bald Eagle populations were reduced to a mere vestige of their former numbers until DDT was banned. Osprey and Bald Eagles have rebounded, and the outlook for raptor conservation is good today. But many raptors can still pick up DDT in South America where its use remains legal, and thousands of Swainson's Hawks have been poisoned by misguided pesticide use in Argentina. Habitat loss remains a threat for Snail Kite and American Kestrel, and all raptors still need our strong watchdog efforts.

See also

Brown Pelican, page 62

HAWK MOUNTAIN

During migration a birder can see, in one day, a number and variety of hawks which might take years to see otherwise. Then, many secretive, forest-dwelling species such as the Sharp-shinned Hawk and Broad-winged Hawk leave the sheltering woods and fly in the open. More importantly, during both spring and fall migrations, raptors concentrate along "leading lines." Excepting Osprey, Peregrine, and Merlin, hawks are not "designed" to fly over water. Most follow lakeshores and coastlines. Shorelines concentrate raptors all over America, from the Marin headlands of California to the Florida Keys. Lakeshore routing creates the large autumn flight at Duluth, Minnesota, and the spring numbers at Braddock Bay, New York. In fall at Cape May, New Jersey, raptors following the Atlantic coastline south, encounter land's end at the tip of the Cape May Peninsula, and fill the skies. The result is spectacular hawk-watching when blustery cold fronts both trigger migration and steadily push migrants toward the coast.

Mountain ridges are another form of geographical leading line; raptors will follow north-south oriented ridgelines. Here updrafts create a "free ride," where hawks can sail along without resorting to time- and energy-consuming flapping. This phenomenon occurs from the Sandia Mountains of New Mexico in spring to the Bridger Mountains of Montana and the Wellsville Mountains in Utah in fall.

The northeast to southwest-oriented Kittatinny Ridge in the Appalachian chain provides one of the most remarkable places for hawk-watching. Hawk Mountain, Pennsylvania, lies on the last ridge of the Kittatinny, and hawks, faced with the Piedmont flatlands before them, hug this last ridge and its updrafts which speed their migration. Hawk Mountain Sanctuary near Kempton, Pennsylvania, is not only the legendary spot where hawk counting began, but also the birthplace of hawk conservation, when in 1934 Maurice Brown climbed to the ridge to begin to silence the gunners of autumn, who killed hawks for target practice. Springing from such humble beginnings, hawk counting at Hawk Mountain has become a major conservation tool to monitor the health of raptor populations.

American Kestrel: *Falco sparverius*, L 10.5 ", W 23", russet back and tail, double black stripes on face, often hovers

FALCONS

Known to rural residents by its old name of "Sparrowhawk," the American Kestrel male (above) is one of the more dapper of falcons, clad in salmony pink and slaty blue, with dark and light markings throughout the head and body plumage. The name Sparrowhawk, taken from an Old World accipiter species, is a misnomer, as kestrels prey largely on small mammals hunted from perches such as power lines and fenceposts. These accomplished mousers were popular with farmers during the European settlement of North America; to have a pair nesting in the eaves of one's barn was considered a blessing. With the increased use of rodenticides, and modern farming (which reduces waste grain available to rodents), the kestrels have become scarce over much of their former range, a decline reflected in the diminishing numbers counted at hawk-watches in the East. Where traditional and organic farming is practiced, in areas such as Pennsylvania farmed by Amish and Mennonite families, kestrels thrive and readily accept nest-boxes built for them.

Range of American Kestrel

CLASSIFICATION

Falcons are hawks, yet they differ considerably from buteos and accipiters, and are in the family Falconidae. Six falcon species are found in North America, and one other, the Eurasian Kestrel, is a near-annual vagrant, in the far Northeast or western Alaska. Another species, the Crested Caracara, is resident in Florida, the Gulf Coast, and the Southwest. The Crested Caracara is a tropical species, and though closely related to other falcons, it is an oddity—a wide-winged eagle-like bird that is mainly a scavenger. It is the one North American falcon that does not look or act like other falcons. All falcons are birds of open country, fields, marsh, meadow, prairie, and tundra, and avoid woods and dense vegetation.

STRUCTURE

Excepting the caracaras, falcons are long-winged hawks with long, broad tails. Their wings are distinctly pointed, with narrow, tapering tips. They use fast-powered, flapping flight to a greater degree than buteos and accipiters, although they soar frequently. A major morphological feature of falcons, compared to other raptors, is the notched beak which enables them to kill their prey by severing or crushing the neck vertebrae. They also have large, powerful feet and long toes, with strongly curved sharp talons. In a stoop, their feet deliver strong blows to knock down or disable prey.

PLUMAGE

Falcons are among the more boldly marked hawks, with a strong facial pattern. The Aplomado Falcon and the American Kestrel are particularly colorful and dramatically marked. The American Kestrel and Merlin are sexually dimorphic, that is the male plumage is different from that of females. All falcons show notable sexual size dimorphism with larger females than males. Juvenile plumages are easily discernable in most falcons, including the Crested Caracara.

FEEDING BEHAVIOR

In summer, the American Kestrel feeds on insects, grasshoppers, and dragonflies and in winter over much of its range on mice and small birds. The Aplomado Falcon also has a varied diet. Merlin, Peregrine, and Gyrfalcon feed almost exclusively on birds, the Merlin taking small birds such as swallows, and the Gyrfalcon taking larger prey such as ptarmigan and ducks. The Prairie Falcon feeds on ground squirrels and birds. The Crested Caracara is a scavenger on items from earthworms to large carcasses, yet at times, will catch and kill live prey, such as nestling birds.

VOCALIZATION

Falcons are among the most vocal of raptors, particularly around their nests. The American Kestrel's clear *killy killy killy* cry echos across Pennsylvania farm fields, Iowa prairie, and California desert, and the Peregrine's harsh, mechanical scolding echoes off Arctic cliffs, western mountains, and downtown office buildings. The Crested Caracara, though, is generally silent.

BREEDING BEHAVIOR

Unlike most other raptors, falcons do not build their own nests. American Kestrel are cavity nesters, in trees, nest boxes, or under the eaves of buildings. Merlin use cliff ledges, crevices, and tree cavities, or usurp an old crow's nest. Peregrine, Prairie Falcon, and Gyrfalcon are cliff nesters. The nest is generally no more than a scrape, sometimes with a few sticks or a bit of decorative foliage added. However, Crested Caracara do build their own stick nests, usually low in a tree or shrub.

Falcons have large clutches, three or four eggs, and both parents attend and feed the young. Peregrines are known for their vigorous nest defense. After fledging, American Kestrels remain in distinct family groups, even into the fall migration journey.

BREEDING RANGE

The American Kestrel is the most widely distributed falcon, ranging from Alaska to Florida and Mexico. The Prairie Falcon is a westerner only, breeding on ledges of the high plains and prairies. The Merlin is mostly a Canadian breeder, found in the United States only in Maine and the northern Rockies. Peregrines are widespread in the West and are even found in cities, where they nest on bridges and tall buildings. Most

Peregrines breed in the high Arctic on cliff tops from Alaska to Canada and throughout the Old-World Arctic. The Gyrfalcon is a robust bird of the far north, breeding on Arctic cliffs in the Northern Hemisphere.

MIGRATION

Except for Crested Caracara, which is resident, and Aplomado, which can be nomadic, all

Crested Caracara

North American falcon species are highly migratory. Arctic-breeding Peregrines traverse the planet to the tip of South America (although some city populations are resident, with only the young migrating). All eastern falcons are coastal during migration, and the Peregrine makes substantial overwater migrations. The Gyrfalcon is the least migratory, with at least some birds remaining near the northern nests in winter, where ptarmigan are their principal and perhaps only food.

WINTER RANGE

Except for Gyrfalcon, falcons go south. Merlin and American Kestrel winter in Central America, and Prairie Falcons leave the northern plains for the Southwest. Arctic breeding Peregrines winter throughout South America.

OBSERVING FALCONS

During migration, places such as Fire Island, New York, see waves of falcons, American Kestrels, Merlins, and Peregrines sweeping down the surf-line. The prime spots for Peregrines are Cape May, New Jersey, Cape Charles, Virginia, and Padre Island, Texas, where over a thousand are seen. Washington State's Skagit Flats has a couple of wintering Gyrfalcons, and Sault Ste. Marie, Michigan, and Duluth, Minnesota, host a Gyr or two in winter.

STATUS AND CONSERVATION

Falcons have a similar conservation history as hawks and eagles. DDT victimized Peregrine and Aplomado Falcons. Peregrines have made a strong comeback, and Aplomado Falcons are being reintroduced. American Kestrel numbers are of concern, but Merlin populations are growing. In all, falcons still require watchdog efforts.

OTHER SPECIES FIELD NOTES

■ **Eurasian Hobby**
Falco subbuteo
L 12.25" W 30.25"
White cheeks; thin, dark moustachial stripe

■ **Aplomado Falcon**
Falco femoralis
L 15-16.5 " W 40-48"
Dark flanks, pale, buffy orange belly, eyebrows join at back of head

■ **Crested Caracara**
Caracara cheriway
L 23" W 50"
Large head with red facial skin, long legs, white patches in wings

■ **Eurasian Kestrel**
Falco tinnunculus
L 13.5" W 29"
Single dark facial stripe

■ **Merlin**
Falco columbarius
L 12" W 25"
Slate blue above, barred tail; female browner

■ **Prairie Falcon**
Falco mexicanus
L 15.5-19.5 " W 35-43"
Pale brown above, dark wing linings, weak mustache

■ **Peregrine Falcon**
Falco peregrinus
L 16-20" W 36-44"
Black crown, nape and heavy mustache form "helmet"

■ **Gyrfalcon**
Falco rusticolus
L 20-25" W 50-64"
Heavy falcon with weak mustache

See also

Owls, page 207
Shrikes, page 268

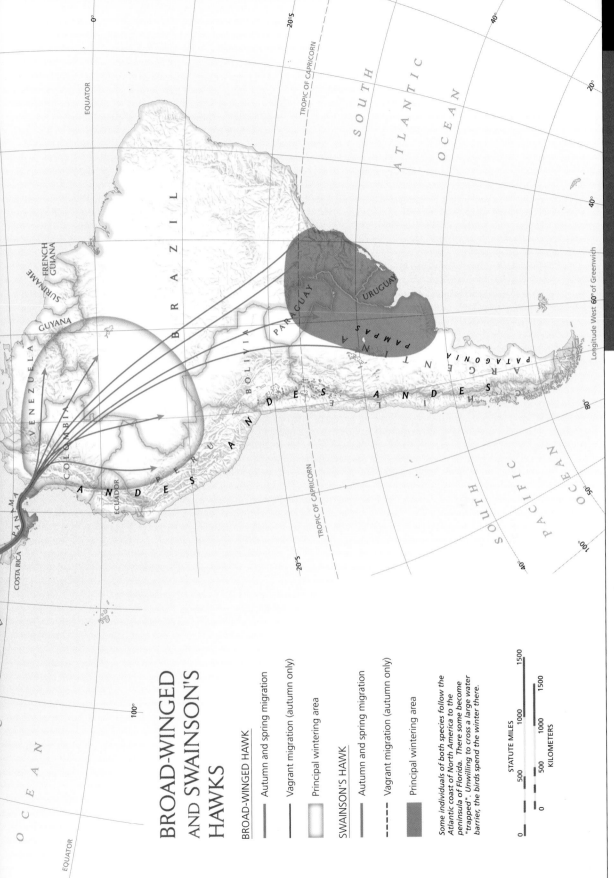

BROAD-WINGED AND SWAINSON'S HAWKS

BROAD-WINGED HAWK

—— Autumn and spring migration

—— Vagrant migration (autumn only)

Principal wintering area

SWAINSON'S HAWK

—— Autumn and spring migration

- - - Vagrant migration (autumn only)

Principal wintering area

Some individuals of both species follow the Atlantic coast of North America to the peninsula of Florida. There some become "trapped". Unwilling to cross a large water barrier, the birds spend the winter there.

STATUTE MILES

0   500   1000   1500

0   500   1000   1500

KILOMETERS

119

CHACHALACAS, GROUSE, QUAIL

Jerry Uhlman

Throughout North America there are 22 species of game birds, or "ground-walkers" as they are sometimes called, and they are found in diverse habitats from arid deserts and prairie grasslands to alpine areas above tree-line. These poultry-like species of gallinaceous birds include Plain Chachalaca, pheasants, partridges, grouse, turkeys, as well as New World Quail.

Gallinaceous species have thick, fleshy breasts and are prized and hunted by small predators such as foxes and raptors, and humans who stalk game birds during the fall hunting season. Three species have been introduced to North America, including Chukar, Gray Partridge, and Ring-necked Pheasant, and were brought to the United States from Asia and Europe to supplement native game bird quarry. Unregulated hunting during the past century nearly decimated several game species, and most of the North American game birds still are objects of open (but regulated) hunts from south Texas into the northern Canadian provinces.

Generally, game birds are wary and employ various techniques to conceal themselves and avoid detection. These species prefer to hide in dense grass or brush and run or freeze when alarmed, but will burst into flight to the nearest cover when surprised. Their wingbeats are loud and very rapid.

The species often live together in flocks, called coveys, which vary in size during the year. Often, coveys consist of family members but may also include unattached adult males or females. During late fall and winter coveys grow in size and males are more tolerant of each other, but when spring breeding season arrives, pairs establish a territory that they defend against intruders.

Many of the gallinaceous male birds have elaborate courtship behaviors, and they gather together in large groups to display and attract one or more mates. During the mating season, skin patches and air sacs become colorful and prominent as a method to attract a mate. The smaller New World Quail have less dramatic displays, but springtime brings considerable posturing and chasing among males.

While nestbuilding is not elaborate, it is usually undertaken by the female with great secrecy and stealth so she can remain undetected during incubation. Nests are built in shallow depressions on or near the ground. Hatchlings are precocial, that is, mobile at birth and generally able to forage and feed themselves, but are especially vulnerable to predation from larger birds and mammals.

Three species have been introduced from Asia and Europe to North America as game birds: Chukar, Gray Partridge, and Ring-necked Pheasant. For years, the species have been reared on game farms and introduced to private preserves. All three species have moved far beyond their original preserve boundaries and established substantial flocks in the western and midwestern portions of the United States, as well as in southern Canada. Ring-necked Pheasants and Gray Partridges are commonly spotted along roadsides and farmlands of the Midwest, but Chukars are more elusive and a challenge for birders to find on the slopes of the Rocky Mountain states.

Wild Turkey: *Meleagris gallopavo*, male L 46", female L 37", dark, iridescent overall, bare head

WILD TURKEY AND ALLIES

The largest North American game bird, the Wild Turkey (above) has an easily recognizable physical structure and plumage with dark, iridescent purple, green and brown plumage, and a bald, reddish head. Males have a long tuft of feathers that dangles from their chest. Turkeys will take flight when alarmed, but they are considered to be ground-birds of grain fields and forest edges. The species is communal, often moving in small family flocks, and occurs throughout the United States, except in the high altitudes of the Rocky Mountain and Appalachian ranges, and is easily seen in the Midwest along country roadsides. As ground feeders, turkeys forage for seeds, nuts, and acorns, and feed in farmfields on leftover grain. They nest in a natural or scraped depression and raise a large brood, typical of game birds subject to heavy predation. The species stay on their range year-round, and their population has steadily increased through the cooperation of conservation and sports hunting organizations.

Range of Wild Turkey

CLASSIFICATION

Larger game birds fall within the taxonomic classification of Galliforme birds that includes at least two distinct families: Cracidae and Phasianidae. Recent evidence seems to indicate that New World Quail are also a separate family of Gallinaceous birds (Odontophoridae), but some authorities still consider quail species to be a subfamily of Phasianidae birds.

Throughout the world, there are about 250 gallinaceous species. In North America, the Cracidae family includes a single species, the Plain Chachalaca, a tropical resident of extreme south Texas. The Phasianidae family includes 15 species found in North America, including Chukar, Gray Partridge, Ring-necked Pheasant, Wild Turkey, Ruffed, Spruce, and Blue Grouse, White-tailed, Rock, and Willow Ptarmigan, Greater Prairie-Chicken, Lesser Prairie-Chicken, Sharp-tailed, Gunnison Sage-, and Greater Sage-Grouse.

Gallinaceous birds have similar physical characteristics and behaviors that generally include round, plump bodies with short necks, ground-pecking while foraging and reliance on legs rather than wings for escape. Most species are wary of humans and seek brushy habitats where they can conceal themselves.

STRUCTURE

Gallinaceous birds have short rounded paddle-like wings and muscular breasts. Most sport a long hind toe, thick downcurved bills, and powerful legs. Several of the grouse species and Ring-necked Pheasants have a spiny spur or claw on the lower leg above the hind toe, and ptarmigans have dense, stiff feathers that cover the lower legs and feet to insulate against their snowy alpine habitat.

The species vary greatly in size, from 37 inches (Wild Turkey) to 12 inches in length (Gray Partridge). Chukars and White-tailed Ptarmigan are smaller birds that range in length from 12 to 14 inches. Mid-size birds, such as Ruffed, Sage, and Sharp-tailed Grouse, White and Willow Ptarmigan, and Greater and Lesser Prairie-Chickens range in length from 15 to 18 inches. Largest of the game birds are Ring-necked Pheasants, Wild Turkeys, Blue Grouse, Plain Chachalacas, and Gunnison Sage- and Greater Sage-Grouse which range in length from 20 (Blue Grouse) to 37 inches (Wild Turkey). For most species, males and females are similar in size, but sage-grouse males are noticeably larger with males measuring up to 28 inches in length and females 22 inches.

Game birds, along with a number of other species, have food storage pouches called crops, so food can be quickly eaten, thus reducing the amount of time needed to forage. Stored food can be digested later in the gizzard with the aid of grit and pebbles, and potential exposure to predators is minimized.

Gallinaceous birds rely on their strong, muscular legs rather than wings to escape predators. When confronted with an enemy, most species freeze to conceal themselves or run to brushy cover and only fly with rapid wingbeats when flushed. The primary and secondary wing feathers are longer at the wingtips and body, so a distinct notch can be seen when the birds are in flight.

PLUMAGE

Most gallinaceous species have various earth tones of tan, brown, and gray that help them blend into their grassy or brushy habitats. Their body and wings have barred or scaled feather patterns without much observable color. However, several are elaborately adorned with vivid, iridescent feather patterns and appendages.

Probably the most ornate game bird, the Wild Turkey is a mix of barred feather patterns of muted green, chocolate brown, and dark reddish orange, with a nearly naked ruddy head, a crimson wattle and a long blackish tuft of feathers hanging from the breast. Ring-necked Pheasants are the most brightly colored, with iridescent orange, gold, mocha brown, and purple. The male has a bluish green neck with a white band, a head with a dark green crown, and vivid, red face patches.

Plumage is often associated with breeding behavior, but it can also serve as concealment, as with the three ptarmigan species. As a method of camouflage, the birds undergo several molts with seasonal change, thus blending into their rocky and snowy alpine habitats. During the summer, when they migrate to lower altitudes to forage, their barred feather patterns adopt a brown or rufous tone. With the arrival of winter and snow, a gradual molt turns feather colors first to blotchy white and brown, then to nearly pure white.

FEEDING BEHAVIOR

Game birds are often referred to as seedeaters because most prefer grains and seeds when available. The ground-walkers slowly wander through their respective ranges moving wherever a food source is adequate. Their search for a plentiful supply is often determined by weather such as drought, flooding, and snow.

Gallinaceous birds feed also on weeds, buds, berries, acorns, corn, and insects. Most species forage on the ground in search of food among the soil and ground-cover vegetation, but several species scour trees for leaves. Grouse look for buds, fir, and hemlock needles, and Plain Chachalaca for leaves and plant shoots.

Unusual for game bird species, the Wild Turkey diet may include frogs and lizards, and both Gunnison Sage- and Greater Sage-Grouse eat sagebrush leaves along with seeds, buds, and flowers.

OTHER SPECIES FIELD NOTES	
■ **Plain Chachalaca** *Ortalis vetula* L 22" Long, lustrous, dark green tail, noisy	■ **White-tailed Ptarmigan** *Lagopus leucurus* L 12.5" White tail in all seasons
■ **Chukar** *Alectoris chukar* L 14" Boldly barred black-and-white flanks	■ **Rock Ptarmigan** *Lagopus mutus* L 14" Winter male has black line from bill through eye, black tail
■ **Gray Partridge** *Perdix perdix* L 12.5" Grayish-brown overall, rusty face and throat	■ **Willow Ptarmigan** *Lagopus lagopus* L 15" Male's mottled summer plumage is redder than other ptarmigans
■ **Ring-necked Pheasant** *Phasianus colchicus* Male L 33" Female L 21" Long pointed tail, iridescent bronze overall, female mottled brown	■ **Greater Prairie-Chicken** *Tympanuchus cupido* L 17" Heavily barred with dark brown, cinnamon and pale buff
■ **Himalayan Snowcock** *Tetraogallus himalayensis* L 28" Whitish face and throat with chestnut stripes	■ **Lesser Prairie-Chicken** *Tympanuchus pallidicinctus* L 16" Male displays orange-red neck sacs
■ **Ruffed Grouse** *Bonasa umbellus* L 17" Black ruffs on sides of neck, dark band near tip of tail	■ **Sharp-tailed Grouse** *Tympanuchus phasianellus* L 17" Underparts scaled, pointed tail held vertically in display
■ **Spruce Grouse** *Falcipennis canadensis* L 16" Black tail with chestnut tip, red comb above eye of male	■ **Gunnison Sage-Grouse** *Centrocercus minimus* Male L 22" Female L 18" tail strongly white-banded
■ **Blue Grouse** *Dendragapus obscurus* L 20" Males have yellow-orange comb above eye, females are mottled brown above, plain gray belly	■ **Greater Sage-Grouse** *Centrocercus urophasianus* Male L 28" Female L 22" Blackish belly, long pointed tail is mottled

Ring-necked Pheasant

VOCALIZATION

Gallinaceous species have a variety of vocalizations for mate attraction and courtship, territorial defense, and calling alarm or to each other when feeding.

The Plain Chachalaca calls its namesake "cha-cha-lak," often at sunrise and sunset, as well as during the breeding season. Similarly, Chukars call a rapid "chuck-chuck-chuck" and Wild Turkeys have the familiar "gobble." Most game birds, though, have similar vocalizations characterized by clucking, cackling, and hooting.

Some of the most unusual vocalizations occur during courtship displays when grouse and prairie-chickens strut and run at each other with fanned tail feathers and brightly colored cheek air sacs, all the while making deep, resonant booming and cackling sounds. Greater Sage-Grouse, too, display with puffed air sacs that make a bubbling or popping sound as they deflate.

BREEDING BEHAVIOR

Perhaps one of the most vivid and unique characteristics of the game bird species is their courtship behavior. Grouse and prairie-chickens make the most colorful displays. Greater and Lesser Prairie-Chickens have separate midwestern ranges and both species hold courtship displays on a "lek," a level patch of ground with scant prairie grass, where male birds congregate for communal mating rituals.

Often prairie-chickens are joined by Sharp-tailed Grouse in flocks of 30 or more that gather in the early morning hours to display before females at the lek edges. With brilliant cheek air sacs puffed out, the males dance, strut, stomp, and leap into the air in mock combat. With erect, fanned tails, their rushes at each other, while fierce-looking, stop short of serious fighting. Females mate with dominant males. Game birds use various displays to attract mates, including neck and tail feather fanning and drumming on fallen logs.

Game bird nests are made in natural depressions in the ground or are built by scraping a shallow bowl in the soil with feet and wings. The shallow depressions are located in thick brushy cover or near a fallen log or rock. Nests are lined with feathers, grasses, dead leaves, moss, and pine needles, depending on the habitat.

Because of potential loss to predation by hawks, owls, foxes, and other small mammals, most gallinaceous species have large broods that reach maturity quickly. Most species lay between 7 and 13 eggs, Plain Chachalacas lay the fewest, two to four, and Wild Turkeys have 6 to 20. Eggs tend to be olive-yellowish, cream colored or tan, and the eggs of several species are marked with dark brown blotches. Incubation generally takes roughly three weeks, and the chicks are able to forage and fend for themselves soon after hatching.

BREEDING RANGE

Game bird species remain on their ranges year-round, where courtship, mating, nestbuilding, and fledging occur. During nonbreeding seasons gallinaceous species are less territorial, and the birds often forage for food and roost in groups. The Plain Chachalaca has the smallest breeding range in extreme south Texas near the Rio Grande. This tropical bird prefers thick forests and chaparral thickets for its habitat. The ranges of Chukar and Gray Partridge species overlap in the northern Rocky Mountain states, but Chukars are also found in the central and southern portions of the mountain

ATTWATER'S PRAIRIE-CHICKEN

This darker and slightly smaller race of the Greater Prairie-Chicken once numbered in the millions in its pristine coastal prairie habitat along the Gulf of Mexico. Today, there are fewer than 60 birds remaining, and now the Attwater's Prairie-Chicken is among the most endangered birds in North America. The last confirmed record of the now extinct Atlantic Coast subspecies of the Greater Prairie-Chicken, the Heath Hen, is from a 1931 sighting in Massachusetts. The storied mating behavior of Prairie-Chickens was once part of the spring ritual throughout our native tallgrass prairies. Now, only a few males gather on their leks, or booming grounds, to strut and prance and dance to lure the perfect mate. True of many prey species, Attwater's Prairie-Chicken is a prodigious egg producer, laying from seven to 17 eggs in its ground nest tucked in the tall grass. A ground feeder, it consumes mainly seeds, leaves, and insects as it clings to existence in the Attwater's Prairie-Chicken National Wildlife Refuge in Colorado County just west of Houston, Texas.

range to southeastern California. The Gray Partridge range extends along the southern Canadian provinces from Ontario to the Pacific. Wild Turkeys and Ring-necked Pheasants range widely across the United States and into the southern Canadian provinces. Turkeys are widely distributed, except in the central Rocky Mountains, whereas pheasants are found in the Pacific Northwest, upper Midwest, and Northeast. Ring-necked Pheasants inhabit open farmland and brushy field edges, whereas Wild Turkeys prefer open forest and brushy vegetation near cropland edges.

Ruffed and Spruce Grouse have similar ranges across Canada and Alaska, extending into the United States along the Rocky Mountains. The Ruffed Grouse range also dips southward along the Appalachian Mountain range to Georgia. Blue Grouse are found in the west, north to Alaska and south through the mountain ranges of California and northern New Mexico. The grouse species are woodland birds that inhabit dense forests with thick brushy cover but can often be sighted near forest clearings.

The ptarmigan species are alpine birds whose ranges are in Canada and Alaska. White-tailed Ptarmigan range along the western portion of British Columbia and southern Alaska, and can be found southward into the northern Rocky Mountains to

Greater Prairie-Chicken

Colorado. Rock and Willow Ptarmigan species reside in the northern Canadian provinces and throughout Alaska. The three species inhabit the rocky tundra of mountain slopes and canyons.

The ranges of Sharp-tailed Grouse and Greater Prairie-Chicken species overlap, and birds of the two species can often be found foraging and performing courtship displays together on the tallgrass prairies of their shared range. The range of Greater Prairie-Chickens is small, mainly on isolated portions of the midwestern states of South Dakota, Nebraska, and Kansas. In contrast, Sharp-tailed Grouse are found throughout the upper midwestern states as well as central Canada and Alaska. One of the smallest ranges of the game birds belongs to Lesser Prairie-Chickens, found within a small arc of shortgrass prairie from southeast Colorado into southwest Kansas, through the Oklahoma and Texas Panhandles into southeast New Mexico.

The Greater Sage-Grouse and Gunnison Sage-Grouse have distinct ranges that nearly join. Whereas Greater Sage-Grouse are found from eastern Montana to western Nevada, Gunnison Sage-Grouse inhabit a relatively small area in southern Colorado and Utah. The two species are found in desert sagebrush terrain.

MIGRATION

Game birds are not migratory, compared to birds that fly great distances when seasons change. They wander only throughout a defined geographical range in search of food. Flock movement can also be triggered by natural occurrences such as drought, flooding, and extreme weather.

WINTER RANGE

The birds reside on their range year-round despite seasonal changes. Grouse and ptarmigan leave high elevations in the winter to find adequate food sources and seek shelter from adverse weather.

OBSERVING LARGER GAME BIRDS

While some species seem nearly tame, others require diligence to find. Ring-necked Pheasants are easily spotted along midwestern fields, and Northern Bobwhites often visit suburban backyard feeders. Plain Chachalacas are found at south Texas parks and wildlife refuges. It will take persistence to locate the alpine Willow and White Ptarmigans or Spruce Grouse. Greater and Lesser Prairie-Chickens and Sharp-tailed Grouse can be viewed from bird blinds located at state or national forests within their ranges. Because most game birds live on desolate or distant ranges, birders often seek help in finding them from local birders who live near the range of a target game bird or from a professional guide.

STATUS AND CONSERVATION

The populations of most game bird species have declined in past decades as their habitats shrank in size. Cattle overgrazing in the West, conversion of both shortgrass and tallgrass prairie to cropland, and deforestation have taken a toll on game bird habitats. One species, Attwater's Prairie-Chicken, a subspecies of the Greater Prairie-Chicken, is considered to be North America's most endangered bird. Fewer than 100 birds remain in three Texas counties near the Gulf Coast. Three others are threatened and may be listed as endangered in the near future: Lesser Prairie-Chicken, Gunnison Sage-Grouse, and Greater Sage-Grouse.

See also

Pigeons, Doves, page 187
Greater Roadrunner, page 203

Northern Bobwhite: *Colinus virginianus,* L 9.75", mottled reddish brown, white throat and eye stripe in male, buff in female

NEW WORLD QUAIL

A small rufous-colored game bird, typical of quail species with its barred and scaled back, wings, and undersides, and famous for its characteristic "bob-white" call, the Northern Bobwhite (above) is found throughout the Southeast and Midwest, the largest range of all North American quail. Males have a prominent white eyebrow, and female's have a less noticeable buff-colored one. Bobwhites prefer farmland and open woodlands with plentiful underbrush, and would rather run than fly when alarmed. A ground-feeder, it forages for seeds, grains, insects, and leaf buds. A bobwhite nest is a mere scrape on the ground lined with grasses or moss, for a clutch of roughly a dozen eggs. After hatching, chicks are immediately able to walk and feed. To escape predation, the bobwhite family stays in a tight flock. The number of Northern Bobwhites has decreased sharply, especially in the East, and aggressive efforts are underway by conservation groups to preserve and restore habitat.

Range of Northern Bobwhite

CLASSIFICATION

The taxonomic classification of New World Quail is unclear. Recently, Gambel's, California, Mountain, Montezuma, and Scaled Quail, and Northern Bobwhite have been considered a distinct family, but some authorities continue to classify them as subspecies in the Phasianidae family. New World Quail of the Odontophoridae family are closely related to them. There are 36 species of quail worldwide, six in North America. The Odontophoridae family is distinct for its teeth or notches on the lower beak, a characteristic that other gallinaceous birds do not have. These quail also do not have a spur or claw on the lower leg as other gallinaceous species do. Whereas partridges and grouse are in the same order and have similar appearances, the two groups differ in that quail are smaller, have shorter beaks, more slender tarsi, primary wing feathers longer than secondaries, and no bare areas around the eye. Quail are better flyers and are considered to be less social species than partridges and grouse.

STRUCTURE

New World Quail are the smallest of the game birds and range from roughly 9 to 11 inches in length, with the Montezuma the smallest and Gambel's Quail the largest. The family of quail has squat and rounded bodies, with a thick, chunky breast. They rely on strong legs to propel them when alarmed and do not fly great distances. The birds will take flight when flushed and head for the nearest cover to escape.

PLUMAGE

All quail are noted for a prominent crest, head plume, or face marking. Mountain Quail have a long plume that curves backward, while Gambel's and California Quail have plumes that curl forward. Northern Bobwhite and Scaled Quail have head crests, and Montezuma Quail, once known as Harlequin Quail, have a pied, or striped, face pattern. All quail tend to have a scaled or barred feather pattern on their breasts, often extending to the wings and back. The birds have a combination of brown body feathers: tan, buff, bronze, and mocha. Mountain and California Quail, have bluish gray breast feathers with rufous neck patches, and the Northern Bobwhite is more russet in color that other quail species.

FEEDING BEHAVIOR

New World Quail forage throughout their ranges by pecking and scratching the ground among the vegetation and soil. Quail typically hunt for seeds, grain, grasses, plant leaves and buds, acorns, and insects.

VOCALIZATION

Quail species cackle and grunt, especially when feeding, but use two- to four-note calls during breeding season, when defending territory, or separated from family flocks. Mountain Quail have a long descending call. Montezuma Quail have a plaintive downward whistle, but the most distinctive call is the Northern Bobwhite's with its clear two-note *bob-white* vocalization.

Gambel's Quail

BREEDING BEHAVIOR

New World Quail species remain on their ranges year-round, where courting, breeding, and nesting occur. During breeding season, when mate selection takes place, couples separate from their flock and seek a suitable site for nestbuilding. The nests consist of a shallow scrape made in the ground with feet and wings or are made in natural depressions in the ground. Depending on the habitat and terrain, the nests are lined with feathers, grasses, dead leaves, moss, and pine needles. The Montezuma Quail usually builds a dome over the nest, and Gambel's Quail may use abandoned nests of other desert birds such as thrashers and Cactus Wrens.

Quail broods are large compared with other birds to counteract the possibility of heavy predation. The number of eggs in a quail clutch varies from 9 to 15, with Montezuma and Mountain Quail laying fewer eggs than other quail species. Incubation lasts for 21 or 22 days. Hatched chicks are relatively independent and able to walk and forage within hours.

BREEDING RANGE

Quail species are most diverse and abundant in the southern United States and Mexico. All species have western or southwestern ranges except the Northern Bobwhite, which is found throughout the eastern and midwestern portions of the United States. The Northern Bobwhite remains on a localized territory to breed in its preferred habitat. The breeding range of Gambel's Quail includes southeastern California, southern Arizona, and New Mexico, extreme west Texas, and southern Utah and Nevada. California Quail breed in Pacific coast states, as well as Idaho, Nevada, and northern Utah, extending into British Columbia. Mountain Quail range up to an altitude of 10,000 feet at tree-line throughout California, Oregon, and Washington, and into Idaho.

With the smallest range in North America, Montezuma Quail breed mainly in southeast Arizona and southwest New Mexico, with several small, highly localized areas in southwest Texas. Scaled Quail breed in the deserts and grasslands of western Texas, New Mexico, the eastern edge of Arizona, and the extreme southern edges of Nebraska and Colorado.

MIGRATION

Quail are not considered migratory. They occupy a particular area, often determined by habitat and food sources and move about the area throughout the year.

WINTER RANGE

Gallinaceous species reside on their range year-round despite seasonal changes. Mountain and California Quail leave high elevations in the winter.

OBSERVING NEW WORLD QUAIL

Observing quail species can be both challenging and frustrating. The birds avoid humans, and their brown feathers camouflage them well. Mountain Quail are particularly secretive and may require the skill of a local professional guide to locate them.

STATUS AND CONSERVATION

The New World Quail have healthy numbers that are not in jeopardy. However, the numbers of Montezuma and Mountain Quails have fallen over the past few decades because of forestry management and cattle grazing. The most dramatic decline occurred in the Northern Bobwhite population across North America. A steep drop has taken place over the past few decades in the eastern and southeastern portions of its range because of habitat loss. Restoration programs are currently underway to assure recovery of the Northern Bobwhite species.

OTHER SPECIES FIELD NOTES

■ **Gambel's Quail**
Callipepla gambelii
L 11"
Teardrop-shaped plume, chestnut crown and sides

■ **California Quail**
Callipepla californica
L 10"
Teardrop-shaped plume, scaled underparts

■ **Mountain Quail**
Oreortyx pictus
L 11"
Two long, thin plumes, chestnut throat outlined in white

■ **Montezuma Quail**
Cyrtonyx montezumae
L 8.75"
Plump, rounded head is highly patterned in male

■ **Scaled Quail**
Callipepla squamata
L 10"
White-tipped crest, scaly underparts

See also

Rails, page 132

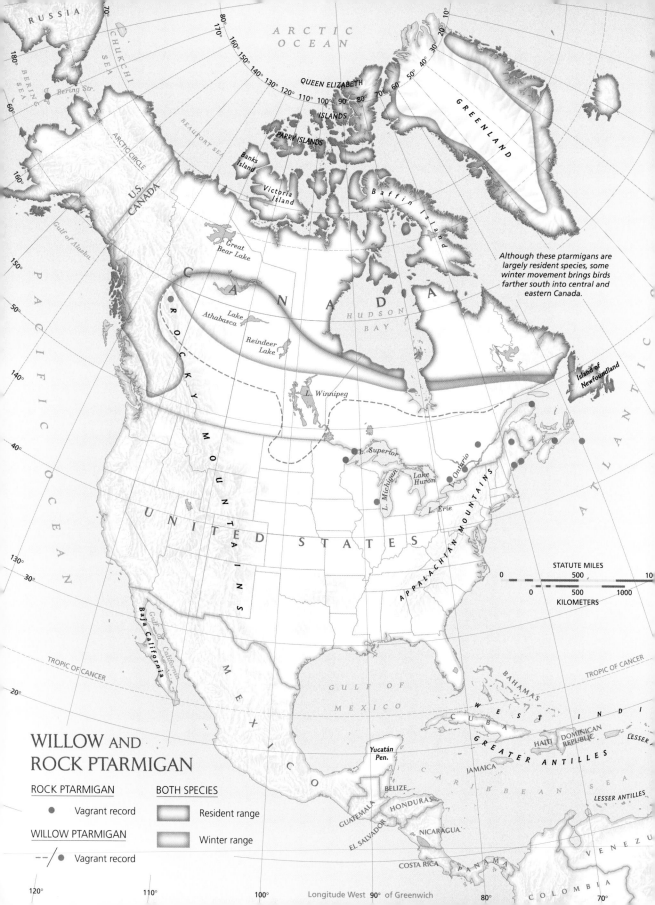

Although these ptarmigans are largely resident species, some winter movement brings birds farther south into central and eastern Canada.

WILLOW AND
ROCK PTARMIGAN

ROCK PTARMIGAN

● Vagrant record

WILLOW PTARMIGAN

- - - / ● Vagrant record

BOTH SPECIES

Resident range

Winter range

STATUTE MILES
0   500   10

0   1000
KILOMETERS

Longitude West 90° of Greenwich

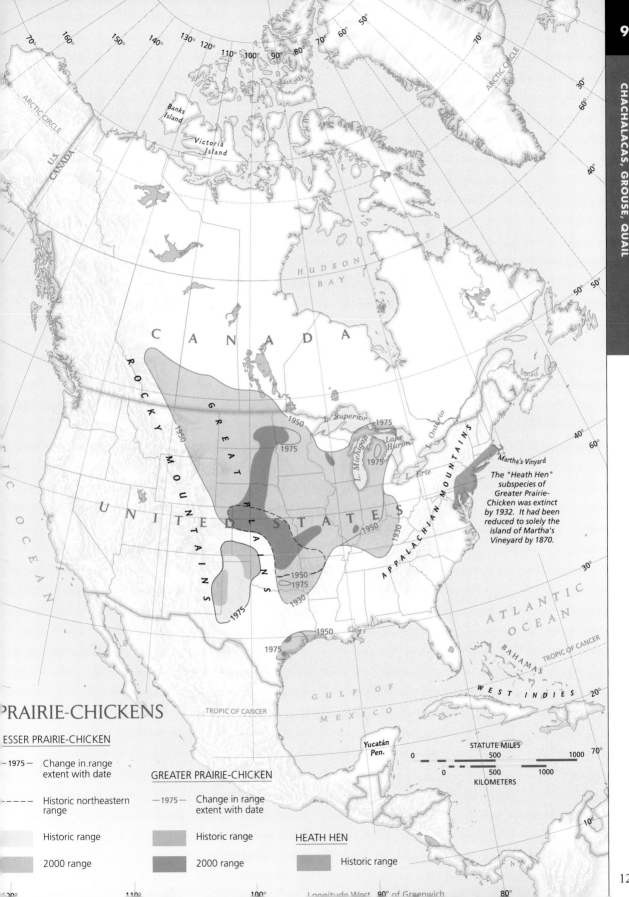

The "Heath Hen" subspecies of Greater Prairie-Chicken was extinct by 1932. It had been reduced to solely the island of Martha's Vineyard by 1870.

PRAIRIE-CHICKENS

ESSER PRAIRIE-CHICKEN

—1975— Change in range extent with date

- - - - Historic northeastern range

Historic range

2000 range

GREATER PRAIRIE-CHICKEN

—1975— Change in range extent with date

Historic range

2000 range

HEATH HEN

Historic range

STATUTE MILES
0   500   1000

0   500   1000
KILOMETERS

129

RAILS, LIMPKINS, CRANES

Within the order Gruiformes are some of the continent's most sought-after bird species: the rails and their allies, cranes, and the enigmatic Limpkin. Birders enjoy this diverse group for a variety of reasons. The enormous gatherings of hundreds of thousands of Sandhill Cranes on Nebraska's Platte River valley harken back to a time of seemingly limitless wildlife on the Great Plains, whereas the few hundred endangered Whooping Cranes that winter in coastal Texas are prized both for their great beauty and rarity. Rails are masters of concealment in marshes, and though easy to hear, they can be difficult to see—their elusiveness makes them all the more of interest, particularly the small Black and Yellow Rails, which are rarely seen. Coots and moorhens are larger members of the rail family, Rallidae, and much more confiding and conspicuous than their smaller relatives. Their fascinating feeding and breeding behavior is readily observable. The closely related Purple Gallinule, a bird of southern marshes, is clad in almost unbelievable hues: The adult is a vivid, glossy purple below, with greenish back and wings, long saffron yellow legs, and a bill of powder blue, scarlet, and yellow—truly the "Painted Bunting" of the rail family. The unusual Limpkin, essentially a giant rail, is restricted in range to Florida and Georgia; its strident calls are almost unearthly, unlike the call of any other North American bird.

Rails fascinate students of birdlife because of their incredible powers of flight and radiation through the continents and islands of the world. When flushed from a marsh, the average rail seems ungainly, almost helpless in flight, with long legs dangling and wings beating quickly before it drops

Edward S.
Brinkley

back into the grasses. But this impression could not be more misleading. Rails have made it to the most remote, inhospitable oceanic islands and adapted to conditions that support only a few passerines and nesting seabirds. Consider that the most frequent North American vagrant to South Africa is the gaudy Purple Gallinule. Workers on oil-drilling platforms in the Gulf of Mexico sometimes wake up to the spectacle of dozens of "purple chickens" standing on the rig. Like many North American species, the Purple Gallinule is a trans-Gulf migrant that tries to make the crossing as quickly as possible, in about 36 hours, but wind shifts sometimes cause "fallouts" of this and other species on ships and oil rigs there. Most North American rails are only short-distance migrants, moving from Canada into the southern United States on migration. The Sora, for instance, is a small crake that nests from the northern tier of the U.S. well up into the Canadian tundra. Fitted with radio transmitters, Soras have been clocked in nocturnal migration at an average flight speed of 59 miles per hour.

Unfortunately, rails in many settings, particularly on small islands, are vulnerable to changes in environment, especially the introduction of mammalian predators, such as rats, mongooses, cats, and dogs, which can wipe out ground-nesting species in only a few years. No fewer than 23 species of rail have been made extinct by the arrival of humans and animals, and at least 45 species are currently listed as vulnerable, threatened, or endangered worldwide. The world's cranes are in similar straits: A majority of the world's crane species (ten) are considered threatened, some critically.

(Left) Sandhill Crane

Purple Gallinule: *Porphyrula martinica,* L 13", pale blue forehead shield, red-and-yellow bill

RAILS AND THEIR ALLIES

The most colorful marsh bird that is related to the Common Moorhen, the Purple Gallinule (above) swims and dives, wades and dabbles throughout its habitat. The chicken-like species is a common marsh and wetland resident in Florida whose summer range extends along the Gulf Coast south into Mexico and north through Louisiana into Arkansas. The male Purple Gallinule is particularly colorful with a red, yellow-tipped beak, an iridescent blue neck and chest, a blue head patch above the bill, dark green wings, bright yellow legs and white rump feathers. Gallinules are most often seen swimming through heavy vegetation and walking across patches of lily pads. The species feeds on wild rice, other grains and seeds, and frogs and aquatic insects found in marsh shallows. A Purple Gallinule pair conceals its nest in dense marsh vegetation and uses grasses for a cup-like nest suspended above the water. Hatchlings from a brood of seven or eight can swim right away, and are often cared for by offspring from the previous year.

Range of Purple Gallinule

CLASSIFICATION

Rails and their allies—the moorhens, coots, swamphens, and gallinules—are all grouped in a single family, Rallidae, within the order Gruiformes, which also includes the cranes, in the family Gruidae, and Limpkin, in the family Aramidae. The crakes are rails in the strict sense, usually small rails with short, thick bills, but the term is not applied consistently. The Black Rail, sometimes called Black Crake, has many subspecies throughout the Americas, and some of these races might be split as distinct species in the future, though research on this most mouse-like of birds is difficult. Clapper Rail also has multiple subspecies, one of which, the Light-footed Clapper Rail of California, is endangered. The closely related King Rail is sometimes considered a subspecies of Clapper Rail because of the tendency of the two species to hybridize, but differences in plumage and voice suggest that these large rails are distinct species.

STRUCTURE

A glance at a field guide's illustrations of rails and their relatives provides a good overview of the distinctions among these birds. Gallinules, coots, and moorhen are chunky, long legged, and short billed, whereas the larger rails, King and Clapper are about the same size but have long, thin bills. Virginia Rail is a pint-size version of the King; the Yellow and Black Rails and the Sora are crakes, with small, tubby bodies and short bills. The body structure, including the legs and bill, is adapted to particular kinds of foraging. Rails with long bills are able to probe into crevices and holes for their prey, and short-billed species tend to pick food from the surface and often take more plant matter than the long-billed species. Most rails have legs and feet looking like a chicken's, well adapted for terrestrial life at the water's edge, but rails also swim fairly well. Coots' feet are different in having long, flexible lobes on the toes, which permit them not only to swim well in open water but also to dive in pursuit of aquatic vegetation below the water's surface; they are the only rails with the ability to dive and stay submerged to feed. The extraordinarily long toes of the Purple Gallinule allow it to clamber around on floating vegetation and in reed beds, even to perch in trees; it swims much less frequently than the similar Common Moorhen. The Limpkin is designed with a long bill and long legs, which are highly specialized adaptations for foraging on its chief prey, the apple snail. In general, marsh-dwelling rails and crakes have bodies that are more streamlined than open-water species (the moorhens, coots, gallinules), and rails are able to flatten themselves laterally to move between dense marsh vegetation, hence the expression "skinny as a rail."

PLUMAGE

Most members of the family Rallidae which dwell in marshes and other closed habitats are cryptically colored to blend into their environment. King, Clapper, and Virginia Rails all have upperparts streaked and mottled with straw-colored and dark feathers, perfect camouflage in marsh grasses; their undertail coverts, flanks, and lower bellies have a darker "ruptive" coloration of dark and light stripes. Black and Yellow Rails match their environs even more precisely and, indeed, the young of all North American rails and allies are black, much like Black Rails, the ideal color for hiding unseen in the shadows beneath dense marsh grasses. In North American context, bright colors are limited to the Purple Gallinule and the even larger Purple Swamphen, an Old World species with a small but viable breeding population introduced in Florida. The soft parts (bill and legs) of the Common Moorhen also sport bright colors.

Sora

FEEDING BEHAVIOR

Rails and their allies take a variety of plant matter and invertebrate prey in their diets, which apparently vary seasonally with the availability of different sorts of food. Many different food items have been reported in rails' diets, including amphibians, small reptiles, and even carrion. With the exception of coots, which make shallow dives to take plant matter, rails are surface seizers, taking food from exposed mud or from the water's surface in the manner of other waterbirds. Species with longer bills are able to exploit areas beneath the marsh or muddy surface, such as the holes of fiddler crabs, a favorite prey item of Clapper Rails in salt marsh environments. Most rails have been considered nocturnal foragers, but recent studies of North American species indicate that they may forage all through the day, especially when feeding young. When paired during the breeding season, rails may occasionally forage together with mate or young, but for most of the year, they are solitary foragers. Coots again are the exception here, as they may form large flocks, sometimes in the many thousands, in productive foraging areas during the winter. The disadvantage to such large congregations becomes clear during outbreaks of disease such as cholera, which can spread rapidly through coot flocks and kill thousands in short order.

VOCALIZATION

Rails produce a remarkable array of sounds, some of which are rather poorly known. The most commonly heard calls are those associated with the establishment, maintenance, and defense of breeding territories. In Clapper and King Rails, this call is a descending crescendo of "clapping" sounds, deeper and more grunting in the larger King Rail. The Virginia Rail gives a scaled-down but still quite loud version of this call but also has twittering calls and a rhythmic "kidick" call, repeated several times. The Yellow Rail utters mostly an erratic series of ticking sounds, much like the clicking of two stones together. Black Rail's calls are many and varied, with the "kik-kee-derr" territorial call being the most familiar; it also gives a series of growls, a duetting that sounds much like Least Grebes chattering, and a bouncy "kyew!" call (apparently only the female does this). The Sora sounds a little like any other species of

---

OTHER SPECIES FIELD NOTES

■ **Limpkin**
Aramus guarauna
L 26"
Chocolate brown overall, streaked with white, long bill

■ **King Rail**
Rallus elegans
L 15"
Rich cinnamon underparts, black-and-white barred flanks

■ **Clapper Rail**
Rallus longirostris
L 14.5"
Races variable, grayer and duller than King Rail

■ **Virginia Rail**
Rallus limicola
L 9.5"
Gray cheeks, rich chestnut wings

■ **Sora**
Porzana carolina
L 8.75"
Short, thick, yellow bill, black face

■ **Yellow Rail**
Coturnicops noveboracensis
L 7.25"
Deep, tawny yellow above with wide dark stripes

■ **Black Rail**
Laterallus jamaicensis
L 6"
Blackish, white speckling, chestnut nape

■ **Corn Crake**
Crex crex
L 10.25"
Short brownish bill, chestnut wing patch

■ **Common Moorhen**
Gallinula chloropus
L 14"
Red forehead shield, slaty plumage with white flank stripe

■ **American Coot**
Fulica americana
L 15.5"
Reddish-brown forehead shield, whitish bill with dark band near tip

■ **Eurasian Coot**
Fulica atra
L 15.75"
Forehead shield and bill entirely white

North American rail, with its loud, descending whinny call, audible for miles, and its sharp "ker-wheer!," also high in pitch. Moorhens, gallinules, and coots utter a variety of trumpeting calls, some soft, others loud, most sounding quite gravelly and raucous.

BREEDING BEHAVIOR

The breeding behavior of wild rails is difficult to study, but some insights have been gained through study of captive rails, which appear to have monogamous bonds for the most part, though both polyandry (a single female with multiple males) and polygyny (a single male with multiple females) have been documented. Rails are highly territorial during the breeding season, and some even maintain winter territories, especially the larger species. To attract a mate, the male calls repeatedly from a territory and often struts and cocks its short tail when a female is present. In some species, the male may feed and preen the female. Nests are constructed of marsh vegetation, deeply concealed by the rails but often out in the open in the case of coots and moorhens, which build floating nests. Most species lay six eggs, but clutches up to 13 have been recorded, some of these perhaps the result of brood parasitism (the dumping of one female's eggs into another's nest). The black chicks hatch asynchronously and are fed and brooded by the parents until fledging.

American Coot

BREEDING RANGE

Rails are found in all mainland United States (though Sora has only the tiniest of toeholds in southeastern Alaska), with Sora and Virginia Rail being by far the most widespread, followed by American Coot and Common Moorhen. The other species have greater species habitat requirements: Clapper Rails are limited to salt marsh in the outermost coastal plain, for instance, and Black Rails also favor these habitats but have small interior populations at scattered localities. Most Yellow Rails breed in Ontario and parts of southern Québec, Saskatchewan, and Manitoba, with a few in the northernmost United States.

MIGRATION

The migration of rails is still something of a mystery to ornithologists. Some rails are sedentary within their ranges and appear not to migrate at all, but most North American species move at least some distance to wintering areas. Some species are now known to have traditional stopover sites on migration. Soras, for instance, congregate by the thousands for several weeks in the vast marshes of the upper Chesapeake Bay in Maryland before moving on in migration to the coasts of South Carolina through Florida. Other species make long-distance movements, such as Purple Gallinules to the Caribbean and northern South America, and Black Rail has been detected as a trans-Gulf migrant on the oil-drilling platforms in a recent study. Because rails migrate at night, their migratory behavior is little-known, but like other migrants, they appear to wait for favorable tailwinds before departing. Some species, such as Clapper Rail, vocalize while migrating, giving night-active bird-watchers a glimpse into what species are moving overhead.

WINTER RANGE

Winter quarters for the majority of true rail species include the extensive marshes of the southern and especially coastal southeastern United States, where King, Clapper, Virginia, Black, and Yellow Rails, as well as Sora, can all be found, along with coot, moorhen, and (in southern Florida) Purple Gallinule. In some states, all of these birds are considered game birds, hunted by boats pushed by long poles through the marshes. Clapper Rails are most often taken in such hunts.

OBSERVING RAILS

One of the most widespread species of rail in North America is also by far the most easily observed: American Coot, which is known across much of Canada and Mexico and the lower 48 states. These birds have adapted well to human-altered habitats, accepting even borrow pits and sewage lagoons when foraging, and some coots are so inured to human activity that they rest on suburban lawns and steal food from picnickers. No other species of rail is quite so birder friendly, although Common Moorhens and Purple Gallinules, found mostly in the southern and eastern U.S., can be easy to observe at the marsh margins, with a little patience. Virginia Rail and Sora are the two species of true rail found in the lower 48 states and most of Canada, and nearly everyone who lives away from the coastal plain of the Southeast is within a half-day's drive of a marsh that holds one or both birds. To see one of these birds during the breeding season requires patient observation of an open area at marsh's edge, where eventually, the birds will make an appearance to preen, feed, bathe, or swim. Some bird-watchers play tape recordings of the male's call, which usually results in seeing the male very quickly, but this practice can be disruptive of the bird's daily activities if it is done too often. Even with common species such as these, it is important to use discretion if considering the use of audio lures to see birds.

Even where they are abundant, as in the middle Atlantic coastal marshes, Clapper Rails can be maddening to see well, but watching the edges of salt marshes, especially where they are cut through by canals, is usually profitable, especially during the breeding season, when they are most active and most vocal. Making a sharp, repeated clucking or clapping sound similar to the male's call with one's mouth is usually enough to lure a male into the open; the best time to try such an imitation is early during the breeding season, April through June. The same is true for the related King Rail, which nests mostly in freshwater or brackish marshes. Yellow Rail, which nests in prairie marshes north into the tundra in Canada, can likewise be lured into view by taking two quarters (or two small rocks) and tapping them together in the irregular Morse-code-like pattern of the male's call (again, discretion is important with this scarce species). Observers in the continent's interior have discovered in recent years that Yellow Rails forage at migration stopover sites in rice fields—in Louisiana and Arkansas in October. When the farm machinery moves through these fields to harvest, Yellow Rails may flush out in front of them in some numbers. For Black Rail, those who know this will-o'-the-wisp well say that the best time to see numbers of them is when the tides are highest, and these tiny birds are forced by rising water out to the edges of the marsh. They also will respond to tape recordings of the male's calls, but their status as state endangered makes this impermissible in some areas.

Finding a species of rallid other than the regular North American breeders might be called the "holy (g)rail" of birding, something that happens once in a lifetime, if ever. Though known throughout the world as long-distance vagrants, rails' secretive behavior means that they are rarely detected by bird-watchers. Of the 22 North American records of Corn Crake (a European species), for instance, several were found dead or brought in by cats, and the same is true of the few records of the tropical Spotted Rail, Paint-billed Crake, and Azure Gallinule, each with one or two North American records. A few Old World crakes have made it to the Western Hemisphere: Spotted Crake has reached the Caribbean island of St. Martin, whereas Baillon's Crake is known from one record at Attu in the Aleutian chain of Alaska. Vagrant Eurasian Coots have been detected from the continent's corners in northeastern Canada (four records) and in the Pribilofs (one record). It is unclear that a pure Caribbean Coot, a species that apparently often hybridizes with American Coot, has ever made it to North American shores, and variation in American Coots' frontal shields presents a problem for the field identification of this threatened West Indian species.

LIMPKIN

The Limpkin is the last remaining member of the formerly wide-spread family of Aramidae, thought to be most closely related to rails and to sungrebes, another tropical family within Gruiformes. Limpkins in North America are found only in Florida and southeastern Georgia, in marshy areas where their chief prey, large apple snails (of the genus *Pomacea)* are found in abundance. They share this dietary preference with another specialist, the Snail Kite. Limpkins are somewhat retiring birds, and the first indication of their presence may be the eerie, piercing wails delivered by both sexes. Once hunted to near extirpation in Florida, the population has increased and stabilized in recent years.

STATUS AND CONSERVATION

Rails and their allies in North America must contend not just with atmospheric conditions that alter their habitats, drying marshes and ponds that were once ideal nesting or wintering areas, but also with man-made changes to these habitats, particularly the draining and degradation of wetlands. For some species, up to 90 percent of past habitat has been eliminated during the European settlement of North America, especially in the continent's interior. Introduction of large waterfowl—such as Canada Geese and Mute Swans—into wetlands appears to be detrimental to populations of nesting rallids as well, as these enormous birds tend to be aggressive toward any other birds in their large territories when nesting.

See also

Whooping Crane: *Grus americana*, L 52" W 87", white overall, black primaries.

CRANES

The rarest crane species, found in only a handful of sites in North America, the Whooping Crane (above) has long black legs, a white back and wings with black-tipped primaries, a yellowish bill, and a crimson red crown that extends along the throat. Only roughly 400 birds remain in zoos and restoration programs. The birds winter in south Texas and breed in northern Canada. Migratory birds often accompany Sandhill Cranes, stopping on Nebraska's Platte River sandbars midway along their journey, feeding on crabs, shrimp, frogs, and snakes.

Range of Whooping Cranes

CLASSIFICATION

Both North American cranes, the Whooping and the Sandhill Crane, are classified in the family Gruidae, subfamily Gruinae, and genus *Grus*. As many as six subspecies of Sandhill Crane have been described, but the subspecies are difficult or impossible to distinguish in the field in most cases. Other species of crane have been noted in the wild in North America—the Common Crane (*Grus grus*) in many states, the Demoiselle Crane (*Anthropoides virgo*) in California and British Columbia—but it is not yet clear how many of these records pertain to escapees from zoos or bird collections. Reports of other species of crane in North America are known to be of former captives.

STRUCTURE

Cranes resemble herons or egrets superficially, with long bills, legs, and necks, but are larger birds, with "bustles" of feathers (mostly tertial feathers) at the rear and red plumage in the head of adults: In flight, cranes keep their long neck extended, while herons and allies mostly retract the neck during extended flights.

PLUMAGE

As a rule, typical cranes have simple plumages in blacks, whites, and grays, with touches of red in the head in many species. The Sandhill Crane is predominantly gray, often with rust tones in the upperparts (especially in juveniles), a pale cheek, and a red "poll" in the adult. The Whooping Crane is mostly white with black primaries and more red in the head.

FEEDING BEHAVIOR

Cranes are opportunists and omnivores that pick food from the surface of wetlands or farm fields while walking slowly, alert for predators. The Sandhill Cranes take grain and seeds as well as fruit, insects, and small vertebrates. The Whooping Cranes also have a varied diet that includes many marine invertebrates such as crabs, mast such as acorns, and a host of small reptiles, fish, and amphibians.

VOCALIZATION

Cranes make loud, ringing, rolling bugling-calls that have a rough or grating quality. These calls are delivered often in flight, sometimes from great heights and more frequently and intensely during the birds' spectacular courtship displays.

BREEDING BEHAVIOR

The courtship of cranes is complex and includes elaborate displays with stereotyped movements of head, neck, and wings, with high leaps that look to humans like the most audacious ballet moves. These "dances" are frequently performed by subadults that have yet to pair and can even be seen in migratory staging areas before birds have arrived on the nesting grounds. Cranes appear to be monogamous for life, as is true of many large birds, and pairs establish traditional territories that are defended both in breeding and nonbreeding areas. Sandhill and Whooping Cranes build nests typical of the family, a mound of moist vegetation in a marshy area, in which they lay two eggs in most cases. The parents take turns incubating the eggs for about a month, though the female does more nocturnal incubation than the male. The young are born downy and are precocial, able to move about on their own within a few hours of hatching. Fledging of the young birds takes as much as four months in Whooping Cranes, and young cranes spend their first winter and spring with their parents, both in migration and on the wintering grounds.

BREEDING RANGE
Sandhill Cranes nest in wetlands from eastern Siberia, through Alaska, into most of Canada, and sparingly in the United States around the Great Lakes and in the northwestern states. Whooping Cranes nest only in Wood Buffalo National Park, in northern Alberta and the Northwest Territories, Canada.

Common Crane

MIGRATION
The migration of Whooping Cranes is astonishingly constant: they fly along a narrow path from nesting to wintering grounds, pausing on the long route mostly in the late afternoon to forage or rest, particularly if the weather is bad. Sandhill Cranes fly along a much broader front but have traditional staging areas across the interior of the continent, and these places have become very popular for ecotourists. The small populations of Sandhill Cranes in the Gulf Coast states and Georgia are essentially nonmigratory.

WINTER RANGE
Sandhill Cranes winter chiefly in a large area from southern and western Texas into New Mexico and

Mexico, as well as in western and southern California. Whooping Cranes winter only in the coastal bend of Texas, where a small tourist industry has developed to show these birds to the public.

OBSERVING CRANES
As some of the most stately of North American birds, it is little surprise that both Sandhill and Whooping cranes attract tens of thousands of visitors per year, many of them novice bird-watchers or even generalist naturalists. In Nebraska and New Mexico, large birdwatching festivals are planned around the migration and wintering of Sandhill Cranes, which congregate in numbers comparable only to those of certain waterfowl. In coastal Texas, a dozen different operators offer small-boat excursions to watch wintering family groups of Whooping Cranes, which have become so accustomed to their admirers that they never take flight at the approach of "Captain Ted" or the other veteran pilots.

STATUS AND CONSERVATION
Although the Sandhill Crane is not considered threatened as a species, several of its subspecies are endangered: the race nesting in Cuba and the race that nests in coastal Mississippi and vicinity (roughly a hundred individuals of that race were reintroduced there from captive breeding programs). The Whooping Crane is one of the most critically endangered birds in the Americas, with scarcely more than 200 birds left in the wild, up from a mid-century low of only 15 individuals. For several decades, conservationist biologists have taken one of the two eggs from Whooping Crane nests—as the parents typically raise only one young per year—and used the extra egg in various attempts to rebuild both the wild and the captive populations of the species. Cross-fostering experiments involved placing the eggs into the nests of wild Sandhill Cranes, which migrated from Idaho to New Mexico. These Whooping Cranes did survive but did not pair with one another, however, and the last individual from this experiment disappeared in 2002. In Florida, efforts to reintroduce a nonmigratory population have shown promise, despite high mortality from bobcat depredation in the early years, and the Whooping Cranes there have begun to breed.

OTHER SPECIES FIELD NOTES
■ **Common Crane**
Grus grus
L 44-51" W 79-91"
Blackish head and neck with broad white stripe
■ **Sandhill Crane**
Grus canadensis
L 34-48" W 73-90"
Overall gray, red skin on crown

See also

Herons, Egrets, page 71
Ibises, Storks, Flamingos, page 81

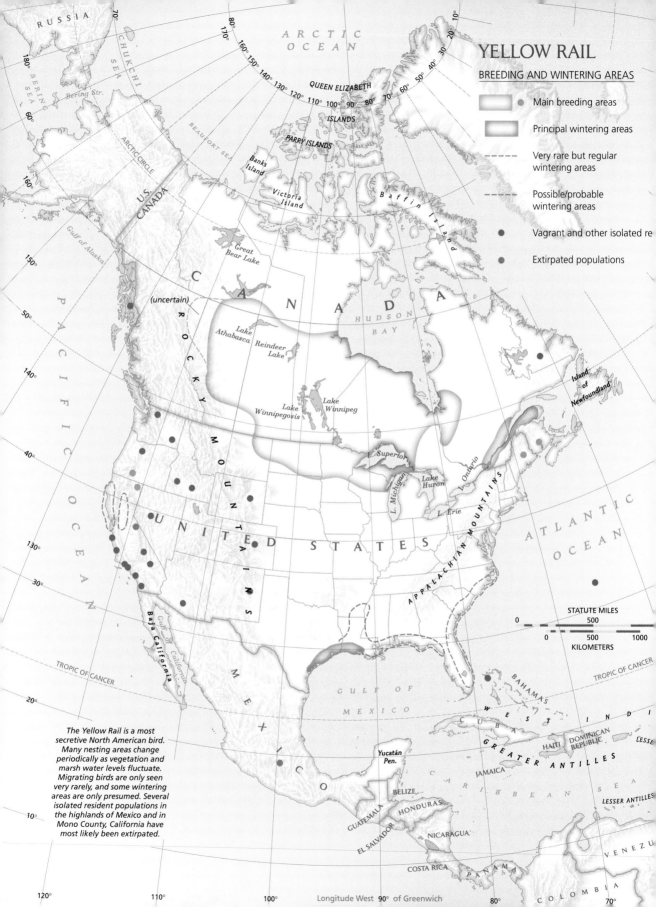

YELLOW RAIL

BREEDING AND WINTERING AREAS

▢ ●	Main breeding areas
▢	Principal wintering areas
- - - -	Very rare but regular wintering areas
- - - -	Possible/probable wintering areas
●	Vagrant and other isolated re
●	Extirpated populations

ARCTIC OCEAN

RUSSIA

CHUKCHI SEA

Bering Str.

BERING SEA

QUEEN ELIZABETH

ISLANDS

PARRY ISLANDS

Banks Island

Victoria Island

Baffin Island

BEAUFORT SEA

ARCTIC CIRCLE

U.S. CANADA

Gulf of Alaska

PACIFIC OCEAN

C A N A D A

Great Bear Lake

HUDSON BAY

(uncertain)

Lake Athabasca

Reindeer Lake

Lake Winnipegosis

Lake Winnipeg

ROCKY MOUNTAINS

Island of Newfoundland

L. Superior

Lake Michigan

Lake Huron

L. Ontario

L. Erie

U N I T E D   S T A T E S

APPALACHIAN MOUNTAINS

ATLANTIC OCEAN

M E X I C O

Gulf of California

Baja California

TROPIC OF CANCER

GULF OF MEXICO

Yucatán Pen.

BELIZE

GUATEMALA

HONDURAS

EL SALVADOR

NICARAGUA

COSTA RICA

PANAMA

BAHAMAS

CUBA

HAITI

DOMINICAN REPUBLIC

JAMAICA

GREATER ANTILLES

W E S T   I N D I

CARIBBEAN SEA

LESSER ANTILLES

VENEZUELA

COLOMBIA

TROPIC OF CANCER

STATUTE MILES
0 — 500

0 — 500 — 1000
KILOMETERS

The Yellow Rail is a most secretive North American bird. Many nesting areas change periodically as vegetation and marsh water levels fluctuate. Migrating birds are only seen very rarely, and some wintering areas are only presumed. Several isolated resident populations in the highlands of Mexico and in Mono County, California have most likely been extirpated.

Longitude West 90° of Greenwich

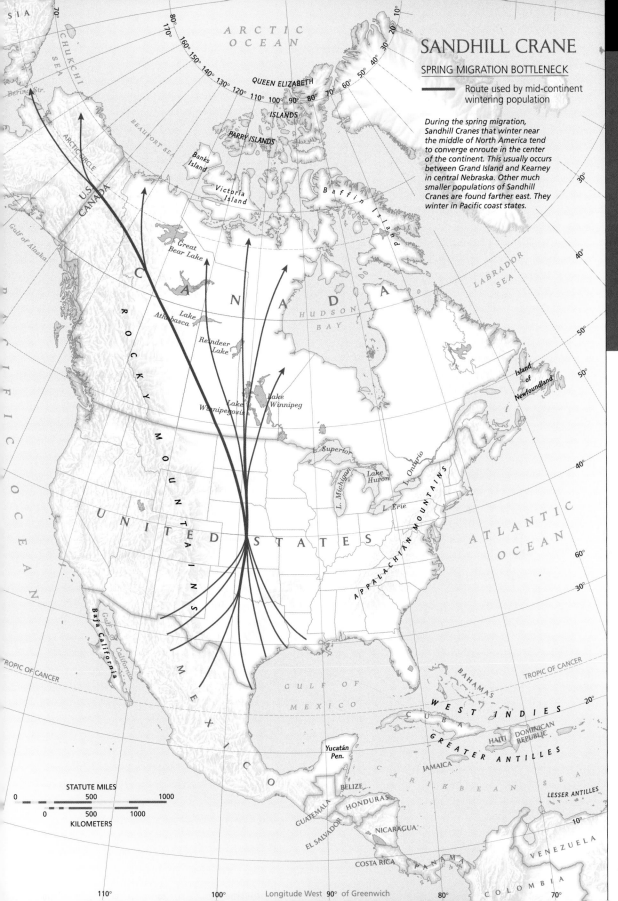

SANDHILL CRANE

SPRING MIGRATION BOTTLENECK

—— Route used by mid-continent wintering population

During the spring migration, Sandhill Cranes that winter near the middle of North America tend to converge enroute in the center of the continent. This usually occurs between Grand Island and Kearney in central Nebraska. Other much smaller populations of Sandhill Cranes are found farther east. They winter in Pacific coast states.

STATUTE MILES
0   500   1000
0   500   1000
KILOMETERS

Longitude West 90° of Greenwich

PLOVERS, JACANAS, OYSTERCATCHERS

Henry T. Armistead

This varied group consists of three families: lapwings and plovers (the Charadriidae; 16 North American species), oystercatchers (Haematopodidae; three species) and the highly distinctive jacanas (Jacanidae; one species). Of these, seven species are primarily birds of Old World Arctic areas and are unlikely to be encountered outside of Alaska, Labrador, or Newfoundland.

The exotic Northern Jacana has sometimes bred in south Texas. It is notable for its extremely long toes that enable it to walk on lily pads and other freshwater, surface-aquatic vegetation as is found in the oxbow-like *resacas* of the Rio Grande. Recent records are mostly of wandering juveniles. Sex roles are reversed. Males build nests, brood, and attend chicks. Females are larger, more aggressive, have as many as four mates, and actively defend nesting territories. Jacanas are gallinule-like in appearance, habits, and habitat. The Northern Jacana has a blackish head and neck, reddish-brown body, and bright yellow bill, a frontal shield at the base of the bill, and carpal spurs at the bend of the wings.

Oystercatchers are large, stocky, gull-size shorebirds with thick legs and big, bright red bills they use to locate and pry open their favorite marine foods, especially mussels and other shellfish, worms, and other invertebrates found in tidal areas, but seldom do they eat oysters. The all-black Black Oystercatcher inhabits the West Coast from Alaska's Aleutians south well into Mexico in Baja California. The American Oystercatcher is expanding in the East from the coast of southern New England to Yucatan, as well as on the Pacific Coast from Panama north to Mexico. The similar Eurasian Oystercatcher has only been encountered twice in Newfoundland in the spring. The latter two species have dark upperparts, white underparts, and a conspicuous white wing stripe. Oystercatchers emit piercing whistles, especially during courtship displays when they utter rapidly repeated piping calls as they walk, run, and fly in tandem, sometimes joined in flight by other, neighboring pairs.

Plovers are shorebirds with roundish heads and bodies, large eyes, and short bills. They have a thrush-like manner of feeding, characterized by short runs and stops, then dips to grab food that is located by sight. Plovers' whistled calls are musical, often described as querulous or plaintive, evocative of the wild areas they live in.

North America has 16 species of plovers. Of the five primarily Eurasian species, the Common Ringed Plover, European Golden-Plover, and Eurasian Dotterel are seldom seen in America except in the Arctic. The Killdeer is our most familiar plover and enjoys a wide distribution. Piping and Wilson's Plovers are beach-nesting birds, as are Snowy Plovers, which also breed in interior, western alkaline areas. The Piping Plover has attracted great publicity as an endangered species. Its preference for beaches, and consequent conservation efforts limiting access to these, brings it into conflict with people who use beaches for recreation. It is surprising to learn that there are actually more Piping Plovers breeding in sandy areas of the prairie states and provinces than on the Atlantic or Gulf Coasts.

(Left) Black Oystercatcher

Killdeer: *Charadrius vociferus*, L 10.5", double breastbands, loud piercing call

PLOVERS AND JACANAS

A common member of the plover family, the Killdeer (above) is widespread across much of the United States and Canada with breeding grounds that extend into southern Alaska. The Killdeer has a mottled chocolate-brown back, white chest and belly with two neck rings, a short dark bill, and a reddish eye ring. It is often confused with the Semipalmated Plover, which has only one neck ring and is smaller. Unlike most plover species that prefer mudflats and beaches, Killdeers are frequent visitors to inhabited areas and can often be seen in grassy or fallow fields, city parking lots, and other areas in close proximity to humans. They mainly feed on insects that are found in fields or grassy areas with short vegetation. Nests are shallow depressions scraped in the sand to hold three or four eggs. Unlike other plovers and shorebirds that travel great distances to wintering grounds in the Southern Hemisphere, Killdeers have a year-round range across much of the United States.

Range of Killdeer

CLASSIFICATION

Plovers and lapwings belong to the family Charadriidae, comprising 67 species and ten genera. There are 24 lapwing species, all of the genus *Vanellus*. The Northern Lapwing, common and widespread in the Old World (over 200,000 pairs in Britain and Ireland), is the only one ever seen in North America with barely 30 records, most in the Northeast in late fall and early winter. Three other lapwings are endemic to South America, the other 20 are in south Asia, Australasia, and especially Africa.

The remaining 43 Charadriidae are plover species, found as breeders worldwide except for Antarctica, the Greenland ice cap, the interior portions of some major deserts, the Himalaya, and sections of boreal forests in Canada and Russia. North American plovers belong either to the genus *Pluvialis* (four species: Black-bellied and the golden-plovers) or *Charadrius* (11 species). The greatest plover diversity is in temperate regions. They are thought to have originated in the Southern Hemisphere where there are several species with unusual bill shapes and plumages, but North American species are quite generalized.

The extraordinary jacanas consist of eight species (six genera) and enjoy a pantropical distribution, with some species extending into subtropical areas such as Mexico, northern Argentina, northern Australia, and eastern China. Most are found in South America, the southern half of Africa, and southern Asia. These spectacular swamp denizens are highly colored with extremely long toes and claws. Formerly a rare breeder in south and central Texas, our only jacana, the Northern Jacana, shares the genus *Jacana* with the Wattled Jacana, widespread in eastern South America.

STRUCTURE

Plovers and lapwings are notable for their upright posture, round heads, large eyes, thick necks, short or spiky bills, and medium-length legs. They are small or medium-size, compact birds. Excellent, swift flyers, they have long pointed wings. Only the somewhat bizarre lapwing has broad and rounded wings and sports a prominent crest. Some plovers, especially tropical ones, have nasal salt glands to rid the body of excess salt.

Jacanas are the odd ones of this grouping, bearing a chicken, rail, or gallinule-like appearance, but DNA research and other evidence confirms they are properly classed with shorebirds. Their almost unbelievably long toes and claws, combined with legs that are merely long, enable them to walk on and nest among lily pads and other floating, freshwater vegetation, much of it as exotic looking as the birds. Jacanas have stubby tails (except for the appropriately named Pheasant-tailed Jacana of south Asia), generalized wings, tending toward broad and rounded, and medium-length, pointy bills. Rounding off the morphology of this species, the Northern Jacana also has bony wingspurs.

PLUMAGE

Most North American plovers (11 species) belong to the genus *Charadrius*. These birds characteristically have white underparts, often with a black breastband, some black markings on the head, brownish upperparts, and varyingly prominent white wing stripes visible in flight. The breastbands disrupt their plumage pattern, breaking up the bird's contour somewhat, lending it a cryptic quality. Legs and bill are most likely to be brownish, blackish, or yellow—in that order— eyes are black. Most of the markings are less pronounced in females and juveniles. The Killdeer has two black breastbands, except for juveniles which for a short time have but one. The Eurasian Dotterel and Mongolian Plover are exceptions, too. They have considerable reddish brown underparts, are very rare south of Alaska, and hard to find even in Alaska, although the former probably breeds sparingly in the north

American Golden-Plover

of the state. The four *Pluvialis* plovers are champion long-distance migrants with sleek, long, pointed wings, but otherwise they conform to a generalized plover shape. In breeding, or alternate plumage, they show mostly black underparts with a prominent white area extending from the flanks and the side of the breast and neck up to, behind, and finally over the eye. Upperparts are a complex white, mottled with golden barring (in the case of the Black-bellied Plover blackish barring). In nonbreeding, or basic, plumage, they lose most or all of the black and the barring, becoming much plainer with brownish or grayish streaked or patterned underparts.

The Northern Lapwing is a much stockier plover with unusually broad, rounded yet long wings (especially the primaries), and is dark above, light underneath with a black breast and a conspicuous crest. It is a large bird with a pigeon-like flight manner.

The Northern Jacana has a rufous body and inner wings, yellow bill, and frontal shield above the bill, and black breast, neck, and head. In flight, the secondary and primary flight feathers are a spectacular yellow, and the almost unbelievably long toes, claws, and legs trail behind the tail. Females are bigger than males.

FEEDING BEHAVIOR

Plovers and lapwings locate food by sight in contrast to sandpipers, which probe for their food. Therefore, most plover food, often moving prey, is located on top of the substrate, in low grasses and other ground vegetation. These birds have large eyes. Typically plovers and lapwings feed deliberately, running short distances, sometimes only a few steps, then stopping with their head held high, all the while looking for food. Then they lower the head, pause again, and seize the prey by pecking. This manner of hunting is similar to the way American Robins and other thrushes hunt.

Most of the food consists of a variety of small invertebrates—worms, small mollusks, shrimp, insects and their larvae, and eggs, small crabs, spiders, and sometimes also berries, less frequently seeds. They feed in the day but also forage at night, especially when there is sufficient moonlight. Plovers and lapwings are not as gregarious as sandpipers, which often feed in close proximity in large flocks. Plovers and lapwings usually form smaller, more loosely grouped or dispersed assemblages. Plovers sometimes engage in foot-trembling or stamping, using their feet alternately, perhaps to simulate the

---

OTHER SPECIES FIELD NOTES

■ **Black-bellied Plover**
Pluvialis squatarola
L 11.5"
Black-and-white plumage, breeding male has frosty crown

■ **American Golden-Plover**
Pluvialis dominica
L 10.25"
Breeding male has bulging white patch on side of neck, black underparts

■ **Pacific Golden-Plover**
Pluvialis fulva
L 9.75"
White stripe on side of neck continues onto flanks

■ **European Golden-Plover**
Pluvialis apricaria
L 11"
Plump body, white underwings

■ **Snowy Plover**
Charadrius alexandrinus
L 6.25"
Pale above, thin dark bill, partial breast band

■ **Piping Plover (Endangered)**
Charadrius melodus
L 7.25"
Pale above, orange legs

■ **Wilson's Plover**
Charadrius wilsonia
L 7.75"
Long, very heavy black bill, broad breast band

■ **Semipalmated Plover**
Charadrius semipalmatus
L 7.25"
Dark brown back, small bill

■ **Common Ringed Plover**
Charadrius hiaticula
L 7.5"
Broad breast band, distinct white eyebrow

■ **Mongolian Plover**
Charadrius mongolus
L 7.5"
Bright rusty red breast

■ **Little Ringed Plover**
Charadrius dubius
L 6"
Conspicuous yellow eye ring

■ **Mountain Plover**
Charadrius montanus
L 9"
Unbanded white underparts

presence of a mole. This causes some prey to rise to the surface of the ground, whereupon the plover grabs it. They defend their feeding territory against others of the same species. Plovers will ingest grit and drink by lowering their bill so it is horizontal to the water's surface. They often consume items high in calcium in the breeding season.

Jacanas feed on insects and other invertebrates they find on the surface and the underside of floating aquatic vegetation or close to the water's surface. Much less frequently they eat small fish and plant matter, including seeds. Jacanas will investigate flowers of aquatic plants previously disturbed by other marsh birds. Their weight causes water plants to submerge slightly and disturb invertebrates. When a prey moves, the jacana grabs it with a quick thrust of its bill.

VOCALIZATION

The pleasant plover calls are evocative of the open areas they inhabit, with frequent melodious whistles imbued with a poignant, querulous, lyric quality. Some plovers engage in impressive aerial displays in the breeding season, accompanied by more complex vocalizations. In some species a dozen or more kinds of calls have been noted in addition to a species' primary call, including calls for distraction, warning, distress, maintaining contact, territorial defense, and numerous other purposes. Jacanas call frequently during displays and when in flight. Their calls are described as repeated, harsh squawking with other strident notes often interspersed.

BREEDING BEHAVIOR

Plovers nest on the ground in open terrain. Their nest is a simple scrape or depression on the ground, be it on sand, tundra, grass, or gravel sites. The nests holds usually three or four eggs. Plovers are monogamous. Both sexes incubate the eggs and tend to the young. Eggs hatch in three to four weeks. The precocial, cryptically patterned young can fly three to four weeks later. Most plovers raise but one brood, although Killdeer as well as Mountain and Snowy Plovers sometimes have two broods. Plover pairs nest by themselves, sometimes semi-colonially. The male takes care of most territorial defense. *Pluvialis* plovers and lapwings engage in elaborate aerial flight displays. Jacanas are as bizarre in their breeding habits as they are in appearance. Females lay two or three clutches, sometimes more, for each of their mates. Their breeding displays are equally flamboyant with the female enjoying polyandry and doing most of the solicitation.

BREEDING RANGE

The Northern Jacana breeds in Mexico, Central America and the Greater Antilles in the West Indies. The *Pluvialis* plovers—Black-bellied and golden-plovers—are Arctic breeders, nesting almost exclusively on islands of the high, primarily western Canadian Arctic, Canadian mainland areas south of these, and in northern and western Alaska. The Semipalmated Plover is also an Arctic breeder but with a greater breeding range than the *Pluvialis* plover, extending east to Newfoundland, west to the Aleutians, and south into the Canadian muskeg. Killdeer and Mountain Plovers breed in open interior areas, the Killdeer throughout North America from the subarctic to deep into Mexico, the Mountain Plover in the western areas from south Alberta and Manitoba due south into New Mexico. Snowy Plovers nest in sandy or alkaline

NORTHERN JACANA

Science fiction could not conceive a more unlikely bird. The vocal jacana has extremely long toes and claws, enabling it to walk on lily pads and freshwater aquatic vegetation. Sharp, bright yellow wing spurs, used in displays and defense, project at the bend of the wings from the carpal bones. The flashy wings with bright yellowish flight feathers are often raised during displays and after alighting. The polyandrous females are bigger than males and have as many as four simultaneous mates, which defend their respective territories against each other. Males build nests, incubate, and tend young. The Purple Gallinule is one of the jacana's prime predators, eating its eggs and chicks. Accidental in Arizona, vagrants to southern Texas, they are common in Mexican and Central American lowlands with well-vegetated freshwater lakes and swamps.

areas in the interior West or on southern, coastal beaches. Wilson's Plovers breed in beach areas of the Southeast. Piping Plovers summer in sandy areas of the north and central East Coast as well as interior areas of the prairie states and provinces.

MIGRATION

The *Pluvialis* plovers perform epic migrations from their Arctic breeding grounds, especially the golden-plovers. American Golden-Plovers fly in fall from the high Arctic 2,500 miles or more south nonstop over the Atlantic and winter in the Argentine pampas, returning in spring through interior prairies; it is one of the most dramatic migrations of any animal. Likewise, Pacific Golden-Plovers fly 2,000 miles or more nonstop from Alaska to various Pacific islands. Most *Charadrius* plovers are medium-length migrants withdrawing south to temperate or subtropical wintering areas. Northern Jacanas do not migrate, but dry seasons lead them to wander, and juvenile dispersal is even more pronounced. Most lapwings, except for the Northern Lapwing, are not highly migratory.

WINTER RANGE

Most of the *Charadrius* plovers, our small, light-bellied species, withdraw from breeding areas via medium-distance migrations of several hundred miles to win-

Semipalmated Plover

tering ranges on southern beaches, including Mexico and the West Indies. The Arctic nesting Semipalmated Plover is an exception, wintering anywhere on coasts from Virginia and California south as far as Argentina and Chile. Killdeer winter throughout the United States (except the northern and north-central states), Mexico, Central America, and northern South America. The golden-plovers are champion long-distance migrants. American Golden-Plovers winter on grasslands and the pampas in southern South America. Pacific Golden-Plovers' far-flung wintering range extends from Hawaii to the South Pacific and south Asia. Jacanas do not migrate. Northern Lapwings overwinter in their breeding range in western and southern Europe and the Middle East, but most migrate outside their breeding range, to southern Europe and North Africa, the Middle East, India, and China.

OBSERVING PLOVERS AND JACANAS

Plovers are easy to observe in the windswept areas they favor, be they beaches, tundra, alkaline flats, low grasslands, or other open, often semibarren terrain. Getting to these places is sometimes a minor challenge. Once

there, distance can be another problem, so a telescope is desirable. As ground nesters they are especially vulnerable to predation so birders should be circumspect. As migrants and wintering birds they need to feed, rest, and preen their plumage to make it flight efficient. Shorelines, mudflats, low-grass prairie habitat, and wet dirt fields are all good places to observe plovers. Look for jacanas in subtropical, open, freshwater areas with luxuriant growths of lily pads and other emergent aquatic vegetation.

STATUS AND CONSERVATION

Beach-nesting species such as Wilson's, Snowy, and Piping Plovers are variously listed as threatened or endangered in several states and on federal level. These three scarce, declining species, each with limited breeding ranges, often consisting of narrow beach strips, are greatly impacted by human activity in coastal areas including collateral disturbance by dogs, foxes, and other natural predators. Alteration of interior western grasslands by agriculture, planting of tall grasses, and elimination of native grazing animals has impacted the uncommon Mountain Plover, which prefers open areas with low growth. Burning of grasslands and restricted commercial activity during the breeding season has benefited this unique, declining species. Because of their fondness for gravelly areas Killdeer are especially susceptible to death by vehicle. Their affinity for farmlands exposes them to agrochemicals, but they remain widespread and common, although periodically reduced by severe winters. The numbers of *Pluvialis* plovers—widely dispersed as Arctic breeders, migrants, and on wintering grounds—are difficult to assess. Predation on Arctic birds decreases when there are periodic, big increases of lemmings that are preferred prey. Extensive "eat-outs" of tundra vegetation by the burgeoning Snow Goose population may actually favor Semipalmated Plovers and some other Arctic breeding species. Jacana populations are presumed to be healthy but can be threatened by wetlands draining. In the western Palearctic, Northern Lapwings have expanded their range northward and remain widespread and abundant. They decline in very cold winters, and their numbers have fluctuated markedly.

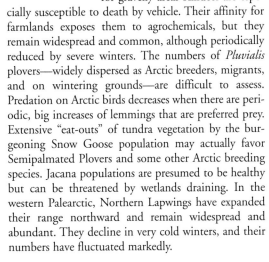

See also

Greater Yellowlegs, page 152
Wilson's Phalarope, page158

American Oystercatcher: *Haematopus palliatus,*
L 18.5", black head, large red-orange bill, white underparts

OYSTERCATCHERS

The American Oystercatcher (above) is a large wading bird that inhabits the Atlantic seaboard and Gulf Coast. Its year-round range stretches from Texas to the Mid-Atlantic states, with breeding grounds that extend into northern New England. The species has a white belly and chest, brown neck and back, with brown wings accented by a white stripe. Oystercatchers can be found on sandy beaches or coastal rocky outcrops, and feed in shallow water on clams, oysters, and mussels. Their feeding technique is unique. The birds hammer or stab the shellfish with their chisel-shaped bill to crack an opening in the shell. They sever the shellfish's constrictor muscle, then pry the shell open. American Oystercatchers nest on open beaches but may also use man-made structures equipped with sand or small pebbles. Nests are shallow depressions that hold two to four eggs. Parents feed hatchlings for nearly two months until the chicks are strong enough to open shellfish on their own.

Range of American Oystercatcher

CLASSIFICATION

The world's eleven oystercatcher species belong to the family Haematopodidae. All are members of the genus *Haematopus*. The Canarian Black Oystercatcher, formerly of the Canary Islands off northwest Africa, is unverified since 1913 and probably extinct. Some experts consider it to have been the same species as either the Eurasian or the African Black Oystercatcher. Few oystercatchers have had subspecies designated. Most species are found in the Southern Hemisphere. Only four species populate the New World. Structurally similar, the world's oystercatchers are considered by some taxonomists to represent a superspecies comprised of four or five closely allied species.

STRUCTURE

These are large, robust, stolid shorebirds with long, stout, laterally compressed, bright reddish orange bills, and long, dull pinkish, stout legs. The eyes are bright yellow or red with even brighter red or reddish orange eye rings. The color of the bills, eyes, and legs (aka soft parts) increases in intensity during the breeding season. Oystercatchers are 17 to 18 inches long, the size of a duck. As with many shorebirds, females are bigger, with respect to bill, wing, and leg length as well as mass and weight. They live in coastal, marine environments and have salt glands above the eyes that drain excess salt from the circulatory system. The wings are long and pointed, the tails short. The powerful bill is adapted for opening the shells of bivalve mollusks as well as dislodging and seizing other shellfish and marine invertebrates.

PLUMAGE

Almost as uniform in plumage as in structure, the world's oystercatchers all either have totally black or blackish brown plumage such as the Black Oystercatcher or are all black but with white underparts and a conspicuous white wing stripe such as the American Oystercatcher. The black-and-white birds are sometimes referred to as the pied species and colloquially as "sea-pies" in the Old World. Males tend to have marginally blacker plumage and brighter soft part coloration than females. Grown juveniles are somewhat duller than adult females.

FEEDING BEHAVIOR

These big shorebirds primarily walk or run in the intertidal zone, probing with their strong bills in sand and mud for worms, knocking off limpets and chitons from rocks, or seizing shellfish, especially bivalves, which their dagger-like bill can open. They consume a wide variety of marine invertebrates. Oystercatchers do not probe as much as many shorebirds. They locate most food by sight, especially in beds of shellfish, and consume mussels, clams, worms, small crabs, and many other small invertebrates, but rarely oysters. Shellfish are either hammered or pried open.

VOCALIZATION

The vocal oystercatchers are easily located by their piercing, repeated whistles and loud, piping calls, which are important components of their courtship flights, or when a couple engages in side-by-side running or slightly rotating in place on the ground. These piping courtship calls begin in late winter and extend into the breeding season. Neighboring oystercatchers sometimes join in when a couple starts this loud calling. A single, loud whistle is given as a contact or pairing call. They also make certain calls in defense of their territory.

BREEDING BEHAVIOR

These attractive, engaging birds make frequent, ritualized courtship flights and displays of running and rotating in place as described above. Those flights are often notable for their shallow, rapid wingbeats. The nest is a scrape or bowl-shape area in sand, grass, rock, or on gravel or shell piles above the high tide line in the expansive, open coastal areas they favor. They can lay one to four eggs, but usually only two or three. These hatch in 24 to 29 days. The young are capable of flight after about five weeks. Both sexes incubate and attend the precocial young. Oystercatchers are monogamous and raise one brood annually.

BREEDING RANGE

The Black Oystercatcher is a permanent resident from Alaska's Aleutian islands south to south-central Baja California, Mexico, and favors rocky, tidal shorelines. The American Oystercatcher breeds on coasts from Massachusetts south along most of the Atlantic and Gulf Coasts to Yucatan, as well as from most of Baja California and the Sea of Cortez south to Panama, and is a year-round resident in most of its range, where it is found mostly on sand, mud, and shell flats.

MIGRATION

Since they are largely resident species, oystercatchers' migrations are poorly understood. In winter American Oystercatchers withdraw from their New England and Long Island ranges. They also winter in areas of the Gulf and Pacific Mexican Coasts where they do not

Black Oystercatcher

breed. Interior records of our oystercatchers are almost unheard of in contrast to the Eurasian Oystercatcher.

WINTER RANGE

Their winter range is mostly identical to the breeding range as noted above. Oystercatchers often assemble in groups of scores or even hundreds in the winter. In recent decades the American Oystercatcher has expanded its wintering range from Virginia north to include all of coastal New Jersey and southern New England. Black Oystercatchers are hardy enough to overwinter in Alaska's Aleutians, sometimes even the Pribilofs.

OBSERVING OYSTERCATCHERS

Oystercatchers are easily seen, especially at low tide, in many American saltwater coastal areas. Query local bird clubs and consult bird-finding guides and the results of Christmas Bird Counts to determine where they are common, since there are long stretches of coast where they may be absent. Familiarize yourself with their loud, whistled calls from the several good commercial recordings available.

STATUS AND CONSERVATION

Oystercatcher populations seem to be stable or even increasing in some areas. Black Oystercatchers are estimated at about 11,000, most of these occurring from British Columbia northward. There are about 17,000 American Oystercatchers on the Atlantic coast from Florida north. Human disturbance in coastal areas and the presence of dogs, rats, and foxes is detrimental. Rising sea levels affect their breeding grounds within feet of the high tide line. Dredge spoil areas sometimes benefit oystercatchers, especially in the East, but pollution, chemicals, and oil spills contaminate their prey.

OTHER SPECIES FIELD NOTES

■ **Black Oystercatcher**
Haematopus bachmani
L 17.5"
Dark overall, large red bill

See also

American Avocet, Black-necked Stilt, page 154
Shorebird bill comparison, page 157

Pacific Golden-Plovers
winter in a broad area
ranging from South
Asia to Australia and
Oceania. Large
numbers winter in
Hawaii.

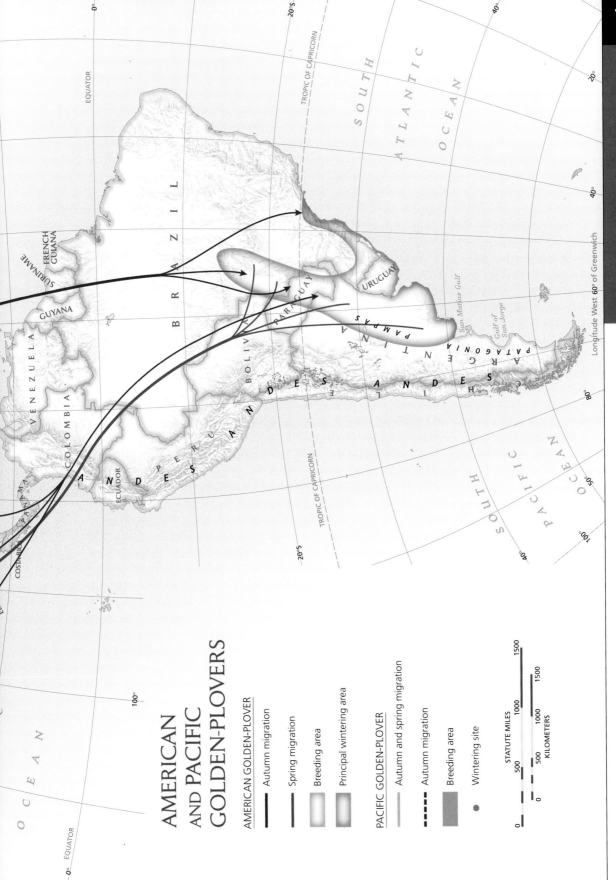

AMERICAN
AND PACIFIC
GOLDEN-PLOVERS

AMERICAN GOLDEN-PLOVER

— Autumn migration

— Spring migration

Breeding area

Principal wintering area

PACIFIC GOLDEN-PLOVER

— Autumn and spring migration

--- Autumn migration

Breeding area

• Wintering site

STATUTE MILES

0   500   1000   1500

0   500   1000   1500
KILOMETERS

STILTS, AVOCETS, SANDPIPERS

Almost every beach is sometimes populated by sandpipers "playing tag with the waves." If for no other reason, sandpipers are birds familiar to everyone. Also known as shorebirds or waders, they inhabit open areas including shorelines, tundra, lakesides, grasslands, and mudflats.

Their habit of forming flocks and their vocal nature ensure they are conspicuous, although their coloration is usually drab. Shorebirds generally have long legs and bills, bestowing on many an attractive elegance. They feed energetically in mud, sand, shallows, and grasslands, searching for invertebrates, small fish, and sometimes, vegetable matter.

North America has 67 species; many are Arctic nesters. The 28 largely Palearctic species are seldom seen in America outside Alaska. Most are encountered as migrants. Some Pectoral Sandpipers fly several thousand miles east from central Siberia, cross the Bering Sea, then go south through Alaska to Argentina. Bar-tailed Godwits fly 7,000 miles nonstop from Alaska to Australasia. Some Red Knots migrate 9,000 miles one way.

Most shorebird nests have four large eggs. After having flown from Argentina to the Arctic, Baird's Sandpiper lays four eggs in four days that can be 120 percent of the female's body mass. Young shorebirds hatch well-developed and are precocial—able to walk and feed soon afterward. Many sandpipers have elaborate and vocal aerial displays. Adult sandpipers leave their natal areas before the young. Most July and August migrants are adults. Juveniles come in late August or later. Early southbound fall birds appear in late June, especially Least Sandpipers,

Henry T. Armistead

Short-billed Dowitchers, and Lesser Yellowlegs. The last ones to straggle through on their northbound voyage in spring are usually the Semipalmated and White-rumped Sandpipers.

Birders refer to some shorebirds by their habitat preference. "Grasspipers" include Long-billed Curlew, Pectoral, and Upland Sandpipers. "Rockpipers" are Rock and Purple Sandpipers, Surfbird et al. Except for Sanderling and a few others, sandpipers prefer mud or wet grassy areas to sand. American Woodcock is unusual in its affinity for dense thickets and damp scrubby areas where it forages for earthworms. The tip of its bill is prehensile and tactile, enabling it to seize worms when probing below ground.

Small shorebirds, known as "peeps" after their calls, present one of birding's most daunting identification problems. By examining a combination of leg color, primary feather projection past the folded wing in relation to tail length, upperparts coloration, bill shape, vocalizations, habitat, and the when-and-where of their distribution, most can be sorted out.

Many female sandpipers have longer, curvier bills than males. Young birds have shorter bills than adults, especially long-billed species such as godwits, avocets, and curlews. The normally longer, curvier bill of Western Sandpiper may not be any longer or curvier in autumn for a male juvenile than the characteristically shorter, stouter bill of an adult female Semipalmated Sandpiper.

Extraordinary shorebirds include Solitary Sandpipers which nest in boreal forests where they appropriate abandoned nests of American Robins, Rusty Blackbirds, and other passerines.

(Left) Willet

Greater Yellowlegs: *Tringa melanoleuca,* L 14", legs yellow to orange, long bill, slightly upcurved

STILTS, AVOCETS, SANDPIPERS

Many shorebird species feed and rest on mudflats and tidal pools, especially during migration, and one of the most frequently seen shorebirds across North America are the Greater Yellowlegs (above). This species is recognized by its long, bright yellow legs and dark, slightly upturned bill. The plumage appears to be similar to other shorebird species, with a brownish mottled back and white underside, but the yellow legs are distinctive. Greater Yellowlegs usually are found singly or in pairs; their characteristic three- or four-note cry of "tew-tew-tew" is the species' trademark. Both Greater and Lesser Yellowlegs bob and teeter when feeding, but the Greater is generally less active as it feeds on aquatic worms, insects, and small fish. Greater Yellowlegs breed across northern Canada and southern Alaska where pairs nest in shallow depressions on the ground. They usually have broods of four chicks that can fend for themselves soon after hatching. After the breeding season, the species migrates to wintering grounds along the Atlantic and Pacific coasts and the extreme southern portion of the United States.

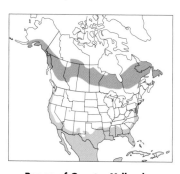

Range of Greater Yellowlegs

CLASSIFICATION

These distinctive birds compose a group of approximately 93 species. Their taxonomy is an evolving process dependent on research, especially biochemical studies involving DNA-DNA hybridization and protein electrophoresis analysis, as well the more traditional area of morphology, but also behavior, including vocalizations. Along with plover, oystercatchers, and jacanas they are generally referred to as shorebirds in the Americas, as waders in the Old World.

Stilts, avocets, and sandpipers belong to the order Charadriiformes, a sprawling, diverse taxon that also includes plovers, oystercatchers, jacanas, gulls, terns, jaegers, skimmers, and our Northern Hemisphere answer to the penguins, the alcids.

Stilts and avocets are large, pied shorebirds with long legs and bills. They belong to the family Recurvirostridae, best represented in the Australasian Region. There are four avocet species worldwide, each with widely separated ranges, all members of the genus *Recurvirostra.* They are found on all continents except Antarctica. Stilt classification is much less clear with taxonomists recognizing anywhere from three to seven species. The Black-winged Stilt complex is considered by some experts to include five subspecies, found on six continents and including North America's Black-necked Stilt and the Hawaiian Stilt. Others see these to be as many as five distinct species.

The world's approximately 86 species of sandpipers (26 genera) are readily categorized into nine groupings, sometimes referred to as tribes, here considered from those with most North American species to the least. Some of these names are somewhat contrived but are convenient categorizations gaining in popular usage. Sandpipers do not have a great subspecific variation although Short-billed Dowitcher (especially), Dunlin, Rock Sandpiper, and Red Knot each have several races, some identifiable in the field with care.

The calidridines (*Calidridini*) compose 24 species, most are members of the genus *Calidris.* These are small to medium-size shorebirds with moderate-length bill and legs. They breed at northern latitudes and include the small, hard-to-identify peep species, such as Least, Semipalmated, and Western Sandpipers. Calidridines are mostly generalized in shape, bland and brownish, but they include the distinctive Dunlin, Purple Sandpiper, Stilt Sandpiper, Sanderling, the knots, and the bizarre Ruff; "mudpipers" would be a good, general name for this group.

Of the 18 species of tringines (*Tringini*) 15 have been seen in North America. These average larger than the more compact calidridines. Familiar representatives are the yellowlegs, Spotted Sandpiper, Willet, and the tattlers. Nine of our tringines belong to the genus *Tringa.* They have a slightly more southern breeding

OTHER SPECIES FIELD NOTES

■ **American Avocet**
Recurvirostra americana
L 18" Long, recurved bill

■ **Black-necked Stilt**
Himantopus mexicanus
L 14" Black-and-white
plumage, long red legs

■ **Willet**
*Catoptrophorus semi-
palmatus*
L 15" Black-and-white
wing pattern in flight

■ **Lesser Yellowlegs**
Tringa flavipes
L 10.5" Yellow legs

■ **Common Redshank**
Tringa totanus
L 11" Orange legs

■ **Common Greenshank**
Tringa nebularia
L 13.5 Greenish legs

■ **Spotted Redshank**
Tringa erythropus
L 12.5 Bill droops at tip

■ **Wandering Tattler**
Heteroscelus incanus
L 11" Dark gray above,
barred underparts

■ **Gray-tailed Tattler**
Heteroscelus brevipes
L 10" Dark gray above,
finely barred underparts

■ **Green Sandpiper**
Tringa ochropus
L 8.75" White rump

■ **Wood Sandpiper**
Tringa glareola
L 8" Heavily spotted

■ **Solitary Sandpiper**
Tringa solitaria
8.5" White below, bold
white eye ring

■ **Spotted Sandpiper**
Actitis macularia
L 7.5" Spotted underparts

■ **Common Sandpiper**
Actitis hypoleucos
L 8" Brown above, dark
barring and streaking

■ **Terek Sandpiper**
Xenus cinereus
L 9" Upturned bill

■ **Eskimo Curlew** *Numenius
borealis*
L 14" Downcurved bill

■ **Whimbrel**
Numenius phaeopus
L 17.5" Striped crown,
downcurved bill

■ **Little Curlew**
Numenius minutus
L 12" Streaked head

■ **Bristle-thighed Curlew**
Numenius tahitiensis
L 18" Stiff thigh feathers

■ **Long-billed Curlew**
Numenius americanus
L 23" Long, decurved bill

■ **Far Eastern Curlew**
*Numenius madagas-
cariensis*
L 25" Long decurved bill

■ **Eurasian Curlew**
Numenius arquata
L 22" White rump and
wing linings

■ **Black-tailed Godwit**
Limosa limosa
L 16.5" Mostly black tail

■ **Hudsonian Godwit**
Limosa haemastica
L 15.5" Upcurved bill,
black wing linings

■ **Bar-tailed Godwit**
Limosa lapponica
L 16" Long upcurved bill

■ **Marbled Godwit**
Limosa fedoa
L 18" Long upcurved bill,
cinnamon wing linings

■ **Ruddy Turnstone**
Arenaria interpres
L 9.5" Black-and-white
head and bib

■ **Black Turnstone**
Arenaria melanocephala
L 9.25" Striking black
and white wings in flight

■ **Surfbird**
Aphriza virgata
L 10" Black tail band

■ **Rock Sandpiper**
Calidris ptilocnemis
L 9" Black breast patch

■ **Purple Sandpiper**
Calidris maritima
L 9" Orange-yellow legs
and base of bill

■ **Great Knot**
Calidris tenuirostris
L 11" Black breast

■ **Red Knot**
Calidris canutus
L 10.5" Chestnut face
and breast

■ **Sanderling**
Calidris alba
L 8" Prominent wing
stripe in flight

■ **Dunlin**
Calidris alpina
L 8.5" Black belly patch

■ **Curlew Sandpiper**
Calidris ferruginea
L 8.5" Mottled chestnut
back

■ **Semipalmated Sandpiper**
Calidris pusilla
L 6.25" Straight black bill

■ **Western Sandpiper**
Calidris mauri
L 6.5" Bill tip droops

■ **Least Sandpiper**
Calidris minutilla
L 6" Thin bill, yellow legs

■ **White-rumped Sandpiper**
Calidris fuscicollis
L 7.5" Long primaries
project beyond tertials

■ **Baird's Sandpiper**
Calidris bairdii
L 7.5" Long primaries

■ **Long-toed Stint**
Calidris subminuta
L 6" Split eyebrow

■ **Little Stint**
Calidris minuta
L 6" Rufous cheeks

■ **Temminck's Stint**
Calidris temminckii
L 6.25" White outer tail
feathers, yellow legs

■ **Red-necked Stint**
Calidris ruficollis
L 6.25" Rufous on face
and breast

■ **Spoonbill Sandpiper**
Eurynorhynchus pygmeus
L 6" Spatulate bill

■ **Broad-billed Sandpiper**
Limicola falcinellus
L 7" Upper mandible
droops at tip

■ **Pectoral Sandpiper**
Calidris melanotos
L 8.75" Dark streaks on
breast, white belly

■ **Sharp-tailed Sandpiper**
Calidris acuminata
L 8.5" Buffy breast, eye-
brow flares behind eye

■ **Upland Sandpiper**
Bartramia longicauda
L 12" Small head, long
neck, large dark eyes

■ **Buff-breasted Sandpiper**
Tryngites subruficollis
L 8.25" Prominent dark
eye on buffy face

■ **Ruff**
Philomachus pugnax
Male L 12" Female L 10"
Rufous to black ruffs on
breeding males

■ **Short-billed Dowitcher**
Limnodromus griseus
L 11" White on belly

■ **Long-billed Dowitcher**
Limnodromus scolopaceus
L 11.5" Reddish below
with dark bars

■ **Stilt Sandpiper**
Calidris himantopus
L 8.5" Chestnut on cheek

■ **Wilson's Snipe**
Gallinago delicata
L 10.5" Stocky; very long
bill, striped head

■ **Common Snipe**
Gallinago gallinago
L 10.5" Buff overall

■ **Pin-tailed Snipe**
Gallinago stenura
L 10" Pale edges on
scapulars

■ **American Woodcock**
Scolopax minor
L 11" Chunky; long bill

■ **Jack Snipe**
Lymnocryptes minimus
L 7" Bobs while feeding

■ **Wilson's Phalarope**
Phalaropus tricolor
L 9.25" Stripe on face

■ **Red-necked Phalarope**
Phalaropus lobatus
L 7.75" Chestnut patch
on front and side of neck

■ **Red Phalarope**
Phalaropus fulicaria
L 8.5" Black tip on yellow
bill, reddish underparts

American Avocet
Recurvirostra americana, L 18", long, recurved bill

A large, strikingly black-and-white patterned shore-bird with a long, sharply recurved bill, long bluish legs, and the only avocet in the world to undergo an annual color change, the American Avocet acquires its rich cinnamon head and neck as pair bonds form in early spring. Noted for its scything feeding method, avocets often move in a loose line sweeping their slightly open bills in a side-to-side motion, lightly brushing the muddy bottom for small fish and invertebrates. Both visual and tac-tile feeders, their bills are so sensitive that they defend against intruders with their feet and wings rather than their bill. The females have shorter, but curvier bills than the males. Avocets tolerate the cold very well, wintering regularly as far north as Pea Island National Wildlife Refuge on North Carolina's Outer Banks, even in frigid and icy conditions.

Black-necked Stilt
Himantopus mexicanus, L 14", long red legs, long black bill

Black-necked stilts are the dandies of the shorebird world. Tall and elegant with long, red, pencil-thin legs, and a long needle-like black bill, their glossy black-and-white plumage lends them a graceful, dignified, formal air. Once disturbed, howev-er, a quietly feeding flock is instantly transformed into a chaotic mob, flailing, yelp-ing and loudly whistling, sent tumbling into the skies on the wings of unbridled panic. The Black-necked Stilt is a warm-weather bird, and large numbers inhabit shallow-water impoundments and western alkaline flats in areas such as California's Salton Sea and Utah's Great Salt Lake region. They are partial to freshwater and feed on insects, shrimp, small fish, and frogs. Though sensitive to contami-nants such as concentrations of selenium resulting from farm-ing operations, the population is increasing and expanding its range northwards.

range than calidridines, flock together less, and are extremely vocal, hence the name tattler for some. "Marshpipers" might be an appropriate group name, although they are occasionally referred to as shanks after their sometimes distinctive legs.

The nine American curlew species are all of the genus *Numenius* save the shorter billed Upland Sand-piper which is *Bartramia*. Four are rare strays from Eurasia. The Eskimo Curlew may be extinct. These are large, beautifully mottled, brown birds with long, down-curved bills. The world's four godwits are placed in the genus *Limicola*. They are large shorebirds with spectacular, long, slightly upturned bills. The Black-tailed is a rare vagrant here. The world's three phalaropes are compact, small shorebirds, good swim-mers of the genus *Phalaropus*. Turnstones belong to the genus *Arenaria*. As with godwits and phalaropes, North Americans can also see the planet's two turnstone species at home, the Ruddy and the Black.

Of the 19 snipe species, only one is found in North America, the Wilson's; two others are accidental in Alaska. Until recently the Wilson's was considered conspecific with the Old World's Common Snipe. It and all but three of the other 18 are classified in the genus *Gallinago*. Snipes, dowitchers, and woodcocks are closely allied, as are godwits and curlews. America's two dowitcher species are of the genus *Limnodromus*. There is a third species found in Asia. All are mottled brownish with long, straight bills.

Which leaves us with the redoubtable, bug-eyed woodcocks. Six species grace the world, all of the genus *Scolopax*, most found in Southeast Asia. The American Woodcock is widespread in the East, with about eight records there for the accidental Eurasian Woodcock.

STRUCTURE
Sandpipers' bodies are compact with short necks and a somewhat chesty appearance. Many are long-distance migrants, helped along by their ample wing length and sharp, pointed wings. Excellent flyers, they are a chal-lenging prey item for such masters of the air as Merlins and Peregrine Falcons. Sandpiper tails are short, almost inconsequential, although in birds at rest the projec-tion of the wings' primary feathers past the tail is a key to identification in a few species.

In most species the bills are spiky, stout, and strong, yet lengthy, variously adapted to probing in mud or sand, grabbing small prey in shallow water, opening or breaking small mollusks, or snatching insects and worms depending both on the species and habitat. Sandpipers' bills are extremely variable in direct relation to their main prey items, the habitats they feed in, and their manner of feeding.

The curlews and godwits have remarkably long bills, enabling them to probe deep into invertebrate burrows and mud. The American Woodcock probes far into soft, wet mud for earthworms. Yellowlegs and stilts have medium-length, spiky bills with which they variously capture small fishes or probe in mud. Avocets' bills, and those of godwits, Greater Yellowlegs, and Terek Sandpiper are upturned. Bills of curlews, Curlew Sandpipers, stilts, Least, Western, and Purple Sandpipers, and Dunlins curve downward, also known as being decurved, or else merely droop somewhat. Most of the rockpipers—turnstones, Purple and Rock Sandpipers, Surfbirds and the tattlers—have stout, medium-length bills adapted for dealing with shellfish. Other sandpipers' bills are more generalized, mostly straight but still longish.

Sandpiper bills are sometimes prehensile—some of them able to grab with flexible tips—not just by opening and closing the bill, especially the woodcock. Bills of some probing species have sensitive chemoreceptors perceptive to changes in smell, pressure, and touch. Consequently such species are better able to feed at night, than species that feed by sight.

Sandpipers' legs are almost as varied as the bills, ranging from the unbelievably long legs of stilts to the short legs of the peep and other calidridines. In between

Marbled Godwit

are the longer, often colorful legs of the tringines, medium-length legs for medium-size sandpipers.

The woodcock, an exception in every other way, has short legs in keeping with its squat body. Shorebirds often look one-legged but seldom are. Usually they are roosting on one leg so the other can be drawn into its plumage to conserve body heat.

PLUMAGE

Most sandpipers have brownish, dun-colored (hence Dunlin) upperparts often infused with reddish, blackish, or grayish overtones combined with white, buffy, light, or at least lighter colored underparts. Many sport a white stripe on the wing, usually at the base of the secondary and primary feathers, often visible only in flight.

A few, most notably Ruddy Turnstone and Dunlin, have dramatically brighter plumage in the breeding season. This is also true, although somewhat more subtly, of the Ruff; godwits; stilt; Spotted, Western, Curlew, and Rock Sandpipers; Red Knot; avocets; Sanderling; and some of the rarer stints. Much of the difference is the appearance of rufous in the early summer (alternate) plumage. But many sandpipers

have only subtle differences year-round in their plumage, accompanied by increased barring or streaking of the underparts in alternate plumage. Soft parts, especially bill (particularly the base) and leg color, tend to brighten for the breeding season.

The uncommon Ruff males develop elaborate, puffy breast and head plumage for breeding display that may be variously reddish, black, or whitish, sometimes seen in July on North American strays. Also exceptional are the phalaropes. The females are more brightly colored than the males.

Determination of plumage is helpful in shorebird identification. Juvenile plumage, typical of late summer, tends to have fresh, fully realized feathering, often with pale, bright edges on the upperparts. Feathers on the wings (except for the primaries and secondaries) tend to be shorter and more rounded. Nonbreeding (basic) plumage is generally lacking in rufous coloration, streaking and barring, blander than in juveniles or breeding adults. Breeding (alternate plumage) birds tend to have more rufous coloration, more barring or streaking on the underparts.

Confusing the issue are birds molting from one plumage to another, having qualities shared by two plumages simultaneously, as well as feather wear, causing individuals in the same plumage to vary significantly. Still another problem is individual variation, when birds of the same age in a flock can be in various stages of molting from one plumage to another, or are simply duller or brighter than their cohorts at an identical stage in their plumage. Regardless, many sandpipers are subtly beautiful. A juvenile in fresh plumage can be as lovely as any adult at the height of the breeding season.

FEEDING BEHAVIOR

Most shorebird feeding could be described as "down and dirty." Sandpipers feed mostly on a wide array of invertebrates—worms, insects, mollusks, small crabs, and fishes—in muddy, sandy, or shallow water. Less frequently some species will feed on berries, seeds, and other vegetable matter. Prey items are gleaned or seized on substrate surfaces or obtained by probing just beneath the surface.

Sandpipers will often feed in agricultural fields, especially if they are recently ploughed or otherwise mostly barren dirt. In coastal areas this is often the case during rains or abnormally high tides.

Snipes, woodcocks, and dowitchers feed by probing with their long, straight, stout bills. Dowitchers feed with such energy they earned a special colloquial name from market hunters, who called them "sewing machines." Such probing feeders make more use of their tactile senses than surface-feeding species, which rely primarily on sight. The shorter billed sandpipers feed more by seizing visible prey, mostly in damp areas, the edges of freshwater ponds and lakes, and coastal intertidal zones, less frequently by shallow probing. Species feeding in firmer substrates tend to have shorter, straighter bills.

Stilts and avocets feed in deeper water than most shorebirds, enabled by their long legs. Stilts seize small fishes in such settings with remarkable dexterity. Yellowlegs also feed on small fishes. Stilt Sandpipers will favor deeper water, sometimes submerging their heads while searching for food.

Phalaropes are the most aquatic feeders of all away from their terrestrial breeding grounds. They spin and turn while sitting on the water's surface, which agitates the water. The resulting upwelling effect brings minute organisms closer to the surface where they are grabbed by these energetic feeders. Red-necked and Red Phalaropes winter at sea favoring wrack lines with abundant, floating vegetation.

Least Sandpiper

Curlews use their long, decurved bills to probe, especially into burrows of small crabs and shrimp as well as worms and other invertebrates. Godwits feed mostly by probing and will eat plant tubers and a variety of invertebrates.

Many shorebirds feed more in freshwater areas in the summer, less in the intertidal or other waterline areas they may favor at other seasons, enabling them to occupy a wider geographic area for nesting purposes. In such settings flies and other insects, as well as their larval and pupal stages, are fair game, often gleaned from shallow groundwater areas and ponds.

More terrestrial species, especially in the breeding season, such as Long-billed Curlew and Spotted, Buff-breasted, and Upland Sandpipers consume more adult insects than most other shorebirds.

VOCALIZATION

For many birders the clear, pure call of the Black-bellied Plover is evocative of a thousand wild shorelines and resonating with the attractive musical qualities of other shorebird vocalizations. Most sandpiper call notes are simple, consisting of one to three or more notes, often repeated. Many times they are whistled but can be emphatic or grating and rough, such as the harsh, hoarse, reedy *churk* of the Pectoral Sandpiper.

Many sandpipers engage in aerial displays, behavior typical of other, unrelated bird groups that frequent open habitats, accompanied by what are termed actual songs. The richest array of other sounds is also heard in breeding areas with many calls only heard there, such as contact notes between pairs, calls by parents to chicks, threat notes, and other unique vocalizations.

Flight displays are seldom seen outside the Arctic breeding areas where most sandpipers nest, except for Wilson's Snipe and American Woodcock. Snipes have more tail feathers than other shorebirds, and in their winnowing displays, made during impressive dives, the wind rushing over their tail feathers produces a series of owl-like *hu, hu, hu* notes. Woodcocks perform a crepuscular flight display accompanied by complex chippering notes, then dive snipe-like, straight down to the ground.

But for most lower or middle-latitude birders, the call notes of sandpipers are the vocalizations that will be familiar. These are loud, and often repeated, and serve as contact calls, alarm notes, signals of aggression, and other purposes. Most birds utter more vocalizations than there is space in field guides to detail. For example, the Stilt Sandpiper, famous for its elaborate aerial display whose last notes resemble somewhat the braying of a donkey, has more than ten discrete vocalizations.

The yellowlegs and some other tattlers (tringines) are especially loud and vocal. Flush them and these sentinels will sound off, piping provocatively, warning any other shorebird of the perceived danger. Approach the sub-Arctic nesting territory of a Lesser Yellowlegs and the naturalist will be vocally hounded without letup. Willet are especially loud and vocal to any trespasser in their nesting grounds. Avocets and stilts are also very vocal and loud on their territories.

BREEDING BEHAVIOR

Except for the unique Solitary Sandpiper, which uses old nests of medium-size land birds (e.g. American Robin) in the northern boreal forest, all other sandpipers, stilts, and avocets are ground nesters, most of them favoring Arctic or subarctic climes.

For the majority of sandpipers and also the stilts and avocets it may be said: They are monogamous; have clutches of four eggs; both sexes incubate and tend the young; eggs hatch in 18 to 30 days; and young are precocial and can fly at 20 to 30 days of age, although curlews can take over 40 days before they are airborne. Similarly most species are single brooded and breed in their second calendar year of life, larger species delaying until the third or fourth calendar year.

The exceptions are interesting. Polyandry is found with the Spotted Sandpiper, the three phalarope species, and Sanderling (sometimes). Why the White-rumped Sandpiper is polygynous, whereas its many close-relative peep species are not, is a curiosity. Several other species are promiscuous or polygynous, including Pectoral and Buff-breasted Sandpipers, as well as American Woodcock, none of which form pairs. As a result, with these four latter species only females incubate and tend young.

The three phalaropes are also exceptional, exhibiting numerous sexual role reversals. Phalarope females are more highly colored than males, court and display to attract them, and then leave the incubating and care of young to the male. Females are also larger than males in body mass as well as bill and wing length. Phalaropes are polyandrous.

Many sandpipers engage in elaborate, charming courtship displays, often aerial with special songs and atypical, mannered wingbeats. Also associated with nesting are distraction displays to confuse predators, including the "rodent-run" display wherein the bird puffs out its feathers, droops its wings, and runs along the ground squeaking like a rodent, as well as threat postures to intimidate territorial intruders. Another common practice is for courting males to raise one, or two wings while on the ground to draw attention.

Pectoral and White-rumped Sandpipers have complex breeding behavior. They puff out their breast feathers (the reason for the Pectoral's name) and inflate their unusual breast sacs which produce remarkable noises employed in courtship. Buff-breasted Sandpipers are especially complex (one author recognized 17 distinct courtship behaviors). This species performs on leks, as do Ruffs. Leks are communal display grounds where males strut their stuff, used by prairie-chickens and some other gallinaceous birds.

BREEDING RANGE

The majority of sandpipers breed in the Arctic and subarctic, especially in western expanses of these regions. Of species under consideration here, only these have a substantial part of their breeding range in the lower 48 states: American Avocet, Black-necked Stilt, Willet, Spotted and Upland Sandpipers, Long-billed Curlew, Marbled Godwit, American Woodcock, Wilson's Snipe, and Wilson's Phalarope. Among these, the majority also enjoy a primarily western distribution, except for the woodcock, which is confined to the eastern half of temperate North America.

Only the Willet, woodcock, snipe, and Spotted and Upland Sandpipers breed extensively in the East. The others and the Willet breed in wetland and grassland areas of the Great Basin and the prairies and provinces of the West, although the two sandpipers' ranges extend well up into the subarctic.

Examples of birds breeding at northern latitudes with primarily western ranges include: Bristle-thighed and Eskimo Curlews (if, indeed, the latter still persists), Bar-tailed Godwit, Black Turnstone, Wandering Tattler, Surfbird, Rock Sandpiper, Western Sandpiper, and Long-billed Dowitcher. Of these only the latter two (and possibly Eskimo Curlew) occur regularly in the East.

BILL COMPARISON

American Avocet
Recurvirostra americana
L 18", long, recurved bill

Avocets feed in deeper water than other shorebirds, swinging their long, curvy bills back-and-forth in a scythelike manner, as do yellowlegs and stilts. The female's bill is slightly shorter, but more strongly recurved. Avocets feed on insect larvae, small crustaceans, other invertebrates, and fish. They favor alkaline lakes, briney ponds, and coastal areas.

American Woodcock
Scolopax minor
L 11", chunky, long bill

The short-legged woodcock's long, straight, stout bill is adapted to probing deep into damp earth for its favorite sub-surface prey items, especially earthworms and millipedes, and is also used to seize beetles, flies, and ants. The upper bill is flexible, enabling it to seize prey inches below ground. The species' eyes are set far back on the head allowing it to see almost directly behind while still feeding.

Long-billed Curlew
Numenius americanus
L 23", long, downcurved bill

Our largest shorebird, the Long-billed Curlew uses its elegant, long, decurved bill to probe deep into burrows and holes for shrimp and crabs on its wintering grounds, as well as for earthworms in its breeding range. Its diet is varied and includes flying insects, other grassland invertebrates, the eggs and young of small ground-nesting birds, and in the fall it feeds heavily on berries to build up fat before migration.

Other Arctic or subarctic breeders less exclusively confined to the western Arctic include Whimbrel; Lesser Yellowlegs; Hudsonian Godwit; Ruddy Turnstone; Red Knot; Sanderling; Dunlin; and Pectoral, White-rumped, Baird's, Stilt, and Buff-breasted Sandpipers. Almost all of them breed from Hudson Bay longitudes westward, but they also occur in the East in migration. Notable are sandpipers nesting in the high Arctic, some among the most northern of breeding birds, including Baird's Sandpiper and Red Phalarope (to northern Ellsemere Island and northwestern Greenland) as well as Red Knot, Purple Sandpiper, and Ruddy Turnstone (to northern Greenland).

MIGRATION

Shorebird migrations rank with the most impressive of any bird. Some fly nonstop for periods of 60 hours or over 2,000 miles, although many others are merely medium-distance migrants. Bar-tailed Godwits are believed to migrate nonstop for up to 7,000 miles from Alaska to Australia and New Zealand.

A suite of sandpipers migrate from high Arctic or subarctic areas to southern Argentina and Chile. These include the Hudsonian Godwit and Eskimo Curlew, in addition to the White-rumped, Buff-breasted, Pectoral, Upland, and Baird's Sandpipers. Several of these perform an elliptical migration, launching south from New England and the Maritime Provinces in the fall, returning north through America's prairies and plains in the spring.

Equally impressive are species that migrate back and forth from Alaska to points far south to island wintering areas in the Pacific, such as Bar-tailed Godwit,

Bristle-thighed Curlew, Ruddy Turnstone, and Wandering Tattler. Ruddy Turnstones and Sanderlings migrate south to beaches from the temperate Northern Hemisphere to most of the Southern Hemisphere, including such remote places as the Falkland Islands.

Several species have important staging areas along the way where significant percentages of their world populations assemble, including Hudsonian Godwit and Red Knot, as well as Red-necked and Wilson's Phalaropes. American Woodcocks sometimes appear at Cape May, New Jersey, and Cape Charles, Virginia, in numbers unreplicated anywhere else.

Often overshadowed by the spectacular migration of the Argentine migrants are other species that are primarily middle-distance migrants. Though many migrate "only" to Mexico or the southern United States, others continue to central or southern South America, including Willet; Least, Semipalmated, and Solitary Sandpipers; Whimbrel; Red Knot; and Greater and Lesser Yellowlegs. The three phalaropes migrate deep into the Southern Hemisphere, the Red-necked less so than the other two.

By contrast a few species, or at least some of their population, migrate to their overwintering coastal ranges far to the temperate Northern Hemisphere such as Surfbird, Rock Sandpiper, Black Turnstone, and Wandering Tattler on Pacific coasts, and Dunlin, Black-bellied Plover, Purple Sandpiper, Ruddy Turnstone, and Sanderling on the Atlantic. Many species become more coastal at the end of their migration, exploiting the greater availability of invertebrates in milder, saltwater tidal areas, moving from freshwater or tundra locations to tidal shorelines.

WILSON'S PHALAROPE

A trans-equatorial migrant, the Wilson's Phalarope breeds in the wetlands of interior North America, and winters in the highlands of western South America, some birds moving as far south as Tierra del Fuego. The female phalarope has the more colorful plumage and competes with other females for mates. She may breed sequentially with several males. After laying her eggs in a shallow scrape, she deserts her mate, leaving nest completion and incubation duties to the male. Wilson's, the largest and most terrestrial of our three phalaropes, lack the lobed toes of their more aquatic cousins. Loss of breeding habitat in prairie wetlands seems to have caused a recent and dramatic range expansion with nesting birds being found as far north as Alaska and as far east as Massachusetts. After breeding, Wilson's gather near western saline lakes where they undergo a "molt migration" in preparation for their non-stop flight to the saline lakes in the highlands of western South America.

WINTER RANGE

In general, sandpiper species breed in North America's interior or Arctic areas. If they also winter in our area, they seek southern and temperate coasts. The most northerly wintering American sandpipers on the Pacific coast include Rock Sandpiper, Dunlin, Black Turnstone, and Surfbird, which linger north to the rocky coasts of southern Alaska; the Rock Sandpiper—the northernmost—winters along the broad fetch of the Aleutian islands. On the Atlantic coast the Purple Sandpiper is the winter champion, populating rocky shores as far north as the southern half of Newfoundland.

The opposite extreme are species with no individuals wintering north of Central America. These include the Argentine wintering group. The wintering grounds of Alaska-breeding Bar-tailed Godwit and Bristle-thighed Curlew are equally far south in the middle and southern reaches of far-flung Pacific Ocean islands. Phalaropes also winter far to the south, Wilson's in interior southern South America. Red and Red-necked Phalaropes are Arctic circumpolar breeders and winter at sea, Reds off Chile as well as West and southern Africa, Red-neckeds off Chile and Peru, southern Arabia, east of Indonesia and north of New Guinea in the southwest Pacific.

Fortunately some 30 sandpiper species winter in the southern U.S. Christmas Bird Counts regularly find 20 to 25 or more shorebird species in parts of the Southeast, and the Texas and California coasts. Some of these include the dowitchers; snipe; yellowlegs; Willet; Marbled Godwit; Long-billed Curlew; Sanderling; avocets; stilts; Ruddy Turnstone; Dunlin; and Spotted, Western, and Stilt Sandpipers, albeit several of these in small numbers. The farther north on the Pacific and Atlantic coasts, the fewer shorebird species there are. Interior areas are rather bereft of these birds in winter except in the southern states.

OBSERVING SANDPIPERS, STILTS, AND AVOCETS

Coastal tidal areas, whether sand, mud, or rock, wetlands with exposed mud, sand, and low grasses, and grasslands with low grasses and damp areas are the optimal habitats for seeing sandpipers. Agricultural fields, especially if they have freshly exposed soil and are wet, can be excellent. At interior locations wet fields and the shorelines of reservoirs, rivers, and lakes, especially if they are receding (as in times of drought), are important places to check.

To see the birds, telescopes and high-power binoculars are necessary because of the vastness and remoteness of these places. Contact with local bird clubs and acquisition of regional bird-finding guides (such as are sold by the American Birding Association) will help.

In tidal areas, shorebirds are more concentrated at half-tide at a few local roost areas. At low tide they will disperse over the flats. On a falling tide they eagerly gather as waters recede, excited at the prospect of fresh food, since they have probably not eaten for several hours. Superior sites include Washington's Skagit Flats, the Delaware Bay, coastal Texas (especially the Bolivar Flats near Galveston), California's coastal bays, parts of the Bay of Fundy, the Cheyenne Bottoms in Kansas, and coastal Florida. Many national wildlife refuges have impounded areas where shorebirds are seen to best effect, especially in May, July, and August. Observers in the Arctic tundra in early summer will see sandpipers in their breeding plumage finery, complete with elaborate courtship displays and unique vocalizations.

Red-necked Phalarope

STATUS AND CONSERVATION

The remote breeding grounds of many shorebirds in Arctic and subarctic regions afford them significant protection.

Sandpipers, especially long-distance migrants, are vulnerable at areas of concentration by human disturbance, oil spills, or other chemical contamination, and perhaps by rising sea levels. In much of Latin America, unregulated shooting threatens them. Over-harvesting of horseshoe crabs, whose eggs are vital to spring migrants along the Delaware Bay, is probably one of several reasons Red Knots and Sanderlings have declined in recent decades. Widespread destruction of grasslands has adversely affected Upland Sandpipers and Marbled Godwits. Habitat destruction may be a major reason for the serious decline of American Woodcock.

Subsistence hunting threatens some large Arctic shorebirds such as Bar-tailed Godwits, although their global population is still estimated at a surprising 1,200,000. The Eskimo Curlew, whose vast flocks once filled the skies, never recovered and may be extinct. Closely regulated hunting still exists for Wilson's Snipe and American Woodcock.

Recent shorebird research resulted in the development of the Western Hemisphere Shorebird Reserve Network, the U.S. Shorebird Conservation Plan, and the International Shorebird Survey.

See also

Killdeer, page 142
Northern Jacana, page 144
Oystercatchers, page 146

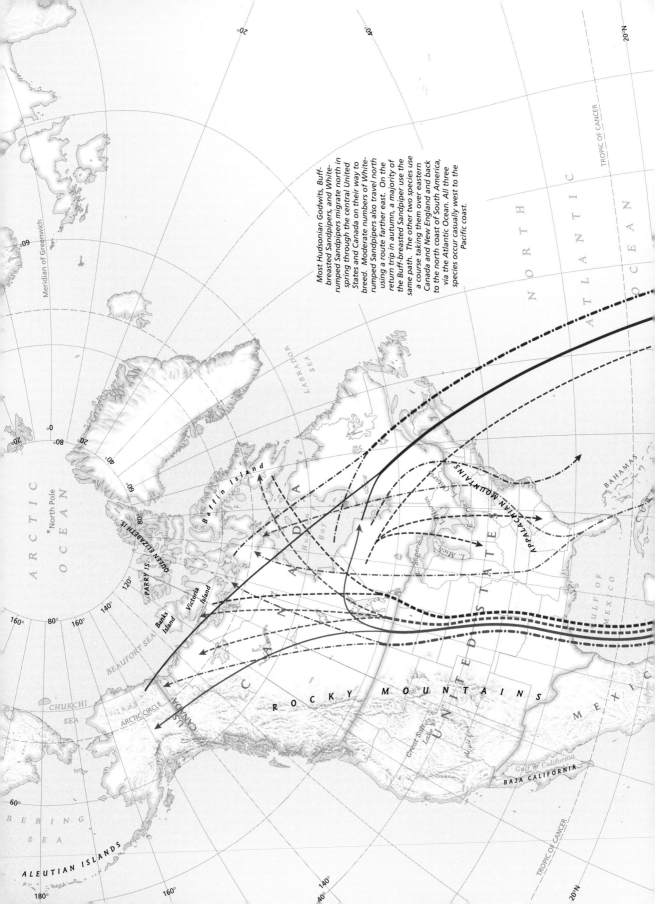

Most Hudsonian Godwits, Buff-
breasted Sandpipers, and White-
rumped Sandpipers migrate north in
spring through the central United
States and Canada on their way to
breed. Moderate numbers of White-
rumped Sandpipers also travel north
using a route farther east. On the
return trip in autumn, a majority of
the Buff-breasted Sandpiper use the
same path. The other two species use
a course taking them over eastern
Canada and New England and back
to the north coast of South America,
via the Atlantic Ocean. All three
species occur casually west to the
Pacific coast.

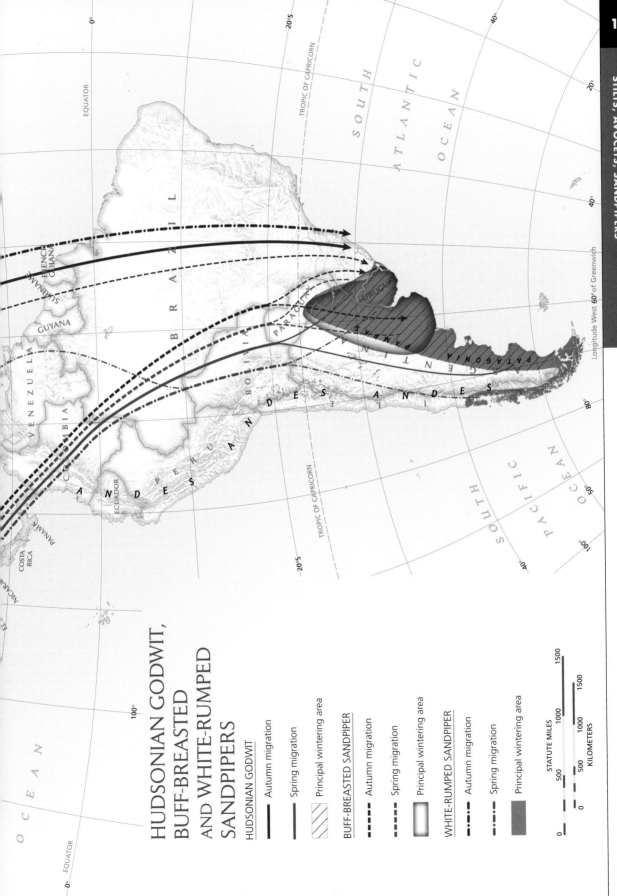

HUDSONIAN GODWIT, BUFF-BREASTED AND WHITE-RUMPED SANDPIPERS

HUDSONIAN GODWIT
— Autumn migration
— Spring migration
▨ Principal wintering area

BUFF-BREASTED SANDPIPER
—·— Autumn migration
—·— Spring migration
▢ Principal wintering area

WHITE-RUMPED SANDPIPER
—··— Autumn migration
—··— Spring migration
▨ Principal wintering area

STATUTE MILES
0   500   1000   1500

KILOMETERS
0   500   1000   1500

SKUAS, GULLS, TERNS

The Larids comprise a familiar, varied, and cosmopolitan suborder, broken into four families: skuas and jaegers; gulls, terns, and skimmers. These are medium to large birds with a moderate range in shape. Gulls are easily recognizable because of their close association with humans. To many they symbolize the ocean and the beach. All birds in this group are found around water ranging from pelagic waters to marshes, mudflats, and inland lakes. Gulls are plentiful where there is an abundance of waste. In winter they may reside at landfills and wastewater treatment facilities. Gulls and terns are adorned in white and gray as adults, but exhibit more browns and grays as young birds. Skuas and skimmers are darker, showing combinations of dark gray, brown, and black that are offset by paler or white areas.

George Armistead

Though the taxonomy, especially of gulls and skuas, is far from well understood, there are about 104 species of larids in 15 genera found across the globe and of these, 52 species in 11 genera are known from North America. Of these, 46 species either breed or are found regularly on the continent, but others including Black-tailed and Yellow-legged Gulls, Large-billed, White-winged, and Whiskered Terns, and Black Noddy occur only as vagrants.

Gulls, terns, and skimmers nest in colonies, which can number in the thousands. Skuas tend to have solitary nests and defend territories aggressively by driving out intruders. Jaegers and skuas are cosmopolitan, breeding in the Arctic, or Antarctic in the case of South Polar Skua, and wintering pelagically. While all three jaegers breed in Arctic North America, South Polar and Great Skua only visit the continent during their nonbreeding season. Gulls concentrate their nesting in the northern United States and Canada or coastally, but then move south in the fall, with a few moving further south than Central America. Terns are more evenly distributed as breeders in North America, and Black Skimmers breed just along the Atlantic and southern Pacific coasts.

Though birds in this group are generally familiar, they present considerable challenges when it comes to their identification. The Black Skimmer is an obvious, gaudy, and awkwardly proportioned bird that really cannot be confused with anything else, but terns, gulls, and skuas can be difficult. Gulls, particularly the larger species, demonstrate much intraspecific variation and regularly hybridize with other large gull species. Combine this with varying differences in size and structure between males and females of the same species, and try to determine which species, or combination of species, you are looking at. Gulls present something of a paradox in that they are often found in large numbers where birders can study them at close range, but the complexity of the group dictates that a relatively high number of well studied birds will go unassigned. Terns in North America are more often encountered on their breeding grounds so that identification is more straight forward, but migrants and vagrants can be difficult to study as views may be fleeting, and several species are similar. Skuas, by contrast, are fairly easily identified as adults, but often a birder's first experience with a skua or a jaeger may be on a pelagic trip offshore where individuals may be distant and rapidly moving, or they may be young birds that are much more difficult to identify.

(Left) Least Tern

South Polar Skua: *Stercorarius maccormicki,* L 21" W 52", barrel-chested, white bar at base of primaries, overall gray-brown

SKUAS

One of several seabird species that are sometimes spotted off the Atlantic and Pacific coastlines, the South Polar Skua (above) is a heavy-set, thick-necked species with broad wings that have a white bar at the base of the primaries. Birds appear grayish-brown in color, with darker wings and lighter underbellies. When spotted, the species is often far from land, but vagrants have been seen near Atlantic and Pacific beaches and the Alaskan coast. Skuas are usually solitary except during breeding season or where fish concentrations attract a number of species. South Polar Skuas forage for squid, fish, crabs, and other mollusks, and edible debris from isolated coastal military bases. Sometimes the species chases other birds to steal their food, and skuas prey on chicks of other seabirds. They breed on the South Shetland Islands and along the coast of Antarctica, and nonbreeding birds range throughout the Pacific, Atlantic, and Indian Oceans. Juveniles take several years to reach adult plumage. Their population is stable.

Range of South Polar Skua

CLASSIFICATION

There are at least seven species of two genera in the family Stercorariidae. Five have occurred in North America. Skuas and jaegers are closely related to the gulls and share a similar overall shape but are stronger fliers with stronger bills. Despite appearances, the recent research indicates that the Pomarine Jaeger is a closer relative of the larger skuas than it is to the jaegers.

STRUCTURE

Skuas are broad, chesty birds and are well built for their nomadic lifestyle with stout, hooked bills and short legs. Their legs are insulated and aid in heat retention in the cold climes they frequent. Adult jaegers have tail streamers that increase in length with age, and these are thought to aid in aerial displays for mate attraction, and in reinforcing pair bonds, with males averaging slightly longer tails than females. Their physique makes them an intimidating, foreboding bunch, as they are strong, capable of rapid acceleration, and agile. Female skuas are bigger than males.

PLUMAGE

The dark browns of the larger skuas aid in camouflage, as they do in immature jaegers, most of which show barring on the underparts and often paler fringes to the upperparts. Many adult jaegers are countershaded, showing paler creamy, white breasts and dark brown or gray upperparts. Polymorphism is featured prominently among this group with some individuals in certain species appearing wholly dark and others pale. Some young Long-tailed and even some Parasitic Jaegers are only a pale, straw-colored tan, whereas the darkest Pomarine Jaegers and South Polar Skuas are a cold, dark blackish-brown. Great Skuas tend to exhibit warmer tones in their plumage. In each of these species both dark and light morphs and intermediate plumages exist, and they do so in adult, immature, and male and female plumages. The Parasitic Jaeger shows the greatest variation, and dark ones are more common in the southern part of their range with paler birds outnumbering them at more northerly latitudes. Breeding pairs throughout often consist of one dark and one light adult. The idea that the dark plumage of these birds aids in their camouflage is further reinforced by the fact that kleptoparasitism is more heavily employed by Parasitic Jaegers in the southern part of their breeding range where a greater proportion of them tend to be dark morphs.

FEEDING BEHAVIOR

These birds are bullies, but are so tough, elegant, and masterful in flight that they quickly win over the respect of their observer. To watch any skua or jaeger induce its victim to give up its hard-earned prey after a twisting, turning, arcing, and swerving chase is enthralling. The larger skuas often aim their attacks from above, and sometimes from considerable heights, diving in a falcon-like manner in an effort to drive their victim to the water, while jaegers tend to stay low, seeking to surprise. Victims are usually gulls, terns, or alcids, and Great Skuas may attack gannets as well.

Parasitic Jaegers

This group does not consist solely of pirates, though. While piracy is commonplace at sea for nonbreeding jaegers and visiting skuas, some catch fish and other prey of their own. Feeding strategies change somewhat in the breeding season, when these birds scavenge carrion and obtain food directly through predation on berries, eggs, fish, small birds, and small rodents, especially lemmings. The smaller and sleeker Long-tailed Jaegers attack the lemmings aerially, hovering above and then diving onto them. Parasitic and Pomarine Jaegers are too broad-winged to catch lemmings this way and usually dig them out of their holes instead.

VOCALIZATION

This group is not especially vocal, and calls are limited. Most vocalizations indicate agitation because a person is entering their breeding territory or because of a battle with another bird for food. Like gulls, the larger skuas and Pomarine Jaeger, and to a lesser degree the smaller jaegers, perform a long call on the breeding grounds, to establish themselves in a territory or in response to a mate. For the skuas and Pomarine Jaeger this consists of a few to a dozen laughing cries, each of which last only a second or two. The long call given by the smaller jaegers is more plaintive and whining.

BREEDING BEHAVIOR

Monogamy is the norm, with most birds mating for life and exhibiting strong site fidelity, but Pomarine Skuas may choose new mates and territories each year,

and this is probably due to fluctuations in lemming population. Once they chose a territory, they form a nesting scrape, sculpted by both members of the pair. A normal clutch size is one or two eggs. Though breeding territories may be small, these birds maintain individual territories and do not nest colonially. Nonbreeding skuas, may form "clubs" at watering holes near breeding grounds, where other birds come to drink and bathe. The oldest stercorarid known was a 34-year-old Great Skua.

BREEDING RANGE

South Polar Skuas breed in Antarctica. Great Skuas breed in the northeast Atlantic. The three jaegers are Holarctic, and breed on the Arctic tundra near water.

MIGRATION

Great Skuas migrate south in winter to mid-Atlantic waters and as far south as Brazil. South Polar Skuas return via the Atlantic and Pacific to their breeding grounds in the austral summer in Antarctica. The jaegers leave their breeding grounds, migrating through the oceans to their wintering areas. The Long-tailed Jaeger migrates farthest, moving down to sub-Antarctic waters while the other two jaegers spend their winter in more tropical or temperate waters.

WINTER RANGE

All skuas and jaegers spend their winter pelagically, often near fishing vessels or other areas where they can exploit groups of feeding birds.

OBSERVING SKUAS AND JAEGERS

These birds are often encountered at sea, jaegers in the Arctic. Because skuas do not breed in North America, they are only found on pelagic trips; Great Skua only in the Atlantic. Jaegers are slightly easier to observe. If you enter their breeding grounds, they are aggressive toward intruders, diving repeatedly as they give little barking calls. In migration and wintering at sea they may perform much as the skuas, frequenting boats that attract other hungry birds looking for handouts.

STATUS AND CONSERVATION

None of these species are subject to an imminent threat or drastic declines.

OTHER SPECIES FIELD NOTES

■ **Great Skua**
Stercorarius skua
L 22" W 54"
Barrel-chested, white at base of primaries, streaked above overall ginger-brown

■ **Pomarine Jaeger**
Stercorarius pomarinus
L 21" W 48"
Heavy body, twisted spoon-shaped tail streamers

■ **Parasitic Jaeger**
Stercorarius parasiticus
L 19" W 42"
Pointed tail streamers

■ **Long-tailed Jaeger**
Stercorarius longicaudus
L 22" W 40"
Lightly built, long, pointed tail streamers, two-tone wings

See also

Albatrosses, Shearwaters, Storm-Petrels, page 39
Frigatebirds, Tropicbirds, Boobies, page 51
Gulls, page 166

Laughing Gull: *Larus atricilla* L 16.5" W 40", breeding adult, black hood, black outer primaries

GULLS

Often considered to be noisy and aggressive, the Laughing Gull (above) is a successful breeder that ranges along the Gulf Coast and Atlantic coast into New England. The species looks like other black-headed gulls and has a drooping bill, gray back, white chest and belly, and grayish-white wings with black tips. The bird gets its name from a characteristic vocalization that sounds like "ha-ha-ha-ha", given when feeding or during courtship. Laughing Gulls eat various aquatic scraps such as decayed fish and crabs as well as flying insects and garbage on the beach. The breeding season of Laughing Gulls and horseshoe crabs coincide, and large gull flocks congregate along Mid-Atlantic beaches to feed on a concentration of eggs deposited in the wet sand by migrating horseshoe crabs. Gulls are colonial nesters, and their nests, made of grasses and aquatic plants, are placed on the sand close to each other. Typically there are three to four chicks that are cared for by both parents. Although they attract predators, Laughing Gulls have steadily increased in number.

Range of Laughing Gull

CLASSIFICATION

Worldwide there exist about 50 species of gulls and these tend to be concentrated in temperate areas of the northern and southern hemisphere. Gulls, and especially the large white-headed gulls, are a complex group. Five genera and 27 species are found in North America. Ivory Gull (*Pagophila*), Sabine's Gull (*Xema*), and Ross's Gull (*Rhodostethia*) are in their own genus, and the two Kittiwakes (*Rissa*) are separated into their own. The remaining birds are all of the genus *Larus* and are further subdivided into either the small hooded gulls including Little, Bonaparte's, Black-headed, Laughing, and Franklin's Gulls, or the larger white-headed gulls.

The Herring Gull, perhaps more than any other bird, has tested the parameters of the biological species concept. This bird interbreeds with the Yellow-legged Gull in some parts of Europe, but does not in other areas of overlap. Some studies show that the distance between the two species genetically approximates that between many gull species, yet other studies indicate that the Lesser Black-backed Gull is still a closer relative to the Yellow-legged Gull. The picture is muddled, and still more research is necessary to clarify the relationships. The Iceland Gull has variously been considered conspecific with or (as it is currently) separate from Thayer's Gull. Thayer's Gull interbreeds with the North American form of Iceland Gull called Kumlien's Gull. These forms may merely reflect clinal variation of a single group over the North American Arctic, but the amount of hybridization within contact zones is similar to that between Herring and Glaucous Gulls and between Glaucous-winged and Western Gulls so that drawing the line between species is a difficult task. Recent research has shown that the North American form of Herring Gull (*L.a. smithsonianus*) shows a substantial difference in genetics from European populations and is more closely allied to other North American species such as California, Iceland, Thayer's, and Glaucous Gulls so that some are considering whether a split might be advisable.

STRUCTURE

Though their identification may be difficult, as a group, gulls possess an instantly recognizable form. Whether it's a small hooded gull or a white-headed gull, most observers know a gull when they see one. These birds range in size from medium to large and are heavily built with longish, broad wings, legs of moderate length with webbed feet, and a long, stout, slightly hooked bill. Gulls have medium long, rounded tails except in Ross's Gull, which has a wedge-shaped tail, and Sabine's Gull which has a notched tail. White-headed gulls have larger bills, which show a stronger angle at the gonys than the small hooded gulls, a result of different feeding strategies. Head shape varies between species and intraspecifically, with some heads appearing small and rounded and others large and blocky.

California Gull

PLUMAGE

Most gulls combine gray, black, and white in their plumage, with younger birds exhibiting a range of browns. Young birds usually have a black or dusky-colored bill, and adults' range from yellow to mildly orangish-yellow. Winter plumaged adults often show grayish-brown head streaking and most white-headed gulls show a red spot on the bill at the gonys that is brightest in the breeding season, thought to stimulate nestlings to feed. Heerman's Gull is the only North American gull that diverges from the typical adult gull pattern of white below and gray above, instead it is almost wholly dark with adults being an ashen, steely gray below and dark slaty-gray above with a red bill. Adults also show an unusual tail pattern with mostly black tail, save a white terminal tail band. Young Heermann's Gulls

are browner with duskier colored bills. Male gulls are larger than females with similar plumage. Some gulls require four years to reach maturity, smaller gulls just two. An example of the latter is Franklin's Gull which is also one of the few species breeding in North America that undergoes a complete molt twice a year. Attaining adult plumage is a gradual process for larger gull species which are either "three year" or "four year" gulls. Those that take this long to mature undergo several changes in their appearance before reaching adulthood and may show as many as eight different, increasingly adult-like, plumages. These different plumages make identification more problematic, but once one has learned how to "age" gulls, it becomes easier to identify them.

FEEDING BEHAVIOR

Gulls are resourceful feeders and well suited for a variety of foraging strategies. Perhaps more opportunistic than any other group of birds, gulls can scavenge a large host of items including seeds, fruit, grains, grasses, shellfish, mollusks, dead fish and fish remains, and will prey on marine invertebrates,

OTHER SPECIES FIELD NOTES

■ **Heermann's Gull**
Larus heermanni
L 19" W 51"
Red bill, white head

■ **Franklin's Gull**
Larus pipixcan
L 14.5" W 36"
Black hood

■ **Bonaparte's Gull**
Larus philadelphia
L 13.5" W 33"
Dark hood, black bill

■ **Black-headed Gull**
Larus ridibundus
L 16" W40"
Dark brown hood,

■ **Little Gull**
Larus minutus
L 11" W 24"
Black hood, underwings

■ **Ross's Gull**
Rhodostethia rosea
L 13.5" W 33"
Black collar, rosy tint

■ **Ring-billed Gull**
Larus delawarensis
L 17.5" W 48"
Yellow bill with black ring

■ **Mew Gull**
Larus canus
L 16" W 43"
White head, yellow bill

■ **California Gull**
Larus californicus
L 21" W 54"
White head, yellow bill

■ **Black-tailed Gull**
Larus crassirostris
L 18.5" W 47"
Yellow bill with black ring

■ **Band-tailed Gull**
Larus belcheri
L 20" W 49"
Bill has black and red tip

■ **Kelp Gull**
Larus dominicanus
L 23" W 53"
Black back, greenish legs,

■ **Herring Gull**
Larus argentatus
L 25" W 58"
Pink legs, yellow bill

■ **Yellow-legged Gull**
Larus cachinnans
L 24" W 57"
Square head, yellow legs

■ **Glaucous Gull**
Larus hyperboreus
L 27" W 60"
Translucent primaries

■ **Iceland Gull**
Larus glaucoides
L 22" W 54"
Pale eyes and wingtips

■ **Thayer's Gull**
Larus thayeri
L 23" W 55"
Dark eyes, rounded head

■ **Yellow-footed Gull**
Larus livens
L 27" W 60"
Yellow legs and feet

■ **Western Gull**
Larus occidentalis
L 25" W 58"
White head, pink legs

■ **Glaucous-winged Gull**
Larus glaucescens
L 26" W 58"
White head, gray mantle

■ **Slaty-backed Gull**
Larus schistisagus
L 25" W 58"W yllow
Pink legs, yellow eyes

■ **Lesser Black-backed Gull**
Larus fuscus
L 21" W 54"
White head, yellow legs

■ **Great Black-backed Gull**
Larus marinus
L 30" W 65"
Black mantle, pink legs

■ **Black-legged Kittiwake**
Rissa tridactyla
L 17" W 36"
Yellow bill, black legs

■ **Red-legged Kittiwake**
Rissa brevirostris
L 15" W 33"
Coral red legs

■ **Sabine's Gull**
Xema sabini
L 13.5" W 33"
Dark gray hood, yellow bill tip, tricolored wings

■ **Ivory Gull**
Pagophila eburnea
L 17" W 37"
Adult, pure white plumage, black bill with yellow tip

arthropods, fish, nestlings of other species, rodents, and some birds. The Great Black-backed Gull takes birds including Pied-billed Grebe, Manx Shearwater, Atlantic Puffin, and American Coot. During the breeding season, gulls may vary their diet, depending on the abundance of foods. Grains and fruits are less desirable, but may be consumed if there is little else to eat. In winter these birds are found near bodies of water or along the coast where their diet will become more pescivorous or at landfills where foods may be scavenged. Gulls may be engaged in jaeger-like chases in which they pirate food from other birds. This activity can occur anywhere but is often seen offshore where large groups of gulls may follow or congregate around fishing boats to collect scraps and discarded offal.

VOCALIZATION

Gulls are a vocal bunch calling frequently wherever they are, but especially when feeding and nesting. A visit to a gull colony can be deafening with birds calling, croaking, and crying incessantly. The long call of a gull is one of the most recognized bird sounds, consisting of a series of laughing croaks that begins with a short, gruff note and falls into an accelerated set of "kheeyaahh"-type sounds. This call is thought to help in pair-bond maintenance, or to get the attention of a mate or young, or to declare a territory. These birds have several other calls when they are fighting for or have found food, or when they become aware of a threat. Individuals will utter contact calls to each other while flying in tandem.

BREEDING BEHAVIOR

Gulls breed on the ground, often in large colonies that can be comprised of several species. Bonaparte's Gulls are an exception, they construct stick-nests high in spruce trees, often isolated from others of the same species. Occasionally Herring Gulls, too, will maintain a solitary nest. Kittiwakes nest in colonies of thousands along cliff edges. Pair bonds are monogamous. Clutches of three to four eggs are most common, and both members of a pair will incubate for the requisite 22 to 26 days. Fledging occurs at four to seven weeks. An unusual phenomenon that occurs among several gull species including Ring-billed, California, Herring, Western, and probably more, are nests tended by pairs or trios of females. These arrangements occur when females are unable to find a male to pair with, but are successful in soliciting copulation and so team with another female or females to maintain a nest. The scarcity of breeding males may be a result of differing survival rates, but in some cases was known to be a consequence of DDT use in the area.

BREEDING RANGE

Gulls tend to nest coastally, in the Arctic, or in the wetlands of the northern United States and Canada. Some species are strictly coastal, such as the Laughing or Western Gull, while others such as Herring Gull may nest along the coast, around the Great Lakes, or at an interior wetland. Still others such as Glaucous, Thayer's, Iceland, Sabine's, and especially Ivory Gull breed only in the far north.

MIGRATION

A few gulls move hardly at all and are essentially resident, but most perform some sort of movement, heading for milder climes in winter, and some species journey thousands of miles. Western Gulls are largely sedentary and are only rarely seen away from the Pacific Coast, but Franklin's Gulls leave their Canadian breeding grounds and spend the winter in southern South America. Franklin's Gulls

BLACK-LEGGED KITTIWAKE

Although some Black-legged Kittiwakes have red legs, similar to their near relative the Red-legged Kittiwake, leg color is still a helpful field identification mark. The dressy Black-legged has a pearl-gray mantle and wings with the tips of the primaries so sharply defined that they appear to have been dipped in black ink. Its uniformly yellow-green bill is longer than that of the Red-legged. Among the most pelagic of gulls, the Black-legged Kittiwake breeds mainly on seacliffs along the Canadian and Alaskan coasts on ledges so small it must face the wall with its back to the sea and its tail projecting over the edge. During the summer most kittiwakes move south out to sea with few coming to shore. The species feeds mainly on small fish near the surface, and unlike other gulls, does not forage at landfill sites.

are the longest distance migrant of the gulls, but Sabine's Gulls also migrate far from their breeding range in the Arctic to the tropical waters south of the equator in western South America and western Africa. Others like California, Ring-billed, and Herring Gulls leave their nesting areas in the interior and space themselves out along the coast. Other birds breeding in the Arctic may move only as far as the pack ice pushes them, lingering along its edge for the winter. Often directed movements of large groups of gulls will happen during the evening, but groups of migrating gulls can also be seen in the early morning hours or late in the afternoon. All gulls are subject to wandering long distances away from their normal haunts and even some mostly sedentary species such as Kelp and Black-tailed Gull have shown up several times in North America.

WINTER RANGE

Especially in winter, gulls concentrate along the coast. Smaller gulls such as Bonaparte's will flock together in large groups offshore. In most species, adults move shorter distances than immature gulls, with younger birds wintering in greater numbers in the more southerly regions of a species' range. However, vagrant gulls seem fairly evenly proportioned between young (especially first year) and adult birds. This may be the result

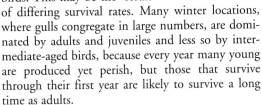

Bonaparte's Gull

of differing survival rates. Many winter locations, where gulls congregate in large numbers, are dominated by adults and juveniles and less so by intermediate-aged birds, because every year many young are produced yet perish, but those that survive through their first year are likely to survive a long time as adults.

OBSERVING GULLS

Some species in this group are hard to see almost anywhere. Ivory and Ross's Gulls usually require special trips to see them, but a pelagic trip, a tour of the coast, or a visit to a local landfill can be a great way to observe lots of gulls of several species. Although certain individuals will confound an observer and defy identification, most can be identified fairly easily.

STATUS AND CONSERVATION

Given the group's proclivity to frequent aquatic areas they face the same risks as other organisms that inhabit these areas such as those posed by the development and water level management of wet-

land areas, pollution, and contaminants including pesticides. DDT used in the 1960s and 1970s had a feminizing effect on gull embryos that prevented males from reproducing and resulted in populations that were abnormally high in females. Eventually, these effects on a Great Lakes population of Herring Gulls reduced their productivity to 10 percent of what it had been. Of the gulls found in North America none are facing an imminent threat but some birds may be at risk due their restricted breeding range. The Red-legged Kittiwake is deemed vulnerable because at the two perhaps most prosperous breeding colonies of its seven total breeding sites, the birds have declined by 50 percent. Heermann's Gull while healthy in total numbers at the current time has 90 percent of its breeding population concentrated on an island in the Sea of Cortez. This precarious situation has led to this bird's near-threatened status. Franklin's Gulls breed in marshes in the interior West of the United States and southern central Canada, and their dependence on this habitat that is so prone to human manipulation of water levels, development, and contamination may put them in a dangerous position. However, accompanied by a general increase in food at landfills, wastewater treatment plants, and offal from fishing boats and processing plants, several species have shown dramatic increases in recent decades including the Ring-billed, Laughing, Great Black-backed, Lesser Black-backed, and Herring Gulls. Ring-billed Gulls have increased to such a degree that they are now being detected increasingly in parts of Europe, where they were formerly only a rare vagrant. The proliferation of Great Black-backed and Herring Gulls, particularly along the East Coast, has caused concern in the areas which these gulls are colonizing, where entire tern colonies and some other breeding birds such as shorebirds, have vanished altogether. The gulls drive the terns away from the breeding sites, and when the terns attempt to breed, their eggs and young are preyed upon by these domineering species. The increase in the Lesser Black-backed Gull in the past two decades is perplexing as they have yet to be detected breeding in North America.

See also

Auks, Murres, Puffins, page 177
Frigatebirds, Tropicbirds, Boobies, page 51

Forster's Tern: *Sterna forsteri*, L 14.5" W 31", long, forked tail with white outer edges, mostly orange bill

TERNS

Of the North American tern species, the Forster's Tern (above) has the largest wintering range in the United States along the Gulf Coast and portions of both Atlantic and Pacific coasts. As with most tern species, Forster's Tern plumage is generally whitish-gray, with a full black cap. The birds often give a one-note call while feeding over water or during the breeding season. The species inhabits marshes, lakes, and coastlines where abundant fish and insects can be found, but the birds often range well inland. When feeding, birds pass back and forth over the water's surface searching for small fish. When prey is spotted, terns dive straight down and plunge beneath the surface to capture it. In the spring, the species migrates to breeding grounds in the Midwest, Pacific Northwest, and southern Canada. Forster's Terns are colonial nesters that scrape a shallow depression in the sand and produce a small number of hatchlings. Parents in a colony often join together to fiercely defend their young against predators.

Range of Forster's Tern

CLASSIFICATION

Terns are represented by 44 species of 10 genera worldwide. In North America 19 species of four genera have occurred and of those, 15 breed on the continent every year. Terns are most closely allied to the gulls, but fill a different set of niches as birds that feed mostly on fish, but hunting more on the wing, than as scavengers. Of the terns commonly encountered in North America 13 are of the genus *Sterna*. The Black Tern belongs to the *Chlidonias* group along with the vagrant Whiskered and White-winged Terns, and these species are often referred to as Marsh Terns. The two noddies are of the genus *Anous* and the vagrant Large-billed Tern is the sole member of the genus *Phaetusa*. Scientists have variously placed Royal and Elegant Terns (the crested terns) in the genus *Thalasseus* or in *Sterna*, and some also separate out the larger-billed species, Gull-billed and Caspian Tern in their own genera as *Geochelidon* and *Hydroprogne* respectively.

The skimmers are comprised of three species in the world, all in the genus *Ryncops* with their closest relative being the gulls and terns. The only species in North America is the unmistakable Black Skimmer.

STRUCTURE

Terns are elegantly proportioned, with a rather sleek, slender build with short legs and long pointed wings. Bill and tail shape vary. Certain species have long, swallow-like tails and slim pointed bills, and others have shorter thick bills and shorter, slightly notched tails. Terns are quick and buoyant and graceful in the air.

Black Skimmers are vaguely tern-like in shape, with short legs, but more robust for their size with long, angular wings and a bill that is unique in its appearance. The bill is long (especially in males) with the lower mandible considerably longer than the upper. The tail is short and slightly notched.

PLUMAGE

Sterna terns are largely white with gray mantles and wings; in breeding plumage, with black caps. Exceptions to this are Sooty and Bridled Terns, sometimes referred to as "tropical terns." They are darker with blackish or gray-brown upperparts and white below. Juvenile Sooty Terns are almost entirely dark, appearing rather like a noddy. The Brown Noddy is a rich chocolate brown with a grayish-white cap, and the Black Noddy is similar but smaller, finer-billed, and blacker overall with a more well defined cap. The marsh terns show the greatest change in plumage from breeding to non-breeding plumage, changing from largely black in summer to a dark gray and white or mostly white winter plumage. Bill color in terns varies from bright red to pale yellow and black. Adult skimmers are a striking contrast in black and white. The upperparts are a rich black and the underparts a clean, bright white. The bill is a bright orange on the base and black on the outer third. Juveniles show a muted and duskier bill pattern and are paler, checkered above, where adults are purely black.

Black Tern

FEEDING BEHAVIOR

Terns are aerial feeders, hovering and plunge diving into water to catch small fish. Food comes from aquatic habitats, be it sea, beach, marsh, mud flat, river, or inland lake and can include crustaceans, and occasionally small toads or frogs. The latter may be taken by Gull-billed Terns which feed by hawking insects over fields and marshes. Some terns engage in piracy, chasing members of the same species until a captured prey item is turned over.

Skimmers are nocturnal feeders, but they also feed during the day in estuaries, coastal waters, and tidal bays, and even at inland lakes such as the Salton Sea. Their food is mostly fish, and to a lesser degree crustaceans, and is obtained by flying low over water, dropping the lower mandible into the water, and skimming it. Skimmers drag their lower mandible until they come into contact with some prey and then snap down their maxilla to snatch it out of the water. They may feed in tandem with a mate, or other bird, or solitarily.

VOCALIZATION

Terns are a vocal group, especially when feeding or around the nesting colonies, and their calls have a harsh, scratchy tone. On the breeding grounds they have a greater variety of calls than at other times of the year, including chattering scolds and rattles and "kik" or "keik" notes that warn other birds that they are intruding on a territory, or that are given in greeting a mate. Males also have a copulation call they give when they are mating. Male and female skimmers make yelping barks when at the nesting colony, defending a territory, sitting on a beach or mud flat, or in alarm, or response to a threat.

BREEDING BEHAVIOR

Terns form monogamous pair bonds and usually nest in colonies on small islands or marshes, often with strong site fidelity, though the latter is dependent on the habitat. Birds which nest on sandbars, such as Least Terns, may relocate regularly due to the disappearance or formation of new bars. Pair bonds are formed through ritualized calling and aerial displays, and often

---

OTHER SPECIES FIELD NOTES

■ **Sandwich Tern**
Sterna sandvicensis
L 15" W 34"
Slender black bill tipped with yellow

■ **Elegant Tern**
Sterna elegans
L 17" W 34"
Long, thin, reddish-orange bill

■ **Royal Tern**
Sterna maxima
L 20" W 41"
Large orange-red bill

■ **Caspian Tern**
Sterna caspia
L 21" W 50"
Thick orange to coral red bill, slightly forked tail

■ **Roseate Tern**
Sterna dougallii
L 15.5 " W 29"
Mostly black bill, long forked tail

■ **Gull-billed Tern**
Sterna nilotica
L 14" W 34"
Stout black bill, slightly forked tail

■ **Common Tern**
Sterna hirundo
L 14.5" W 30"
Long forked tail with dark outer edges, red bill tipped in black

■ **Arctic Tern**
Sterna paradisaea
L 15.5" W 31"
Long forked tail, gray underparts, short legs

■ **Aleutian Tern**
Sterna aleutica
L 13.5" W 29"
White forehead, black cap, bill and legs

■ **Least Tern**
Sterna antillarum
L 9" W 20"
White forehead, orange-yellow bill

■ **Black Tern**
Chlidonias niger
L 9.75" W 24"
Mostly black with dark gray back, pale underwings

■ **White-winged Tern**
Chlidonias leucopterus
L 9.5" W 23"
Whitish upperwing coverts, black wing linings

■ **Bridled Tern**
Sterna anaethetus
L 15" W 30"
White forehead extends past eye, brownish-gray upperparts

■ **Sooty Tern**
Sterna fuscata
L 16" W 32"
White forehead reaches eye, blackish above

■ **Black Noddy**
Anous minutus
L 13 5" W 30"
Black overall, small white crown

■ **Brown Noddy**
Anous stolidus
L 15.5" W 32"
Overall dark gray-brown, extensive whitish-gray cap

■ **Large-billed Tern**
Phaetusa simplex
L 14.5" W 36"
Stout yellow bill, striking tricolored upperparts

■ **Black Skimmer**
Rynchops niger
L 18" W 44"
Lower mandible longer than upper

begin with a male landing near a female and offering her a fish. They will take to the air together, simultaneously performing a "fish-flight" that is characterized by high soaring glides on stiff wings. Once mates are chosen, males continue to hunt fish while females remain at the territory to defend it. The male will return to feed her and, if he is judged to be a suitable provider, copulation ensues. Nests are small depressions, or scrapes, or in the case of the noddies, constructed of small sticks, feathers, and often fused together by their excretions. Clutch sizes vary from one to three eggs and depend on food availability. If the clutch size exceeds this number, it may indicate the presence of multiple females tending a nest. Nest duties are shared by males and females, and incubation varies from three to four weeks. If a person intrudes on a nesting area during this time, especially after chicks hatch, terns will defend their territory aggressively by diving on and screeching at the intruder. First breeding in terns typically occurs in a bird's second year.

Skimmers are monogamous and pair bonds may last several years or more. Copulation occurs usually at night after the male has presented a female with a fish or a substitute gift such as leaf or twig. Nests are a scrape in the sand, sculpted by both members of the pair. Only one brood is attempted per season, and nest duties are shared with both sexes performing roughly equally in incubation and feeding of young. Incubation lasts three weeks, with chicks being semi-precocial, wandering from the nest after three to five days and fledging within about a month.

Sooty Tern

BREEDING RANGE

Terneries occur at or near wetland habitats in North America from the monstrous Sooty Tern and Brown Noddy colonies in the Dry Tortugas, Florida, to inland marshes where Black Terns nest, and the sparse colonies of Aleutian Terns in western Alaska. The Forster's Tern is the most widely seen tern on its breeding grounds while others are far more restricted in their breeding range. The Bridled Tern is known to have nested but a few times in the Florida Keys, and the Brown Noddy is restricted to the Dry Tortugas within North America but both nest in huge colonies abroad. One of the more unusual breeding distributions occurs in the Roseate Tern, which is found nesting along the coast from New York to Nova Scotia, but also in the sub-tropical waters of the Florida Keys; between the two regions it is only a scarce, if regular migrant.

The Black Skimmer is found breeding from Massachusetts south to Texas and into Mexico, and along the southern coast of California and the Sea of Cortez. Skimmer colonies are constructed on beaches, sandbars, spoil banks, or in salt marshes.

MIGRATION

The terns perform some sort of seasonal movement, whether it is a nomadic wandering, a post-breeding dispersal northward, a migration from the interior to the coast, or a long journey from the northern to the southern hemisphere. The more tropical species move less, though young Sooty Terns will—after fledging from the Dry Tortugas—cross the Caribbean to South America before turning east to cross the Atlantic to reside in the waters off western Africa. There they will remain for several years before reaching sexual maturity and returning directly across the Atlantic to breed, so that once a juvenile leaves its natal colony in the Dry Tortugas it may not touch land again for several years. Common Terns undertake a fairly long migration, breeding along the East Coast and interior marshes of central and eastern North America, then moving south into Central and South America. Surely the most impressive migration of the group, however, and perhaps the most amazing migrant bird in the world is the Arctic Tern. This species, the heavyweight champ of bird migration, is a circumpolar breeder of the high Arctic, nesting in such northerly spots as the north slope of Alaska, Ellesmere Island, northern Greenland, and Svalbard Islands. From its breeding grounds the Arctic Tern then moves, mostly pelagically, all the way south to the waters of Antarctica, and then back again in the spring. This may entail a journey of some 30,000 miles or more.

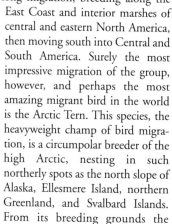

Skimmers breeding in the northerly part of their range from Massachusetts to Virginia leave for warmer waters in winter, moving into Florida, and perhaps the Caribbean and Central America. Birds breeding further south are not believed to undertake much movement of any distance. Vagrants have strayed as far north as Newfoundland and occasionally far inland.

WINTER RANGE

Terns winter either coastally or pelagically. The winter range of the Aleutian Tern is still only partially realized with a few sightings at this season from the waters around the Philippines.

The skimmers winter along the coast from North Carolina south to Florida. The Gulf Coast and southern California populations, however, are believed to be sedentary.

OBSERVING TERNS

Terns can be very difficult to identify and especially when they are away from their breeding grounds. Breeding colonies are probably the best place to see a lot of terns and may afford the opportunity to observe and hear well one or several species. In migration, terns congregate at inland lakes, along rivers, and especially along the coast, where with the aid of a good telescope one may be permitted the opportunity to study several species simultaneously. Pelagic boat trips to deep waters offshore may net lucky observers a chance to see Arctic, Common, and Roseate Terns in migration. These species provide the most significant identification challenges. Important characteristics to pay attention to include the overall color and structure of the bird, tail length, bill structure and pattern, primary pattern, and general style of flight.

Skimmers are striking birds and are usually obvious when present. They are found in large open areas near the coast, sitting or flying, sometimes in large groups, on beaches, sand spits, or mud flats.

STATUS AND CONSERVATION

Most terns are subject to annual fluctuations because of their dependence on ephemeral and unstable habitats such as sandbars and small islands. Food availability on the breeding ground also limits the productivity of a nesting season. The Least Tern (recently split from Little Tern) is protected at the state level throughout much of its range, with interior and coastal California populations being especially vulnerable, numbering only in the hundreds. This bird has faced considerable declines because of pressure from recreational human activities where it breeds. Their young are also vulnerable to predation by Ghost Crabs. In recent years, the coastal Least Terns have found some relief in the form of gravel-topped buildings that have provided suitable breeding grounds. Other threats to terns include overfishing, competition with increasing and expanding gull populations, pollution and water contamination, mismanagement of water levels for marsh-nesting species, and habitat loss because of development.

In the 19th century, terns were subject to dramatic declines, and some entire colonies were wiped out because of hunting and harvesting of their eggs. While this practice no longer exists in North America, it still does in parts of Africa and South America, and this is thought to be a contributing factor to the decline of the Roseate Tern in both Neararctic and Palearctic populations. Few species are on the increase, but one is the Sandwich Tern, and the South American form called the "Cayenne" Tern is spreading north into the West Indies; it has been detected on a number of occasions in North America as well.

Skimmers were harvested in large numbers in the 19th century, although this is no longer a problem for them, they are prone to many of the same dangers that threaten the terns. The biggest threats to skimmers are contamination through polluted waters, ingestion of contaminated prey, and loss of habitat.

See also

Frigatebirds, Tropicbirds, Boobies, page 51

Herons, Egrets, page 71

BLACK SKIMMER

This large, tern-like bird of sheltered bays and coastal marshes possesses a red, black-tipped bill, the lower mandible of which is longer than the upper, unlike that of any other bird. Using its long, pointed wings to glide low over the water, it drops its lower mandible to slice the surface as it skims along, foraging for small fish and minnows. It is a tactile feeder; when its bill touches a fish, the upper bill, or maxilla, instantly snaps shut capturing the prey. The Black Skimmer also has a unique pupil that contracts to a narrow, vertical, cat's-eye-like slit, thought to protect the eyes from the bright sunlight glaring off the water's surface. Its large eye is surrounded by black feathers and is often invisible. Though skimmers are active day feeders, especially during the nesting season when chicks must be fed, they often forage at dawn and dusk, and even at night. The highly social Black Skimmer nests in large colonies on barrier islands and salt marshes, often sharing the site with tern colonies to take advantage of the defensive tactics of these aggressive breeding birds.

SOOTY TERN, ARCTIC TERN AND RED-NECKED PHALAROPE

SOOTY TERN MOVEMENTS FROM DRY TORTUGAS NESTING COLONY

Area frequented by adults

Multi-year "wintering" area of young birds

Migration route of first-year birds east and recently matured birds west

Nesting area

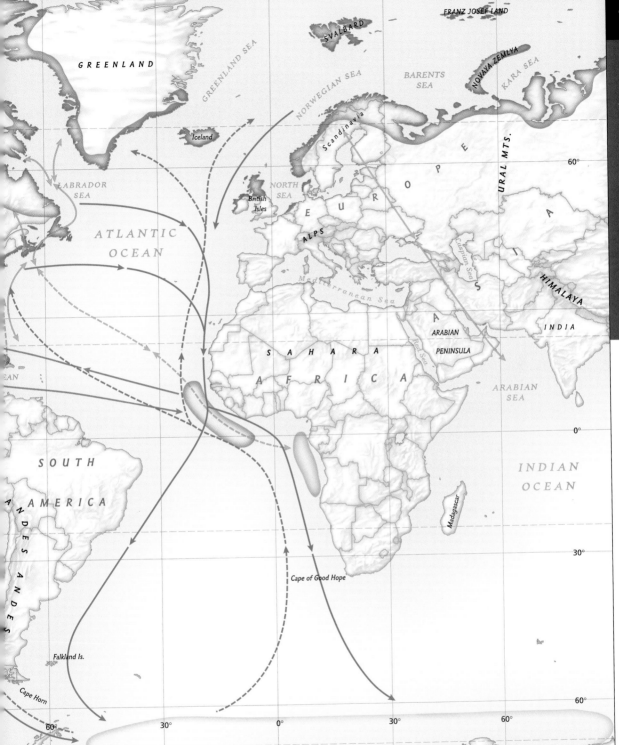

GREENLAND

GREENLAND SEA

SVALBARD

FRANZ JOSEF LAND

NOVAYA ZEMLYA

BARENTS SEA

KARA SEA

NORWEGIAN SEA

Scandinavia

LABRADOR SEA

Iceland

NORTH SEA

British Isles

E U R O P E

URAL MTS.

ATLANTIC OCEAN

ALPS

Caspian Sea

HIMALAYA

60°

Mediterranean Sea

SAHARA

ARABIAN PENINSULA

Red Sea

INDIA

A F R I C A

ARABIAN SEA

0°

SOUTH

AMERICA

INDIAN OCEAN

Madagascar

30°

A N D E S

Cape of Good Hope

Falkland Is.

30°

Cape Horn

60°

60°

30°

0°

30°

60°

60°

ARCTIC TERN MIGRATION

PRINCIPAL RED-NECKED PHALAROPE MIGRATION

Arctic Tern nesting range — Fall migration

Wintering area – – – – Migration (uncertain)

Arctic Tern wintering area – – – – Spring migration

Migration

AUKS, MURRES, PUFFINS

Jonathan Alderfer

The alcids (or auks) are a small, diverse family of seabirds, unfamiliar to many birders. Going to sea or visiting the remote oceanic islands where alcids breed is the best way to see most species. Alcids have an exotic appeal to birders because they are so difficult to observe and identify. Some have fantastically shaped, colorful bills and ornamental head plumes, otherwise their plumage is monochromatic.

There are 23 species of alcids in the world, and 21 have occurred in North America. The center of alcid abundance is the Bering Sea region of the North Pacific—only the Razorbill and Atlantic Puffin are unrecorded from the Pacific Ocean. Tragically, the Great Auk of the North Atlantic, a flightless species, became extinct by the 1850s.

Most species are colonial nesters, sometimes spectacularly so. Least Auklets and Dovekies can occur in single colonies of more than a million pairs. Remote islands near productive fishing areas are valuable alcid real estate often shared by different species, each occupying a different niche. Buldir Island in the Aleutian chain claims the record for alcid diversity, with 12 different species breeding there.

Most birders glimpse their first alcid on an organized pelagic trip. Offshore trips can be a daunting experience and good views of these species are unusual. The typical experience is of a smallish bird flying rapidly away from the boat or diving underwater at a close approach. With persistence and luck, better looks are possible, and these become treasured birding memories. In the Pacific there are a few breeding species observable year-round as far south as southern California, especially around Channel Islands National Park. In the Atlantic, the southernmost breeding sites of Razorbills, Black Guillemots, and Atlantic Puffins are in Maine—all of them can be seen on a summer whale-watching trip. Black Guillemots are even seen from shore, in places like Acadia National Park. To experience the full glory of alcid diversity and abundance, however, you must travel to their Arctic breeding islands, such as St. Lawrence Island or the Pribilofs in Alaska. Organized tours make these trips feasible for birders of all levels. The views of their breeding cliffs, alive with murres, auklets, and puffins, are extraordinary.

A fair share of mystery has been associated with the alcid family. The nest of the Marbled Murrelet remained undiscovered until 1974. A closely related species, the Long-billed Murrelet which breeds in the Russian Far East, has been found to wander far from its home—vagrants have turned up as far away as Florida and recently one was found on Lake Zurich in Switzerland. Ancient Murrelets have also turned up as vagrants on lakes and reservoirs throughout the interior of North America. The reasons for their wanderlust have not been determined. More easily explained, alcids are at times storm driven to inland bodies of water—Dovekies, for instance, have turned up in "wrecks" on the Great Lakes.

Alcids are not birds for the casual observer. Travel to their northern breeding islands will put you in some of the remotest and wildest locations on Earth. Further south, alcids can be hard to see and harder still to identify as they hurtle off toward the horizon, and you try to focus your binoculars, while on a rocking boat. It's quite a challenge.

(Left) Tufted Puffin

Atlantic Puffin: *Fratercula arctica,* L 12.5", massive, brightly colored bill

AUKS, MURRES, PUFFINS

The most spectacular species among the alcids is the Alantic Puffin (above), a foot-long bird with bright orange feet and massive, orange bill, found in northern New England and the Canadian Maritimes. This aquatic species has a black back and neck collar, a white face and underparts, and an orange eye ring. The birds catch fish by floating on the water's surface, tipping forward to dive and using their wings to pursue prey underwater. Puffin feeding and breeding grounds are widely separated. They breed on islands or rocky coasts and travel great distances to find schools of fish. The nests are burrows dug under boulders or usurped from burrowing animals. A breeding pair produces a single chick and both parents share feeding duties. Because of the long distances involved, puffins carry several fish at once in their bill to their hatchling. The Atlantic Puffin population suffered heavy predation from Herring and Black-backed Gulls and rats, and has declined sharply. The species was reintroduced on Maine and Canadian islands.

Range of Atlantic Puffin

CLASSIFICATION

The alcids (family Alcidae) form a distinct taxonomic group of 23 species worldwide. Superficially they resemble the loons and grebes of North America, but they are not closely related to them. They are instead classified as part of the large order Charadriiformes, which includes all the shorebirds, gulls, and terns. Even more strikingly, they resemble the penguins and diving-petrels of the Southern Hemisphere with which they share similar body structure, plumage coloration, and the ability to use their wings for underwater propulsion. Although they are not closely related, these remarkable similarities are the result of a similar evolutionary response to similar environments and lifestyles—an example of convergent evolution. Subspecies variation is limited—14 of the 23 species are classified as monotypic (there are no subspecies). The widespread murres and guillemots show the most subspecific diversity.

STRUCTURE

Alcids are so marvelously adapted for their marine life that they come onshore only to breed. They have short, narrow wings to propel them rapidly underwater in pursuit of their prey. In fact, they are said to fly underwater. And they have short legs with large, webbed feet that act as rudders to steer them. Their heavy, compact bodies are covered with dense waterproof plumage. Auks, murres, and puffins have strong bones to withstand the great pressure of deep dives. Common Murres have been caught in gill nets set at depths of more than 500 feet.

The heavy bodies of alcids combined with their small wings result in their typical flight style—very rapid (up to 50 miles per hour) and usually low over the ocean—resembling a football on whirring wings. For some of the larger species, becoming airborne can be challenging, and long, running starts are necessary. After feeding, some individuals may become especially heavy and temporarily incapable of flight—these birds will attempt to escape any close approach by diving. Once airborne, most alcids are strong fliers, and birds traveling to their feeding grounds often form large "commuter" flocks, especially in the Bering Sea. Some species, especially murres, fly together in long lines known as "trains."

The extinct Great Auk adapted to its watery existence so completely that it became flightless, although it must have been a superbly capable, underwater "flier." In fact, the Great Auk (*Penguinus impennis*) is the "original penguin," after which those other underwater fliers, the penguins of the Southern Hemisphere, were named. Very little is known of the Great Auk's biology or life history, but museum specimens (80 specimens of birds and eggs exist) have allowed ornithologists to study its structure and skeleton. Outwardly, the Great Auk resembled an oversize Razorbill, except that its wing bones were much heavier and proportionately shorter. From the study of fossilized bones, it is known that flightlessness was not unique to the Great Auk; for example, the long-extinct Lucas Auk was an even larger, flightless bird with more massive bones. On land, most alcids are quite clumsy. With their legs set far back on their body, they typically stand with the lower legs (tarsi) flat on the ground. Puffins and a few other alcids stand upright on their toes and can be very agile on land.

Alcid bills are highly variable and structurally adapted to the type of food each species pursues. In addition, a number of species, especially the puffins, grow ornamental bill plates before the breeding season. In the puffins these bill plates are very colorful and increase the showy bulk of the bill, which is used in courtship interactions. The aptly named Rhinoceros

Common Murre

Auklet grows a horn-like appendage on the top of its bill, and many of the Bering Sea auklets also grow ornamental bill plates. A few species may even grow small plates around the eyes and have fleshy appendages above them—hence the name Horned Puffin. These bill ornaments are "deciduous"—meaning they are shed after the breeding season and grown anew each year.

PLUMAGE

Most alcids are studies in black and white—dark above and white below (countershaded)—which minimizes their visibility to both predators and prey. Two species, the Marbled and Kittlitz's Murrelets, are more cryptically plumaged with mottled browns and grays in summer, which distinguishes them from other murrelets. These two solitary species nest in exposed locations, and they need additional camouflage for protection. There is only a slight variation in size between the sexes, and their plumages are identical. In most species,

OTHER SPECIES FIELD NOTES

■ **Dovekie**
Alle alle
L 8.25"
Black breast, white underparts, small bill

■ **Common Murre**
Uria aalge
L 17.5"
Long, slender, pointed bull, streaked flanks

■ **Thick-billed Murre**
Uria lomvia
L 18"
Thick, short bill with pale stripe

■ **Razorbill**
Alca torda
L 17"
Massive, arched bill with white band

■ **Black Guillemot**
Cepphus grylle
L 13"
Large white wing patch, white underwings

■ **Pigeon Guillemot**
Cepphus columba
L 13.5"
Black bar on white wing patch, dark underwings

■ **Long-billed Murrelet**
Brachyramphus perdix
L 11.5"
Pale oval patches on sides of nape in winter, pale underwings

■ **Marbled Murrelet**
Brachyramphus marmoratus
L 10"
White collar in winter, dark underwings

■ **Kittlitz's Murrelet**
Brachyramphus brevirostris
L 9.5"
White face in winter

■ **Xantus's Murrelet**
Synthliboramphus hypoleucus
L 9.75"
Variably white in face, white underwings

■ **Craveri's Murrelet**
Synthliboramphus craveri
L 8.5"
Long bill, dusky-gray wing linings, partial collar

■ **Ancient Murrelet**
Synthliboramphus antiquus
L 10"
White streaks on head and nape, yellow bill

■ **Cassin's Auklet**
Ptychoramphus aleuticus
L 9"
Gray overall, pale eyes, plump body

■ **Least Auklet**
Aethia pusilla
L 6.25
Tiny size, white, bristly feathers on forehead and lores, white chin

■ **Parakeet Auklet**
Aethia psittacula
L 10"
Broad, upturned orange bill, white plume behind eye

■ **Whiskered Auklet**
Aethia pygmaea
L 7.75"
Three white plumes on face, black plume on forehead

■ **Crested Auklet**
Aethia cristatella
L 9"
Black crest curves forward over bright orange bill

■ **Rhinoceros Auklet**
Cerorhinca monocerata
L 15"
Pale horn at base of bill, two white plumes on side of face

■ **Horned Puffin**
Fratercula corniculata
L 15"
Fleshy horn extends up from eye, massive, mostly yellow bill

■ **Tufted Puffin**
Fratercula cirrhata
L 15"
Golden tufts droop over back of neck, orange bill

the plumage of the juveniles resembles the adult's winter plumage. A full bill-size and any ornamental plumes are acquired over the first few years of life.

Two, distinctly different plumages—breeding and winter—are worn by most species each year. In general, winter plumages are characterized by more whites, especially on the head and throat, and the loss or reduction of any ornamental plumes. Some species such as Xantus's Murrelet and Cassin's Auklet look nearly the same year-round. Other species such as the Marbled Murrelet and the guillemots radically alter their appearance in different seasons; most species fall somewhere in between. The complete post-breeding molt—going from breeding to winter plumage—results in a period of flightlessness because all the primary feathers are dropped simultaneously (except in the auklets). This molt usually takes place at an offshore location before any winter dispersal or migration is undertaken.

Atlantic populations of the Common Murre exhibit an interesting plumage variation—the bridled morph—which does not occur in Pacific Ocean birds. Bridled-morph birds have a white eye ring with a short white spur (the bridle) extending behind it. Bridled morphs interbreed with non-bridled birds in varying percentages at different colonies. As a general trend, bridled-morph percentages increase—up to 50 percent—in more northerly colonies, which may indicate that they are more cold tolerant.

FEEDING BEHAVIOR

The alcids are extraordinary divers with the ability to "fly" underwater in pursuit of prey. Diving depths depend on prey location, but the larger species generally forage at greater depths and concentrate on fish species like capelin and sandlance. Many of the smaller auklets feed heavily on planktonic copepods and crustaceans such as krill. In the Bering Sea where species diversity is great and food competition could be a problem, each species exploits a particular marine niche. For instance, Whiskered Auklets frequent violent tidal rips while Least Auklets favor downstream areas where they make shallower dives in calmer water. These plankton-feeding species have distensible throat pouches to carry masses of food back to their chick. Fish-eating species, such as murres, usually carry a single fish, but the puffins have developed the remarkable ability to capture and carry many small fish at a time. Foraging distances from the breeding colonies vary, but alcids often fly considerable distances to reach favorable locations—30 miles or more is not uncommon.

VOCALIZATION

Alcid vocalizations consist mostly of calls, whistles, and low growls, heard at colonies—the birds being generally

MARBLED MURRELET

Newsflash: First Marbled Murrelet Nest Discovered
For much of the 20th century, no ornithologist or birder had been able to locate a nest of a Marbled Murrelet. The National Audubon Society was even offering a hundred-dollar reward to the finder of the first documented nest. There were glimpses of mystery birds seen at dawn or dusk, flying over old-growth forests, up to 50 miles inland. Perhaps they nested on inland mountaintops or on the forest floor. The speculation ended in 1974, when a tree trimmer in California's Big Basin Redwoods State Park discovered a nest—148 feet above the ground on an old-growth Douglas fir. This North American bird species had finally yielded up its secret. Since then, the protection of Marbled Murrelets (and Spotted Owls) has been instrumental in the preservation of the ancient, temperate rain forests of the Pacific Northwest.

silent at sea. Occasionally birders on pelagic boat trips will hear the contact calls of Xantus's Murrelets, which go to sea with their downy chicks. Marbled Murrelets are probably the most vocal alcids at sea, giving their high-pitched calls, "keer...keer...keer" while swimming or in flight.

BREEDING BEHAVIOR

Most alcids return to their breeding sites one to two months before laying their single egg. This time is spent cementing the pair bond, and taking possession of, and preparing, the nest site. Nest locations vary from species to species; they can be in the open, on rock ledges, or hidden in crevices, or in underground burrows. Alcids do not actually construct a nest, although they may shift around some nearby pebbles and other debris. The burrowing species—the puffins, Ancient Murrelet, and Cassin's Auklet—make deep, extensive excavations, and the puffins have well-developed claws to help them dig. Nest-site fidelity is high. Most individuals return to the same or nearby ledges or burrows used the previous year. Alcids are monogamous breeders, and most pairs remain together for their entire breeding life. "Divorce" is rare, apparently most often associated with nesting failure.

Courtship display is well developed and in some species involves their elaborate plumes and colorful bills, which both sexes exhibit. For instance, Atlantic Puffins engage in "billing," in which a bird approaches its partner in a stylized "low profile walk," all the while swinging its bill back and forth. The ritual reaches its climax with both birds knocking their bills together for up to a minute. Other displays include "skypointing" with the bill and "pelican walking," in which a bird struts with high steps, showing off its large orange feet and signaling burrow ownership. Crested and Whiskered Auklets are even perfumed with a noticeable, citrus-like odor.

Most species lay a single, large egg, although the guillemots and some murrelets lay two. Incubation lasts from 27 to 46 days, and most alcid chicks hatch covered with down. Alcid chick-rearing strategies are unusually variable for such a small family. Three general strategies have been identified:
1) The Dovekie, guillemots, some murrelets, auklets, and puffins tend their chick at the nest site for 27 to 55 days, until it is almost full-grown. Once fledged, the young bird flies to sea and is independent of its parents.
2) In some species—the Razorbill and murres—the chick goes to sea with the *male* parent when it is partially grown. After hatching, the young bird stays at the nest-site for 15 to 23 days. Then, in a highly synchronized exodus, the young birds—only about 25 percent adult size and flightless—make their way to the sea. This may involve hurtling off high cliff faces and running a gauntlet of predators, but the chicks are very resilient and many successfully negotiate these perils. At sea, the male parent cares for the young bird for the next four to eight weeks.
3) In a few, closely related species, the Ancient, Xantus's, and Craveri's Murrelets—and very unusual in a seabird—the chicks (usually two) go to sea with both parents in attendance. The newly hatched, downy chicks are very active and well developed, with almost adult-size legs and feet. Under cover of darkness, two-day-old chicks depart their forest burrows like tiny, windup toys—heedless of obstacles and unrelenting until they reach the sea. After negotiating the surf, they

Craveri's Murrelet

start calling loudly and reunite with their parents. The entire family then leaves the area and heads out to sea. Paddling steadily, the family can cover 20 miles or more on the first day. Both parents attend the chicks until they are fully grown.

BREEDING RANGE

The alcid family has a circumpolar breeding distribution in the cold waters of the Northern Hemisphere. This distribution mirrors that of their Southern Hemisphere counterparts, the penguins. While breeding, alcids are very vulnerable to mammalian land predators and, as a consequence, they seek out remote predator-free islands or sheer sea cliffs, preferably close to productive feeding areas, for nest sites. Ideal locations are a very limited commodity, and in some areas this has resulted in the formation of immense colonies, often harboring a variety of species.

The center of alcid abundance and diversity is in the North Pacific and Bering Sea. Large populations also occur in the North Atlantic, Arctic Canada, and along the coast of Greenland, although species diversity is greatly reduced. The two murre species occur abundantly in both oceans.

Two uncommon murrelet species, the Xantus's and Craveri's, have the most southerly breeding ranges. The southernmost one—Craveri's Murrelet—breeds only on small islands in the Sea of Cortez in Mexico. The Xantus's Murrelet breeds on the Channel Islands off southern California, and south to a few islands off Baja California. With a total population of between 6,000 to 10,000 birds, the Xantus's Murrelet is our rarest alcid, even so, it is regularly seen on pelagic trips off southern and central California. In the summer months, parent birds accompanying their downy chicks are sometimes encountered.

Two other species of murrelet—Marbled and Kittlitz's—are solitary nesters. Unique among seabirds, the Marbled Murrelet nests high up in old-growth trees in the Pacific Northwest. The tiny Kittlitz's Murrelet has its own, equally unusual solution. It flies as much as 20 miles inland, to nest on alpine mountain slopes with scattered snowfields. About 95 percent of the estimated world population of 20,000 birds breeds in Alaska.

MIGRATION

Post-breeding dispersal away from the breeding colonies is highly variable. Different populations or age classes of the same species may undertake different journeys. Three general strategies have been identified:

1) short-distance dispersal within the birds' breeding range; 2) longer distance dispersal, generally southward, in response to adverse ocean conditions such as pack ice or low food availability; 3) lengthy migrations that may involve a rapid exodus to a particularly favorable wintering location.

In most cases, the alcids tend to confine their migratory wanderings to the food-rich waters of the continental shelf. By contrast, small numbers of southerly breeding Craveri's and Xantus's Murrelets actually move north after breeding.

BEAKS FOR FISHING

Atlantic Puffin
Fratercula arctica
L 12.5", massive, colorful bill

The massive, brightly colored bill of the Atlantic Puffin, our only East Coast puffin, takes about five years to fully develop. A master fisher, it forages while "flying" underwater propelled by its wings, collecting up to a dozen small fish per foray, and cleverly managing to clamp them each in turn crosswise in its bill. Puffins fish within the first 50 feet of water, but are known to dive to 200 feet.

Least Auklet
Aethia pusilla
L 6.25", knobbed, red bill

The smallest member of the auk family—at 6.25"—the Least Auklet is about the same size as a Tufted Titmouse. An agile underwater forager, it has a stubby, knobbed, dark red bill with a pale tip that it uses to capture small shrimp, copepods, and plankton found in the cold, preferably turbulent waters and tide rips around Alaskan and Bering Sea islands. Usually seen far offshore in huge flocks, Least Auklets move in advance of the winter ice, though few range as far south as Washington State.

Common Murre
Uria aalge
L 17.5", long, pointed bill

The long, slender, pointed bill of the Common Murre is yet another shape used by the adaptable auks, and like the Atlantic Puffin, it specializes in pursuing fish underwater in cool northern waters. Found in the North Atlantic and Pacific, it is more abundant in its western range, and most often seen nesting on sea cliffs, standing upright and looking somewhat similar to a penguin. The Common and Thick-billed Murres are the largest living auks.

WINTER RANGE

The alcids are cold-water specialists. Many birds, particularly adults, tend to spend the winter as close to their breeding areas as open water and available food allow. In the Atlantic Ocean, Dovekies may winter as far north as the edge of the pack ice, or they may move to productive waters further south, such as the Grand Banks off Nova Scotia. Rare stragglers have been recorded as far south as Florida. Cold-water adaptation and the lack of truly long-range migrations have kept the alcids restricted to the Northern Hemisphere.

Young birds often disperse farther from the breeding colonies than adults of the same species. These immatures account for many of the records of out-of-range birds. They also are more likely to be displaced by large or prolonged storms, and "wrecks" of birds may even end up at inland locations.

OBSERVING ALCIDS

Seeing auks, murres, or puffins can be difficult. A few species, notably Black and Pigeon Guillemots, are coastal species that can regularly be spotted from northern Atlantic and Pacific shores.

Seeing most other species requires a trip to sea or a visit to their breeding colonies. In the northeastern United States, summer day-trips are available to places like Machias Seal Island, off the coast of Maine, to observe breeding Atlantic Puffins and Razorbills.

A visit to the immense and spectacular breeding islands in the Bering Sea—especially St. Lawrence Island or the Pribilof Islands in Alaska—is best arranged through a bird-tour company. Otherwise, offshore boat excursions or pelagic trips are a birder's best bet. These day trips are relatively inexpensive and usually feature knowledgeable leaders—check for trip availability with the local Audubon Society or on the Internet. As a general rule, winter is the best season for observing alcids in most locations, especially in the Atlantic Ocean, south of Maine.

The identification of most species is straightforward, but only if they are well seen. Since many observations are complicated by a rocking boat, large waves, bad weather, or great distance—or all of the above—the actual situation may present real challenges. Some poorly seen birds will be unidentifiable.

Calm seas are a great advantage because simply locating a small, dark, swimming bird can be almost impossible in heavier seas. Once a bird is located, a slow approach is best—a disturbed bird may simply dive rather than fly off—this is helpful because flight identification is more difficult, especially if the fleeing bird is headed directly away from the boat, which is usually the case. A distant bird in flight can sometimes be easier to identify, because it can be followed with binoculars and offers a longer observation period.

Noting differences in flight styles can be helpful in making a proper identification, especially on distant birds whose plumage field marks are obscured. For instance, distant Cassin's and Rhinoceros Auklets can appear quite similar, but the more erratic, twisting flight of Cassin's Auklet—more like a spiraling-football—is distinctly different from the low, straight-ahead flight of the Rhino Auklet

A number of alcid species are high on the wish-list of many bird-watchers—some of those species are briefly detailed below.

All of the Bering Sea auklets live in remote locations, but only the Whiskered Auklet is particularly difficult to find. These birds are not rare—rough estimates put the population at more than half a million birds—but none of their colonies are accessible. Scattered colonies of Whiskered Auklets exist on remote and restricted Aleutian Islands and on even more remote Russian islands.

Die-hard bird-watchers with adequate funds can head for Dutch Harbor, Alaska, located in the central Aleutians, to look for the Whiskered Auklet. A flight from Anchorage or the ferry from Kodiak will get visitors there. Unfortunately the ferry passes through the best locations for Whiskered Auklets in the middle of the night; however, fishing boats can be chartered for day trips in Dutch Harbor, and some of the captains know where the auklets can be found.

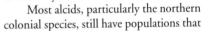

Crested Auklet

A world away, in the waters off southern and central California, two species of murrelet—Craveri's and Xantus's—are highly sought after. Craveri's Murrelets nest on islands in the Sea of Cortez, Mexico, and small numbers of the birds wander into North American waters after breeding. However, you have to be very lucky to find one.

Xantus's Murrelets are more common—they nest on the Channel Islands off southern California, but to avoid predators, they only make nocturnal nest visits. Offshore sightings are regular in summer and fall. The *hypoleuca* subspecies of Xantus's Murrelet is a distinctive race with a whiter face. It breeds on islands off Baja California and, as with Craveri's Murrelets, small numbers wander north after breeding.

The Long-billed Murrelet, which until recently was considered a subspecies of the Marbled Murrelet, nests in the Russian Far East and is an infrequent visitor to North America. On rare occasions this species has been found in fall and winter on lakes and reservoirs scattered across the continent. These extraordinary sightings are red-letter events, and the news is quickly made known on birding hotlines and the Internet.

STATUS AND CONSERVATION

Historically, the alcid family has not fared well when coming into contact with human activities. The fate of the extinct Great Auk was already sealed in the early 1800s when fishermen slaughtered them for fish bait, feathers, and oil.

Before being exploited by egg harvesters in the late 1800s, the Farallon Islands off San Francisco were home to more than a million pairs of Common Murres—by 1911 there were fewer than 17,000 pairs left. Today, after being protected for many years, their numbers have slowly rebounded, but only to about 80,000 pairs. On a worldwide level, direct exploitation for meat and eggs has decreased, but large numbers of murres, puffins, and Dovekies are still hunted in places such as Canada, Iceland, and western Greenland. Up until 1987, a packing plant in Greenland produced canned murre meat for export.

Other present-day threats are more varied—predators like Arctic Foxes that were introduced for fur-farming, have wreaked havoc on many breeding islands for these birds. Oil spills around those same islands and coastlines can be deadly—as much as 10 percent of the world population of Kittlitz's Murrelet was lost as the result of the Exxon Valdez accident in 1989. Gill-nets trap and drown uncounted, but possibly significant numbers of alcids—the full facts are hard to come by.

Most alcids, particularly the northern colonial species, still have populations that number in the millions. The Least Auklet is probably the most abundant alcid with a population estimated at more than 20 million birds.

By contrast, Xantus's and Craveri's Murrelets have small worldwide populations. Xantus's, numbering fewer than 10,000 birds, are especially at risk—their breeding range is centered on the Channel Islands off southern California, a major shipping area. An oil spill there could be devastating.

Fortunately, many alcid populations establish their nesting grounds well away from the most detrimental of human activities. The removal of introduced predators from some breeding islands has been very beneficial and more work is underway. With closer regulation of the fishing, shipping, and logging industries and the continued decline in direct exploitation, the future of most species will be secure.

See also

Shearwaters, page 42
Storm-Petrels, page 46
Diving Ducks, page 100
Sandpiper bill comparison, page 157

GEON
~~G~~UILLEMOT AND
~~CR~~AVERI'S
~~MU~~RRELET

~~PIGE~~ON GUILLEMOT

- Late summer and early fall migration

Principal breeding range

Principal wintering range

~~CRAV~~ERI'S MURRELET

- Late summer and early fall migration

- Post-breeding limits

Resident range

~~Large~~ numbers of Craveri's Murrelet
~~move~~ north off the California coast
~~after t~~he breeding season. After the
~~open~~ water season from August to
~~Octobe~~r they then return south for the
~~winter~~. In fall and winter, it is believed
~~that m~~ost of the U.S. pacific coast
~~Pigeon~~ Guillemot population migrates
~~north~~ to the Puget Sound region.

~~STATU~~TE MILES

500

500

~~KILOM~~ETERS

DOVEKIE AND
~~A~~TLANTIC PUFFIN ▶

~~WI~~NTER RANGE AND WANDERING

~~West~~ern section of normal winter range

Dovekie wanderings - - - - - - ●

~~Atlan~~tic Puffin wanderings - - - - - - ●

~~D~~ovekies move south and offshore during
~~the~~ non-breeding season. Rarely, some
~~in~~dividuals or small groups can be found
~~in~~land following a strong late autumn or
~~early~~ winter storm. Atlantic Puffins also
~~move~~ offshore in the winter, and some
~~also~~ shift south off the mid-Atlantic coast.
~~T~~hey have been found casually inland.

STATUTE MILES

0   500

0   500

KILOMETERS

PIGEONS, DOVES

Of the more than 300 species of the family Columbidae found in the world, 16 appear in North America. Of those, 13 species are native to the continent; the remaining three were introduced here. The most recent arrival is the Eurasian Collared-Dove. These birds fanned out from Florida after arriving there from the Bahamas, where they were released in the 1970s. Rock Doves were brought from Europe in the early 1600s and quickly spread out across the continent. First released near Hollywood, California, around 1917, the Spotted Dove, a native of Asia, spread through urban areas, but it has shown little expansion beyond southern California. The Oriental Turtle-Dove, also a native of Asia, is only a casual spring and summer visitor to the Aleutians, appearing rarely as far south as Vancouver Island.

The strong, fast-flying pigeons and doves of North America are small- to medium-size birds, ranging in length from the Common Ground Dove at 6.5 inches to the Band-tailed Pigeon at 14.5 inches. Although a few species are denizens of deep woodlands, the vast majority inhabits more open terrain—grasslands, deserts, fields, and a variety of edge environments. Many species seem to benefit from moderate human contact, Rock Doves, for example, thrive in urban and suburban neighborhoods along with Mourning Doves, which also appear abundantly in agricultural areas and open natural habitats. Although the terms "pigeon" and "dove" have no scientific standing, the former is often applied to the larger family members with square or rounded tails and the latter to the smaller species with pointed tails.

Certain structural and behavioral traits set them apart from other families. With the exception of the

Phil George

Northern Fulmar, columbids are the only North American birds able to drink water through suction. They dip their bill in the water and draw it into their throat. Other birds scoop up water and point their bill skyward to let the water run down.

Large crops let columbids store copious amounts of food in a short time, thus the birds can forage quickly and move to safety to process what they have ingested. If food and water are plentiful, they may spend more time roosting and digesting than in active foraging.

Their strong-shafted feathers are only loosely fastened to the skin and detach easily. This "quick release" trait may have developed as an aid in escaping the grasp of hawks or other predators.

Most other birds fuel the development of their hatchlings by providing animal proteins and fats in whole or predigested form. Since pigeons and doves consume little animal matter, they have developed an alternative. They produce "pigeon milk"—a creamy substance in the parents' crop lining. Richer in fats and proteins than either cow or human milk, it supplies all the nutrients columbid squabs require. Both sexes produce this milk for the hatchlings for their first five days to two weeks. During that time they also introduce seeds and fruits. Young birds insert their bill at the side of the parent's mouth to receive the milk. Flamingos and Emperor Penguins are the only other birds to produce a similar substance.

Although the females lay only one or two eggs per clutch, they tend to have more than one brood per year. Rock and Mourning Doves have as many as six or more broods. Multiple, smaller clutches allow parents to produce more offspring and better care for them, increasing the survival rate of the hatchlings.

(Left) White-winged Doves

Mourning Dove: *Zenaida macroura*, L 12", long, pointed tail, slender body

PIGEONS, DOVES

Of the family Columbidae, the Mourning Dove (above) is a common and familiar bird that feeds on scattered seeds from backyard feeders. The trim-bodied, long-tailed Mourning Dove has black spots on the upper wings and a pinkish wash below. The species can be found throughout most of the United States year-round, and the southern Canadian provinces during the summer. These doves prefer open habitat, often choosing urban and suburban sites

Range of Mourning Dove

for feeding and nesting. Mourning Doves are generally ground-feeders that forage for grains and other seeds, grasses and insects. The species' call is a short, soft "who-o-o," sometimes repeated several times. A dove pair builds a flimsy nest of loose twigs and grasses that is often placed in a tree fork or hidden in dense vines. Similar to some wren species, Mourning Doves sometimes choose nesting sites close to human habitation, such as front porch eaves and trellis vines. The species may have several broods during a breeding season, each one consisting of two or three chicks. Although the species remains year-round in the U.S., some flocks gather in the fall to migrate southward to wintering grounds in Mexico and Central America. A very successful breeder, the Mourning Dove species is robust.

CLASSIFICATION

The pigeons and doves of the world, the family Columbidae, are the only living members of the distinct order Columbiformes that also includes the now extinct family Raphidae. The flightless Dodo of Mauritius Island in the Indian Ocean and other members of this family were extirpated by humans who prized them as food—the same fate meted out to the famed Passenger Pigeon whose flocks blackened the skies over North America until humans hunted them to extinction. Of the roughly 40 columbid genera and 300 species known worldwide today, 16 species in six genera appear in North America.

STRUCTURE

All pigeons and doves possess a small head, short neck, and short legs that contribute to a somewhat stocky appearance. As they forage on the ground, they move at a short-stepped, "pigeon-toed," stodgy gait made all the more ungainly by a head that bobs fore and aft. They have a short bill, often with a swollen, naked cere—a patch of thick featherless skin—at the base of the upper bill. Soft at the base and hard at the tip, these bills are adapted for gathering seeds from the ground and picking fruit and nuts from trees and shrubs rather than for crushing, chiseling, or tearing their food.

PLUMAGE

Although some of their Old World, South American, and Asian counterparts are brilliantly colored, less flashy tones of brown, tan, and gray predominate for most North American columbids. Many show scaling or barring on the wings and tail, whereas others have showy iridescent patches on the nape of the neck. Within a species there is little color variation except for the Rock Dove which ranges from black and white through mottled browns, rusty reds, and tans to slaty blue-gray. Columbid feathers often have a dry or powdery appearance, since the preen gland is small or absent in pigeons and doves, and they cannot oil their feathers as other birds do. In most species there is little difference in coloration between the sexes. In those species where differences do exist—White-crowned Pigeon, Mourning Dove, Common and Ruddy Ground-Doves, and Ruddy and Key West Quail-Doves—the variations are so subtle that they are not reliable as sexual field marks. Juveniles tend to be lighter in color than adults or lack some of the collars, mottling, or iridescence they will acquire after their first molt. Many of the heavier shafted feathers of pigeons and doves are only rather loosely attached to the skin so they may be easily detached. This quick-release trait may have developed as an aid in escaping the grasp of hawks or other predators or to help avoid being snared in thickets.

FEEDING BEHAVIOR

Columbids are mainly vegetarians, but some will eat an occasional earthworm or insect. Red-billed, Band-tailed, and White-crowned Pigeons rarely come to the ground to forage and spend most of their time eating nuts, fruits, and berries from trees and shrubs. White-winged Doves get most of their water from cactus fruit and flowers and, like most columbids, are ground feeders. While most columbids feed in small to medium flocks especially when breeding, in pairs, the White-tipped Dove is uncharacteristically solitary, rarely gathering in groups of three or more. Mourning, Spotted, Inca, Common Ground-, Rock and even White-tipped Doves will come to backyard feeding stations. They glean the ground for spilled seeds and will land on feeders, if tops and shelves permit. A few, especially Rock Doves, will consume bread crumbs and popcorn, sometimes out of human hands.

Most pigeons and doves, especially those that eat large quantities of dry seeds, pick up grit and small pebbles to aid the grinding of hard materials in their muscular crops. Perhaps because pigeons and doves must drink a lot of water—as much as 10 to 15 percent of their body weight per day—to help process the grains they eat, they have developed the ability to draw water through their bill and mouth directly into their throat and stomach. Doves and pigeons can forage in the open quickly and then move to relative safety, away from exposure to predators, to process what they have ingested. Thus, in areas of ample food and water, individuals may spend more time roosting and digesting than in active foraging. In the arid Southwest many columbids reduce their exposure to the broiling sun by getting food and water quickly, eating fleshy cactus fruits and flowers, then retiring to shadier spots.

VOCALIZATION

Although there are distinctive species variations, all members of this family utter low-frequency cooing sounds. Species with extended breeding seasons are often heard during most of the year. All males have an advertising song that is repeated for a long time. Females of some species have a similar, softer variation of the male's call.

Band-tailed Pigeon

BREEDING BEHAVIOR

Columbids tend to be monogamous throughout any given breeding season, and some such as the Rock Dove may pair for life. Males often call during courtship displays, in which the male struts around the female while puffing out his breast and neck feathers. Some species perform flight displays that include exaggerated wing flapping during which the wings may strike each other, creating a loud clapping sound, as well as glides with splayed tail and wings held in a V-shape above the body. Often pairs will perch side by side and rub their beaks together in a "billing" display.

It takes two to four days for pigeons and doves to build simple platform nests with stiff twigs that some species line with rootlets or pine needles. The male gathers the materials and presents them to the female, who actually builds the nest. Built on the ground or more than 80 feet up in shrubs, trees, cactuses, or on cliffs, or buildings, or on top of already existing nests,

---

OTHER SPECIES FIELD NOTES

■ **Band-tailed Pigeon**
Columba fasciata
L 14.5"
Broad gray tail band, white band on nape

■ **Red-billed Pigeon**
Columba flavirostris
L 14.5"
Dark overall, red bill with yellow tip

■ **White-crowned Pigeon**
Columba leucocephala
L 13.5"
White crown patch

■ **Rock Dove**
Columba livia
L 12.5"
Multicolored city pigeon

■ **Zenaida Dove**
Zenaida aurita
L 10"
White trailing edge of wing

■ **Spotted Dove**
Streptopelia chinensis
L 12"
Spotted collar

■ **Eurasian Collared-Dove**
Streptopelia decaocto
L 12.5"
Black collar, pale gray-buff plumage

■ **White-winged Dove**
Zenaida asiatica
L 11.5"
White wing patches

■ **Oriental Turtle-Dove**
Streptopelia orientalis
L 13.5"
Streaked neck patch, scaly pattern above

■ **Common Ground-Dove**
Columbina passerina
L 6.5"
Chestnut primaries in flight, scaly breast

■ **Ruddy Ground-Dove**
Columbina talpacoti
L 6.75"
Black lines on scapulars, chestnut primaries in flight

■ **Inca Dove**
Columbina inca
L 8.25"
Conspicuously scalloped, long tail with white sides

■ **White-tipped Dove**
Leptotila verreauxi
L 11.5"
White-tipped tail, large size

■ **Key West Quail-Dove**
Geotrygon chrysia
L 12"
White line under eye, pale underparts

■ **Ruddy Quail-Dove**
Geotrygon montana
L 9.75"
Buffy line under eye, cinnamon underparts

a nest may be used repeatedly, resulting in a buildup of fecal matter. Since many species breed in loose colonies with individual nests in close proximity, individuals don't defend large territories. Only the space surrounding the nest is vigorously defended. Columbids use aggressive posturing and rapid blows from the wing to drive off potential predators.

On average only one or two white, unmarked eggs are laid per clutch, but most pigeons and doves lay several clutches a year. Rock and Mourning Doves may breed during much of the year, producing as many as six or more clutches. Multiple, smaller clutches allow parent birds to produce a lot of offspring, increasing the survival rate.

Both male and female incubate—the male taking daytime duty, the female incubating at night. After 12 to 14 days for most species, 16 to 20 for the larger ones, the chicks need almost a full day to hatch. The altricial young, nearly naked of down and feathers, eyes still tightly shut, and utterly helpless, are fed by both parents within hours of hatching.

Most birds of other families fuel the development and growth of their hatchlings by initially providing animal proteins and fats in whole or predigested form. Since pigeons and doves consume little animal matter, they have developed an alternative high protein, high fat food for their young—a milky substance called pigeon or crop milk that is richer in fats and proteins than either cow or human milk. Both parents produce the

Red-billed Pigeon

substance as the primary hatchling diet for the first five days to two weeks. Then seeds and fruits are introduced. Young birds insert their bill at the side of the parent's mouth to receive the mixture. Flamingos and Emperor Penguins are the only other birds capable of producing a similar substance.

The young of the larger species such as the Band-tailed, Red-billed, and White-crowned Pigeons may take up to 30 days to fledge; the young of most others leave the nest after 11 to 18 days. The fledglings rely on their parents for food for as long as 40 days. If the parents are preparing for a subsequent clutch, the male parent fulfills most of the feeding duties. As the flying and foraging skills of the young increase, they begin to spend more time with other adolescents or join mixed flocks of feeding adults and other immatures.

BREEDING RANGE

Of North America's 13 species, the Mourning and Rock Doves are the most ubiquitous, breeding coast to coast, from southern Canada throughout the United States, south into Mexico and the Greater Antilles.

There are a few reports of Mourning Doves breeding as far south as Costa Rica and Panama. Rock Doves have been reported mating even in northern South America.

Rock Doves, our nearly ubiquitous park pigeons, were the earliest columbid immigrants to the New World. Brought to America's Atlantic coast from Europe in the early 1600s, they quickly spread out over the continent. The most recent arrival is the Eurasian Collared-Dove. After a small captive flock was released in the Bahamas in the 1970s, the species soon reached southern Florida, where it was breeding by the early 1980s. The flock has since fanned out across the United States. Now common along the Gulf Coast as far west as eastern Texas and as far north as North Carolina, it has been spotted frequently even in New Jersey, Pennsylvania, Delaware, and New York. There are also reported sightings in lower Wisconsin, Minnesota, and South Dakota, and there appear to be local populations in Colorado, New Mexico, and California. Not included in field guides printed before 1987, this import now seems to be expanding and thriving throughout North America much as the European Starling has done. First released near Hollywood in about 1917, the third immigrant, the Spotted Dove, is a native of Asia, which spread through urban areas, but its numbers have never been high, and it has shown little expansion beyond the introduction sites in California. The Oriental Turtle-Dove of Asia is a casual spring and summer visitor to the Aleutian Islands of Alaska, only rarely appearing as far south as British Columbia's Vancouver Island.

Most of the native North American columbids seem to prefer warmer climates and, with the exception of the Band-tailed Pigeon—which breeds along the Pacific coast into Washington State and British Columbia—the birds rarely breed farther north than the bottom tier of the United States. While some columbids, the White-tipped Dove, Red-billed, and White-crowned Pigeons, and the Ruddy Ground-Dove, for example, may be common in the West Indies or south through Mexico, they breed only as far north as the extreme southern tips of Texas and Florida. Breeding populations of Key West Quail-Dove and Zenaida Dove were apparently extirpated in the United States by the mid-1900s: The Key West Quail-Dove is now reported as only a casual visitor to south Florida and the Keys. Since records have been kept, there are only five reports from Florida and one from Texas of sightings of the highly tropical Ruddy Quail-Dove.

EURASIAN COLLARED-DOVE

Introduced into the Bahamas in 1974, the Eurasian Collared-Dove is a large, adaptable dove that had found its way to Florida by the end of the decade. Partial to human activity, it is often seen in suburban yards and at backyard feeders. The species is also a regular visitor to farms and fields where it feeds on seeds and grain. An overall pale, buff-colored dove with white-edged dark primaries and the distinctive black collar on the back of its neck, it tends to travel in small groups, or singly, and has increased its range north into the Carolinas, west into New Mexico, and has followed the Mississippi River into Montana. This recent visitor to Florida is now a common resident in North America.

MIGRATION

Although most columbids withdraw, at least slightly, from the northernmost reaches of their ranges, the White-crowned Pigeon, Band-tailed Pigeon, Mourning Dove, and White-winged Dove are the only North American columbids thought to be migratory.

Though primarily diurnal migrants, there is mounting evidence that some Mourning Doves may be nocturnal in their movements. On a single rainy night, more than a thousand Mourning Doves, apparently confused by a high-powered light on a military base, simply flew into the ground and perished. Large numbers of this species frequently are found among the dead in similar kills near brightly lit, tall buildings, spotlights, and communications towers.

Mourning Dove migration begins when immatures withdraw from Canada and the northern reaches of the U.S. and spread out south across the species' breeding range. Northern adult males follow, then the females. Adult males tend to winter farther north than females and immatures, perhaps assuring them a shorter return to claim prime breeding territory during spring migration. By comparison, the adult White-winged Doves are the first to leave the breeding area, to be followed by the immatures.

Even though most columbids do not migrate, all possess an incredible homing instinct, allowing them to navigate their way back to their home territory, regardless of where and how far away they might be taken. Detailed, long-term studies of this amazing ability of pigeons and doves has provided most of what we know about avian navigation using sun, moon, the stars, visual clues, and the Earth's magnetic fields.

WINTER RANGE

Columbids from the more northerly areas rarely migrate beyond the southern reaches of their species' normal breeding range. This limited movement yields a mix of migratory and nonmigratory individuals where breeding and wintering ranges overlap.

OBSERVING PIGEONS AND DOVES

Given that many species of pigeons and doves are comfortable near humans, most are easy to observe. In spite of this familiarity, there is much yet to be understood. Citizen-scientist birders can help by volunteering to participate in Project Pigeon Watch organized by the Cornell Laboratory of Ornithology to help document variations in coloration, color preferences for mates, and breeding displays internationally.

STATUS AND CONSERVATION

Mourning and White-winged Doves and Band-tailed and White-crowned Pigeons are hunted throughout their ranges. Although as many as 70 million Mourning Doves—with an estimated population in the hundreds of millions—are thought to be shot each hunting season, those losses appear to be quickly replenished, and this species seems to remain stable. Hunting of the other three species, coupled with human encroachment on specialized habitat, has put them in danger. The White-crowned Pigeon is listed as threatened in Florida and, along with the Band-tailed, is on the WatchList prepared by Partners in Flight and the National Audubon Society. Without some protection, especially in Mexico, Central America, and the Caribbean, these two along with the White-winged Dove are likely to become endangered.

See also

Chachalacas, Grouse, Quail, page 12

EURASIAN COLLARED-DOVE

RANGE EXPANSION

— Approximate northern limit of range expansion

— Additional populations resulting from local release

Away from the southeastern U.S., Eurasian Collared-Doves are irregularly distributed.

2003
1998
1989
1986
1975
1998
2003

STATUTE MILES
0   500   1000
0   500   1000
KILOMETERS

Longitude West 90° of Greenwich

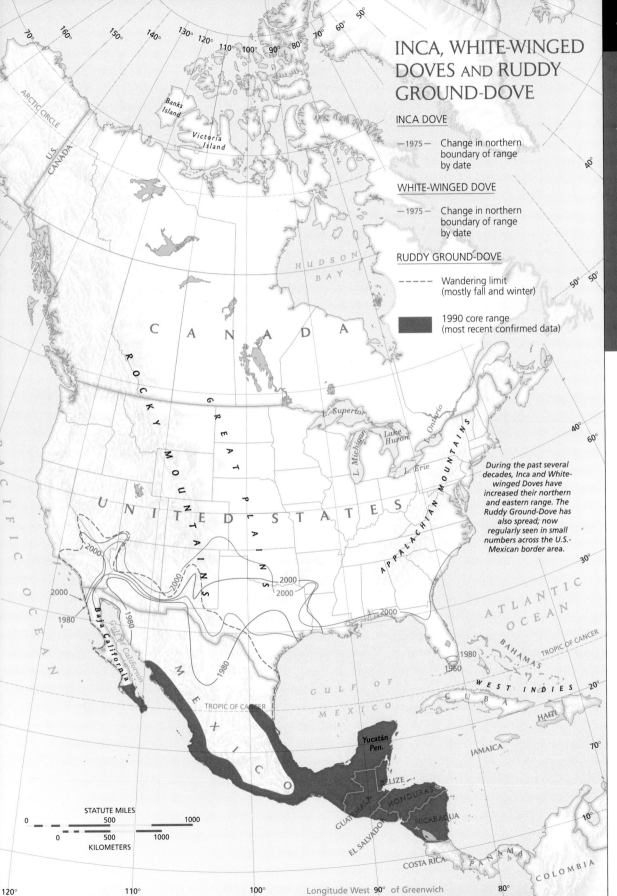

INCA, WHITE-WINGED DOVES AND RUDDY GROUND-DOVE

INCA DOVE

—1975— Change in northern boundary of range by date

WHITE-WINGED DOVE

—1975— Change in northern boundary of range by date

RUDDY GROUND-DOVE

- - - - Wandering limit (mostly fall and winter)

█ 1990 core range (most recent confirmed data)

During the past several decades, Inca and White-winged Doves have increased their northern and eastern range. The Ruddy Ground-Dove has also spread; now regularly seen in small numbers across the U.S.-Mexican border area.

ARCTIC CIRCLE

U.S.
CANADA

Banks Island

Victoria Island

C A N A D A

HUDSON BAY

R O C K Y   M O U N T A I N S

G R E A T   P L A I N S

U N I T E D   S T A T E S

A P P A L A C H I A N   M O U N T A I N S

L. Superior
L. Michigan
Lake Huron
Ontario
L. Erie

2000
2000
2000
2000
2000
2000
1980
1980
1980

PACIFIC OCEAN

Baja California
Gulf of California

M E X I C O

TROPIC OF CANCER

GULF OF MEXICO

1980
1960

ATLANTIC OCEAN

BAHAMAS
TROPIC OF CANCER

W E S T   I N D I E S
CUBA
HAITI
JAMAICA

Yucatán Pen.

BELIZE
GUATEMALA
HONDURAS
EL SALVADOR
NICARAGUA
COSTA RICA
P A N A M A
COLOMBIA

STATUTE MILES
0   500   1000

0   500   1000
KILOMETERS

PARAKEETS, PARROTS

Parrots are easily recognized as parrots. As popular cage birds traded, kept, and bred throughout the world, they are familiar to all of us. One of the misconceptions about parrots is that their bright and gaudy colors make them conspicuous. It is true that these bright colors—predominantly green in New World species—make parrots highly visible in cages, but as arboreal birds in the wild, they blend into the foliage amazingly well. We are also mistaken in thinking of parrots as birds of tropical forests. Although many species do occur in these habitats, other parrots occupy savannas, high mountain woodlands, oceanic islands, and—especially in Australia—cool temperate woodlands, deserts, and grasslands.

Kimball Garrett

Parrots represent a uniform and well-defined group, the order Psittaciformes, with no known close affinities to other birds; they are usually placed near the pigeons and/or cuckoos because of a few shared characteristics, but their true relationships are uncertain. There are some 350 species in the world, but the only species that naturally occurred in North America north of Mexico were the extinct Carolina Parakeet and the Thick-billed Parrot. An additional 14 species are found within 300 miles of the United States border in Mexico and the Caribbean.

In North America the present-day parrot fauna is an artificial one comprised of introductions, generally accidental. Populations thrive mainly in urban and suburban regions of California, southern Florida, and southern Texas. One temperate species, the Monk Parakeet, tolerates colder climates, and introduced populations occur in many eastern and midwestern states and in Oregon, as well as Texas and Florida. Parrots thrive in these areas by adapting to a highly modified landscape with often tropical vegetation that provides food and shelter throughout the year.

Parrots are highly social birds, with flock cohesion and social hierarchies aided by a wide range of cacophonous vocalizations. In the morning they commute to productive feeding areas, which supply fruits, seeds, nectar, or other vegetarian fare, and return late in the day to traditional, though shifting, roost sites. Social pre-roosting behavior can involve an almost comical array of interactions, mutual preening, and displays. Most parrots are monogamous, and are seen in close pairs even within larger flocks. Nearly all parrots are cavity nesters, though the Monk Parakeet builds a large communal stick-nest structure.

As conspicuous and noisy as parrots are in the cage and aviary settings in which most of us observe them, studying wild populations can be far more difficult. We most often see parrots in flight as they commute among feeding areas or to and from their roost sites. Learning the various shapes and flight styles of parrots, along with their vocalizations, is thus of paramount importance in field identification. Foraging parrots can be surprisingly quiet, and most of our species blend in closely with green foliage. One of the best opportunities for studying parrots is at their pre-roosting gatherings—they are conspicuous and noisy in such situations and often perch openly, albeit in low, late afternoon light.

Nearly a third of the world's parrot species are considered to be at risk of global extinction. In the New World, parrots have suffered especially from habitat modification, harvesting of birds for the pet trade, and direct persecution and hunting.

(Left) Green Parakeets

Monk Parakeet: *Myiopsitta monachus*, L 11.5", gray face and underparts

PARAKEETS, PARROTS

Of the few species of parrots and parakeets that make their home in North America, the Monk Parakeet (above) is one of the most ubiquitous. For more than 50 years Monk Parakeets have been popular cage birds in the United States, captured and imported from the mountains of South America. There have been numerous escapes or releases of the pet birds, and growing flocks of Monk Parakeets have successfully adapted to our climate and environment. Colonies of this species are found widely across the U.S., dwelling in cities as well as rural areas, particularly in Florida. The parakeets have a green back, light gray chest and nape, and blue wing tips. The free-flying escapee is the only parrot species that is not a cavity nester. Monk Parakeet pairs build a stick platform and dome that can be a single nest or part of a larger communal group, attached to a neighbor's nest. Nesting sites are often in deciduous trees, but pairs may also choose silos, fire escapes, and utility poles as sites to raise a small brood. The species is nonmigratory and has gradually increased its range, with a vigorous growing population.

Range of Monk Parakeet

CLASSIFICATION

The parrots—family Psittacidae—and the closely related cockatoos, make up the order Psittaciformes. Separate lineages of true parrots occur in Australia, New Guinea, Africa, southern Asia, and the New World. All but one of the parrot species that are naturalized in North America, and the two species that formerly occurred naturally, belong to the New World group—now considered a subfamily, the Arinae—which includes macaws, amazons, and other parrots, and conures and other parakeets. The exception is the Rose-ringed Parakeet of Old World (Indian) origin that is established in California and Florida; another Old World Parrot, the Budgerigar of Australia, had a large, introduced population around Tampa, Florida, but few now remain. There are some 350 species of parrots worldwide, about 150 are native to the New World.

STRUCTURE AND PLUMAGE

Parrots are easily recognized by their strongly hooked bills, bare cere covering the external nostrils in most groups, strong jaw musculature, fleshy tongues (brush-tipped in the lores for nectar-feeding), loose plumage, and short legs with a zygodactyl toe arrangement (two toes forward, two backward). Their plumage color is varied, but the true parrots of the New World subfamily Arinae, are predominantly green with red, yellow, blue, white, or other markings.

FEEDING BEHAVIOR

The parrots native in North America are strictly arboreal, and their diet is mostly vegetarian, consisting of fruits, seeds, nuts, buds, and nectar. The Thick-billed Parrot specializes on pine seeds. Our introduced species avail themselves of a great range of food items, largely from exotic, non-native plants. Parrots are agile and acrobatic foragers, using the bill to help climb among branches. They adroitly manipulate food items with their feet, bill, and tongue. Since their food supply is patchy and continually shifting, they typically commute various distances from their roosts or nests.

VOCALIZATION

Parrots have complex vocal repertoires that include not only loud screeching, cawing, and grating calls, but some whistles and other more musical vocalizations. They can be remarkably quiet when resting or feeding but even more remarkably noisy when engaging in social interactions or flock cohesion behaviors.

BREEDING BEHAVIOR

Parrots are generally monogamous and may have long-term pair bonds; within flocks, birds are routinely seen in closely associating pairs. Most are cavity nesters, using old woodpecker cavities, which the parrots can enlarge, and artificial cavities. In contrast, the Monk Parakeet builds a large, communal stick nest on utility poles, light standards, or branches. Parrots lay two to five white eggs, the Monk Parakeet up to eight. The altricial young do not fledge for about six to eight weeks.

BREEDING RANGE

Most parrots, including the naturalized populations in the United States, are nonmigratory. They are resident in urban and suburban areas of central and southern Florida, southern California, and in the urban areas of the Rio Grande Valley of Texas. The Monk Parakeet is more cold tolerant, with populations in at least ten states. On a global scale, natural populations of parrots are found throughout the southern continents and northward in subtropical and temperate habitats to northern Mexico, northern India, and southernmost China.

STATUS AND CONSERVATION

The only species ever to occur widely in the U.S., the Carolina Parakeet has been extinct since around 1930; it formerly ranged throughout the Southeast and Midwest, occurring as far north as New York, Michigan, and South Dakota. The causes of this species' extinction clearly included the loss of wooded bottomland habitats, as well as shooting and other direct persecution. The introduction of various exotic avian diseases has recently been proposed as another major factor in its demise. The Thick-billed Parrot, a pine-seed specialist that still lives locally in the mountains of western Mexico, was a former visitor and possibly a sporadic breeder in the border ranges of southeastern Arizona and southwestern New Mexico; it has undergone a serious decline in its Mexican range due to habitat loss, trapping, and shooting, though it still breeds within sight of the U.S. border. A reintroduction program in Arizona in the late 1980s was unsuccessful.

Up to a third of the parrot species worldwide are considered to be at some degree of risk of global extinction. A major drain on parrot populations is the exploitation (especially of nestlings) for the pet-bird industry; although this bird trade is increasingly regulated or prohibited by international conventions and the laws of various nations, parrot capture for the pet trade remains a significant problem. Parrots are also endangered by habitat loss or modification, the introduction of exotic predators (which has especially impacted populations endemic to islands), and direct persecution (often because parrots are considered crop pests).

As non-natives, the populations of Red-crowned Parrots, Monk Parakeets, Mitred Parakeets, Yellow-chevroned Parakeets, and perhaps a dozen other parrot species currently residing in the United States have few conservation protections. In some cases such measures may even negatively affect native species or agricultural crops. However, nearly all of these populations are restricted to urban and suburban habitats, and their conservation impacts are generally not thought to be of great significance.

Orange-winged Parrot

OTHER SPECIES FIELD NOTES

■ **White-winged Parakeet**
Brotogeris versicolurus
L 8.75"
White outer secondaries

■ **Yellow-chevroned Parakeet**
Brotogeris chiriri
L 8.75"
Yellow-green body color, no white in wing

■ **Dusky-headed Parakeet**
Aratinga weddelli
L 11"
Green breast shades to yellow belly, gray head

■ **Black-hooded Parakeet**
Nandayus nenday
L 13.75"
Black face and bill, red thighs

■ **Green Parakeet**
Aratinga holochlora
L 13"
Large, all green

■ **Blue-crowned Parakeet**
Aratinga acuticaudata
L 10"
Blue face, bicolored bill

■ **Mitred Parakeet**
Aratinga mitrata
L 13.75"
White eye ring, red forehead

■ **Red-masked Parakeet**
Aratinga erythrogenys
L 13"
Mostly red head, red leading edge to wing

■ **Thick-billed Parrot**
Rhynchopsitta pachyrhyncha
L 16.25"
Red forehead, marginal coverts, thighs, heavy black bill

■ **Rose-ringed Parakeet**
Psittacula krameri
L 15.75"
Yellow-green plumage, very long tail, thin collar

■ **Red-crowned Parrot**
Amazona viridigenalis
L 13"
Red crown

■ **Orange-winged Parrot**
Amazona amazonica
L 12.25"
Yellow forehead, blue facial stripe

■ **Lilac-crowned Parrot**
Amazona finschi
L 13"
Pale lilac crown, red forehead

■ **Yellow-headed Parrot**
Amazona oratrix
L 14.5"
Large, with yellow head

■ **Budgerigar**
Melopsittacus undulatus
L 7"
Barred upperparts, long tail

See also

Red-whiskered Bulbul, page 338

North Pole

ARCTIC OCEAN

Meridian of Greenwich

60°

80°

40°

20°

0°

20°

40°

60°

80°

Baffin Island

LABRADOR SEA

QUEEN ELIZABETH IS.

PARRY IS.

Victoria Island

Banks Island

BEAUFORT SEA

CHUKCHI SEA

ARCTIC CIRCLE

CANADA

U.S.

BERING SEA

ALEUTIAN ISLANDS

180°

160°

140°

120°

100°

80°

60°

40°

20°

L. Athabasca

Reindeer Lake

Lake Winnipeg

L. Manitoba

Hudson Bay

CANADA

ROCKY MOUNTAINS

UNITED STATES

Great Salt Lake

Gulf of California

BAJA CALIFORNIA

MEXICO

L. Superior

L. Huron

L. Mich.

L. Erie

L. Ontario

APPALACHIAN MOUNTAINS

GULF OF MEXICO

NORTH ATLANTIC OCEAN

BAHAMAS

CUBA

TROPIC OF CANCER

20°N

1980's
1974
1967
1968
1969
Late 1960's
1989
1980

TROPIC OF CANCER

20°N

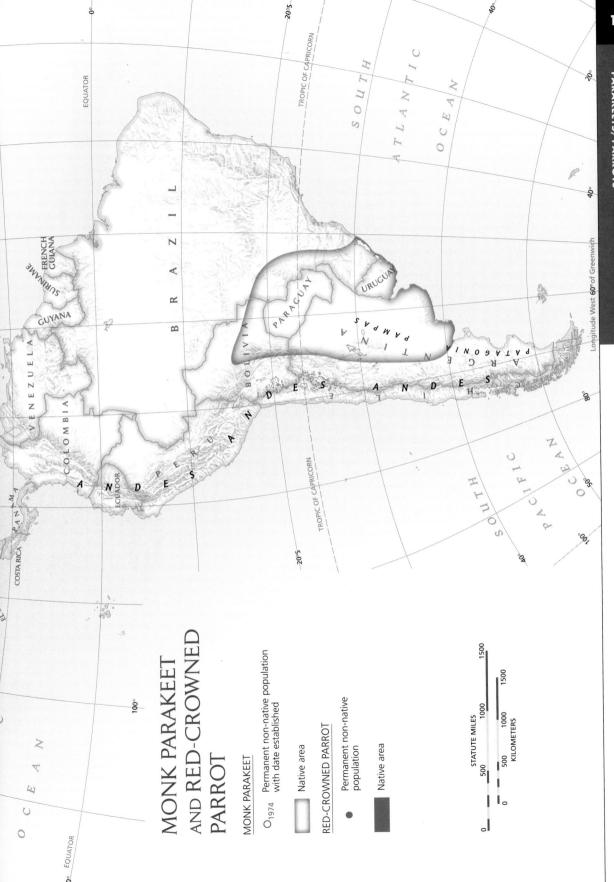

MONK PARAKEET AND RED-CROWNED PARROT

MONK PARAKEET

O 1974   Permanent non-native population
         with date established

         Native area

RED-CROWNED PARROT

●   Permanent non-native
         population

         Native area

STATUTE MILES
0   500   1000   1500

KILOMETERS
0   500   1000   1500

CUCKOOS

Cuckoos and their near-est of kin—the anis and roadrunners—are well known in bird lore for their fascinating behaviors, though much of popular legend is exaggerated or erroneous. Plain in plumage, the birds of the family Cuculidae exhibit foraging techniques that make them both interesting and conspicu-ous: Anis ride on the back of cattle, looking for ticks; roadrunners dash through south-western backyards in search of lizards; and cuckoos often attend suburban outbreaks of tent caterpillars. But the two cuckoos that nest across most of North America do not, as do many Old World species, habitually lay their eggs in other birds' nests, nor do they prey upon other birds' eggs or announce the coming of rain when they call. And roadrunners, for all their energetic foraging, rarely come into contact with cartoon coyotes.

There are about 142 species of cuculids in the world, and of these, eight or nine have occurred in North America; two of these species, the Oriental (Horsfield's) and Common Cuckoos, only as vagrants from the Old World. The center of cuculid diversity lies in the Old World tropics, but many species are found through Central and South America as well.

Cuckoos and their relatives in North America build sloppy-looking stick nests, and most pairs nest independently, though communal nesting is seen in anis and sometimes in Yellow-billed Cuckoos. These nests are usually well-hidden structures. Most observers know these birds chiefly from their unusual calls or from close-at-hand encounters, as most species in the family tend to be confiding and observ-able at close range. The two most widespread mem-bers of this group, the graceful Black-billed and

Patricia Sutton

Yellow-billed Cuckoos, nest in a wide swath across eastern North America. Their local abundance is often tied to the availability of their chief prey—caterpillars and other insects—and they are thus patchy in distribution. Both species migrate to the New World tropics in autumn, returning in late spring to most latitudes. They are often some of the last birds of spring to arrive, nesting later than many other Neotropical migrants, especially near the northern edge of their breeding range. Mangrove Cuckoos, whose range barely enters North America in south-ernmost Florida, specialize in tropical lowland habi-tats; some of their populations are also migratory, but these movements are not well understood.

Roadrunners and anis bear little outward resem-blance to the cuckoos. The Greater Roadrunner's large size and ground-racing habits make it singular among North American birds, and its omnivorous diet permits survival in some of the harshest envi-ronments in the Southwest. Groove-billed and Smooth-billed Anis, both confined to the southern-most parts of North America, are coal black and sport an enormous, exaggerated maxilla (the upper part of the bill), presumably an adaptation to feeding on a diversity of insects and seeds, but also a tool that can be used to part the dense vegetation in which they often forage. Roadrunners, true to reputation, can be elusive in the field, slinking around desert washes and canyons, but the sharp-eyed traveler to their southwestern stronghold can hardly fail to spot one along the roadside, even from busy interstates. Anis and the Mangrove Cuckoos, by contrast, often require a dedicated search in habitats that are scarce and dwindling in the United States; all three are common south of the border.

(Left) Smooth-billed Ani

Yellow-billed Cuckoo: *Coccyzus americanus,* L 12",
rufous primaries

CUCKOOS

A shy species that usually dwells in dense canopies, the Yellow-billed Cuckoo (above) has a brown back, pale gray or white chest and belly, and long tail feathers that are white-tipped and have three pairs of white ovals. A bright yellow bill and unique three-note vocalization of "kulp-kulp-kulp" are characteristics of the species. The bird ranges throughout the eastern and midwestern United States. Cuckoos are forest birds that inhabit marsh and swamp edges with plentiful tangles and vines, or orchards and streamside groves of deciduous trees. Cuckoos comb vegetation for their preferred food of caterpillars but will also prey on frogs, lizards, cicadas, and other insects. Their nest on a horizontal tree limb is lined with grasses and moss and holds four or five chicks.

Range of Yellow-billed Cuckoo

CLASSIFICATION

Cuckoos and their allies (family Cuculidae) form a distinct taxonomic group of 142 or so species worldwide; they have no close relatives and are part of the order Cuculiformes, which contains only one other living family, the turacos, Musophagidae. Fossil cuckoos date back 37 million years, making this an ancient family. The three North American cuckoos in the genus *Coccyzus* (Black-billed, Yellow-billed, and Mangrove) are placed in the subfamily Coccyzinae, with Old World cuckoos in Cuculinae, anis in Crotophaginae, and roadrunners in Neomorphinae. Analyses of DNA differences suggest that these subfamilies should be considered full families.

STRUCTURE

Cuculids are streamlined, medium-size birds with long tails and long, slightly decurved bills, which in the case of the anis are outsized. Their feet are zygodactylous in arrangement, meaning they have two toes forward and two posterior, unlike passerines or perching birds. The legs of anis and arboreal cuckoos are short and used for perching, whereas the terrestrial roadrunner has powerful legs adapted for high-speed pursuit of prey. The migratory species have rather long, narrow wings compared to the sedentary species, such as the ani and roadrunner, which have shorter, more rounded wings.

PLUMAGE

New World cuckoos are brownish above and pale below, with a dark mask around the eyes and sometimes a bit of rufous in the base of the primaries, as in the Yellow-billed Cuckoo. Sexes are similar. Immature plumage is also similar to that of adults, though tail pattern and soft-part colors are different. In roadrunners and anis, sexes and ages look alike: heavily streaked in roadrunners, virtually all black in anis. Subspecies variation is minimal except in Mangrove Cuckoos, whose Caribbean and Central American taxa are distinctive, with varying intensity of coloration below. Old World cuckoos have different morphs or color forms; both Oriental and Common Cuckoos have a gray and a rufous (or hepatic) morph. Both have been recorded in North America.

FEEDING BEHAVIOR

Each subfamily differs in its manner of foraging, though all rely on keen vision to detect prey. Cuckoos sit quietly and peer around in slow motion, watching the leaves and branches for caterpillars and other insects. When they spy prey, cuckoos move swiftly to pick the item and "soften" and dispatch it by striking it against a limb, which also serves to empty the insect's gut. They eat hairy caterpillars, shunned by most birds, and regurgitate the hairs as a pellet. Where tent caterpillars are found in eastern North America, cuckoos seem to converge out of thin air to clean out dozens from a web in one sitting. They may drop to the ground to take invertebrates or small frogs.

Anis move in gangs of several birds through scrubby underbrush and pasture, feeding on insects and spiders, but also on fruit and seeds. The Groove-billed Ani associates with cattle, darting along the ground and seizing insects flushed by the animals or taking external parasites such as ticks. The Greater Roadrunners' pursuit of prey is clocked at speeds of over 19 miles per hour. They spot prey—whether rodent, lizard, or scorpion—and run it down, matching the prey's tight turns by using tail and wings for steerage. Roadrunners take insects, small birds, and nestlings, and some have learned to forage at flowers or bird feeders, snapping up unwitting hummingbirds attracted to the nectar; many roadrunners take prickly pear cactus (Opuntia) fruit when available. To observe a pair of roadrunners ambush and kill a rattlesnake is to witness one of the more impressive performances in the bird world.

Greater Roadrunner

VOCALIZATION
Vocalizations are simple but distinctive and form a memorable part of the dawn chorus. Cuckoo calls consist of a repeated, sometimes accelerating series of "cu" or "kuk kuk kuk" sounds, more plaintive and pleasant in the smaller Black-billed Cuckoo and guttural and grating in larger species, though call types overlap. Black-billed and Yellow-billed Cuckoos also give distinctive nocturnal flight calls during migration. Anis give high, whistling, querulous calls, descending in Groove-billed. Roadrunners sing a mournful series of "ooo" notes during nesting season.

BREEDING BEHAVIOR
Courtship display is simple. In cuckoos, the male calls while offering food to the female. During copulation, this food is often transferred to the female from above. Male roadrunners also offer food during copulation, but offer an elaborate display beforehand, with repeated rushes made at the female, wings, crest, and tail raised. The male then wags his tail from side to side while facing the female and gives a whirring call before jumping into the air and onto the mate.

Although in North America cuckoos are not nest parasites, they occasionally lay eggs in other birds' nests to be reared by the other species. Such behavior is observed when prey is abundant. Sometimes the cuckoos return to the nest and feed their and the other birds' young.

BREEDING AND WINTER RANGE
Cuckoos, anis, and roadrunners occupy most temperate and tropical habitats in North America. The cuckoos winter exclusively in South America.

MIGRATION
Black-billed and Yellow-billed Cuckoos migrate over long distances, traveling to South America. Common and Oriental Cuckoos migrate far as well, and their appearance in the spring months in western Alaska, on offshore islands, can be attributed to an overshooting of their breeding range. In the autumn, records of young birds in Alaska are thought to be reverse migrants whose orientation is 180° off course. Groove-billed Anis withdraw from the northernmost parts of southern Texas, returning in May. On occasion, reverse migrating anis turn up in the southern Great Plains, Midwest, or East, with most records referring to Groove-billed Anis. Roadrunners do not migrate.

STATUS AND CONSERVATION
Black-billed and Yellow-billed Cuckoos have declined by 45 percent in the East, according to Breeding Bird Survey data, and this decline should be monitored. In the West, the Yellow-billed Cuckoo, with perhaps 50 pairs in California, merits listing as endangered.

OTHER SPECIES FIELD NOTES

■ **Mangrove Cuckoo**
Coccyzus minor
L 12"
Black mask, buffy underparts

■ **Black-billed Cuckoo**
Coccyzus erythropthalmus
L 12"
Reddish eye ring, brown primaries

■ **Greater Roadrunner**
Geococcyx californianus
L 23"
Long, heavy bill, bushy crest

■ **Common Cuckoo**
Cuculus canorus
L 13"
Belly narrowly barred with gray

■ **Oriental Cuckoo**
Cuculus saturatus
L 12.5"
Belly barred with gray

■ **Smooth-billed Ani**
Crotophaga ani
L 14.5"
Black plumage, smooth hump on upper bill

■ **Groove-billed Ani**
Crotophaga sulcirostris
Black plumage, grooved upper bill

See also

Blackbirds, Orioles, page 400

ARCTIC CIRCLE

70°   160°   150°   140°   130°   120°   110°   100°   90°   80°   70°   60°   50°   40°

ARCTIC CIRCLE

60°

ARCTIC CIRCLE

U.S.
CANADA

Gulf of Alaska

150°

60°

140°

50°

HUDSON
BAY

C A N A D A

40°

L. Superior

R
O
C
K
Y

G
R
E
A
T

Lake
Huron

L. Michigan

L. Erie

L. Ontario

ATLANTIC

30°

M
O
U
N
T
A
I
N
S

P
L
A
I
N
S

U N I T E D   S T A T E S

A
P
P
A
L
A
C
H
I
A
N

M
O
U
N
T
A
I
N
S

OCEAN

130°

P
A
C
I
F
I
C

Gulf of California

Baja California

M
E
X
I
C
O

O C E A N

120°

40°

30°

TROPIC OF CANCER

20°

Yucatán
Pen.

GUATEMALA

BELIZE

HONDURAS

EL SALVADOR

NICARAGUA

COSTA RICA

PANAMA

GULF   OF

MEXICO

CUBA

BAHAMAS

WEST   INDIES

JAMAICA

HAITI

DOM.
REP.

TROPIC OF CANCER

COLOMB

10°

120°   110°   100°   Longitude West 90° of Greenwich   80°

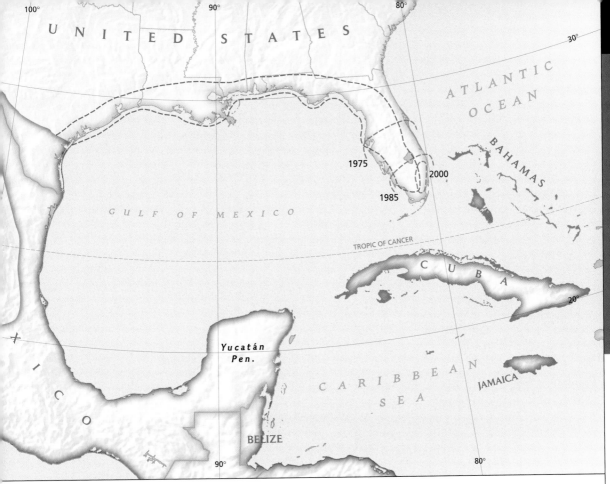

CUCKOOS

MIGRATION AND WANDERING

—— Yellow-billed Cuckoo migration

------ Limits of Yellow-billed Cuckoo regular autumn wandering

—— Black-billed Cuckoo migration

The Yellow-billed Cuckoo is a widespread migrant. The Black-billed Cuckoo is a circum-Gulf migrant. Small numbers of Yellow-billed Cuckoos also wander north in the fall, particularly in the Northeast.

▲ SMOOTH-BILLED ANI & GROOVE-BILLED ANI

SMOOTH-BILLED ANI

▭ Regular range

------ Range reduction

GROOVE-BILLED ANI

▭ Regular range

------ Fall and winter wandering

Anis, particularly Groove-billed, occur casually far to the north of their normal range in the fall.

STATUTE MILES
0 — 500
0 — 500
KILOMETERS

STATUTE MILES
0   200   400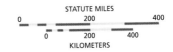
0   200   400
KILOMETERS

OWLS

Throughout recorded history, owls have played a major role in mythology, folklore, art, and literature, perhaps to a degree rivaled only by eagles. Few but the most technical and jaded researchers would argue that owls are mysterious. Their comings and goings in the dark of night are, by their very nature, unfathomable. Their nocturnal habits combine with their allure and mythology to render them inscrutable, and owls remain one of the most desirous and popular groups of birds for most birders. Indeed, owls probably have a bigger fan club of nonbirders than any other group of birds.

Patricia Sutton

Many myths surround owls, and much misinformation persists. While owls, along with nightjars, are the most nocturnal of all groups of birds, they are far from fully nocturnal. Some species of owls such as the Burrowing Owl and Short-eared Owl are quite active during daylight. It is important to note, however, that they are not completely diurnal either, but are more often crepuscular, hunting in the dim light of dawn and dusk. It is usually only during the breeding season (while feeding young) or during overcast days (which simulate dawn and dusk), that Burrowing and Short-eared Owls are particularly active during midday hours. On the high Arctic breeding grounds, with 24 hours of daylight in summer, Snowy Owls may be active around the clock—yet are mainly active at dusk and throughout the night on their wintering grounds.

It is a myth that owls cannot see during daylight. They see perfectly well in sunshine. It is also probably untrue that they can see as well during the darkest of nights as they can during daytime or in bright moonlight. Under many conditions, and certainly on the darkest nights, owls use hearing to a great degree to locate prey, and their exceptional hearing ability is every bit as remarkable as their keen vision. Another myth is that owls are "wise." They are certainly competent, able, and efficient exploiters of their habitat and environment, but probably no smarter than other birds, and probably not nearly as intelligent as some corvids or parrots.

Owls are predators at or near the top of the food chain, but small owls always need to be alert for and wary of larger owls. A Great Horned Owl will prey on all the other owl species in its territory if given the opportunity.

Owls are most closely related to nightjars, Whip-poor-wills, nighthawks, and their kin. Despite a similar predatory lifestyle and similar plumage and features, owls are not closely related to hawks and eagles. An owl's resemblance to a hawk is an example of convergent evolution, wherein the birds have developed similar features (coloration, talons, beak) in response to similar conditions and lifestyle, but from far different origins and ancestors.

All species of owls in North America are easily recognizable as such, but they are a diverse group. The Elf Owl, our smallest owl, is 5.75 inches tall with a wingspan of 13 inches, and may weigh as little as 1.4 ounces. Compare that with our heaviest owl, the Snowy Owl, which can weigh more than 4 pounds, and with the Great Gray Owl, which may have a wingspan of 52 inches. The Elf Owl will feed mainly on moths; the Snowy Owl feeds on animals as large as Snowshoe Hare and even Canada Geese. All owls share a mysterious aura, and despite all we have learned from owl researchers, few would not agree that owls are among our most interesting, exciting, and evocative birds.

(Left) Great Horned Owl

Barn Owl: *Tyto alba*, L 16", pale, heart-shaped face, strong facial disk

OWLS

The Barn Owl (above) of the family Tytonidae is a bird of prey that hunts primarily by sound at night. Barn Owls are found throughout most of the United States except in the upper Midwest. The species has a heart-shaped white face, chest, and belly, with a cinnamon-colored, barred back. Barn Owls typically fly low over their preferred hunting habitat of marshes, woodlands, and meadows, using one upward-pointing and one downward-pointing ear to search for prey, which they catch in their talons. They eat insects, bats, and snakes, but mice and other rodents are also an important part of the species' diet. Barn Owls have elaborate courtship displays of chasing, calling to each other, and presenting food by the male to the female. Nests are built in various sites such as tree hollows, barn rafters, and burrows or cliff holes. Breeding success is dependent on food sources, and when prey is plentiful broods are large. Barn Owls remain year-round on their range that stretches across the U.S. southward into Mexico.

Range of Barn Owl

CLASSIFICATION

Owls are widespread in most habitats around the world and are found on all continents except Antarctica. There are about 212 recognized species worldwide, with 19 species found breeding in North America. Three other species have occurred as vagrants. The migratory Oriental Scops-Owl, an Asian species, has occurred in the Aleutian Islands, and the tropical Mottled Owl and the Stygian Owl have both been found in the Rio Grande Valley of Texas. All owls are in the order Strigiformes, and are divided between two families, Tytonidae, the Barn Owls and related species, and the Strigidae, the true owls.

Tytonidae, the Barn Owls and related species, have a narrow skull and a distinctly heart-shaped face and strong facial disks. These disks function to funnel sound to the hidden asymmetrical ear openings. Barn Owls lack the ear tufts that many members of the true owls have. Strigidae, the true owls, show wider, rounded heads and varying degrees of facial disks. Some have asymmetrical ear openings. Most, but not all, have ear tufts and movable feathers used mainly for camouflage and at times in displays. True owls occupy almost all habitat types, from deep forests to open grassland.

Owls are most closely related to the Caprimulgidae, the nighthawks and nightjars. DNA evidence suggests a close evolutionary relationship, but owls differ mainly in their long legs and powerful feet. Owls resemble hawks in many ways, but are not closely related. Owls have forward facing eyes, an outer toe that can rotate backward, and nostrils located in front of the cere. Owls do not have a crop, as hawks do.

North American owls are readily recognized as such, and their plumages are mostly variations on a theme. They are easy to identify when seen but, being secretive and mostly nocturnal, the trick is in finding them.

STRUCTURE

Owls are well designed for their predatory lifestyle. They have strong feet, long toes, and sharp talons suitable for catching, holding, and carrying prey. They have strong, downturned or hooked beaks similar to those of hawks. All owls have large, blunt, rounded heads with large eyes set in the front of the skull, unlike all other birds. Their eyes are huge, proportionally the largest of all birds. Due to the density of cells in the retina, owls see an estimated 10 to 100 times better than humans in dim light. They also see perfectly well in daylight. Their forward-facing eyes give owls overlapping fields of vision, and hence greater depth perception, but an owl's eyes are fixed, immovable in their sockets. To see to either side, an owl must turn its head. Extra vertebrae in the neck allow its head to rotate up to 270 degrees in each direction.

Owls have exceptional hearing, due to a flattened facial disk that reflects sound back to their hidden, yet large and highly sensitive ears. In some owl species, the ears are arranged asymmetrically, with one higher than the other. This asymmetry helps them triangulate on their prey. The so-called "ears" of Great Horned Owls, Long-eared Owls, and others are not ears, but simply hornlike tufts of feathers thought to aid in the overall camouflage of a roosting owl.

Owls flap and glide in silence, made possible by the soft, velvety covering of the flight feathers. On most owls, the leading (front) edge of the primaries (outer wing feathers) is serrated or fluted. This comb-

Eastern Screech-Owl

like edge, combined with the velvety upper surface of each feather, serves to muffle the sound as the wing passes through the air. Silent flight not only allows an owl to approach and surprise its prey unheard, but also allows for noninterference with the owl's own hearing on which it is so dependent for hunting. Some of the more diurnal owl species, such as the pygmy-owls and the Burrowing Owl, do not have serrated primaries—proving that they depend primarily on vision to detect prey. For most owls though, hearing plays an equal role with vision in the capture of prey, which is often hidden from sight under leaf litter or snow cover. An owl's frequency range is similar to that of the human ear, but its hearing is much more acute.

Owl feet are said to be zygodactyl, meaning the outer toe can rotate or pivot back and forth. By this spreading of the toes, an owl's powerful feet actually form a symmetrical "web" which helps it to snare running prey or secure struggling animals.

PLUMAGE

Owls have a mottled and muted plumage that helps camouflage them during the daytime. Their streaked and barred patterns disappear into the dappled sunlight and shade of dense vegetation. Owls show a mix of blacks, grays, browns, and reddish browns. The exceptions are the Barn Owl, which is pale below and slightly dimorphic, males being decidedly paler than females, and the Snowy Owl, whose distinctive white plumage blends with its chosen northern range in all seasons but summer. The white coloration of Snowy Owls no doubt has both a camouflage and a stealth function. A few owls, such as Snowy and Saw-whet Owls, show a distinct juvenile plumage, but the fledged young of most species closely resemble the parents.

When approached, owls often display a cryptic posture, elongating the body into a non-owl-like profile, and look much like tree bark, or a branch, limb, or stump. Upon relaxing, they lower themselves, fluff out, and appear round and plump. For the birder, seeing the elongated posture is an indicator that the owl is feeling threatened and that it is time to back away, before the bird flushes and is exposed to daytime threats.

The various screech-owls and the Flammulated Owl show different color morphs. For example, a pair of Eastern Screech-Owls may include one red morph and one gray morph individual, and a single brood of

---

OTHER SPECIES FIELD NOTES

■ **Short-eared Owl**
Asio flammeus
L 15"
Bold breast streaks

■ **Long-eared owl**
Asio otus
L 15"
Long, close-set ear tufts

■ **Great Horned Owl**
Bubo virginianus
L 22"
Large ear tufts, white throat

■ **Barred Owl**
Strix varia
L 21"
Dark barring on breast

■ **Great Gray Owl**
Strix nebulosa
L 27"
Large, ringed facial disk

■ **Spotted Owl**
Strix occidentalis
L 17.5"
White spots on head, back, and underparts

■ **Snowy Owl**
Nyctea scandiaca
L 23"
Large, white plumage

■ **Eastern Screech-Owl**
Otus asio
L 8.5"
Small, two color morphs, pale bill

■ **Western Screech-Owl**
Otus kennicottii
L 8.5"
Small size, dark bill

■ **Whiskered Screech-Owl**
Otus trichopsis
L 7.25"
Small size, pale bill, small feet

■ **Flammulated Owl**
Otus flammeolus
L 6.75"
Very small, red and gray plumage

■ **Ferruginous Pygmy-Owl**
Glaucidium brasilianum
L 6.75"
Long, reddish tail, black nape spots

■ **Elf Owl**
Micrathene whitneyi
L 5.75"
Very small, very short tail

■ **Northern Pygmy-Owl**
Glaucidium gnoma
L 6.75"
Long, dark brown tail, black nape spots

■ **Northern Saw-whet Owl**
Aegolius acadicus
L 8"
Reddish streaks below

■ **Northern Hawk Owl**
Surnia ulula
L 16"
Falconlike profile

■ **Boreal Owl**
Aegolius funereus
L 10"
Black-bordered facial disk, spotted forehead

■ **Burrowing Owl**
Athene cunicularia
L 9.5"
Long legs, terrestrial

young may contain a mix of both morphs. A red morph bird will remain red for life, and there are no intergrades. A brown morph of the Eastern Screech-Owl is also recognized.

FEEDING BEHAVIOR

Owls are true predators and highly opportunistic. All are carnivorous and feed on a variety of animal prey, including insects, spiders, scorpions, earthworms, crabs, snails, fish, birds, and mammals. The size of the owl is usually an indicator of prey size. The Elf Owl feeds primarily on insects. Screech-owls in warm seasons will feed widely on moths and other insects, but in winter mostly on mice, voles, and shrews. The Great Horned Owl has been called the "winged tiger" and will eat a variety of prey, including animals larger and heavier than itself, such as jackrabbit, skunk, opossum, and raccoon. Great Horned Owls will readily take other owls and hawks. An owl's large size doesn't always mean large prey items. The huge Great Gray Owl has fairly small and weak feet, and it preys mainly on mice and voles. The Northern Hawk Owl takes many birds and is known to feed on prey as large as grouse and ptarmigan.

Owls dissect larger prey, but usually eat smaller prey where caught and consume it whole. An owl's digestive juices are not as acidic as a hawk's, so it can't digest bones. Instead, an owl's digestive system compacts the fur, bones, and skull into a compact "pellet." An owl regurgitates several pellets a day, usually about 12 hours after the prey is eaten. For the birder, these pellets are a clue to an owl's whereabouts and favorite roost sites and, when dissected, a clear guide to its diet. Prey remains in pellets provide exacting evidence on prey species, availability, and foraging patterns.

Owls use a variety of hunting techniques. Most fly from hidden daytime-roost sites to adjacent hunting areas. Barn Owl roost sites and nest sites may be several miles from their favored feeding sites. Most owls hunt (listen and look for prey) from perches, waiting and then dropping down on or flying low toward unsuspecting prey. Great Gray Owl and Northern Hawk Owl commonly use their amazing hearing to detect unseen prey active in runways beneath snow cover. Some owls routinely give chase to prey, particularly other birds. Northern Hawk Owl and Short-eared Owl can hover hunt, not unlike an American Kestrel.

A few owls routinely soar and the Short-eared Owl commonly does so during daytime, both during migration and over hunting territory. The Short-eared Owl does little if any hunting while soaring, hunting instead while coursing low over favored grasslands, in a style much like the Northern Harrier. Barn Owls also commonly hunt by coursing over open fields.

VOCALIZATION

The varied calls of owls, emanating from the dark of night, are intriguing and often mysterious. Birders can more often hear than see owls. Although classic owl calls are easily recognized, many birders do not realize how many more varied calls most owls use.

Owls are extremely vocal birds and have a variety of calls. Prior to the breeding season they advertise their territory to warn other like owls away. Typically monogamous, a pair of owls will stay in touch throughout the night, and occasionally during the day, through specific purpose calls. A few owl species' calls might be

HOW TO SPOT AN OWL

The best way to look for owls—such as the Northern Saw-whet Owl at left—is during the day. This is a rigorous quest, but one with its own rewards. There are many clues. Most searchers seek owl pellets and the owls' distinctive "whitewash," the excrement below a favored perch. Look at all nearby vegetation for the telltale shape of a secreted, hidden owl. Search within the densest cover; owls normally perch within the thickest vegetation they can find. Owls hide during the day to avoid predators and challengers such as hawks, ravens, and even agitated songbirds. Evergreens are best, and cedars and junipers are preferred spots for owls to hide during the day.

If you spot clues, scan ahead with your binoculars before stepping closer and potentially flushing the owl from the safety of its daytime roost. Listen for the telltale scolding of chickadees, jays, and other songbirds. Use them as your eyes and ears. They will more often find an owl than you; their alarm might be caused by a Screech Owl nearby. Remember, if you have seen owl signs such as whitewash or pellets, try again.

characterized as the classic hoot, but most whistle, screech, hiss, or grunt. The Eastern Screech-Owl rarely screeches; its normal call is a clear, tremulous whistle. Some owls are aptly named. The Northern Saw-whet Owl's call is like the sharpening or whetting of a saw with a file. A Barred Owl has a clear "who-cooks-for-you" hoot, but also wails, whines, squeals, and even has an eerie "laugh." Recent studies of nesting Barred Owls, using cameras and microphones in nest boxes, have shown that Barred Owls routinely use up to ten different calls, each for a specific purpose.

Researchers use owl calls for a number of purposes. The responses of owls to tape playback of their calls are routinely used for census, status and distribution, and territorial studies. Vocalizations also offer clues as to the relationships of owl species. In all owls, vocalizations are inherited and of great taxonomic interest. Owls usually show little of the variation in geographic dialect so often seen in other groups of birds. There is little variation among individuals, but the calls of males differ from those of females.

Northern Pygmy-Owl

BREEDING BEHAVIOR

Vocalizations are no doubt used far more than visual displays, yet owls use food presentation, mutual preening, and bill rubbing in their courtship displays. Whereas nomadic or migratory species likely choose new mates each nesting season, some species of resident owls, such as Spotted Owls, screech-owls, and Great Horned Owls are monogamous and probably mate for life.

Over most of North America the ubiquitous Great Horned Owl may be the earliest bird to nest each season. In the Northeast, Great Horned Owls will begin nesting in late January or early February, and snow-covered females have been seen sitting on their nests. They may nest so early to take advantage of winter-stressed prey and a springtime surfeit of food (frogs, baby birds, and young rabbits, to name a few). The female Great Horned Owl does most of the brooding, while the male delivers food to her. Peak vocalization for such an early nester occurs in November and December. Owls are mostly silent when on the eggs and while the young are vulnerable in the nest. Near the fledging date, vocalization becomes more active.

Snowy Owls and Short-eared Owls nest on the ground, and Burrowing Owls nest underground. Barn Owls typically nest in buildings, caves, crevices, mine shafts, abandoned wells, and silos, under bridges and even in nooks in large piles of hay bales. Smaller owls frequently use natural holes in trees or man-made nest boxes. Most of the larger owls will use either abandoned or appropriated large nests of sticks built by other birds. The Great Horned Owl will utilize an old Great Blue Heron, raven, hawk, magpie, Osprey, or even Bald Eagle nest as its own. Owls never build nests, but use the last season's hand-me-down nests.

Young owls often leave the nest long before they have fledged. They climb about the nest tree or even nearby trees, at times calling loudly to be fed. This behavior is called "branching" and occurs when the owlets outgrow the nest or when the stick nest begins to fall apart from the trampling of the young birds.

Clutch size often varies widely with prey availability. Snowy Owls may not nest at all in lean years or may lay six to eight eggs in years when lemming populations explode. Owls are attentive and caring parents, and many will vigorously defend their nest and young. The young are dependent on the adults for many weeks after fledging, and both parents care for and feed the young.

BREEDING RANGE

Owls breed virtually everywhere in North America. Snowy Owls nest on high Arctic tundra, and Elf Owls are found only on the southern fringe of the United States. Great Horned Owls use every habitat, from the fringe of the northern boreal forest, south to the borderland deserts, and onward to Argentina. In most regions of North America, Great Horned Owls and screech owls (Western and Eastern) are comfortable in suburban and even urban surroundings. The Barn Owl is one of the world's most cosmopolitan birds, found throughout North and South America, Europe, Africa, Asia, and Australia.

Often several species of owls may be found in the same habitat and even have overlapping territories. They can coexist by partitioning the food resources or by partitioning the area into microhabitats with each using a slightly different area. A Barred Owl, for example, will feed on a different mix of prey items than a Great Horned Owl. Both may eat mice and voles, but the Great Horned Owl will take a higher percentage of rabbits and squirrels and the Barred Owl a higher proportion of reptiles and amphibians.

Although owls may share habitats, larger owls do eat smaller owls. This is especially true of the Great Horned Owl. All the other owls, from Northern Saw-whet Owl to Barred Owl, living in a Great Horned Owl's territory must be ever alert to the threat of predation.

MIGRATION

Although many owls are resident, living in one area their entire lives, others are migratory and some highly so. In North America, the Barn, Short-eared,

Long-eared, Burrowing, Flammulated, and Northern Saw-whet Owls are considered regular migrants. The Flammulated Owl of the West nests north into southern Canada, but winters in central Mexico.

Some owls are irregular migrants and referred to as irruptive species. In winters of food abundance, few or none will migrate, but in years of poor food resources, many will head south, sometimes far beyond their normal range. Great Gray, Northern Hawk Owl, and Boreal Owl are classic irruptive species, responding to population fluctuations of their rodent prey. Many rodents are cyclical with peaks of superabundance and crashes when there are few, if any, to be found. Saw-whet, Short-eared, and Long-eared Owls are normally migratory, yet sometimes vacate the northern sections of their range in big numbers (a true irruption), if prey species populations crash. The Snowy Owl is another irruptive species, but is also known to be nomadic, moving around over huge distances in search of abundant food. Snowy Owls hatched in Alaska have been found nesting in Siberia in following seasons. Irruptions or "invasions" of northern owls are a major highlight for birders.

During migration, owls select habitats most like their breeding areas, if available. Owls follow migratory leading lines, much like hawks, and concentrate at geographical bottlenecks. Long-eared and Northern Saw-whet Owls concentrate in good numbers around Cape May, New Jersey, during fall migration, where many are captured, banded, and released by the Cape May Owl Banding Project. In spring, owls concentrate on the south shore of the Great Lakes, and saw-whets and others are found and banded in good numbers at places like Whitefish Point, Michigan, on the Lake Superior shoreline, and at Braddock Bay, New York, on Lake Ontario.

WINTER RANGE

Migratory owl species may not move far in winter, but far enough that snow cover does not preclude hunting opportunity. Most movements are dictated by prey availability. In much of the Northeast, good numbers of wintering owls (migrants from the north) are found where vole populations are high (this can be either a regional or highly local phenomenon). High numbers of migrants follow good breeding seasons; data from the network of saw-whet owl banding stations have clearly documented this trend. Wintering owls, some-

times hundreds or a thousand miles from their nest sites, often are attracted to and select a habitat similar to their breeding habitat. Snowy Owls gravitate to beaches, dunes, marshes, prairies, and even airports in winter, all spots which clearly replicate their open-country Arctic tundra breeding habitat.

Owls are often gregarious, both during migration and in winter. Long-eared Owls form communal roosts, with often three or four in one tree and even several dozen in the same grove of evergreens. Both saw-whet owls and Barn Owls form loose assemblages with often five or six in the same grove of trees. In winter, Short-eared Owls form large communal daytime roosts on the ground in open marsh or meadow areas. It is believed that mutual defense against predators is the reason for these groupings.

Snowy Owl

OBSERVING OWLS

Owls are more often heard than seen. Particularly during the breeding season, the owl seeker should be content to hear their complex and fascinating repertoire of sounds rather than chance disturbing them by trying to see them. Short-eared Owls and Burrowing Owls, being open-country birds and partly diurnal, are the owls most frequently observed. During irruptions, Northern Hawk Owl, Great Gray Owl, and Snowy Owl are sometimes seen in daylight. The terrific system of birding hotlines and list serves shared on the Internet can offer specific directions to both concentrations and individual birds.

Over much of North America, the Great Horned Owl is often a birder's first owl. In nesting season, they may usurp last season's Red-tailed Hawk, Osprey, or Great Blue Heron nest; some of these nests may be out in the open where they can be watched. In late winter or early spring, the birder should check all known large stick nests to see if a Great Horned Owl pair has claimed one. If an active nest is found, you can often watch the young grow over time, and at dawn and dusk witness food deliveries to the female or young. If on eggs, the female will sit very low in the nest and almost be impossible to see. As the eggs hatch and the young grow, she will sit higher on the nest, brooding the owlets, until she is easily in plain view. Eventually the young will become so large that the female roosts nearby, often hidden from view. The male has been in attendance all along, but concealed. Always watch an active nest from a respectful distance with a spotting scope so as not to cause any disruption. Because the Great Horned Owl is one of the most common, it is a good owl for the beginner to observe.

In more southerly areas, owl numbers swell in winter when "snowbirds" from the north supplement the local residents. In fall, migrant owls from the north (Northern Saw-whet, Long-eared, and Short-eared Owls) move south and are drawn to good feeding habitats like coastal salt marshes, freshwater marshes, fallow fields, and pastures, where they will pass the winter before migrating back north in spring. Owls hunt at night and hide by day in available nearby cover such as evergreens, honeysuckle tangles, overhangs, and hollow trees. Searching for their daytime roost sites can be productive if one follows up valuable clues such as piles of pellets, fresh whitewash dripping down through branches, or scolding crows or songbirds. Wintering saw-whet and Long-eared Owls may favor a particular daytime roost site for several weeks or even months at a time, coming back to the same spot on the same branch to hide each day.

STATUS AND CONSERVATION

Large owls were often shot by hunters, farmers, and game managers. The Great Horned Owl, bold and aggressive, is well known for its attempts to take unpenned chickens, ducks, or guinea fowl, and in some areas remains unpopular. Unfenced poultry is like a supermarket to a hungry owl.

The Spotted Owl is a federally listed threatened species in the United States, an endangered species in British Columbia, and remains at the center of extreme controversy in the Pacific Northwest. The Spotted Owl is dependent on extensive old-growth forest for its survival and is a high-profile icon for the protection of the ancient temperate rain forests of the Northwest. It is championed by conservationists and reviled by many logging interests. Elsewhere, Barn, Short-eared, Long-eared, and Burrowing Owls are documented as declining in many parts of their range, victims of either outright habitat loss (as is the case of Burrowing Owls in Florida) or habitat change and alteration. Short-eared Owls are disappearing along with their native grassland and prairie habitats, and Barn Owls in many regions seem to be victims of mechanized agriculture, a process that leaves little in the way of fallow fields.

Efforts to reintroduce Barn Owls to some areas of the Midwest were initially unsuccessful, due to the absence of a strong rodent prey base to support the birds. Mechanized agriculture and heavy use of pesticides and herbicides meant that there were too few small mammals for the Barn Owls to feed on. Midwestern states that have since been successful with reintroduction programs have secured funding to pay

BURROWING OWL

Burrowing Owls are ground dwellers. They are birds of open country, active during the day, and one of the easiest of all owls to watch. They perch during the day at or near the entrance to their underground nest sites. Look for them on the ground, on fence posts, or on low trees. Burrowing Owls may dig some cavities on their own, but usually nest in abandoned dens of other animals such as foxes, skunks, armadillos, ground squirrels, and prairie dogs. There are populations in central and south Florida; otherwise Burrowing Owls are western birds, found on the plains from Texas west to California, and northward into the Canadian prairies. The birds are migratory, withdrawing south far into Mexico in winter. A tropical species, Burrowing Owls are also widespread in Central and South America.

farmers to leave fallow fields. The Barn Owl has responded well in many regions to the provision of nest boxes. As old barns disappear, replaced by metal structures, Barn Owls find little access. The provision of entrances and enclosed boxes inside likely structures, where nearby hunting habitats still exist, has been successful. Nocturnal banding programs, of both resident and migrant owls, are expanding since researchers are now able to share information through the Internet.

The Ferruginous Pygmy-Owl and the Elf Owl are two other species of concern. Both are tropical species, have small ranges in the U.S., and could be sensitive to habitat loss, disturbance, or change.

See also

Hawks and Eagles, page 110
Nighthawks, Nightjars, page 217

~~B~~ARRED OWL

~~NOR~~THWESTERN
~~RAN~~GE EXPANSION

~~197~~5 — Historic boundary
of resident range

Modern resident range

~~B~~arred Owl first spread west across
~~the b~~oreal forest of western Canada.
~~The e~~xpansion continued south along
~~the P~~acific coast to northern California.

BOREAL, ▶
GREAT GRAY,
AND HAWK OWLS

BOREAL OWL

Exceptional single record ●

GREAT GRAY OWL

Exceptional single record ●

HAWK OWL

Exceptional single record ●

ALL FEATURED SPECIES

Limit of typical invasion   – – – – –

Limit of rare or casual   – ‐ – ‐ –
occurences

Combined eastern
resident range

Generally, these Owls are permanent
residents of the northern boreal and
montane forests, with only individual
birds moving south in winter. Every few
years, in response to low prey levels,
more substantial numbers are forced to
move. Small numbers can be seen very
rarely out of their normal Pacific
Northwest range. They are more
commonly seen east of the Rockies.

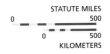

STATUTE MILES

0   500

0   500

KILOMETERS

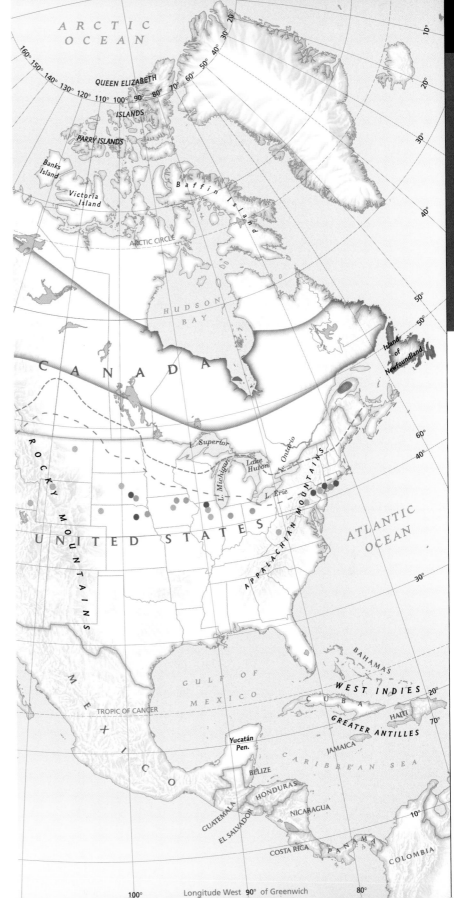

NIGHTHAWKS, NIGHTJARS

Edward S.
Brinkley

Nightjars—including Chuck-will's-widow, Whip-poor-will, Common Poorwill, Common Pauraque, and Buff-collared Nightjar (or Cukacheea)—are strictly nocturnal birds known to most people by their ringing, repetitive songs, heard at dusk and through the night. Their colorful names are onomatopoeic of these calls, which figure in the poetry and music around the world wherever nightjars are found. One species, the Jungle Nightjar, is an East Asian bird known in our area only from one Alaska specimen. The North American nighthawks—Antillean, Common, and Lesser—are, by contrast, often active by day and at dusk, foraging over cities and fields for insects on the wing and migrating in large, loose flocks in the daytime. Collectively, the nightjars and nighthawks are often called "goatsuckers" because of the folk belief that they drink goats' milk at night. No one is certain how this belief arose, but it could be because goats inhabit open areas frequented by foraging nightjars, and shepherds would be likely to flush these birds at night from areas where their flocks are present. As is the case with the owls, some cultures consider these nocturnal birds to be omens or agents of evil, but in most cultures, they are appreciated and celebrated for their vocal repertoire.

Nightjars are rarely seen away from their natural nesting habitat except during migration. Throughout their ranges, both in the breeding areas and wintering grounds, nightjars spend much of the day roosting singly in concealed locations, often on the ground, where their plumage makes them almost impossible to detect. Even during migration, which exposes these concealment artists to many unpredictable forces, the nightjars, in particular, are rarely observed. Their retiring habits make them of great interest to birdwatchers, who seek them out mostly during spring, when their territoriality, and thus vocalizing, is at a peak. Some people use a tape recording of the male's song to bring the bird into view, but it is often possible to find the open-country species such as the Chuck-will's-widow on roadsides at night.

Nighthawks are rather easily observed compared to their close relatives the nightjars. Some people mistake them for large bats, probably because they notice them at dusk, hence the local name of "bullbat" for the Common Nighthawk. The display of the Common Nighthawk is often seen in broad daylight: The male flies high into the sky, then plummets to earth, its wings producing a jarring sound like a buzz saw as it nearly strikes the ground, then pulls up steeply from the dive, in a spectacular U-shape arc. This display marks territory but is also used to threaten predators or trespassers, including humans. At many points on the North American continent, the fall migration of this species is an eagerly awaited turning point in the season.

Birders gather along ridges, lakeshores, and coastlines to observe this normally solitary species gather into flocks of hundreds (formerly thousands) and dance across the sky, their deep, bounding, erratic wingstrokes more reminiscent of a seabird than a land bird. The nighthawks usually migrate between August and September, at the same time that many species of warbler, vireo, thrush, cuckoo, and tanager are also heading to winter quarters in the New World tropics.

(Left) Lesser Nighthawk

Common Nighthawk: *Chordeiles minor*, L 9.5", white bar across primaries farther from wing tip

NIGHTHAWKS, NIGHTJARS

One of the most widespread, primarily nocturnal species, the Common Nighthawk (above) breeds throughout most of the United States and Canada. The species has darker brown plumage in the East, compared to paler, gray coloration in the Midwest, and has long, tapered wings with a prominent wing patch. The nighthawk's mottled and barred plumage provides effective camouflage when roosting during the day along tree branches or on the ground. The birds have a streamlined body and are capable of agile aerial displays when feeding at dusk. Nighthawks feed largely on insects while in flight, and often may be seen feeding near bright city lights to which insects are drawn. When feeding, the lower jaw drops and creates a wide opening capable of scooping in large moths and even small birds. Breeding Common Nighthawks scrape a shallow depression in the ground, or nest on rooftops, shaping a site among gravel and nearby debris. There are usually two hatchlings in a brood and both parents care for the young.

Range of Common Nighthawk

CLASSIFICATION

The nightjars and nighthawks (family Caprimulgidae) compose a group of about 89 small to medium-size species worldwide (nine in North America) and form part of the order Caprimulgiformes, which also includes the similarly nocturnal oilbird, frogmouths, potoos, and owlet-nightjars in other families. Fossil birds in this order date back as far as 40 million years ago, into the late Eocene epoch, making this an ancient family. Their nearest relatives, though distant, are the owls. The Jungle Nightjar is placed in the genus *Caprimulgus* (with most North American nightjars) and with all nightjars in the subfamily Caprimulginae. The nighthawks are grouped together in the genus *Chordeiles* and in the separate subfamily Chordeilinae, which is restricted to the Americas.

STRUCTURE

All goatsuckers appear to be rather stocky birds when seen perched but are graceful, streamlined birds when seen in flight, with nighthawks having the most slender, pointed wings and body of the group. Both nightjars and nighthawks have wide bills that open to reveal an enormous gape, capable of capturing large insects. Around these bills are rictal bristles, which both guide prey toward the bill and presumably provide sensory information to the bird. Goatsuckers have large eyes and are capable of foraging even on moonless nights.

PLUMAGE

All nightjars and nighthawks share cryptic plumages in browns, buffs, grays, and rusts, designed to blend in with their surroundings while roosting during the day or while at the nest. Some species have areas of white on the throat, or in the wings and tail, that contrast sharply with the remainder of the plumage, and these areas often play a role in displays during the breeding season.

VOCALIZATIONS

In contrast to their cryptic plumage, nightjars have some of the most memorable songs in the bird world, and nearly all of them have names that reflect the male's territorial song, which is easily rendered using phonemes: "Whip-poor-will" is a good example. The rapid repetition of these songs in the early breeding season at night—together with the nightjars' near-invisibility to casual observers—have given these birds a mythical status. Nighthawks have less varied vocalizations, but their aerial displays, when combined with their simple calls, make them memorable all the same. Goatsuckers make a variety of other sounds, including purrs, growls, and snaps, the latter made by clapping the bill together.

BREEDING RANGE

Nightjars are found in the temperate latitudes, but

only the Whip-poor-will and Common Poorwill are found nesting as far north as southernmost Canada, limited by habitat and the short supply of moths and other insects. The Buff-collared Nightjar and Common Pauraque range just into Arizona and Texas, and the Chuck-will's-widow is restricted to the southeastern U.S. Likewise, among nighthawks, one species, the Common, nests north into Canada, whereas the Antillean is restricted in North America to southernmost Florida, especially the Keys, and the Lesser to the desert Southwest.

Common Pauraque

large areas in search of prey, in high, bounding, erratic flight, while nightjars typically hunt singly from low perches in vegetation or from the ground, returning to the same site on the ground to watch for prey, much as a flycatcher does.

BREEDING BEHAVIOR

North American nightjars and nighthawks are believed to be monogamous and pair for life, but their breeding biology is difficult to study. All are ground nesters and highly territorial, with confrontations between rival males sometimes involving growling sounds and grappling contests. Males attract females by calling from their territories, and pair bonds form following displays in which males stretch out their plumage—wings, tail, or throat—to show off contrasting white markings.

FEEDING BEHAVIOR

All caprimulgids feed on insects, often on moths, but many kinds of flying insects are taken on the wing. North America's largest species, Chuck-will's-widow, at 12 inches, is large enough to prey on small songbirds as well as the largest moths. Nighthawks may range over

MIGRATION

Because the Common Nighthawk can be observed during the day, its migration has been well documented, particularly in the East, where in August and September, large flocks pass by hawk-watching stations. The spring migration occurs over a shorter period and is less concentrated, but large flights can be seen along major lakeshores in the North. Migration of most nightjars is poorly documented. Chuck-will's-widow is known to be a common trans-Gulf migrant in both fall and spring migration, observed on oil rigs and ships in the Gulf of Mexico, or in parks in Florida and Texas.

WINTER RANGE

Because they are exclusively insectivores, all North American species with the exception of Common Pauraque (and in some areas Common Poorwill) migrate to warmer clime; most end up in Mexico and Central America, but the Common Nighthawk winters as far south as northern Argentina. Chuck-will's-widow's winter range takes it to Colombia and the Caribbean Islands. The Common Poorwill stays, but goes into torpor, a state of reduced metabolic activity, when prey is scarce and temperatures low.

OBSERVING NIGHTHAWKS AND NIGHTJARS

A drive in remote and rural backroads on a warm night, often turns up several nightjars resting on the roads, which attract the birds for the retained warmth; they are detected by their bright orange or reddish reflective eyeshine. On some spring and summer nights, nightjars are silent and impossible to detect.

STATUS AND CONSERVATION

No species of caprimulgid in North America is listed as threatened or endangered. Data from Breeding Bird Surveys, however, show a recent drop in the populations of Chuck-will's-widow and Common Nighthawk, and these declines deserve attention from conservationists.

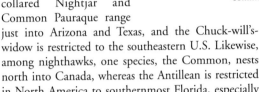

OTHER SPECIES FIELD NOTES

- **Lesser Nighthawk**
  Chordeiles acutipennis
  L 8.5"
  White bar across primaries closer to wing tip

- **Antillean Nighthawk**
  Chordeiles gundlachii
  L 8"
  Best distinguished by voice

- **Common Pauraque**
  Nyctidromus albicollis
  L 11"
  Long, rounded tail and wings

- **Chuck-will's-widow**
  Caprimulgus carolinensis
  L 12"
  Whitish necklace below buffy throat

- **Whip-poor-will**
  Caprimulgus vociferus
  L 9.75"
  Dark throat, white necklace

- **Buff-collared Nightjar**
  Caprimulgus ridgwayi
  L 8.75"
  Buffy bar across nape

- **Common Poorwill**
  Phalaenoptilus nuttallii
  L 7.75"
  Short, rounded wings and tail

See also

Owls, page 207
Swifts, page 223

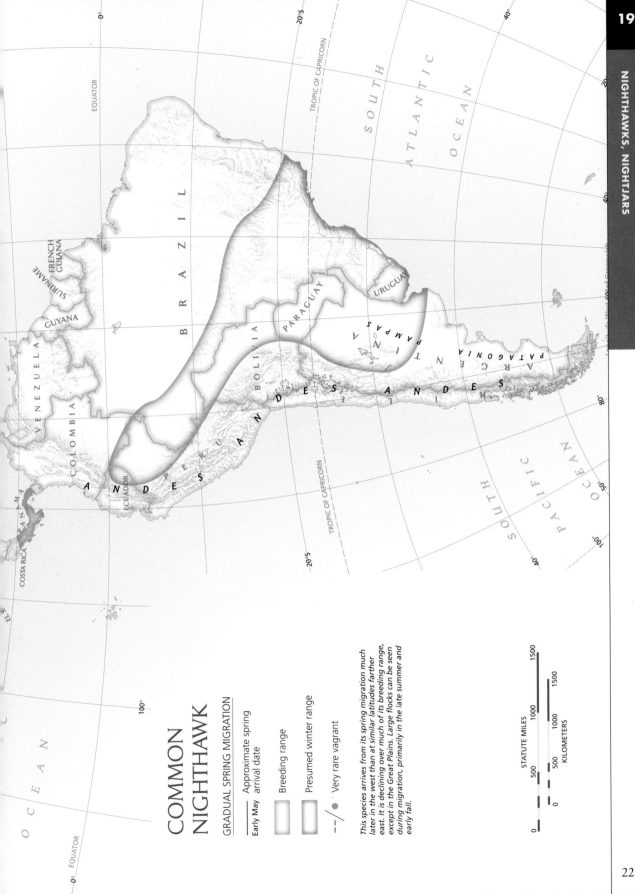

COMMON NIGHTHAWK

GRADUAL SPRING MIGRATION

Early May Approximate spring
            arrival date

[ ] Breeding range

[ ] Presumed winter range

--- / • Very rare vagrant

This species arrives from its spring migration much later in the west than at similar latitudes farther east. It is declining over much of its breeding range, except in the Great Plains. Large flocks can be seen during migration, primarily in the late summer and early fall.

STATUTE MILES

0   500   1000   1500

KILOMETERS

0   500   1000   1500

EQUATOR

TROPIC OF CAPRICORN

SOUTH ATLANTIC OCEAN

SOUTH PACIFIC OCEAN

VENEZUELA

GUYANA

SURINAME

FRENCH GUIANA

COLOMBIA

ECUADOR

PERU

BRAZIL

BOLIVIA

PARAGUAY

URUGUAY

ARGENTINA

PAMPAS

PATAGONIA

ANDES

PANAMA

COSTA RICA

EL SALVADOR

20°S

40°

60°

80°

100°

0°

SWIFTS

Despite appearances, the swift family, or Apodidae, are related closely to hummingbirds, not swallows. Of the approximately one hundred species of swifts worldwide, four species appear in North America: the Chimney Swift east of the Rocky Mountains, and the Black Swift, the White-Throated Swift, and Vaux's Swift in the west. The White-collared Swift, a tropical species, appears as an accidental along the coast of southeast Texas and Florida.

Howard Robinson

The most widely distributed of the swifts is the Chimney Swift, which ranges from the East Coast to the Rocky Mountains. An important reason for the bird's widespread distribution is its relationship with civilization. Chimney Swifts used to nest and roost in hollow trees. Once chimneys, barns, and the like became available, and as the number of hollow trees declined, Chimney Swifts opportunistically adapted to the man-made structures and expanded their range.

The other three swifts live in the West. They nest in steep seaside and canyon cliffs, in caves, behind waterfalls, and in hollow trees. Because of their inaccessible nesting sites, swifts have been difficult to study, and much about their lives is unknown.

Currently, the Driftwood Wildlife Association of Driftwood, Texas, sponsors a nest-site research project in which it monitors the effectiveness of experimental nest and roost sites for the declining population of Chimney Swifts. The group has initiated a citizens' science project called A Swift Night Out that encourages birders to observe how many Chimney Swifts and Vaux's Swifts enter known roosts and to submit their counts to a central data-collection point.

The scientific name for Apodidae, means "without feet." Though that is not literally true, their legs and feet are so poorly adapted to life on the ground that swifts do not perch during the day. Typically, they spend daylight hours in flight, snagging insects and ballooning spiders, drinking water and bathing, and, except for Black Swifts, gathering nestbuilding materials on the fly.

The inaccessible nesting sites of the four species of swift in North America have played to their advantage, protecting them from most predators, including human beings. For some species in Asia, though, the nests of Edible-nest Swiftlets, for example, are aggressively harvested by people supplying the food industry with the ingredients for bird's nest soup. This multimillion dollar business is so threatening that naturalists fear the Edible-nest Swiftlets will become extinct within five to ten years. Fourteen swift taxa are included in the World List of Threatened Birds.

Apart from their fast, "fidgety" flight patterns, swifts in North America are acclaimed for their magnificent roosts. In preparation for and during migration, swifts gather at night in impressive roosts, which they use over and over again. One Chimney Swift roost in south-central Kansas has been estimated to harbor as many as 10,000 birds. Smaller roosts are more common. A large roost of Vaux's Swifts in Washington State numbers around 500 birds, and a winter roost of White-throated Swifts may contain 400 to 500 birds.

Roosts are not for nesting. At times, a breeding pair may cohabit with other swifts in a roost, but roosts generally are made up of nonbreeding birds. Roosting will conserve warmth on cold days and enable the birds to preserve reserves of fat or gain weight in preparation for migration. Chimney Swifts, for example, may add up to 50 percent of their body weight when roosting before migrating.

(Left) Black Swifts

Chimney Swift: *Chaetura pelagica,* L 5.25", dark plumage, cigar-shaped body

SWIFTS

The most common swifts in the eastern half of the United States and southern Canada are the sooty-colored Chimney Swifts (above). The species can be seen soaring over forested, open, and urban sites and are known for their evening circular flights overhead. Swifts have a high-pitched chirp. They roost, supported by small spines on their tail, in large groups in chimneys and steeples. Their primary food is insects caught in flight. They nest in chimneys or under the eaves of abandoned farm buildings and build nests by breaking off small twigs with their feet and carrying them to the nest site. The twigs are cemented together by saliva to make a small cup. A swift pair raises a brood of four or five that fledge in two weeks. A diminishing insect food source in the fall brings on migration as far south as Peru.

Range of Chimney Swift

CLASSIFICATION

Of the approximately 90 species of swifts worldwide, four species regularly breed in North America. The Apodidae family is a member of the superorder Apodimorphae, which comprises two orders: the Apodiformes, which include the swift family (Apodidae) and the treeswift family; and the Trochiliformes, which include the hermits and typical hummingbirds. The American Ornithologists Union's list of North American swifts and hummingbirds contains the following species of Apodidae: the Cypseloidinae, which includes the Black Swift (*Cypseloides niger);* the Chaeturinae, which includes the Chimney Swift (*Chaetura pelagica)* and the Vaux's Swift (*Chaetura vauxi);* and the Apodinae, which includes the White-throated Swift (*Aeronautes saxatalis).*

STRUCTURE

The swifts' primary feathers are unusually long, due to the structure of their wing bones, which differ from those of passerine birds—swallows and martins, for example—and which allow swifts to attain speeds approaching 100 miles per hour. Chimney, Vaux's, and Black Swifts have anisodactyl feet (three toes facing forward and one toe facing backward), which is the most common type of foot among songbirds. In White-throated Swifts, the toes are opposed laterally in groups of two, and the two inner and outer sets move together to grasp surfaces and nesting materials.

FEEDING BEHAVIOR

Swifts' feed on the wing, plowing through swarms of flying ants, termites, and other insects and spiders, often with their mouths wide open. This soup of prey is referred to as aerial plankton, but swifts do not indiscriminately fill their stomach as they slash through a swarm. They tend to take the largest prey that will fit in their gape, and they avoid stinging insects, although, being opportunists, they feed on beehives when possible. During breeding season, both sexes capture prey, which they glue together into food balls, called boluses, and regurgitate them to the nestlings, even tearing apart the bolus to help the newly hatched cope with the size of the meal.

VOCALIZATION

While perched, the Chimney Swift emits a high pitched chipper call. During flight, this same call is sometimes made so close together that it sounds like a buzz. The vocalization of Vaux's is softer and higher pitched and includes rapid chirping and insectlike twitter. The White-throated Swift's call has been likened to a "scree" or "he he he he," or "tee dee dee dee." Black Swifts make a clicking sound in flight, but they are said to be generally silent.

BREEDING BEHAVIOR

Swifts engage in aerial spectacles during the breeding season. In addition to virtuoso chases, male and female White-throated Swifts cling to each other in flight, a few hundred feet above ground, then free fall, spinning around, and separate only just before reaching the ground. Black Swifts engage in "group chase," in which a leader, followed by as many as six other birds, races in horizontal flight, punctuated by rapid changes in direction; the followers perform in synchrony. Among Chimney Swifts, aerial courtship includes a type of flight called V-ing. As a pair flies horizontally, the bird following raises its wings to form an acute angle. Sometimes the lead bird also V-s, but the action is always initiated by the follower.

The nests of Black Swifts differ from those of the other three swifts and depend on the habitat. Nests constructed on ledges of steep canyon walls near water and waterfalls resemble pads and are made mainly of moss. They are held together by mud, not saliva. At nest sites on seaside cliffs, the birds frequently make slight depressions in mud and use them for nests.

The nests of Chimney, Vaux's, and White-throated Swifts are usually cup- or cone-shaped. Chimney Swifts and Vaux's Swifts use twigs, with the former occasionally gathering pine and juniper needles, and the latter including weed stems and pine needles, cemented together by saliva. Vaux's Swifts rely much more than Chimney Swifts on hollow trees. White-throateds place their nest on ledges or in niches in rocks and buildings. They construct them of grasses, moss, seed down, and feathers. Black Swifts lay one egg. Chimney Swifts average four to five eggs, and the nests

of Vaux's Swifts contain up to seven eggs. The White-throated Swift lays three to six eggs.

Vaux's Swift

MIGRATION

All swifts in North America migrate, though two of the species do not go far. The northern population of Vaux's Swift departs its breeding grounds in southeast Alaska, British Columbia, Washington, northern Idaho, and western Montana for Mexico and Honduras. Other swifts spend winters farther south, though just where is not well known. Black Swifts overwinter in South America, leaving North America in small flocks from late August to mid-September. Chimney Swifts gather in premigration flocks and fly south in daylight to spend winter east of the Andes in the Amazon Basin of Peru, Ecuador, Colombia, and Brazil, and west of the Andes in Peru and Chile. When Chimney Swifts return in the spring, they travel along three flyways: the Atlantic coastal plain, along the east side of the Appalachian Mountains (the Piedmont flyway), and up the Mississippi River.

OBSERVING SWIFTS

The Chimney Swift may be the most cosmopolitan of our four common swifts, often seen over the eastern half of the United States, especially in the evening as it forages above city parks and ponds. The Black, Vaux's, and White-throated are western species seen inhabiting the open sky throughout daylight hours.

STATUS AND CONSERVATION

Although they are not in danger, three of the four species—the Chimney, Vaux's, and White-throated Swift—seem to be declining in population. Likely causes for the loss are pesticide residues ingested with food and, for the Chimney, and Vaux's Swift, the replacement of open, rough-textured chimneys with capped, smooth-walled chimneys.

OTHER SPECIES FIELD NOTES

■ **Black Swift**
Cypseloides niger
L 7.25"
Large size, blackish overall

■ **Vaux's Swift**
Chaetura vauxi
L 4.75"
Pale rump and breast

■ **Common Swift**
Apus apus
L 6.5"
Dark plumage, long, thin wings, pale throat

■ **White-collared Swift**
Streptoprocne zonaris
L 8.5"
White collar, very large size

■ **White-throated Swift**
Aeronautes saxatalis
L 6.5"
Black and white below

■ **White-throated Needletail**
Hirundapus caudacutus
L 8"
White throat and undertail coverts

■ **Fork-tailed Swift**
Apus pacificus
L 7.75"
Long, forked tail, white rump

See also

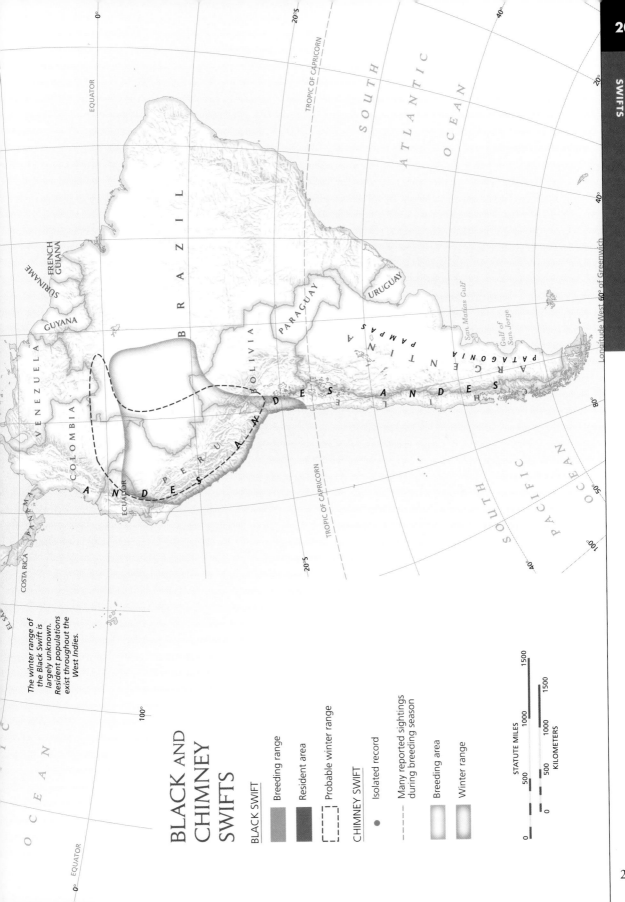

Longitude West 60° of Greenwich

SOUTH ATLANTIC OCEAN

EQUATOR

TROPIC OF CAPRICORN

B R A Z I L

SURINAME
FRENCH GUIANA
GUYANA
VENEZUELA
COLOMBIA
PANAMA
COSTA RICA
ECUADOR
PERU
BOLIVIA
PARAGUAY
URUGUAY
ARGENTINA
PAMPAS
PATAGONIA
CHILE
A N D E S

San Matías Gulf
Gulf of San Jorge

TROPIC OF CAPRICORN

SOUTH
PACIFIC
OCEAN

OCEAN

EQUATOR

The winter range of the Black Swift is largely unknown. Resident populations exist throughout the West Indies.

BLACK AND CHIMNEY SWIFTS

BLACK SWIFT

Breeding range

Resident area

Probable winter range

CHIMNEY SWIFT

● Isolated record

Many reported sightings during breeding season

Breeding area

Winter range

STATUTE MILES
0   500   1000   1500

KILOMETERS
0   500   1000   1500

HUMMINGBIRDS

Hummingbirds are among the most familiar and beloved birds in North America. Their flashy plumage, fearless nature, and willingness to take advantage of garden flowers and feeders have earned these tiny dynamos a following far out of proportion to their size. Although their charisma may entrance the casual observer, it can overshadow a complexity that challenges birders and ornithologists alike. Their rapid, darting flight and confusing plumages complicate field identification, and their propensity to wander means a rare hummingbird can show up almost anywhere. Despite their mass appeal, many aspects of their intimate lives still hold surprises for the researcher.

Sheri Williamson

One key to their popularity is their bold, pugnacious personality. Incredible speed and agility give hummingbirds the audacity to look a human in the eye from a few inches away and drive off competitors many times their own size. Sugar-rich nectar fuels their supercharged metabolism, and anyone who has observed them quarreling and jousting over a choice patch of flowers knows that hummingbirds are ruthless competitors for this limited resource. Modern observers often mistake savagery on such a small scale for playfulness, but Native American traditions have long associated hummingbirds and their defensive and aggressive postures with warfare.

Though nectar-feeding birds are found throughout the tropical regions of the world, hummingbirds are unique to the Americas.

The center of species diversity is in equatorial South America, where the Andes Mountains divide the arid Pacific slope from the lush forests of the Amazon River Basin. More than 150 different species of hummingbirds have been recorded in Ecuador alone, a country that is about the size of the state of Nevada.

North America can claim a mere fraction of this diversity; only 14 species of hummingbirds are well-established breeders north of Mexico, whereas another eight occur as rare breeders or irregular visitors. Only one species, the Ruby-throated Hummingbird, nests east of the Mississippi River and is casual west to California, but a surprising number of hummingbirds of other species occur in eastern North America as visitors or winter residents.

Though no match for the tropics in species diversity, the southwestern border region, from western Texas through southeastern Arizona, offers outstanding opportunities to observe these fascinating birds. Each spring and summer at feeding stations in the "sky island" mountains of southeastern Arizona, visitors can enjoy up to 15 different species of hummingbirds, including the striking Magnificent, White-eared, and Lucifer Hummingbirds. Fewer species inhabit the Rocky Mountains, the Sierra Nevada of California, and the Texas coast along the Gulf of Mexico, but these major migration corridors see astounding numbers of hummingbirds during the fall migration.

Most residents of North America need look no further than their own backyards to find hummingbirds. Sugar feeders and nectar plants provide needed refueling stops for migrants, even in cities. Gardeners can create a nesting habitat in their backyards in the most barren urban setting with a little wildlife-friendly landscaping. However familiar or exotic the habitat, hummingbirds offer a glimpse of life on the edge.

(Left) Costa's Hummingbird

Ruby-throated Hummingbird: *Archilochus colubris,*
L 3 .75", red throat, black chin

HUMMINGBIRDS

The widely distributed Ruby-throated Hummingbird ranges from Florida into the southern Canadian provinces. Males have iridescent, dark green heads, a ruby-red throat, and green and brown bodies, but females lack the bright red tones. The species is a common backyard bird throughout its range and seeks out hummingbird feeders. The birds feed on flower nectar but will also prey on small spiders and other insects. In the spring, male hummingbirds arrive well before females to claim and defend a breeding territory. Their migration to and from wintering grounds leads roughly 700 miles directly across the Gulf of Mexico. Males are aggressive with each other, sparring and jousting for a prime site. Once a mating pair chooses a site, the female builds a nest on a small tree limb and raises one or two young by herself. Ruby-throated Hummingbirds have increased in number over the past decade, perhaps because of the rising popularity of backyard feeders and a longer breeding season that permits two broods.

Range of Ruby-throated Hummingbird

CLASSIFICATION

At approximately 330 species, the hummingbird family, Trochilidae, is the second largest bird family in the New World. Taxonomists traditionally place hummingbirds in the order Apodiformes along with swifts (family Apodidae), based on certain anatomical similarities. Recent biochemical discoveries and DNA hybridization studies seem to confirm a relationship between these groups but also suggest that hummingbirds diverged from the swift lineage early enough to merit their own order, Trochiliformes.

The unrelated sunbirds of Africa and Asia (order Passeriformes, family Nectariniidae) are convergent with hummingbirds in their nectar-feeding habits and their brilliant, iridescent plumage.

STRUCTURE

The principal characteristic that sets hummingbirds apart from all other birds is their mode of flight. Hummingbirds are among the most adept aerialists of all birds and the only ones capable of sustained hovering. Their unique anatomy allows the wings to rotate in a figure-eight stroke, beating the air with the top and bottom surfaces of the wings alternately and allowing the birds to remain virtually stationary in midair. The wings of the Black-chinned Hummingbird beat around 50 times per second in hovering flight; during the male's diving courtship displays, the wings beat even faster.

Hovering flight is an elegant, if energy-intensive, solution to the problem of harvesting the nectar of flowers, an ecological niche dominated by insects. In fact, their unorthodox mode of flight and diminutive size give hummingbirds the distinction of being the only birds more often confused with insects than with other birds.

The aptly named Bee Hummingbird of Cuba is the smallest bird in the world, weighing in at less than 0.07 ounces (2 grams), and most North American hummingbirds weigh between 0.1 and 0.14 ounces (3 and 4 grams), slightly more than a penny. Not all are so small, however. Many tropical species, including the Magnificent and the Blue-throated Hummingbirds of the southwestern United States, are the size of warblers. The largest of all, the Giant Hummingbird of South America, is similar in size to an Orchard Oriole and may represent the upper-size limit possible for a hummingbird.

Their extreme lifestyle requires other adaptations, including modifications of the bill and tongue. The bills of most hummingbirds are long probes adapted for feeding from deep, tubular flowers. The thin, translucent tongue can extend up to twice the length of the bill and has a forked tip edged in a delicate fringe that acts like a mop. The edges of the tongue curl inward, forming two partial tubes tiny enough to draw in liquid by capillary action. The tongue is anchored in front of the eyes, and muscles wrapped around the skull flick it in and out of the bill tip at rates of up to 13 licks per second. Most birds drink by tipping their head back and letting gravity do the work, but hummingbirds can drink continuously from any angle. The distensible crop can store a third or more of the hummingbird's body weight in nectar for later processing.

Xantus's Hummingbird

A huge heart pumps blood and oxygen to flight muscles that may be 50 percent larger than those of other birds. The muscle fibers themselves are packed with mitochondria, subcellular structures that power metabolic processes. Hummingbirds have proportionally fewer feathers than other birds, which helps to dissipate the heat generated by their high metabolism. Hovering reduces the need to perch and climb, so to save weight the feet and legs are greatly reduced in size and almost useless for walking.

PLUMAGE

Though reduced in number and size compared to other birds, hummingbird feathers can be spectacular. The flashing, jewel-like colors seen primarily in the throat and crown of adult males are created by the internal structure of the feathers.

Beneath the transparent outer layer of the barbule are stacks of flattened granules of the ordinary blackish pigment melanin. Each granule, called a platelet, is packed with dozens of microscopic air bubbles that act like tiny mirrors. Light reflects and refracts as it passes through these layers, and interference effects cancel out some wavelengths while amplifying others. This effect creates the pure colors that reach the observer's eye. Unlike pigments, these structural colors can change dramatically depending on the angle at which they are viewed. The gorget of a male Rufous Hummingbird appears scarlet, seen from straight on, shifting to a coppery orange and lemon yellow before the color disappears entirely. Seen in poor light, the male's gorget may appear black.

The females of most North American species are more cryptically colored than the males, which helps them avoid detection as they care for the eggs and their young. In many tropical species, including the Violet-crowned Hummingbird and the Plain-capped Starthroat, both males and females are very similar in plumage.

OTHER SPECIES FIELD NOTES

■ **Green Violet-ear**
Colibri thalassinus
L 4.75"
Violet patches on face and breast

■ **Green-breasted Mango**
Anthracothorax prevostii
L 4.75"
Purple outer tail feathers

■ **Buff-bellied Hummingbird**
Amazilia yucatanensis
L 4.25"
Buff belly, chestnut tail

■ **Berylline Hummingbird**
Amazilia beryllina
L 4.25"
Chestnut rump, wings, tail

■ **Bahama Woodstar**
Calliphlox evelynae
L 3.75"
Broad white collar

■ **Violet-crowned Hummingbird**
Amazilia violiceps
L 4.5"
Violet crown

■ **Lucifer Hummingbird**
Calothorax lucifer
L 3.5"
Purple throat, downcurved bill, long tail

■ **Broad-billed Hummingbird**
Cynanthus latirostris
L 4"
White undertail coverts, mostly red bill

■ **White-eared Hummingbird**
Hylocharis leucotis
L 3.75"
Broad white ear stripe, green breast

■ **Blue-throated Hummingbird**
Lampornis clemenciae
L 5"
White malar and eye stripe

■ **Xantus's Hummingbird**
Hylocharis xantusii
L 3.5"
Buff underparts, white ear-stripe

■ **Magnificent Hummingbird**
Eugenes fulgens
L 5.25"
Purple crown, white spot behind eye

■ **Plain-capped Starthroat**
Heliomaster constantii
L 5"
Striped head, very long bill

■ **Black-chinned Hummingbird**
Archilochus alexandri
L 3.75"
Black throat with purple below

■ **Costa's Hummingbird**
Calypte costae
L 3.5"
Violet crown and gorget

■ **Anna's Hummingbird**
Calypte anna
L 4"
Rose head and throat

■ **Broad-tailed Hummingbird**
Selasphorus platycercus
L 4"
Rose-red throat, wingbeats produce whistle

■ **Calliope Hummingbird**
Stellula calliope
L 3.25"
Tiny size, carmine streaks on throat

■ **Rufous Hummingbird**
Selasphorus rufus
L 3.75"
Rufous back and belly

■ **Allen's Hummingbird**
Selasphorus sasin
L 3.75"
Green back, rufous belly

FEEDING BEHAVIOR

A hummingbird's metabolism and appetite are prodigious. They have the highest basal metabolic rate of any bird, and in hovering flight they burn energy at nearly ten times the maximum possible rate for a human athlete. To meet their energetic needs, hummingbirds may drink one-and-one-half times their body weight in nectar every day, which translates to between one quarter and three quarters of their weight in sugars. The digestive system is both rapid and efficient, extracting up to 99 percent of the sugar in a meal of nectar in 15 minutes or less.

Hummingbirds and the flowers they pollinate have each evolved to meet the other's needs. Typical hummingbird flowers have a narrow, tubular corolla with nectar at the bottom, accessible only to a long bill or tongue. The flowers lack fragrance, because hummingbirds do not use their poorly developed sense of smell to locate food. The nectar inside the flower is rich in sucrose, the same sugar for which sugarcane and sugar beets are grown.

Like humans, hummingbirds prefer this complex sugar over simpler ones abundant in the nectar of insect-pollinated flowers. Bright colors, usually in shades of red, orange, and pink, attract the hummingbirds' attention, while subtle changes in color or pattern may communicate nectar availability. In some cases, flowers that exhibit this suite of characteristics may be visited by insects but are pollinated only by hummingbirds. This relationship is far from exclusive from the birds' side. Any flower that offers abundant, sugar-rich nectar may be visited by hummingbirds, no matter what its color or shape.

If its bill is a poor match for a flower's shape or size, a hummingbird may be able to extract the nectar by probing between the bases of the petals or taking advantage of holes chewed in the base of the flower by wasps or bees. Taking nectar while bypassing the pollination mechanism amounts to thievery, but this is common feeding behavior for many of the shorter-billed hummingbirds.

When nectar is in short supply, tree sap can be a vital source of sugars and other nutrients. Ruby-throated Hummingbirds drink from wells drilled by sapsuckers in early spring and lick droplets of sap that ooze from acorn cups in fall migration.

Hummingbirds have two common strategies to assure an adequate supply of nectar. Territorialism is most successful when a nectar source is rich and localized enough to provide more energy than it takes to defend it from competitors. When resources are less concentrated, hummingbirds may "trapline," which means visiting widely spaced flowers (or feeders) along a regular route.

Small hummingbirds often adopt a third strategy, becoming "parasites" on nectar sources within the territory of a larger, more aggressive bird. Some species pursue one of these strategies consistently, whereas others are adaptable enough to switch from one strategy to another as resources and competition dictate.

A hummingbird's tremendous demand for energy cannot always be met. During inclement weather, when nectar is in short supply, or when storing energy for migration is a priority, hummingbirds can minimize energy consumption by entering torpor, a hibernation-like state in which body temperature, heart rate, and respiration are greatly reduced.

Nectar is basically a solution of sugars and water

RUFOUS HUMMINGBIRD

These coppery-colored bullets, known as Rufous Hummingbirds, breed from southern Oregon and northwestern Wyoming to southeastern Alaska. They are common late summer migrants throughout the West.

Males may spend more than half their lives in migration between the breeding grounds and their winter homes in Mexico. These monumental journeys require frequent refueling along the way. Their highly aggressive temperament allows migrating Rufous Hummingbirds to get the nectar they need by driving off competitors up to three times their size. Battles are punctuated by raucous chatter and the shrill, metallic wing trill of adult males.

Female and immature male Rufous Hummingbirds are virtually indistinguishable from Allen's Hummingbird, and bird-watchers often refer to them as "Rufous/Allen's." Adult males, however, can be safely separated by the shape of their tail feathers.

that provides much-needed calories but little else of nutritional value. To supply their other needs, hummingbirds must become predators. Small insects and spiders are snatched from midair, gleaned from bark and leaves, or plucked from flowers during visits for nectar. The need for protein, vitamins, and minerals is greatest in nestlings, which are fed largely on invertebrates to provide the range of nutrients necessary for proper development. Breeding females also have special needs and may feed on mineral-rich wood ash to ensure strong eggshells.

VOCALIZATION

Hummingbirds are surprisingly noisy, with species-specific vocabularies of chirps, shrieks, and snarls heard during conflicts over feeding or breeding rights, also described as twittery calls or chattering "chase notes" when driving off intruders. These vocalizations tend to show limited variation and are probably innate, but males of most species sing songs, the complexity of which has only recently come to light. Hummingbirds are now known to be among the few groups of animals capable of learning and repeating sounds. In species such as Anna's and Blue-throated Hummingbirds, an individual's song develops over time and may incorporate various phrases and elements learned from neighbors, even other species.

Broad-tailed Hummingbird

Not all sounds made by hummingbirds are vocal. The modified wing feathers in adult males of some species—most notably the slotted outer primaries of the Broad-tailed Hummingbird—make a characteristic buzz, hum, or whistle as the wings move rapidly in flight. These may serve a function similar to song, which is usually lacking or poorly developed in these species.

BREEDING BEHAVIOR

Male hummingbirds typically combine sounds and visual displays to delineate territory and advertise to receptive females. Dizzying aerial displays may be directed at either rivals or prospective mates, whereas more intimate side-to-side shuttle displays are generally reserved for the females. The mating act itself is brief and may take place on a branch, on the ground, or in flight.

Once mating is complete, the female retires to her nesting territory to incubate her two eggs and raise the young alone. The nest is a cup formed of soft plant fibers and animal hair, often camouflaged on the outer surface with lichens, leaf fragments, or other plant parts. Strong, sticky strands of spider silk serve as the main structural element of the nest, holding its components together and binding it to its support. Nest construction is substantially complete before mating, but the female continues to add material to the lining after the eggs are laid. The incubation and nestling periods are relatively short, ranging from 30 days to 45 days. Many hummingbirds in the southern part of the breeding range in the United States manage to raise three broods per season. The female may begin a new nest while a previous nest is still active, alternating between feeding older nestlings and incubating a new clutch of eggs.

Hybridization in hummingbirds occurs with surprising frequency and can confuse identification. Floresi's Hummingbird (*Selasphorus floresii*), originally described in 1861 by John Gould from a specimen collected in southern Mexico, was included in the 1895 edition of the American Ornithologists' Union's *Check-List of North American Birds* based on a specimen seen in a San Francisco taxidermy shop. The entry was removed soon after it was determined to be a hybrid between Anna's and Allen's Hummingbirds.

BREEDING RANGE

In North America, hummingbirds breed in forest, woodland, desert, and chaparral habitats as far north as southern Québec in the East and southeastern Alaska in the West. Only the Ruby-throated Hummingbird nests east of the Mississippi River, while five to ten species nest in the "sky islands" region along the Mexican border from western Texas through southeastern Arizona. The mild winter climate of the Mojave and Sonoran Deserts and Pacific coast allow year-round residency and early nesting by Anna's and Costa's Hummingbirds.

MIGRATION

Although many tropical hummingbirds are relatively sedentary, most species that breed in temperate climates migrate to take advantage of seasonal resources. The Rufous Hummingbird makes one of the longest migrations relative to body size of any bird, with individuals from the northern edge of the species' breeding range in southeastern Alaska traveling at least 2,700 miles to reach the winter range in Mexico. Spring migration begins in January and mostly follows the Pacific coast. The return route may shift farther inland to take advantage of the abundance of summer flowers along the Rocky Mountain flyway. Like most hummingbirds, male Rufouses typically migrate earlier than females; the first southbound males arrive in northern Mexico by early July.

The Ruby-throated Hummingbird makes an equally astounding migration. Each spring, these little birds, weighing about 0.1 ounce (3 grams) in "fighting trim," fatten up to nearly twice that weight on their wintering grounds in Central America and southern Mexico. In March and April, thousands of Ruby-throated Hummingbirds gather along the northern edge of the Yucatán Peninsula. From there, they cross the Gulf of Mexico to reach the southeastern United States, a nonstop flight of more than 500 miles across the water. During the fall migration, most individuals seem to follow a less dangerous overland route following along the Gulf Coast.

Contrary to the persistent notion that feeders must be taken down to force hummingbirds to migrate, migration is not dependent on food supply. Highly migratory species such as Rufous and Calliope Hummingbirds undertake their dramatic continent-spanning journeys when their internal clocks tell them to do so. Abundant nectar resources, whether natural or artificial, actually help speed the journey by shortening the predeparture fattening process and reducing the number and duration of refueling stops along the way.

Not all North American hummingbirds migrate in the traditional north-south fashion. As in many tropical species, the seasonal movements of Anna's and Costa's Hummingbirds are more limited. At the end of their winter-through-spring breeding season, many individuals move up into the mountains to escape the summer heat and drought in the lowlands, returning in the fall. Like several other southwestern species, the Costa's Hummingbird is a partial migrant, vacating the northernmost parts of its breeding range in winter. Some Buff-bellied Hummingbirds undertake a reverse migration—nesting as far south as the central Gulf Coast of Texas—and migrate slightly north in the fall to winter as far east as western Florida.

The Allen's Hummingbird is unique among the North American species in having two distinct subspecies with dramatically different migration strategies. One of these species nests along the Pacific coast from southern California to extreme southwestern Oregon and winters primarily in south-central Mexico. The other species occupies a year-round range in California south of the breeding range of the migratory subspecies. Originating on the Channel Islands off the coast of southern California, this subspecies is a relative newcomer to the mainland around Los Angeles and is expanding its populations both inland and along the coast.

Costa's Hummingbird

WINTER RANGE

Inadequate supplies of nectar and insects force most North American hummingbirds to abandon their breeding ranges during the winter. The Ruby-throated Hummingbird is the only species in the United States to winter as far south as Central America; the western migratory species winter mainly in central and southern Mexico. In recent years, year-round feeding stations and gardens have created a winter haven for hummingbirds in the southeastern United States. Hundreds of Rufous Hummingbirds, along with smaller numbers of Black-chinned, Calliope, Allen's, Broad-tailed, Buff-bellied, and other western species, can be found each winter from coastal and southern Texas eastward to the Carolinas. Even southernmost Florida, which is oddly devoid of nesting hummingbirds, hosts wintering Ruby-throated and Rufous Hummingbirds as well as occasional individuals of other species. The same phenomenon has allowed Anna's Hummingbird to expand its year-round range northward to British Columbia, and it is now also common year-round on the southeastern end of Vancouver Island in Canada.

Occasionally a hummingbird will linger in an area where its long-term survival is in doubt. Controversial approaches to this dilemma include removal of feeders to force the birds' departure and capture and relocation to a more hospitable climate. Most authorities favor continuing to provide support to the hummingbirds in the form of feeders but otherwise allowing nature to take its course.

OBSERVING HUMMINGBIRDS

Hummingbirds are among the best loved birds in North America, in part because watching them is an easy, largely backyard occupation. Though attracting hummingbirds can be as simple as hanging out a feeder filled with sugar water, many enthusiasts go to great lengths to create an appealing backyard habitat. Some gardeners grow special nectar plants that bloom throughout the season, establish a source of moving water for bathing, and plant lush trees and shrubs to provide an environment for shelter and nesting. Both native hummingbird-pollinated flowers and noninvasive exotics can be incorporated into plantings, ranging from simple flowering window boxes to elaborate ornamental landscapes.

For birding travelers, one of the best areas for watching hummingbirds is southeastern Arizona. Though fair numbers of Anna's and Costa's Hummingbirds are present year round, the diversity of species for which this area is famous is best appreciated from late April through September. Diversity peaks in July and August, when summer rains create a "second spring" complete with a bounty of wildflowers. Southbound migrants overlap with local breeding species and occasional wanderers from Mexico, and feeding stations may host 12 to 15 species of hummingbirds, from the elfin Calliope to the warbler-sized Magnificent and the noisy Blue-throated. Fall migration is also the time when the spectacle of tens of thousands of southbound hummingbirds draws bird-watchers to migration hot spots such as the Rocky Mountains, the Sierra Nevada of California, and the Mississippi Flyway. Migrating Ruby-throated Hummingbirds pass along the Texas coast by the thousands in September, taking advantage of native wildflowers, lush public and private gardens, and feeding stations.

STATUS AND CONSERVATION

Beloved as they are, hummingbirds are subject to the same threats of habitat loss as many other birds. A few tropical species are found in areas as small as a single island, river valley, or mountain slope, making them highly vulnerable to even limited habitat disturbance.

The International Union for the Conservation of Nature lists eight species as critically endangered, threatened, or vulnerable. Though no hummingbird in the United States is currently in such dire straits, relatively little is known about population size and trends for most species. Population monitoring methods that have been developed for other birds, however, often undercount hummingbirds, and specialized monitoring programs are erratic in geographic coverage and lack coordination.

An additional challenge to understanding hummingbird populations is the species' antisocial tendencies. Hummingbirds will spread out as far as available resources will allow, and an abundance at feeding stations has been shown to be in inverse proportion to availability of natural nectar.

Many North American species have adapted to life in suburbia, but most still depend on tropical habitats for part of each year. They must not only have an appropriate nesting and wintering habitat but migratory corridors between the two. Any significant interruption of these routes places their migration in jeopardy. Large-scale threats include residential, agricultural, and commercial development, logging, loss of riparian vegetation to dambuilding, aquifer depletion, replacement of natural desert vegetation with exotic grasses for grazing, and aerial spraying for fruit flies, gypsy moths, and other insect pests.

Even in national parks, wildlife preserves, and other protected areas, the quality of the hummingbird habitat can be degraded by air and water pollution, exotic plants and animals, and land management policies. Suppression of natural forest fires slows recycling of nutrients and limits the growth of nectar plants that require sunny openings in the tree canopy. Life in cities and suburbs, as well as rural landscapes, comes with its own dangers, ranging from pesticides and free-roaming house cats to collisions with windows and transmission towers.

CALLIOPE HUMMINGBIRD

Weighing less than a penny, the Calliope Hummingbird is the smallest bird found north of the Mexican border. The daggerlike, wine red gorget feathers of the male can be extended in an impressive "sunburst" display during territorial or courtship encounters.

These elfin creatures nest in mountain forests, ranging from northern Baja California, Mexico, to central British Columbia, Canada. Most Calliopes winter in tropical southwestern Mexico, but a few cross the Great Plains in the fall to winter in parks and gardens along the coast of the Gulf of Mexico. Occasionally, fall vagrants wander even farther off the typical compass heading for their species. In November 2001, two young male Calliope Hummingbirds gained national media attention when they took up temporary residence in a park in upper Manhattan.

See also

Swifts, page 223

BLACK-CHINNED, BROAD-TAILED, AND CALLIOPE HUMMINGBIRDS

BLACK-CHINNED HUMMINGBIRD
Breeding range

BROAD-TAILED HUMMINGBIRD
Breeding range

CALLIOPE HUMMINGBIRD
Breeding range

ALL FEATURED SPECIES
Historic winter range

Recent winter range extension

- - - - - Rarely but regularly sighted in fall and winter

Beginning in the 1980's, reports of "western" hummingbirds east of their normal range greatly increased. This may be the result of increased observer awareness, greater interest in the feeding of hummingbirds, and an actual expansion of some species' winter range.

ARCTIC CIRCLE

U.S. CANADA

Gulf of Alaska

PACIFIC OCEAN

C A N A D A

R O C K Y   M O U N T A I N S

G R E A T   P L A I N S

U N I T E D   S T A T E S

A P P A L A C H I A N   M o u n t a i n s

L. Superior
L. Michigan
Lake Huron
L. Ontario
L. Erie

ATLANTIC OCEAN

Baja California

Gulf of California

TROPIC OF CANCER

M E X I C O

GULF OF MEXICO

Yucatán Pen.

BAHAMAS
TROPIC OF CANCER

W E S T   I N D I E S
C U B A
HAITI   DOM. REP.

JAMAICA

BELIZE
GUATEMALA   HONDURAS
EL SALVADOR   NICARAGUA
COSTA RICA   P A N A M A   COLOMBIA

STATUTE MILES
0   500   1000

0   500   1000
KILOMETERS

Longitude West 90° of Greenwich

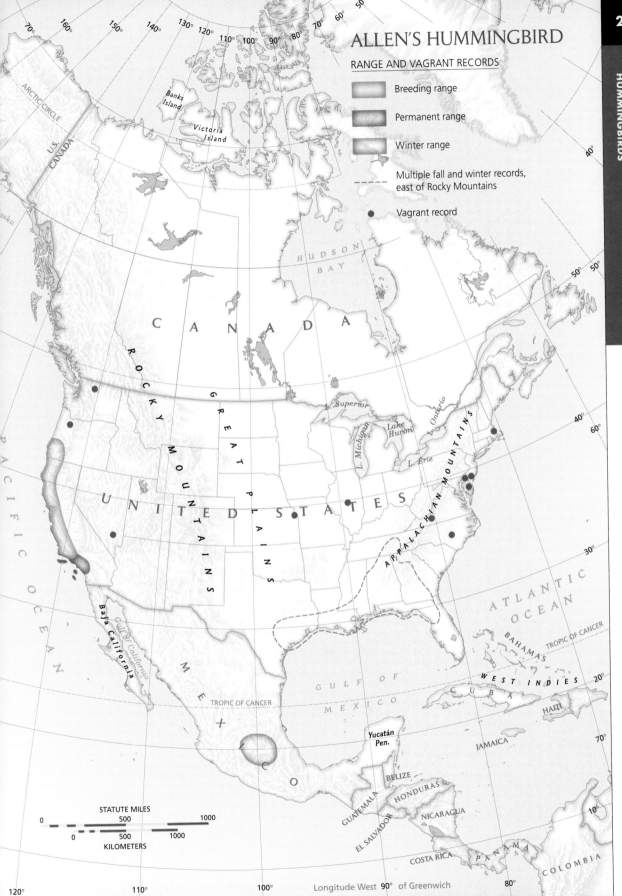

ALLEN'S HUMMINGBIRD

RANGE AND VAGRANT RECORDS

Breeding range

Permanent range

Winter range

Multiple fall and winter records, east of Rocky Mountains

● Vagrant record

ARCTIC CIRCLE

U.S.
CANADA

Banks
Island

Victoria
Island

Alaska

HUDSON
BAY

C A N A D A

R O C K Y   M O U N T A I N S

G R E A T   P L A I N S

U N I T E D   S T A T E S

L. Superior

L. Michigan

Lake
Huron

Ontario

L. Erie

A P P A L A C H I A N   M O U N T A I N S

PACIFIC   OCEAN

Baja California

Gulf of California

M E X I C O

TROPIC OF CANCER

G U L F   O F
M E X I C O

Yucatán
Pen.

BELIZE

GUATEMALA

HONDURAS

EL SALVADOR

NICARAGUA

COSTA RICA

PANAMA

COLOMBIA

ATLANTIC
OCEAN

BAHAMAS

TROPIC OF CANCER

W E S T   I N D I E S

C U B A

HAITI

JAMAICA

STATUTE MILES

0   500   1000

0   500   1000

KILOMETERS

Longitude West **90°** of Greenwich

120°   110°   100°   80°

TROGONS, KINGFISHERS

Jonathan
Alderfer

The trogon and kingfisher families are the sole North American representatives of two orders—Trogoniformes and Coraciiformes. These two families (and two orders) are distantly related to each other; both consist primarily of arboreal perching birds. The two orders have few species in North America, reaching their full diversity in tropical habitats around the world.

The representative species that do reach North America are distinctive, even charismatic birds. Cave Creek, the Chiricahuas, Madera Canyon, the Huachucas, and Ramsey Canyon are place names that conjure up visions of trogons and other special birds of Arizona's "sky islands"—mountain ranges surrounded by desert that are extensions of habitat and birdlife more typical of Mexico. Sulfur-bellied Flycatcher, Rose-throated Becard, Red-faced Warbler, Flame-colored Tanager, and Yellow-eyed Junco are colorful "Mexican" species, but trogons always head the list of hoped-for birds. Elegant Trogons are richly attired in carmine red, metallic green, and burnished copper tones, but can stay well hidden in the forested canyons where they nest. Even so, most first-time visitors get a good look at them by following the sound of their distinctive "co-ah, co-ah, co-ah" calls.

The other trogon species seen in the sky islands has been recently renamed as a quetzal—the Eared Quetzal. Its voice, plumage, and behavior more closely resemble the quetzals of Middle and South America. The Eared Quetzal is not as flamboyant as the Resplendent Quetzal, a bird sacred to the Aztecs and the Mayas with a two-foot "tail," but it is a quetzal nonetheless. Eared Quetzals are rare. First discovered in the Chiricahuas in 1977, they are probably year-round residents in small numbers. Nobody knows how many are in Arizona because only a small percentage of the habitat is visited on a regular basis. The first Eared Quetzal nest was found in 1991 in Ramsey Canyon.

Kingfishers are mundane by comparison. They hunt for fish by plunge diving and are dressed in simple colors. The Belted Kingfisher is a widespread, well-known species. These pugnacious, territorial birds have a strident rattle call and challenge all intruders—even humans. Belted Kingfishers are distributed coast to coast and from Texas north to Alaska, wherever they can find clear water and suitable earthen banks in which to excavate nesting tunnels. Northern breeders migrate south as far as Central America when icebound waters make food unavailable.

The two other species found in North America—Ringed and Green Kingfishers—are specialty birds. Ringed Kingfishers are found only in the Rio Grande Valley in Texas. Big and loud, they favor open perches and resemble oversize Belted Kingfishers, except for their more rufous underparts. Green Kingfishers are just the opposite. The tiny Green sits quietly on streamside rocks or on low branches overhanging the clear water where it fishes. Green Kingfishers are a challenge to find—listen for its "tick, tick, tick, tick" call and look for the movement of its twitching tail. Green Kingfishers are found in some of the same river habitat as Ringed Kingfishers—the stretch of Rio Grande below Falcon Dam is reliable for both species. Farther afield, Greens occur along the streams and rivers of the Edwards Plateau in Texas and along a few creeks and rivers in southeast Arizona.

(Left) **Ringed Kingfisher**

Elegant Trogon: *Trogon elegans,* L 12.5", yellow bill, white breast band

TROGONS

A year-round resident in extreme southeastern Arizona, the Elegant Trogon (above) is a colorful, long-tailed bird. Males have a bright red chest, metallic green head, broad yellow bill, and long barred tail. Elegant Trogons mainly eat fruit and insects that they gather by swooping above vegetation, hovering and plucking prey or berries that are carried to a tree branch to eat. The species is sedentary and perches, barely moving, for long periods of time. During breeding season, males become animated, flying among trees and calling to attract a mate with their head tilted straight up. Trogons nest in tree cavities, often abandoned by woodpeckers, which are located in large sycamore trees along riparian streamsides. The nest cavity is lined with grass, feathers, and debris found nearby, and a pair produces two or three hatchlings. The species is rare in the United States and most trogons return to Mexico during the winter months. In Mexico, Elegant Trogons are numerous, but the status of the species has not been closely monitored to understand the impact of hunting, pesticide usage, and habitat loss.

Range for Elegant Trogon

CLASSIFICATION

The trogons and quetzals—family Trogonidae—are a distinctive family of 39 tropical species occupying their own order—Trogoniformes. They are further divided into three subfamilies that reflect their geographical distribution in the Americas (25 species), Africa (three species), and Asia (11 species). Two species—Elegant Trogon and Eared Quetzal (formerly Eared Trogon)—have reached the Mexican borderlands of Arizona, New Mexico, and Texas.

STRUCTURE

All trogon species are similar to one another in structure: medium-size arboreal birds with compact bodies, short necks, and long, broad tails with graduated feathers. Their short bills have a curved culmen and a notched (or toothed) cutting edge, useful for plucking fruit in flight, subduing large insects, and assisting in nest hole excavation. Stiff rictal bristles surround the bill and assist in guiding food to the mouth. Strong flight muscles power short, rounded wings—a compact shape, helpful during flights around dense vegetation. Their large eyes are well adapted to the reduced light of their forest haunts.

Trogons have small feet and exceptionally short legs (tarsi) that render them incapable of normal walking, but help to reduce their flight weight. The first and second toes point backward, the other two point forward (heterodactyl)—an arrangement that is anatomically distinct from similar toe positions in other bird groups, such as woodpeckers or parrots. Trogons perch in an upright posture with their long tails pointing downward. They require horizontal perches because their short legs cannot compensate for angled ones.

PLUMAGE

The plumage of trogons and quetzals displays a stunning combination of brilliant colors and intricate patterns. In the Americas, the dark upperparts feature greens, blues, or blacks, and the underparts are various combinations of red, yellow, and orange, often with a white chest band. From below, the tails of the different species display dizzying, black-and-white patterns, formed by bars and vermiculations of varying sizes and intensity. The graduated length of the individual tail feathers enhances the effect. A barred or vermiculated wing panel, lacking in the quetzals, sets off the dark wings. The "ears" referred to in the Eared Quetzal's name are wispy feathers that extend behind the eye.

Males and females differ in plumage coloration. Overall, females are less gaudy—the head and upperparts are often brownish, and the colors of the underparts are less intense. Juveniles resemble females. Juvenile Elegant Trogons are identifiable by their white-spotted wing coverts and tertials.

FEEDING BEHAVIOR

The quetzals primarily eat fruit, obtained by "hover gleaning". This involves spotting a food item while perched, followed by a short sally, and ending in a brief hover or momentary stall during which the item is plucked from the vegetation. Trogons tend to target larger items—fruits with pits, large caterpillars, moths, and beetles. Because they consume large food items, they spend long periods perching motionless between feeding forays. They swallow fruits with pits whole and reguritate the seeds, an important method of seed dispersal for some tropical trees. The red, berry-like fruits of the madrone make up a significant part of the Eared Quetzal's winter diet in Arizona. Birds may glean food while perched or catch large flying insects in flight.

VOCALIZATION

Elegant Trogons make croaking or frog-like calls, described as "co-ah, kyow," or "kwah" and a series of "oink" or "quowm" calls. Eared Quetzal calls are different—a loud, up-slurred squeal "squeeeee-chuk," and a less common crescendo of quavering whistles.

BREEDING BEHAVIOR

Trogons are monogamous hole-nesters, establishing or renewing a pair relationship each breeding season. Males establish territories, advertise for females, and defend nests by undertaking extended bouts of singing. A proper nest hole is of paramount importance to attracting a mate. In Arizona, Elegant Trogons favor old Northern Flicker holes in dead or dying sycamores or the male may excavate a new hole in a well-rotted tree.

Eared Quetzal

Elegant Trogons lay two or three whitish eggs, quetzals pale blue eggs. Both sexes participate in incubation, which lasts about 20 days. The female assists the male in providing food to the nestlings. Young birds fledge in another 20 to 30 days, and are fed by the parents until their flight feathers are fully grown. Some juveniles continue to accompany their parents for a more extended period.

BREEDING RANGE

Elegant Trogons breed in the middle elevations of mountain ranges in southeastern Arizona—the "sky islands" that connect like stepping-stones to mountain ranges in Mexico. They have bred sparingly in the adjacent Peloncillo Mountains of New Mexico, but are not well known there. The core range of the Elegant Trogon is in Mexico and extends south to Panama. In Arizona, Elegant Trogons favor mixed oak woodlands and riparian forests with sycamores. In recent years, Eared Quetzals have occupied some of the same "sky islands" of Arizona—but remain rare in North America. They favor higher elevations and dryer forests intermixed with pines. The first Eared Quetzals were discovered in October 1977 in the Chiricahua Mountains, and the first nest in 1991 in the Huachuca Mountains. The core range of the Eared Quetzal is the Sierra Madre Occidental of Mexico.

MIGRATION AND WINTER RANGE

Most Elegant Trogons in North America are believed to move south into northern Mexico during the winter months, but a few individuals stay. Most Eared Quetzals in Arizona are probably resident there, though they may wander after breeding. The few records of Elegant Trogons from the Rio Grande Valley and Big Bend area of Texas involve wanderers from Mexico.

OBSERVING TROGONS

Elegant Trogons are one of the most sought-after specialty birds of southeast Arizona. They are most active early and late in the day, but spend long periods perched quietly. Learning their distinctive calls is the best way to locate a bird. Trogons can swivel their head like an owl, lending their calls a ventriloquial quality. They often perch with their bright underparts turned away from an intruder.

Eared Quetzals are even more difficult to locate. Listen for their calls, and check with the Arizona birding hotlines or local birders for any current sightings.

STATUS AND CONSERVATION

Elegant Trogons and Eared Quetzals in North America are at the northern edge of their normal range, and numbers fluctuate from year to year. The number of nesting failures—whether the result of natural predation or human disturbance—can be high. Birders are duty-bound not to do anything to aggravate the situation, such as using tapes or approaching nest sites. In Mexico, the primary threats come from human activities.

OTHER SPECIES FIELD NOTES

■ **Eared Quetzal**
Euptilotis neoxenus
L 14"
Blackish bill, dark plumage

See also

Northern Flicker, page 248

Belted Kingfisher: *Ceryle alcyon,* L 13", slate-blue breast band, white belly

KINGFISHERS

The only kingfisher species that is a year-round resident throughout the United States, the Belted Kingfisher (above) is a large blue-gray waterside species with a shaggy crest, white neck ring, and long spearlike bill. The female has a rufous breast band. Kingfishers prefer a habitat that is partially wooded near water such as lakes, streams, and lagoons. The species breeds throughout most of the continental U.S., Canada, and southern Alaska. Their characteristic vocalization is a chatter or rattle, often given when alarmed and in flight. The species eats fish, frogs, and insects, and often hovers above prey before plunging into water to capture it. A kingfisher pair builds a nest in a mudbank by using their bills to loosen soil and their feet to extract it, creating a tunnel and underground chamber as a nesting site. A pair produces a brood of five to seven hatchlings. After breeding in Canada and Alaska, kingfishers migrate back to the U.S. and wintering grounds far into Mexico. The population of Belted Kingfishers has declined in past decades and continues to shrink, primarily because of habitat loss.

Range of Belted Kingfisher

CLASSIFICATION

The kingfishers—family Alcedinidae—are a cosmopolitan family of 93 species. They are placed in the ancient order Coraciiformes with seven other families, and are most closely related to two New World families—the todies and motmots. Only three kingfisher species—Belted, Ringed, and Green—inhabit North America. Above the species level, current taxonomy is unsettled. Some experts favor splitting the kingfishers into three separate families.

STRUCTURE

Kingfishers are compact, large-headed birds varying from small to medium in size. The three North American kingfishers eat fish captured by aerial plunge diving. Adaptations to this style of feeding include the ability to hover, a large heron-like bill for capturing prey, and eyes adapted to see in air and underwater. The kingfishers have short legs, well suited to tunnel-nesting birds, and walk with a shuffling gait. Their small but sturdy feet and sharp claws allow them to perch with confidence. The forward-facing toes are partially joined (syndactyl), forming a broad, flattened sole.

The wings are relatively broad with pointed tips, and kingfisher flight is strong and direct with regular wingbeats. Short flights tend to be low over the water, but longer flights can be higher. Most flights made by Belted and Ringed Kingfishers end at open, often conspicuous perches. Green Kingfishers are more retiring and favor low perches with overhanging vegetation.

PLUMAGE

The plumage is rather subdued, a palette of steel blue, deep green, rufous, and white. Males and females are distinguishable by plumage differences, by the distribution of rufous on the underparts and the pattern and number of chest bands. Juveniles resemble adult females and attain adult plumage in their second year. Belted and Ringed Kingfishers have prominent, shaggy crests that often appear double peaked, and a small white spot between the eye and the bill (supraloral spot). When agitated or threatened, these feathers can be erected. The Green Kingfisher has an inconspicuous crown, restricted to the hindneck.

FEEDING BEHAVIOR

The three North American species specialize in capturing small fish by plunge diving, although they supplement their diet with other aquatic animals and flying insects. All three species spend long periods on perches overlooking the clear waters where they hunt. Prey is located either from a perch or while in flight, and attacked from the air. The headfirst dives are sometimes preceded by a brief hover, as the bird lines up its target. Hunting kingfishers appear to compensate for the distortion of the water, the anticipated direction of any escape maneuvers, and the depth of the prey. If the water is shallow, the wings remain partially open, limiting the dive to a few inches. Deeper dives are on a streamlined, high-speed entry. They do not swim, and take flight directly after surfacing. The birds carry fish crosswise to a perch and subdue larger items. The prey is repositioned before being swallowed headfirst.

VOCALIZATION

Kingfisher song is undeveloped, but some soft warbles occur during courtship. Belted and Ringed Kingfishers produce loud, drawn-out rattle calls all year long. These calls are territorial and are given in response to intruders. Green Kingfishers are quieter, producing a subdued series of clicking or ticking notes.

BREEDING BEHAVIOR

Kingfishers are monogamous, establishing or renewing a relationship each breeding season. Courtship rituals establish and maintain the pair bond. These include display flights, feeding of the female by the male, and a variety of vocalizations. Kingfishers are highly territorial, defending their home range aggressively. Pitched battles between males include loud vocalizing, aerial chases, and, in some cases, grappling with their bills with such persistence that the entangled birds fall into the water.

Green Kingfisher

The three North American kingfishers construct tunnel nests, digging into vertical, earthen banks near suitable watery habitat, or use road cuts or rotted trees. This work is carried out by both sexes, but the male does most of the tunneling. Tunnels vary in length—ranging from two to ten feet or more—depending on the species and conditions. No additional material is used to the enlarged nest chamber in the tunnel.

They lay three to eight white eggs. Both sexes share the incubation. The eggs hatch in four to six weeks, and the young fledge four to five weeks later. They may remain with the parents for an additional two to three weeks, as they learn to fish for themselves.

OTHER SPECIES FIELD NOTES

■ **Ringed Kingfisher**
Ceryle torquata
L 16"
Rust-colored belly, large size

■ **Green Kingfisher**
Chloroceryle americana
L 8.75"
Green above, white collar, small size

BREEDING RANGE

The Belted Kingfisher's breeding range extends across North America—from the southern states north to the tree limit of Canada and Alaska. Ringed and Green Kingfishers have large breeding ranges that cover much of Central and South America, but extend into North America near the Mexican border. Ringed Kingfishers are limited to the Rio Grande Valley of Texas. Green Kingfishers occur on the Edwards Plateau of Texas and small numbers are resident in southeast Arizona.

MIGRATION

Belted Kingfishers require unfrozen water for fishing and are migratory over much of their northern range. Migrating birds follow coastlines, lakeshores, and rivers, and can be observed in passage at these locations. Ringed and Green Kingfishers are nonmigratory, although juveniles disperse to establish their own territories.

WINTER RANGE

Belted Kingfishers occupy their southern breeding range year-round. Farther south, migratory birds winter throughout Mexico, Central America, and the Caribbean. Kingfishers are solitary at this time of year, but continue to maintain territories.

OBSERVING KINGFISHERS

Belted Kingfishers are common and easily observed. The typical call is easy to learn and often the first clue that a kingfisher is in the area. Similar calls, though, are made by the Hairy Woodpecker. Perched kingfishers have a distinctive silhouette—big head, large bill, and compact body—a help in identifying distant birds. Ringed and Green Kingfishers are harder to see. The lower Rio Grande Valley is the most reliable location for observing them. Ringed is much larger than Belted and selects higher perches, check their distinctive underparts. The Green Kingfisher is diminutive and retiring—look for it in sheltered areas, perched close to the water.

STATUS AND CONSERVATION

Recent Breeding Bird Surveys document a substantial decline in the Belted Kingfishers. Stream channelization, acid rain, decreasing water clarity, and human disturbance are contributing factors. The shooting of Belted Kingfishers at fish farms and hatcheries is a concern.

See also

Loons, Grebes, page 244
Northern Gannet, page 56
Osprey, page 110

BELTED KINGFISHER

RANGE AND VAGRANT RECORDS

Breeding range

Resident range

Winter range

• Vagrant record

STATUTE MILES

0   500   1000   1500

KILOMETERS

0   500   1000   1500

WOODPECKERS

Twenty-five species of Woodpeckers have occurred in North America. Two, the Eurasian Wryneck and the Great Spotted Woodpecker, are widespread Eurasian species represented by only one and seven records, respectively, in western Alaska. The others are largely resident, nonmigratory species, many not found south of the border with Mexico. With their often black-and-white plumage and stiff, jerky movements, woodpeckers have a formal persona many find appealing. The striking Red-headed Woodpecker, the only species with an all-red head, was the inspiration for the cartoon character, Woody Woodpecker.

Most woodpeckers are primarily black and white with some red on the head (often lacking in females), especially the eight of the genus *Picoides*. Such birds have a general pied appearance with black-and-white barred "zebra" backs. Three *Melanerpes* species (Gila, Golden-fronted, and Red-bellied) fit this description but have pale tan or grayish underparts. The flickers are exceptional, being mostly brown overall, and are untypical ground feeders, searching for ants as their favorite prey.

In contrast with their name, most woodpeckers find food in ways that supplement foraging underneath tree bark. Nuts, berries, fruit, acorns, flying insects, seeds, small vertebrates, and invertebrates living on plant surfaces or on and in the ground compose important segments of many woodpeckers' diets, which may also include grains and, rarely, bird eggs. Many regularly come to feeders for suet or sunflower seeds. Some such as Acorn and, to a lesser extent, Red-headed Woodpeckers hoard nuts and acorns in tree trunks and even telephone poles.

The four sapsuckers fashion rows of sap wells in smooth-barked trees, holes they peck through the bark to areas of xylem and phloem, which they defend against others of their own species. They feed on the consequent sap flow and the insects it attracts, sometimes dipping the insects in the sap as a sauce. The sap wells are important to hummingbirds and other birds, which often nest nearby.

Henry T. Armistead

Pecking per se remains important for all woodpeckers. Nonvocal sounds, especially drumming on hard wood, are important for announcing territory, mate attraction, maintaining the pair bond, or simply as a contact mechanism. Often both sexes drum. Drums are apparently distinctive for each species although they are variable. The rolling tattoo drum of the familiar Downy Woodpecker on spring mornings is astoundingly loud for our smallest woodpecker. Woodpeckers' old, abandoned tree cavity homes are widely used by many birds and other animals, including Wood Ducks, Great-crested Flycatchers, flying squirrels, and many other creatures, sometimes referred to collectively as secondary cavity nesters.

Because of the great impact of their drumming and other pecking activities, woodpeckers' physiology and anatomy have been the subject of study to determine how their heads sustain such impacts. Adaptations include rather long, stiff tails that help support the bird as it works its way foraging or excavating nest cavities on trees and cactuses. The Black-backed and Three-toed Woodpeckers have only three toes, two fore and one aft. Some other species are zygodactyl with two toes pointed forward, two backward. Some have long, coiled tongues that help them obtain grubs and other invertebrates which may be deep inside tree trunks.

(Left) Pileated Woodpecker

Northern Flicker: *Colaptes auratus,* L 12.5", black bib, spotted breast

WOODPECKERS

The second largest species of North American woodpeckers, the Northern Flicker (above) is a year-round resident across the United States with breeding grounds throughout Canada and most of Alaska. Only the Pileated Woodpecker is larger. The flicker has a brown barred back, light gray chest with black speckles, and a dark crescent under the throat. A white rump is visible during its loping flight. Northern Flickers eat berries, seeds, and insects that are caught in midair, but ants, found while foraging on the ground, compose nearly half of the species' diet. During courtship, a pair often displays with synchronized bobbing and repeated calls.

Range of Northern Flicker

CLASSIFICATION

The distinctive woodpeckers belong to the family Picidae, which comprises approximately 217 species worldwide consisting of 28 genera. Picidae in turn are part of the order Piciformes that also includes toucans, barbets, jacamars, puffbirds, and honeyguides. The richest assemblages of woodpeckers populate the New World tropics. As with many bird groups, taxonomy is now in a state of flux because of revolutionary DNA studies, so numbers cited above may change slightly as relationships are subject to future divination, an evolutionary process in its own right. North America's 23 breeding species consist of six genera.

Nine species, primarily black-and-white birds, belong to the genus *Picoides,* including the Downy and Hairy Woodpeckers, two of our most widespread and familiar species. The four sapsuckers have their own genus, *Sphyrapicus.* Until recently they were considered but two species, Williamson's and Yellow-bellied Sapsuckers, but in 1983 the latter superspecies was split into three species, the eastern Yellow-bellied and two western forms, the Red-breasted and the Red-naped. The three illustrate a clinal tendency—an increased amount of red on the head as one goes from the easternmost to the westernmost species.

Six other woodpecker species are of the genus *Melanerpes,* including the Red-bellied Woodpecker of the Southeast as well as the striking Red-headed Woodpecker. Flickers are members of the genus *Colaptes.* Sole North American representatives of their respective genera are the mythic Ivory-billed (genus *Campephilus*) and the nearly as lordly Pileated (genus *Dryocopus*) Woodpeckers. These two genera are represented elsewhere by ten more and six more species, respectively, *Campephilus* being restricted to the Western Hemisphere, but *Dryocopus* verging on being nearly cosmopolitan.

STRUCTURE

Woodpeckers primarily inhabit areas with trees to which they are well adapted. Their stiff tails brace them against tree trunks, taking some of the strain off their short, strong legs, and sharp claws. Their chisel bills enable them to extract grubs, worms, and other invertebrates from underneath the bark and to excavate nesting cavities. Many woodpeckers have long, pointed tongues, sometimes with bristles, barbs, and sticky fluid, that help them secure their prey out of recessed areas in bark or holes made by boring insects.

The tongues are variously wrapped around the skull and/or eye and can in some cases be extended several inches. The bone and muscle structure of woodpeckers' heads are adapted to absorb shock when they peck and drum against hard wood just as the feet, tail, and bill have evolved to support a lifestyle that is spent primarily in an upright posture against tree trunks.

The shock-absorbing qualities of their body build have inspired research by anatomists and physiologists.

PLUMAGE

Our most familiar, widespread, and common woodpecker, the appealing little Downy, exhibits plumage characteristics found in many others of the order Piciformes, especially the eight, usually small *Picoides* species. The Downy is primarily black and white with pale underparts, a barred or pied appearance in the back and wings; the males sport a small red patch toward the back of the head.

Red-headed Woodpecker

These characteristics hold true in three similar species of the Southwest, the Nuttall's, Strickland's, and Ladder-backed Woodpeckers that replace the Downy there.

Males of the mysterious Black-backed and Three-toed Woodpeckers, rare birds of northern boreal forest and the edges of spruce forest burn-outs, have a yellow patch instead of a red one. The six *Melanerpes* species are more varied from each other; they are somewhat larger, less "pied", with more red on the head. The Red-bellied, Golden-fronted, and Gila Woodpeckers are tan or dirty gray-white underneath, with barred black and white upperparts and wings similar to the more pied *Picoides* species. The four sapsucker species, also medium-size, display (except for the striking Williamson's) with generally less sharply delineated black-and-white areas, red on the head, and dirty white underparts. The two flickers differ from all these, being primarily large brown woodpeckers, which allows them to blend into the ground in keeping with their more terrestrial lifestyle. Flickers' bright yellow or salmon-pink-colored underwings and conspicuous white rumps flash strikingly when they fly. The remaining species, the crow-size Pileated and the huge, spectral Ivory-billed (if it even still exists), each the sole representative of its genus in America, are largely black with white wing stripes and much red on the head, with black underparts.

In almost all North American woodpeckers adult females can be distinguished from their mates because they have less or no red on their head. Exceptions include the eastern Northern (Yellow-shafted) Flicker whose female lacks the male's black gape stripe that

OTHER SPECIES FIELD NOTES

■ **Red-headed Woodpecker**
Melanerpes erythrocephalus
L 9.25"
Red head, neck and throat

■ **Acorn Woodpecker**
Melanerpes formicivorus
L 9"
Red cap, white eyes

■ **White-headed Woodpecker**
Picoides albolarvatus
9.25"
White head and throat

■ **Lewis's Woodpecker**
Melanerpes lewis
L 10.75"
Greenish black head

■ **Golden-fronted Woodpecker**
Melanerpes aurifrons
L 9.75"
Golden-orange nape

■ **Red-bellied Woodpecker**
Melanerpes carolinus
L 9.25"
Red crown and nape

■ **Gila Woodpecker**
Melanerpes uropygialis
L 9.25"
Barred rump, brown nape

■ **Gilded Flicker**
Colaptes chrysoides
L 11.5"
Cinnamon crown, paler brown back

■ **Williamson's Sapsucker**
Sphyrapicus thyroideus
L 9"
Black back and crown

■ **Red-breasted Sapsucker**
Sphyrapicus ruber
L 8.5"
Red head and nape

■ **Yellow-bellied Sapsucker**
Sphyrapicus varius
L 8.5"
Red crown and throat bordered in black

■ **Red-naped Sapsucker**
Sphyrapicus nuchalis
L 8.5"
Red patch on back of head

■ **Ladder-backed Woodpecker**
Picoides scalaris
L 7.25"
Buffy underparts, red crown

■ **Red-cockaded Woodpecker**
Picoides borealis
L 8.5"
White cheek patch

■ **Nuttall's Woodpecker**
Picoides nuttallii
L 7.5"
Broad black bar on hind-neck, white underparts

■ **Arizona Woodpecker**
Picoides arizonae
L 7.5"
Solid brown back

■ **Downy Woodpecker**
Picoides pubescens
L 6.75"
Spots on outer tail feathers, small bill

■ **Hairy Woodpecker**
Picoides villosus
L 9.25"
White outer tail feathers, large bill

■ **Three-toed Woodpecker**
Picoides tridactylus
L 8.75"
Barred back, yellow cap

■ **Black-backed Woodpecker**
Picoides arcticus
L 9.5"
Black cap, yellow cap

■ **Ivory-billed Woodpecker (Possibly Extinct)**
Campephilus principalis
L 19.5"
Large ivory bill, white secondaries

■ **Pileated Woodpecker**
Dryocopus pileatus
L 16.5"
White chin, dark bill, black secondaries

extends posteriorly from the bird's bill base. In the Three-toed and Black-backed Woodpeckers, females lack the males' yellow crowns. Sexes are similar or identical in Red-headed and Lewis's Woodpeckers as well as Red-naped Sapsucker. The male and female of the unique Williamson's Sapsucker look so different that for a time early historical authorities considered them to be separate species. There is more difference in appearance between the stylish, black-and-white Williamson's male and the mottled, somewhat moth-eaten-appearing female than there is between an adult male and a juvenile female of any other woodpecker species.

FEEDING BEHAVIOR

Woodpecker feeding behavior varies widely among species and even between sexes of the same species. Depending on the seasonal availability of food, it often varies throughout the year. Most woodpeckers forage in, on, through, or under tree bark for wood-boring and other insects and invertebrates. In the Southwest this includes feeding on prey attracted to cactuses. Some woodpeckers, including the Acorn and Red-headed Woodpeckers, are partial to fruit, acorns, nuts, and other mast. Others, such as the Lewis's, are notable predators on flying insects.

The distinctive White-headed Woodpecker—basically a nearly all-black woodpecker with a conspicuous white head—is specialized and at the same time diverse in its feeding behavior. Although White-headeds feed on invertebrates, especially insects, they are especially fond of the seeds of ponderosa, sugar, and other pines in the mountains of the West Coast states they inhabit. They extract the pine seeds directly from the unopened cones, maintaining distance with their legs so their body feathers do not take on sap, which is often on the cones. White-headeds exhibit further diversity by sometimes drilling horizontal rows of sap wells on tree bark in the manner of the four sapsucker species. As with most other woodpeckers, there are numerous subtle differences between the feeding techniques of the sexes. The White-headeds have relative preferences of tree species, feeding heights, condition of the feeding substrate, and even the pace of foraging.

The closely allied Three-toed and Black-backed Woodpeckers, inhabitants of Subarctic spruce forests, also differ in feeding behavior. The Black-backed feeds mostly by excavating and extracting and is attracted to stands of burned timber. The Three-toed feeds more on the bark surface or just under it and is less dependent on burned-over tracts. Flickers feed much on the ground, especially on ants. Several species, including the Red-headed and Lewis's (named for explorer Meriwether Lewis), store food in granaries, especially the Acorn Woodpecker, notorious for sometimes placing thousands of acorns in a single telephone pole. Ornithologist John V. Dennis patented a woodpecker repellant at the behest of utility companies. Sapsuckers drill hundreds of small holes, known as sap wells, on tree bark, often forming distinctive parallel rows. They, as well as various other birds, especially hummingbirds, eat the sap and the small insects the resulting sap flow attracts. These sap wells do not seem to be deleterious to the trees. Berries and fruits are attractive to some woodpeckers, especially in winter. Downy and Pileated Woodpeckers often consume poison-ivy berries. The Pileated excavates large, easily recognized rectangular

ACORN WOODPECKER

Its intense white eye is a window into the personality of this frenetic but sociable woodpecker of pine-oak western and southwestern canyonlands and coastal oak groves. Seen traveling in small flocks, the Acorn Woodpecker readily visits backyard feeders and even takes sugar water from hummingbird feeders. This colorful bird has a white forehead and cheeks, white wing patches, streaked sides, a light yellow bib, and bright red cap. Small noisy colonies feed mainly on insects, especially ants, and nuts and acorns. Acorn Woodpeckers are noted for creating "granary trees" in the fall by drilling small holes in a dead tree and pounding acorns into them for storage of a winter food supply for the family group. These larder sites are used by succeeding generations year after year in which they have ultimately drilled tens of thousands of storage holes. Nesting is a communal activity in which several adults share in the duties of incubating the eggs and feeding the young. They defend their food stores and nesting territory year-round.

areas in dead and rotten wood, sometimes several inches on the long sides, in search of its favorite prey of carpenter ants and beetle larvae but, as with several *Melanerpes* species, will also eat fruit, nuts, and other mast.

Differential feeding behavior by sex is found in some woodpeckers. Male Downies feed among thinner branches and in annual weeds and cornstalks. Females have more affinity for larger branches and tree trunks. In the closely related Ladder-backed Woodpecker of the Southwest, males and females not only choose different plants but also shift their foraging techniques by season. There is even further variation according to geographical locality. Males have been found to prefer cholla cactuses during the colder months, mesquite in the summer in Arizona, and Joshua trees in California. Males use larger branches, females smaller ones, and they also may forage higher.

California's Nuttall's Woodpecker prefers oaks. Nuttall's females also prefer smaller branches than males and forage higher. The percentage of time that the sexes devote to varied physical foraging techniques (probing, gleaning, or tapping) differs as well. Such division of labor is thought to enable the procurement of a wider variety of prey, a particular benefit in feeding nestlings during the breeding season.

Thus some woodpeckers exhibit a sort of sexual ecological isolation. As with many seemingly uncomplicated animals, woodpeckers and other birds display a high complexity—one is

Red-bellied Woodpecker

tempted to say sophistication—in their feeding and other behavior. Some woodpeckers feed actively in backyards and semi-urban areas. Downy and occasionally Hairy Woodpeckers, and others, are attracted to feeding stations that have suet and fat available. Red-bellied and some other woodpeckers readily accept sunflower and other seeds and peanut butter. The common Downy Woodpecker, in addition to "conventional" woodpecker foods found in tree bark and wood, is often seen feeding on the berries of vines or on cornstalks in agricultural fields.

VOCALIZATIONS

Woodpeckers are more "primitive" than passerines or songbirds. They do not sing but instead have rather simple calls, used variously to express alarm, announce or defend territory, attract a mate, or simply keep in contact or maintain the pair bond. Frequently sharp, metallic, and emphatic, woodpeckers' main calls are a descending rattle (as in the Downy Woodpecker) or a flat rattle (as in the Hairy Woodpecker), reminiscent of the Belted Kingfisher to which woodpeckers are allied.

Other species utter rattles, including the White-headed Woodpecker, usually given in flight or at rest.

Flickers are especially noisy, vocal, and assertive, particularly at the start of the breeding season. At this time an alpha flicker, as with Northern Mockingbirds, can call so continuously one wonders when it takes the time to feed. Some species, such as the Red-bellied, Gila, and Golden-fronted Woodpeckers, and to a lesser extent the Red-headed Woodpecker, emit a whirring call, which rises and falls (except for the Red-headed Woodpecker, whose whirr call is flat), reminiscent of the whirring of wings. Flickers also emit a "wick-er, wick-er, wick-er" call, probably the inspiration for their name.

Woodpeckers also have much nonvocal communication in the form of drumming, often done on hard wood, including sometimes the side of a house. Unlike songbirds both sexes participate in calling and drumming. Sapsuckers and flickers have drumming patterns that are less continuous, more broken-up, than that of other woodpeckers, somewhat Morse-code-like with a pattern of brief interruptions. It is difficult to distinguish most woodpeckers by their drumming, rather easy to sort them out by their calls. The drumming of the Pileated Woodpecker is impressive and easily recognized, a loud striking of hard wood that diminishes in amplitude and increases in frequency as it goes along. This can be heard at distances of a mile or more in calm weather. Woodpecker nestlings make buzzy calls that sometimes draw one's attention to what might be an otherwise unnoticed nest site.

BREEDING BEHAVIOR

Woodpeckers excavate cavities in—usually—dead trees and living cactuses in which they raise young and use for roosting. As with most cavity-nesting birds, the eggs are white. Clutches are usually three to five eggs. Flickers sometimes have much bigger clutches and rarely will nest on the ground. Woodpeckers are monogamous although a few species, such as Red-cockaded and Acorn Woodpeckers engage in cooperative breeding wherein young from previous broods assist variously in raising new young (Red-cockaded) or more than one male or female will breed as a group (Acorn). Most of the time woodpeckers will not reuse a cavity from one year to the next. The old cavities are important, being used by a large suite of other birds, mammals, insects, and even snakes, including Wood Ducks, Ash-throated and Great Crested Flycatchers, flying squirrels, Elf, screechowl and other small owls, bluebirds, bees, rat snakes, mice, and many other creatures. Flickers and Pileated Woodpeckers occasionally make

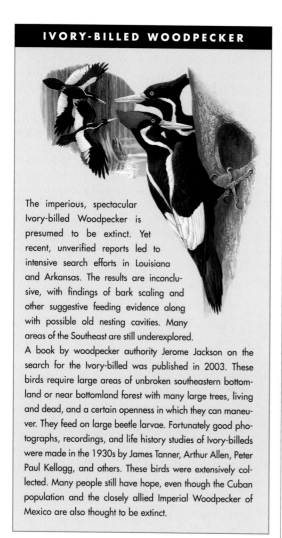

The imperious, spectacular Ivory-billed Woodpecker is presumed to be extinct. Yet recent, unverified reports led to intensive search efforts in Louisiana and Arkansas. The results are inconclusive, with findings of bark scaling and other suggestive feeding evidence along with possible old nesting cavities. Many areas of the Southeast are still underexplored.

A book by woodpecker authority Jerome Jackson on the search for the Ivory-billed was published in 2003. These birds require large areas of unbroken southeastern bottomland or near bottomland forest with many large trees, living and dead, and a certain openness in which they can maneuver. They feed on large beetle larvae. Fortunately good photographs, recordings, and life history studies of Ivory-billeds were made in the 1930s by James Tanner, Arthur Allen, Peter Paul Kellogg, and others. These birds were extensively collected. Many people still have hope, even though the Cuban population and the closely allied Imperial Woodpecker of Mexico are also thought to be extinct.

widely, pairs can be spaced out so that they populate their range somewhat sparsely. Most species are nonmigratory, and their breeding range and winter range are largely congruent. Obviously these birds require substantial woodlands with both sizable living and dead trees or, in the case of some Southwest birds, extensive cactus stands, especially saguaros, used by Gila and other woodpeckers. Among the most widespread are the flickers, Downy, and Hairy Woodpeckers, all of which breed from central Alaska east to Newfoundland and south throughout almost all of the United States. Others have restricted ranges, the Red-cockaded is restricted to old-growth longleaf and loblolly pines with various disjunct populations, some of them covering extensive areas in the Southeast.

Several species are restricted to northern areas, including Yellow-bellied Sapsucker, Three-toed, and Black-backed Woodpeckers. Still others are primarily montane, such as the former three birds in temperate latitudes, Williamson's, Red-breasted, and Red-naped Sapsuckers, and White-headed Woodpecker. In the U.S. the Strickland's Woodpecker is found mostly in small areas of Arizona and New Mexico, the Nuttall's in California. The common Red-bellied Woodpecker is widespread throughout the greater Southeast. Now that the formerly great unbroken expanses of pinelands in the Southeast are fragmented into thousands of separate forests, Red-cockaded Woodpeckers are primarily restricted to an existence of disjunct clans in the few areas where there are unlogged stands of the 80- or 90-year-old trees they require. Other woodpeckers, with the exception of the Ivory-billed, are not as highly specialized in their ecological requirements.

MIGRATION

Although most are nonmigratory, some woodpeckers are prone to wandering within their normal range (e.g. Pileated Woodpecker) or to vertical migrations down from high montane areas in winter (some sapsuckers). Flickers, especially eastern ones, being largely insectivorous, are highly migratory, passing some East Coast concentration points such as Cape May, New Jersey, and Cape Charles, Virginia, by the hundreds, or even thousands, on some optimal fall days. The Yellow-bellied Sapsucker, also dependent on insects as well as the free flow of tree sap, is the most migratory of all. Good flyers, they leave their North Woods breeding areas to winter from the Southeast to Panama and the West Indies, and even Bermuda. The three western sapsucker species are also migratory but not as markedly so. Some are partial, short-distance migrants, as is the Lewis's Woodpecker, fond of ponderosa pine country, but pulling out of British Columbia and the Northwest in winter. Fully 14 species are nonmigratory. Probably because so many woodpecker species are nonmigratory,

nesting cavities in utility poles. Flickers are also notorious for drumming on the side of houses and making cavities there as well.

The Red-cockaded Woodpecker is remarkable in its use of live trees where it excavates holes that may be used for years. Sap exudes from around Red-cockaded excavations and is thought to repel predators, especially snakes. Woodpecker young fledge in 24 to 30 days. Incubation takes 11 to 14 days. Both sexes incubate and assist the young. Usually there is but one brood a year.

BREEDING RANGE

Woodpeckers are found nearly worldwide with the exception of Australasia, the polar regions, the largest severe deserts, and numerous islands, including Madagascar. North America's most diverse genera, *Picoides*, *Colaptes*, and *Melanerpes*, are also well represented beyond our borders, especially in the Americas. Although many woodpecker species are distributed their flight manner is unimpressive. Most exhibit a labored, undulating flight style. Several wingbeats propel them up, then they stop flapping and undulate down, rather deeply so. Often their wings make a whirring sound. An experienced observer in a familiar setting can often tell a Downy Woodpecker is approaching when they hear the labored sound their wings make. An exception is the Pileated Woodpecker whose flight does not labor much. Instead its wings perform an arching, rowing, somewhat crow-like, irregular beat that sends it along in a straight line, often high above the forest, calling as it goes.

WINTER RANGE

As noted above, only some flickers and Yellow-bellied Sapsuckers perform long-distance migrations, though some Red-naped and Williamson's Sapsuckers migrate as far as south-central Mexico from their U.S. Rocky Mountain breeding areas. Another partial migrant is the Red-headed Woodpecker, whose northern and western populations travel to the Southeast in winter. Most range maps in the standard bird guides will show them to be permanent residents throughout their distribution.

OBSERVING WOODPECKERS

Most are easily seen within their ranges, although species such as the Three-toed, Black-backed, and Red-cockaded Woodpeckers and the sapsuckers can be quiet, subtle, and

Williamson's Sapsucker

cryptic. Some, dependent on temporary habitat, such as the Three-toed and Black-backed (recently burned spruce forest) and Red-headed (newly lumbered areas with numerous dead snags), will seem numerous for a few years, then move on to more optimal habitat. But many woodpeckers are vocal, drum frequently, or can be heard pecking, and are, therefore, easy to locate, often flying from one woodlot or tree to another. The rare and declining Red-cockaded Woodpecker is best seen by going to known locations where its clans still persist. Woodpeckers are easiest to locate in the early breeding season. Listen for their pecking and drumming but be aware that the considerable pecking of chickadees, titmice, and nuthatches can sometimes confuse the issue. As with finding any other bird, local bird club contacts and guides are indispensable.

STATUS AND CONSERVATION

Historically the larger woodpeckers were often shot as inviting targets, for food, or because their nut, grain, or fruit-eating preferences made them presumed pests. Many woodpecker populations seem stable, although

their widespread distribution, their vocal manner, and often conspicuous behavior can make their apparent, perceived abundance misleading. With increasing fragmentation of woodlands woodpeckers face an uncertain future. Flickers have decreased markedly in the East, perhaps due to the effects of chemicals on their favorite prey—ants—as well as cavity competition by starlings. The suitability of invasive, non-native ants such as the fire ant, widely distributed throughout the Northern Flicker's southeast range (especially in winter) as flicker prey as well as the effects of these invaders on native ant species complicate the flickers' future.

The lumbering of old-growth bottomland forests in the Southeast has led to the probable extinction of the magnificent Ivory-billed Woodpecker, the devastation of mature pinelands to the alarming decrease of Red-cockaded Woodpecker. Red-bellied Woodpecker has increased and expanded its range into the northern states of the East in the last century. In much of its range the Pileated Woodpecker has increased recently. If sufficient forest areas (including stands of large cactuses in the Southwest) are maintained and woodpeckers are not too heavily impacted by starlings, most species should fare adequately.

The dynamic development of areas of the southwestern United States is of concern, especially for the Gila Woodpecker, the Gilded Flicker, and other birds that depend on the saguaro cactus. If these desert woodpeckers decline, other creatures that use the old woodpecker nesting holes will be affected also.

The future of the Red-cockaded Woodpecker, which favors mature loblolly and longleaf pines in the Southeast, is uncertain. These unique birds require extensive, semi-open stands of large pines 80 years old or more. Lumbering practices do not favor the retention of such stately trees. Many such stands are found on military reservations, state and national forests, and national wildlife refuges, where their retention and would seem to be a given—as long as the enlightened management policies remain in effect. With their pinelands so fragmented, Red-cockadeds persist largely in disjunct populations, out of contact with their congeners. Attempts are underway to relocate birds into some areas where they have declined, including beefing up the pathetic remnant population with breeding-age males at the extreme north end of their historic range in Virginia, where there are some 20 remaining birds.

See also

Nuthatches, Brown Creepers, page 304

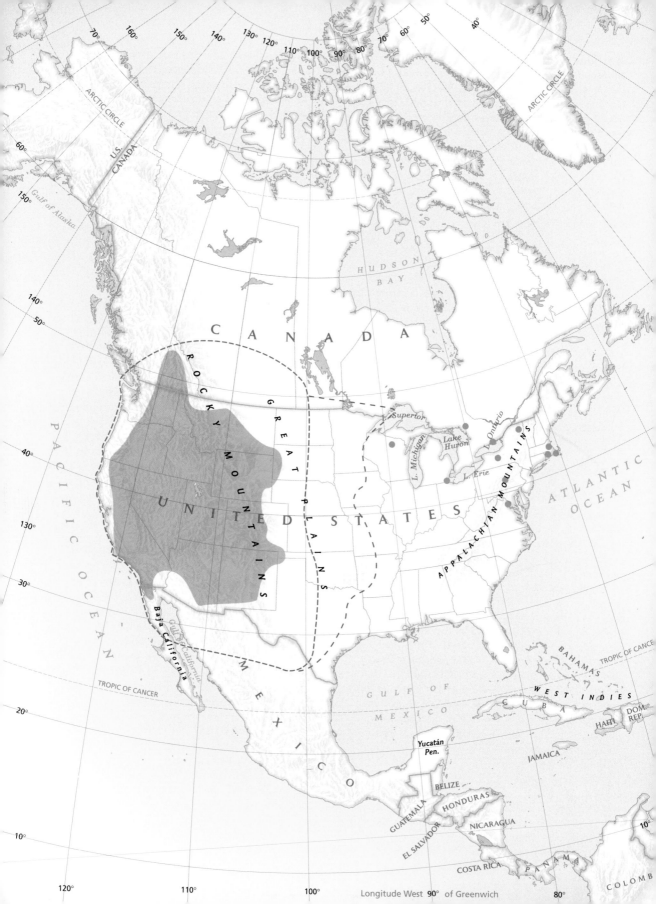

ARCTIC CIRCLE

70°

160°

150°

140°

130°

120°

110°

100°

90°

80°

70°

60°

50°

40°

ARCTIC CIRCLE

60°

U.S.
CANADA

150°

Gulf of Alaska

HUDSON
BAY

C   A   N   A   D   A

50°

40°

PACIFIC   OCEAN

140°

50°

ROCKY   MOUNTAINS

GREAT   PLAINS

L. Superior

L. Michigan

Lake
Huron

L. Ontario

L. Erie

APPALACHIAN   MOUNTAINS

ATLANTIC

OCEAN

U   N   I   T   E   D   S   T   A   T   E   S

130°

30°

Gulf of California

Baja California

M   E   X   I   C   O

TROPIC OF CANCER

BAHAMAS

TROPIC OF CANCER

20°

GULF   OF

MEXICO

C U B A

W   E   S   T   I   N   D   I   E   S

HAITI

DOM.
REP.

JAMAICA

Yucatán
Pen.

BELIZE

GUATEMALA

HONDURAS

10°

NICARAGUA

EL SALVADOR

COSTA RICA

PANAMA

COLOMB

10°

120°

110°

100°

Longitude West 90° of Greenwich

80°

VIS'S
OODPECKER

DERING RANGE

Isolated record

◦— Small numbers appear
irregularly in fall and winter

— Limit of straggler wandering

▪ Combined breeding, resident,
and winter ranges

ecies travels irregularly in fall and
Some years moderate numbers
south of its breeding range;
only a few make the journey. A
anderers are found somewhat
ly in the central Great Plains and
rn Mexico. Some even make it to
t Coast.

E MILES
500
500
TERS

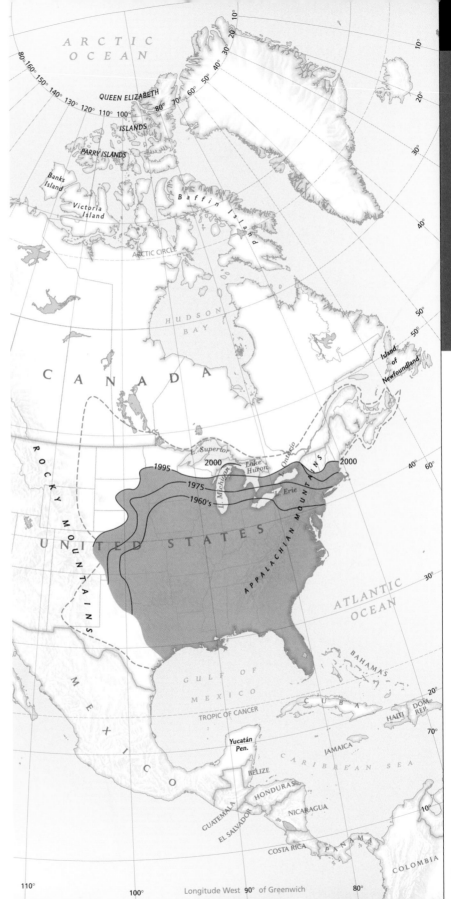

RED-BELLIED ▶
WOODPECKER

NGE EXPANSION & WANDERING

Historic range limit —1975—
with date

Limit of fall and winter - - - - -
wandering

Modern resident range

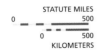

STATUTE MILES

0   500

0   500
KILOMETERS

TYRANT FLYCATCHERS

Christopher Wood

When bird-watchers think of flycatchers, only the confusing genus of unremarkably colored Empidonax flycatchers may come to mind. Although many flycatchers are characterized by dull shades of olives, browns, and pale yellows, it is difficult to define a typical flycatcher in a family of over 400 species. Flycatchers tend to perch upright; they have broad-based bills usually with a hook at the tip; most have bristles near the base of the bill; and many species sally after insect prey. But that is where similarities end. Although many birders prefer to forget about those unidentified greenish flycatchers they saw in the course of a day, few forget the first time they saw a brilliant male Vermilion Flycatcher.

Tyrant flycatchers are a large New World family of some 425 species. The greatest diversity and abundance occurs in the New World tropics, with 208 species recorded in Ecuador alone. Forty-three species of tyrant flycatcher are known to have occurred in North America. Thirty-five species of ten genera are native breeders; the other eight species are considered casual or accidental.

Watching flycatchers can provide hours of enjoyment. No matter where you live in North America, chances are high that you have a few flycatchers nesting nearby. Only the High Arctic lacks nesting flycatchers. Since most species perch for relatively long periods, bird-watchers can usually study these birds with binoculars or scopes. Empidonax flycatchers are generally a bit more hyperactive, tending to fly from perch to perch, actively flicking their wings and tail. But even empids, as this confusing genus is often referred to, are easier to follow than a warbler high in the canopy.

Empidonax flycatchers are a notoriously difficult group to identify. Two of the other most difficult identification challenges are Couch's versus Tropical Kingbird and Eastern versus Western Wood-Pewee. Yet identification of members of these species may be straightforward, *if* the bird is vocalizing. There is probably no other group of birds in North America for which vocalization is more important for identification than flycatchers, and serious birders carefully study vocalizations, structure, and plumage. Even with hundreds of hours of experience, bird-watchers may leave some birds identified only as "Empidonax species" or "Tropical/Couch's Kingbird." And if it gets a bit frustrating, there are always Scissor-tailed and Vermilion Flycatchers to enjoy.

Flycatchers are best enjoyed by birders who are more interested in behavior than identification. Even a single species can provide interesting observations. Eastern Kingbirds, aptly named *Tyrannus tyrannus,* actively defend nests and territories and will drive off invaders the size of a Red-tailed Hawk. Watching several nest areas closely reveals that Orchard Orioles seem to nest in close proximity to Eastern Kingbirds—probably because of the kingbirds' tenacious defense of their nest. The observer will notice that kingbirds are feeding almost exclusively on insects during the summer. When birders think they know everything about kingbirds, they may venture to the birds' wintering grounds in South America and see that their behavior changes completely. There Eastern Kingbirds form large flocks and consume quantities of fruit. Careful observers may find similar contrasting behaviors in other flycatchers.

(Left) Great Crested Flycatcher

Eastern Kingbird: *Tyrannus tyrannus,* L 8.5", white-tipped tail

TYRANT FLYCATCHERS

The Eastern Kingbird (above) of the tyrant-flycatcher family is a common species that prefers open fields with small forest stands and is easily observed on fence wires and treetops. The species ranges throughout the United States, except for California and the Southwest, as well as much of Canada. An Eastern Kingbird can be identified by its dark gray head, back, and tail, its pale gray or white breast, and its white-tipped tail feathers. Its cousin, the Western Kingbird, is similar in size but has a lighter gray back and yellow belly. The species feeds almost exclusively on flying insects and leaves its perch to catch prey in midair. Kingbirds have a raspy call when feeding or defending territory that sounds like "z-e-e-r." Eastern Kingbird pairs build a cup-shaped nest that is placed near the end of a horizontal tree branch, lined with weeds, moss, and feathers. Eastern Kingbird parents will remove alien eggs that are placed in their nests by Brown-headed Cowbirds.

Range of Eastern Kingbird

CLASSIFICATION

Passerines are classified into two suborders: Oscines and Suboscines. The only family of Suboscines that is found north of Mexico is the tyrant flycatcher (family Tyrannidae). The Suboscines do include several other mostly neotropical bird families unfamiliar to many North American birders who have not ventured to the tropics.

While all passerines have a syrinx adapted for singing, the syringeal morphology of the Suboscines is simpler, which often results in vocalizations that are not as spectacular as those of some Oscines. Suboscines further differ from Oscines in mitochondrial DNA organization. The structure of a small bone in the ear that transmits sounds is distinctive. Suboscine songs are apparently innate, unlike Oscines which learn songs.

For field purposes in North America, tyrant flycatchers may be divided into four groups that correspond with currently recognized subfamilies: Tropical flycatchers (Tyrannulets, Elaenias, and allies); *Empidonax* and allies (pewees, phoebes, Vermilion Flycatcher, and Tufted Flycatcher); kingbirds, *Myiarchus* and allies; and the becards and tityras. Asian flycatchers which reach western Alaska, such as the Gray-spotted and Red-breasted Flycatchers, are not closely related to Tyrant Flycatchers and are classified as Old World Flycatchers.

When observing an unfamiliar flycatcher, a birder's first step is to determine to which group or subfamily the bird belongs. Most subfamilies are distinctive, and with only a bit of practice a birder can quickly determine them. Structure and behavior offer important clues. The following sections describe the four major groups of flycatchers, and flycatcher-like birds found in the United States and Canada.

Elaeniinae (tropical flycatchers) is a large and diverse subfamily of small to medium-size flycatchers found in scrub, second-growth, edge, and humid forest in the neotropics. They feed largely on insects but consume some fruits. Nests are varied; some are cup-shaped and others long and pendulous. Most species are sedentary. Only the Northern Beardless-Tyrannulet of this subfamily is a regular in North America; its range extends into south Texas, southeastern Arizona, and the southwestern corner of New Mexico. This odd tropical flycatcher is somewhat similar to an *Empidonax* flycatcher, but smaller, with a shaggy-looking head and stubby bill. Two other species have been recorded as accidentals: one record of Greenish Elaenia from High Island, Texas, in May 1984, and one of Caribbean Elaenia from Escambia County, Florida, in April 1984.

Fluvicolinae includes several species that are found in North America including the *Empidonax* flycatchers, pewees, phoebes, and the Vermilion Flycatcher. These small to medium-size birds tend to be dull colored, perch upright, and are found mostly in forests, along

OTHER SPECIES FIELD NOTES

■ **Greater Pewee**
Contopus pertinax
L 8"
Slender crest

■ **Olive-sided Flycatcher**
Contopus cooperi
L 7.5"
Sides and flanks olive-brown

■ **Eastern Wood-Pewee**
Contopus virens
L 6.25"
Pale throat, darker breast, greenish back

■ **Western Wood-Pewee**
Contopus sordidulus
L 6.25"
Yellow base of lower bill, olive back

■ **Cuban Pewee**
Contopus caribaeus
L 6"
White crescent behind eye

■ **Acadian Flycatcher**
Empidonax virescens
L 5.75"
Large empid with long wings

■ **Yellow-bellied Flycatcher**
Empidonax flaviventris
L 5.5"
Short tail, big head, yellowish throat and belly

■ **Alder Flycatcher**
Empidonax alnorum
L 5.75"
Prominent eye ring, identify by voice

■ **Willow Flycatcher**
Empidonax traillii
L 5.75"
Lacks prominent eye ring, identify by voice

■ **Least Flycatcher**
Empidonax minimus
L 5.25"
Small empid with large head, short wings

■ **Hammond's Flycatcher**
Empidonax hammondii
L 5.5"
Tiny bill, long wings

■ **Gray Flycatcher**
Empidonax wrightii
L 6"
Gray above, long bill with dark tip

■ **Dusky Flycatcher**
Empidonax oberholseri
L 5.75"
Short primary projection, long tail

■ **Pacific-slope Flycatcher**
Empidonax difficilis
L 5.5"
Teardrop eye ring, separate from Cordilleran Flycatcher by range

■ **Cordilleran Flycatcher**
Empidonax occidentalis
L 5.75"
Teardrop eye ring

■ **Buff-breasted Flycatcher**
Empidonax fulvifrons
L 5"
Cinnamon-orange breast, small size

■ **Northern Beardless-Tyrannulet**
Camptostoma imberbe
L 4.5"
Bushy crest, whitish eyebrow, tiny size

■ **Eastern Phoebe**
Sayornis phoebe
L 7"
Dark head and tail, lacks wing bars

■ **Black Phoebe**
Sayornis nigricans
L 6.75"
Black head and breast

■ **Say's Phoebe**
Sayornis saya
L 7.5"
Tawny undertail coverts

■ **Vermilion Flycatcher**
Pyrocephalus rubinus
L 6"
Bright red and dark brown

■ **Brown-crested Flycatcher**
Myiarchus tyrannulus
L 8.75"
Pale gray throat and breast, large size

■ **Great Crested Flycatcher**
Myiarchus crinitus
L 8"
Dark gray throat and breast, rich yellow underparts

■ **Ash-throated Flycatcher**
Myiarchus cinerascens
L 8.5"
Whitish-gray throat and breast, dark tips to underside of tail

■ **La Sagra's Flycatcher**
Myiarchus sagrae
L 8"
Mainly white underparts, little rufous tail

■ **Dusky-capped Flycatcher**
Myiarchus tuberculifer
L 7.25"
Pale yellow belly, little rufous tail

■ **Cassin's Kingbird**
Tyrannus vociferans
L 9"
Dark brown tail with pale tip, dark gray breast

■ **Western Kingbird**
Tyrannus verticalis
L 8.75"
Pale gray breast, dark tail with white sides

■ **Couch's Kingbird**
Tyrannus couchii
L 9.25"
Thick, broad bill, greenish back

■ **Tropical Kingbird**
Tyrannus melancholicus
L 9.25
Long, thinner bill, olive-gray back

■ **Fork-tailed Flycatcher**
Tyrannus savana
L 14.5"
Long, black tail streamers

■ **Gray Kingbird**
Tyrannus dominicensis
L 9"
Gray above, black mask

■ **Thick-billed Kingbird**
Tyrannus crassirostris
L 9.5"
Very large bill

■ **Scissor-tailed Flycatcher**
Tyrannus forficatus
L 13"
Long outer tail feathers, salmon pink belly

■ **Piratic Flycatcher**
Legatus leucophaius
L 6"
Blurry streaks below, dark mask across face

■ **Variegated Flycatcher**
Empidonomus varius
L 7.25"
Larger than Piratic, rufous edge on tail

■ **Great Kiskadee**
Pitangus sulphuratus
L 9.75"
Black and white head, yellow belly

■ **Sulphur-bellied Flycatcher**
Myiodynastes luteiventris
L 8.5"
Streaked above and below, bright rufous tail

■ **Rose-throated Becard**
Pachyramphus aglaiae
L 7.25"
Rosy throat on male

edges, and in scrubby habitats. They feed largely on insects. Nests are cup-shaped. Most species are migratory. Nineteen species are regular in the U.S. and Canada. There are two records of Tufted Flycatcher from Texas. Reports of Cuban Pewee from Florida are currently under review by the American Birding Association (ABA) Checklist Committee.

Tyranninae (kingbirds, *Myiarchus,* and allies) is comprised of medium-size to large rather brightly colored flycatchers that are found in open habitats and forest edges. Many species are migratory. Kingbirds tend to perch horizontally, whereas *Myiarchus* perch upright. Most build cup nests, but *Myiarchus* nest in cavities. Fourteen species are regular in the U.S. and Canada. Nutting's Flycatcher, La Sagra's Flycatcher, Piratic Flycatcher, and Variegated Flycatcher are accidental north of the Mexican border. Fork-tailed Flycatchers are casual in the U.S. and Canada but are now of nearly annual occurrence.

The placement of Becards and Tityras (and a few other neotropical species) is still uncertain. The American Ornithologists' Union (AOU) recently placed them in the superfamily Tyranniodea, but not necessarily within the family Tyrannidae. Rose-throated Becard is the only regularly occurring species in the ABA area. It is found only from May to September in the southeastern corner of Arizona; it is irregular in south Texas at any season. Like other becards, it has a large head and a slight crest. The nest is a bulky globular structure with the entrance near the bottom. The only other species known to have occurred north of the Mexican border is the Masked Tityra—the sole record being from Bentsen-Rio Grande Valley State Park in Texas, during February and March 1990.

STRUCTURE

Tyrant flycatchers tend to perch upright and have a broad flattened bill with a hook on the tip of the mandible. Rictal bristles at the base of the bill are thought to possibly inform the bird of the position or movement of prey in the bill, or perhaps protect the eyes. The one exception in North America is the Northern Beardless-Tyrannulet. Otherwise, with some 425 species, tyrant flycatchers are a diverse group, and structure differs by genera and species.

Understanding structure is a critical part of flycatcher identification. Wood-Pewees appear similar to *Empidonax* flycatchers, but have longer wings, and longer bills. Subtle differences in bill size and shape are important for identifying *Myiarchus* flycatchers.

LEAST FLYCATCHER

The first step when identifying an Empidonax flycatcher—such as the Least Flycatcher at left—is to make sure that it is actually a bird of that family. Both Wood-Pewees and Greater Pewees are often confused with Empids, but such confusion need not occur. Empidonax flycatchers are active birds that frequently change perches and flick their wings and tail. Pewees, by contrast, sit for a long time. They may spread their wings and tail after landing, or to preen, but they do not engage in the quick tail and wing flicks that are characteristic of empids. Pewees also have longer wings and tails. Once you start dealing with empids, watch known-identity birds on the breeding grounds that have been identified by song. Watch them for a time and under a variety of lighting conditions. Don't stop after you have seen one or two birds, but look carefully at as many of the same species as you can. Pay attention to the exact shape of the bill. Some species such as Willow Flycatcher have broad bills, others such as Hammond's have narrow bills. The pattern of the lower mandible is often important. Study the wings, in particular the primary projection (how far the primaries extend past the end of the tertials). Eye ring, throat color, and upperparts coloration are also important to note. Listen to any vocalizations, particularly call notes, which are frequently given in migration and will prove useful to know. As shown here, appearance changes based on age, molt, and season, as well as individual variation.

1st fall

worn fall adult

spring

Whereas the Great Kiskadee is unmistakable in the U.S., several other species appear quite similar in Central and South America, and these are best separated by a combination of structure, overall size, bill size and shape, as well as plumage and vocalizations.

Many of the best clues for distinguishing similar species are based on structure. Hammond's Flycatcher has longer primary projection than the similar Dusky Flycatcher. Both La Sagra's Flycatchers and Ash-throated Flycatchers occur as vagrants to Florida. By paying close attention to structure of *Myiarchus* flycatchers, you may be able to note the smaller size, with a relatively larger head, longer bill, and shorter wings of a La Sagra's Flycatcher.

Structural variations are based on characteristics in the ecology of different species. Pewees have evolved long wings that help with long-distance migration, and the aerial hawking of pewees is fast, powerful and, on average, longer than that of other flycatchers. The Dusky Flycatcher is shortwinged and a short-distance migrant. It is an aerial forager, but its sallies are short, and the species frequently hovers.

PLUMAGE

Flycatcher plumage is subtly colored. Males and females are typically identical. The bright red of an adult male Vermilion Flycatcher is an obvious exception. The female Vermilion Flycatcher more closely resembles other members of this family, characterized by shades of dull greens, pale yellows, and washed-out grays or browns. The flycatchers' dull plumage reduces their visibility to predators and prey. The brilliant yellow bellies of many southwestern kingbirds are stunning, but to identify the species, you often have to focus on shades of gray on the head, structural clues, and vocalizations. Juveniles appear similar to adults with subtle differences in plumage, molt, and feather shape.

Open country birds such as kingbirds and Vermilion Flycatchers tend to be more brightly colored than those of the forest interior. Two species—Scissor-tailed and Fork-tailed Flycatchers—have evolved long tails. In each species, the males have longer tails than the females; but without a systematic study of the genus, it is impossible to tell if these characteristics have evolved once, or twice independently.

Molt timing differs among some species of flycatchers and provides a way to distinguish some difficult species in the fall. The challenging pair of Hammond's and Dusky Flycatchers differs in their molt timing, with

the former molting on their breeding grounds and the latter molting on their wintering grounds. On fall migration, Hammond's Flycatchers are in fresh plumage and relatively bright and contrasty, whereas Dusky Flycatchers are worn, pale, and dull.

FEEDING BEHAVIOR

As their name suggests, tyrant flycatchers eat a variety of insects including flies, spiders, grasshoppers, butterflies, dragonflies, cicadas, wasps, ants, and even mollusks and fish. Many species eat at least some fruits, usually in migration or on the wintering grounds. Most tyrant flycatchers sit on a perch and wait until they spot an insect, then go after it. Some species such as Olive-sided Flycatchers, sally out to grab a flying insect and return to the same or another prominent perch. Others, such as Gray and Least Flycatchers, often fly from a perch, hover, and strike prey. Vermilion Flycatchers frequently

Western Wood-Pewee

fly from a perch and pounce on or capture prey on the ground. Dusky-capped Flycatchers will feed in that style or hover while picking insects from leaves or twigs in the shady interior of a tree. Northern Beardless-Tyrannulets use their short warblerlike bill to glean stationary prey from foliage and branches, more in the manner of a vireo than a typical flycatcher.

Behavior can also play an important role in identification. One of the best ways to distinguish pewees from *Empidonax* flycatchers is by observing feeding behavior. Pewees generally remain perched, actively looking about, but without any wing or tail flicking. When prey is spotted, they fly out and generally return to the same perch. *Empidonax* flycatchers are much more active. Most species flick their wings and/or tail. After sallying after prey, they frequently return to a different perch. The distinctive downward tail movement of the Gray Flycatcher is much more reminiscent of a phoebe than any other *Empidonax,* and this distinctive behavior makes this one of the easiest Empids to identify in the field.

VOCALIZATION

Most Oscine flycatchers have fairly simple vocalizations without musical elements present. Calls are frequently heard throughout the year. Unlike the Oscines, tyrant-flycatcher songs are innate, and the song of any species of flycatcher varies little between geographical areas. Several species of tyrant flycatchers, including all the *Myiarchus* flycatchers, have dawn songs sung by the males just before and at dawn. Although males and

Vermilion Flycatcher

females use components of dawn songs during the day, dawn songs themselves are arrangements of these elements into predictable patterns and occur chiefly in the early morning and to a lesser extent near evening and when it is cloudy.

Many species found in more open habitats, such as kingbirds, have developed courtship displays involving aerial flights. One of the most impressive is that of the Vermilion Flycatcher in which the male flies some 40 feet or more above the ground with methodical, exaggerated wingbeats, puffing out his bright red breast and crown feathers. The display culminates in a song of buzzy twitters near the peak of the flight before he flutters down to his perch.

Vocalizations are extremely important for flycatcher identification. Willow Flycatcher and Alder Flycatcher are so similar that they were considered one species, Trail's Flycatcher, until the 1970s, when they were determined to be a separate species, in large part because of differences in songs and call notes.

BREEDING BEHAVIOR

Most tyrant flycatchers are thought to be monogamous, but on rare occasions a male may pair with two females. Genetic studies also reveal that in at least some species such as Eastern Phoebe, a male other than the male attending the nest may father one or more of the offspring. Timing of nesting varies considerably between species. Great Crested Flycatchers often have nests with eggs by mid-April—one record has a nest with eggs as early as March 14, in Massachusetts. Alder Flycatchers are the last flycatchers to arrive on the breeding grounds, and they don't lay eggs until late June.

Nests among the tyrannids are diverse. *Myiarchus* flycatchers, such as the Brown-crested Flycatcher, build nests in cavities; *Empidonax* flycatchers build cup nests; phoebes and Cordilleran Flycatchers often build nests on man-made structures; becards build large globular

nests usually at the end of a long hanging branch. Some flycatchers such as Eastern Kingbirds actively defend their nests. Greater Pewees often chase jays and other potential nest predators away, and some observers suggest that warblers and other small birds preferentially nest close to this species to gain protection.

BREEDING RANGE

Tyrant flycatchers breed throughout the New World in almost every available habitat. The familiar Say's Phoebe of the open West breeds as far north as the Arctic tundra of Alaska, Yukon, and Northwest Territories, where it is apparently limited by the availability of nest sites. The ranges of several species extend only into the border states of the southwestern U.S. Some species of flycatchers that occur only as rarities in the U.S. breed in South America. The spectacular Fork-tailed Flycatcher that occurs almost annually in the U.S. breeds from Mexico south to the Falkland Islands, but most of the well-documented records of Fork-tailed Flycatcher appear to be of the migratory South American race. The Variegated Flycatcher is another austral migrant that breeds throughout much of South America, but there are records in North America from Tennessee, Maine, and Ontario.

MIGRATION

Most flycatchers which breed in North America are migratory. In general, flycatchers are nocturnal migrants, although some kingbirds and closely related species engage in diurnal migration. Scissor-tailed Flycatchers may be seen in large, loose flocks that can number into the thousands, particularly in coastal areas that concentrate migrants such as near Cardel in the Mexican state of Veracruz. Some species such as Olive-sided Flycatcher, which move from boreal forests in Canada to the Andes in Colombia or Ecuador, travel thousands of miles. Most phoebes travel short distances. Unlike many neotropical migrants, the majority of flycatchers do not cross the Gulf of Mexico, but follow the Mexican coastline. Flycatchers tend to move later in the spring and earlier in the fall than many other birds. Yellow-bellied and Alder Flycatchers are particularly late migrants and are frequently seen in early June. Throughout the West, many birders have hung up their binoculars for the summer before a stray of one of these species has shown up in late May or early June.

WINTER RANGE

Most flycatchers spend the winter south of the U.S. border, and two-thirds of North American breeders depart the breeding range entirely. Most neotropical migrant flycatchers winter in Mexico and Central America. Of the nonvocalizing pewees, the Western Wood-Pewee is probably the only passerine that breeds solely in western North America and winters almost exclusively in South America.

Several flycatchers winter in the southern U.S. Eastern Phoebes winter widely in the East. Great Crested and Scissor-tailed Flycatchers, along with Western Kingbirds, winter regularly in south Florida. Vermilion Flycatchers and Say's and Black Phoebes winter widely in the Southwest. Southeastern Arizona also regularly hosts wintering Ash-throated, Dusky, Gray, and Hammond's Flycatchers and Northern Beardless-Tyrannulets. Tyrannulets and Great Kiskadees are residents in south Texas.

OBSERVING TYRANT FLYCATCHERS

During the warmer months, flycatchers are not particularly difficult to find. Most places in North America have at least one species of phoebe, which often nests on homes, buildings, and other human-made structures and arrives earlier and departs later than others in this family. Since most flycatchers stay perched for relatively long periods, it is easy to enjoy prolonged studies with binoculars or a scope. Flycatchers provide an excellent subject for photography or video.

Flycatchers often conjure images of heat and humidity, but that needn't be the case. An excellent place to study flycatchers during the summer is in Alberta where one can find all but four of the breeding North American Empidonax flycatchers. The Dusky Flycatcher occurs alongside the Yellow-bellied in Jasper National Park. Hammond's Flycatcher is also readily found in Jasper, while Pacific-slope Flycatcher is easily found on the south side of Lake Minnewanka Dam at Banff National Park of Canada.

For the greatest variety of flycatchers north of Mexico, birders must go to Arizona and Texas. These are wonderful places to see the more brightly colored species and to study the challenging Myiarchus flycatchers. While there, listen for a loud descending series of clear notes that may reveal the plain Northern Beardless-Tyrannulet—the sole breeding member of the large tropical subfamily Elaeniinae that regularly reaches the U.S. Rose-throated Becards are also most reliably found in southeastern Arizona in summer.

STATUS AND CONSERVATION

Worldwide, Birdlife International classifies 25 tyrant flycatchers as threatened and 23 species as near threatened. The most threatened bird is the southwestern subspecies of Willow Flycatcher, *Empidonax traillii extimus*, which is a federally listed endangered species. Concentrations of this subspecies are found in areas of nonnative tamarisk, which creates a dilemma for conservation biologists who would otherwise want this invasive, exotic plant removed.

Contopus flycatchers (Olive-sided Flycatcher, both Wood-Pewees, and Greater Pewee) may have a high risk of decline, in part because the genus has the lowest reproductive rate of all North American passerine genera. The Olive-sided Flycatcher, in particular, is thought to experience widespread declines based on Breeding Bird Survey (BBS) data. While the reasons for this decline are conjectural, deforestation on the wintering grounds—particularly in the Andes—is of specific concern. On the breeding grounds, fire-suppression reduces forest openings on which this species depends. The surveys also indicate a significant decrease over the last 25 years in the abundance of Eastern Wood-Pewee. Studies suggest that high populations of White-tailed Deer may lead to lower breeding populations of this species due to damage of the intermediate canopy caused by overbrowsing. Western Wood-Pewees also appear to be declining, perhaps from loss of riparian habitat and changes on migration and winter grounds.

See also

Shrikes, Vireos, page 267

SCISSOR-TAILED FLYCATCHER

Hardly your stereotypical dull flycatcher, the Scissor-tailed Flycatcher is immediately recognizable by its long tail and pearly gray upperparts. Like most other kingbirds, the species prefers open areas. The birds breed in savannas with scattered trees and shrubs, as well as in rural areas, pastures, parks, and towns in the south-central United States and northeastern Mexico. Scissor-tailed Flycatchers are partially diurnal migrants. Along parts of the Gulf Coast during fall, observers may witness hundreds or even thousands flying past in a single morning as they move toward their wintering grounds in southern Mexico and Central America.

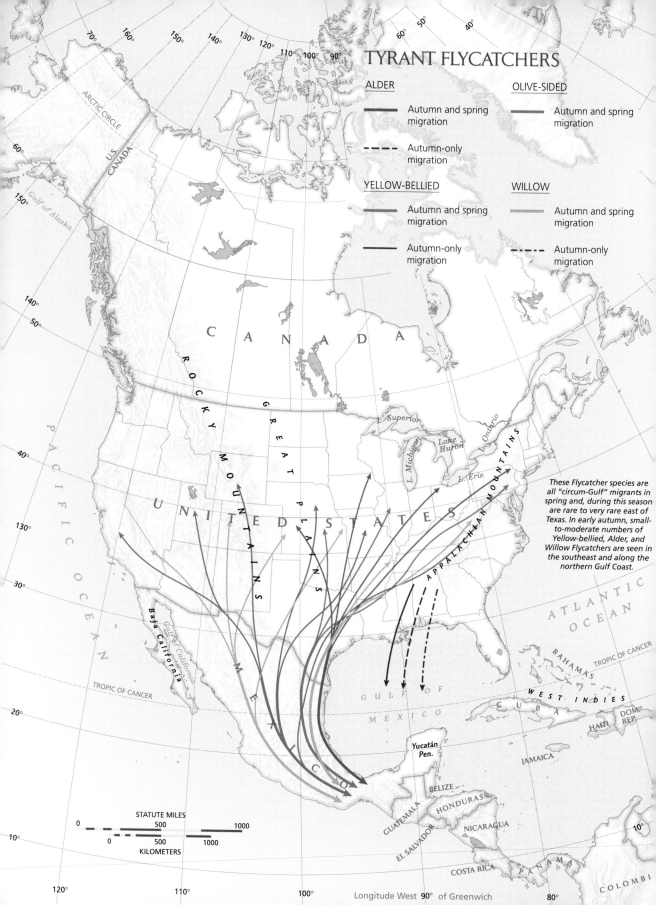

TYRANT FLYCATCHERS

ALDER

—— Autumn and spring migration

- - - Autumn-only migration

OLIVE-SIDED

—— Autumn and spring migration

YELLOW-BELLIED

—— Autumn and spring migration

—— Autumn-only migration

WILLOW

—— Autumn and spring migration

—·—·— Autumn-only migration

These Flycatcher species are all "circum-Gulf" migrants in spring and, during this season are rare to very rare east of Texas. In early autumn, small-to-moderate numbers of Yellow-bellied, Alder, and Willow Flycatchers are seen in the southeast and along the northern Gulf Coast.

STATUTE MILES
0   500   1000

0   500   1000
KILOMETERS

Longitude West 90° of Greenwich

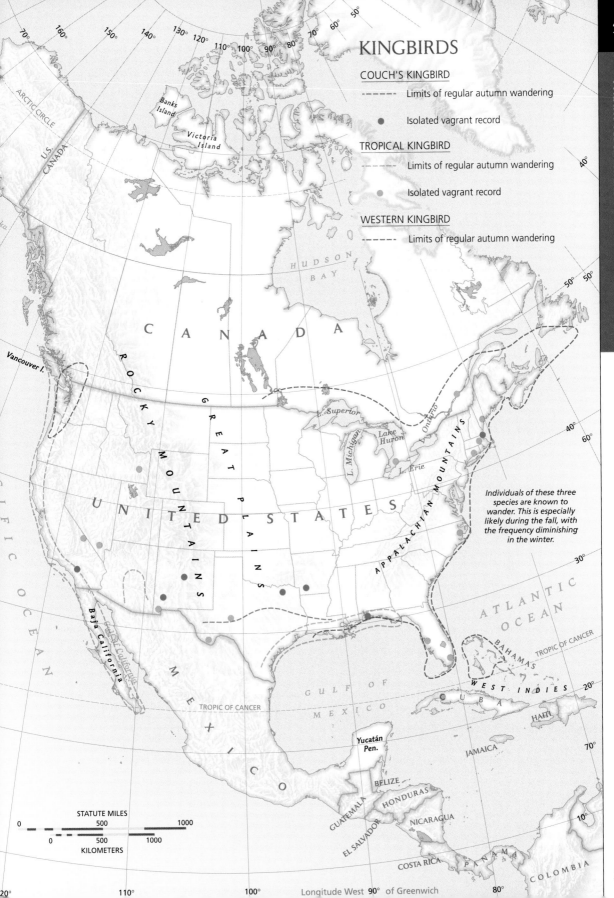

KINGBIRDS

COUCH'S KINGBIRD

- - - - Limits of regular autumn wandering

● Isolated vagrant record

TROPICAL KINGBIRD

- - - - Limits of regular autumn wandering

● Isolated vagrant record

WESTERN KINGBIRD

- - - - Limits of regular autumn wandering

*Individuals of these three
species are known to
wander. This is especially
likely during the fall, with
the frequency diminishing
in the winter.*

STATUTE MILES

0   500   1000

0   500   1000

KILOMETERS

Longitude West 90° of Greenwich

SHRIKES, VIREOS

Shrikes and vireos comprise two closely related families, Laniidae and Vireonidae, respectively. The shrikes are represented in North America by two regularly occurring species of the widely distributed world genus *Lanius,* the Loggerhead Shrike and the Northern Shrike. The Brown Shrike, an east Asian long-distance migrant also in the genus *Lanius,* has occurred eight times as a vagrant to North America.

Brian Sullivan

Vireos are represented in North America by 13 regularly occurring species, and two vagrants, the Thick-billed Vireo and the Yellow-green Vireo, which was recently split from the Red-eyed Vireo. This diverse and widely distributed family breeds in a variety of habitats in North America and typically winters in Central and South America.

Current research indicates that shrikes and vireos may be related to a primal family of crows and jays that originated in Australia, but that debate has not been settled.

The shrikes are unique among passerines for their raptorlike aspect, including a stout upright perching posture, large hooked bill, and predatory hunting style. Both species prey on a wide array of food items including insects, rodents, and songbirds, the last sometimes larger than the shrikes themselves. Shrikes and vireos both possess hooked beaks, but the shrike's beak is larger and notched, similar to a falcon's.

Historically referred to as butcherbirds, due to their habit of impaling prey items on barbed wire, thorns, or other sharp objects, shrikes have long been the subject of interest and wonder to birders and scientists alike. The two species of North American shrikes cover a continent-wide breeding distribution.

The aptly named Northern Shrike occurs at higher latitudes than the more southerly breeding Loggerhead Shrike. The Northern Shrike is also widely distributed in northern Europe and Asia, where it is known as Great Gray Shrike.

Vireos are an important and familiar component of North America's avifauna. Birders may encounter large numbers of certain species in local migrant traps during fall and spring, such as Warbling Vireos in the West and Red-eyed Vireos in the East. However, they may be forced to trek into the hottest or most remote areas of the United States in search of several other representatives of this family such as the endangered Black-capped Vireo and the elusive Gray Vireo.

Like the shrikes, vireos occur in a wide range of habitats—from the White-eyed Vireo, specializing in secondary deciduous scrub habitat in the East, to the mangrove-nesting Black-whiskered Vireo of Florida, and the Philadelphia Vireo of northern latitudes and early- to mid-successional forests.

Vireos are typically drab passerines, characterized by their short, blunt, faintly hooked bills, and bluish legs. Only one species, the Black-capped Vireo, is sexually dimorphic, while most others show little to no plumage differences between the sexes. Vireos are often detected moving methodically through the trees gleaning insects, in association with feeding flocks of migrating passerines.

The shrike populations are mysteriously in decline, due mainly to habitat change and loss. Vireo populations vary widely, some of which are stable, whereas others, such as the Black-capped Vireo, are endangered, threatened primarily by habitat loss and parasitism by Brown-headed Cowbirds.

(Left) Yellow-throated Vireo

Loggerhead Shrike: *Lanius ludovicianus*, L 9", whitish underparts, black mask meets across bill

SHRIKES

One of the most wide-ranging shrikes across the lower United States and into Mexico, as well as Canada, the Loggerhead Shrike (above) is a species that prefers open fields that are dotted with shrubs and small trees. Loggerhead shrikes are smaller and grayer than Northern Shrikes and have a smaller, less hooked bill. Sometimes confused with mockingbirds because of their gray and white plumage, Loggerhead Shrikes have a thin black mask across the eyes that mockingbirds lack. Shrikes commonly perch atop a short tree or bush at the edge of an open field to hunt for prey. They mainly feed on insects but also take small birds and rodents and often store their prey by impaling it on a sharp tree limb or thorn. A Loggerhead Shrike pair builds a nest of twigs lined with bark in a bush or tree with dense foliage. A brood often consists of five or six young that are cared for by both parents. Loggerhead Shrikes have seriously declined in the Northeast and Midwest because of habitat loss of open meadows and the increase of suburban sprawl.

Range of Loggerhead Shrike

CLASSIFICATION

The shrikes—family Laniidae—are in the order Passeriformes a large and diverse group of birds containing all passerines, or perching birds, including warblers, sparrows, and buntings. Although shrikes superficially resemble raptors in size, shape, and habits, they are taxonomically unrelated, and the resemblance may be a case of convergent evolution, whereby both groups have evolved to occupy a similar niche.

STRUCTURE

Shrikes are medium-size, long-tailed passerines well adapted to take larger vertebrate prey items. They are characterized by having a large head (hence the name Loggerhead), stout hooked bill for seizing and tearing, relatively plump, round bodies, and long, graduated tails. Their characteristic perched silhouette is often referred to as resembling the shape of a lollipop. In flight they appear short-winged and long-tailed; both species have characteristic white wing patches at the primary bases. Their flight is low and bounding, undulating between wing beats, very different overall from that of the similarly plumaged Northern Mockingbird.

PLUMAGE

The two species of North American shrikes are dapper birds, clad only in gray, black, and white. Both species are similar in appearance, having gray backs and heads, the latter with a characteristic black mask stretching back from the bill base through the auriculars. The width of this mask can be a useful feature for separating these two species—Northern having a narrow black mask and Loggerhead typically having a more broad and distinct mask. Both species have black wings, and mainly white underparts. Northern Shrikes typically show faint gray barring below as adults, whereas Loggerheads are unmarked below. Both species' long, graduated tails are primarily black with white tips. There are no sex-related differences in plumage; however, there are marked age-related differences. Juvenile Northern Shrikes are generally washed with brown throughout their first fall and spring, appearing barred below with pale brown and sometimes appearing rusty overall. Juvenile Loggerhead Shrikes are also tinged in brown—although this fades by early fall—and sometimes they are marked with weak, grayish barring below.

FEEDING BEHAVIOR

Shrikes are primarily perch hunters, sitting for long periods in the open in search of terrestrial prey. Typically, shrikes make short sallies or stoops on prey items from a favored perch, often returning to the same perch for prolonged periods. Loggerhead Shrikes are more adept at catching insects, a main staple of their diet, and can be seen foraging aerially on calm days. Shrikes commonly store prey when it is abundant, impaling prey on sharp spikes, or forks in trees, for consumption later. Larders can contain several prey items, the sight of which may be considered gruesome by someone unfamiliar with the species. While not possessing the powerful talons of a raptor needed to secure prey for tearing, shrikes often rip apart impaled prey items with their powerful bills and neck muscles.

VOCALIZATION

Shrikes have an array of vocalizations ranging from a pleasant, almost warbling song, to harsh alarm and begging calls. They are both loud species, and are easily detected when vocalizing; breeding songs can be soft in tone. Both species also use begging calls in courtship and pair bonding. Begging calls of juveniles are similar.

BREEDING BEHAVIOR

Both shrikes build bulky, cup-shaped stick nests in small shrubs or trees. Breeding displays can be intricate, but typically consist of various offerings from male to female, coupled with head bowing and wing fluttering. The female typically begs for food during pair bonding.

BREEDING RANGE

The Northern Shrike breeds across the taiga belt stretching from Alaska to Labrador. It is a bird of forest edge and boggy areas requiring small trees and shrubs for nesting. The Loggerhead Shrike breeds over a wider area, stretching from Florida through the prairie states as far north as southern Canada, and as far west as the California coast. Two subspecies, *anthonyi* and *mearnsi,* occupy the California Channel Islands. Loggerhead Shrikes breed in more open habitats than Northern Shrikes, often using isolated trees and shrubs for their nest.

MIGRATION

Northern Shrikes occur year-round in part of their breeding range, but more typically this species moves south to winter in southern Canada and the northern United States. They periodically undergo southward invasions, when large numbers occur at the southern

limit of this species' range; typically a large proportion of these birds are juveniles. Loggerhead Shrikes are resident across the majority of their breeding range, however, populations breeding in the northern portion of this species' range are medium-distance migrants. Those breeding in the upper prairie provinces winter in Texas and Mexico, whereas information for western and eastern migrants is limited. Both species are thought to be diurnal migrants, although neither can be seen at typical migrant traps. They move only short distances stopping to feed for up to several days.

WINTER RANGE

Northern Shrikes winter across a wide area including central Canada and the upper reaches of the lower 48 states. Loggerhead Shrikes are more variable, the majority being resident over much of their range; however, northern populations winter in areas south and east of normal breeding areas in Mexico. Winter range of the western migrant subspecies remains poorly known. Northern migrants also augment resident populations in winter, as on the central plateau of Mexico.

Brown Shrike

OBSERVING SHRIKES

Shrikes are conspicuous and easily seen throughout most of the year. They can be found perched atop trees and along roadside fences, often in the fashion typical of the American Kestrel. Shrikes hunt from exposed perches and subsequently are readily spotted. During inclement weather, both species will spend long periods perched in dense cover, easily escaping detection. Once considered common, Loggerhead Shrikes are increasingly difficult to see across much of their range. Northern Shrikes are difficult to find in their scattered, remote breeding locations; however, on migration and during invasion years they can be found with relative ease across much of the northern U.S. and southern Canada.

STATUS AND CONSERVATION

Northern Shrikes have generally escaped contact with humankind on their remote breeding grounds, and consequently little is known about their conservation status. Nearctic populations of this species appear steady, or perhaps in slight decline, but trends are viewed with skepticism for a variety of reasons. This species' natural rarity and remote breeding locations make long-term monitoring difficult, and its propensity for poorly understood irruptive dispersal to the south makes the analysis of Christmas Bird Count data difficult.

See also

Vultures, Eagles, Hawks, Falcons, page 107

Acorn Woodpecker, page 250

OTHER SPECIES FIELD NOTES

■ **Brown Shrike**
Lanius cristatus
L 7.5"
Brown upperparts, black mask

■ **Northern Shrike**
Lanius excubitor
L 10"
Lightly barred underparts, black mask separated by bill

Red-eyed Vireo: *Vireo olivaceus*, L 6", gray crown with dark border, green back

VIREOS

Often the only bird singing during hot, midsummer days, is the Red-eyed Vireo (above), a common forest-canopy bird, difficult to see but easily recognized by its unique sing-song "here-I-am, where-are-you." Its characteristic ruby-red eye has a white stripe above and a darker one along the eye line. This foliage-foraging species ranges throughout most of the United States and Canada except for the Southwest and lower Pacific Northwest. Vireos may eat fruits and berries but favor leaf-dwelling insects and caterpillars in deciduous forests. Red-eyed Vireos choose a nesting site on horizontal tree limbs, and the female lines the nest with grasses and other forest understory debris. During incubation the male often feeds the female, and both parents care for their small brood. Red-eyed Vireos are migratory birds that winter in Central and South America. Although common in the eastern United States, the species may be in decline elsewhere in its range because of deforestation in both the Northern and Southern Hemisphere.

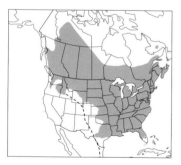

Range of Red-eyed Vireo

CLASSIFICATION

The vireos—family Vireonidae—are included in the order Passeriformes, comprising the large and diverse group of birds containing all passerines. As recently as 1997 the American Ornithologists' Union split the Solitary Vireo complex into three species, Plumbeous, Cassin's, and Blue-headed Vireos, so that in North America we currently have 13 regularly occurring species. The Thick-billed and Yellow-green Vireos were split from the Red-eyed Vireo and are occasional visitors to the southernmost United States. Vireos, as distinctly different in appearance as the Yellow-throated and the Blue-headed, are known to hybridize, and their feather patterns and morphology are similar. But scientists argue that in spite of these shared features they are separate species. A firm definition of species may never be settled upon in the scientific community, so we may see more splits in this family in the future. Vireos have been shown to be genetically similar to shrikes; however, the two groups outwardly share few noticeable features. Vireos superficially resemble warblers and kinglets, but they form a distinct group based on structure, most notably bill shape and leg color.

STRUCTURE

Vireos are small passerines, roughly comparable in size to warblers and sparrows, with notably thick, blunt, and mildly hooked bills, appropriate both for capturing insects by gleaning or flycatching, and for eating fruits and berries. Vireos are shaped much like warblers, but they are more heavily built, and often appear rather stout and short-tailed. Vireos range in size from the small, 4 1/2 inch-long Black-capped Vireo to the relatively large Black-whiskered Vireo at about 6 1/4 inches long. The thick blue legs of vireos are an excellent field mark and can be useful in the separation of similarly plumaged species such as Hutton's Vireo and Ruby-crowned Kinglet. The blunt bill shared by all vireos is a good field mark when comparing them with species that often cause confusion such as warblers and kinglets.

PLUMAGE

Vireos are generally plain birds with subtle markings, but several species can appear striking in the field. They vary in plumage from largely yellow (White-eyed Vireo), to all gray (Gray Vireo), to smartly patterned with dark caps, yellow underparts and green backs (Black-capped and Blue-headed Vireo). The Yellow-throated Vireo is the only vireo with a bright yellow throat and breast and white belly. In general, vireos fall into one of three plumage categories: relatively monochromatic, plain birds of one general color; birds with eye lines, dark backs, and paler underparts; and birds with spectacles, darker heads and backs, and pale underparts. Only the Black-capped Vireo is truly sexually dimorphic—with males having dark black heads replaced by dark gray on females—and displays delayed-plumage maturation, with first-year males still having gray, rather than black napes. There are no marked age-related differences in plumage; some species can be aged on the basis of eye color. Possible yet difficult to detect in the field, juvenile White-eyed and Red-eyed Vireos have brown eyes throughout their first year, turning white and red respectively, during their second year.

Blue-headed Vireo

fruit eating. Required moisture seems to be derived from food, but the White-eyed Vireo has been seen to collect dewdrops. Vireos typically forage more slowly and methodically than warblers, moving about thickets and trees with a stealthy, deliberate pace. Bell's Vireos have been observed holding a hard-bodied insect with a foot while hammering it with their bill to soften it up before eating it. A few species are quite active in their foraging techniques. The Bell's Vireo, for instance, often flicks its wings while feeding, in a manner akin to that of the similarly plumaged Ruby-crowned Kinglet. The Blue-headed often prefers to sally, or pick insects off a twig or leaf while in flight, consuming over half its food this way. Vireos are generalists in terms of foraging resources. Several species such as the Gray Vireo are known to change their diet from primarily insects during the breeding season to fruits and berries during fall and winter. There are two main reasons for this change. The first is the decline in the insect population with the onset of cooler weather. The second, and more important, reason is that fruit is high in carbohydrates that are converted to fat, the fuel of migration, and fruit is relatively easy to digest. In preparation for migration, birds engage in a behavior known as hyperphagia, or overeating, to store fat to fuel the long flight ahead, often increasing their body weight by 30 to 50 percent or more. In the East, it is not uncommon to encounter many Red-eyed Vireos foraging on berries in a single tree during fall migration.

FEEDING BEHAVIOR

Vireo feeding habits are as diverse as the group itself. They are adept at aerial foraging, insect gleaning, and

OTHER SPECIES FIELD NOTES

- **Black-capped Vireo**
  Vireo atricapillus
  L 4.5"
  Black head, white spectacles

- **White-eyed Vireo**
  Vireo griseus
  L 5"
  White iris, yellow spectacles

- **Thick-billed Vireo**
  Vireo crassirostris
  L 5.5"
  Large, stout bill, broken spectacles

- **Yellow-throated Vireo**
  Vireo flavifrons
  L 5.5"
  Yellow throat and spectacles

- **Bell's Vireo**
  Vireo bellii
  L 4.75"
  One bright wing bar, varies geographically

- **Hutton's Vireo**
  Vireo huttoni
  L 5"
  Pale lores, heavy bill

- **Gray Vireo**
  Vireo vicinior
  L 5.5"
  Plain gray plumage, white eye ring, long tail

- **Blue-headed Vireo**
  Vireo solitarius
  L 5"
  Blue-gray hood, green back, white spectacles

- **Plumbeous Vireo**
  Vireo plumbeus
  L 5.5"
  Gray head and back, white spectacles

- **Cassin's Vireo**
  Vireo cassinii
  L 5"
  Dull blue-gray hood, white spectacles

- **Yellow-green Vireo**
  Vireo flavoviridis
  L 6"
  Yellow-green face, bright yellow undertail

- **Black-whiskered Vireo**
  Vireo altiloquus
  L 6.25"
  Dark malar stripe, green-brown back

- **Philadelphia Vireo**
  Vireo philadelphicus
  L 5.25"
  Dark eye line, yellowish breast

- **Warbling Vireo**
  Vireo gilvus
  L 5.25"
  White eyebrow, pale face pattern and lores

VOCALIZATION

The vocalizations of vireos are well known to birders. For the experienced ear, it can be easy to pick out the simple repetitive phrases of the vireos amid the pre-dawn cacophony. Being able to tell just which species of vireo is singing is another matter. Several species, such as Red-eyed, Philadelphia, and Blue-headed Vireos, sound very much alike, and it takes a keen ear to learn to distinguish each species. Key differences are found in tone and pitch, as well as the quality, being either smooth or sweet, or having varying degrees of a burry quality. White-eyed nestlings beg with peep sounds that grow louder with age. Fledglings begin to chatter like adults, and young birds are singing within one month. The aptly named Warbling Vireo captured the heart of one Dawson back in 1923, who described it as "Fresh as apples and as sweet as apple blossoms...." It does sing a sweet warbling song, ending in an emphatic up-slurred note, a key difference from the otherwise similar song of the Purple Finch. The male is known to persist in song even while dutifully incubating the eggs. Or, speaking of the Red-eyed Vireo,

Bradford Torrey said in 1889, "I have always thought that whoever dubbed this vireo the 'preacher' could have had no very exalted opinion of the clergy." Bell's, Black-capped and White-eyed Vireos also have grating, jumbled, agitated phrases run together in a hyper-sounding, displeasing song. White-eyeds are known for continuing to sing during the heat of the summer, while all other birds are quiet, trying to stay cool. Vireos make harsh, scolding calls when agitated, often in the presence of other birds, human disturbance, or predators. They are often among the noisiest of passerines in a mixed species flock, particularly when agitated.

BREEDING BEHAVIOR

White-eyed Vireo females seem to choose male partners as they wander from one male's territory to another until finding a mate that meets their requirements. Males are usually first to arrive in the nesting area and pair bonding takes place within a day or two after the arrival of the females. In most cases vireos are monogamous for the breeding season. The female Blue-headed will chase intruding females and males from her nesting territory. Courtship and pair displays are limited in vireos, and consist mainly of chasing events initiated by either sex, nest building, or copulatory displays in which there is a substantial amount of wing fluttering, similar to shrikes. However, the male Red-eyed Vireo will often chase a female, even pinning her to the ground to emphasize his decision, and both sexes are known to aggressively peck during courtship. Males also offer food as enticements. All vireos nest above ground level in trees and occasionally in shrubs, building characteristic, suspended cup nests, placed in the forks of branches often near the outer edge. Females tend to choose the nest site and both participate in nest construction. In Volume 168 of the *Birds of North America* Steve L. Hopp describes the construction of a White-eyed Vireo nest: "Nest building begins several days after pairing. Both adults participate, collecting spider and caterpillar silk, attaching it to forked branches, creating a cup of lacework caterpillar silk or until a wad of webbing fills the fork. Birds then attach plant matter inside and out and shape cup with their bodies by settling into the mass and rocking or shifting their weight. Female alone lines nest. Nest building takes three to five days." This is typical of the vireo nest-building process.

BREEDING RANGE

Vireos breed singly in a variety of habitats across North America. Some species, like the Hutton's Vireo, are specialists, found only in restricted ranges of the West Coast region. The Gray Vireo inhabits only the hot, arid regions of California, Arizona, New Mexico, and Texas, and the endangered Black-capped Vireo breeds only in isolated areas of Texas and Oklahoma. Some species, such as the Philadelphia and Blue-headed Vireos, exploit the generous insect hatches available during the northern Canadian summer at relatively high latitudes and undertake long-distance migrations to winter in Mexico and Central America. Others are tropical in distribution, such as the Black-whiskered Vireo, which breeds among the hardwood forests and mangrove thickets bordering the south Florida coasts. The Red-eyed Vireo is one of the most common songbirds in eastern North America. Its breeding range extends to the Pacific Northwest and into northern Canada. It is absent in the more arid Southwest. The Warbling Vireo has the greatest breeding range of all North American vireos, extending east to west and north into Canada and south into Mexico. It is absent

BLACK-CAPPED VIREO

The Black-capped Vireo, listed as federally endangered by the U.S. Fish and Wildlife Service, breeds in some of the hottest and most remote areas in the United States. Its last remaining stronghold is the Edwards Plateau of central Texas; its former range extended throughout similar habitat in Kansas and Oklahoma. The Black-capped Vireo has lost ground due to suppression of fire in its favored early successional habitat, primarily composed of scrub oak, and the proliferation of Brown-headed Cowbird parasitism. At Ft. Hood, Texas, research and conservation efforts are underway to stabilize and protect the Black-capped Vireo. Small satellite populations of this species are being discovered in some areas of its former range, but it is still in jeopardy. Innovative conservation tactics are being tested, and the vireos are responding positively to human-altered habitat and to Brown-headed Cowbird control measures, suggesting a positive direction for the recovery of this species.

only from the Southeast. As a family, vireos breed across the entire North American continent.

MIGRATION

Vireos range from being resident to being medium- and long-distance migrants. Hutton's Vireo is resident throughout its range, and is considered to be the only nonmigratory vireo in the United States. Individuals are known to migrate into Mexico, and some move from higher breeding elevations into lower zones, restricting their movement within preferred evergreen forests that provide insect foraging year-round.

Overall, the migratory movements of the Hutton's Vireo are poorly understood. The majority of vireos are medium-distance migrants, wintering in the southern United States, Mexico, and Central America, many with resident tropical populations. These may include: Bell's, Warbling, Black-whiskered, Yellow-green, Thick-billed, Cassin's, Plumbeous, Blue-headed, Black-capped, Yellow-throated, Gray, and White-eyed Vireos. Two species, the Philadelphia and Red-eyed Vireos, are true long-distance migrants. The Philadelphia Vireo winters in southern Central America and the Red-eyed winters in the Amazon Basin of South America. Vireos are nocturnal migrants, moving long distances at night with many other species of migrant passerines. In the spring, they move north with the wind, following a passing warm front, and in the fall, they follow a cold front south. Like most passerines, vireos tend to migrate at a height of 2,000 to 6,500 feet, changing altitude for more favorable wind conditions when necessary. Many fly below 2,000 feet, as is evidenced by the number killed in collisions with communications towers and office buildings each year. Many cross the Gulf of Mexico during migration, whereas others use the mainland Mexico flyway and can be seen in numbers in fall and spring at local migration hot spots.

WINTER RANGE

Most North American vireos winter in Central America, except for three species: The Yellow-throated and Black-whiskered Vireos winter in the north of South America, and the Red-eyed Vireo travels to the Amazon Basin. Several species are hardy and winter in relatively cool habitats in the southeastern United States. The Blue-headed Vireo is found with increasing regularity on central Atlantic Christmas Bird Counts, a testament to this species' hardy nature and its ability to forage widely. Hutton's Vireos are resident in their western breeding range; however, they may undertake poorly understood migratory movements.

Warbling Vireo

OBSERVING VIREOS

Vireos are relatively common overall and can often be seen on migration in mixed flocks of passerines. In the spring and fall birders should look for these birds as they forage methodically in a variety of habitats. Some species are more active when foraging, flicking wings and foraging from the air for both insects and fruits. On the breeding grounds, vireos are rather shy and are more readily heard than seen.

During the winter, most vireos attend large foraging flocks comprised of both local species and migrants. Abundant, although not often seen is the Philadelphia Vireo. Its song is similar to the Red-eyed Vireo, and it shares its range with the Red-eyed, which overwhelms it in sheer numbers. Listen carefully, and look twice when you think you've identified a Red-eyed Vireo. The occurrence of individuals of each species is linked both to migratory pathways and each species' population status. The Bell's Vireo, one of the few birds to be described as "indistinct," is decidedly plain and must be identified by voice and range, as well as sight, when possible. Birds that are in decline such as the Black-capped Vireo are harder to find on migration than those that are considered common. Always look for that blunt, slightly hooked bill and those bluish legs.

STATUS AND CONSERVATION

Vireos as a group are generally stable. Most species have shown slight increases over the past few decades—a conclusion based primarily on the findings of the Breeding Bird Survey. Two taxa, the Black-capped Vireo and the subspecies Least Bell's Vireo, are listed as federally endangered; both species are negatively affected by habitat alteration and its resulting biological consequences. Parasitism by Brown-headed Cowbirds is a major concern to both species. Alteration of riparian habitat is of concern for the Least Bell's Vireo, whereas alteration of successional habitat through fire suppression threatens the Black-capped Vireo.

Brood parasitism by Brown-headed Cowbirds is probably the main danger. Studies of the abundant Red-eyed and White-eyed Vireos show that from about 25 percent to more than 70 percent of nests are parasitized by cowbirds. The populations of Cassin's Vireo of the Pacific Northwest are benefiting from the undeveloped and cowbird-free lands where they breed. The general outlook for vireo survival is quite positive.

See also

Warblers, page 358

BLUE-HEADED VIREO

- - - - - Autumn migration
          western limit

  Breeding range

Winter range

CASSIN'S VIREO

- - - - - Autumn migration
          eastern limit

Breeding range

Winter range

*Vagrant Blue-headed Vireos have been
recorded west to the Pacific coast.
Cassin's Vireo has been reported as a
vagrant as far as eastern Texas and
Louisiana, with additional records in New
York, Quebec, and south-central Alaska.*

STATUTE MILES
0   500

0   500
KILOMETERS

YELLOW-GREE
VIRE

WANDERING RA▶

Breeding range

Rarely but regularly   - - -
used breeding range

Casual vagrant   - - -
                     /

*Yellow-green Vireos nest only sou▮
the U.S. border except for a rarely
area in south Texas. It does occur fa▮
north as a autumn casual vagrant.
species is a reverse migrant, hea▮
north in the fall instead of south. S▮
birds end up along the U.S.-Me▮
border in the spring or sum▮
overshooting their ra▮*

STATUTE M▮
0

0
KILOME▮

70° 160° 150° 140° 130° 120° 110° 100° 90° 80° 70° 60° 50° 40° 70°

30°

60°

ARCTIC CIRCLE

Banks
Island

Victoria
Island

Baffin Island

LABRADOR
SEA

40°

U.S.
CANADA

HUDSON
BAY

50° 50°

C A N A D A

R
O
C
K
Y

G
R
E
A
T

40° 60°

L. Superior

M
O
U
N
T
A
I
N
S

P
L
A
I
N
S

L. Michigan

Lake
Huron

Ontario

U N I T E D   S T A T E S

A
P
P
A
L
A
C
H
I
A
N
M
O
U
N
T
A
I
N
S

L. Erie

ATLANTIC
OCEAN

30°

Bermuda

30°

P
A
C
I
F
I
C

O
C
E
A
N

Baja California

Gulf of California

M
E
X
I
C
O

GULF   OF

MEXICO

BAHAMAS

TROPIC OF CANCER

TROPIC OF CANCER

20°

W E S T   I N D I E S

C
U
B
A

HAITI

G R E A T E R   A N T I L L E S

JAMAICA

70°

Yucatán
Pen.

BELIZE

GUATEMALA

HONDURAS

10°

EL SALVADOR

NICARAGUA

P A N A M A

COSTA RICA

COLOMBIA

CROWS, JAYS, MAGPIES

Bold, raucous, aggressive, and obviously intelligent, the members of the family Corvidae have long been thought by humans to play unique roles in the grand scheme of things. From ancient times the all-black crows, ravens, choughs, and rooks have been thought to be messengers bearing ill tidings of death, loneliness, and despair—as in the poem by Edgar Allan Poe "The Raven." The magpies are reputed to be thieves in Europe, known for their fondness of shiny items, including silver teaspoons; and Italian composer Gioacchino Rossini even named an opera *The Thieving Magpie.* The jays are also viewed as bold, puckish pranksters frequently stirring up trouble.

Philip
Brandt
George

Supporting these human-ascribed attributes, long-term observations of, and scientific experiments with their foraging skills, adaptability to human intrusions, group activities, and seemingly myriad vocal communications testify to their high avian IQs. That they have excellent memories is suggested by the caching corvids' ability to relocate most of their stashes days, weeks, and sometimes months after storing hoarded food.

Having learned that where there are humans, there is likely to be food, many corvids hang out around places where people congregate or dump their refuse. The Tamaulipas Crow of eastern Mexico, otherwise fairly rare within the borders of the United States, can be seen regularly picking through the contents of a landfill outside of Brownsville, Texas. Some of the jays have learned that campfire smoke, the noise of ax on wood, or the crack of gunfire indicate the presence of humans and, therefore, possibly food.

Highly social birds, most of the Corvidae seem to understand that there is strength in numbers. They often help members of their flock by doing sentry duty as others forage, joining their fellows to mob intruders and would-be predators, and roosting in large numbers to share heat during cold nights.

American Crows seem able to "count" up to three or four, whereas ravens and magpies can apparently do even better, going as high as seven. Common Ravens have shown real problem-solving skills: Faced for the first time with food dangling on a string from a branch, they quickly assess the problem, perch on the limb, and use their feet and bill to grasp the string and pull the food upward "hand over hand," until they can pin it to a perch with their strong feet, so they can eat it.

As clever and cunning as they seem to be, corvid intelligence may have been overestimated at times. It has been suggested that American Crows drop large nuts onto highways for passing cars to break open. Since they do drop nuts on pavement to crack them, whether automobiles are present or not—just as Northwestern Crows open shellfish by dropping them onto rocks—the helpfulness of the vehicles is probably a serendipitous event, not part of the crow's conscious scheme.

The corvids of North America, consisting of one species of jackdaw, four crows, two ravens, one nutcracker, two magpies, and ten species of jays, are medium- to large-size birds, ranging in length from the Green and Pinyon Jays at 10.5 inches to the powerful Common Raven at 24 inches. Wherever they are found, they are a delight to watch.

Blue Jay: *Cyanocitta cristata,* L 11", crest, black necklace

CROWS, JAYS, MAGPIES

One of the more common species of this family, the Blue Jay (above) is found in the midwestern and eastern regions of the United States and southern Canada, in habitats ranging from deciduous and pine forests to backyards and local parks. Blue Jays are pale blue and gray with a long tail that is barred with bright and dark blue stripes. Jays have a black collar and dull blue head crest. Blue Jays are noted for their loud, piercing call particularly when alarmed. The species is often seen in small family groups that feed together. Jays mainly feed on insects, nuts, and berries but also raid nests for eggs and nestlings of smaller species. During spring, males pursue a single female and, after landing, prominently display with bobs and two-note vocalizations. Blue Jays are tree nesters; they build nests of twigs and discarded human-made objects, and raise a brood of four or five hatchlings. Jays often roam in large feeding flocks in the fall. Their numbers have grown because of increased backyard feeding.

Range of Blue Jay

CLASSIFICATION

The family Corvidae contains some of the largest birds of the order Passeriformes—the so-called perching or songbirds. Only some of the Australian lyrebirds with their long, ornamental tails are longer from beak tip to tail tip than some of the ravens. This family is divided into two subfamilies: The Corvinae includes crows, ravens, nutcrackers, jackdaws, and rooks, while jays, magpies, and choughs compose the Garrulinae. One or more of the Corvidae's hundred odd species in 24 genera are found virtually everywhere on the globe except in Antarctica. Among the 20 species in eight genera occurring in North America, only the Old World choughs and rooks are unrepresented. The blue-hued jays and the Brown Jay are unique to the New World, while the Gray Jay, looking much like a large chickadee with its small bill on a large, rounded head, is the only representative of the Old World jays.

STRUCTURE

The wings of magpies and jays are proportionally shorter than those of crows and ravens, but all are rounded and, like those of most passerines, have ten primary feathers. The crows and especially the ravens often have pronounced gaps or slots between the primaries that generate the extra lift needed by larger birds allowing them to soar for long distances in search of food. Except for the magpies, whose tails make up slightly more than half of their overall length, most corvids have medium-length, rounded tails. Their strong legs—long for passerines, but proportionally shorter than those of most other groups—are well suited for ground foraging. All but the Pinyon Jay, whose genus name, *Gymnorhinus,* means "naked nose," have bristles that cover and protect the nostrils and may also serve as tactile sensors. Most corvids have strong, sometimes stout bills that allow for a smorgasbord diet. Only the Clark's Nutcracker and Pinyon Jays have thin, chisel-like bills superbly adapted to extract seeds from pine cones. Many jays have special bone structures in the jaw that brace the lower mandible, permitting the bill to be held partially open so that only the lower mandible strikes to open an acorn or other heavy seed.

PLUMAGE

Whereas crows and ravens are usually jet black overall, most jays sport bright plumage of blues and greens—only the Brown Jay is uncharacteristically drab. The Blue and Steller's Jays have prominent crests, and magpies are boldly patterned in black and white with iridescent green and blue highlights. A recent arrival to the northeastern United States, the Eurasian Jackdaw is basically black all over, but has a gray nape, gray ear patches, and pale grayish eyes. The sexes of all corvids are similar in appearance. Although the male Corvinae tend to be larger than the females, size is a tricky field mark for determining gender in the wild.

FEEDING BEHAVIOR

Jays and the chisel-billed nutcrackers concentrate on pine seeds and acorns, and magpies, crows, and ravens show an inclination toward animal foods, but all of the corvids are truly omnivorous, opportunistic feeders. "Specialized generalists," they eat a variety of insects, small mammals (American Crows have been observed snatching hairless, newborn squirrels from their nest), carrion, birds and birds' eggs, seeds, and fruit. All hide food for later consumption. Many species periodically check on their stores, either to ascertain the condition of the food or to re-familiarize themselves with the location. Although Clark's Nutcracker is the champion hoarder, some jays may hide thousands of individual nuts and seeds in a given year.

The Gray Jay uses its sticky saliva to help "glue" food in crevices and under tree bark. Such caching helps with plant dispersal since some forgotten or uneaten seeds may germinate and help revitalize forests. Crows and ravens often bury excess carrion to be uncovered later. Their heavy, broad bill is not built to open a carcass—these birds must wait until another predator or an automobile has torn through the hide before they can dine—but they are well suited to ripping open plastic garbage bags to discover what might be inside. Crows, magpies, and the two scrub-jays are also known to hoard shiny nonfood items like aluminum foil, shards of glass and china, and sometimes even forks, spoons, and knives. All corvids are to some degree nest predators, devouring the eggs and nestlings of other birds. When feeding on the ground, the Pinyon Jay hops along while all the others walk.

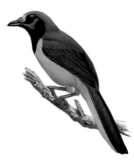

Green Jay

OTHER SPECIES FIELD NOTES

- **Steller's Jay**
  Cyanocitta stelleri
  L 11.5"
  Crested, blue-black overall
- **Gray Jay**
  Perisoreus canadensis
  L 11.5"
  Mostly white face, small bill, no crest
- **Clark's Nutcracker**
  Nucifraga columbiana
  L 12"
  Black wings with white panel
- **Western Scrub-Jay**
  Aphelocoma californica
  L 11"
  Bluish band on chest
- **Island Scrub-Jay**
  Aphelocoma insularis
  L 12"
  Large bill, dark blue, only on Santa Cruz Island
- **Florida Scrub-Jay**
  Aphelocoma coerulescens
  L 11"
  Whitish forehead, only in Florida
- **Mexican Jay**
  Aphelocoma ultramarina
  L 11.5"
  Lack white eyebrows of Scrub-Jays, chunky shape
- **Pinyon Jay**
  Gymnorhinus cyanocephalus
  L 10.5")
  Blue overall
- **Brown Jay**
  Cyanocorax morio
  L 16.5"
  Sooty brown, pale belly
- **Green Jay**
  Cyanocorax yncas
  L 10.5"
  Green, blue, and yellow with black breast
- **Black-billed Magpie**
  Pica hudsonia
  L 19"
  Black bill, long tail
- **Yellow-billed Magpie**
  Pica nuttallii
  L 16.5"
  Yellow bill
- **Eurasian Jackdaw**
  Corvus monedula
  L 13"
  Gray nape and ear patches
- **Tamaulipas Crow**
  Corvus imparatus
  L 14.5"
  Small, glossy black
- **American Crow**
  Corvus brachyrhynchos
  L 17.5"
  Long, heavy bill
- **Northwestern Crow**
  Corvus caurinus
  L 16"
  Smaller than American, identify by range
- **Fish Crow**
  Corvus ossifragus
  L 15.5"
  Smallish head, long tail, identify by voice
- **Chihuahuan Raven**
  Corvus cryptoleucus
  L 19.5"
  White-based neck feathers, smaller than Common Raven
- **Common Raven**
  Corvus corax
  L 24"
  Wedge-shape tail, very large size

VOCALIZATION

Although classified as songbirds, none of the corvids has a song that might be considered melodious. Loud and noisy—a tendency noted in the scientific name for the magpie and jay subfamily, Garrulinae, meaning pointlessly and annoyingly talkative. They utter a variety of sounds, including raucous territorial and predator alerts, rattling noises, clicks, and bell-like tones.

Most corvids seem capable of learning and mimicking the sounds uttered by other birds and some animals. Crows in captivity have been known to imitate human speech, a feat not recorded in the wild, and Blue Jays are so adept at copying the cries of hawks common to their area that sometimes even experienced birders must pay close attention to determine which is calling. Rather noisy and raucous during most of the year, corvids tend to become quiet when nesting. Near the nest they produce only softer, more musical notes when in close communication with others of their species, but these quieter interchanges are rarely heard by birders in the field.

BREEDING BEHAVIOR

While courting, the males of many species will feed the females as they sit side by side or engage in bowing and other ritualized movements. Spectacular feats of diving, soaring, chasing, and tumbling are often observed as ravens and crows begin to form pairs. Some species, especially Mexican Jays, nest in loosely associated colonies in which several pairs share a single territory. As each pair builds its own nest, a female may lay eggs there and in the nests of others and thus any one nest may contain the eggs of several different females. Most of the other Corvidae, however, nest as isolated pairs. Both sexes help build nests that vary from open cups to globular masses with a side entrance. They usually plaster the inside of the structure with mud or dung and then line the nest with hair, wool, bark strips, and fine plant material. Most corvids build their nests in trees and shrubs, but ravens will sometimes settle on rocky ledges and outcroppings. Most corvids produce only one brood of four to six eggs a year, although Blue Jays and American Crows may have two or more broods in the southern part of their ranges. The male frequently brings food to the incubating female. The clutches hatch synchronously and the altricial young are covered in a fine down. Only newborn jays are totally bare—giving rise to the expression "naked as a jaybird."

Family structures can be rather complex in some species. Among Florida Scrub-Jays, Mexican Jays, and some populations of American Crows, juveniles from the previous year or other nonbreeding adults may stay around to help the parents protect and feed their young. Among the Corvidae, the Gray Jay is unique, breeding during the cold, late winter and early spring rather than during the brief, warmer northern summer.

BREEDING RANGE

While species like the Common Raven, American Crow, and Blue Jay breed across large sections of the continent, others breed in restricted areas. The Island Scrub-Jay is found only on the small, six-mile-square Santa Cruz Island off the coast of southern California. Small tracts of fragmented, fire-sustained, scrubby oaks in central Florida are the specialized home of the Florida Scrub-Jay. The Yellow-billed Magpie limits itself to the oaks, rangelands, and foothills of northern and central California's Central Valley and the coastal valleys south to Santa Barbara County. The Northwestern Crow breeds in a narrow coastal strip from the northwest corner of Washington state up into Alaska.

MIGRATION

Although some corvids withdraw from parts of their

ISLAND SCRUB-JAY

Until recently, the Florida, Western and Island Scrub-Jays were considered to be one species, but being geographically separated, they have been split into three separate species. A slightly larger, more robust and larger billed bird than either the Florida or Western, the Island Scrub Jay is restricted to Santa Cruz Island, one of the Channel Islands off the coast of southern California. More wary than the other species, this richly colored bird with bright blue undertail coverts is often seen perched low in the shade of a scrub oak, probably defending its individually held territory. A cooperative breeder, it takes several years for a young bird to acquire the territory needed for nesting.

breeding ranges in winter, especially when weather conditions become too harsh or food is scarce, none is truly migratory. Those populations of Blue Jays, American Crows, and Common Ravens that inhabit the northernmost reaches of their breeding ranges usually withdraw southward for the winter. Steller's and Western Scrub-Jays, Clark's Nutcrackers, and Black-billed Magpies often move to lower elevations as the weather turns colder. Fish Crows may move from inland locations toward warmer coastal areas, and small flocks of Tamaulipas Crows sometimes move northward out of higher elevations in Mexico to lower and warmer areas of southern Texas. All of these movements are thought to be diurnal.

WINTER RANGE

The Gray, Green, Brown, Florida Scrub-, Island Scrub-, and Mexican Jays, along with Yellow-billed Magpies and Northwestern Crows remain on their breeding grounds year-round. Those populations of species that do change location in winter rarely move far outside their individual species' overall breeding range, and often overlap with permanent resident populations.

During the nonbreeding months, some corvid species, especially the crows and ravens tend to gather in large flocks from which they seem to derive a number of possible benefits. As the flock forages in the surrounding area, some individuals, perched high in trees, serve as sentries, rarely searching for food for themselves while on duty. Upon spotting a predator, they sound an alarm so the others may hide or fly away. Frequently, whether the perceived enemy is an owl, a hawk, or even a marauding cat, a group will form to harass or "mob" the intruder with dive-bombing flights and raucous calls. Crows especially gather in large roosts at night. More than one million crows are known to have gathered in separate roosts in Oklahoma and Kansas. Such "murders," as the groups are called, apparently serve several purposes. More eyes make it more probable that potential predators, especially Great Horned Owls, will be sighted. Perhaps because owls prefer to hunt in the dark and are less tolerant of human presence, crows frequently roost near well-lighted parking lots and building complexes. The heat generated by hundreds or thousands of these birds in such close proximity may actually make cold nights easier to withstand. Such

American Crow

roosts may also serve as information gathering places since individuals unsuccessful during the day's foraging may recognize more successful crows and follow them to better feeding grounds the next day. American Crows are known to fly as far as 50 miles from the roost site in a day in search of food.

OBSERVING CORVIDS

Rambunctious, gregarious, and bold in the nonbreeding season, corvids are usually easy to spot within their respective ranges. One or more species appears in every North American habitat, including the forbidding deserts of Mexico, the southwestern U.S., and the icy, high Arctic. Since most species seem to be relatively comfortable around humans, it is easy to witness the boldness of crows, ravens, magpies, and jays as they fly, walk, and hop around fast food restaurants, picnic tables, or campsites to glean whatever edibles might be left behind. Their penchant for brazenly stealing tasty tidbits and shiny objects from under the nose of humans has earned the Gray Jay and Clark's Nutcracker the nicknames of "robber jay" and "camp

robber." Gray Jays have not adapted as easily to developed areas, but they will gravitate to human activities in remote areas, taking bait from traps, following the sound of gunfire to get at fallen prey, moving toward the smoke of a campfire, or tracking down the sound of chopping wood in the hope of finding food.

STATUS AND CONSERVATION

Only two members of North American Corvidae are thought to be in any real danger at this time. Although the Island Scrub-Jay is common on Santa Cruz Island off the coast of California, there is concern for the future of the species: Whenever a small population is isolated, as is this bird, weather extremes, especially during breeding season; virulent epidemics; or human intervention and development could produce a catastrophic decline in that population. The Florida Scrub-Jay is presently classified as threatened and threats are thought to be more imminent since this bird is finicky and insists on a specialized scrub habitat in Florida that has become fragmented. Given that a Florida Scrub-Jay rarely wanders more than half a mile from its hatch site, it rarely is willing to explore far enough from home to find other islands of the right kind of scrub. Parking lots, malls, new roads, and housing developments continue to whittle away at the scrub country pockets and threaten habitat.

Populations of the other corvids appear to be either stable or expanding. The populations of the Yellow-billed Magpie, the Tamaulipas Crow, and others that inhabit limited ranges appear stable, human encroachment into their preferred habitats may present future danger. Although some species seem to have declined in population following initial human contact, most have rebounded. Common Ravens suffered from the initial fragmentation of eastern forests, but their numbers have exploded in the 1990s either due to the regrowth of those forests or an increasing tolerance of human activity. Lovers of edge environments between forest and open space, American Crows and the jays seem to have benefited from that forest fragmentation. Crows were among the first avian species to be hit by the West Nile Virus but it remains to be seen what impact the recent outbreak will have on their population.

See also

Blackbirds, Orioles, page 400

When food supplies fail in fall
and winter, most western
Corvids (jays, magpies, ravens,
and crows) wander out of the
normal range. They may turn
east and south, or at lower
elevations than the birds are
normally found. Records
showing Scrub-Jays well out of
their range may represent
escaped captive birds.

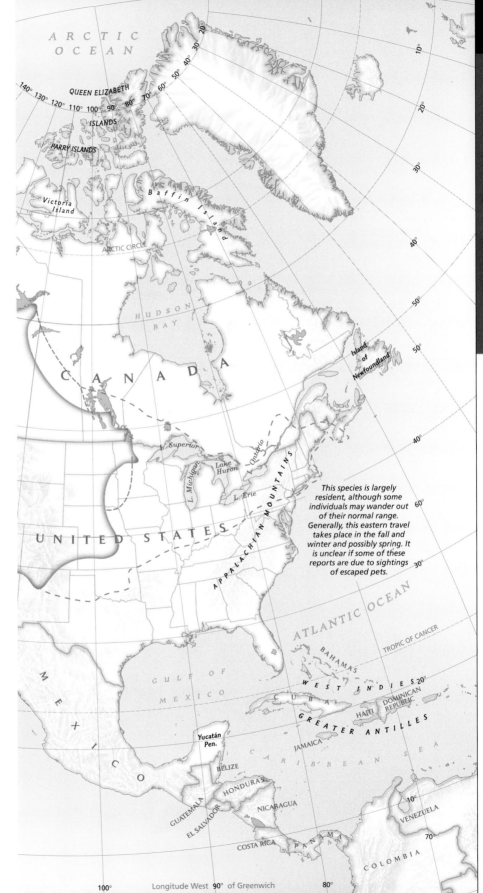

NYON, ELLER'S JAYS D WESTERN RUB-JAYS

ON JAY

Resident range

- - Limits of wanderings

Single record

ER'S JAY

Resident range

- Limits of wanderings

Single record

ERN SCRUB-JAY

Resident range

···· Limits of wanderings

Single record

TE MILES

500

500

ETERS

◄ BLACK-BILLED MAGPIE

BLACK-BILLED MAGPIE

Resident range

Regular winter wandering range

Casual occurences

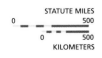

STATUTE MILES

0   500

0   500

KILOMETERS

This species is largely resident, although some individuals may wander out of their normal range. Generally, this eastern travel takes place in the fall and winter and possibly spring. It is unclear if some of these reports are due to sightings of escaped pets.

ARCTIC OCEAN

QUEEN ELIZABETH ISLANDS

PARRY ISLANDS

Victoria Island

ARCTIC CIRCLE

Baffin Island

HUDSON BAY

CANADA

Island of Newfoundland

Superior

L. Michigan

Lake Huron

Ontario

L. Erie

APPALACHIAN MOUNTAINS

UNITED STATES

M E X I C O

GULF OF MEXICO

Yucatán Pen.

BELIZE

GUATEMALA

HONDURAS

EL SALVADOR

NICARAGUA

COSTA RICA

PANAMA

ATLANTIC OCEAN

BAHAMAS

TROPIC OF CANCER

W E S T   I N D I E S

CUBA

HAITI

DOMINICAN REPUBLIC

GREATER ANTILLES

JAMAICA

C A R I B B E A N   S E A

VENEZUELA

COLOMBIA

LARKS

Larks are ground-dwelling passerines characterized by brown, buff, and off-white plumages; juvenile plumage has buff edges to the upperparts. While rather dull in plumage, larks have captivated humans for centuries with their impressive aerial songs. Percy Bysshe Shelly's poem, "To a Skylark," is among the best known poems in western literature and has made the flight song of the Sky Lark familiar to many who have never seen or heard this species. In fact, song flights of other species are often referred to as "skylarking." Several species of larks are also able to mimic other birds.

Christopher Wood

Of the 91 species of larks in the world, only the Horned Lark is a widespread native breeder in North America. This species is common in open habitats including tundra, agricultural fields, and deserts. In the New World, Horned Larks occur from the Arctic to central Mexico, with an isolated population in Colombia's Eastern Andes. The sole additional species found in North America is the Sky Lark, a Eurasian species introduced to Vancouver Island (and the Hawaiian Islands). The Asian subspecies of Sky Lark, *Alauda arvensis pekinensis*, has occurred as a vagrant to Alaska and California and it was recently recorded breeding on the Pribilof Islands, Alaska.

The Horned Lark is highly variable, with some 41 described subspecies in the world, 21 of which occur in North America. Grinnell and Miller, in their work on California bird distribution, recognized 13 subspecies in California alone. Subspecies differ in size and plumage color with the latter factor correlating strongly with soil color. Birds from the red-soil areas of the Central Valley of California have reddish backs; desert-breeding subspecies have pale upperparts; birds of the wet Pacific Northwest are darker-backed. Arctic subspecies are migratory and have longer wings than nonmigratory subspecies.

Horned Larks are easy to see in open areas throughout North America, but are most widespread in the West. In the East, this species is often found at airfields and agricultural fields and in the winter along beaches and sand dunes. During the breeding season, Horned Larks are territorial and use defended areas for feeding, courtship, and nesting. By midsummer, juvenile Horned Larks often gather in small flocks of 10 to 25 individuals. Adults start flocking in fall, and are sometimes joined by longspurs, pipits, and/or Snow Buntings. It is not unusual to see flocks of several hundred Horned Larks in the winter, particularly when snow covers large areas, thus limiting available feeding areas. As snow melts, flocks disperse into smaller groups. In winter, larks are frequently observed feeding along roadsides, fields, ocean beaches, and airfields.

After many unsuccessful attempts at introducing this species to North America, Sky Larks were successfully introduced to the southern part of Vancouver Island and the nearby Fraser River delta in 1903. Those on the mainland died out, but with additional introductions on Vancouver Island, the species became established around Victoria and the Saanich Peninsula in the 1940s. The species reached a high of about 1,000 birds in the 1950s and 1960s. Urbanization and changes in habitat use reduced their numbers, and by 1996 only some hundred birds were found on the Saanich Peninsula. About 10,000 Sky Larks on the Hawaiian Islands are also the result of an introduction.

(Left) Horned Lark

Sky Lark: *Alauda arvensis*, L 7.25", slender bill, slight crest

SKY LARKS

Eurasian Sky Larks were introduced to British Columbia, Canada, from Europe in the early 1900s and were found much later in San Juan Island off the Washington State coastline near the Canadian border. The surviving population is non-migratory, and most birds remain on a small range that consists of agricultural fields planted with mixed vegetables not far from Victoria, B.C. Sky Larks are brown-streaked longspur- or sparrow-sized birds that feed on insects and grubs clinging to vegetable greens. They are skulkers that hide in field rows, flush when approached, and quickly settle into nearby vegetation. The species often moves in small flocks when feeding. During breeding season, Sky Lark males soar into the air and sing a long melodious song before disappearing into vegetation. They nest in holes in fields that have been abandoned by burrowing animals, or in natural shallow depressions hidden by ground cover. A Sky Lark pair will have three to five eggs that, as ground-nesters, are vulnerable to predators.

Range of Sky Lark

CLASSIFICATION

Larks (family Alaudidae) form a distinct taxonomic group of 91 species worldwide, most of which are found in Africa and Eurasia. Many larks bear a superficial resemblance to pipits and longspurs and occasionally pose identification challenges. California's first Sky Lark was identified for several days as a Smith's Longspur. Another problem in spring and summer concerns juvenile Horned Larks, which appear sufficiently like Sprague's Pipit that they are frequently identified as such by unsuspecting birders.

These mistakes are understandable; larks, pipits and longspurs are all found in open areas and have plumages characterized by buffs, tans, usually some black, and other earthy colors. The elongated hind claw of the Horned Lark is also shared by longspurs and several pipits. Larks are not closely related to pipits or longspurs. Since all of these species are found in similar habitats, they face similar evolutionary pressures; the presence of similar plumage and an elongated hind claw is an example of convergent evolution, rather than indicating a close taxonomic relationship. Eastern and Western Meadowlarks are closely related to blackbirds and orioles, not larks.

STRUCTURE

Larks are the product of open habitats. They have long wings that help them fly in often windy environments. They run on short legs, unlike many birds that hop. Their short, stout bill is well adapted to foraging on a varied diet of seeds and insects from the top of soil and from short vegetation. Larks use their bill and feet with long hindclaws to create shallow depressions where they roost and also to dig their nest. Northern populations of Horned Larks have longer wings than sedentary subspecies of the south. Males are considerably larger than females within any one subspecies.

PLUMAGE

Lark plumages are rather subdued with earthy colors that help them blend into their environment. Males and females are similar, but are often separable under good viewing conditions and in the hand. Males are on average more brightly colored. Larks have one complete annual prebasic molt that occurs on the breeding grounds. Horned Larks are variable with some 21 subspecies in the United States and Canada. Pyle (1997) groups these into three subspecies groups: a small Western rufous group, a large pale Western group, and a dark variable-size Eastern group. There is considerable variation within these groups. Male Horned Larks usually have darker more well defined black areas on the chest and head, whereas female Horned Larks typically have more subdued facial patterns, with "horns" that are short or lacking.

FEEDING BEHAVIOR

Larks feed in a variety of open habitats, preferring short grasslands, tundra, deserts, and agricultural lands during the breeding season. Both North American species eat a variety of insects, but feed primarily on seeds and grains. Horned

Horned Lark

Larks form large flocks outside the breeding season that may number into the hundreds, particularly when snow cover reduces available feeding areas.

VOCALIZATION

Flight songs are a conspicuous aspect of lark courtship displays and have captured human hearts and minds for centuries. Most larks, including the two North American species, have songs that are delivered in flight and from the ground. The Sky Lark has a song that can last up to 30 minutes, making it the longest song of any North American species. Male Sky Larks in Eurasia are known to mimic other birds, both in flight and while singing from the ground.

BREEDING BEHAVIOR

Since most species are found in open areas, many larks have developed impressive song flights. While known for flight displays, most species also sing from the ground or from perches. Horned Larks breed in a large range, encompassing the high Arctic, alpine tundra, arid deserts, and agricultural fields. Horned Larks are one of the first species to start breeding in much of North America with pair formation occurring in non-migratory subspecies as early as January. Nest building begins in March in Illinois and Kansas. As with many other passerines, females build the nest and do most of the incubating; both sexes feed the young.

BREEDING RANGE

The breeding range of most larks is in Europe, Asia, and Africa. The Horned Lark is the only widespread breeding lark in North America, where it is found throughout much of the continent in open habitats. The species is less common in the East and absent from the southeastern U.S. during the breeding season. Within North America, Sky Larks are now confined to four small areas of the Saanich Peninsula on southeastern Vancouver Island; a pair of the Asian subspecies, *pekinensis*, recently bred on the Pribilof Islands, Alaska.

OTHER SPECIES FIELD NOTES

■ **Horned Lark**
Eremophila alpestris
L 6.75-7.75"
Variable plumage, black horns on males

MIGRATION

Most of the world's 91 species of larks are sedentary, but several, including some subspecies of Horned Larks in North America, are migratory. Three northern subspecies of Horned Larks are migratory, leaving in September and October and returning to Alaska and northern Canada in April and early May. Northern populations of three other subspecies move south in late fall and early winter. Southern subspecies are sedentary, but occasionally wander south. Populations that inhabit high elevation alpine habitats are likely to move to nearby lowlands in the winter. Introduced populations of Sky Larks in the U.S. and Canada are nonmigratory, but the Asian subspecies, *pekinensis*, is migratory; vagrants of this subspecies have occurred in California and Alaska.

WINTER RANGE

Horned Larks largely move south of Canada and join local populations of Horned Larks. During these times it may be possible to see flocks of two or more subspecies of Horned Larks. Individuals and small flocks show up irregularly along the Gulf Coast as far southeast as northern Florida.

OBSERVING LARKS

Horned Larks occur throughout most of North America, so finding them is not difficult. For birders interested in subspecies identification, Horned Larks can present a challenge; much remains to be learned. The easiest place to see Sky Larks is at the Victoria airport on the Saanich Peninsula, Vancouver Island.

STATUS AND CONSERVATION

Breeding Bird Survey and Christmas Bird Count data suggest that the population of Horned Larks has declined in parts of the Midwest, but the species appears stable in most of its range. The Horned Lark population increased greatly during the settlement of North America, as a result of cutting forests, opening habitat that allowed populations to expand in the Midwest and the East. Some decline in these regions is the result of agricultural lands reverting to deciduous forests. Introduced Sky Larks have declined drastically in the past 30 years, largely due to habitat loss and changes in farming practices; only about a hundred birds remain on the Saanich Peninsula. Worldwide, several species of African larks are of the most serious conservation concerns. All eight species of African larks classified by BirdLife International are listed as Globally Threatened.

See also

Sparrows, page 378

VAGRANCY & INTRODUCED POP

● Record of natural vagrants, presumably from Asia

● Resident population of introduced birds from Europe

STATUTE MILES
0　　　　　　　　　500
0　　　　500
KILOMETERS

ARCTIC OCEAN

RUSSIA

CHUKCHI SEA

BERING STR.

BERING SEA

70°

180°

60°

160°

150°

50°

40°

30°

20°

130°

120°

110°

100°

170°

160°

150°

140°

130°

120°

110°

100°

90°

80°

70°

60°

North Slope

Brooks Range

ARCTIC CIRCLE

BEAUFORT SEA

Alaska Range

Kodiak Island

Gulf of Alaska

CANADA

ROCKY MOUNTAINS

Vancouver I.

UNITED STATES

PACIFIC OCEAN

TROPIC OF CANCER

MEXICO

HORNED LA

RANGE AND VAGRA

Summer range

Resident range

Winter range

Rare to casual winter visitor and vagrant

Isolated record (Asian subspecies)

STATUTE

0

0

KILOM

ARCTIC
OCEAN

CHUKCHI
SEA

Bering Str.

BEAUFORT SEA

QUEEN ELIZABETH

ISLANDS

PARRY ISLANDS

Banks
Island

Victoria
Island

Baffin Island

ARCTIC CIRCLE

ARCTIC CIRCLE

SIA

U.S.
CANADA

Gulf of Alaska

C A N A D A

Great
Bear Lake

Great
Slave Lake

HUDSON

BAY

Lake
Athabasca

Reindeer
Lake

Vancouver I.

R O C K Y

Island
of
Newfoundland

Lake
Winnipeg

G R E A T

L. Superior

Lake
Huron

L. Michigan

Ontario

L. Erie

M O U N T A I N S

P L A I N S

U N I T E D   S T A T E S

A P P A L A C H I A N   M O U N T A I N S

ATLANTIC

OCEAN

PACIFIC

Baja California

Gulf of California

M E X I C O

TROPIC OF CANCER

TROPIC OF CANCER

O C E A N

GULF   OF

MEXICO

BAHAMAS

W E S T   I N D I E S

CUBA

HAITI

DOMINICAN
REPUBLIC

P.R. U.S.

G R E A T E R   A N T I L L E S

JAMAICA

Yucatán
Pen.

BELIZE

GUATEMALA

HONDURAS

EL SALVADOR

NICARAGUA

COSTA RICA

PANAMA

C A R I B B E A N   S E A

LESSER ANTILLES

VENEZUELA

COLOMBIA

70°

80°

170° 160° 150° 140° 130° 120° 110° 100° 90° 80° 70° 60° 50° 40° 30° 20° 10°

10°

20°

30°

40°

60°

50°

50°

40°

30°

60°

20°

10°

110°

100°

Longitude West 90° of Greenwich

80°

70°

SWALLOWS

With very long wings and streamlined bodies, swallows swoop and soar gracefully, spending hours on the wing capturing small flying insects. A homogeneous family of aerial songbirds, its 90 species are distributed throughout the world—absent only from the polar regions, New Zealand, and most oceanic islands. The well-known Barn Swallow is truly cosmopolitan, with six subspecies distributed around the globe—breeding in North America, Europe, China, and Japan and wintering in Central and South America, southern Africa, India, and Southeast Asia.

Jonathan Alderfer

Swallows are gregarious birds, and most species show little fear of man. Over thousands of years, many species have adapted to using human-made structures for their nest sites. People have generally welcomed this association. They are attractive birds, and their prodigious appetite for insects is appreciated. From observing marked birds, we know that many return year after year to the same nests, to build new nests, or rebuild the previous year's nest.

Being dependent on insect food, most North American swallows are highly migratory. In late summer, after nesting is over, some species gather in large premigration flocks. These flocks can reach immense proportions—hundreds of thousands of birds may roost together at night in favored coastal marshes or reed beds, where they cling to plant stems. When cold weather and lack of insects force them to move south, they may disappear abruptly. Medieval Europeans believed that the swallows had disappeared into the mud to hibernate. In fact, their journey had just begun. Many European species spend the winter months in southern Africa. North American swallows also undertake long-distance migrations. Purple Martins and Cliff Swallows journey to southern South America. Spring migration is a drawn-out process; some species arrive at their nesting sites extremely early. For the many people who have erected birdhouses and martin apartments, the arrival of these birds is an eagerly anticipated harbinger of spring. The popular belief is that swallows return to their summer homes on precise dates—the most famous being the March 19 arrival of Cliff Swallows at the old Mission of San Juan Capistrano in California. The truth is that the date depends on the weather—swallows need a prolonged warm spell accompanied by a hatch of flying insects before they can survive in northern climes—and arrival dates vary from year to year.

Swallow identification is not particularly difficult, although the general public often confuses swallows and swifts. Some challenges await the active birder—such as identifying birds in a mixed species flock as they swirl and dart over a lake or marsh, or separating the "brown-plumaged" swallows in fall. Most North American birders share similar identification challenges because six of our eight breeding species are distributed from coast to coast. Even the two species that have more restricted ranges—the Cave Swallow (most abundant in Texas) and the Violet-green Swallow (western mountains)—have healthy populations and are easily observed in the proper habitat and season. Rounding out the family are some rarities: the Bahama Swallow (occasional in south Florida), the Common House-Martin (accidental in Alaska and on St. Pierre and Miquelon), and four species of martins native to the Caribbean and areas farther south (all extremely rare in North America).

(Left) Tree Swallow

Barn Swallow: *Hirundo rustica,* L 6.75", long forked tail

SWALLOWS

The Barn Swallow (above) has a summer range throughout most of North America. It is the only swallow with a long, forked tail and has an iridescent cobalt blue back and a buffy, burnt-orange chest. Upon reaching northern breeding grounds, Barn Swallows begin collecting mud and water for nestbuilding. They may place their nest in a culvert, on beams under bridges, or on a barn, or outbuilding. This colonial species builds its bowl-shaped nest—made of mud and grass and lined with feathers—only inches away from its neighbor, yet the male will vigorously defend this small area from intruders. Barn Swallows skim pond or lake surfaces to snatch flying or floating insects. In the fall, the birds leave North America for lengthy treks to their wintering grounds in Central and South America, as far south as Argentina.

Range of Barn Swallow

CLASSIFICATION

The swallows—family Hirundinidae—are a well-defined family of aerialist songbirds without any truly close relatives. Swallows were once thought to be related to swifts because of their similar lifestyles and body types. Early ornithologists soon determined that the two groups are not closely related. Worldwide there are about 90 species of swallows and martins. Only eight species breed in North America and another six species have turned up as vagrants. By contrast, swallow-rich Africa has more than 40 breeding species and is probably the continent where the family originated. The common English names—swallow and martin—have no taxonomic significance, for example, our Bank Swallow is also known by its British name conversely as Sand Martin.

STRUCTURE

Swallows are beautifully adapted for life in the air. Their long, saber-tipped wings and substantial tails allow them to stay aloft for extended periods of time and to maneuver with grace and efficiency. They have short wide bills with a large gape, flanked by stiff bristles to facilitate the capture of their prey—flying insects. Their feet and legs are small, and they walk with a weak, shuffling gait. Like all songbirds, they perch easily and are often seen on overhead wires. In size, they range from about 4.75 inches (Bank Swallow) up to 8 inches (Purple Martin).

PLUMAGE

Swallow plumage is typically metallic blue or green above and white or buff below. Two species, the Northern Rough-winged and Bank Swallows, are brown above—possibly an adaptation to nesting in cavities or burrows.

Male Purple Martins are unusual in having completely dark plumage. Some species have contrasting flank patches or breastbands, while others exhibit distinctive patches of color on the forehead or rump that help in their identification.

The Barn Swallow has an exceptionally long, forked tail with white patches. This species is the only North American swallow with a classic "swallowtail." When fanned out, this long tail allows for remarkable maneuverability, but it is usually closed into a single point during direct flight.

Sexual variation is minimal in most species. In North America, only the Purple Martin has obvious differences between male and female plumage. Juveniles are duller than adults, but are otherwise quite similar. However, Tree Swallows and Purple Martins take two or more years to acquire full adult plumage. The subadults are distinguished by their browner or paler coloration.

FEEDING BEHAVIOR

Because swallows are aerial insect-feeders, which hunt their prey by sight, they are rather similar to each other in structure and feeding behavior. Unlike swifts, another group of aerial insect-feeders, the swallows have strong jaw muscles that allow them to snap their bills shut and subdue larger or harder prey such as small beetles and flying ants. Purple Martins take the largest prey—up to the size of butterflies and dragonflies. Swallows are capable of drinking, and even bathing, on the wing, by skimming just above the water's surface and dipping their bill, or breast, into the water.

Foraging altitude and habitat can vary from species to species, but there is substantial overlap, especially during migration. Purple Martins, and Cliff and Violet-green Swallows usually forage over land at higher altitudes than other swallow species. By contrast, Barn Swallows favor low-altitude foraging over fields and open country. Northern Rough-winged Swallows prefer low-altitude foraging over lakes, rivers, and other freshwater habitats. A favorite feeding tactic is skimming back and forth over open water, capturing emerging insects, or even picking them from the water's surface. The diet of most species is variable, exploiting any abundant insect prey, but some colonial species, such as Cliff and Bank Swallows, specialize on smaller, swarming insects. Some species add airborne spiders to their diets. Where different species nest in

Violet-green Swallow

the same area, each tends to specialize in different prey species or favors different habitats or feeding elevations.

Among all the world's swallows, only the Tree Swallow regularly feeds on plant material, particularly small berries. In the southern United States, Tree Swallows have a special fondness for waxy bayberries, having developed the specialized ability to digest them. These food adaptations allow Tree Swallows to migrate north sooner and linger there later in fall, than swallows that are solely dependent on insects.

VOCALIZATION

Although they are songbirds, the swallows are not known for their vocal prowess. Most vocalizing consists of a simple twittering; during the breeding season it often starts well before dawn. In migration, when mixed flocks may be encountered, subtle differences in their call notes can be helpful in picking out less common species.

BREEDING BEHAVIOR

Swallows can be categorized either as cavity-nesting or mud-nesting species. They vary from being highly colonial, to loosely so, and solitary. Over many generations, the swallow family has come to rely more on human-provided nest sites than any other family of birds in North America. Of all swallow species, the Purple Martins of eastern North America are the most dependent on this association. Most swallows lay from three to eight, white or lightly spotted eggs, that hatch about 14 days later. The young birds fledge about three weeks after that; Purple Martins need four weeks.

The cavity-nesting species—the Purple Martin, Tree, Bank, Rough-winged, and Violet-green Swallows—nest in natural holes and crevices, self-dug burrows, or man-made birdhouses. After constructing their nests, some species—especially Tree, Violet-green, and Barn Swallows—diligently search for white feathers to line the nest cup. So desirable are these feathers that, with a little conditioning, the birds can be coaxed into swooping down and taking them directly from a person's hand.

The mud-nesting species—Cliff, Cave, and Barn Swallows—construct either open cups or, in the case of the Cliff Swallow, completely enclosed gourd-like structures. Mud is carried to the nest site, mouthful by mouthful, by both sexes. Mud nests must be protected from the elements, and nest sites vary from natural (caves, overhanging cliffs) to human-made structures (bridges, culverts, barns, house eaves).

The highly colonial, mud-nesting Cliff Swallow has evolved an unusual, two-tiered breeding system.

OTHER SPECIES FIELD NOTES	
■ **Tree Swallow** *Tachycineta bicolor* L 5.75" Greenish blue above, white below	■ **Bank Swallow** *Riparia riparia* L 4.75" Brownish breastband with center spike
■ **Bahama Swallow** *Tachycineta cyaneoviridis* L 5.75" White underwing coverts	■ **Cliff Swallow** *Petrochelidon pyrrhonota* L 5.5" Squarish tail, buffy rump, dark throat
■ **Violet-green Swallow** *Tachycineta thalassina* L 5.25" White on cheeks extends above eye	■ **Northern Rough-winged Swallow** *Stelgidopteryx serripennis* L 5" Brown above, whitish below
■ **Purple Martin** *Progne subis* L 8" Purplish blue	■ **Cave Swallow** *Petrochelidon fulva* L 5.5" Buffy throat and ear coverts
■ **Common House-Martin** *Delichon urbica* L 5" Glossy blue above, mostly white below	

Some birds in a given colony are intraspecific brood parasites; that is, they lay their eggs in the nests of neighboring Cliff Swallows. A parasitic individual will enter a nearby nest, sometimes toss out an existing egg, and lay her own egg in that nest—all in less than a minute. Some parasitic birds have even been seen carrying their own eggs to neighboring nests in their beaks. These parasitic Cliff Swallows may make up 25 percent of a colony and are very successful breeders—they raise their own broods, in addition to the eggs they lay in other nests. It is unknown whether these parasitic individuals are genetically different or are responding to environmental stimuli.

BREEDING RANGE

As a family, swallows breed throughout North America, with the exception of the northernmost Arctic. The various swallow species are adapted to a wide variety of habitats and, because of their abundance and close association with man, they are familiar birds to the general public. Of the more common species, the Cave Swallow has the most restricted breeding range in North America. It only breeds in Texas and New Mexico on a regular basis, with a small population of a different subspecies in south Florida.

The breeding range and population status of Cave Swallows in North America is undergoing a transformation. More than 30 years ago, Cave Swallows were considered a rare species in North America—nesting locally in south-central Texas and around Carlsbad Caverns National Park in New Mexico. They favored limestone caves and sinkholes for nesting.

In 1972, a University of Texas survey team discovered that Cave Swallows had colonized an extensive system of Texas highway culverts and were actually much more common than previously thought. Twenty years later, in the early 1990s, wandering Cave Swallows were observed as far north as Cape May, New Jersey. They were seen mostly in November, not in large numbers, perhaps a few each year, and experts were wondering what was going on. Then in November 1999 Cave Swallows turned up all over the East, even in southern Canada. There were more than a hundred birds in Cape May (including a flock of 30), 90 in Ontario, 35 in Connecticut, and smaller numbers in other eastern states. Although the 1999 invasion was clearly related to a southern storm that moved north from Texas, the numbers were unprecedented.

PURPLE MARTIN

Unique to North American birds, Purple Martins of the common, eastern race (*subis*) are completely dependent on humans to provide them with nesting sites. Some time in the distant past, Native Americans discovered that Purple Martins could be attracted to hanging gourds or calabashes that had been hollowed out. These attractive and sociable birds were desirable company and the tradition became widespread among the tribes of eastern North America. European colonists took up and expanded the practice; in addition, the clearing of forested land provided more of the open habitat favored by martins. Over hundreds of generations the martins prospered under this arrangement and eventually abandoned natural nest sites in favor of human-provided housing. Today hundreds of thousands of nest sites, mostly in the form of apartment-style nest boxes, are provided. Early each spring, the regular return of the first martins is an eagerly anticipated event. To find out more contact the Purple Martin Conservation Association at www.purple-martin.org.

Purple Martins from the Rocky Mountains westward belong to a different subspecies (*arboricola*). These western birds are mostly solitary nesters and use natural tree cavities or old woodpecker holes for nesting—not martin houses.

Could this have happened if the Cave Swallows in Texas had not colonized the state's highway culverts and improved their breeding success? Other questions, as well, remain unanswered.

Some of the East Coast records definitely belong to a different subspecies—the one from the Caribbean that breeds sparingly in south Florida. In a "normal" year, are these birds that are making their way up the coast north to Cape May and beyond? No one knows for certain, but birders along the eastern seaboard will be scrutinizing all November swallows in the years to come.

MIGRATION

All North American swallows are migratory, some highly so. They are diurnal, or daytime, migrants and large groups may be encountered in the spring and fall. In late summer, large concentrations of birds may gather before migration in favorable coastal and inland marshes; premigration flocks of Tree Swallows estimated at more than half a million birds have occurred. Lakes, rivers, and other water impoundments are reliable locations for observing migrating swallows; often flocks can be seen resting in long rows on power lines. In the spring, some adult males are very early migrants, to claim and defend a prime nesting territory. On occasion, they succumb to a late-season snowstorm or starve from lack of available insect food.

Cliff Swallow

WINTER RANGE

Dependent on a reliable source of flying insects for food, North American swallows must winter south of their breeding range, except those that breed in the southernmost United States. Even there, swallows are generally scarce in winter—the species most likely to be seen is the Tree Swallow. Most North American swallows spend the winter months farther south, in Central or South America.

Purple Martins undertake some of the longest migrations. Most Purple Martins spend the northern winter in South America, with some individuals penetrating well into the Amazon Basin and others travelling as far south as coastal northern Argentina.

OBSERVING SWALLOWS

Being an abundant species of open spaces, swallows are often encountered by birders and are not difficult to identify. Nest sites can be easy to locate and offer long and satisfying observations. At the other end of the spectrum, fall flocks that have a mixture of adults and young birds of a variety of species can be challenging. The so-called "brown swallows" (Bank Swallows, Rough-winged Swallows, and juvenile Tree Swallows) are particularly difficult to separate. During observations you should concentrate on breast pattern, general shape, and flight characteristics. One clue, for instance, is that Bank Swallows have a distinct breastband; they are noticeably small and compact, and fly with rapid, shallow wingbeats.

Six swallow species are casual or accidental in North America. Three martins—Cuban, Gray-breasted, and Southern Martins—have not been recorded in North America for more than one hundred years. The Brown-chested Martin (two records in the East) and the Common House-Martin (eight records, mostly in Alaska) have been recorded more recently. The Bahama Swallow is casual in south Florida and may have nested there at some point, but the bird is not seen every year. The Bahama Swallow has a very small world population, which is roughly estimated at 2,500 pairs.

In an unusual event, a Mangrove Swallow (*Tachycineta albilinea*), native to Mexico and Central America, was seen and photographed in Florida in November 2002. If accepted by the Florida and national record committees, it will become the first record of that species for North America.

STATUS AND CONSERVATION

All eight swallow species which breed in North America remain abundant and are easily observed by the active birder. In fact, human activities—from land clearing, to highway and bridge construction, and providing nest boxes—have benefited some species. On the other hand, the destruction of marshes and swamps, and the loss of open land to housing sprawl have had a negative impact on some populations. Protection of traditional, premigration roosting sites may be an important conservation goal.

Purple Martin populations are in decline throughout the United States. In the West the reason is probably because of loss of habitat. In the East Purple Martins may be losing in the fierce competition with European Starlings and House Sparrows for space in nesting boxes.

See also

Nighthawks, Nightjars, page 217
Swifts, page 223

PURPLE MARTIN

GRADUAL SPRING MIGRATION

Approximate arrival
date in spring

The southwestern population
arrives much later than its
eastern counterpart.

May 15
April 10
May 15
May 1
April 15
April 1
March 15
March 1
April 1
February 15
May 1
February 1
Feb. 15
February 1
January 15

STATUTE MILES
0   500   1000
0   500   1000
KILOMETERS

Longitude West 90° of Greenwich

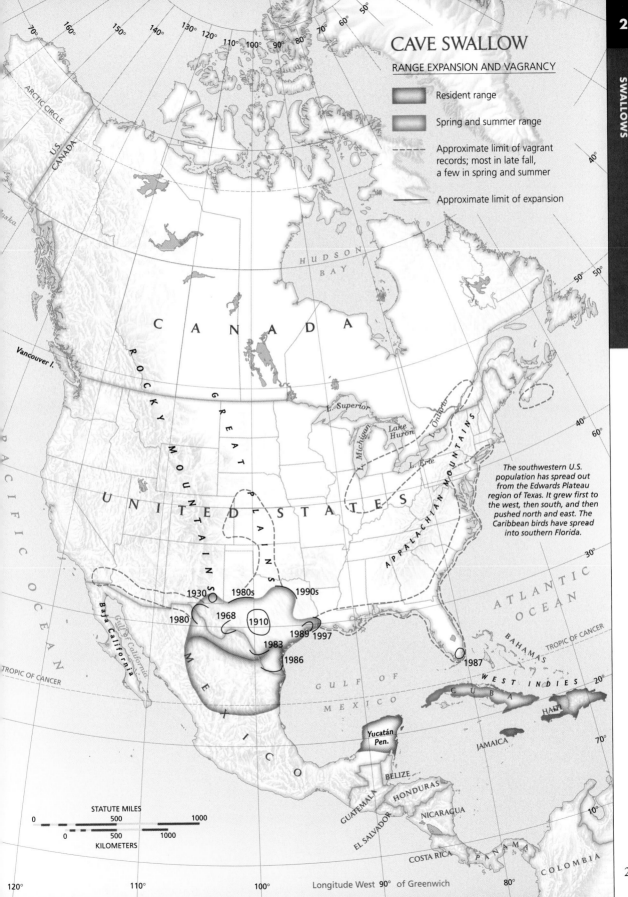

CAVE SWALLOW

RANGE EXPANSION AND VAGRANCY

Resident range

Spring and summer range

- - - - Approximate limit of vagrant
records; most in late fall,
a few in spring and summer

———— Approximate limit of expansion

*The southwestern U.S.
population has spread
out from the Edwards Plateau
region of Texas. It grew first to
the west, then south, and then
pushed north and east. The
Caribbean birds have spread
into southern Florida.*

ARCTIC CIRCLE

U.S.
CANADA

Alaska

PACIFIC OCEAN

Vancouver I.

ROCKY MOUNTAINS

GREAT

HUDSON BAY

C A N A D A

L. Superior

Lake Michigan

Lake Huron

L. Ontario

L. Erie

APPALACHIAN MOUNTAINS

U N I T E D S T A T E S

P L A I N S

ATLANTIC OCEAN

BAHAMAS   TROPIC OF CANCER

Baja California

Gulf of California

TROPIC OF CANCER

1930s   1980s   1990s

1980   1968   1910

1989 1997

1983

1986

1987

GULF OF MEXICO

W E S T   I N D I E S

C U B A

HAITI

M E X I C O

JAMAICA

Yucatán Pen.

BELIZE

GUATEMALA

HONDURAS

EL SALVADOR   NICARAGUA

COSTA RICA   PANAMA

COLOMBIA

STATUTE MILES

0   500   1000

0   500   1000

KILOMETERS

CHICKADEES, NUTHATCHES, ALLIES

Christopher Wood

This chapter includes five families of birds that at one time or another were thought to be closely related: Paridae, Remizidae, Aegithalidae, Sittidae, and Certhiidae. In North America, the family Paridae (Chickadees and Titmice) is composed of twelve species of parids. Many, like the beloved Black-capped Chickadee, are widespread and familiar species. A handful has small ranges in North America including the Gray-headed Chickadee—probably the species that is most difficult to see of all species that regularly breed in North America. The family Remizidae (Penduline Tits) includes but a single North American species, the Verdin, which is found in the arid southwest. The drab-colored Bushtit is the only member of the family Aegithalidae (Long-tailed Tits) that occurs in North America. The four North American species of nuthatches belong to the family Sittidae. The final family, Certhiidae, also includes a single well-known North American species, the Brown Creeper.

There is still a fair share of mystery surrounding this group. The Siberian Tit, found only in remote parts of Alaska, Yukon, and the Northwest Territories, is probably the most difficult regular breeding species to see in North America because of its largely inaccessible breeding grounds. In the past decade two species were split—Plain Titmouse into Juniper and Oak Titmouse—and more recently, Black-crested Titmouse was split from Tufted Titmouse. Further species questions surround the widespread White-breasted Nuthatch, which shows considerable geographic variation in vocalizations as well as differences in plumage.

This group includes some of North America's most beloved birds. The Black-capped Chickadee is the state bird of both Maine and Massachusetts. Nuthatches, creepers, and chickadees are frequent visitors to feeders, particularly in the fall and winter where many species of nuthatches and creepers gather seeds to store in caches for retrieval later. Food caches are particularly important for several species that remain in extremely cold environments with short days during the winter. Gray-headed Chickadees, or Siberian Tits as they were formerly called, routinely winter north of the Arctic Circle, and many Black-capped and Boreal Chickadees remain far to the north.

Nest structures differ considerably between several of these families. Parids usually nest in cavities, either natural, such as those created by woodpeckers, or man-made nest boxes. Creepers build a cup nest behind tree bark. Bushtits build a tightly woven hanging gourd-shaped nest with an entrance near the top. Verdins build a large spherical stick nest with an entrance on the side. Nuthatches nest in natural cavities, woodpecker holes, or similar structures.

Most species are nonmigratory, or have rather limited movements. Several species, however, such as the Red-breasted Nuthatch and Black-capped Chickadee irrupt somewhat regularly at least from portions of their range to move further south for no more than a hundred miles, much to the delight of bird-watchers to the south. More research is needed to determine if severe large-scale drought may reduce food supplies and trigger dispersal of several montain species.

Black-capped Chickadee: *Poecile atricapilla,* L 5.25",
ragged-edged black bib, frosty wing panel

CHICKADEES AND ALLIES

Of the two chickadee species in North America, the Black-capped (above) is primarily a northern bird that ranges from New England to northern New Mexico and northward to western Alaska. It is the larger of the two chickadees and can be distinguished from the Carolina Chickadee by range and song, with a two-note whistle rather than the four-note song. The species prefers high altitude habitats where its range may overlap with Carolina Chickadees. Black-capped Chickadees feed on seeds and tree-dwelling insects and often join feeding flocks of similar-size species that forage through forests and meadows. These birds seek out backyard feeders and relish sunflower seeds. Black-capped Chickadees are cavity nesters that excavate a suitable site in rotten wood or seek a nestbox or natural cavity for nest building. Moss, wood chips, and various discarded man-made materials are used for lining. A chickadee brood usually consists of six to eight hatchlings that are fed by both parents. The species remains year-round on their range.

Range of Black-capped Chickadee

CLASSIFICATION

The taxonomy of parids (chickadees and titmice), family Paridae, has changed considerably over the decades. Although it is agreed upon that chickadees and titmice are closely related, the relationships of the long-tailed tits (including Bushtit in North America) and Penduline Tits (including Verdin in North America) are less clear. Once considered part of Paridae, each of these groups is now thought to be in a separate family. In fact, some experts suggest that the long-tailed tits (Family Aegithalidae) are actually more closely related to gnatcatchers than to chickadees and titmice.

Until recently all Parids were classified under the genus *Parus,* but recent studies looking at DNA-DNA hybridization resulted in placing the parids into several genera. Two genera occur in North America, *Poecile* (all the North American chickadees) and *Baeolophus* (all the titmice). Species limits within the Parids have also changed. Juniper Titmouse and Oak Titmouse were once considered to be one specie—the Plain Titmouse. Most recently, the Black-crested Titmouse of central Texas was split from the widespread Tufted Titmouse. Carolina Chickadee and Black-capped Chickadee have also sometimes been considered as a single species. Despite occasional hybridization between the two species, and more frequent song learning of the "other" species, the Black-capped Chickadee appears more closely related to the Mountain Chickadee than the Carolina Chickadee, and is best treated as a separate species.

STRUCTURE

Parids are small to medium-size passerines with a short stout bill and short, very strong legs and feet. The stout bill helps parids pound seeds into crevices for storage, and to open a variety of seeds. Parids may place seeds into crannies to simply hold the seed and make it easier to open, as is the case when a chickadee grabs a sunflower seed from a feeder, or when it leaves the seed for retrieval several months later. Specialized leg muscles help chickadees cling to the end of branches, hang upside down, and obtain food in difficult to reach places. Parid wings are short and rounded, and the tail is rather long and squared or slightly notched. Chickadees and Titmice avoid flying long distances at any one time and seem to prefer to take short flights from tree to tree.

PLUMAGE

Most North American parids are hued in shades of grays and browns. North American chickadees have a dark cap and a black or brown throat. The flanks of the Tufted and the Black-crested Titmouse and several chickadees can be a rather bright buff, cinnamon, or even chestnut in color, and it is the flanks that are usually the brightest part of North American parids. The Oak Titmouse and the Juniper Titmouse are exceedingly plain. The Bridled

Titmouse is the most distinctive North American parid with an unmistakable harlequin-like facial pattern.

Several species appear quite similar and are difficult to identify. The Boreal Chickadee looks much like the Gray-headed Chickadee, but has a smaller cheek patch, shorter tail, and uniformly gray wing coverts. The Black-capped Chickadee and the Carolina Chickadee also appear somewhat the same, and separation is best determined by range. The Oak Titmouse and the Juniper Titmouse are also undifferentiated in their plain plumage; luckily they only overlap on the Modoc plateau in northern California.

Hybrids between the Black-capped and the Mountain Chickadee, the Black-capped and the Carolina Chickadee, and the Tufted and the Black-crested Titmouse are not unusual in areas where these species overlap. A hybrid Mountain x Black-capped Chickadee looks like a Black-capped Chickadee on one side and a Mountain Chickadee on the other side. Geographic variation between subspecies is weak and clinal for most

Boreal Chickadee

species. The Black-capped, Mountain, Chestnut-backed, and Boreal Chickadees exhibit moderate variations between subspecies, but even with these species, variation is clinal where the ranges of subspecies meet.

FEEDING BEHAVIOR

Parids eat a wide selection of seeds, berries, and insects. Particularly during the breeding season, titmice and chickadees eat a variety of caterpillars, moths, beetles, aphids, other insects, and spiders. Bridled Titmice often feed on acorn pulp and search for snout beetles growing inside acorns. Gray-headed Chickadees will apparently consume carrion and have been observed feeding on a dead cow. Most species are often observed hanging upside down to reach food. Many parids are favorites at feeding stations. A chickadee or titmouse usually flies in and grabs a large seed from the feeder. The bird then flies off with the seed in its bill and either eats the seed or places it in a cache. Some caches may be temporary, but many of these storage sites are important for parids that winter in cold and harsh environments.

During the nonbreeding season most parids travel in small flocks and form the center of mixed species flocks. Some of the most conspicuous flocks of tits in the northern United States and southern Canada are dominated by Black-capped Chickadees. These flocks may include permanent flock members during the nonbreeding season as well as roving chickadees that float between different flocks. Oak and Juniper Titmice are territorial year round and do not form flocks. Gray-headed Chickadees are also different from most parids in that flocks are typically composed only of family groups.

VOCALIZATION

The best way to locate chickadees and nuthatches is by listening to parid vocalizations. Their sounds are a familiar year-round component of most North American woodlands. Bird-watchers learn to listen for flocks of parids because titmice and chickadees often flock with other species such as kinglets, nuthatches, creepers, warblers, and vireos. At times flocks of agitated parids may reveal the presence of a small owl or other predator that is being mobbed by the birds; again other species may join the mobbing or at least fly in and investigate. Most species have a fairly wide array of vocalizationsl. For example, the Black-capped Chickadee has at least 15 different kinds of vocalizations; the Boreal Chickadee has 13 major calls or call complexes; and the Tufted Titmouse has 10 groups of calls. All North American chickadees have a call that sounds at least vaguely like "chick-a-dee," but these are quite variable and may require some imagination to hear. The Boreal, Gray-headed, Chestnut-backed, and Mexican

---

OTHER SPECIES FIELD NOTES

- **Bridled Titmouse**
  Baeolophus wollweberi
  L 5.25"
  Distinct crest, black-and-white face pattern

- **Oak Titmouse**
  Baeolophus inornatus
  L 5"
  Grayish-brown, short crest

- **Juniper Titmouse**
  Baeolophus ridgwayi
  L 5.25"
  Pale gray, short crest

- **Tufted Titmouse**
  Baeolophus bicolor
  L 6.25"
  Gray crest, black forehead

- **Black-crested Titmouse**
  Baeolophus atricristatus
  L 5.75"
  Black crest, pale forehead

- **Carolina Chickadee**
  Poecile carolinensis
  L 4.75"
  Smooth-edged black bib, gray wing panel

- **Mexican Chickadee**
  Poecile sclateri
  L 5"
  Dark gray flanks

- **Mountain Chickadee**
  Poecile gambeli
  L 5.25"
  White eyebrow

- **Chestnut-backed Chickadee**
  Poecile rufescens
  L 4.75"
  Chestnut back and rump

- **Gray-headed Chickadee**
  Poecile cincta
  L 5.5"
  Gray-brown above

- **Boreal Chickadee**
  Poecile hudsonica
  L 5.5"
  Chestnut brown flanks, dark wings

- **Verdin**
  Auriparus flaviceps
  L 4 .5"
  Yellow head and throat

- **Bushtit**
  Psaltriparus minimus
  L 4.5"
  Gray above, pale below, long tail

Verdin
Auriparus, L 4.5″, gray-brown above, ashy-gray below, yellow forecrown, chin and throat, chestnut shoulder patches

This nonmigratory desert dweller is known for building a surprising number of conspicuous nests, including smaller roosting nests built in all seasons and continually maintained. The brood nest is a hollow sphere constructed of small, thorny twigs and lined with leaves, grass, and feathers with the entrance hole located low on the side. Valuable nesting material is often stolen from other Verdins. One of our smallest songbirds, this active, vocal insect gleaner also feeds on flower nectar and from hummingbird feeders.

Bushtit
Psaltriparus minimus, L 4.5″, gray plumage; brown crown on coastal birds, brown earpatch on interior population

A small bird with a long tail that travels in flocks and gleans insects from trees and bushes, the Bushtit is so inconspicuous that it may not be observed until a group streams from a foraging site in a long, continuous, undulating file. The birds often fasten their pendulous, gourd-shaped nest with spider webs to clumps of mistletoe, orienting it so the incubating chamber at the bottom of the sack receives the warming rays of the morning sun. Unmated males and other adults are known to assist in raising chicks. Some adults, mainly males of the extreme Southwest, have a black mask or earpatch.

Chickadees lack a whistled song typical of other chickadees. Most species, however, are quite vocal year round, although the species becomes less conspicuous and noisy during nesting.

Parids are inquisitive and often respond to imitations of their songs and pishing. The birds frequently will fly in quite close and give a variety of calls. Once a few chickadees or titmice arrive, you can usually expect a few more species to be attracted.

BREEDING BEHAVIOR

Chickadees and titmice generally form pair bonds in the fall, and they remain together in a winter flock. After flocks break up in late winter, both sexes defend the territory. The Boreal Chickadee and the Carolina Chickadee, as well as several other parids, may mate for life. The breeding behavior of the Mexican Chickadee and the Gray-headed Chickadee in North America is only poorly known.

Parids nest in cavities, including old woodpecker holes and other natural crevices, and many species will use nesting boxes. Tufted Titmice and Black-capped Chickadees will even nest in fence posts in open pastures, as long as these are surrounded by more appropriate habitat. Typically only females develop a brood patch and incubate eggs. Although the males of Black-capped Chickadees have been noted with partial brood patches, there is no evidence they ever incubate. Males frequently feed the incubating female. Chickadees and titmice keep a clean home, and once the young hatch, it is common to see one of the parents fly out with a fecal sac. Both parents feed the young until the juveniles disperse. Pairs of Tufted Titmice may be assisted by a "helper" bird, usually one of their offspring from a previous year.

BREEDING RANGE

Parids are generally found in wooded habitats year round. During the breeding season, chickadees and titmice require trees that are large enough to have natural cavities or old woodpecker holes. Most habitats rarely support more than one or two breeding species of parids. Similar species are usually separated by habitat types, but do come into contact in some places. Whereas Oak and Juniper Titmice are both found in dry habitats, Oak Titmice generally breed in warm oak or oak-pine woodlands. Juniper Titmice, by contrast, are found at higher elevations and are most commonly found where juniper is prevalent with large, older trees with cavities for nesting. Black-capped and Carolina Chickadees overlap in the Appalachians, where Black-capped Chickadees are typically found at higher elevations. In places where the Black-capped Chickadee overlaps with the Mountain Chickadee and the Boreal Chickadee, the Black-capped is usually found in deciduous patches.

The Gray-headed and Mexican Chickadees have very

limited ranges in the United States and Canada. The Gray-headed Chickadee is the only parid found in both the New World and the Old World, and it also has one of the most inaccessible breeding ranges of any North American species, with much of the range above the Arctic Circle. Gray-headed Chickadees are the sole parid in this area and are found in narrow belts of willow and spruce along rivers in habitat that is otherwise tundra. The Mexican Chickadee has one of the most restricted ranges north of the United States border; it breeds in the Chiricahua Mountains of southeastern Arizona and the higher peaks of the Animas Mountains in southwestern New Mexico.

MIGRATION

Parids are mostly sedentary and no species is a long-distance migrant. A few species may move short distances, but it is difficult to discern breeders from migrants and winterers because of the short distances they typically travel. Mountain Chickadees sometimes move to lower elevations in the winter, at times well over a hundred miles. Numbers fluctuate from year to year, probably based on available food, but in most years migrating Mountain Chickadees are found as far east as Morton County, Kansas, a distance of at least a hundred miles from the nearest breeding location.

Carolina Chickadee

Most of the migrant Mountain Chickadees are birds in their first fall or winter. Some Bridled Titmice move to riparian communities at lower elevations. In southeastern Arizona, Bridled Titmice move to riparian corridors in late September and return to higher elevations by mid-April. Boreal Chickadees also stage periodic irruptions outside the breeding range in fall, winter, and spring.

Irruptions often occur during different years in different areas, but usually coincide with major movements of other birds. For instance, Boreal Chickadees wander to the south, typically during "good" flights of Black-capped Chickadees—but not all significant movements of Black-capped Chickadees are matched by flights of Boreal Chickadees. At least in parts of the West, significant movements of Mountain Chickadees and Pygmy Nuthatches to the plains may correlate with movements of corvids, finches, and even hummingbirds. Several mountain species are known to disperse during extreme drought conditions.

WINTER RANGE

Gray-headed Chickadees—the Siberian Tits—routinely winter north of the Arctic Circle. Their remote range makes it very difficult to learn much about the details of their winter range and behavior. Northern species such as the Black-capped, Boreal, and Gray-headed Chickadees must contend with short days, extremely cold temperatures, and long nights. Under these conditions, parids can lower their body temperature to save energy. Food that was stored in the fall becomes particularly important.

OBSERVING PARIDS

Generally it is easy to observe most parids. Several species are regulars at bird feeders, including the Carolina Chickadee, the Black-capped Chickadee, and the Mountain Chickadee, as well as the Tufted Titmouse and the Black-crested Titmouse. Finding the Gray-headed Chickadee in North America, on the other hand, is very challenging, and typically bird-watchers find themselves on a bush plane, on remote wilderness roads, or fording some river, and in most instances in some combination of these situations.

Movements of Black-capped Chickadees are apparent in several regions. Locations that funnel or trap birds along some of the Great Lakes can be particularly good. At the top of the list is White Fish Point, Michigan, where Black-capped Chickadees migrate through each year. Boreal Chickadees are also present almost every year at White Fish Point, and in some years spectacular movements of Black-capped and Boreal Chickadees occur.

STATUS AND CONSERVATION

Compared to many other families of birds, parids are not at risk. Only one species is classified by Birdlife International as threatened anywhere in the world, the White-naped Tit, which is endemic to tropical dry scrub forest in India, and is listed as vulnerable. Three other tits, two in the Philippines and one in Taiwan, are also considered near threatened.

The Oak Titmouse is the only parid on the Audubon WatchList. Habitat loss as a result of increasing suburban sprawl is the greatest threat to this species. A fungal disease in parts of California has also killed several thousand oaks within the range of the Oak Titmouse. While this is not a direct threat, some land managers combat the spread by removing dead or dying oaks, which titmice use for nesting.

Gray-headed Chickadees in Eurasia are vulnerable to habitat loss, caused almost exclusively by commercial logging. In the United States and Canada, trees within the range of the Gray-headed Chickadee are too small, scattered and stunted for commercial logging operations.

See also

Kinglets, Gnatcatchers, page, 314

White-breasted Nuthatch: *Sitta carolinensis*, L 5.75", black cap, white face

NUTHATCHES, ALLIES

The most wide-ranging bird of this family, the White-breasted Nuthatch (above) is a sleek, elongated black-and-gray bird with rufous patches on the rump or flank, a white throat, and a prominent black crown. The species is common throughout the United States and southern Canada, usually found in mixed deciduous and pine forests. Nuthatches often forage in pairs or with a feeding flock, particularly during the winter. They are distinguished by their food-gathering behavior of climbing headfirst down trees and combing tree trunks and branches for insects and nuts, rather than hopping from limb to limb like other birds. Nuthatches are cavity nesters that seek abandoned woodpecker holes or natural cavities in decaying trees. A nuthatch pair builds a nest of twigs lined with feathers, hair, or fur. A typical nuthatch brood has six to eight young, cared for by both parents. The species is nonmigratory and stays year-round on its range. Nuthatches may roam widely in winter in search of food and often descend to lower altitudes to avoid severe winter storms.

Range of White-breasted Nuthatch

CLASSIFICATION

Nuthatches are widely thought to have a close relationship with Sittidae, but the relationships of creepers are poorly understood. The American Ornothologists' Union considers the Brown Creeper to be the only New World member of the tree-creeper family Certhiidae, comprised of six species in the genus *Certhia* and the Spotted Creeper (*Salpornis spilonotus*). Others using DNA-DNA hybridization suggest that creepers may be part of a much larger family of some 100 species that would also include wrens, gnatcatchers and gnateaters. Of the 25 species of nuthatches found in the world, four are North American species.

STRUCTURE

Nuthatches are small and compact birds. Their bill is strong, rather long, straight, and pointed. They have short legs with strong feet and long claws they use for climbing up and down tree trunks. The wings and tail are short. Creepers are immediately recognizable as such. They are small with a long, graduated tail composed of 12 stiff and pointed rectrices they use for support when climbing. Their wings are short and rounded. The legs are short with long claws. The bill is medium long, slender, and noticeably decurved.

PLUMAGE

Most nuthatches have blue-gray upperparts. The crown is brown or black, and most species have a dark eye line. Pygmy and Brown-headed Nuthatches are similar in appearance, but only present identification challenges when an individual wanders out of range. Birds up to one year can usually be separated from adults by plumage characteristics until the end of spring. The sexes are also similar, but male and female Red-breasted and White-breasted Nuthatches can be separated by plumage. Male Red-breasteds have darker black crowns than females that contrast more with upperparts. The crown and nape of White-breasteds is more uniformly black on males; the crown on females has some gray feathers and contrasts with the blacker nape. Nuthatch hybrids are unknown in North America. The Red-breasted Nuthatch is monotypic, and Brown-headed Nuthatches show weak variation between the two subspecies. Pygmy and White-breasted Nuthatches show more variation between subspecies.

FEEDING BEHAVIOR

Creepers and Nuthatches all climb trees, but foraging styles differ. Nuthatches move up and *down* branches and trunks, using only their strong legs for support. Nuthatches glean food from bark crevices, and they may make small holes. Brown-headed and Pygmy Nuthatches forage in clusters of pine needles at the tip of branches; they occasionally fly to the ground to feed. Their diet is similar to that of creepers, but nuthatches consume more nuts and store food in caches. Several species frequent bird feeders. Nuthatches gather in small flocks during the nonbreeding season, often with chickadees, kinglets, and creepers. As is true for chickadees, calling nuthatches may reveal the presence of a mixed flock, so it pays to track down these birds during the nonbreeding season.

Creepers, like woodpeckers, use their tail for support and cannot climb head down. They are often seen on tree trunks, spiraling their way upward looking for insects, particularly eggs and pupae hidden in the bark. Once a creeper finishes with a tree, it flies toward the next tree and spirals up. Creepers sometimes visit bird feeders where they feed on suet or peanut butter.

Brown Creeper

VOCALIZATION

White-breasted Nuthatches and Brown Creepers exhibit geographic variation in vocalizations between different subspecies, which is not completely understood. Call notes of White-breasted Nuthatches differ between birds in the East, Rocky Mountains, Great Basin, coastal California, and Mexico; these differences may suggest that more than one species is involved. Songs of Eastern, Western, and Mexican Brown Creepers differ. While experts focus attention on regional differences in songs and calls, many people struggle just to hear the high-pitched sound of the Brown Creeper, the call notes of which are often confused with the Golden-crowned Kinglet.

BREEDING BEHAVIOR

Nuthatches, like chickadees, build nests in cavities. Some Brown-headed and Pygmy Nuthatches have helper adults that assist in nest building and feeding the young; Brown-headed Nuthatches have rarely more than one helper, but Pygmy Nuthatches have up to three. Helpers of both species are typically first-year males. Creepers build an unusual half-cup nest of twigs, bark strips, and moss, tucked between tree bark

and the trunk. Nests can be up to seven feet off the ground.

BREEDING RANGE

All but the White-breasted Nuthatch prefer habitats with a significant conifer component. The Brown-headed Nuthatch is endemic to the southeastern United States where it is found in pine forests. The Brown Creepers require mature forests with large trees. They are found in bottomland forest in the East and forests in the North and West.

MIGRATION

Nuthatches are largely nonmigratory. Some White-breasted Nuthatches move south each fall. Portions of Kansas and Colorado lack breeding White-breasted Nuthatches, so those that regularly appear in fall, winter, and spring are migrants. In these areas, mountain birds (*Sitta carolinensis nelsoni*) typically outnumber the eastern White-breasted Nuthatches (*S.c. carolinensis* including *S.c. cookei*), but both subspecies are regular migrants. The northern populations of Red-breasted Nuthatches move south each year, and some mountain breeders move to lower elevations; other populations are irruptive. In large flight years, hundreds of these birds can move through an area (e.g. Gaspé Peninsula of Quebec) in a few hours. The Pygmy and Brown-headed Nuthatches are largely sedentary, but both species have appeared well out of range. The Brown Creepers regularly move south in the fall and may be seen in small flocks during migration.

WINTER RANGE

The winter range of nuthatches is generally similar to the breeding range, although the Red-breasted Nuthatches may travel as far south as Louisiana, Georgia, and northern Florida.

OBSERVING NUTHATCHES AND ALLIES

All five species are easily observed in appropriate habitats. All but Brown-headed Nuthatches are regularly seen at bird feeders.

STATUS AND CONSERVATION

The Brown-headed Nuthatch is the only nuthatch or creeper on the Audubon WatchList with a 2.2 percent population decline between 1966 and 2001.

OTHER SPECIES FIELD NOTES

■ **Brown Creeper**
Certhia americana
L 5.25"
Streaked brown with white underparts

■ **Red-breasted Nuthatch**
Sitta canadensis
L 4.5"
White eyebrow, rusty underparts

■ **Pygmy Nuthatch**
Sitta pygmaea
L 4.25"
Pale nape spot, gray-brown cap

■ **Brown-headed Nuthatch**
Sitta pusilla
L 4.5"
Pale nape spot, brown cap

See also

Woodpeckers, page 247
Warblers, page 358

WRENS, DIPPERS

Most often seen scurrying and flitting about in shrubs and brush or rock piles, on or near the ground, wrens often appear to be in a great rush to get somewhere or to find something. Their family name, Troglodytidae, derives from the Classical Greek words *trogle* and *dytes* meaning "hole" and "diver" respectively, and it describes well the wren family's penchant for ducking deep into bushes and tangles for cover when threatened.

Philip
Brandt
George

They are small- to medium-size birds, ranging in length from the tiny Winter Wren, which measures about 4 inches, to the much larger Cactus Wren at 8.5 inches. Usually clad in reddish to grayish browns on the back and head, many sport striping, barring, or spotting on their tails. They are stocky birds with short, rounded wings and a tendency to "cock" their stubby tails in an upright position. The variety and volume of their song belie their small size. The extensive repertoire of some wrens bedevil at times even the most experienced birders. Often the song is so loud, especially in the Carolina Wren, that the observers wonder at how such a tiny bird can conjure such volume.

A unique head shape and location, coupled with a slender, slightly down-curved bill, allows wrens to search for prey deep into nooks and crevices in dead wood, tree bark, and under rocks—places unavailable to other birds.

A rare practice among other birds, several wren species often enter the nests of their own and other species, not to eat, but rather, expressly to destroy the eggs. Some scholars hypothesize that the resulting decrease in young in the territory may reduce competition for food and nesting sites, and fewer active nests might make the area less attractive to predators.

Superficially at least, the sooty- to slaty-gray American Dippers, with their thickset shape, short wings, busy demeanor, and frequently cocked tails, resemble large, stocky wrens. Dipper song is highly variable and often bubbly like that of wrens, and like some wrens, they too prefer to build their domed nests with side openings in crevices. In spite of these apparent similarities, wrens and dippers are not close relatives.

The term "dipper" seems to refer to the nearly constant bobbing of the bird's body and tail and the extending or stretching of the wings. These movements may help in communications with other dippers in the noisy environment, help locate prey by offering constantly changing angles of view, or show how fit they are and thus deter predation. Local names for the American Dipper include "Water Ouzel," stemming from the Anglo-Saxon word *osle,* meaning "blackbird."

The American Dippers have developed traits that make them the only truly aquatic passerines, capable of swimming on the surface, diving, and even walking along the bottom of streams in search of prey. Adaptations in plumage, eyes, wings, legs, toes, and nostrils permit dippers to forage in currents that can knock down an adult human. The birds are good indicators of water quality, because they seem to thrive only where their habitat remains fairly pristine. They have declined, however, where streams have become polluted. Although dippers compete with trout for certain types of food, the degree of competition between the two has not been established, and ornithologists and fly-fishermen have joined hands to help preserve the habitat shared by bird and fish.

(Left) *Marsh Wren*

House Wren: *Troglodytes aedon*, L 4.75", Brown, faint eyebrow, plain underparts

WRENS, DIPPERS

One of the smallest wren species in North America, second to the Sedge Wren, the House Wren is found throughout the United States and lower portions of Canada. Probably the drabbest of all wren species, House Wrens lack the bold eye-stripes and rich chocolate-brown barring and markings of other species. House Wrens, especially males, are distinguished by their characteristic bubbling and whistling song, often given in rapid succession by males when searching for a partner in the springtime and defending the pair's territory. This species is also known for its penchant for human tolerance, often nesting in gardens or backyards.

Range of House Wren

House Wrens primarily are insect eaters, spending much of the day foraging among leaf-litter and scouring bushes for small insects. A wren pair builds a nest together but the male often begins construction at a number of sites before a preferred location is chosen. The females lays five or six eggs in a grass-and-feather lined nest. In the fall, House Wrens migrate to the lower southeastern and southwestern states as well as Mexico for the winter.

CLASSIFICATION

The wrens of the family Troglodytidae are said to have originated in North America and gradually spread to Central and South America, where they reached their greatest diversity. Only nine of the more than 70 recognized species are known to breed in North America. The diminutive Winter Wren is the only member of the family to have spread out from the New World by crossing the Bering Strait from modern Alaska eons ago: It now appears throughout Asia and Europe. Wrens are apparently more closely related to the Old World warblers than any other avian family.

The American Dipper is the only one of the world's five known species that appears in North America. Although the dipper has been placed in taxonomies near the wrens, DNA studies indicate that the dipper is more closely related to thrushes than wrens, yet it has no close relative in North America.

STRUCTURE

Wrens are smallish, stocky birds with short tails and wings—a form that allows them to move about readily in the closed-in, shrubby, and rocky habitats most of them prefer. Their spinal columns are connected to a point far back on the skull rather than directly beneath it as in most other songbirds. Most wrens' skulls show some of degree of lateral flattening. In addition, all wrens possess longish, decurved bills. These traits, most exaggerated in the Cactus Wren, allow wrens to reach deeper into crevices than most other species with which they may compete for food.

Dippers, the only songbirds that swim, exhibit a number of unique traits that assist them in their semi-aquatic lives. Rather long legs, with strong toes like those of other perching birds, help dippers achieve sure footing as they forage along stream bottoms. With blood capable of storing more oxygen than nonaquatic birds, dippers can remain submerged up to 20 seconds and reach depths of up to 20 feet or more. A moveable flap seals off the nostrils when the bird submerges and a well-developed nictitating membrane protects the eyes. Strong iris-sphincter muscles allow dippers to alter the curvature of the lens for better vision above and below the water. Their short wings are efficient for flight and also serve as paddles for "flying" underwater. Their wings are so powerful that the birds can take flight from beneath the surface. Dippers possess a dark, long, laterally flattened bill that is slightly hooked and notched at the end, a useful tool for flipping rocks and exploring crevices in the search for food.

PLUMAGE

Wren coloring tends toward reddish-browns and brownish grays with varying amounts of black, gray, white, or brown streaking, barring, and spotting.

Several species, especially the Carolina, Bewick's, Cactus, Marsh, and Sedge Wrens, display a prominent white "eyebrow" or supercilium. The sexes look alike. All wrens, like other passerines, go through a complete molt in the fall. While most songbirds undergo a partial molt in the spring, Marsh and Sedge Wrens have a complete molt at that time. Ornithologists believe that this second feather replacement may be required given the wear and tear of living among the thick, abrasive shrubs and grasses of their marshy habitats. No other species of North American wren molt in the spring.

Carolina Wren

Whereas adult dippers wear various shades of dark grays and black and have a dark bill, juveniles show lighter-toned mottling on the throat, breast, and belly, and have a pale bill. As an adaptation to the cold waters in which they forage, dippers possess twice as many contour feathers as most songbirds and a preen gland proportionally ten times larger than that of other passerines. Drawing oils from the large gland at the base of their tail, they frequently preen their feathers for up to 10 minutes at a time, to maintain the waterproofing and insulating properties of their plumage. Unusual among birds, dippers have a border of small white feathers around their dark eyes that flash when they blink, sometimes up to 50 times a minute, perhaps a signal to other dippers or a discouragement to predators.

OTHER SPECIES FIELD NOTES

■ **Winter Wren**
Troglodytes troglodytes
L 4"
Stubby tail, barred belly

■ **Carolina Wren**
Thryothorus ludovicianus
L 5.5"
White eye stripe, buffy underparts

■ **Bewick's Wren**
Thryomanes bewickii
L 5.25"
Long, flitting tail

■ **Cactus Wren**
Campylorhynchus brunneicapillus
L 8.5"
Dark crown, white eyebrow, spotted breast

■ **Rock wren**
Salpinctes obsoletus
L 6"
Buffy tail tips

■ **Canyon Wren**
Catherpes mexicanus
L 5.75"
White throat and breast, rufous belly

■ **Marsh Wren**
Cistothorus palustris
L 5"
Streaked back, long bill

■ **Sedge Wren**
Cistothorus platensis
L 4.5"
Streaked crown and back, short bill

■ **American Dipper**
Cinclus mexicanus
L 7.5"
Sooty gray, short tail

FEEDING BEHAVIOR

North American wrens and dippers are solitary creatures, foraging alone or in pairs, yet some wrens will join a mixed flock of chickadees, nuthatches, and creepers. Although the House Wren frequently seeks food at a variety of levels, even high in the trees, most wrens forage much lower down or on the ground. Wrens feed primarily on insects and other invertebrates, spiders, snails, and millipedes. The Cactus and the Carolina Wrens also eat small lizards, and the latter may occasionally consume a tree frog. Winter, Bewick's, and Carolina Wrens add some fruits, berries, and seeds to their diets, especially in winter, and the Cactus Wren consumes up to 20 percent of similar plant matter.

Like the wrens, the American Dipper feeds primarily by probing into crannies and under rocks for its prey, but the dipper is the only songbird that swims. While dippers may occasionally "hawk" a flying insect in the air, they seem to prefer to hunt while swimming and diving. They often find prey on or just below the surface of the water, but more commonly they hunt beneath the surface and along the bottoms of fast-water streams and rivers. Some enter the water by wading in from shore and diving from the surface, others perch at surface-level, or dive from a low flight over the water. From underwater, they seek out the larvae of various flies, mosquitoes, and midges and also eat worms, water bugs, and beetles or take clams, snails, fish eggs, and some trout fry less than 3 inches long.

VOCALIZATION

Renowned singers, all wrens possess a varied repertoire of musical phrases and songs. Perhaps because they have less need to impress potential mates, the larger, more monogamous Canyon and Cactus Wrens have as few as three songs, whereas the songbooks of the smaller, more polygynous wrens are much larger—western Marsh Wrens may sing up to 219 different songs. The nature and make-up of wren songs vary from species to species, ranging from the hoarse, disorganized tones of the Cactus Wren to the melodic, bubbly song of the House and Carolina Wrens. Most wrens are year-round performers, singing to establish and defend their territories, and to attract mates and renew pair bonds.

Along mountainous streams, a rattling call, loud enough to be heard over the splash and gurgle of waterfalls and fast-moving brooks and similar to a high-pitched version of the call of a Belted Kingfisher, usually announces the presence of an American Dipper. Both male and female dippers sing all year long, and song is used to attract mates and establish both springtime breeding and winter feeding territories. Unlike other songbirds, however, dippers don't sing to advertise or defend a territory once established. Their song consists of a series of musical phrases similar to those of the more melodic of the wrens. Each phrase is repeated two to four times before the next phrase voiced.

BREEDING BEHAVIOR

The Troglodytidae—a term sometimes translated as "cave dwellers"—are primarily cavity nesters. Some wren species apparently prefer to line cavities in trees, rocks, cliffs, nest boxes, or even old shoes, hats, cans, and teapots. Others build their cup nests in covering crevices, fissures, low vegetation, or even on the ground, depending on their respective habitats. Still others create their own cavities using twigs and grasses to construct globular nests with side entrances. Dippers construct similar, sometimes football-shaped nests, also with side entrances, on some inaccessible ledge or among upturned tree roots at streamside, a beam under a bridge, or even behind a waterfall. Wren nests, commonly made of woven twigs and grasses, are usually lined with soft materials like down, plant fiber, feathers, and even fur or hair. To construct their nest, female dippers, sometimes with help from their mates, use moss and soft grasses, although some rootlets and twigs may be woven in as well.

American Dipper

Within their breeding territory, most male wrens begin construction of a number of nests, only one of which a female will choose and line in preparation for laying her eggs. Most of the extra nests will never be used. This building exuberance seems to serve multiple purposes. Female wrens may view nest-building abilities as a sign of a quality male. While one or more of the extra nests may be used for roosting, the extras may serve also as decoys for predators.

During courtship the males of several wren species spread their wings and raise or spread their tail while singing to gain the attention of a female. A visiting female is often chased, as if she were an intruder, but a churring call announces that she is an interested female. The male may then hop stiffly about her and then fly to, and sing around, one or more of the many nests he has begun, inviting her to inspect them. She shows acceptance of a site—and the male—by bringing materials to finish the nest.

A courting male dipper often struts about a potential mate, singing as he stretches his neck, head, and bill skyward and spreads his drooping wings. Sometimes the female will imitate him, and the display

may end with the two jumping upward, breasts touching. To signify acceptance of a male as a potential mate, a female may approach him in a crouched, pleading stance, in a chick-like request to be fed. A flight-chase series of complex aerial maneuvers throughout their territory may ensue.

They are territorial creatures. All wrens and dippers defend their breeding territory and many attempt to preserve an all-purpose territory year-round. Although loud, agitated vocalizations are a male's primary defense, a male wren may also crouch low and extend his bill aggressively toward the intruder. If the outsider doesn't yield, the conflict may escalate to a flight chase or even a fight. Highly territorial in breeding season, but less so in winter, dipper pairs take a more aggressive approach toward homeland defense, flying directly at the intruder and chasing it out of their territory.

While the large Cactus Wren typically produces only three eggs per clutch, the rest of the wrens and the American Dipper usually lay an average of four to six. Both groups average two broods a year. The females incubate the eggs until they hatch, usually after about two to three weeks. Both parents feed the altricial wren and dipper chicks until they fledge. Fledgling dippers can swim and dive almost immediately. The young of both groups will be ready to repeat the cycle the following year.

BREEDING RANGE

Wrens breed in a variety of habitats virtually in every part of North America. Winter Wrens seem to prefer the moist coniferous forests of the north, even along the Pacific Coast of Alaska and into the Aleutians. Few other wrens appear as far north as southern Canada. Canyon and Rock Wrens nest in the canyonlands of western and southwestern states, while the Cactus Wren settles in the prickly world of the Sonoran and Chihuahuan Deserts. Marsh and Sedge Wrens breed in the thick grasses and brush in or near wetlands. Most other wren species prefer to nest in thick, shrubby undergrowth in edge environments such as the edges of forests or lakes.

American Dippers breed along the rocky streams of the Western mountains from Central Alaska to Panama. Usually found at elevations ranging from 2,000 to 10,000 feet, dippers seem to prefer swift, cold water, often in narrow canyons, but sometimes, especially in Alaska, may be found in flatter areas and even near sea level.

MIGRATION

Migration patterns for wrens are highly variable. Carolina, Canyon, and Cactus Wrens are usually permanent residents in their breeding ranges. Bewick's and Rock Wrens are partial migrants, the former leaving the eastern part of their range and the latter moving out of only the northern reaches of their breeding territory. Marsh, Winter, Sedge, and House Wrens are highly migratory, abandoning their breeding grounds almost entirely and moving to the southernmost states and farther south. For these last four, nocturnal migration seems to be the norm.

The American Dipper usually remains on its breeding territory all year long.

WINTER RANGE

Most wrens winter in their summer ranges and most of those that do migrate usually winter in the southern United States and Mexico. House and Sedge Wrens prefer Central and South America.

Only the icing-over of streams or depletion of food resources will drive the American Dipper to move to lower elevations or slightly south for the winter.

OBSERVING WRENS AND DIPPERS

In the field, wrens are usually heard long before they are seen. Since they sit only rarely still, usually while singing, movement in dense shrub is often the first visible sign of their presence. While some wrens such as the Carolina, House, and Cactus are fairly bold, occasionally offering good long "looks" to birders, others, like the Winter, Marsh, and Sedge Wrens, are secretive, visible often only in brief glimpses through heavy tangles of undergrowth, reeds, or grasses. The noisy, bubbling brook environments of the dippers reduces the value of their vocalizations for locating them. Their sometimes almost frenetic movements may catch the birder's eye first as the birds scurry in and out of the water, foraging, or flashing eye rings as they preen on shore or on a rock in mid-stream.

STATUS AND CONSERVATION

Only one subspecies of wren, the Appalachian Bewick's Wren, appears to be in any real danger. Expanding populations of House Wrens have moved into the Bewick's Wren's eastern range competing for food resources and nesting cavities. The draining of marshes and wetlands for urban and agricultural development in both their breeding and wintering ranges may eventually have an impact on populations of the Marsh and Sedge Wrens, although no significant declines have been documented. Breeding Bird Survey reports indicate a possible decline in Rock and Cactus Wren populations, but suggest a significant increase in the Carolina, Winter, and House Wrens.

Given their preference for remote areas, American Dippers have not been well documented and good data are hard to come by. Silting in and pollution of streams can destroy the invertebrate populations causing dippers to abandon those areas. Pollutants can also negatively affect reproductive success, and young. Dippers have proved adaptable to living along creeks and streams in urbanized areas in part due to the additional nest sites provided by bridges.

See also

Kinglets, Gnatcatchers, Allies, page 317

AMERICAN DIPPER

Lovingly referred to by John Muir, and many of us still today, as the Water Ouzel, the American Dipper derives it name from its habit of constantly bobbing and dipping its entire body when moving about on land. Even more fascinating is its predilection for feeding underwater, often in turbulent, mountain streams, even plunging into the current from shelf ice in sub-zero winter temperatures. In passerines, the skin between feather tracts is bare, but the dipper has adapted to its tough environment by covering these tracts with heavy, insulating down, and it grows one to two thousand more contour feathers than other passerines. Even its eyelids are completely covered by feathers, white ones that flash when it blinks. Dippers feed mainly on acquatic insects, fish eggs and even small fish captured by diving underwater and walking along the stream bottom as it forages. Dives last about fifteen seconds and feeding sessions may last up to one hour. The cheery dipper can be heard singing between feeding bouts in the dead of winter.

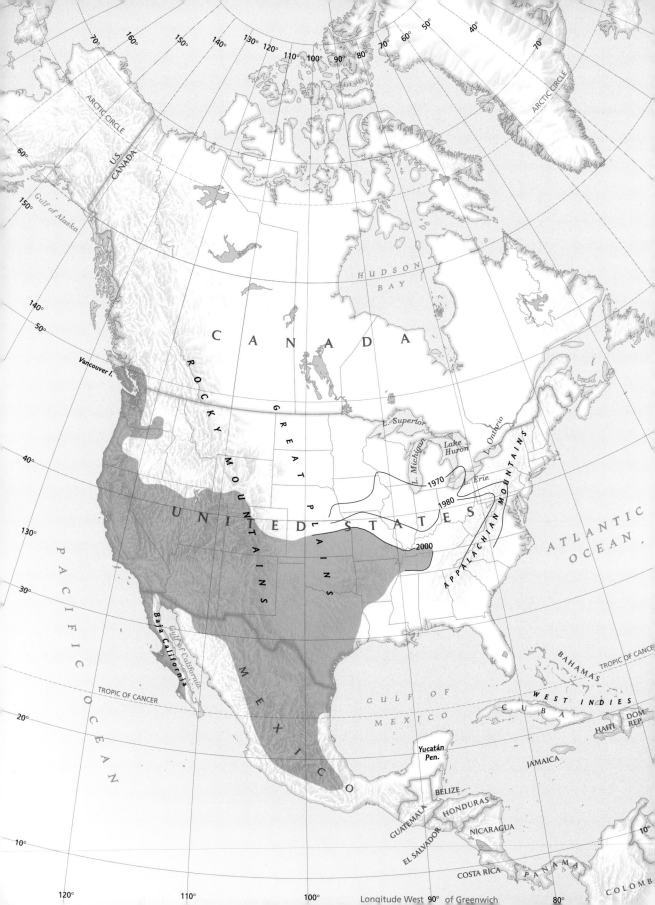

ARCTIC CIRCLE

70°

160°   150°   140°   130°   120°   110° 100°   90°   80°   70°   60° 50°   40°

ARCTIC CIRCLE

70°

60°

U.S.
CANADA

150°

Gulf of Alaska

HUDSON
BAY

140°

50°

C A N A D A

Vancouver I.

R
O
C
K
Y

G
R
E
A
T

L. Superior

L. Michigan

Lake
Huron

L. Ontario

40°

M
O
U
N
T
A
I
N
S

P
L
A
I
N
S

1970

L. Erie

1980

A
P
P
A
L
A
C
H
I
A
N

M
O
U
N
T
A
I
N
S

ATLANTIC
OCEAN

U N I T E D   S T A T E S

130°

30°

2000

PACIFIC

Baja California

Gulf of California

M
E
X
I
C
O

BAHAMAS

TROPIC OF CANCER

TROPIC OF CANCER

20°

GULF   OF

W E S T   I N D I E S

C U B A

MEXICO

HAITI   DOM.
REP.

O C E A N

Yucatán
Pen.

JAMAICA

BELIZE

GUATEMALA   HONDURAS

10°

EL SALVADOR   NICARAGUA

COSTA RICA   PANAMA   COLOMB

120°   110°   100°   Longitude West 90° of Greenwich   80°

WICK'S WREN

RANGE REDUCTION

Combined range
(breeding, resident, and winter)

70 — Historic range limit
with date

STATUTE MILES

| | 500 |

500

KILOMETERS

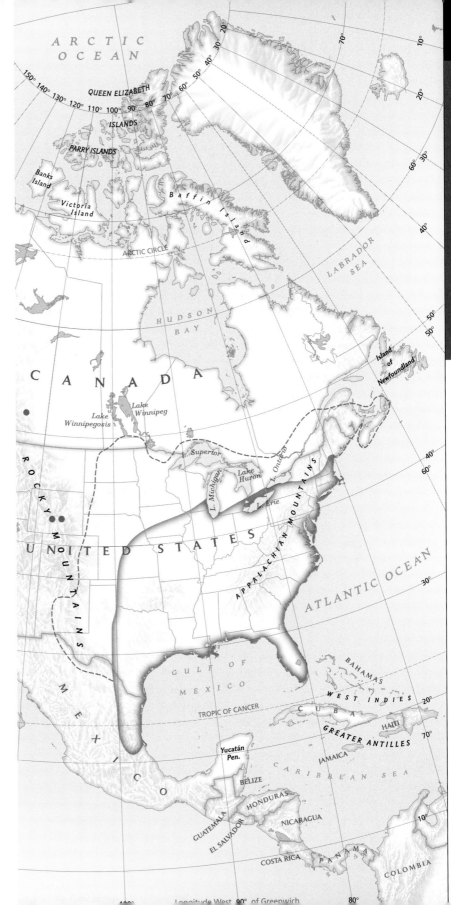

CAROLINA WREN ▶

RANGE AND WANDERING

Resident range

semi-regular wanderings ─ ─ ─

Isolated vagrant record ●

*The northern range of the Carolina Wren
expands and contracts with the severity
of winter weather. Ice and snow may be
particularly important factors. Wanderers
farther to the north are often found at
suet feeders during the winter.*

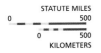

STATUTE MILES

0   500

0   500

KILOMETERS

KINGLETS, GNATCATCHERS, ALLIES

The Golden-crowned and Ruby-crowned Kinglets (family Regulidae) are the only North American representatives of an Old World family whose nearest relatives are the so-called Old World warblers (family Sylviidae, which includes the gnatcatchers of the New World) and the Old World flycatchers (family Muscicapidae). These three families have sometimes been merged with thrushes and other families into Muscicapidae; their many similarities lend them to synoptic treatment, whatever their taxonomic arrangement. Largely insectivorous, these species vary tremendously in their foraging methods.

Edward S. Brinkley

Within these three families, only the Blue-gray, California, and Black-tailed Gnatcatchers, the Arctic Warbler and the two kinglets breed in North America regularly. On a few occasions the Black-capped Gnatcatcher has been recorded nesting in extreme southern Arizona, and at least once in a mixed pair with a Blue-gray Gnatcatcher. The remaining 14 species known from North America—seven Old World flycatcher species and seven Old World warbler species—have been documented as vagrants from West Coast states, chiefly Alaska, and then only during the spring and fall migration. With increased scrutiny of the offshore islands of Alaska in the autumn, more records of Eurasian vagrants of the Muscicapidae and Sylviidae should be made.

Some species in this group are sedentary such as Black-tailed and California Gnatcatchers, but most are known either as medium-distance (North American kinglets) or long-distance migrants (the species that breed farthest north such as Arctic Warblers and other mostly Eurasian species); the long-distance migrants show up farthest out of range, as attested by the appearance on St. Lawrence Island, Alaska, of the Willow Warbler, Spotted Flycatcher, and Lesser Whitethroat in fall 2002—all species that had never before been recorded in North America and two of which nest no closer than 2,500 miles away.

The greatest commonality among the world's 400-plus sylviids, regulids, and muscicapids is their relatively active foraging strategy when searching for arthropods and insects in their respective habitats. Old World warblers, gnatcatchers, and kinglets are among the most active species. The gnatcatcher's twitching tail and the Ruby-crowned Kinglet's flicking wings are only the most familiar of foraging habits. Such quick movements possibly function to startle insect prey, but they are performed so habitually that their ultimate significance is still something of a puzzle. Other techniques include flycatching (from perches and from the ground), ground-foraging, and hover-gleaning, in which the kinglet or warbler hovers, usually at the tip of a light branch, to pick off food.

In size, structure, and appearance, the Old World warblers and Old World flycatchers resemble their counterparts in the New World, the parulids and tyrannids. An important difference between the Old World warblers and the similar wood-warblers is the number of functional primaries: ten in sylviids, nine in parulids. Genetic studies, however, confirm that they are not close relatives, and their similarities are the product of convergent evolution.

(Left) Ruby-crowned Kinglet

Blue-gray Gnatcatcher: *Polioptila caerulea*, L 4.25",
blue-gray above

GNATCATCHERS

A common breeding bird throughout the eastern and southern United States, the Blue-gray Gnatcatcher is a small species that is easily distinguished by its high-pitched buzz when feeding or on breeding territory. Both males and females have a prominent eye ring and a long tail with white feathers along the outer edges, which are easily seen in flight. Blue-gray Gnatcatchers feed almost exclusively on small insects and spiders that they find while scouring deciduous tree limbs and leaves, but they also capture prey in flight. The species breeds as far north as the Canadian border, and a gnatcatcher pair builds a cuplike nest made of plant fibers, spider webs, moss and lichen. The pair raises two broods of three or four young, often recycling nest materials for the second brood. These small birds migrate to wintering grounds along the southern Atlantic coastline, the Gulf Coast, and Mexico. The population of Blue-gray Gnatcatchers has increased and is thriving across the U.S. compared to Black-tailed and California Gnatcatchers, two western species that have declined because of habitat loss.

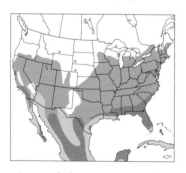

Range of Blue-gray Gnatcatcher

CLASSIFICATION

As in many other cases, the classification of birds currently arranged in the families Sylviidae, Muscicapidae, and Regulidae has changed significantly in recent time and is almost certain to shift in the near future, as studies into the genetic make-up of these species refine our understanding of their relationships. The family Sylviidae, for instance, was one of several that was merged into the family Muscicapidae, which contained the fascinating babblers (now family Timaliidae, with Wrentit the only North American representative) as well as many other largely Old World families. When a distinctive group is combined into another, larger family, it retains some identity as a subfamily, and the name thus became Sylviinae (the suffix '-nae' marking the group as subfamily rather than family). Currently, however, only the Old World warblers are included in Sylviinae, which is now a subfamily within Sylviidae, whose other subfamily is Polioptilinae, the gnatcatchers and gnatwrens. The taxonomic tide may change yet again, as the gnatcatchers and gnatwrens receive more scrutiny. Most observers who have watched gnatwrens in the field may have thought that they form a sort of link between wrens and gnatcatchers. Preliminary studies suggest that this hunch could be correct.

Currently the Sylviidae encompass some 285 species of Old World warblers, gnatcatchers, and gnatwrens, with only five species having nested in North America (four gnatcatchers and the Arctic Warbler) and seven species known only as very rare vagrants, mostly to Alaska: Dusky Warbler, Willow Warbler, Wood Warbler, Yellow-browed Warbler, Lesser Whitethroat, Middendorf's Grasshopper-Warbler, and Lanceolated Warbler.

The kinglets (family Regulidae) were also once included in the family Sylviidae, and though there are still lingering questions as to whether the Old World warblers are the closest relatives of the kinglets, recent studies confirm that kinglets are distinctive enough genetically to merit classification in their own family. Currently, the world's six (or seven) kinglets are categorized in the genus *Regulus,* despite the several differences of Ruby-crowneds from the others in the group. Some authorities suggest that the Madeira Firecrest is a full species, *Regulus madeirensis,* but this proposal has not yet been widely accepted.

The Old World flycatchers (family Muscicapidae) are a large group of Eurasian and African birds, some 120 or more worldwide, that are mostly drab in coloration. Their relationship to other groups are still unsettled, though it seems likely that the Old World thrushes are closely related to them. As with many such large families, the question of species limits is still very much open, and there are proposals to recognize some subspecies as full species.

STRUCTURE

Birds of the families Sylviidae, Muscicapidae, and Regulidae are all small, relatively slender birds with delicate, pointed bills. The length of the tail varies from relatively long for the body, as in gnatcatchers, to quite short in the kinglets; the same is true of leg length, which is longest in the gnatcatchers. Relative wing-length tends to be longest in the long-distance migrants, especially the northern Eurasian breeders. The Old World warblers resemble North American Vermivora species to a degree, but most are more delicately built; and the sylviids have ten, rather than nine, functional primaries. The Old World flycatchers that stray to North America are rather small birds, closer

in size to Empidonax flycatchers than to the larger tyrannids. Most species have rictal bristles that can be seen at close range such as the North American flycatchers', but the bills are smaller in proportion.

Golden-crowned Kinglet

PLUMAGE

The plumages of sylviids, muscicapids, and regulids vary a great deal, but are generally plain. Gnatcatchers' colors range from grays to sky-blues above and mostly gray or white below, with tails patterned in gray, black, and white. Kinglets all tend to be olive above and mostly pale below, with pale wingbars, but the markings around their eyes and especially on their crowns lend them their names of "little kings." When agitated, the Ruby-crowned raises a stunning set of scarlet erectile feathers that fan out to the rear. Because this feature is usually concealed, it is startling to see such vivid color emerge from such a plain bird. Likewise, the Golden-crowned Kinglet can display a brilliant neon-tangerine crown patch from within its saffron-colored, black-bordered crown, an equally arresting and seldom-seen display.

Some of the vagrant Old World flycatchers that have reached North America are brownish above and mostly pale below: the Asian Brown Flycatcher, Spotted Flycatcher, Siberian (Sooty), and Gray-spotted Flycatcher all look relatively similar to the untrained eye. However, the also-rare Red-breasted, Mugimaki, and Narcissus Flycatchers have more than a touch of color. The face of the Red-breasted Flycatcher is a soft dove gray, surrounding and setting off an intensely rufous throat-patch, whereas the Narcissus Flycatcher and Mugimaki Flycatcher have stunning black-and-white patterns above and either rich gold and orange (Narcissus) or vivid, pale orange (Mugimaki) below. Discovery of any of these flycatcher species, whether drab or colorful, makes for a red-letter day of birding in North America.

FEEDING BEHAVIOR

Old World warblers, flycatchers, gnatcatchers, and kinglets share broad overlap in diet, as most species take insects, spiders, and other arthropods, as well as their eggs. The warblers, gnatcatchers, and kinglets tend to be gleaners, meaning they pick their prey from the surfaces of bark and leaves, often from tiny recesses, where their slender, sharp bills allow them access. Most of the gleaning is arboreal, from the canopy through the lowest bushes. The Ruby-crowned Kinglet can sometimes

OTHER SPECIES FIELD NOTES	
■ **Golden-crowned Kinglet** *Regulus satrapa* L 4.25" Orange crown patch, striped face	■ **Dusky Warbler** *Phylloscopus fuscatus* L 5.5" Pale eyebrow, brown eye line, flicks wings
■ **Ruby-crowned Kinglet** *Regulus calendula* L 4" Red crown patch, plain face	■ **Arctic Warbler** *Phylloscopus borealis* L 5" Long, buffy eyebrow, pale legs
■ **Black-capped Gnatcatcher** *Polioptila nigriceps* L 4.25" Black cap, graduated tail	■ **Narcissus Flycatcher** *Ficedula narcissina* L 5.25" Overall black and yellow
■ **Black-tailed Gnatcatcher** *Polioptila melanura* L 4" Black cap, prominent eye ring, whitish underparts	■ **Siberian Flycatcher** *Muscicapa sibirica* L 5.25" Diffuse streaks on breast
■ **California Gnatcatcher** *Polioptila californica* L 4.25" Black cap, indistinct eye ring, gray-brown underparts	■ **Red-breasted Flycatcher** *Ficedula parva* L 5.25" White patch on black tail
■ **Lanceolated Warbler** *Locustella lanceolata* L 4.5" Streaked , flicks wings, skulks	■ **Gray-spotted Flycatcher** *Muscicapa griseisticta* L 6" Streaked below, very long wings
■ **Middendorff's Grasshopper-Warbler** *Locustella ochotensis* L 6" Wedge-shaped tail with white tip, skulks	■ **Asian Brown Flycatcher** *Muscicapa dauurica* L 5.25" Gray wash on chest, shorter wings

be seen in company with other birds in field settings, taking insect prey from the ground or old cornstalks or the like. Kinglets are also proficient at gleaning while hovering briefly, a form of foraging known as "hover-gleaning." All three groups, however, rarely pass up the chance to snap up a slow-moving insect, such as a mosquito, while in flight. Short sallies out from vegetation are commonly seen in all but the most retiring species such as Middendorf's Grasshopper-Warbler, a vagrant to North America. Old World Flycatchers occasionally glean insects from vegetation, but forage mostly by flying from a perch, usually in a bush or tree but also from the ground.

VOCALIZATION

The rollicking, syncopated song of the Ruby-crowned Kinglet, one of the most impressive sounds of the boreal forest, can sometimes be heard in the nonbreeding season, especially in spring; they are easily located by their "ji-dit" call during most of the year. Other kinglets have high-pitched, sibilant songs and calls, similar to the Brown Creeper in tonal quality and sometimes confused with that species' song and call. The Blue-gray and other gnatcatchers have lispy, chickadee-like calls and odd, jumbled songs that can include, rather incredibly, scratchy imitations of other birds' songs and calls. Their status as mimics, like that of siskins, comes as a surprise to most birders, who are familiar mostly with the European Starling and members of Mimidae as imitators.

BREEDING BEHAVIOR

Kinglets and gnatcatchers are rather different in their breeding biology. Both species are territorial, and both appear to be monogamous, at least within one nesting cycle or season. In kinglets, the female constructs a hanging nest of lichen, moss, bark, twigs, and spider webs and incubates clutches of up to 12 eggs, an enormous number for such a tiny bird. In gnatcatchers, both male and female build a small, cup-shaped nest resembling a hummingbird nest, with lichen and spider webs on the outer portion; if a second brood is to be raised, the male quickly builds a second nest, often salvaging materials from the first. Male gnatcatchers help incubate, though they do not have a brood patch. Clutch size is smaller in gnatcatchers than in kinglets, usually around four eggs. Ruby-crowned Kinglets have only a single brood per year, but Golden-crowneds are sometimes double-brooded.

Young gnatcatchers and kinglets are altricial, that is, they are born naked and unable to see. The young are fed for about two weeks on the nest and another three weeks afterward—a shorter period if a second brood is started. Both gnatcatchers and kinglets breed at one year of age.

The Arctic Warbler builds a covered nest on the ground, usually near the base of a willow or other vegetation, with only a small side-hole as entrance. The female incubates the clutch of four or five eggs for about two weeks, while the male feeds her on the nest. Both parents feed the young for several weeks.

BREEDING RANGE

The North American kinglets nest chiefly in Canada and the high elevations of the United States, except for the Ruby-crowned Kinglet which nests also in Alaska. The Blue-gray Gnatcatcher complements this distribution, nesting mostly in the United States and mostly in the lowlands. The breeding range of the Arctic Warbler

ARCTIC WARBLER

The Arctic Warbler (Phylloscopus borealis) is the only species of the Old World warbler family that breeds in North America in western and central Alaska. It has a long, yellowish-white eyebrow, which often curves upward behind the eye, and straw-colored legs and feet. The species sports a square tail, olive upperparts, and a pale wing bar on the tips of the greater coverts. The Arctic Warbler's stout bill is thicker and straighter than the Orange-crowned Warbler's. The species nests in thick willow habitats in Alaska and builds a dome-shaped nest on the ground, similar to that of the unrelated Ovenbird, but with the entrance on the side of the nest. Only the female Arctic Warbler incubates the eggs. The species is a "trans-Beringian" migrant, which means that after the nesting season, it migrates across the Bering Sea into Siberia to its wintering grounds in southern Asia. Only a few other North American nesters—such as the wagtails—perform this kind of migration.

is much more remote, overlapping only with the Ruby-crowned Kinglet in central and western Alaska.

MIGRATION

During migration, the gnatcatchers are relatively early migrants, moving between late August and September, with a trickle of birds migrating later. The kinglets are later migrants, beginning in late September in most places in the United States and migrating well into early November or even later, though the bulk of the migration occurs in October. Both kinglets and gnatcatchers can be found in unusual habitats during migration. The Arctic Warbler's migration takes it across the Bering Sea and Chukchi Sea into Siberia, where it moves southward toward wintering areas in southern Asia.

WINTER RANGE

The two kinglets in North America retreat from the Canadian portion of their breeding ranges to the United States in winter. The Golden-crowned Kinglets may winter near the Canadian border in mild years, but the less hardy Ruby-crowned Kinglet stays mostly in the South, the Southwest, and the Pacific Coast. The Golden-crowned Kinglet is renowned for being able to maintain normal body temperature in subfreezing conditions, the smallest species able to do so. The Blue-gray Gnatcatcher withdraws almost entirely from its North American breeding range in winter, remaining only in Florida, southern Texas, and southern California, with smaller numbers in other southeastern states. Most Blue-gray Gnatcatchers winter in Mexico and Central America, and the other gnatcatchers in North America do not appear to make large-scale seasonal movements out of breeding range, though some clearly do wander during the nonbreeding season. Arctic Warblers winter mostly in southeastern Asia, the Philippines, the Moluccas, and the East Indies.

Black-capped Gnatcatcher

OBSERVING GNATCATCHERS, KINGLETS, AND THEIR ALLIES

Kinglets nest in areas mostly remote from human population centers, but on migration and in the winter, they are common in most of the United States and Canada. The Ruby-crowned Kinglet is perhaps more easily located than the Golden-crowned, as it tends to forage more regularly in mixed-species feeding flocks in winter, which are usually composed of chickadees, titmice, warblers, woodpeckers, creepers, and wrens. The Ruby-crowned Kinglet tends to be more of a habitat generalist, whereas the Golden-crowned Kinglet sticks mostly to forested areas, usually conifers, in winter. It can be a strain on the neck to watch a small flock of Golden-crowneds work through the top of a 100-foot pine tree, but they do sometimes forage at eye-level in young conifers.

Gnatcatchers are likewise fairly easy to observe on the continent, but as most Blue-gray Gnatcatchers migrate south for the winter, the nesting season, from April to August, is the best time to see them in much of their large range. Areas near water are often good places to look for this species. Black-tailed and California Gnatcatchers, which are more restricted in their ranges, may require some planning to find, especially the rather rare California Gnatcatcher, a threatened species limited to a small part of the continent. Both gnatcatchers inhabit rather dry habitats, which they share in winter with nonbreeding Blue-grays. It takes luck and a big investment of time searching the arid, hackberry-lined canyons of southernmost Arizona, to find a Black-capped Gnatcatcher there—the one place from which all United States records are known.

Of the Old World flycatchers and warblers, only the Arctic Warbler nests in the United States, mostly in heavy thickets of willow in Alaska; it can be found readily with some persistence in places such as Denali National Park, as well as in less accessible areas.

To see any of the other Old World warblers or flycatchers noted above would entail an expensive holiday on one of the remote western Aleutian islands or St. Lawrence Island during the migration and a fortuitous wind to blow a vagrant from Siberia. Even with weeks of watching and waiting in such places, a waif is never a sure bet.

STATUS AND CONSERVATION

In North America, the California Gnatcatcher is the only species in these three families that is listed as federally threatened. Its habitat, which is limited to coastal chaparral in southern California and the state of Baja California in northwestern Mexico, has been cleared on a large scale for housing and other human structures. In many places, small fragments of this habitat remain but are too small to support even one pair of nesting birds. Their population is perilously low, estimated at about 5,000 pairs.

See also

Wrens, Dippers, page 309

Wrentit, page 329

ARCTIC WARBLER

Breeding range in U.S.

—— Regular migration route

● Isolated vagrant record
east and south of Alask

LANCEOLATED WARBLER

● Vagrant record south o

DUSKY WARBLER

● Vagrant record south o

*The Arctic Warbler breeds in Alaska an
in southeast Asia. Individual birds are k
wander to the east and south far out o
breeding range. Several other species b
in Asia, the Lanceolated Warbler and t
Warbler, have also occurred multiple ti
western Alaska.*

STATUTE MILES
0   500
0   500
KILOMETERS

BLUE-GR
GNATCATCH

RANGE EXPAI

Historic northern range   —
limit with date

Combined range
(breeding, resident, and winter)

STATUT
0
0
KILON

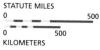

Longitude West 90° of Greenwich

THRUSHES, BABBLERS

Thrushes can be found on every continent, with 300 species worldwide. Though their plumage color and pattern differ strikingly between subfamilies, thrushes are fairly uniform in body shape and bill morphology: large, liquid eyes, relatively unspecialized forceps-like bills, a single annual molt, and pleasingly plump contours. Most have spotted breasts in juvenile plumage; the *Catharus* and *Hylocichla* thrushes bear spots throughout their lives. The diet of all North American thrushes consists of invertebrates and small fruits. They do much of their foraging on the ground, sorting through leaf litter on shaded forest floors or plunge diving after insects from a low perch.

Julie Zickefoose

Most thrushes are monogamous, building substantial, sturdy nests on or near the forest floor or on a branch higher in the canopy. The subfamily Sialinae, which includes the three North American bluebirds, are cavity nesters, much to the delight of enthusiasts who are able to attract them with artificial nest boxes.

Most people have grown up with a fairly intimate acquaintance with the thrush. The American Robin, the largest, most abundant North American thrush, has followed the watered lawn, with its plentiful earthworm prey base, westward across the continent. Only parts of Florida, Texas, and the Southwest, where the soil is too sandy to support the introduced common earthworm, lack robins. The robin's simple yet evocative "cheerily cheerio" song meshes well with the thunk of basketballs and the drone of lawnmowers in suburban neighborhoods all across North America; yet they also hide their nests in mountaintop spruce and fir forests, where they are as wary as any hermit thrush.

Oddly enough, the American Robin is the only member of its genus, *Turdus*, that breeds in large numbers. The closely related Clay-colored Robin, which looks like an American Robin that has been washed too many times, breeds sparingly in south Texas. Turdine thrushes are strong, deep-breasted flyers, and some species are apt to show up well out of their normal ranges in Asia, Europe, Central and South America.

When a bird-watcher mentions thrushes, the *Catharus* thrushes—smallish, spot-breasted songsters of the deep forest—are in the mind's eye. Surprisingly little-known, the Veery, Gray-cheeked, Bicknell's, Swainson's, and Hermit Thrushes are more often heard than seen. The Wood Thrush, now in the genus *Hylocichla,* will likely be grouped into genus *Catharus* in time. Their secretive ways hide them from scientist and bird-watcher alike. Their voices—seemingly disembodied, like the spirit of the forest itself—float through the branches at dawn and dusk, thrilling and transfixing human listeners with their ethereal beauty.

Birders who have traveled to the cloud forests of Central America may have heard the spine-tingling, pure notes of a solitaire. The Townsend's Solitaire ranges into the conifer-dominated mountains of the western United States. This slender, gray bird with flashing white outer tail feathers and a startled white eye ring nests beneath rocks and logs, and sallies after flying insects in a most unthrushlike way.

Thrushes have something for everyone, from the familiar American Robin to the woodland *Catharus* species that delight us with flutelike songs. While robins and bluebirds nest readily in our yards and meadows, the furtive and mysterious woodland thrushes bring out the Zen in any bird-watcher. Watch closely for them during spring and fall migrations.

(Left) Eastern Bluebird

American Robin: *Turdus migratorius*, L 10", brick red breast

THRUSHES

The most well-known and largest of the thrushes is the American Robin (above). Most people know a little about this bird—that it commonly frequents grassy suburbia, that it eats earthworms, or that it is an early spring migrant—although the American Robin is more interesting than this bare summary indicates. Not all robins migrate, however. Individuals return repeatedly in the

Range of American Robin

spring to the same breeding grounds, but in the fall they disperse widely, with few members of winter flocks having come from the same breeding areas. In addition to using the "head-cock" and "bill pounce" techniques of spotting, then catching, prey on the ground, robins glean foliage for butterflies,

damselflies, and the like, and even take prey in flight. They consume fruit—more in fall and winter than in summer—and eat both plant and animal matter in the summer. This ability to feed by several methods is one of the secrets to the robin's success, enabling it to live in habitats ranging from forests with smallish trees (recessional after fires or cutting), to woodlands where trees and shrubs are interspersed with short grasses, and lawns in suburbia.

CLASSIFICATION

Thrushes occur all over the world, with 54 genera and 300 species in the family. The Muscicapidae is a large family, and recent DNA-hybridization studies suggest that it may be divided into three subfamilies: Turdinae (true thrushes), Muscicapinae (Old World flycatchers and chats), and Sialinae (bluebirds). Differences in plumage, foraging, and nesting behavior between the three subfamilies are significant. Whereas most of the Turdinae are modestly colored, medium-size ground-feeders which build open-cup nests, the Muscicapinae include small, boldly patterned wheatears, chats, and Old World flycatchers, most of which nest in crevices or tree cavities, and sally after flying insects. The three species comprising the Sialinae, or bluebirds, are in a class of their own: They are brilliantly colored cavity nesters known only from North America.

STRUCTURE

There is a fair range of body size in North American thrushes, from the 5.5-inch Bluethroat of Alaska to the 10-inch American Robin, our largest thrush. Specializations are subtle; most of the ground-feeding wheatears, robins, and *Catharus* and Wood Thrushes have long, strong legs, straight, forceps-like bills, and large, light-sensitive eyes. The thrush tarsus, or unfeathered part of the leg, has a single long scute, rather than a series of scutes, a condition referred to as a "booted tarsus." Wings are long and breast muscles well developed on these long-distance migrants. The bluebirds, on the other hand, have shorter, weaker perching legs and finer bills, and are better adapted to drop foraging, seizing insects spotted from a high perch. Townsend's Solitaires are unique among North American thrushes in having short legs, a long, white-paneled tail and slender build—well suited to flycatching from exposed perches.

PLUMAGE

Most thrushes are modestly arrayed in earth tones of brown, gray, olive, buff, and rust, blending well with the leaf litter on forest floors. The general plan for *Catharus* and *Hylocichla* thrushes is a unicolored dorsal surface and a spotted breast. The majority of thrush species sport spotted breasts in juvenile plumage, though this may change to a solid color in adult plumage. Bluebirds, which resemble no other thrushes, have densely spotted breasts when they leave the nest. Similarly, American Robins have spotted breasts only as juveniles; their gray, black, and brick red color scheme is repeated, with many slight variations, in the genus *Turdus* worldwide. The Northern Wheatear, like its European cousins, is all flash patterns, with bold black-and-white geometrics in wings and tail. The Varied Thrush of Pacific coastal forests has exquisite, intricate wing patterns in slate and orange that recall a Native American blanket. Vibrant color finally takes hold in the tiny Bluethroat and the three North American bluebird species, which sport pigment-free structural blue coloration—caused by light refracted from prism-like oil droplets in the feathers—that can only be described as heavenly.

Western Bluebird

FEEDING BEHAVIOR

All thrushes feed on insects (mostly soil arthropods) and animal matter (snails and invertebrates), as well as small fruits and berries. Many short-distance migrants such as robins and Hermit Thrushes manage a nearly complete changeover from animal protein to fruit when autumn arrives. Their rapid metabolism ensures that seeds pass quickly through their digestive tract, making them effective dispersers of the seeds of fruiting trees and shrubs.

Robins and *Catharus* hop on the ground, watching for insects and invertebrates, often picking up and tossing leaf litter to reveal their prey. The Swainson's,

Hermit, and Wood Thrushes do a fair amount of gleaning above ground, examining leaf surfaces for hidden insects and larvae. The woodland thrushes have a foraging behavior in which they rapidly vibrate their feet on soil, which may serve to stir invertebrates out of hiding. Some experts have speculated that this pattering imitates rainfall, bringing invertebrates to the surface. The Swainson's Thrush earned the name "mosquito thrush" from its habit of flycatching in the lower forest canopy.

Solitaires take flycatching to new heights, sallying after insects from exposed perches. Wheatears combine the two foraging strategies, hopping, running, and flying after prey, their black-and-white wings flashing like semaphores. Bluebirds tend to still-hunt from elevated perches, dropping to the ground to seize crickets, grasshoppers, and spiders. Their large eyes are incredibly acute, and Eastern Bluebirds have been observed pouncing on insect prey spotted from 130 feet away. Mountain Bluebirds, which live in treeless grassy

OTHER SPECIES FIELD NOTES

■ **Wrentit**
Chamaea fasciata
L 6.5"
Cream-colored eye, long tail

■ **Siberian Rubythroat**
Luscinia calliope
L 6"
Ruby red throat

■ **Bluethroat**
Luscinia svecica
L 5.5"
Blue throat

■ **Red-flanked Bluetail**
Tarsiger cyanurus
L 5.5"
Bluish tail, orange flanks

■ **Northern Wheatear**
Oenanthe oenanthe
L 5.75"
White tail with black terminal band

■ **Stonechat**
Saxicola torquata
L 5.25"
Black head, orange on breast

■ **Eastern Bluebird**
Sialia sialis
L 7"
Blue upperparts, orange breast and throat

■ **Western Bluebird**
Sialia mexicana
L 7"
Purple-blue upperparts and throat

■ **Mountain Bluebird**
Sialia currucoides
L 7.25"
Blue above, pale blue below

■ **Townsend's Solitaire**
Myadestes townsendi
L 8.5"
Gray plumage, white eye ring, buffy wing stripe

■ **Wood Thrush**
Hylocichla mustelina
L 7.75"
Boldly spotted throat and breast

■ **Veery**
Catharus fuscescens
L 7"
Reddish above, weakly spotted breast

■ **Gray-cheeked Thrush**
Catharus minimus
L 7.25"
Gray-brown above, spotted breast, plain gray face

■ **Bicknell's Thrush**
Catharus bicknelli
L 6.25"
Warmer brown, especially tail, than Gray-cheeked

■ **Swainson's Thrush**
Catharus ustulatus
L 7"
Distinct buffy spectacles

■ **Hermit Thrush**
Catharus guttatus
L 6.75"
White eye ring, reddish tail

■ **Varied Thrush**
Ixoreus naevius
L 9.5"
Orange underparts, black breast band

■ **Eyebrowed Thrush**
Turdus obscurus
L 8.5"
White eyebrow, buffy flanks

■ **Dusky Thrush**
Turdus naumanni
L 9.5"
Scaly spotted breast

■ **Fieldfare**
Turdus pilaris
L 10"
Gray head and rump, white underwings

■ **Redwing**
Turdus iliacus
L 8.25"
Rusty red flanks and underwings

■ **White-throated Robin**
Turdus assimilis
L 9.5"
White throat crescent

■ **Rufous-backed Robin**
Turdus rufopalliatus
L 9.25"
Reddish back and wing coverts

■ **Clay-colored Robin**
Turdus grayi
L 9"
Buffy and olive-brown plumage

■ **Aztec Thrush**
Ridgwayia pinicola
L 9.25"
Boldly patterned black-and-white plumage

expanses, add hovering to their repertoire of foraging behaviors, looking much like miniature kestrels as they hang suspended on rapidly beating wings, then dive on insects. The Mountain Bluebird has been described as the "most anomalous thrush"; it is the most insectivorous of all North American thrushes, taking only 8 percent of its diet in fruit, and it is unusual in its choice of grasslands for preferred habitat.

VOCALIZATION

Just as the American Robin was named for the beloved, albeit distantly related European Robin, the Hermit Thrush has been called the American Nightingale. If there is one characteristic for which thrushes are known, it is their song. An eerie voice of old-growth western forests is the shy Varied Thrush, with its bold plumage of slate and rust. The species' single, drawn-out notes at varying pitches ring throughout dark, moist woodlands. Stunningly little is known of this big, beautiful thrush—its migration habits and its mating system are as shrouded in mystery as the coastal redwood forests it inhabits.

Mention of thrush vocalizations would be incomplete without giving due credit to the tiny Bluethroat, which is the only thrush to use mimicry in its song. Laplanders call this species "a hundred tongues." Mimicry is sometimes a resort of birds that live, as the Bluethroat does, in dense, low-visibility habitats. Needing a continuous, varied song for advertising and territorial defense, birds such as Bluethroats, Yellow-breasted Chats, White-eyed Vireos, and thrashers "borrow" from their neighbors' songs.

The *Catharus* thrushes (the genus name means "pure" in Latin) are able to sing a note from each of the two chambers of the forked syrinx, effectively harmonizing with themselves, and creating breezy, melodic, and stirring songs rivaled by no other North American bird. The Veery has been described as "whistling down a well," while the Hermit Thrush sings a swirling melody that chimes like tiny silver bells. Swainson's and Gray-cheeked Thrushes spiral melodies up the scale, in contrast to the Veery's downward-whirling lay.

The slightly congested, hurried warbling of a bluebird on the first warm morning of spring brings a delicious foretaste of summer. Even the less elaborate songs of the thrushes can evoke a powerful response in people. The favorite birdsong of renowned ornithologist George Miksch Sutton was the very simple "cheerily cheerio" of the American Robin, heard as a thunderstorm rolled away.

BREEDING BEHAVIOR

Most North American thrushes rely on advertising song for their breeding displays. Having no plumage specializations such as crests or flash patterns, most thrushes tend to take action rather than passively display their plumage. Flight pursuits are a common element of thrush courtship. Veery males pursue females, and even sing duets with them in early bonding before accepting and finally mating with them. Male American Robins strut on the ground before females, tails spread and wings drooping. Male bluebirds, with vivid color on their side, make floating butterfly and wing-waving displays beside a chosen nest site. The Varied Thrush, with its zigzag wing patterns, has tail-cocking and bowing displays that show them to full advantage.

One of the most interesting aspects of thrush biology is the array of nest sites chosen in each of the subfamilies. True thrushes—robins and *Catharus*—are open-cup nesters, constructing substantial nests on tree

Mountain Bluebird

branches, or tucked under shrubbery. Solitaires, Wheatears, and Bluethroats prefer to hide their nests under rocks, roots, or in crevices—a probable evolutionary step toward cavity nesting. Bluebirds are wholly dependent on the nest cavities chiseled out by woodpeckers, but will also accept artificial nestboxes.

Open-cup nesters have the shortest nestling periods; robins, *Catharus* thrushes, and solitaires leave the nest after 13 days. By contrast, cavity nesters enjoy better protection from predators, and can afford a longer nestling period; bluebirds are rarely ready to leave before 16 days, and may linger until day 21. By then, however, they can fly right out of the nest, and are much less vulnerable to ground predators than the open-cup nesters.

BREEDING RANGE

Thrush diversity is highest in the northeastern United States and Canada; most of the *Catharus* thrushes breed in New England and north of it. The West also has an array of beautiful thrushes; the Western and Mountain Bluebird, Townsend's Solitaire, and stunning Varied Thrush join the Veery, Swainson's, and Hermit Thrushes in breeding west of the Rockies. In general, the northern tier of North America has the greatest diversity of breeding thrushes.

A glance through a European field guide shows the Black-and-white Stonechat, which sometimes makes a cameo appearance as a vagrant in North America. Europe also hosts an array of wheatears—small, boldly patterned thrushes with upright posture and a preference for open, rocky country. Alaska lays claim to breeding

Northern Wheatears, as well as to a related jewel—the Bluethroat. This small, fawn-colored thrush has a gorget of blue, black, and red to rival any hummingbird's. From its dense habitat of dwarf tundra shrubs, it sings long, varied songs packed with imitations of other birds.

Bicknell's Thrush, a species newly split from the Arctic-breeding Gray-cheeked Thrush, has the most restricted range—mountaintops in northern New England and maritime Canada. Once thought to be a disjunct population of the Arctic-breeding Gray-cheeked Thrush, the Bicknell's Thrush is getting more attention in recent years. Ornithologists are only beginning to look into its unique lifestyle and the possible reasons for its endangered status. Only the adaptable American Robin breeds all across North America, from the Yukon to the Mexican border. Other members of the genus *Turdus*, such as the Eyebrowed (*T. obscurus*). and Dusky (*T. naumanni*) Thrushes, White-throated (*T. assimilis*) and Rufous-backed (*T. rufopalliatus*) Robins, and the Fieldfare (*T. pilaris*) and Redwing (*T. iliacus*) appear in North America only as occasional, albeit thrilling, vagrants. Fieldfares and Redwings may show up in migrating flocks of American Robins, which should always be scanned for rarities. The boldly pied Aztec Thrush occasionally visits the southwestern United States from its Mexican haunts.

MIGRATION

Being dependent on insects for much of their diet, all thrushes migrate to some extent as cold weather reduces prey. Migrations range from the altitudinal movements of Townsend's Solitaires and some Mountain Bluebirds, in which birds forsake higher elevations as winter progresses, to the short-distance, or facultative migration of the Eastern Bluebird and Hermit Thrush, which tend to fly only as far south as they need to find food. The Northern Wheatear, on the other end of the spectrum, makes an awe-inspiring journey, as the only breeding passerine in North America which winters on another continent. It leaves Alaska each autumn for sub-Saharan Africa, 13,000 miles each way. Almost as impressive is the flight of the Gray-cheeked Thrush, which leaves the Arctic taiga for northeast Mexico.

Species which migrate long distances have longer primary wing feathers than do short-distance migrants. Many gorge on fruit prior to embarking on migratory flights, building up fat which will fuel trans-Gulf crossings. Scientists track these flocks on Doppler radar, where bright green blips on the screen sometimes coalesce into solid fronts—waves of birds moving on ancient pathways, unseen under cover of night.

Most thrushes migrate singly or in small flocks by night, though the bluebirds undertake their short-distance migrations by day. Many so-called nocturnal migrants are actually crepuscular, doing much of their flying in the evening before midnight. American Robins are unique in migrating in flocks of hundreds; Mountain Bluebirds may travel in flocks of up to 50 birds. These lovely birds survive the winter on the insects and small fruits they locate on open grasslands.

WINTER RANGE

Classic long-distance Neotropical migrants such as the Veery, Swainson's, Gray-cheeked, Bicknell's, and Wood Thrushes may occupy an extensive breeding range in North America, only to concentrate in comparatively

---

BABBLERS

The drab gray Wrentit *(Chamaea fasciata)* of the family Timaliidae is North America's only representative of the babbler family, an Asian and African group that includes such exotic jewels as mesias, minlas, sibias, and yuhinas. A startled yellow eye, and a bouncy, year-round song compensate for what "the voice of the chaparral" lacks in plumage color.

This weak flier has been called North America's most sedentary bird. Males select a territory once in their lives, defending it against unrelated individuals. Monogamous and mating for life, a Wrentit may never travel more than 1,300 feet in any direction in its 12 years of life. Wrentits raise one brood of three to four young per season, and may be found in small family groups later. Confined as it is to the highly threatened coastal scrub from Washington's Columbia River south to Baja California, this little babbler bears watching as an irreplaceable American species.

limited regions of the West Indies, Central, and South America. The abundance of these species is closely linked to the fragmentation and degradation of both their breeding and wintering habitat. Swainson's Thrushes, for instance, winter in primary rain forest in Veracruz, precious little of which remains. In Costa Rica, however, they are more common in secondary (cutover) forest. In the United States, certain breeding populations of Swainson's Thrushes have gone inexplicably extinct, and perhaps the answer lies in where the populations attempt to spend the winter. Those which arrive on the wintering grounds to find their forests cut and burned may not survive their migration. Not surprisingly, long-distance eotropical migrants are showing overall declines not suffered by shorter-distance migrants such as the Hermit Thrush, Townsend's Solitaire, and the three bluebirds, which winter mainly in the southern United States.

OBSERVING THRUSHES

American Robins occur wherever people water lawns. Robins will sometimes construct their grass-and-mud nests under eaves and on windowsills, and many a fledgling has been "kidnapped" by suburban children, as robins often leave the nest before they are able to fly. Young robins have a comparatively long period of dependence on their parents, and can be seen following them about on lawns, shrilling for food. Many robins depart northern latitudes in autumn, and their mass return, when all-male flocks suddenly dot golf courses and lawns, is one of the most welcome signs of spring.

Eastern, Western, and Mountain Bluebirds will nest in boxes erected in suitable open habitat, and are quite tolerant of human intervention as the boxes are monitored. Bluebirds have far greater nesting success when their boxes are checked regularly, to eliminate wasps, parasites, and competing species such as the introduced House Sparrow. Many people who claim not to have seen a bluebird since childhood are simply overlooking these birds on roadside fence posts and powerlines. A pair of binoculars will magically turn an undistinguished dark silhouette into a vision of celestial blue.

Most thrushes are not so accessible and cooperative. Furtive and shy, they are better known by voice than by sight. Patience is key to getting more than a glimpse of the woodland *Catharus* group, and sitting quietly, even concealed, is a good tactic. Most of these birds are crepuscular singers, and it is easiest to locate them in the hours around dawn and dusk (when light is poorest). Powerful, light-gathering binoculars of 7x50 or 8x50 power help penetrate the forest gloom to reveal skulking thrushes. Bird-watchers occasionally luck into "fallouts" of migrating thrushes, especially during adverse weather conditions in the spring. Early morning fog and rain, which keep birds from flying, may fill a woodlot with hopping Swainson's Thrushes and Gray-cheeked Thrushes.

Once in a birder's sights, telling the *Catharus* thrushes apart can be a challenge. Wood Thrushes are the largest and most heavily marked, with round, black spots on snowy white underparts, running all the way down the flanks. Veeries share the Wood Thrushes uniformly warm brown upperparts, but are only faintly and smudgily spotted on the upper breast. Hermit Thrushes have a warm rufous tail that contrasts with the cooler brown of the back and wings. They have a habit of raising, then slowly lowering the tail, and often flick their wings, voicing a low, dry *chup*. A small thrush seen in temperate zone woodlands in winter is likely to be a Hermit. Swainson's Thrushes can be distinguished by their dull olive-brown backs and wide, buff-colored spectacles, which give them a surprised look. If you are looking at a small *Catharus,* and can't distinguish much of anything, it may be a Gray-cheeked or even a rare

NIGHT MIGRATION

Why would a bird choose to fly long distances at night? Soaring birds such as hawks depend on thermal updrafts created by the sun's warmth on land; birds that must flap their wings tend to migrate at night. Most songbirds, such as the Wood Thrush, above, take off about 45 minutes after sunset, flying continuously until midnight, then land to rest. Thrushes, tanagers, warblers, vireos, cuckoos, orioles, and others feed during the day, resuming their flight the following night. At the end of the trans-Gulf flight, daylight may catch them near the coastline.

Researchers Frank Moore and Paul Kerlinger theorize that small birds may also prefer migrating at night because of the cooler air. Starlings, whose normal body temperature ranges from 100°F to102°F, may have temperatures of 105°F to 111°F during these powered flights. Cool nights help birds lose heat in flight, and the birds will encounter less turbulence.

Bicknell's Thrush. It's best to resort to a field guide for these two species; even experts prefer to have the birds in hand when making an identification.

STATUS AND CONSERVATION

The plump, fox brown Wood Thrush, its breast boldly spangled with black spots, has become a poster child for vanishing neotropical migrants throughout the Americas. More than any other, its absence from traditional breeding grounds has been noticed by birdwatchers. A forest without Wood Thrushes has lost an intangible mystery and beauty, and we are poorer for it. One of the species' wintering areas in Veracruz, Mexico, had only 30 percent as many Wood Thrushes in 1985 as it had in 1960. Its lovely song is becoming a rare treat, as Wood Thrushes undergo local extinctions in smaller woodlots in the eastern United States It seems fairly certain that habitat fragmentation on both the breeding and wintering grounds is a major cause of this and other thrush species' drastic decline. The Brown-headed Cowbird, an open-country nest parasite which lays its eggs in most thrush nests, compromises its host's nesting success, and is given an entry into woodlands by logging roads, clearcuts, and housing developments. Though they will breed in lots only an acre in size, wood thrushes enjoy much better nesting success in 250-acre woodlots or larger. The Wood Thrush's wintering grounds, the primary broadleaf evergreen forests from Mexico to Panama, are being rapidly felled and fragmented.

Hermit Thrush

Little is known about our more secretive thrushes. Ornithologists have not yet divined the mating system of Varied Thrushes; nor do they understand the nature of their short-distance migration. Birds from more northerly populations may leapfrog over or even replace southern birds in winter, pushing them farther south, but this is only speculation. We also do not know whether the flashily patterned, ten-inch-long Varied Thrush is monogamous or not.

Ornithologists do not yet know where in northern South America Veeries spend the winter. Swainson's Thrushes are inexplicably disappearing from former breeding strongholds in the American West, and are suffering low nesting success (not attributable to Brown-headed Cowbird parasitization) throughout their range. Wintering ground deforestation may hold the answer to the perplexing, male-biased sex ratio among the endangered Bicknell's Thrush. Preliminary capture studies suggest that male and female Bicknell's Thrushes winter in different areas of the Greater Antilles, possibly skewing survivorship in favor of

males. Haiti, for example, has only 1.5 percent of its original forest cover; the Dominican Republic has only 10 percent. If female Bicknell's Thrushes are attempting to winter in a place that is being deforested, while the wintering grounds of male thrushes are intact, this could help explain why scientists in Vermont observed from two to four males feeding the brood of a single female—at 75 percent of the nests observed. Three-quarters of broods surveyed had multiple fathers. Clearly, such a skewed sex ratio does not bode well for the long-term survival of this species.

Acid rain from industrial pollution fallout is being implicated in the large-scale death of balsam fir and spruce forests on mountaintops in the northeastern United States and maritime Canada. Not only does this destroy habitat for sensitive species such as the Bicknell's and Swainson's Thrush, but evidence from British studies suggests that it affects the birds' invertebrate prey base as well. Snails, an important supplement to many thrushes' diets, may not be able to form shells, and thus survive, where acid rain adversely affects calcium in the soil.

Cooperative international efforts to protect what is left of the wintering area of thrushes are ongoing, and long overdue. It is important to think of neotropical migrants as species which are shared with Central and South America where they overwinter. Most of a migrant's year is spent in passage to and from the wintering ground. Breeding, especially above the Arctic Circle, can be a brief, two-month interlude in a life spent on the wing.

Thrush population trends are not all downward, however; the American Robin, for one, is holding its own throughout the suburban landscape. Heartening, too, is the restoration of the Eastern Bluebird. Populations dipped dangerously low in the 1970s, hit by hard winters in the southern U.S. and poisoned by pesticides such as DDT. The North American Bluebird Society and its 45 state, regional, and provincial affiliates dedicated to helping all three bluebird species, collectively have over 11,000 members. Perhaps 17,000 nest boxes are registered by such organizations nationwide. Populations of Eastern and Mountain Bluebirds are on a strong upswing.

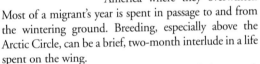

See also

Kinglets, Gnatcatchers, Allies, page 317

Accentors, Wagtails, Pipits, page 345

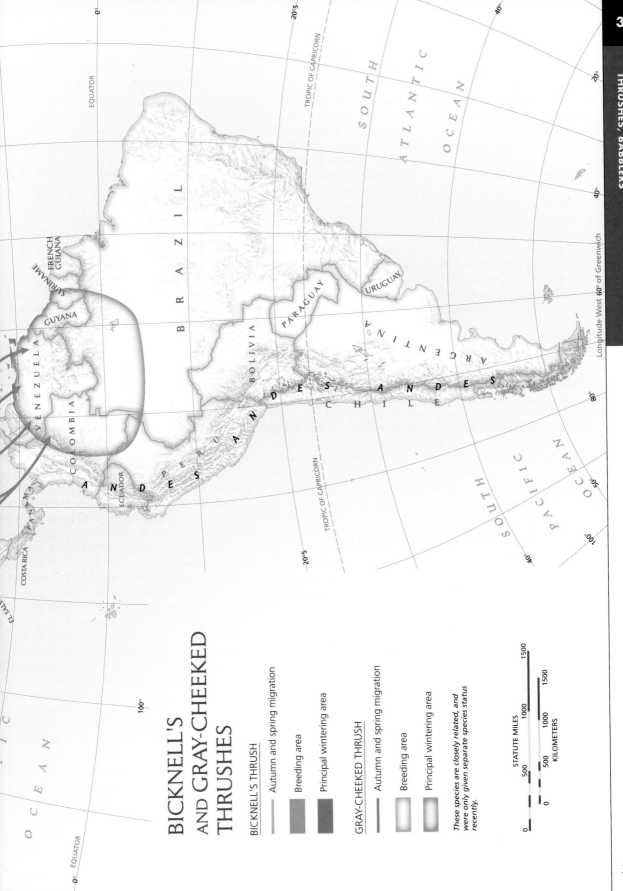

EQUATOR

SOUTH ATLANTIC OCEAN

BRAZIL

FRENCH GUIANA
SURINAME
GUYANA
VENEZUELA
COLOMBIA
ECUADOR
PERU
ANDES
BOLIVIA
PARAGUAY
URUGUAY
ARGENTINA
CHILE
ANDES

PANAMA
COSTA RICA
EL SALV

TROPIC OF CAPRICORN

SOUTH PACIFIC OCEAN

Longitude West 60° of Greenwich

OCEAN

BICKNELL'S AND GRAY-CHEEKED THRUSHES

BICKNELL'S THRUSH

— Autumn and spring migration

Breeding area

Principal wintering area

GRAY-CHEEKED THRUSH

— Autumn and spring migration

Breeding area

Principal wintering area

These species are closely related, and were only given separate species status recently.

STATUTE MILES
0   500   1000   1500

KILOMETERS
0   500   1000   1500

THRASHERS, BULBULS, STARLINGS

Whereas thrashers, catbirds, and mockingbirds are strictly New World birds, bulbuls, starlings, and mynas are Old World birds, four species of which have been imported to the Western Hemisphere.

Widespread in Asia and Africa, only one of the more than one hundred species of bulbuls of the family Pycnonotidae appears in North America. Red-whiskered Bulbuls with their cheery, melodic song (their species name, *jocosus*, means "full of fun"), contrasting black, white, and red coloration, and distinctive crests have long been popular cage birds. A handful apparently escaped captivity near Miami, Florida, in the mid-20th century, and by 1961 they were known to be nesting in a 25-square-mile area just south of the city. Ten years later their population was estimated at 250 birds. They seem to prefer suburban areas planted with a variety of exotic fruit-bearing shrubs and trees.

Of the more than one hundred species worldwide of the family Sturnidae, only the European Starling and the Crested, Common, and Hill Mynas appear in North America. Like the bulbuls, all four sturnids were introduced to this continent by humans—the starlings from Europe and the mynas from Asia. The Common Myna has been increasing in numbers since it was introduced into southern Florida in the early 1980s. The Hill Myna has been reported in both southern Florida and in the Los Angeles, California area, but the populations are apparently small. After the Crested Myna was released into the Vancouver, British Columbia, area in the 1890s, its population blossomed into the thousands by the 1920s but then began to decline.

Philip Brandt George

Fewer than one hundred birds were reported in the 1990s and only two in 2002. Ironically, this decline may be due in part to the success of another 1890s Sturnidae invader. About 60 European Starlings were released into New York City's Central Park and, adapting to the new environment, the population spread out, exploding as it went. By out-competing local species for nesting cavities everywhere they go, starlings may be contributing to the decline of several species including their West Coast Crested Myna cousins. Unlike the other Sturnidae imports that are reliant on human-influenced habitats, the European Starling has proven itself adaptable to a variety of natural environments.

The catbirds, mockingbirds, and thrashers of the family Mimidae are unique to the New World, breeding from southern Canada to the deserts of Patagonia in Argentina. Of the more than 30 known species, only ten are reported to breed in North America. Three of those, the Gray Catbird, Northern Mockingbird, and Brown Thrasher, breed in a variety of habitats across the continent. Six others limit themselves mainly to the more arid parts of the southwestern United States and northern Mexico; and the Bahama Mockingbird is only a casual visitor to southern Florida. Most mimids live up to their family's name, which comes from the Latin *mimus* meaning "mimic" or "imitator." Called by some the mockingbird or the mockingthrush family or the "mimic thrushes," they are capable of reproducing the songs, grunts, and other noises of not only other bird species but of mammals, humans, and sometimes even machines.

(Left) Sage Thrasher

Northern Mockingbird: *Mimus polyglottos,* L 10", white wing patches

THRASHERS AND BULBULS

The most popular and widespread bird of this order is the Northern Mockingbird (above). It is the official bird of five states and a year-round resident in most of its range, which includes all of the United States. Mockingbirds are mimics that learn as many as 200 or more song types, or acoustically distinct sounds. Males have a spring and a fall repertoire, with only one percent of the song types shared between them. They apparently sing mainly to attract females and stimulate them to mate rather than to combat other males. Both sexes have four types of calls they use in such circumstances as relieving a mate at the nest and mobbing. The Female defends the couple's territory against mockingbirds of the same sex. Highly pugnacious, mockingbirds defend their territories not only against other birds, but also against dogs, cats, and even humans, who frequently enter their territory. Mockingbirds are highly reproductive. Monogamous during the breeding season, couples produce up to four broods per season.

Range of Northern Mockingbird

CLASSIFICATION

Mockingbirds, catbirds, thrashers—family Mimidae—and bulbuls (Pycnonotidae) are all members of the order Passeriformes—the so-called perching or songbirds. Like all North American songbirds, except the tyrant flycatchers and cotingas, they belong to the suborder Passeres—known also as Oscines. They posses a unique muscle in the syrinx that helps with complex song production, and they are anisodactyl—having feet with three toes pointing forward and one toward the back.

The Mimidae have been thought by many to be relatives of the thrushes (family Turdidae) with which they share some characteristics and habits: Both families feed primarily on the ground; build bulky, cup-shaped nests; and produce complex and melodic song. By other characteristics, given their decurved bills and propensity for ground foraging in thickets and underbrush, they have been thought to resemble the wrens. DNA-DNA hybridization studies, however, indicate that although current taxonomies list the Mimidae and the Sturnidae—starlings and mynas—as separate families, the two are so closely related that many scholars feel they could be included in the same family.

Despite a superficial resemblance to some of the flycatchers and waxwings, the bulbuls' closest relatives, according to DNA-DNA hybridization data, may be the Old World warblers, kinglets, and swallows.

STRUCTURE

The Mimidae possess bills of varying lengths and degrees of curvature. Some such as Northern Mockingbirds and Gray Catbirds, for example, have relatively short, straight bills, others such as Curve-billed and Crissal Thrashers have quite long, decurved bills. All are well adapted for rummaging through ground surface matter or digging in the soil for food.

Overall, the mimids are longish, medium-size songbirds ranging from the European Starling-size Gray Catbird at 8.5 inches to the Northern Flicker-size California Thrasher at 12 inches. Possessing longer tails, they tend to appear sleeker than the thrushes. Rictal bristles projecting from the base of the beak presumably protect the nostrils from ground litter and dust particles. Their relatively short, rounded wings with ten primary feathers are ideal for flight in the close, shrubby entanglements they prefer. Primarily ground feeders, they have fairly long, strong legs which are ideal for lengthy walks in search of prey.

PLUMAGE

Unique among the mimids, the Northern Mockingbird frequently flashes myna-like, white wing patches and flicks open its white-edged tail as it forages on the ground. Some experts suggest these displays are to discourage predators, others claim they serve as intraspecies communications, still others think they might serve to scare up hiding prey. The Northern Mockingbird is plumed primarily in patterned shades of gray, and the Gray Catbird has russet undertail coverts and a black-capped head on an otherwise gray body; the rest of the

Brown Thrasher

Mimidae appear mostly in shades of brown. The Brown Thrasher is the rustiest hued of them all, and it—along with the Long-billed and Sage Thrashers—shows heavy streaking on the light breast. Such streaking is virtually absent in the other thrashers.

FEEDING BEHAVIOR

The Mimidae eat beetles, grasshoppers, flies, and caterpillars, but also spiders, snails, and earthworms. Some of the larger thrashers prey on small lizards and fish. In fall and winter, the mimids increase the amounts of seeds and berries in their diet. In the nonbreeding season, fruit intake may make up as much as 50 percent of the diet of the Northern Mockingbirds and Gray Catbirds. The desert thrashers have adapted well to their arid existence—with little expenditure of energy, some, especially the Curve-billed and Bendire's Thrashers, get much of their water and food from the

cactus fruits and flowers they consume. By contrast, fruits are the main fare of the Red-whiskered Bulbuls, although they also fly-catch and glean larvae and adult insects from plants. Preferring small fruits and berries, they rarely puncture large fruit but wait until they ripen and split open.

All of these birds are predominantly ground or near-to-the-ground feeders and tend to forage alone or in pairs. Gray Catbirds and Northern Mockingbirds usually forage by walking along on their strong legs, gleaning from the surface. Northern Mockingbirds often flash their wing patches in conspicuous movements, perhaps to startle insects into the open. The larger thrashers often do much heavier work in search of food. Most will at least sweep their bill back and forth, scattering leaf litter and even gravel in the pursuit of food. The Le Conte's Thrasher can pick up and throw items one-and-one-half times its body weight. Some longer-billed thrashers probe deep into the soil. Curve-billed Thrashers routinely dig holes up to two inches deep, and Le Conte's Thrashers can go to more than three inches deep.

VOCALIZATION

Although their happy, exuberant song makes them desirable as cage birds, Red-whiskered Bulbuls are not among the mimics. Whether or not thrashers imitate sounds—some never do, others only occasionally, still others constantly—almost all produce ebullient, multi-phrased, repetitive song, loud and rich in variety, sometimes accompanied by sharper chips, clucks, and rattling noises. Whereas the Brown Thrasher uses mimicry often in its song and the Gray Catbird got its name from copying the mewing of cats, by far the best mimic is the Northern Mockingbird. One such bird was heard to imitate 32 different species of birds within a ten-minute period. "Mockers" have been known to include the sounds of frogs, crickets, cats, dogs, the squeak of an ill-oiled wheel, and the clanging of a piano. Captive mockingbirds can imitate and repeat human sounds and household noises as well.

BREEDING BEHAVIOR

Mimids are monogamous in any given season, although there have been reports of Northern Mockingbird males mating with several females. Migrants such as the Gray Catbird must form a new bond at the beginning of each breeding season. Among the nonmigratory species, such as Le Conte's, Curve-billed, and California Thrashers, pair bonds may last for several years, and it is thought that Le Conte's Thrashers may even pair for life.

OTHER SPECIES FIELD NOTES

■ **Gray Catbird**
Dumetella carolinensis
L 8.5"
Chestnut undertail coverts, black cap

■ **Bahama Mockingbird**
Mimus gundlachii
L 11"
Streaked neck and flanks

■ **Brown Thrasher**
Toxostoma rufum
L 11.5"
Reddish-brown above, streaked below

■ **Long-billed Thrasher**
Toxostoma longirostre
L 11.5"
Grayis -brown above, streaked below

■ **Sage Thrasher**
Oreoscoptes montanus
L 8.5"
Straight bill, white cornered tail

■ **Bendire's Thrasher**
Toxostoma bendirei
L 9.75"
Mottled breast

■ **Curve-billed Thrasher**
Toxostoma curvirostre
L 11"
White tips on tail, spotted breast

■ **California Thrasher**
Toxostoma redivivum
L 12"
Pale eyebrow, dark streaked cheeks

■ **Crissal Thrasher**
Toxostoma crissale
L 11.5"
Chestnut undertail patch, dark malar streak

■ **Le Conte's Thrasher**
Toxostoma lecontei
L 11"
Pale with dark tail

■ **Red-whiskered Bulbul**
Pycnonotus jocosus
L 7"
Red ear patch and undertail coverts

For most of the Mimidae, courtship and pair bonding is carried out with little fanfare. Since they can form pair bonds in any season, courting among several of the nonmigratory thrashers consists of little else but song. Among Brown Thrashers, for example, the entire process may consist of one or both birds picking up and dropping some leaf litter or twigs in front of the other. Male catbirds and the other thrashers may sing and then posture in front of females by puffing themselves up while raising and lowering their head. Both male and female may offer a stick or leaf to its potential partner, and the male may feed the female. The most elaborate courting rituals occur among Northern Mockingbirds. In looping flight displays, the male leaves a perch in mid-song, rises in the air, and then floats back to the point of origin while spreading his wings to show off the white patches. Or, the male may face his potential mate and then leap in the air, flashing his white tail and wing patches, while singing. Occasionally the female will mimic the move, and they end the maneuver by bumping breasts in midair.

Although the mimids all build woven cup or basket nests, how the site is selected, and which partner begins and ends the construction varies from species to species. Brown Thrasher pairs share the duties of choosing the location and gathering the materials, but actual construction is the female's lot. Northern Mockingbird males build the basic nest platform but the female lines it. A male Gray Catbird may supply a bit of material, but most of the task of building and lining the nest falls to his mate. Depending on the habitat, nests are constructed in low shrubs or small trees in dense growth that offers some protection. In the Southwest they build cup nests of coarse matter beneath a canopy of cactus spines and heavy, spiny undergrowth that adds protection not only from predators but also from the sun. While some mimids will reuse a nest in a season if the first brood fails, none are known to return and reuse a nest the following season.

On average, the mimids lay three to five eggs per clutch. Both males and females incubate and then feed the altricial young. Many species are vigorous in their defense of territory, nest, and young. Gray Catbirds and Northern Mockingbirds are notorious for dive-bombing and even grabbing bits of scalp or hair from intruders.

BREEDING RANGE

During the past 50 years, the Northern Mockingbird,

RED-WHISKERED BULBUL

By temperament the Red-whiskered Bulbul was always extremely adaptable to human activity in its native India and southeast China, and is now a noisy, sociable, and popular cage bird around the world. In the early 1960s escaped birds established wild populations near Miami, Florida, and Los Angeles, California, and though not rapidly expanding, they have remained stable. At about the same time both Red-whiskered and Red-vented Bulbuls were released on O'ahu in the Hawaiian Islands. This population has grown and spread at an extraordinary rate, and has since been released on or carried to other islands in the archipelago. The frugivorous bulbuls require a warm, tropical habitat that provides berry- and fruit-bearing vegetation year-round. Flocks of Red-whiskered Bulbuls will raid orchards and commercial flower and vegetable farms damaging these products to the extent that the U.S. Department of Agriculture now prohibits their importation. Throughout their range, bulbuls are nonmigratory, thus enjoying an extended breeding season and raising two to three broods per year. In the nonbreeding season these gregarious birds gather in large, vocal communal flocks and are quite content in the gardens and parklands of the suburbs where they are most likely to be seen. About the size of a bluebird, the Red-whiskered Bulbul with its sharply pointed crest, crimson undertail coverts, and crimson, hairlike "whiskers" behind its eyes is easily identifiable. The full impact of this introduced species on native birds is not fully known.

always common and widespread in the southern United States and northern Mexico, has expanded its range. Once rare above the Mason-Dixon Line, it now appears regularly in the East as far north as Newfoundland and appears to be advancing northward into Canada across the plains and mountain states. Mockers have been reported casually as far north as Alaska.

Whereas Northern Mockingbirds are generalists, living in a variety of habitats, Brown Thrashers and Gray Catbirds—widespread in the eastern two-thirds of North America—prefer second-growth woodlands and edge environments with dense shrub and undergrowth.

Most of the rest of the Mimidae are residents in a variety of niche habitats, ranging from wet, dense thickets to deserts, sagebrush, and chaparral lands in the West and southwestern states. Although their ranges overlap, the differing habitat preferences of Curve-billed, Bendire's, Crissal, and Le Conte's Thrashers reduce competition among them for nesting sites and food. Large, fleshy desert cactuses and mesquite seem to best serve the needs of the Curve-billed. Bendire's likes the woodier cholla cactus and slightly higher-elevation desert grasslands with some yucca. It will also breed in sagebrush and junipers. Crissal Thrashers prefer mesquite thickets along desert washes. They, too, range into juniper shrublands at higher elevations. The most restricted in habitat tolerance is Le Conte's Thrasher, which seems to breed only in the sparsely vegetated, sandy desert of extreme southern Nevada, California, and Arizona.

Gray Catbird

MIGRATION

Of the thrashers and bulbuls, only the Gray Catbird is a true migrant that abandons its breeding grounds in the fall for more southerly realms, migrating across the Gulf of Mexico at night. The Red-whiskered Bulbul and Curve-billed, Long-billed, California, Crissal, and Le Conte's Thrashers are largely permanent residents on their breeding grounds. Northern Mockingbirds and Brown, Bendire's, and Sage Thrashers are partial migrants—the northern poplations move south but southern populations remain in place. The Brown Thrashers that do migrate, do so at night, and they are often found in "tower kills" when, on foggy or rainy nights, the lights from radio towers or high-rise buildings distract or confuse nocturnal fliers, causing them to tire and drop, or to crash into windows or guy wires. Northern populations of Sage Thrashers, diurnal migrants, frequently move into the desert habitats already occupied by Crissal and Bendire's Thrashers.

WINTER RANGE

Of the mimids, the Gray Catbird is the only neotropical migrant, moving south to Mexico, Central America, and the Caribbean. Small numbers of catbirds may also take up winter residence in the southeastern United States. While the bulbul is a truly permanent resident in its restricted range, several of the more sedentary thrashers relocate a bit during the winter. These movements are often no more than wanderings within the summer range in search of better forage or shifts to the south or to lower elevations in search of warmer weather. Among the partial migrants, many of the southern populations are permanent residents on the breeding range, while the northern populations sometimes join the southern populations or leapfrog to spend the winter farther south. With most of these, there is a central section of the breeding range that is inhabited all year long.

OBSERVING MIMIDAE

Preferring to feed close to the ground, in thickets or heavy vegetation, alone or in pairs, many of the Mimidae can be difficult to locate. Birders can find them by following the thrashing noises they make as they dig around.

Even if the bird cannot be located, its multiphrased song can help lead to an identification. Gray Catbirds tend to jump abruptly from one phrase to another, Brown Thrashers repeat a phrase twice before moving on, and Northern Mockingbirds repeat a phrase at least three times before beginning a new one.

STATUS AND CONSERVATION

While none of the Mimidae is considered to be truly endangered, most are declining in population. Le Conte's, Bendire's, Curve-billed, California, and Long-billed Thrashers are currently on the WatchList of Partners in Flight and the National Audubon Society. Loss of habitat through agricultural development and the growth of metropolitan areas in the West and Southwest have led to the decrease of Curve-billed, California, Le Conte's, Bendire's, and Crissal Thrashers. Reforestation in eastern North America has affected populations of Gray Catbird, Northern Mockingbird, and Brown Thrasher.

See also

Accentors, Wagtails, Pipits, page 345

European Starling: *Sturnus vulgaris*, L 8.5", black with yellow bill

STARLINGS

Of the family Sturnidae, the European Starling (above), introduced into New York in 1890, is exceptionally adaptable. It thrives in a variety of habitats, from urban centers to agricultural regions. Starlings gorge on a tremendous variety of food, ranging from invertebrates—such as snails, worms, millipedes, and spiders—to fruits, berries, grains, seeds, even garbage. They nest in cavities, ranging from crevices in urban settings to woodpecker holes and nesting boxes. The species aggressively takes over the nesting sites of other birds, including Eastern Bluebirds, Wood Ducks, Red-bellied Woodpeckers, Great Crested Flycatchers, and Purple Martins. A highly social species that flies and forages in flocks, starlings also mix into flocks of other species, including Red-winged Blackbirds, Brown-headed Cowbirds, American Robins, Rock Doves, and Common Crows. Because if this adaptability, the starling has increased its range to most of North America.

Range of European Starling

CLASSIFICATION

The European Starling and Hill, Crested, and Common Mynas are members of the Old World family of birds called Sturnidae. The relationship of this family to others is under debate. Since European Starlings often join mixed flocks of icterids—especially blackbirds, cowbirds, and grackles—and share with them the ability to "gape" or forcefully open their beaks to pry into soil or plant matter, the sturnids have often been linked with the icterids. Some scholars have thought, they more closely resemble crows. Recent DNA-DNA hybridization studies, however, indicate that the Sturnidae are so closely related to the Mimidae—mockingbirds, thrashers, and catbirds—that these two may constitute a single family.

STRUCTURE

Although European Starlings often flock with blackbirds, they can be distinguished by their chunkier appearance, shorter tail, and longer, more pointed bill. Special musculature in the jaw allows starlings and many blackbirds to not only grasp prey but to pry apart materials. As the bill pries open, the eyes rotate forward giving the bird binocular vision.

PLUMAGE

The name starling (little star) is thought to derive from the light spots that give the bird a star-studded appearance in the fall. By spring, the starry spots wear off, leaving the bird black, with a rich iridescent gloss of green and purple, and the black bill of fall turns bright yellow. Were the European Starling rarer or more melodious in song, we might appreciate its beauty. The European Starling's cousins, the Hill and Crested Mynas are also glossy black with an ever-changing purple sheen. Only the Common Myna is predominantly brown, but its head is a rich black and, like the other mynas, it has white wing patches that stand out in flight.

FEEDING BEHAVIOR

During spring and summer, ground-foraging European Starlings dine on small insects and invertebrates, preferring beetles, grasshoppers, flies, and caterpillars, but they will also eat spiders, snails, and earthworms. In fall and winter, they spend more time in low shrubs and trees where they find seeds and berries in increasing amounts. Mynas, too, are ground feeders, but they are primarily frugivores with fruit making up to 60 percent of their diet. Insects and earthworms compose most of the remaining 40 percent, although Hill Mynas may also take nectar and small reptiles.

European Starlings live, roost, and forage in large flocks in all but the breeding season. Starlings seem most at home in a wide variety of edge environments, but, like the mynas, also have adapted well to human, suburban environments. All four of the Sturnidae seem to thrive around garbage dumps, farmyards, open groves, and suburban parks. From late summer into winter, small groups of European Starlings forage by day, and many such small groups gather, sometimes with blackbirds, cowbirds, grackles, and American Robins, to form roosts in the tens of thousands.

VOCALIZATIONS

Sturnidae song overall seems chaotic and raucous although at times includes a truly melodic, whistling, warbling phrase. In the spring, European Starlings gather in treetops where they utter a variety of squeaks, chatters, creaks, chirps, and even a wolf whistle. Or, they imitate bobwhite, Killdeer, flicker, phoebe, and wood-pewee calls, as well as sirens, dogs, and cats.

Whereas captive European Starlings mimic household sounds, mynas are so adept at the imitation of those sounds and human speech that they have long been popular cage birds.

BREEDING BEHAVIOR

Unlike the mimids, the sturnids are cavity nesters, willing to nest in rock crevices, holes in banks, and niches in buildings. The male establishes the territory based on the location of a possible nesting site. After beginning construction of the nest, he perches near it and sings while flicking his wings to attract a mate.

Crested Myna

Most Sturnidae are monogamous during a single season, but some European Starling males switch mates for a second brood, especially if the first was not successful. Starlings defend only the immediate area around their nest, and when multiple suitable sites are available, they will nest semicolonially.

Unlike most cavity nesters which simply drop in a few leaves or wood chips, starlings build a nest inside the hole. Linings of anti-parasite, anti-pathogen laden greenery not only help keep the eggs and nestlings warm and dry but protect them from illness and other dangers. The parents remove the hatchlings' fecal sacs, which helps insure the health of the nest. Both parents

incubate the four to six eggs laid per clutch for nearly two weeks and feed the hatchlings for at least 21 days when they fledge and after.

BREEDING RANGE

The invasive European Starling seems ubiquitous, breeding across North America from below the Arctic Circle south to central Mexico. The three mynas breed only near their point of introduction—the Crested near Vancouver, the Common in southern Florida, and the Hill Myna in southern Florida and near Los Angeles.

MIGRATION

The three mynas do not move out of their limited ranges. European Starlings, too, tend to stay put year-round, although some northern birds are diurnal migrants that move south from late September through November and return north from mid-February to early March.

WINTER RANGE

Since none of the Sturnidae are migratory, their winter ranges coincide with their breeding ranges. Some European Starlings shift their range during the winter, but these are only minor shifts in search of better forage.

OBSERVING STARLINGS AND MYNAS

Birders must go to the myna breeding ranges to see them but can enjoy European Starlings everywhere. Their unison, aerial maneuvers that, with no apparent leader, first expand and then retract the flock into a tight ball, serve not only to confuse predators but delight human observers.

STATUS AND CONSERVATION

Of the Sturnidae, only the European Starling is doing well. With a highly variable diet and an ability to adapt to a variety of habitats, the 50 or 60 starlings first released in New York in the 1890s now number around 200 million. These aggressive, invasive newcomers compete successfully for nesting sites with native secondary cavity nesters like Eastern Bluebirds and Great Crested Flycatchers and primary cavity nesters such as Northern Flickers and Red-headed Woodpeckers, posing a real threat to these and other native species.

Given the small populations and limited range, the mynas may not be able to remain viable in the wild.

OTHER SPECIES FIELD NOTES

■ **Crested Myna**
Acridotheres cristatellus
L 9.75"
Bushy crest on forehead

■ **Common Myna**
Acridotheres tristis
L 10"
Yellow patch around eye,
brown back and belly

■ **Hill Myna**
Gracula religiosa
L 10.5"
Yellow wattles and legs,
orange bill

See also

Old World Sparrows, Exotics, page 419

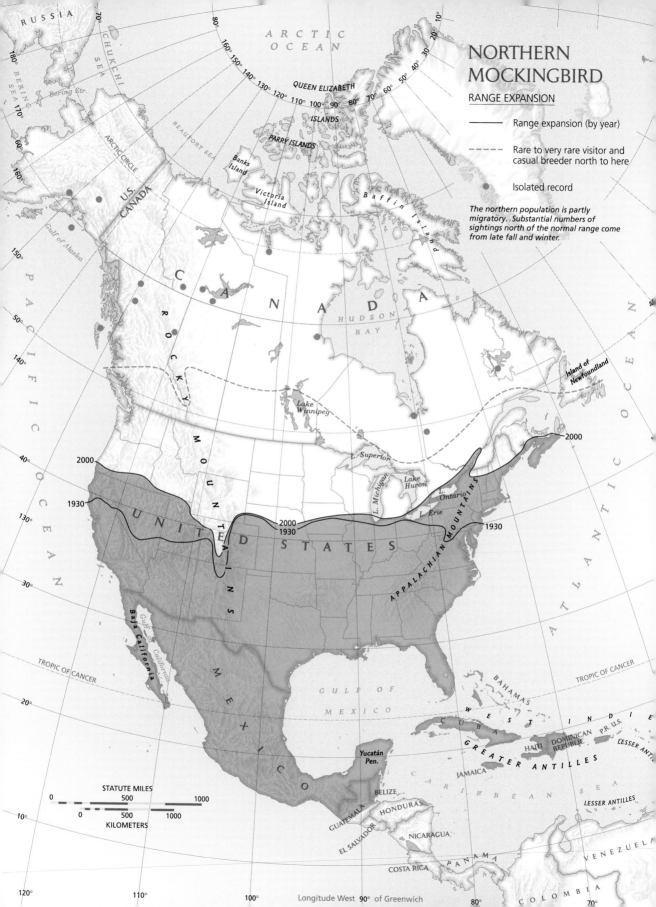

NORTHERN MOCKINGBIRD

RANGE EXPANSION

——————— Range expansion (by year)

— — — — — Rare to very rare visitor and casual breeder north to here

●   Isolated record

The northern population is partly migratory. Substantial numbers of sightings north of the normal range come from late fall and winter.

RUSSIA

ARCTIC OCEAN

CHUKCHI SEA

BERING SEA

Bering Str.

ARCTIC CIRCLE

U.S.
CANADA

Gulf of Alaska

PACIFIC OCEAN

BEAUFORT SEA

QUEEN ELIZABETH
ISLANDS

PARRY ISLANDS

Banks Island

Victoria Island

Baffin Island

C A N A D A

ROCKY MOUNTAINS

HUDSON BAY

Island of Newfoundland

ATLANTIC OCEAN

Lake Winnipeg

L. Superior

Lake Michigan

Lake Huron

L. Ontario

L. Erie

2000

2000

1930

2000
1930

1930

U N I T E D   S T A T E S

APPALACHIAN MOUNTAINS

Baja California

Gulf of California

M E X I C O

TROPIC OF CANCER

TROPIC OF CANCER

GULF OF MEXICO

BAHAMAS

W E S T   I N D I E S

CUBA

HAITI DOMINICAN REPUBLIC

P.R. U.S.

LESSER ANT.

GREATER ANTILLES

JAMAICA

CARIBBEAN SEA

LESSER ANTILLES

Yucatán Pen.

BELIZE

GUATEMALA

HONDURAS

EL SALVADOR

NICARAGUA

COSTA RICA

PANAMA

VENEZUELA

COLOMBIA

STATUTE MILES
0   500   1000
0   500   1000
KILOMETERS

Longitude West 90° of Greenwich

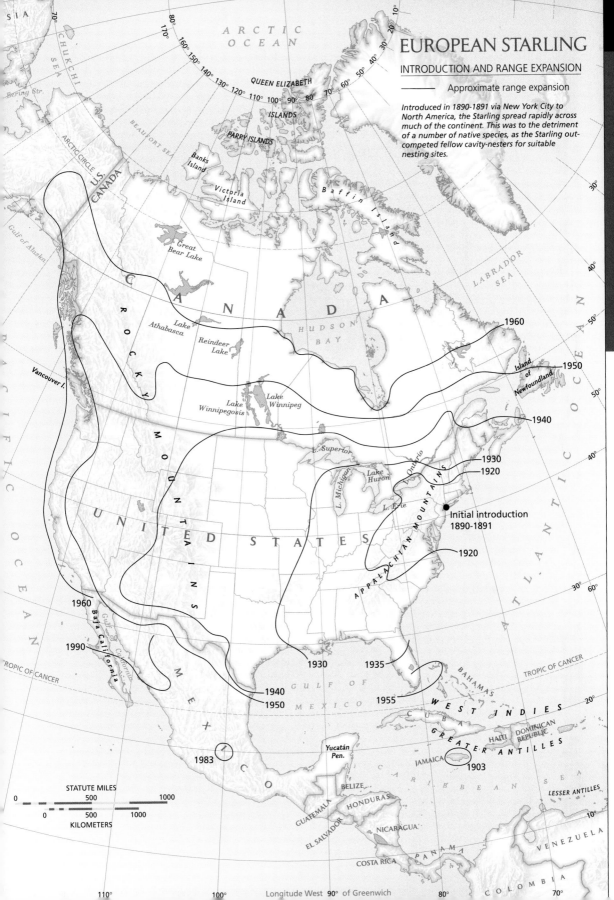

EUROPEAN STARLING

INTRODUCTION AND RANGE EXPANSION

—— Approximate range expansion

Introduced in 1890-1891 via New York City to North America, the Starling spread rapidly across much of the continent. This was to the detriment of a number of native species, as the Starling out-competed fellow cavity-nesters for suitable nesting sites.

Initial introduction
1890-1891

1960
1950
1940
1930
1920
1920

1960
1990
1930 1935
1940
1950 1955
1983
1903

STATUTE MILES
0   500   1000

0   500   1000
KILOMETERS

Longitude West 90° of Greenwich

ACCENTORS, WAGTAILS, PIPITS

Pipits and wagtails (family Motacillidae) are open-country, ground-loving passerines found all over the world, with the exception of Antarctica. Their greatest diversity lies in the Old World, where the taxonomy of this group is changing rapidly, and many forms once considered subspecies are now classified as full species. Of the 65 to 85 species worldwide, eleven are recorded from North America, six of which nest on the continent. Almost all pipits of the world are cryptically clad in browns, buffs, and grays, darker above, paler below, usually with streaking below, whereas wagtails are more strikingly patterned in combinations of black, white, yellow, and gray. Pipits feed on insect matter and small seeds; wagtails are mostly insectivorous but take a variety of other invertebrates throughout the year as well.

Edward S. Brinkley

The most widespread motacillid in North America, the American Pipit (known as Buff-bellied Pipit in the rest of the world), is familiar to most birders from farm fields, where large flocks are recorded throughout most of the United States during the nonbreeding season between October and April. Occasionally, the same fields will hold numbers of Horned Larks, Snow Buntings, longspurs, meadowlarks, or sparrows, making the search for "field birds" a full morning's outing in some areas. Sprague's Pipit, which nests in native prairie in the northern Great Plains, is much less familiar to most birders. It does not gather in flocks in winter and tends to stay well hidden in grassy vegetation, flushing only if approached closely. Birders visiting Texas or the southern reaches of Arizona and New Mexico in winter often make a special search for Sprague's

Pipit. Red-throated Pipit, which nests sparingly in northwestern Alaska, is known otherwise chiefly in winter from California, where it is sometimes found flocking with American Pipits, though it is quite rare there. Of the three nesting North American species, Red-throated is the most brightly plumaged, sporting a rusty or rufous face and throat in breeding-plumaged adult males. On late-spring and summer trips to western Alaska, one stands a good chance of finding this species in the right habitat.

Wagtails rarely visit North America other than Alaska, where Yellow and White Wagtails both breed regularly, and the Black-backed Wagtail (formerly considered a form of White Wagtail) is known to breed at a few locations. These species are "trans-Beringian" migrants, meaning they cross the Bering Sea and Chukchi Sea in early autumn, en route to wintering grounds in southeastern Asia, rather than wintering in North America. All three species, however, are known as vagrants to the Pacific coast, mostly to California, but all are quite rare there. Wagtails are long-distance migrants with a remarkable propensity to show up as vagrants: a Citrine Wagtail even showed up in Mississippi, the only North American record of this Palearctic species. Identification of wayward wagtails, as with pipits, can be tricky, as most species have multiple subspecies, as well as having a variety of plumages that differ by age, sex, and season, so that care is needed in identifying what seems to be a bird out of normal range. With patience—and a careful study of the latest books on field identification—North America's species can all be safely identified.

American Pipit: *Anthus rubescens,* L 6.5" Gray above, streaked buffy underparts

ACCENTORS, WAGTAILS, PIPITS

The American Pipit (above) is a bird of barren tundra during the short northern summer. In the fall, the faint tinkling sound of a flock of American Pipits overhead is often the first sign that these inconspicuous little birds have arrived on their wintering grounds in the southern United States and Mexico. The wintering pipit favors farm fields and short-grass meadows, as well as river and lake margins, where the species gather into large flocks, often joined by other field birds such as Horned Larks or Lapland Longspurs. By contrast, the Sprague's Pipit does not gather into flocks in winter. When foraging, pipits walk briskly on the ground, with a strong gait and bobbing head, in

Range of American Pipit

search of invertebrate prey such as insects and arthropods. Their cryptic plumage, a dull brown above, pale with streaks below, helps to camouflage them in most terrestrial settings, and both predators and birders presumably overlook them until the pipits flush. When a flock flies up, American Pipits almost always vocalize as they wheel about, flashing their white outer tail feathers. Unlike many species of passerine, pipits migrate most commonly during daylight hours.

CLASSIFICATION

The pipits and wagtails form a distinct taxonomic group of at least 65 species worldwide. Pipits might be confused with sparrows or larks, but wagtails' helpful habit of constantly "wagging" or bobbing their tail up and down, combined with their ground-dwelling habits, usually gives away their identity quickly. Motacillids are thought to be related to the accentors, sparrows of the genus *Passer,* weavers, and estrildid finches of the Old World, though this kinship is not altogether certain, and some authorities have proposed a closer relationship with Old World warblers. Interestingly, Sprague's Pipit, which differs in habits, voice, and appearance from Red-throated and American, more closely resembles the pipits of South America than those of North America or Eurasia.

From a North American perspective, classification of the pipits and wagtails might look straightforward, but taxonomists in the Old World have wrestled endlessly with species relationships in motacillids. In the recent past, American Pipit was considered a form of the widespread "Water Pipit," a name still used by some birders for the North American form but properly applied only to *Anthus spinoletta,* the true Water Pipit of the Old World, whose range overlaps with American Pipit in central Eurasia, but the two species apparently do not interbreed there. Because American Pipit has a sizable breeding population in eastern Eurasia, and winters as far west as Israel, European taxonomists prefer the common name Buff-bellied Pipit, most applicable to birds in their alternate or breeding plumage. The "splitting" of pipits has accelerated in Africa as well, especially southern Africa, where several forms have recently been elevated to full-species status. Among the wagtails, Black-backed Wagtail has already been officially split from White Wagtail, and ornithologists in Europe propose dividing Yellow Wagtail into as many as 12 species, depending on the authority. Most such proposals are still tentative and not yet widely accepted, but up-to-date references on how to identify the different subspecies of wagtail continue to be refined, no matter how one categorizes the different forms.

STRUCTURE

The ground-dwelling pipits and wagtails are both slender and streamlined birds with moderately long tails. The wagtails are larger than the pipits and have a much longer tail. The tail of the Yellow Wagtails is noticeably shorter than that of the White and Black-backed Wagtails. The bills of all Motacillids are slender and pointed, similar to warblers' bills, however, their legs are longer and stronger than those of warblers, and the rear toe is long with a long nail, as in other ground-dwelling passerines.

PLUMAGE

Brown above and usually streaky below, pipits are some of the "little brown jobs" of the sort dreaded by some birders, highly prized for their subtlety by others. In truth, when seen well, pipits are handsomely attired, particularly during the breeding season, when the underparts take on a more intense color, ranging from the delicate rose-buff of the Sprague's Pipit to the buffy orange-peach of some American Pipit races, to the brilliant rusty orange of the Red-throated Pipit. Male pipits in alternate plumage are generally more richly colored than females, and subspecies of the American Pipit, for instance, differ in the degree of streaking and the richness of their underparts during the nesting season.

Wagtails are pied in plumage, with starkly contrasting areas of black, white, and gray (White, Black-backed) or yellow, greenish, and gray with black-and-white accents (Yellow, Gray). Immature, female, and nonbreeding plumages are much less stark than those of the adult males in breeding plu-

Gray Wagtail

mage, and these require some study to separate in the field, especially those of the White and Black-backed Pipits, which apparently do hybridize to a limited extent. Some individuals thus might not be safely assignable to species.

OTHER SPECIES FIELD NOTES

■ **Siberian Accentor**
Prunella montanella
L 5.5"
Buffy eyebrow, dark cheek patch

■ **Yellow Wagtail**
Motacilla flava
L 6.5"
Olive above, yellow below

■ **Gray Wagtail**
Motacilla cinerea
L 7.75"
Gray back, yellow below

■ **White Wagtail**
Motacilla alba
L 7.25"
White face and under-parts, gray back

■ **Black-backed Wagtail**
Motacilla lugens
L 7.25"
Black back and breast, mostly white wings

■ **Sprague's Pipit**
Anthus spragueii
L 6.5"
Dark eye stands out in pale face

■ **Olive-backed Pipit**
Anthus hodgsoni
L 6"
Eyebrow orange to white, faintly streaked, olive back

■ **Pechora Pipit**
Anthus gustavi
L 5.5"
Richly patterned back with white lines

■ **Red-throated Pipit**
Anthus cervinus
L 6"
Pinkish-red face and breast

FEEDING BEHAVIOR

American Pipits forage by walking through open habitats, often with a bobbing gait that includes head and tail, and by searching for small seeds, arthropods, and insects on or near the ground. They also feed on emerging insect larvae at water's edge and will even walk into water to take aquatic insects or other invertebrates. On occasion, these pipits flycatch as well. Wagtails forage in much the same manner but are much more active in pursuit of insects, frequently chasing invertebrate prey along the ground or into the air, and often using disturbances created by farm equipment or cattle to their advantage, as they seize insects stirred up by moving mammals or machinery. The Yellow Wagtails also forage by rummaging through leaf litter or other debris, much like a thrush or a sparrow.

VOCALIZATION

The songs of pipits and wagtails, heard only on the nesting grounds, are not familiar to most birders. They consist mostly of harsh, high, often squeaky notes, repeated or modified in series, and lasting from just a few seconds (as in some wagtails) to over 40 minutes (Sprague's Pipit). Pipits tend to deliver their songs in flight display, whereas wagtails sing more often from the ground or from song-perches on the tops of vegetation or buildings. The call-notes of both pipits and wagtails are delivered regularly, largely from birds in flight, but also from perched birds, and have a relatively similar quality within the family, being high in pitch, short in duration, and rather sharp in inflection, whether single- or double-noted. These call-notes can in some cases be used to separate similar species, so they should be listened to and noted carefully in the case of immature birds or vagrant occurrences.

BREEDING BEHAVIOR

Though often gregarious in winter, wagtails and pipits are territorial in the nesting season. Most species form pairs on the nesting grounds, with males singing to attract mates and to mark and defend territories, although females defend territories as well. Socially, motacillids are monogamous, but copulation outside the pair has been observed in wagtails. Both sexes usually participate to some degree in the construction of the cup-shaped nest, which is built on the ground in pipits, and in a variety of settings in wagtails such as in cliff crevices, under debris, in dilapidated buildings, or under shrubs. Pipits and wagtails differ in their nest duties: The pipit females incubate the eggs, whereas wagtails share the incubation (though the female does most of the work). Male pipits feed incubating or brooding females; wagtails do so to a lesser degree. Young pipits are altricial, meaning they are born naked and with their eyes closed, and they are raised in the nest for the first two weeks of life, on average. Parents feed their young for another two or three weeks after they fledge.

BREEDING RANGE

Most motacillids in North America nest in the far north, north of the tree-line, in the Canadian and Alaskan tundra and along the coast. American Pipits also nest sparingly in subalpine meadows above the tree-line in mountain ranges as far south as California and Arizona in the West, and Maine in the East. Habitat use differs subtly among species, with White and Black-backed Wagtails more likely to nest right along riverbanks, coastal cliffs, in villages, and among industrial operations, and Yellow Wagtails nesting more in interior habitats with shrubby vegetation.

MIGRATION

After the nesting season, American and Red-throated Pipits form flocks that migrate, often diurnally, toward winter quarters. Flocks of American Pipits are a familiar sight in agricultural land in virtually all states and provinces at some point during their migration. Because the bulk of American Pipits probably winter within the temperate southern United States, the species is not considered to be mainly a neotropical migrant, despite substantial numbers of the species that winter in southern Mexico and sometimes even farther south. The Sprague's Pipit is noted even less frequently on migration in the Great Plains and as a vagrant to either Pacific or Atlantic coastal states. It is an extreme rarity, probably overlooked because of its cryptic plumage and retiring habits.

Less is known of the migration of wagtails and Red-throated Pipits across the Bering Sea and to their wintering grounds in southern and eastern Asia,. However, diurnal migration in small groups has been observed in the wagtails, and large coastal flocks of Red-throated Pipits in fall suggest that this species follows the outer coast south to wintering areas. Most Alaskan-nesting wagtails probably arrive with Siberian-nesting wagtails in Japan and eastern China in the mid- to late autumn, at latitudes comparable to the passage of Red-throated and American Pipits toward wintering areas. In recent years, American Pipits of the strongly-marked subspecies *japonicus,* which nests in Siberia, have been found among American and Red-throated

Red-throated Pipit

Pipits in California. These long-distance migrants should be looked for in other states and provinces as well.

WINTER RANGE

American Pipits in the East winter from the latitude of Virginia, Tennessee, and Texas south into southern Mexico. In the West, pipits are mostly found in southern New Mexico and Arizona, through much of lowland California, and up the Pacific coastal plain north to Washington. Sprague's Pipit by contrast winters largely in Texas and northern Mexico, with small numbers present in the Southwest and in southern Oklahoma. Red-throated Pipits occasionally overwinter with American Pipits in southern California, but most winter in southern and eastern Asia (where most North American wagtails winter as well), and west into the Middle East.

Both wagtails and pipits are attracted to open habitats. The American Pipits frequent agricultural areas, especially cultivated fields, as well as the shores of lakes and rivers and flat rocky areas. Sprague's Pipits are more wide-ranging in their choice of wintering habitats than of breeding habitats, accepting grassy fields of many sorts, and even shoreline dikes and baseball fields. The Wagtails are versatile foragers and are able to use many human-altered habitats, but they tend to be found in damp areas or sites near water in winter and around coastal areas and rivers, mudflats, and rocky shorelines. In most cases, wintering wagtails are far more likely to be found in close association with human settlements or landfill operations than are pipits.

OBSERVING MOTACILLIDS.

To become familiar with the American Pipit requires little more than driving into the nearest flat farmland where pipits are known to winter (southern states) or stage in migration (central and northern states, southern Canada) and watching for flocks among short-grass or cultivated fields. Winter wheat fields often hold large flocks for long periods in the southern United States.

When in flight, American Pipits show much white in the outer tail feathers, and in most cases, they utter a distinctive, cheerful, rising "pee-PIT!" call, with many individuals calling simultaneously from large flocks. The Horned Lark, common in flocks in the same habitat, has a more melancholy "SEE-tl" call given in the same circumstances. It also has white outer tail feathers, making it a possible source of confusion. Like wagtails, American Pipits tend to bob the tail when standing and foraging, but not to the degree that wagtails do. Unless the birds are close to the road, a spotting scope is useful for appreciation and careful study, though these pipits can be very tame and tolerant of birders at close range. American Pipits on their nesting grounds—on Arctic tundra and subalpine mountaintop meadows—are often even more confiding than in winter. Here they sing a lovely tinkling song while in flight, dropping back to earth after 15 to 30 seconds to continue foraging, apparently oblivious to people nearby.

The male Sprague's Pipit also sings in flight, but from an even greater altitude of up to 360 feet and for a longer period of time, often over a half-hour. At such heights, the bird appears as a dark speck just below the clouds. After delivering its remarkable song, the Sprague's Pipit plummets back to earth and into the vegetation, where it is perfectly camouflaged. Some luck and a spotting scope, however, can turn up one of these pipits after its return to earth, where its cryptic colors are best appreciated. On the wintering grounds, the Sprague's Pipit is mouse-like and most often found when it flushes up at the birder's feet, rising high in the air while delivering its sweet, sharp call-note, then dropping back to earth abruptly many feet away. (This is a different flush behavior as that known from sparrows and other field birds.) As on the nesting grounds, patience is required on the part of the birder.

The search for wagtails and Red-throated Pipits usually entails a journey to remote Alaskan habitats during the nesting season. Whereas the Yellow Wagtail is widespread in coastal northern Alaska as a breeder, the White Wagtail (of the subspecies group *alba*) is mostly found on the Seward Peninsula. In flight, wagtails show a distinctive undulating pattern (as in some woodpeckers or shrikes), with their squeaky, pipit-like calls delivered on the upward part of the "roller-coaster" flight path. To find any of the rarer or vagrant motacillids—Gray Wagtail, Olive-backed Pipit, Tree Pipit, or Pechora Pipit—requires a commitment of much time and a good amount of luck in the western Alaskan islands during the spring and fall migration, but all of these species are easily seen in their regular ranges in Eurasia.

STATUS AND CONSERVATION

Only one species of motacillid, the Sprague's Pipit, has been placed on the National Audubon Society's WatchList, owing to critical declines in populations as the species' native prairie habitat is converted to farmland. The Canadian Wildlife Service lists this species as Threatened, and data from Breeding Bird Surveys support this listing. In the southern United States, Christmas Bird Count data also show a decline in wintering populations of the American Pipit, as former farmland

SIBERIAN ACCENTOR

Probably a close relative to the pipits and wagtails, the beautifully-plumaged Siberian Accentor *(Prunella montanella)*—one of 13 species of accentors worldwide—is the only member of the small family Prunellidae to have reached North America. A few have reached western Alaska during the autumn migration, six of which have been seen on St. Lawrence Island. Exceptional records of single vagrants come from British Columbia in Canada and in Idaho and Washington State. This pattern of vagrancy is seen in only a few other Siberian species, notably Dusky Warbler. A bird of boreal forest through taiga habitat in Siberia, the Siberian Accentor has been little studied on the nesting grounds, but its mating system may be as varied and flexible as that of its well studied, close relative, the Hedge Accentor (Dunnock), which displays every possible combination of strategies, including the rare situation in which both members of a primary pair may make extra-pair bonds with other birds of the opposite sex. Also unusual is the shape of the bill, which resembles that of a wagtail but is wider at the base and more distended through the maxilla. It is thought that the bill shape relates to the species' foraging habits for gleaning small invertebrates and berries.

is converted to suburban neighborhoods and industrial areas. The Alaska-nesting populations of wagtails and Red-throated Pipits have not been studied, but there do exist concerns for habitat loss as a result of global climate change.

See also

Sparrows, Allies, page 379

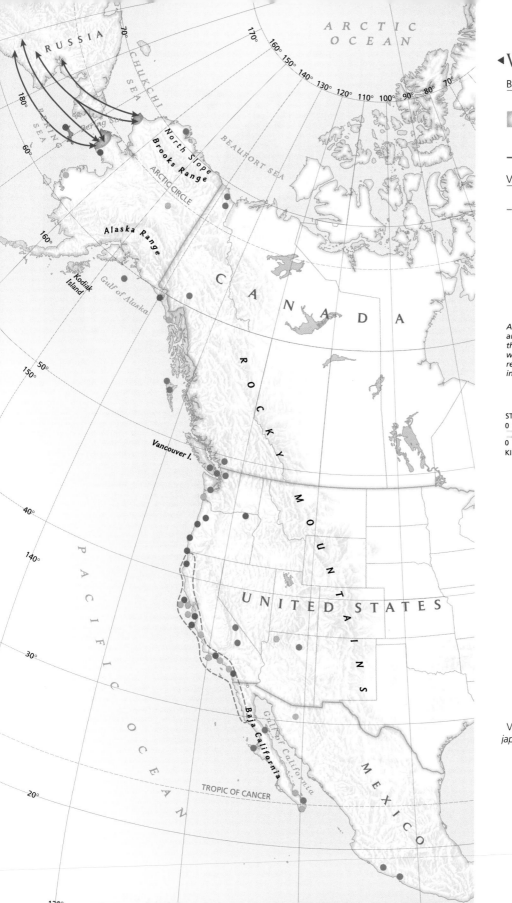

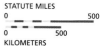

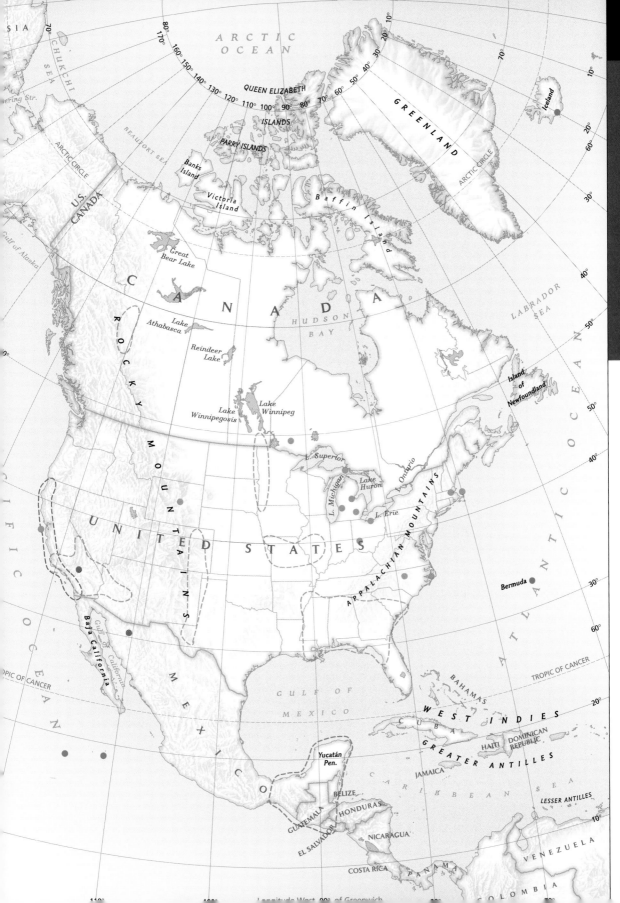

ARCTIC
OCEAN

CHUKCHI
SEA

Bering Str.

QUEEN ELIZABETH

ISLANDS

GREENLAND

Iceland

PARRY ISLANDS

BEAUFORT SEA

ARCTIC CIRCLE

ARCTIC CIRCLE

Banks
Island

Baffin Island

U.S.

CANADA

Gulf of Alaska

Victoria
Island

C   A   N   A   D   A

Great
Bear Lake

HUDSON

BAY

LABRADOR

SEA

R
O
C
K
Y

Lake
Athabasca

Reindeer
Lake

Island
of
Newfoundland

Lake
Winnipegosis

Lake
Winnipeg

L. Superior

M
O
U
N
T
A
I
N
S

Lake
Michigan

Lake
Huron

Ontario

L. Michigan

L. Erie

APPALACHIAN MOUNTAINS

A
T
L
A
N
T
I
C

O
C
E
A
N

U   N   I   T   E   D

S   T   A   T   E   S

Bermuda

P
A
C
I
F
I
C

Baja California

Gulf of California

M
E
X
I
C
O

TROPIC OF CANCER

TROPIC OF CANCER

GULF   OF

MEXICO

BAHAMAS

W   E   S   T   I   N   D   I   E   S

C
U
B
A

O
C
E
A
N

Yucatán
Pen.

G   R   E   A   T   E   R   A   N   T   I   L   L   E   S

HAITI

DOMINICAN
REPUBLIC

JAMAICA

BELIZE

C   A   R   I   B   B   E   A   N   S   E   A

LESSER ANTILLES

GUATEMALA

HONDURAS

EL SALVADOR

NICARAGUA

VENEZUELA

COSTA RICA

PANAMA

COLOMBIA

Longitude West 90° of Greenwich

WAXWINGS, SILKY-FLYCATCHERS

Bird-watchers in North America have the opportunity to see two of the world's three species in the family Bombycillidae: Cedar Waxwings and Bohemian Waxwings. The third species is the Japanese Waxwing of eastern Asia. Waxwings are small birds—Cedars about 7.25 inches; Bohemians 8.25 inches long—but because they often group into large flocks, their presence can be impressive.

A close relative of waxwings, the Phainopepla (one of only four species in the family Ptilogonatidae or Silky-flycatchers) is similar to waxwings in skeleton, musculature, digestive tract, and nesting behavior.

Cedar Waxwings are by far the most common, ranging from southeast Alaska, the southern regions of Canada, and west to east through the United States as far south as northern California and the Gulf states, where they live year-round. By contrast, Bohemian Waxwings spend most of their lives farther north in Canada and Alaska, migrating south only under duress to find food. They appear most regularly in the Rocky Mountain states as far south as Colorado, although they have erupted as far east as the Atlantic region and as far south as New Mexico.

Phainopeplas reside in California, southern Nevada, western and central Arizona, southwest Utah, southern New Mexico, and southwest Texas.

Cedar Waxwings are among the most frugivorous (fruit-eating) birds in North America. Up to 84 percent of their diet is fruit, whereas the diet of the American Robin, a frugivorous thrush, is 57 percent fruit. The Bohemian Waxwing also feeds predominantly on fruit. Before fruit is available, the birds consume sap, flower petals, and insects. Fruits include cedar berries (from which the Cedar Waxwing got its name), mountain ash, chokecherry, mistletoe, peppertree, crabapple, and hawthorn. Phainopeplas are fruit and insect eaters as well, and they are famous for their role in spreading mistletoe, their principal food in winter. The seeds pass undigested through the birds' digestive tract and are dropped onto tree branches in a sticky pulp that glues the seeds to the branches. Phainopeplas even defend patches of mistletoe from other species of birds.

Howard Robinson

The gregarious social nature of waxwings benefits them in their search for food and helps protect them from predators, who may become confused by a rapidly dispersing flock of waxwings. Not strongly territorial, waxwings defend only their nest.

Phainopeplas living in desert habitats vigorously defend territories of less than an acre. Oddly, Phainopeplas living in woodlands establish overlapping home ranges and frequently nest colonially. Aggressive waxwing behavior near the nest has also been interpreted as the male's attempt to guard his mate or the nesting material. Typically, waxwings join in flocks, ranging from a few up to thousands. Phainopeplas form small flocks when migrating and sometimes around fruiting shrubs. During one especially large irruption of Bohemian Waxwings one February, an estimated 10,000 birds invaded Denver, Colorado, and devoured all the fruit on the Russian olives and other plants in the area. There have been anecdotal reports of Cedar Waxwings perched in a row passing a berry from one to another until one of the birds swallows it, but conclusive proof is missing.

(Left) Phainopepla

Cedar Waxwing: *Bombycilla cedrorum*, L 7.25", crest, belly pale yellow

WAXWINGS AND ALLIES

The natty, sleek Cedar Waxwing (above) of the family Bombycillidae is famous for its beauty and its unusual dietary habit, an exceptional reliance on sugary fruit for a temperate-zone species. Cedar Waxwings also eat insects. In fact, they feed their hatchlings large numbers of insects during the first two days of life, before switching the offerings to fruit. From early May and lasting until fruit is available, insects are important food. Overall, insects make up about 12 percent of a waxwing's diet. But it is its reliance on sugary fruit (84 percent of its diet) that distinguishes the Cedar Waxwing and affects so many aspects of its life. The abundance and location of berries influence the waxwing's facultative migration patterns: It moves long distances only when the local fruit supply runs out. The waxwing's breeding season is late in the year, corresponding with the abundance of summer fruit. The waxwing's reliance on patchy sources of fruit correlates to its lack of territoriality during the breeding season and its spectacular sociability during the winter, when members of large flocks feed side by side.

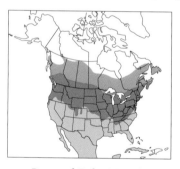

Range of Cedar Waxwing

CLASSIFICATION

Waxwings and Phainopeplas share similarities in skeletal structure, nesting behavior, musculature, and digestive tracts. But just how closely related they are, and how to place them in the taxonomic tree, is controversial. Some experts link them closely to the thrushes and Old World flycatchers, listing the waxwings as Bombycillini, the Palmchat as Dulini, and Phainopeplas as Ptilogonatini in a larger tribe called Bombycillidae. Other experts, including the American Ornithologists' Union (1998 Checklist), place them closer to pipits and starlings and give family status to the Bombycillidae, the Ptilogonatidae, and the Dulidae.

STRUCTURE

Bohemian Waxwings are larger than Cedar Waxwings, averaging 8.25 inches in length to the Cedar's 7.25 inches. The Phainopepla is in between the two waxwings at 7.75 inches in length. All three species have distinctive crests and soft, sleek plumage. Phainopeplas are also distinguished by their red eyes. The digestive tract of Phainopeplas is adapted to efficiently process mistletoe berries, which are low in nutrients.

PLUMAGE

Male Phainopeplas are shiny black with white wing patches that are highly visible in flight; females are gray. Waxwings have gray-brown plumage. The Bohemian Waxwing is grayer than the Cedar Waxwing and has white wing patches and rust-colored undertail coverts. Both species of waxwing have a black tail with a yellow band at the end and red waxy tips on the secondary feathers of the wing. These tips are not feathers, but flattened portions of the feather shafts. Some evidence suggests that these red tips are keys to mate selection: Older waxwings have more and larger red tips on their secondaries—and raise more young—than do immature waxwings. Birds tend to select mates who have similar numbers of these red flags. The yellow bands at the ends of the tail feathers result from carotenoids ingested in the food. Since the early 1960s, an increasing number of Cedar Waxwings have been gorging on the fruits of Morrow's Honeysuckle (an alien species) during the time their feathers are forming. This type of honeysuckle contains red carotenoids that mix with the yellow carotenoids ingested with other fruits, resulting in orange-tipped tail feathers.

FEEDING BEHAVIOR

Cedar Waxwings, Bohemian Waxwings, and Phainopeplas feed on both insects and sugary fruits, whatever is most abundant. Fruit is the largest component of their diet, with insects being favored mainly during nesting. In fall and winter (October through April), Phainopeplas depend almost entirely on mistletoe berries. The volume of insects they ingest increases to about 37 percent of their diet in late spring and summer. Cedar Waxwings are such voracious eaters that they are nicknamed "glutton" or "gourmand."

VOCALIZATION

Flocks of Cedar Waxwings chatter continually, Bohemians twitter. The Bohemian Waxwing's call is coarser and a bit lower pitched than the Cedar Waxwing's. Cedar Waxwings vary the loudness, duration, and other qualities of their notes depending on the purpose of calling: courtship, begging, or contact. The Cedar Waxwing has no song. The Phainopepla's call sounds like a low-pitched, whistled "wurp?" and its song is a brief warble that is seldom heard.

BREEDING BEHAVIOR

Courtship among waxwings is entertaining to witness. Beginning around mid-April and at times lasting through mid- June, Cedar Waxwing mates engage in what is called courtship hopping. While the male and female are on the same perch, the male hops toward the female, then the female hops toward the male, and they continue until they get close enough to touch bills. Once the two mates have met, they may pass food or some other object from one to another: The male gives the item to the female, who hops away from the male and then back toward him, returning the item. This behavior may be repeated several times. The courtship rituals of Phainopeplas also involve exchanges of insects or berries, as well as special flights, chases, and groupings. Exhibiting behavior that is unusual among passerine species in North America, Phainopeplas breed in two different habitats: desert and woodland, at two different times of the year.

Bohemian Waxwings build cup-shaped nests in conifers, 10 to 50 feet above the ground. Cedar Waxwings build their cup-shaped nests lower—usually four to 20 feet above ground. Bohemians lay between four and six eggs, and Cedars between two and six. Phaino-

Bohemian Waxwing

peplas lay two to three eggs in cup-shaped nests some 6 to 15 feet above ground in heavily shaded vegetation.

BREEDING RANGE

Cedar Waxwings breed over a range that extends as far north as southeast Alaska, across southern Canada, and into the United States to northwest California. Bohemian Waxwings breed from western Canada to Alaska. Phainopeplas breed in two different ranges—oak and sycamore canyons and in the deserts of Arizona, California, and Mexico.

MIGRATION

Except for winter irruptions that occasionally take them far east and south, Bohemian Waxwings are short-distance migrants. They can withstand severe cold, so lack of food is thought to be the motive for their irruptions. Cedar Waxwings routinely move southward during winter, but because their movements are irregular, their migration is not well understood. They gather in flocks of 30 to 100, or sometimes thousands, and begin moving south in late August, migrating as far as Costa Rica and Panama. Most Cedar Waxwings end their journeys in Florida, South Carolina, Alabama, Mississippi, Texas, and western states. Spring migrations begin around February, with a second wave taking off in May. Phainopeplas are short-distance migrants, moving out of the Sonoran Desert in spring and returning in fall. They breed in California, Nevada, Utah, New Mexico, Texas, and Mexico.

WINTER RANGE

Phainopeplas spend winter in southern California, Nevada, Arizona, New Mexico, Texas, and Mexico. Bohemian Waxwings usually spend winter in western Canada, but periodically irrupt southward into the U.S. to Colorado, New Mexico, and Maine. Cedar Waxwings are found in southern regions of the U.S. where cedars and other fruit-bearing trees are plentiful.

STATUS AND CONSERVATION

Populations of Cedar Waxwings are increasing across the United States, possibly because they benefit from the regeneration of shrublands in the eastern and central states. Human alterations of the riparian woodlands and the birds' desert habitat have diminished the Phainopepla's population, though not to the point of being threatened.

See also

Accentors, Wagtails, Pipits, page 345

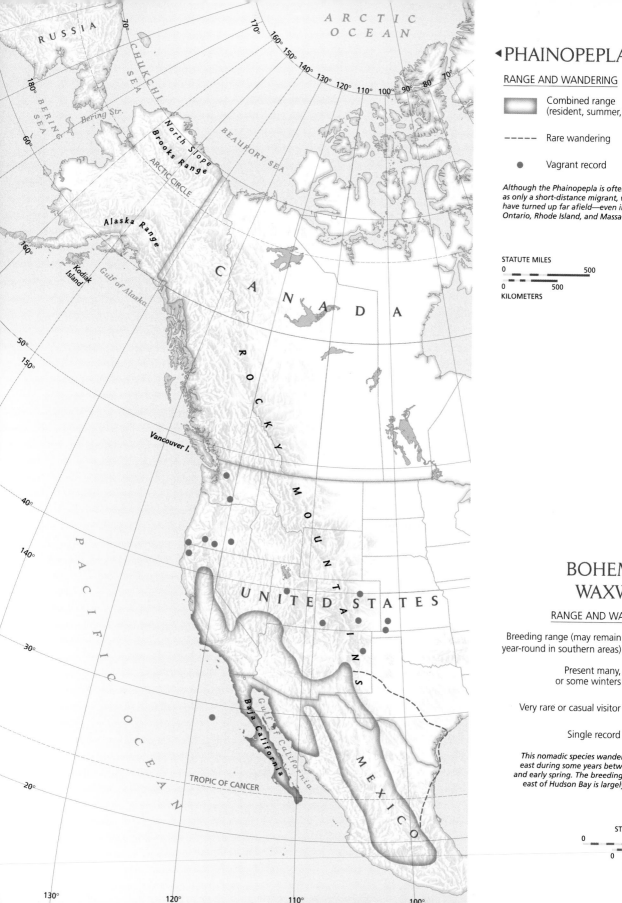

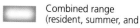
◄PHAINOPEPLA

RANGE AND WANDERING

Combined range
(resident, summer, and

----- Rare wandering

● Vagrant record

*Although the Phainopepla is often thou
as only a short-distance migrant, wande
have turned up far afield—even in Wisc
Ontario, Rhode Island, and Massachuse*

STATUTE MILES
0   500

0   500
KILOMETERS

BOHEMIA
WAXWIN

RANGE AND WANDE

Breeding range (may remain
year-round in southern areas)

Present many,
or some winters

Very rare or casual visitor --

Single record

*This nomadic species wanders sou
east during some years between la
and early spring. The breeding popu
east of Hudson Bay is largely prese*

STATUTE

0

0
KILOM

WOOD-WARBLERS, OLIVE WARBLERS

The warblers, or wood-warblers, as they are usually known, are a large family of small perching birds familiar to most birders. These colorful songsters can spark a lifetime of enthusiasm for birding during spring migration, when the birds' plumage seems to hold every conceivable color, and their songs ring out in every register. Although some birders who look strenuously into the treetops may occasionally complain about "warbler neck," they can easily observe most warbler species in their habitat at the right time of year.

Edward S. Brinkley

Of the roughly 116 species of wood-warblers in the world (family Parulidae), 57 species appear in North America. The remaining species inhabit the warmer climates of Central and South America and the Caribbean Islands.

The similar Olive Warbler, in the separate family Peucedramidae, is believed to be a distant relative of the wood-warblers and is found in the southwestern United States through Central America. There are no other species in that family.

The center of parulid diversity in North America lies in the great swath of eastern Canada and the northeastern United States that includes both broadleaf and boreal forest habitats, home to some 30 species of wood-warblers. During migration, however, places as far apart as Marin County, California; Cheyenne, Wyoming; and Cape May, New Jersey, can hold more than 25 species of wood-warblers under the right conditions. "Warblering" is a particular sort of bird-watching that focuses largely on these birds during the migrations, and its adherents are among the most energetic of birders.

For the aficionado, pilgrimages to central Texas to see the rare Golden-cheeked Warbler and to Michigan to see the Kirtland's Warbler are de rigueur, as are trips to the incomparable spring migration corridors at Point Pelee, Ontario, the upper Texas Coast, and Crane Creek, Ohio.

Most species of warbler are woodland nesters, some nesting on the ground or in underbrush, others high in the canopy. A few species, though, such as the Common Yellowthroat nest in more open habitats such as overgrown fields. Some species are more selective in their nesting habitats than others, and on migration many species can be found foraging in micro-habitats similar to their nesting grounds. During the great migrations in spring and fall, they can sometimes be found by the thousands in traditional "traps" along lakeshores, on peninsulas and headlands, and on barrier islands, sometimes even sitting out on dunes or lawns. These "fallouts" can be predicted by watching the weather, and though usually indicative of some inconvenience for the birds, fallouts showcase warblers' plumages and behaviors like no other phenomenon.

As a widespread and very observable group of birds, warblers make a marvelous point of departure for the beginning birder. Their small size and rapid movements sharpen birding's most basic field skills; their subtle autumn and immature plumages offer identification challenges long after the more striking breeding plumages have become familiar; and their diverse habits and habitats bring the birder into an ever closer relationship with the complex natural history of these remarkable birds.

(Left) **Common Yellowthroat**

Yellow-rumped Warbler: *Dendroica coronata,* L 5.5", yellow rump, throat white, also "Myrtle" or yellow "Audubon's"

WOOD-WARBLERS

Fairly large for wood-warblers of the family Parulidae, the Yellow-rumped Warbler (above) is a blessing for beginning birders because it is so common and, unlike many warblers, it is easy to locate and observe. As it darts about from tree to tree among the branches, it forages for insects during spring and summer and for berries in winter. Although other wood-warblers have yellow rumps, adult

Range of Yellow-rumped Warbler

Yellow-rumped Warblers are easy to distinguish from the others such as Magnolia Warblers and Cape May Warblers, because only they have white-and-black underparts. The Yellow-rumped Warbler actually comprises two groups: the Myrtle Warbler in the East and the Audubon's Warbler in the West. These two groups were considered separate species until research showed that they readily hybridized where their ranges overlapped. Consequently, the two species were lumped together taxonomically in 1973. The two groups are not identical in appearance. For example, the western group has a yellow throat and the Eastern group has a white throat. But both sexes of both groups have yellow rumps, yellow patches on their sides, and white wing bars and tail spots.

CLASSIFICATION

The wood-warblers—family Parulidae—are a group perhaps more distinctive to the ornithologist than to the beginning birder, as they have a strong resemblance to other small woodland birds such as vireos, as well as to the unrelated but very similar Old World Warblers, in the family Sylviidae, which includes our kinglets and gnatcatchers.

Wood-warblers lack the bulbous, slightly hooked bill of the vireos, and their bill and body proportions also differ from the more delicate kinglets and gnatcatchers. Importantly, wood-warblers—or parulids—lack the functional tenth primary of the Old World sylviids. Unlike their Palearctic counterparts, wood-warblers are part of the very large group of mostly American birds known as the nine-primaried oscine passerines, an assemblage of songbirds that includes tanagers, orioles, blackbirds, grosbeaks, and the buntings and sparrows of the New World. In the recent past, all of these birds were combined into the family Emberizidae, but that name is now used only for the New World sparrows; the more nuanced current arrangement includes Parulidae alongside Icteridae (orioles, blackbirds, meadowlarks), Cardinalidae (grosbeaks, cardinals, New World buntings), Thraupidae (tanagers), Coerebidae (Bananaquit), and Emberizidae (New World sparrows) as well as other families within the enormous order Passeriformes, or passerines.

Within the wood-warblers, similar species are grouped by genus, although some of these genera are themselves very similar and apparently closely related; this is especially true of the largest groups in North America, the mostly plain *Vermivora* and the mostly colorful *Dendroica.* The most distinctive species are placed in genera that include no other species, such as Black-and-white Warbler in *Mniotilta,* Swainson's Warbler in *Limnothlypis,* Worm-eating Warbler in *Helmitheros,* Prothonotary Warbler in *Protonotaria,* and American Redstart in *Setophaga.* In between the broadest and narrowest generic classifications, there are many genera that contain only a few species: the retiring *Oporornis* (Connecticut, MacGillivray's, Kentucky, and Mourning Warblers); the ground-loving *Seiurus* (Ovenbird, Louisiana, and Northern Waterthrushes); and the short-tailed, diminutive *Parula* (Northern and Tropical Parulas, Crescent-sided Warbler). When learning about wood-warblers' plumages, habits, and subtly different structures, a birder will find it helpful to know their classification by genus, as genus corresponds in many cases to observable structural features.

One fascinating aspect of wood-warblers' classification is the complex, sometimes contentious, designation of subspecies. Some widespread species, such as Common Yellowthroat, Yellow Warbler, and Orange-crowned Warbler have marked differences across their large ranges, and these differences in populations are countenanced in the many trinomials, or subspecies designations. Some of these forms appear quite distinctly different from one another. The Mangrove Warbler, for instance, a subspecies group within Yellow Warbler, shows a striking chestnut head, lacking in other subspecies groups. The Myrtle Warbler and Audubon's Warbler, once considered distinct species based on strik-

ing differences in plumage and vocalizations, were combined into a single species, Yellow-rumped Warbler, after ornithologists detected inter-breeding where their ranges overlap. Other distinctions are very difficult to detect: the western subspecies of Nashville Warbler, *ridgwayi* (Calaveras Warbler), looks rather similar to the nominate eastern form, though their ranges are disjunct. The same is true of the southeastern *waynei* subspecies of Black-throated Green Warbler (known as Wayne's

OTHER SPECIES FIELD NOTES

■ **Prothonotary Warbler**
Protonotaria citrea
L 5.5" Gold-yellow

■ **Blue-winged Warbler**
Vermivora pinus
L 4.75" Yellow crown

■ **Golden-winged Warbler**
Vermivora chrysoptera
L 4.75" Black ear patch

■ **Tennessee Warbler**
Vermivora peregrina
L 4.75" Gray crown

■ **Orange-crowned Warbler**
Vermivora celata
L 5" Yellow undertail

■ **Bachman's Warbler**
Vermivora bachmanii
L 4.75" Black forecrown

■ **Nashville Warbler**
Vermivora ruficapilla
L 4.75" Gray head

■ **Virginia's Warbler**
Vermivora virginiae
L 4.75" Gray head

■ **Colima Warbler**
Vermivora crissalis
L 5.75" Rufous crown

■ **Lucy's Warbler**
Vermivora luciae
L 4.25" Red crown

■ **Crescent-chested Warbler**
Parula superciliosa
L 4.25" Chestnut crescent

■ **Northern Parula**
Parula americana
L 4.5" Yellow throat

■ **Tropical Parula**
Parula pitiayumi
L 4.5" Dark mask

■ **Chestnut-sided Warbler**
Dendroica pensylvanica
L 5" Chestnut flanks

■ **Cape May Warbler**
Dendroica tigrina
L 5" Chestnut ear patch

■ **Magnolia Warbler**
Dendroica magnolia
L 5" White eyebrow

■ **Black-and-white Warbler**
Mniotilta varia
L 5.25"Black and white

■ **Black-throated Blue Warbler**
Dendroica caerulescens
L 5.25" Black throat

■ **Cerulean Warbler**
Dendroica cerulea
L 4.75" Streaked sides

■ **Blackburnian Warbler**
Dendroica fusca
L 5" Fiery orange throat

■ **Black-throated Gray Warbler**
Dendroica nigrescens
L 5" Striped head

■ **Townsend's Warbler**
Dendroica townsendi
L 5" Black ear patch

■ **Hermit Warbler**
Dendroica occidentalis
L 5.5" Yellow face

■ **Black-throated Green Warbler**
Dendroica virens
L 5" Greenish crown

■ **Golden-cheeked Warbler**
Dendroica chrysoparia
L 5.5" Golden face

■ **Grace's Warbler**
Dendroica graciae
L 5" Streaked back

■ **Yellow-throated Warbler**
Dendroica dominica
L 5.5" White ear patch

■ **Kirtland's Warbler**
Dendroica kirtlandii
L 5.75" Streaked back

■ **Prairie Warbler**
Dendroica discolor
L 4.75" Streaked neck

■ **Bay-breasted warbler**
Dendroica castanea
L 5.5" Black face

■ **Blackpoll Warbler**
Dendroica striata
L 5.5" Solid black cap

■ **Pine Warbler**
Dendroica pinus
L 5.5" Yellow breast

■ **Palm Warbler**
Dendroica palmarum
L 5.5" Chestnut cap

■ **Yellow Warbler**
Dendroica petechia
L 5" Yellow overall

■ **Mourning Warbler**
Oporornis philadelphia
L 5.25" Yellow belly

■ **MacGillivray's Warbler**
Oporornis tolmiei
L 5.25" Bold eye-crescents

■ **Connecticut Warbler**
Oporornis agilis
L 5.75" Bold eye ring

■ **Kentucky Warbler**
Oporornis formosus
L 5.25" Bold spectacles

■ **Canada Warbler**
Wilsonia canadensis
L 5.25"Black necklace

■ **Wilson's Warbler**
Wilsonia pusilla
L 4.75" Black cap

■ **Hooded Warbler**
Wilsonia citrina
L 5.25" Black hood

■ **Worm-eating Warbler**
Helmitheros vermivorus
L 5.25" Striped head

■ **Swainson's Warbler**
Limnothlypis swainsonii
L 5.5" Brown crown

■ **Ovenbird**
Seiurus aurocapillus
L 6" Russet crown

■ **Louisiana Waterthrush**
Seiurus motacilla
L 6" Eyebrow flares

■ **Northern Waterthrush**
Seiurus noveboracensis
L 5.75" Eyebrown even

■ **Common Yellowthroat**
Geothlypis trichas
L 5" Black mask

■ **Gray-crowned Yellowthroat**
Geothlypis poliocephala
L 5.5" Split eyering

■ **Fan-tailed Warbler**
Euthlypis lachrymosa
L 5.75" White tail-tips

■ **Golden-crowned Warbler**
Basileuterus culicivorus
L 5" Yellow crown stripe

■ **Rufous-capped Warbler**
Basileuterus rufifrons
L 5.25" Rufous crown

■ **Yellow-breasted Chat**
Icteria virens
L 7.5" White spectacles

■ **American Redstart**
Setophaga ruticilla
L 5.25" Orange patches

■ **Slate-throated Redstart**
Myioborus miniatus
L 6" Chestnut crown

■ **Painted Redstart**
Myioborus pictus
L 5.75 Red belly

■ **Red-faced Warbler**
Cardellina rubrifrons
L 5.5" Black and red face

■ **Olive Warbler**
Peucedramus taeniatus
L 5.25" Black face patch

Warbler), which has a smaller bill than the nominate but is otherwise similar. Subspecies in many large groups of birds have in recent years been elevated to the level of species by ornithologists, but few suggestions have been made for recognizing new species, though some have advocated a splitting of Yellow-rumped Warbler back into Myrtle and Audubon's Warblers, as well as a reconsideration of species limits among Yellow Warbler forms.

STRUCTURE

With the exception of the cardinal-size, heavy-billed Yellow-breasted Chat, wood-warblers are all rather small songbirds with small, slender, pointed bills and tails of modest length. With patience and close study, one can see differences in warblers' bills, and such differences relate to the foraging techniques used by the various species. Cape May Warbler, for example, has a slender bill that is slightly curved and sharply pointed, perfect for foraging on insect larvae and drinking flower nectar, whereas the bill of the American Redstart is broader and more flattened and is ringed by rictal bristles, perfectly suited for active flycatching but also for many other kinds of foraging by a generalist. The Yellow-rumped (Myrtle) Warbler, which winters much farther to the north than its congeners, also needs a fairly heavy bill, as it feeds largely on myrtle (*Myrica*) berries in midwinter. Warblers' overall structures are affected by other aspects of their natural history as well, such as their migrational strategies. Blackpoll Warblers, for instance, make an epic open-ocean crossing en route to South America, and so their wings are quite long compared to short-distance migrants. A long, strikingly patterned tail, as in Painted Redstart, aids in startling insect prey, as the tail is fanned and flashed while foraging. The structure of legs and feet are similar in most species, rather slender, with all species showing the toe arrangements of passerines—three toes forward and one posterior.

PLUMAGE

Warblers wear several distinctive plumages through their lives, beginning with a juvenile plumage that is held only briefly. Usually much more spotted, streaked, and muted than later adult plumages, the juveniles' first plumage is retained only for a few weeks on the nesting grounds, as they fledge from the nest and follow the adults around, still dependent on them for food. During this time, the young birds molt into their first basic plumage, that is, the plumage of a bird in its first fall and winter season. These plumages are often dull compared to those of the adult birds, and most birders find them to be the most difficult to distinguish from one another. Adult warblers undergo a molt into a basic plumage before the fall migration, and in most

cases, this molt results in a much more subdued plumage than that of the breeding season.

During late winter and into spring, most warblers molt the feathers of the head, body, and (usually) wing and tail coverts, thus replacing their basic plumage with the alternate plumage of spring and summer. These are the plumages on which avid birders fixate, appreciating the range of colors after the long gray winter. Most warblers are countershaded, that is, they are darker above than they are below, but only a minority of North American species are what might be called dull colored in the spring and summer. Even the species whose hues are mostly brown—such as Swainson's Warblers, Worm-eating Warblers, and

KIRTLAND'S WARBLER

The Kirtland's Warbler, one of the rarest warblers worldwide, nests almost exclusively on Michigan's Lower Peninsula, and then only in one type of habitat: stands of young jack pines. When these trees age, the habitat loses the qualities needed by Kirtland's for foraging, and the birds move on in search of younger stands, which are found in areas of recent forest fires. Because such fires were suppressed through much of the 20th century, warbler habitat declined sharply, with the result that this species was reduced to only 167 pairs in 1987. The rise in numbers of the Brown-headed Cowbird, a nest parasite, was calamitous for Kirtland's Warblers during the same period. Modern conservation recognizes the subtle needs of this attractive species and, with a regimen of prescribed burns and cowbird trapping, wildlife biologists have succeeded in elevating the population to a record high 710 singing males in 2002. Studies of this warbler on its wintering grounds in the Bahamas have begun to lay the foundation for a management program in the equally important broadleaf coppice woodlands there.

Ovenbird—have touches of chestnut, buff, lemon, or umber that enhance their aesthetic interest to birders. The gaudier male plumages, of course, are not for the benefit of human audiences but for the wooing of the female warbler, which is in most cases less colorful than the male, owing in part to a greater need for camouflage on the nest. Sexual dimorphism is not apparent, however, in the case of the waterthrushes; and the American Redstart presents an interesting exception in that males in their second calendar year look much more like females (and even breed in this plumage). Such birds are on the low end of the totem pole when looking for territories on both the wintering and the breeding grounds.

FEEDING BEHAVIOR

Birders who have the luxury of observing warblers at length while the birds are feeding, will gradually notice that the birds are predictable in how and where they feed within their environment. Warblers, like other birds, have adapted to specialize in certain habitats, but within these areas, the birds specialize even more in particular micro-habitats. The ground-dwelling warblers provide a good example of habitat partitioning among similar species. Ovenbird, known by the colorful name Betsy Kickup on its wintering grounds in Jamaica, forages for arthropods and insects on the ground by

Ovenbird

moving around in the leaf litter to uncover prey, much as a sparrow does. The waterthrushes, Louisiana and Northern, also forage on the ground, but both prefer wet spots. The Louisiana Waterthrush forages along fast-moving streams, whereas the Northern selects moist patches, puddles, and pond edges. Swainson's Warbler, which often forages on the ground, tends to work areas intermediate between Ovenbirds' and waterthrushes' preferred habitats.

Other wood-warblers specialize in gleaning insects and their larvae from various sorts of branches and leaves (even from clusters of dead leaves) and from different kinds of trees, or even at different heights in trees. Some flycatch, others hover briefly while foraging, and still others, such as Black-and-white Warblers, cling to bark and forage in nuthatch fashion. Some species utilize a variety of habitats at different times of year. The Pine Warbler and Palm Warbler, for example, often feed in fields with bluebirds or pipits in the non-breeding season. Careful research has demonstrated that the foraging niche of a given species can be influenced by the presences of other species in the area. If two warblers with similar foraging strategies are nesting

in the same location, they tend to segregate by micro-habitats, partitioning foraging areas in trees according to height or even inner-versus-outer branches and thereby coexisting.

VOCALIZATION

Wood-warblers have a complex variety of vocalizations that have only recently come under close scientific scrutiny. Most birders learn warbler songs early in their study of birds, and most find it easy to distinguish between the loud, ringing songs of the ground- and thicket-dwelling species from the lisping trills of the canopy foragers. Because many species sing from a conspicuous song perch, birders can quickly learn the typical song of male warblers, though regional and individual variation means that they should be careful when making identifications only by song, particularly with species that have trilled songs that can be confused with those of sparrows' or juncos'.

During the breeding season, male warblers sing to attract mates and to mark and defend territories, much like most other passerines. But almost all species studied carefully appear to have at least two kinds of song, one delivered in the early morning, especially dawn (sometimes at dusk or at night), which is often more complex; the other during the day. The latter is usually the familiar song described in the field guides and on commercial audio recordings of warblers' songs. Though more study is needed, it appears that the "typical" song familiar to most birders, and heard through most of the day, is for the benefit of the female and is vigorously delivered by unmated males, while the less familiar song type is used in territorial definition and defense, directed primarily at other males in adjacent territories. One fascinating observation, of uncertain meaning, is that, on rare occasions, some female warblers sing full male songs or softer versions of male songs.

In the last decade, the call notes and flight calls of wood-warblers have been studied in detail, and although many calls in closely related groups are too similar to be distinguished by the human ear, some species' call notes are readily identifiable in the field by birders, and most can be distinguished by computer analysis. It should be possible in the near future to establish monitoring stations that listen to the night sky, record the nocturnal flight calls given as birds pass overhead, and identify these calls by computer. Such technology would enable scientists to understand many aspects of migration far better than is possible now, with data from observers in the field, from radar studies (which show migrants on the screen but cannot differentiate species), and from banding stations.

BREEDING BEHAVIOR

Warblers, like most passerines, nest in discrete territories rather than in colonies, are largely monogamous, and breed in their second year of life. Males establish and defend territories on the breeding grounds a little before the arrival of the females, and courtship involves intensive singing, some stereotyped posturing display in some species, and rarely courtship feeding. Nest-building and incubation are largely duties of the female, and the male feeds the female while she incubates. Most nests are cup-shaped and placed in a tree, though a few are made on the ground, and two species (Prothonotary and Lucy's Warblers) are cavity nesters.

Hybridization is rare among most species, but among two closely related pairs of species, it is relatively frequent. The Blue-winged and Golden-winged Warblers commonly interbreed, with the result, in many areas, being the loss of genetically pure Golden-winged Warblers. Townsend's and Hermit Warblers also hybridize readily, and the resulting hybrids are called "Heto" Warblers by local birders in the Pacific Northwest.

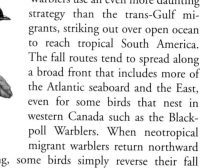

American Redstart

BREEDING RANGE

Warblers are found in all vegetated habitats from the subarctic to the tropical, from just above tree line in the taiga habitats, where Northern Waterthrushes breed, to the Mexican border, where Colima Warblers just enter the United States. Only the most sparsely vegetated, almost barren habitats—such as salt flats and dry sand deserts—lack breeding warblers. The greatest diversity of species is found between the Great Lakes and northern New England, with Appalachia also being an important region and center of warbler diversity.

MIGRATION

With few exceptions, wood-warblers are migratory birds that travel considerable distances between breeding and wintering ranges. Almost all of their traveling is done under the cover of darkness, though some short-distance migrants, such as Palm and Yellow-rumped Warblers, can be seen moving by the thousands during the day. At other times warbler "reorientation" flights continue well after dawn, as birds seek out shelter and areas for refueling for the next flight. Those warblers that do migrate across the Gulf of Mexico, such as the Kentucky, Hooded, and Blue-winged Warblers, usually require more than 12 hours for the flight and so must make their open-water cross-

ing partly during daylight hours. When the birds make landfall, they must locate a habitat that provides both cover and food, which sometimes necessitates "onward" migration after their initial landfall. This is also true of the birds returning across the Gulf in the spring, a time when southern-nesting species (such as the Prothonotary Warbler) regularly overshoot their natal or nesting areas, appearing hundreds of miles north of typical range. Such appearances may indicate the effects of weather or poor navigation, but they could also represent exploratory flights in search of new nesting areas.

Most warblers that nest in North America avoid long, dangerous flights over water in the fall and use the land corridor through Mexico instead. Others such as the Black-throated Blue Warblers move down the Florida peninsula and island-hop to Caribbean destinations. Connecticut and Blackpoll Warblers use an even more daunting strategy than the trans-Gulf migrants, striking out over open ocean to reach tropical South America. The fall routes tend to spread along a broad front that includes more of the Atlantic seaboard and the East, even for some birds that nest in western Canada such as the Blackpoll Warblers. When neotropical migrant warblers return northward in the spring, some birds simply reverse their fall migratory routes, but most species tend to move more rapidly and directly toward breeding areas.

WINTER RANGE

North American species winter from the southern United States through Mexico, Central America, and the Caribbean, with a smaller number of species wintering in tropical South America. Within this enormous area, nearly all vegetated habitats are used by one or more species, and in some areas, especially montane regions, one sees large mixed flocks of warblers foraging together. As on the breeding grounds, some species are more selective in their use of habitat, and many eastern species are known to segregate in their habitat on the wintering grounds by sex and age.

OBSERVING WARBLERS

Spring migration is a restless time of year for birders, as the anticipated return of wood-warblers from tropical wintering grounds has become for many the very embodiment of the season itself. Fall migration is an even better time of year for observing great numbers of warblers, as the migrating flocks not only have adult birds but the young of the year, and their migration proceeds at a more leisurely pace. The more subtly plumaged fall adults and immatures might lack the vivid colors of spring, but they complement the autumn palette of rusts, golds, and browns perfectly.

Birders need not travel long distances in search of warblers, as is the case with other groups of birds. With study, patience, and a bit of luck, your home state or province can produce several dozen warbler species, even in your own backyard or very nearby. The best way for a novice to learn about the migration and nesting of warblers is to join a bird club, Audubon Society, or other group of naturalists, which will have many members attuned to the habits and haunts of warblers. Learning in the context of a field trip is a marvelous way to become familiar with this group, though some patience with oneself will be necessary, as warblers are often restless during migration, flitting about the vegetation with little regard for their fans. Studying a field guide in advance of the trip is the surest way to prepare for the day, and many birders find it useful to listen to recordings of songs and calls, which indicate the presence of warblers far sooner than the eye can detect them. Most areas also have monographs on the avifauna of the state or province, or even a smaller region, that orient the bird-watcher to the relative abundance, breeding status, and migration phenology of all birds in the area.

Armed with a combination of local knowledge, study of the literature, and enthusiasm, new warbler-watchers can soon strike out on their own, watching weather forecasts for conditions favorable to fallouts in their area (often produced, in spring, by precipitation, fog, or northerly winds, especially along lakeshores or coastlines), trekking to remote areas to learn more about nesters and migrants there, and in some cases,

making the great journeys to famous migration sites where warblers can sometimes seem to "drip from every tree." But even the urban birder can find warblers during migration: Try to locate the largest island of green vegetation in an otherwise urban setting. Small parks, cemeteries, and other green spaces can be magnets for birds seeking shelter during their twice-annual movements. In the autumn migration, which is more protracted or drawn-out than the spring, even a half hour in such a spot can yield studies of two dozen or more species—just ask the die-hards who bird New York City's Central Park with great success. The same principle applies to birders seeking out vagrant warblers in the dry Southwest or Southern California, where an isolated grove of trees in an otherwise treeless landscape can hold scores of "lost" migrant warblers. The key to locating such birds is a basic understanding of habitat needs.

In addition to following the relatively predictable arrival of wood-warblers during migration, birders seek out wood-warblers in locations where they should not, theoretically, turn up. Wayward warblers, known as vagrants or accidentals, are of great interest to local birders, as they add spice and a bit of the unexpected, to time in the field. Even in places as far away as western Europe, where neotropical wood-warblers are great rarities, the cachet of these species is tremendous. A Golden-winged Warbler in England drew 5,000 admirers overnight, and a Cerulean Warbler on Iceland is considered one of that island's most sublime vagrants. The causes for birds such as these showing up thousands of miles out of range are not well known. It's clear that in some instances, birds are caught up in weather systems that move them to places contrary to their destination. This happens occasionally in late

BLACKPOLL WARBLER

One of the more impressive migrations in the animal kingdom is the fall passage of Blackpoll Warblers from their breeding grounds in the boreal forests of Canada and Alaska to their winter quarters in northern South America. While most wood-warblers migrating to the tropics use the land corridor of Mexico, or fly across the Gulf of Mexico in a day or so, Blackpolls cross the open Atlantic. After fattening up on the last insects and fruits of summer, Blackpolls move toward the coast of New England and the mid-Atlantic states, where they refuel to an astonishing degree—in some cases, almost doubling their body mass. From here, they jump off the continent, flying southeast, toward Bermuda. Somewhere hundreds of miles off the southeastern United States, they locate the northeasterly winds that bring them, with a minimal expenditure of energy, back toward landfall in northeastern South America.

autumn, for instance, when birds moving south through the Caribbean are swept up by low-pressure systems that deposit them in Nova Scotia instead of northern South America. One theory holds that the birds, rather than fighting a headwind to reach their destination, fly downwind to preserve precious energy reserves, thus ending up far off course. In other cases, scientists argue that the birds' very orientation systems are flawed, so that they fly in a direction opposite of the normal. In many instances, it is impossible to distinguish such "misoriented," "reverse," or "mirror" migrants, as they are called, from birds that have been caught in an adverse weather system. So little is known

about how birds actually orient and navigate that theories about vagrancy are all speculative at this point. Nevertheless, as patterns of vagrancy emerge in the data gathered by bird-watchers, ornithology stands to learn much about the changing distribution of these species, how weather affects migrants, and perhaps even why birds misorient.

STATUS AND CONSERVATION

North America has apparently lost one species of wood-warbler forever. Bachman's Warbler, now believed to be extinct, was an uncommon denizen of the southeastern United States' wooded swamps, particularly those with canebrakes, and has been the subject of intensive searches since its apparent disappearance in the middle of the 20th century. No photographic records of this beautiful warbler have been made since 1962, though reports persisted into the late 1970s in South Carolina. Its demise was almost certainly the product of habitat destruction on both the wintering and breeding grounds, but the species may never have been common. It has even been suggested that an intense period of hurricane activity in the 1800s could have contributed to this species' demise.

Two equally striking other warblers could share the fate of Bachman's Warbler if not given full protection from habitat loss. Listed as federally endangered in the United States are the Golden-cheeked Warbler, which nests in ash, juniper, and oak habitat in central Texas and winters in Central America, and the Kirtland's Warbler, which nests in jack pine habitat on the Lower Peninsula of Michigan and winters in the Bahamas. Although the Golden-cheeked is thought to have a larger overall population than Kirtland's Warbler, its habitat, especially in the greater Austin area in Texas, is under tremendous development pressure. Habitat specialists—such as the Bachman's, Kirtland's, and Golden-cheeked—are typically the first species to show signs of disappearing when humans alter or destroy ecosystems. Although still widespread and relatively common in their respective habitats, the Hermit Warbler, which inhabits old-growth coniferous forests in the Pacific Northwest, and Lucy's Warbler, which is restricted to riparian corridors in the Southwest, are potentially at risk of population declines owing to habitat loss.

The decline of several other species has been carefully documented, and monitoring programs are in place to track their numbers. The National Audubon Society's WatchList features 13 wood-warblers believed threatened by habitat loss and other factors. Of these, the Cerulean Warbler and Golden-winged Warbler are two eastern species with limited ranges and apparently declining, and shifting, populations. A recent four-year study of Cerulean Warblers identified several hundred

OLIVE WARBLER

The Olive Warbler is an unusual species, and its many differences from the superficially similar wood-warblers have led ornithologists to categorize it in a separate family, the Peucedramidae. To the casual observer, the Olive Warbler's foraging habits and structure, including its nine functional primaries, resemble those of wood-warblers, but genetic analyses indicate that the Olive Warbler is not closely related. Its bill is blunt, more like an Old World warbler's than a parulid's, and its eggs are densely spotted with black, unlike the pale, lightly spotted eggs of wood-warblers. When the young are in the nest, adult Olive Warblers do not remove the fecal sacs, but allow the young to defecate on the rim of the nest. This characteristic is also seen in the finches of the family Fringillidae, which may be the nearest relatives.

important breeding sites, with most birds located in the Allegheny Mountains in West Virginia, the Allegheny Plateau in Ohio, and the Northern Cumberland Plateau in eastern Kentucky, West Virginia, and small parts of Virginia and Tennessee into Alabama and Georgia. Smaller numbers were also found in the Allegheny Plateau of west-central Pennsylvania, the southern tier of New York, and in the Midwest. Until this study was done, the Cerulean Warbler's basic distribution was poorly known, which is remarkable in the current golden age of bird study, but both birders and ornithologists are scarce in most strongholds of the species. What was most interesting about this study was that it began to define this enigmatic warbler's habitat requirements, which appear to vary widely, from riparian bottomland forests to a variety of upland forests. Researchers found, however, that sites with breeding Cerulean Warblers have an irregular canopy structure that offers an "internal edge"—a view across the canopy of an individual bird's territory. Although these birds are not specialists within a single narrowly defined habitat, they do appear to need a specific structure of habitat. Studies such as this one bring the modeling of conservation planning onto a much more complex and nuanced level.

Yellow Warbler

The Golden-winged Warbler, another species in steep decline, has also suffered a loss of habitat, but its decline in many areas of core range is thought to be hastened by another factor—competition with, and especially hybridization with, the Blue-winged Warbler. New England and New York are places that just a generation ago held hundreds of Golden-wingeds; these areas now have only Blue-winged Warblers and hybrid Blue-winged x Golden-winged Warblers. The hybrids are so well known that they have their own names: Brewster's Warbler and Lawrence's Warbler. Finding one of these handsome hybrids on the breeding grounds or on migration can be a feather in a birder's cap, but these hybrids indicate a continuing loss of ground for genetically pure Golden-winged Warblers, many of which now sing atypical songs, which is another index of their decline.

Many other populations of warblers have shown steady losses during the past 30 years, detected largely through the Breeding Bird Survey, a long-term monitoring project coordinated through the U.S. Geological Survey. In the Southeast, Prairie and Prothonotary Warblers are good examples of species in decline for similar reasons. In addition to loss of habitat in both the winter and summer quarters, the fragmentation of their habitat into smaller and smaller parcels gives both nest predators (small mammals, snakes, other birds) and nest parasites (especially Brown-headed Cowbirds) greater access to the warblers' nests. A high proportion of nest failures, whether from parasitism or depredation, is calamitous for birds that have short lives (usually under six years) and relatively large clutch sizes (four or five eggs). Careful studies of more widely distributed woodland nesters such as Ovenbirds show a clear correlation between breeding success and extent of intact, unbroken habitat. For this reason, conservationists working with wood-warblers and other woodland species have called for the preservation of large tracts of habitat and for conservation corridors, to allow for gene flow among populations. This modern conceptualization of conservation imperatives has developed in part from long-term studies of wood-warblers.

Because most wood-warblers spend the better part of their year outside the United States, conservation-oriented scientists have also studied the impact of habitat loss on the wintering grounds, particularly in the Caribbean, where tropical forests are being cut at an alarming rate. These islands hold most of the wintering population of Black-throated Blue Warblers and share with the Caribbean slope of Mexico and Central America the bulk of Swainson's and Worm-eating Warbler populations. In western Mexico, where logging of forests is intensive, the wintering Virginia's Warbler is a species of special concern.

In between wintering and breeding areas, most species have traditional stopover sites where they fatten up before continuing their journeys. Such places have only recently been studied under the rubric of "stopover migrant ecology," and the most complete studies so far suggest that these areas are every bit as important for warblers as they are for shorebirds. As on the breeding and wintering grounds, the degradation of habitats in these stopover sites, including not only human alteration but also loss of understory as a result of overgrazing by deer and the spread of exotic plants, is a major focus of ongoing ecological monitoring projects as well.

See also

ARCTIC OCEAN

CHUKCHI SEA

Bering Str.

QUEEN ELIZABETH

ISLANDS

PARRY ISLANDS

Banks Island

Victoria Island

Baffin Island

ARCTIC CIRCLE

ARCTIC CIRCLE

U.S.
CANADA

Gulf of Alaska

Great Bear Lake

Great Slave Lake

Lake Athabasca

Reindeer Lake

HUDSON BAY

LABRADOR SEA

Island of Newfoundland

PACIFIC OCEAN

ROCKY MOUNTAINS

Lake Winnipegosis

Lake Winnipeg

CANADA

C A N A D A

Lake Winnipeg

L. Superior

L. Michigan

Lake Huron

L. Ontario

L. Erie

APPALACHIAN MOUNTAINS

UNITED STATES

U N I T E D   S T A T E S

ATLANTIC OCEAN

Baja California

Gulf of California

TROPIC OF CANCER

TROPIC OF CANCER

GULF OF MEXICO

M E X I C O

Yucatán Pen.

BELIZE

GUATEMALA

HONDURAS

EL SALVADOR

NICARAGUA

COSTA RICA

PANAMA

BAHAMAS

CUBA

JAMAICA

HAITI

DOMINICAN REPUBLIC

GREATER ANTILLES

W E S T   I N D I E S

LESSER ANTILLES

LESSER ANTILLES

CARIBBEAN SEA

VENEZUELA

COLOMBIA

Longitude West 90° of Greenwich

ACKPOLL
ARBLER

MN AND SPRING MIGRATION

— Autumn route

— Spring route

*onally, disoriented birds
in the western U.S. Some may even
he Atlantic and arrive in western
e.*

TE MILES

500

500

ETERS

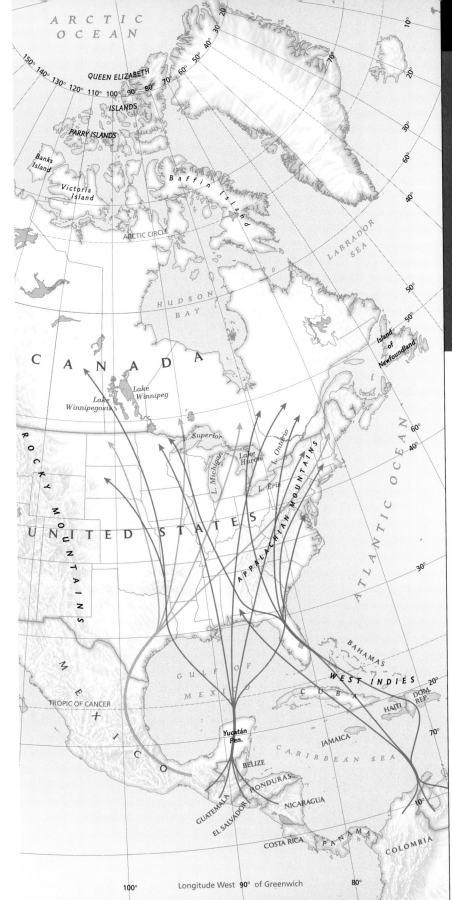

ARCTIC OCEAN

QUEEN ELIZABETH ISLANDS

PARRY ISLANDS

Banks Island

Victoria Island

Baffin Island

ARCTIC CIRCLE

LABRADOR SEA

HUDSON BAY

C A N A D A

Island of Newfoundland

Lake Winnipeg

Lake Winnipegosis

R O C K Y   M O U N T A I N S

L. Superior

L. Michigan

Lake Huron

L. Ontario

L. Erie

A P P A L A C H I A N   M O U N T A I N S

U N I T E D   S T A T E S

ATLANTIC OCEAN

BAHAMAS

WEST INDIES

CUBA

HAITI

DOM. REP.

M E X I C O

GULF OF MEXICO

TROPIC OF CANCER

Yucatán Pen.

JAMAICA

BELIZE

CARIBBEAN SEA

GUATEMALA

HONDURAS

EL SALVADOR

NICARAGUA

COSTA RICA

PANAMA

COLOMBIA

Longitude West 90° of Greenwich

EASTERN ▶
WARBLERS

SPRING MIGRATION

Circum-Gulf route ———

Trans-Gulf route ———

Carribean route ———

*While some warbler species
follow one of these routes,
others use two or even all three.*

STATUTE MILES

0 — 500

0 — 500

KILOMETERS

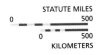

TANAGERS, BANANAQUITS

Approximately 242 species of tanagers (family Thraupidae) live in the world, exclusively in the Western Hemisphere and predominantly in tropical regions. Four of these species are commonly seen in North America: Scarlet Tanagers, Summer Tanagers, Hepatic Tanagers, and Western Tanagers. Another species, the Flame-Colored Tanager, occasionally visits but rarely breeds in southeast Arizona, and a sixth species, the Western Spindalis, occasionally is seen in Florida. The closely related Bananaquit (family Coerebidae) is a casual visitor in Florida from the Bahamas.

Howard Robinson

Scarlet Tanagers spend summers in the eastern United States and Canada and as far west as North Dakota, Nebraska, Kansas, and Oklahoma. Summer Tanagers range from the East Coast through the prairies and southern states into New Mexico and California. The Western Tanager ranges from southern Alaska southward to northern Baja California, and east into such states as Idaho, Montana, Nevada, Utah, Arizona, and New Mexico. The Hepatic Tanager has a much more restricted range—Arizona, New Mexico, west Texas, and Mexico.

In addition to their forest homes, Scarlet Tanagers live in shade trees in suburban parks. Summer Tanagers visit orchards and roadside trees. Hepatic Tanagers appear in parks and gardens in winter. Despite their brilliant color, finding tanagers,is an off-and-on experience because their behavior keeps them mostly out of sight. They tend to be solitary, except in breeding season, and are usually concealed in foliage as they forage for insects and some fruit. Birders are far more likely to hear their songs than to see the birds.

Tanagers socialize actively, and therefore are more easily seen during the breeding season, which begins in May and extends through July—except for the Summer Tanager, which breeds as late as August. As soon as tanagers arrive at their summer breeding grounds, the males establish and defend territories and attract mates aggressively by singing from prominent perches in high trees mostly at dawn. This is the season when they display their splashiest colors. A male scarlet tanager will fly to a perch beneath a female, extend his neck, and droop his black wings to expose the red feathers on his back to the female above him. Because the male's courtship perch usually is only three to six feet from the forest floor, alert birders have a fair chance of spotting the bird. Males frequently pursue females during courtship, bringing them out into the open. Females are attracted to the males with the most conspicuous plumage.

Another reason tanagers are not easily seen is their method of foraging by methodically exploring a tree's inner branches and leaves. Scarlet Tanagers generally feed from 20 to 60 feet above ground. Western and Summer Tanagers feed at the tops of trees. The Hepatic Tanager's feeding habits make it easier to observe: It forages regularly from low in oak trees to the tops of pine trees. Most tanagers, however, do fly out from the foliage to snare flying insects, which makes them intermittently more visible to birders.

Males are far more colorful than females, but a fascinating phenomenon relates to the color of the females: For unknown reasons, their plumage is gradually evolving into brighter coloration, while the males' colors remain the same.

(Left) Summer Tanager

Scarlet Tanager: *Piranga olivacea*, L 7", male red and black

TANAGERS, BANANAQUITS

A common bird of the family Thraupidae in the interior forests of the northeastern and north-central United States, the Scarlet Tanager (above) appears to be stable throughout most of its range. Though the species lives in a wide variety of deciduous and mixed deciduous and coniferous forests, the Scarlet Tanager prefers mature oak forests for breeding. Recent research confirmed that it makes a big difference to the species whether or not these forests are fragmented. Scarlet Tanagers apparently require a minimum of 25 to 30 contiguous acres of forest to sustain a viable population. In fragmented forests, the nests of Scarlet Tanagers are highly susceptible to parasitization by Brown-headed Cowbirds. Scarlet Tanagers are also threatened by predators such as jays and crows, as well as such critters as raccoons and cats, which usually are not found deep in unbroken forests. With this knowledge in hand, land managers can better sustain the forests so that Scarlet Tanagers as well as other species remain common. The related Banaquit is in its own family, the Coerebidae.

Range of Scarlet Tanager

CLASSIFICATION

About 242 species of tanagers (family Thraupidae, subfamily Thraupinae) live in the world today, but only in the Western Hemisphere and predominantly in tropical regions. Four of these species occur in North America: Scarlet Tanagers *(Piranga olivacea)*, Summer Tanagers *(Piranga rubra)*, Hepatic Tanagers *(Piranga flava)*, and Western Tanagers *(Piranga ludoviciana)*. Another species, the Flame-Colored Tanager *(Piranga bidentata)*, occasionally visits but rarely breeds in southeast Arizona; and a sixth species, the Western Spindalis *(Spindalis zena)*, occasionally is seen in Florida. Tanagers are included in a large group of birds known as nine-primaried oscines (songbirds) because their tenth or outermost wing primary is tiny and hidden. Other birds included in this group are wood-warblers, cardinals, buntings, and, by some accounts, honeycreepers. DNA testing has raised issues about relationships within and among the major lineages of New World nine-primaried oscines.

STRUCTURE

The Summer Tanager is a medium-size songbird at 7.75 inches long. The Hepatic Tanager is slightly larger at 8 inches. The Scarlet Tanager, the smallest of the *Piranga* species which breed north of Mexico, is 7 inches long. Male Scarlet Tanagers tend to be larger than females. The Western Tanager measures 7.25 inches. One distinguishing feature of these tanagers is their notched beak, the result of common evolutionary ancestry. The purpose of the notch is not known.

PLUMAGE

The brilliant breeding colors of male tanagers have made these birds favorites among many birders. Varying shades of red—from the Scarlet Tanager's bright scarlet-red through the Summer Tanager's slightly orange or rose red to the Western Tanager's red head atop a yellow-and-black body—distinguish males. Although brightly colored in comparison to females of many bird species, female tanagers are more drab than male tanagers, ranging from an olive tone in Scarlet Tanagers through more yellow-grays in the Hepatic Tanager, to the Western Tanager's greenish yellow nape and rump. Like only one other species of tanager, male Scarlet Tanagers molt in the fall from their bright breeding color into an olive green color that resembles that of the female, though the males are a bit brighter and keep their black wings and tail. Male Scarlet Tanagers metabolically convert yellow carotenoids into red at the beginning of the breeding season. Unique to the *Piranga* tanagers that breed north of Mexico, male Western Tanagers get their color from rhodoxanthin (the same pigment that Cedar Waxwings obtain from honeysuckle berries and that turns their plumage orange). The Western Tanagers probably acquire rhodoxanthin from insects that have obtained it from plants. Tanagers in the East undergo a prebasic molt (when juvenile feathers are replaced by adult plumage) before migrating south for the winter. Tanagers in the West do not begin the prebasic molt until after they have begun fall migration.

FEEDING BEHAVIOR

Piranga tanagers are gleaners and hawkers, moving deliberately and methodically in search of food, mainly insects. Although they sally after flying insects, the major part of their feeding time is spent perching motionless and turning their head slowly to look around, or gradually moving along branches as they inspect bark, leaves, and branches for food, reaching out or lunging forward to take whatever meals they find. They eat a smorgasbord of food: aphids, nut weevils, leaf beetles, cicadas, scale insects, dragonflies, ants, termites, caterpillars of gypsy moths, parasitic wasps, bees, slugs, snails, worms, spiders, millipedes, round-headed wood borers, click beetles, bumble flower beetles, bark beetles, sphinx moths, mulberries, June-berries, huckleberries, blackberries, and whortleberries—to name

Western Spindalis

but a few. Tanagers often mash fruit into juice by rotating it between their mandibles before swallowing.

Summer Tanagers catch so many wasps and bees that one nickname is "bee bird." After snagging a wasp or bee, the tanager returns to its perch and beats its prey against a branch to kill it, then wipes the victim's body along the bark to tear off the stinger before eating its meal. Western Tanagers are known to remove the wings and sometimes the legs and heads of dragonflies before swallowing their prey. Summer Tanagers also prey on wasp and bee nests by either killing (but not always eating) the adults or chasing them away from their nests and breaking the nest apart to consume the wasp larvae and pupae. This predilection for bees sometimes makes the tanagers a nuisance for beekeepers.

For Scarlet Tanagers, the most active feeding times are early morning and late afternoon. Males frequently sing while looking for meals, females less so, saving their singing until they actually eat. Western Tanagers (mostly males) also sing while feeding. Summer Tanagers stay on their perches while singing.

Western Tanagers apparently get enough water from their diet of insects and fruit; they drink infrequently. The same is true of Summer Tanagers. By contrast, Scarlet Tanagers drink from a variety of water sources, including banks of small streams, puddles in roads, and once in a while from birdbaths.

VOCALIZATION

Tanagers sing mostly at dawn, loosing their mellow song from high perches. Summer Tanagers prefer to sing from mid-heights. Often, they use the perches again, perhaps because they mark territory. When males return from their winter ranges, they sing almost continuously through the day. An exception is the male Western Tanager: Some returning males sing as much, but others sing sporadically. Males sing to announce their territory to females and males, and their singing increases in response to a neighbor's song. After establishing its territory, a male sings more often from mid-story perches. After a mate has been selected and especially while the female is incubating, male tanagers sing less often, though Scarlet Tanagers continue to sing throughout the day, with peaks in the morning and evening, until the young hatch. Tanager songs are moderate pitched and resemble the song of thrushes. They emit calls when in distress, when arriving at the nest with food, and during courtship. Calls vary among the *Piranga* tanagers, and even within each species. Scarlet Tanagers call "chip-churr," Summer Tanagers call "pit-ti-tuck" or "pit-t-tuck-i-tuck." Hepatic Tanagers call "tchuk" or "chuck;" and the Western Tanager calls "pit-ick" or "pit-er-ick" and "tu-weep." The song structure of Summer Tanagers is unique. A song comprises one or more groups of two to three phrases and lasts from two to 44 seconds. Female Summer Tanagers sometimes sing, but their song is shorter and more slurred. Much the same is true of female Scarlet Tanagers, whose songs are somewhat less harsh than those of the males. Among Western Tanagers, the female's song is sung more quickly and is more repetitious than the male's song.

OTHER SPECIES FIELD NOTES	
■ **Summer Tanager** *Piranga rubra* L 7.75" Male rosy red year-round	■ **Western Spindalis** *Spindalis zena* L 6.75" Broad black-and-white stripes on head
■ **Hepatic Tanager** *Piranga flava* L 8" Grayish cheek patch	■ **Bananaquit** *Coereba flaveola* L 4.5" White eye stripe and throat
■ **Western Tanager** *Piranga ludoviciana* L 7.25" Male red head and yellow body, wing bars	
■ **Flame-colored Tanager** *Piranga bidentata* L 7.25" Male is flaming orange, wing bars	

If you live in southern Florida and are very, very lucky, or if you visit the Bahamas or other regions in the neotropics, you will see Bananaquits, small birds closely related to tanagers but placed in their own family, Coerebidae. For some unknown reason, although Bananaquits are common at lower elevations throughout a large range, including nearly all the islands in the Caribbean, although they are only vagrants in Cuba. These colorful birds often visit yards, parks, even restaurant tables. Attracted to hummingbird feeders and flowers because they feed on nectar, Bananaquits perch (sometimes hanging upside down) as they eat because they cannot hover. To get at the nectar, a Banaquit either probes small flowers from the front or pierces the sides of large flowers with its decurved bill and extracts nectar with its specially adapted tongue. It also consumes insects and such fruit as ripe bananas.

BREEDING BEHAVIOR

Tanagers are thought to be monogamous, keeping one mate throughout the year, though not the same mate in subsequent years. Unlike the other tanagers in the United States, some male and female Western Tanagers form bonds while on their winter grounds in Mexico and Central America or during migration, arriving together in their breeding range to begin nestbuilding. They have limited courtship displays.

March through June is the optimum time to see tanagers nesting in North America. The males usually arrive first, and after the females arrive, courtship begins. Female tanagers are attracted to the males who exhibit the brightest or most contrasting colors, and they are also drawn to the male's singing. In addition to attracting females, the male's singing announces his claim to territory and discourages other males from intruding.

Female tanagers gather materials from the forest floor within their territory and build the nest, although it is not unheard of for males to accompany them. Building materials include bark strips, grasses, and rootlets or twigs. The nests are a shallow cup-shape and are built near the end of horizontal branches at varying heights: Hepatic Tanagers' nests typically are 6 to 50 feet above ground; Scarlet Tanagers 20 to 59 feet; Summer Tanagers 8 to 34 feet; and Western roughly 6 to 65 feet. The nests of Scarlet and Western Tanagers are so loosely woven that sometimes the eggs are visible through the nest wall. The nests of Summer Tanagers living in the East are similar to those of Scarlet and Western Tanagers, but the nests of those in the West are sturdy, and the eggs cannot be seen from below. Egg laying begins in May, and clutches vary from between three to five eggs. The nests of Scarlet, Summer, and Western Tanagers are preyed upon by jays and crows, chipmunks and squirrels.

BREEDING RANGE

The breeding range of Scarlet and Summer Tanagers partially overlaps over a large area of the Northeast, but the species do not crossbreed. The two tanagers aggressively defend their territories against intrusion from the other species, with the result that their individual territories only occasionally and partially overlap. The degree to which the territories overlap depends on forest composition (or habitat quality), time of year, and age. Where their breeding ranges overlap, Scarlet Tanagers tend to locate their territories in denser habitat than they normally do, and Summer Tanagers settle in areas that are more open than their normal territories. Nevertheless, at least in western Pennsylvania, many young, unpaired male Scarlet Tanagers, called "floaters," move quite a bit within and between forest stands. The breeding ranges of Western and Hepatic Tanagers overlap very little, and where they do, the birds tend to be separated by elevation and habitat. Western Tanagers are distributed widely in the forests of western North America, breeding as far north as southeast Alaska and as far south as northern Baja California. Their preferred altitude ranges from 1,475 feet in Washington to above 7,546 feet in the southwestern states. Hepatic Tanagers in the United States are restricted to extreme southern California, Arizona, New Mexico, and west Texas. They prefer tall trees, especially pine and oak forests at altitudes between 5,250 and 7,546 feet.

MIGRATION

Scarlet, Summer, Western, and Hepatic Tanagers are all neotropical migrants, with the Scarlet Tanager being the most migratory of the four in terms of distance traveled. During the months of August through October, all Scarlet Tanagers depart for northwest South America and cross the Gulf of Mexico. Summer Tanagers depart during September and October and fly to Central America and northern South America. The eastern and central populations of these tanagers are also thought to cross the Gulf of Mexico.

Summer Tanagers form groups of up to 30 individuals prior to departure and also at stopover sites, but whether the groups stay together during migration flights is unknown. Throughout most of their breeding range, Western Tanagers begin their southward journey to Mexico and Central America in late July or August, though some birds leave as late as October. They fly alone or in pairs.

Hepatic Tanagers spend their winters mostly south of the Mexican border. Before migrating north in the spring, many neotropical migrants congregate in the Yucatan Peninsula to gorge themselves. Among them, Summer Tanagers devour high-energy insects and fruit in a frenzy called hyperphagia. The tanagers and other migrants must build enough energy and muscle

Western Tananger

reserve to carry them across the Gulf of Mexico. Tanagers often migrate at night, and consequently they are at risk of fatally colliding with transmission towers and other man-made structures. In the spring, Hepatic Tanagers arrive in their breeding range during April and May. April is the usual arrival date of Scarlet Tanagers, and Summer and Western Tanagers normally return in April to late May.

WINTER RANGE

All species of tanagers that breed in North America migrate south in the fall. Although a few Hepatic Tanagers remain in southeast Arizona during winter, most move to Mexico and farther south. Summer Tanagers depart the United States for Mexico and Central America, Colombia, Venezuela, Trinidad, Ecuador, Peru east of the Andes, Bolivia, northern Chile, northwest Brazil, Guyana, and Suriname. Once there, they live in open and second-growth habitats, including woodland thinned for coffee plantations. Western Tanagers don't travel as far as Summer Tanagers; they overwinter from Mexico to the Central American countries of Guatemala, El Salvador, Honduras, Nicaragua, and Costa Rica, and live in a variety of habitats, including mountain woodlands,

woodlands along river edges, and hedgerows, usually at altitudes between 1,970 and 4,600 feet. Scarlet Tanagers migrate south to areas east of the Andes from Colombia through Ecuador and Peru to Bolivia. Their winter habitat is not well known, but Scarlet Tanagers are thought to live at elevations of 328 feet to 4,265 feet in evergreen forests.

STATUS AND CONSERVATION

Like many neotropical migratory songbirds, tanagers are affected by habitat loss and fragmentation. The Scarlet Tanager is common in the forests of northeastern and north-central North America, and its population seems to be stable throughout most of its range. Nevertheless, populations vary by location: Local populations of Scarlet Tanagers in eastern North America are estimated to have declined at an average rate of 1.2 percent a year from 1978 to 1987. More recently, most states report stable populations, with Illinois and Wisconsin reporting possible declines, and North Carolina, Ohio, and Pennsylvania reporting possible increases.

To understand the phenomenon of forest fragmentation and its effects on tanagers, the Cornell Lab of Ornithology, with sponsorship from the National Science Foundation and the National Fish and Wildlife Foundation, initiated Project Tanager. All across the United States between 1993 and 1996, more than a thousand trained Project Tanager volunteers visited more than 2,000 sites at least twice each during the breeding season to look for evidence of tanager breeding and to record conditions of the forest. The report from the study cautioned against applying the information learned about a single species in a restricted area to other species in other areas, but it confirmed that large forests that have been fragmented by agriculture, road building, dwellings, and so forth become less suitable for breeding birds. Three species of tanager—Scarlet, Western, and Summer Tanager—responded similarly to the fragmentation. A fragmented habitat increases the amount of forest edge, making it easier for cowbirds and other parasites and predators to affect breeding success. The reduced breeding success diminishes the population densities of tanagers in the remaining sections of its breeding habitat.

See also

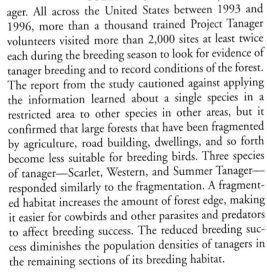

SUMMER TANAGER

MIGRATION AND RANGE

Breeding range

Winter range

- - - - Rare to casual visitor

——— Migration route

● Isolated record

RUSSIA

CHUKCHI SEA

ARCTIC OCEAN

BERING SEA

Bering Str.

QUEEN ELIZABETH ISLANDS

PARRY ISLANDS

Banks Island

Victoria Island

Baffin Island

BEAUFORT SEA

Gulf of Alaska

ARCTIC CIRCLE

U.S.
CANADA

C A N A D A

HUDSON BAY

Island of Newfoundland

PACIFIC OCEAN

L. Winnipeg

L. Superior

L. Michigan

Lake Huron

L. Ontario

L. Erie

ATLANTIC OCEAN

ROCKY MOUNTAINS

U N I T E D   S T A T E S

APPALACHIAN MOUNTAINS

TROPIC OF CANCER

TROPIC OF CANCER

Baja California

Gulf of California

GULF OF MEXICO

BAHAMAS

C U B A

W E S T   I N D I E S

HAITI
DOMINICAN REPUBLIC

LESSER

JAMAICA

G R E A T E R   A N T I L L E S

M E X I C O

Yucatán Pen.

BELIZE

C A R I B B E A N   S E A

LESSER ANTILLES

GUATEMALA

HONDURAS

EL SALVADOR

NICARAGUA

COSTA RICA

PANAMA

VENEZUELA

COLOMBIA

STATUTE MILES

0 ——— 500

KILOMETERS

0 ——— 500 ——— 1000

This "southern" species has a propensity for turning up north of its normal range. This occurs most often in the spring and fall, and occasionally in the winter. At least some of the birds found in coastal California have been of the eastern subspecies *rubra*, rather than the closer southwestern subspecies.

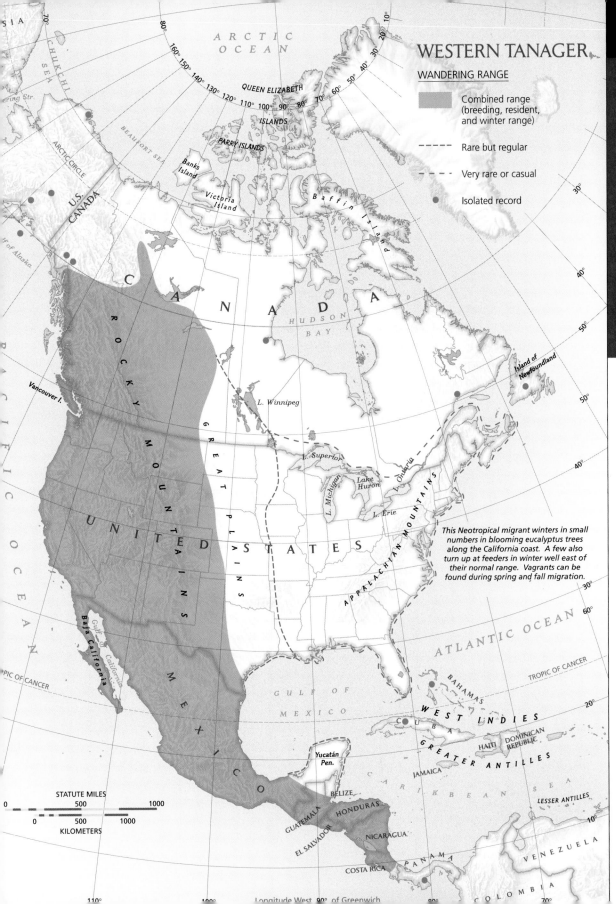

WESTERN TANAGER

WANDERING RANGE

Combined range (breeding, resident, and winter range)

– – – Rare but regular

– – – Very rare or casual

• Isolated record

This Neotropical migrant winters in small numbers in blooming eucalyptus trees along the California coast. A few also turn up at feeders in winter well east of their normal range. Vagrants can be found during spring and fall migration.

SPARROWS, ALLIES

The Emberizids are a diverse group of small birds that may often go unnoticed by the casual observer. To many, the name "sparrow" has connotations of small, furtive, rather plain birds. Even active birders may have problems identifying sparrows. However, birders who spend a little time studying sparrows in the field will discover them to be a wonderfully diverse and attractive group of birds, with the identification challenges offset by the species' subtle beauty. Some Emberizids are highly patterned, with plumages marked in bold saffrons and chestnuts, whereas others exhibit more muted, cryptic coloration. Sparrows are best studied on their breeding grounds, where they typically perch as high as possible (which may be no more than 6 inches off the ground) to sing. Emberizids are small birds with short, stout, conical bills, but they show significant variation in overall size and structure. Most sparrows feed terrestrially, and many species nest on the ground, but they venture to higher perches when agitated or singing.

George Armistead

The world harbors some 319 species of Emberizid in 72 genera. Sixty of these genera have occurred in North America, with 49 genera being regular breeders. This large family includes the towhees, sparrows, longspurs, and *Emberiza* buntings. The center of abundance for emberizids is the New World, but representatives are found on all continents except for Australia and Antarctica.

Eurasia is home to the *Emberiza* buntings, but six species in the group have occurred as vagrants in western Alaska, although the Rustic Bunting and the Little Bunting—these birds of the far north—have been found as far south as California. Only the Snow Bunting and the McKay's Bunting nest in North America.

Sadly, the "Dusky" Seaside Sparrow, considered a subspecies of the Seaside Sparrow, was brought to extinction on its native grounds at Merritt Island National Wildlife Refuge in Florida in 1987. The very rare and local Worthen's Sparrow of Mexico was probably resident in small numbers in southwestern New Mexico where the type specimen was collected at Silver City in 1884. There have been no sightings since, and the species has declined dramatically within its Mexican range, largely because of destruction of its habitat by overgrazing. The Yellow-faced and the Black-faced Grassquits are rare Caribbean vagrants to Florida. Another record of a Yellow-faced Grassquit in south Texas may have come from Central America.

Birders with the goal of seeing all species of North American sparrows will end up traveling through virtually every ecosystem that the continent has to offer. These birds have captured niches in a great variety of habitats that include early stage successional growth woodlots, wood edges and hedgerows, open shrubby areas, chaparral, deserts, grasslands, and marshes.

Some sparrows can be quite confiding, if they are not pressured; others are furtive. Singing males are especially entertaining, with some species demonstrating dramatic song-flight displays. All birds in this group keep discreet breeding territories, with males singing from exposed perches to announce their presence. Much of the sparrows' beauty lies in the subtleties of their plumage, which may be lost on the casual observer; even so—a few species are downright gaudy.

(Left) **Fox Sparrow**

Eastern Towhee: *Pipilo erythrophthalmus*, L 7.5", black above, rufous and white below

TOWHEES

The Eastern Towhee (above) of the large Emberizidae family inhabits brambly fields, hedgerows, and forest breaks with much understory cover throughout the eastern United States and Canada. The name "Towhee," as well as local names such as "Chewink," are onomatopoeic of this sparrow's call—a sprightly, upslurred "cher-EEK." The species is a ground forager and feeds mostly on seeds. In the West, the Eastern Towhee is "replaced" by its close relative the Spotted Towhee, with which it was once combined as Rufous-sided Towhee. The Eastern Towhee is an example of a short-distance migrant that withdraws from the northern parts of its range in late fall and travels perhaps only hundreds of miles, rather than thousands, to the wintering grounds in the Southeast, where local towhee populations are mostly sedentary. Some Eastern Towhees attempt to winter farther north but are forced to migrate south late in the season when snow cover is too extensive for ground foraging. This kind of short-distance movement in response to atmospheric changes is known as facultative migration.

Range of Eastern Towhee

CLASSIFICATION

Formerly four species of towhees of the family Emberizidae were recognized in the United States: the Rufous-sided, Brown, Green-tailed, and Abert's Towhee. The Rufous-sided has since been split into Eastern and Spotted Towhee, and the Brown into Canyon and California Towhee so that we now recognize six species of towhee of the genus *Pipilo*. Hybridization is known to occur occasionally between Spotted and Eastern and also between Spotted and Green-tailed Towhees.

STRUCTURE

Towhees are larger and heavier than most other sparrows, ranging in size from the 7.25-inch Green-tailed to the 9.5-inch Abert's Towhee. They are plump and long-tailed with fairly large, stout bills used for cracking seeds and crushing insects. They have large feet used for scratching in leaf litter on the ground.

PLUMAGE

Browns, greens, and grays adorn the four western towhees with the conspicuous chestnut cap and bright white throat of the Green-tailed being the only bright spots. California, Canyon, and Abert's Towhees are all rather uniform brown birds with more complex markings around the face. The buffy throat of the California Towhee is adorned with a distinct broken ring of dark brown spots appearing rather like a necklace. The Canyon Towhee has a similar necklace, and a dark, central breast spot, much like the American Tree Sparrow, and a subdued warm brown cap. Abert's has cinnamon brown upperparts, paler underparts, pale cinnamon undertail coverts and a black face. They all have a subtle, but beautiful plumage, a study in understated elegance. The Spotted and Eastern Towhees are black, white, and chestnut birds, but the Spotted displays a distinctive arrangement of white spots on the back and wings. All towhees show buffy or brown undertail coverts.

FEEDING BEHAVIOR

During the winter months towhees eat mostly seeds and plant matter. During the breeding season they feed on insects, which compose most if not all the protein for the young. The species obtain food through a foraging technique known as the "double scratch" in which the birds, with their heads held low and tail pointed up, rake both feet over the ground in a synchronized movement that exposes seeds and terrestrial arthropods. Beetles are the mainstay of towhees' diet, and the young are fed on spiders, moths, grasshoppers, caterpillars, and other insects. The California Towhee has been known to feed on fruit in orchards and vegetable gardens. The Canyon Towhee will chase down and even fly after insects. The Eastern Towhee will feed in trees, especially when caterpillars are abundant, and the Spotted Towhee seems to prefer beetles.

VOCALIZATION
Towhees learn their songs—a fact gleaned from studies of isolated Eastern Towhee males raised in captivity, which never sang songs common to the species. Towhees' songs and calls vary greatly, but most contain one or more introductory notes, followed by a

Yellow-faced Grassquit

trill. The secretive and seldom seen Green-tailed Towhee often gives itself away with its distinctive catlike mewing calls. It is sometimes heard singing at night. The Canyon Towhee repeats its double-syllable request of "chili-chili-chili-chili." California and Abert's Towhee are less musical, making a higher and flatter call. Probably the most familiar towhee song is the "drink-your-tea" warble of the Eastern perched out of sight in distant, thick underbrush. Towhees offer high pitched and thin calls, many quite complex and some simple one-note growl-like sounds, nasal mewing calls, and secretive clicks and ticks.

BREEDING BEHAVIOR
Pairs are generally monogamous and maintain a territory together, sharing the duties of feeding and foraging for the young. The female is responsible for nestbuilding and incubation, and the male plays a more prominent role in defending the territory, largely by singing. Females will defend the territory against other females.

OTHER SPECIES FIELD NOTES

■ **White-collared Seedeater**
Sporophila torqueola
L 4.5"
Short, strongly curved bill

■ **Black-faced Grassquit**
Tiaris bicolor
L 4.5"
Black head and underparts, olive above

■ **Yellow-faced Grassquit**
Tiaris olivacea
L 4.25"
Yellow eyebrow and throat

■ **Olive Sparrow**
Arremonops rufivirgatus
L 6.25"
Brown stripes on crown

■ **Green-tailed Towhee**
Pipilo chlorurus
L 7.25"
Olive above with reddish crown

■ **California Towhee**
Pipilo crissalis
L 9"
Buffy, spotted throat

■ **Canyon Towhee**
Pipilo fuscus
L 8"
Reddish crown, breast spot

■ **Abert's Towhee**
Pipilo aberti
L 9.5"
Black face

■ **Spotted Towhee**
Pipilo maculatus
L 7.5"
Spotted back and scapulars, rufous and white below

The accommodating female California Towhee often solicits mating by fluttering her wings and raising her tail while emitting begging calls and offering nesting material in her bill. Pairs may mate for life. Canyon Towhee pairs stay in close visual and physical contact throughout their lives, often staying within inches of each other. The female builds large open cup-nests on the ground or the lower branches of shrubs in dense undergrowth. Broods number between one to three attempts, with three to five eggs per brood.

BREEDING RANGE
The sedentary Canyon and Abert's Towhees are restricted to the arid Southwest; and the California Towhee ranges among the chaparral and riparian uplands of western California and central Oregon. The Green-tailed Towhee breeds in the dry shrublands of the central West, often associated with the recovery of burned-over high-elevation coniferous forests. The Spotted Towhee is a more northerly breeder, ranging into the Great Plains and southern Canada. The only towhee east of the Mississippi is the Eastern Towhee.

MIGRATION AND WINTER RANGE
Some experts consider the Green-tailed to be the only true migratory towhee. It leaves its winter range in southern Mexico in February and makes a leisurely flight to its breeding range in the Northwest, arriving there in May. The Spotted and Eastern Towhees winter in Mexico and the southern U.S. and travel only slightly further north in summer. The three "brown" towhees are sedentary.

OBSERVING TOWHEES
To see all six towhees, a birder would have to undertake a coast-to-coast trek. The birds can be a challenge to find and are most often detected by their call or heard scratching in leaf litter before they are seen. They spend much of their time in the shadows of dense brush, rarely in the open or singing from an exposed perch.

STATUS AND CONSERVATION
Abert's Towhee is a riparian species and is believed to have declined dramatically as the water in the Colorado River Delta has been steadily siphoned off. The Utah towhee population is now believed to be half of what it was 20 years ago. The Eastern Towhee has been in decline since 1966 but still prospers in pine barrens in areas regenerating after fire.

See also

Cardinals, Grosbeaks, Buntings, page 392

Song Sparrow: *Melospiza melodia,* L 5.75-7.5", long, rounded tail, breast spot

SPARROWS

The Song Sparrow (above) is surely one of the most familiar birds of suburban and rural gardens and weedy fields, ranging from southern Alaska and the Canada south into Baja California in the West and to northern Georgia in the East. The species winter mainly in the lower 48 states and northern Mexico. But "familiar" is a relative term, and birdwatchers are often shocked when, traveling far from home, they encounter a sparrow that looks and sounds very different from their local Song Sparrow, yet is nevertheless a Song Sparrow. In different geographic settings the species is highly variable in size, plumage, and song. Eastern and California coastal birds are mostly brownish with some rust in the wings, other western birds are darker and richly rufous throughout, southwestern birds are paler with bright rusty spots. In the early days of American ornithology, these types were considered distinct species, but modern ornithology combines them into one species with different subspecies, most of which are connected through a cline, or gradual gradation, from one form to the next.

Range of Song Sparrow

CLASSIFICATION

Experts have not been able to agree on the exact number of species in the family Emberizidae, ranging up to 319 worldwide. Recently a split occurred in the Sharp-tailed Sparrow, which is now two species and includes the interior and Canadian maritime breeding Nelson's Sharp-tailed Sparrow and the coastal Saltmarsh Sharp-tailed Sparrow. Other variable species such as the Fox Sparrow and the Savannah Sparrow may be subject to splits in the future. Sparrows may seem similar to House Sparrows or finches at first glance, but, in fact, are most closely related to the family Cardinalidae, which includes cardinals, *Passerina* buntings, some grosbeaks, and the Dickcissel. For now, in addition to the six towhees and two buntings, it is reasonably possible to see 33 sparrows, two juncos, and four longspurs in North America.

STRUCTURE

Certain species appear rather long and slender, as those in the genus *Spizella*, including the familiar American Tree and Chipping Sparrows. Others appear shorter and squatter such as the Lincoln's and Song Sparrows of the genus *Melospiza* and the Grasshopper and Henslow's *Ammodramus* sparrows. Still others such as the Fox Sparrow and the Lark Bunting maintain a rather sturdy, stocky build. The medium-distance migrants *Ammodramus* sparrows rarely undertake any long-distance flights on their breeding and wintering grounds, more often remaining within the cover of a grassland or marsh, and thus the species has evolved shorter wings and tail that help it navigate within these close quarters. The *Spizella* sparrows, on the other hand, are medium-distance migrants that will attempt moderate flights just to find feeding areas on their wintering or breeding grounds, and their longer wings and tail and slight build help them in this endeavor.

The Longspurs (genus *Calcarius*) move great distances over vast open habitats and have evolved greater primary projection and long wings that enable them to undertake these longer flights. The *Zonotrichia* sparrows such as the royal looking Golden-crowned Sparrow have developed large feet, and these help them rake the ground and move through leaf litter as they forage for seeds and insects. Bill size varies from fairly small in the *Spizella* to rather large in the Fox Sparrow and the Lark Bunting. Bill size also varies among Savannah Sparrows and Fox Sparrows. Head shape is another noticeable feature showing great variation among the group. The White-crowned Sparrow has a rounded, almost puffy head, whereas *Ammodramus* sparrows such as Grasshopper and Sharp-tailed Sparrows seem to lack a forehead. Sparrows range in size from the diminutive 5-inch-long Le Conte's Sparrow of the *Ammodramus* genus to the larger *Zonotrichia* represented by the bulky 7.5-inch-long Harris's Sparrow.

PLUMAGE

Most sparrows are dressed in various combinations of brown, gray, white, and black. Many species exhibit rich chestnut or pale buffy browns and others pale grays or even rich silver, and

White-throated Sparrow

these browns and grays tend to be offset by white or black areas. The Black-throated Sparrow with its large, rich black triangular throat patch and silvery white supercilium and malar stripes is an elegant study of sparrow colors. Quite a few members show some yellow or buffy orange color around the face such as the golden face patches of the Sharp-tailed Sparrow and the yellow eyebrow stripe of the White-throated Sparrow. In accordance with Gloger's rule, desert and grassland species are more often adorned in paler grays and browns, whereas those found in woodland and marsh habitats wear darker brown plumage. A few species, including the longspurs and the grassland Lark Bunting have a prealternate molt in the spring that greatly alters their appearance, and they show marked sexual dimorphism. In basic, or winter plumage, the Lark Bunting is a dark brown, streaked "sparrow-colored" bird that in the breeding season becomes transformed into a very formal, all-black-bird with a bold, gleaming white wing patch. In most emberizids, adults are similar in plumage. Juveniles are streaky, especially

on the chest, and can baffle birders in this confusing plumage, but during the late summer and fall they undergo their first prebasic molt and achieve a more adultlike plumage. Some species show dramatic geographic variation and may actually compose more than one species. The Sharp-tailed Sparrow is an example of a recent split and was separated into two species: Saltmarsh Sharp-tailed and Nelson's Sharp-tailed Sparrow. The Saltmarsh Sparrow is confined to the salt marshes along the East Coast and the Gulf Coast of Florida. The Nelson's breeds in marshes of interior and maritime Canada but winters also along the East and Gulf Coasts. The Fox Sparrow, Savannah Sparrow, and Song Sparrow are species that show marked geographic variation. In the *National Geographic Field Guide to the Birds of North America* five subspecies of Fox Sparrow, each showing great color variation, are illustrated. The Fox Sparrow has as many as 18 recognized subspecies, but there are at least four easily distinguishable forms that, as some experts contend, could be split and these include: Red Fox Sparrow, Sooty Fox Sparrow, Slate-colored Fox Sparrow, and Large-billed Fox Sparrow. The Large-billed Savannah Sparrow (*P.s. rostratus*) of southern and Baja California is paler and has a large, thick bill whereas *P.s. beldingi* of southern California is darker and has a rather small, fine bill. Some experts maintain that the Large-billed form is a distinct species.

OTHER SPECIES FIELD NOTES

■ **Bachman's Sparrow**
Aimophila aestivalis
L 6"

■ **Botteri's Sparrow**
Aimophila botterii
L 6"

■ **Cassin's Sparrow**
Aimophila cassinii
L 6"

■ **Rufous-winged Sparrow**
Aimophila carpalis
L 5.75"

■ **Rufous-crowned Sparrow**
Aimophila ruficeps
L 6"

■ **American Tree Sparrow**
Spizella arborea
L 6.25"

■ **Field Sparrow**
Spizella pusilla
L 5.75"

■ **Chipping Sparrow**
Spizella passerina
L 5.5"

■ **Clay-colored Sparrow**
Spizella pallida
L 5.5"

■ **Brewer's Sparrow**
Spizella breweri
L 5.5"

■ **Lark Sparrow**
Chondestes grammacus
L 6.5"

■ **Black-chinned Sparrow**
Spizella atrogularis
L 5.75"

■ **Black-throated Sparrow**
Amphispiza bilineata
L 5.5"

■ **Five-striped Sparrow**
Aimophila quinquestriata
L 6"

■ **Sage Sparrow**
Amphispiza belli
L 6.25"

■ **Grasshopper Sparrow**
Ammodramus savannarum
L 5"

■ **Baird's Sparrow**
Ammodramus bairdii
L 5.5"

■ **Henslow's Sparrow**
Ammodramus henslowii
L 5"

■ **Le Conte's Sparrow**
Ammodramus leconteii
L 5"

■ **Seaside Sparrow**
Ammodramus maritimus
L 6"

■ **Fox Sparrow**
Passerella iliaca
L 7"

■ **White-throated Sparrow**
Zonotrichia albicollis
L 6.75"

■ **White-crowned Sparrow**
Zonotrichia leucophrys
L 7"

■ **Golden-crowned Sparrow**
Zonotrichia atricapilla
L 7"

■ **Saltmarsh Sharp-tailed Sparrow**
Ammodramus caudacutus
L 5"

■ **Nelson's Sharp-tailed Sparrow**
Ammodramus nelsoni
L 4.75"

Bird-watchers should study sparrows closely, especially through binoculars, to better appreciate their rare, warm beauty.

FEEDING BEHAVIOR

As a group, sparrows are consummate seedeaters feeding mainly on the ground. The demands of nesting and raising a brood cause sparrows to shift to foraging for insects to get the protein the nestlings need. In the fall, the birds will gradually change their diet back to seeds, berries, and other vegetation. Many species, including Song Sparrow, Olive Sparrow, Fox Sparrow, and the *Zonotrichia*, (Harris's, White-throated, White-crowned, and Golden-crowned Sparrows) double scratch like towhees. This activity can be detected audibly if birders keep their ears open, especially in areas where wintering flocks congregate. Another strategy for obtaining seeds, particularly among juncos and *Spizella* sparrows such as the Chipping, Field, and American Tree Sparrows, is to land atop a reed, and bend it by the force of their weight to the ground so that they can husk the seeds. American Tree Sparrows have been observed beating weeds with their wings, then dropping to the ground to feed on the seeds flailed from the plant. Wetland species such as the two Sharp-tailed and the coastal Seaside Sparrows will probe among the cordgrass, tidal pools, and mudflats in search of insects, spiders, mollusks, and marine worms. In fall and winter, desert species such as the Black-throated Sparrow are granivores, but in spring and summer they feed heavily on insects such as butterfly and moth larvae, dragonflies, walking sticks, and grasshoppers and gain enough water through the insects they ingest so that they do not need to drink water directly.

VOCALIZATION

Most sparrow species learn their songs, and some species such as the White-crowned Sparrow and the towhees produce "regional dialects." In the breeding season males of all species sing from prominent perches at the top of a tree, shrub, or reed, from which they can project their song both to warn other males that the territory is occupied and also to attract females. The females sing only very rarely. Songs in this group range from long, complex, and musical sounds to short and dry or buzzy calls. Many species, including Lark Buntings, longspurs, the *Aimophila*, and *Ammodramus* groups perform great flight displays. The displays performed by Lark Buntings and longspurs are especially dramatic and are often referred to as "skylarking," in which a male ascends in a fluttery flight and—when reaching a peak—begins to sing as he descends while slowly flapping his wings until he reaches the ground or the perch. The songs of these species represent more

pleasing, complex, fluid, and musical sounds than those of other sparrows. Saltmarsh Sharp-tailed Sparrows and Henslow's Sparrows produce far less complex songs. The Henslow's song is simply an overwhelmingly unimpressive "hiccup" that easily escapes notice. Several species including Henslow's, Grasshopper Sparrow, and Clay-colored Sparrow have songs that could be mistaken for insect sounds. Juncos and Chipping Sparrows issue more noticeable dry trills, but the vocalization of the Chipping Sparrows is sometimes closer to the Pine Warbler's song, and the juncos' calls are slightly more melodic and similar to the Longspurs' warbling songs. The Song Sparrows, Fox Sparrows, and *Zonotrichia* sparrows may pipe up on sunny winter days, and their songs are usually characterized by a series of clear whistled notes, sometimes followed by trills or buzzy notes. All sparrows have call notes that they give when agitated and these vary between the families from hard chips to thin "seep"

SAVANNAH SPARROW

Named for the coastal Georgia town where the type specimen was originally collected, the Savannah Sparrow is abundant and distributed throughout North America, breeding coast to coast from the mid-United States north to Canada and Alaska. A bird of open spaces, this sparrow can be found on almost every farm field, meadow, golf course, bog, marsh, beach, or grassy dune, and is as variable in coloration as the worlds it inhabits. The species is streaked, has yellow to whitish eyebrows, and ranges in color from the very dark *beldingi* subspecies of the southern California coastal marshes to the widespread and palest *nevadensis* subspecies. Like most sparrows, the Savannah forages mainly for seeds and berries, changing to an insect diet during the breeding season.

notes. Flight notes can be heard when birds are flushed or during nocturnal migration.

BREEDING BEHAVIOR

Most sparrows have breeding strategies similar to those of towhees, but Smith's Longspurs and Saltmarsh Sharp-tailed Sparrows are exceptions. Smith's Longspurs practice polygynandry in which both males and females are paired to more than one mate. Saltmarsh Sharp-tailed Sparrows are most unusual in practicing a strategy that is very rare in birds termed "scramble competition polygyny." For this reason males travel widely in an effort to inseminate as many females as they can find, and the practice may result in several males attempting to mate with a single female at one time. Females may accept many males in only a short period. This unusual reproductive strategy is observed in the southern part of the species' range, and it demands that males be able to produce sperm rapidly and, indeed, the species has far larger testes than is normal for their size. Cooperative breeding has not been found among sparrows. However, the number of males discovered attending nests with young that they had no part in producing would seem to indicate that extra-pair copulations may be far more common than we now recognize. Less is known about the Harris's Sparrow that breeds west of the Hudson Bay and into the high Arctic. Harris's males arrive on the breeding grounds a few days early, and shortly after the females arrive, they form pair bonds. Mates appear to be monogamous. Even less is known about the breeding habits of the southwest desert-dwelling Black-chinned Sparrow, but pairs seem to be strictly monogamous. More field study is needed. Data gathered in this respect by the birding community in Christmas Bird Counts and Breeding Bird Surveys is invaluable.

Green-tailed Towhee

BREEDING RANGE

The deserts of the southwestern United States are home to many sparrows and represent the northern limit for many species that are largely Mexican in their distribution. The prairies and grasslands of the western United States and Canada are also fertile breeding grounds for a number of species. Compared to the West and Southwest there are relatively few species in the East. The southerly breeding birds tend to be more sedentary. The Lapland Longspur is the most northerly breeder of the emberizids, with birds breeding all the way to Ellesmere Island and into Greenland. The

Harris's Sparrow is one of only a few birds whose breeding range spreads out in northwestern Canada. Within North America, the range of the Olive Sparrow and the White-collared Seedeater are reduced to southern Texas. They are found commonly farther south ranging into Mexico and Central America, though the seedeater is experiencing a decline. Song, Savannah, Vesper, and Chipping Sparrows are the most widespread breeders in the United States and Canada. The Dark-eyed Junco and Fox Sparrow are close behind. The Lapland Longspur (along with Snow Bunting) is one of the few species of emberizids that breeds in both the Old and the New Worlds.

MIGRATION

The migration requirements of sparrows are as varied as the group, but certain patterns relate directly to breeding and nesting. The White-crowned and White-throated Sparrows, both of the genus *Zonotrichia*, breed throughout Canada, into Nunavut—much of what used to be called the Northwest Territories—with the White-crowned breeding as far west as Alaska. Both birds summer in the continental United States when birders have the best opportunity to observe the family. The Baird's and Harris's Sparrows are more restricted in their ranges. The Harris's breeds well into central Nunavut and summers in the central plains to southern Texas. The Baird's breeds in the prairies of the northern United States and southern Canada and winters just across the border in southern Mexico. The gentleman of the southern pine woods, the Bachman's Sparrow, is a short-distance migrant, with some members breeding in Illinois, Ohio, and southern Pennsylvania and moving back in the fall to the Southeast where traveling species join permanent residents in their preferred pine forests. The Lark Bunting is a complete migrant with no year-round residents found in the small area where their breeding and winter ranges overlap around the Texas Panhandle. Most sparrows do migrate to northern breeding grounds where food is abundant in the spring and summer, then move to warmer southern climes in the winter, usually only far enough to find the food they need to survive.

WINTER RANGE

Although none of the emberizids nest in colonies or groups, the social behavior of some species changes in the winter and several will form rather large flocks that forage together. *Spizella* and *Zonotrichia* sparrows are often seen in flocks at this season and may be joined by individuals from other groups such as the *Melospiza* sparrows and towhees. Areas like the Great Plains, the Midwest, and Southeast that support relatively few emberizids during the breeding season provide valuable wintering habitats for many sparrows. Some Mexican species such as the Botteri's Sparrow leave southeast Arizona and southwest New Mexico to winter in Mexico, and the stunningly patterned Lark Sparrow, though widespread throughout the central United States in the spring and summer, winters far into Mexico. Some Lark Sparrows remain year-round in Texas, California, southern Arizona, and New Mexico. We are fortunate to have representatives of this lovely family with us throughout the winter months.

OBSERVING SPARROWS

These birds are furtive, and observers will have a hard time viewing them; even the more commonly encountered species are quick to flush and take cover. Birders will fare no better on the breeding grounds; the sparrows are just as elusive there. The birds' shyness combined with their subtle field marks make their identification a true challenge. Patience will often reward the persistent observer, but many birds will still escape, not only unidentified but undetected. The breeding season is the best time to see some species, when males are more obvious while singing, and pairs are noticeable while out foraging food for their young. Male sparrows may have favorite perches to sing from, and the discovery of one such perch can help an observer obtain a good study of a bird by sitting still and viewing with a pair of binoculars or a spotting scope. Birds in the genus *Ammodramus* such as the Henslow's, Le Conte's, and Grasshopper Sparrow are especially evasive and hesitate to flush, preferring to scamper away on the ground. Indeed, the genus name *Ammodramus* comes from the Latin and means "sand-runner."

Feeding stations can be good starting points for getting to know a few sparrow species. Towhees, juncos, Song Sparrows, Fox Sparrows, White-crowned, and White-throated Sparrows frequent feeders regularly, and once observers have learned to identify a few species, they can better distinguish between these and others that are unfamiliar. Learning to distinguish the songs and call notes will also be a tremendous help when trying to find out if sparrows are present in an area. These birds are generally easier to hear than to see. Walking softly and slowly along the edge of fields, weedy areas, woodlots, and hedgerows is a good way to encounter wintering groups of sparrows. In these places they will venture out from cover to feed on more open ground. They will often respond well to quiet "pishing." When birds do flush, subtle differences in structure and style of flight can be clues as to which genus or species it is. Some sparrows such as those in the genus *Spizella* and the Savannah Sparrow will often fly a long distance when flushed, but some such as the *Ammodramus* species will fly only a few yards before again taking cover and running away.

All birds in this group keep discreet breeding territories with males singing from exposed perches to announce their presence. Birders never tire of coming upon the dressy little Field Sparrow perched atop a grass stalk, singing his plaintive, flute-like accelerating

LE CONTE'S SPARROW

A member of the genus *Ammodramus*, the Le Conte's belongs to the group of sparrows that appear to have no forehead, their crown falling back almost in line with the top of the bill. At barely 5 inches, the Le Conte's is one of the smallest sparrows. The species has a white central crown stripe, a bright, broad golden-orange eye stripe, velvet gray ear patch, chestnut streaks on the nape, and black-and-straw-colored back stripes. The Le Conte's Sparrows are elusive denizens of wet grasslands and marshy meadows, difficult to approach, seldom flushing, and most often scurrying away through the grass like a mouse. In the spring, on their breeding grounds in the central prairies and grasslands of the northern United States and Canada, singing males claim an exposed perch, offering the best viewing opportunity. Le Conte's are short-distance migrants wintering in damp, weedy, grassy fields of the southeastern U.S. Because of their extremely secretive nature, population numbers are unreliable, but seem to be stable throughout their range.

whistle into the evening. Sparrows also utilize a range of habitats from the Artic tundra to boreal forest and arid desert to various wetland and grassland types. The birds have adapted well to evolve into a wide range of habitats and niches. In winter some species form flocks to seek food and protection. Others pass the winter solitarily, while yet others join groups only where food is abundant but otherwise behave independently.

Many people find their first sparrow at the bird feeder in winter. Juncos, birds of the genus *Zonotrichia*, and others of *Melospiza* or *Spizella* are found at feeding stations, and birders can compare the sizes and shapes of different sparrows. Some such as the Song Sparrow have streaked breasts, others such as the Chipping Sparrow remain clean-breasted. Some birds such as the spectacular Lark Sparrow have bold head and face markings, and others such as the Lark Bunting display bold wing bars. Some sparrows give thin "seep" call notes, while others give richer, more emphatic "chip" notes. Valuable time spent studying sparrows in the backyard—before venturing into open habitats such as marshes, grasslands, and deserts, where sparrow identification becomes a greater challenge—will pay off. Sparrows, like so many birds, are a difficult group to get to know, but some patience will reward the observer with some wonderful sightings. There may be no greater reward for diligent study than one day realizing that one has learned to identify the sparrows.

Chipping Sparrow

STATUS AND CONSERVATION

Although no species in this group is currently listed as endangered, sparrows are vulnerable and in obvious need of attention from conservationists. The Henslow's Sparrow is listed as endangered in Canada. The Florida Grasshopper Sparrow and the Cape Sable Seaside Sparrow are two subspecies listed as endangered in the United States. The loss or degradation of suitable habitat poses the greatest threat to the birds in this group. Many emberizids make their home in grasslands, fallow fields, and marshes, and these habitats are prone to alterations that have serious implications on the lives of these birds. Marsh-dwelling species are in an especially precarious position, because diking, flooding, draining, and filling could completely alter their habitat in only a short period of time. Pollution, especially exposure to pesticides, poses a direct threat to the birds in agricultural areas.

One well-known, extirpated taxon, the Dusky Seaside Sparrow, was found only near Titusville,

Florida, which became extinct in June 1987. Some experts contend that were the bird still alive today, this sparrow would be afforded full species status, but mismanagement of its habitat brought an abrupt end to this bird's existence. In an effort to control mosquitoes, the marshes where the Dusky Seaside Sparrow bred were flooded, and after only a few years of regular flooding, the bird was unable to recover from successive years of failed breeding. Only six males remained by the time the cause of the decline was understood.

The Henslow's Sparrow has undergone a dramatic decline in recent decades, and it has been targeted as a major conservation concern. Over the past three decades the species has plummeted at a rate of 7.5 percent per year. The decline is thought to be the result of alteration of successional growth through fire suppression in some areas, draining of wetlands, and a change in farming practices from pasture to monoculture. Loss of habitat is suspected to have affected both the breeding and wintering areas of the Henslow's Sparrow and are thought to have had the same adverse effects on Baird's and Bachman's Sparrow populations which have experienced similar declines. The original, almost continuous open pine forests of the Southeast have fallen to the spread of civilization in the form of highways and housing tracts, depriving the Bachman's of the essential grass and shrub ground cover associated with mature forests. Struggling to survive, this adaptable sparrow is now found in the more open habitat created by clear-cutting and powerline rights-of-way. Ardent bird-watchers are said to have harrassed the birds by playing taped calls, which has caused managers of wildlife preserves to place the rare Bachman's Sparrow habitat off limits to the public because this activity can interfere with successful breeding.

There are 19 species of sparrow on the WatchList developed by the National Audubon Society and Partners in Flight. The list was created to promote conservation of species likely to become endangered, should conservation measures not be taken to help protect or restore certain at-risk species. Frighteningly, 19 percent of the birds on the WatchList consist of emberizids. When one considers that this group comprises just 7 percent of the North American avifauna, it is indeed cause for concern.

See also

Cardinals, Grosbeaks, Buntings, page 393
Finches, page 411
Old World Sparrows, Exotics, page 419

Snow Bunting: *Plectrophenax nivalis*, L 6.75", black-and-white wings, black back

BUNTINGS

The Snow Bunting (above) of the large family Emberizidae nests as far north as there is open ground, far up into northern Canada and Alaska. Most birders encounter them only on the wintering grounds further south, where they inhabit open fields and plains, often in company with Lapland Longspurs or Horned Larks, feeding on seeds and other vegetable matter. Snow Buntings are well adapted to their harsh environment, having a stout, well-insulated body and a shuffling gait low to the ground, which minimizes their exposure to cold. Indeed, on the southern parts of their wintering grounds, Snow Buntings may not appear until snowfalls force them southward, hence the local name of Snowbird (which is also applied to juncos). The related McKay's Bunting nests on several Bering Sea islands; its plumage is similar to the Snow Bunting's except for a white back. The two species sometimes hybridize where found together, a situation that presents a problem for taxonomists, who classify birds as species or subspecies based on evidence of their distinctiveness and their tendency to mate "assortatively," or principally with members of their own kind. Because these buntings inhabit remote areas, the degree to which McKay's and Snow Buntings form mixed pairs is not well known.

Range of Snow Bunting

CLASSIFICATION

The buntings of the family Emberizidae include eight species that occasionally can be found in North America, only two of which make their home in the northernmost corner of Alaska and Canada: McKay's and Snow Buntings. Known as white buntings, McKay's and Snow are closely related and are the only two species in the genus *Plectrophenax*. Some ornithologists believe the McKay's may be a subspecies of the Snow Bunting. McKay's is mostly geographically isolated on Hall and St. Matthew Islands in the Bering Sea, with no subspecies recognized, but hybridization has been recorded on St. Paul Island and St. Lawrence Island. The more abundant Snow Bunting ranges throughout the high Arctic in summer, and six subspecies worldwide have been described based on subtle variation in plumage markings.

STRUCTURE

Snow and McKay's Buntings are similar in size and shape, being rather plump with long wings, shortish tail and legs and conical bills adapted to seed eating.

PLUMAGE

McKay's and Snow Buntings are marked in white and black during the breeding season but display some reddish brown in winter. The breeding male Snow Bunting is entirely black and white, with a white head, chest, and underparts, a black back, central tail feathers, and wing tips. Eyes, legs, and bill are also black. The breeding male McKay's displays black wing tips, scapulars, and a spot on the tip of the central tail feathers. This bird is known to be the whitest of all North American passerines. Both breeding females display a warm brown, chevron-patterned back, and in the summer all adults attain rich, warm buff markings on their head and bodies. Juveniles of both species are a similar streaked buffy gray with a gray head and prominent buffy eye ring.

FEEDING BEHAVIOR

As ground-feeding specialists, these birds obtain seeds and berries in spring and early summer and feed more heavily on insects and spiders in summer and early fall. The Snow Bunting pulls leaves from plants protruding through spring snow cover and forages at the edge of the snowmelt on buds and tender shoots and insects. During the winter, Snow Buntings can be seen in large, mixed flocks of Lapland Longspurs and Horned Larks feeding among the weedy stubble of grain fields and on sand dunes and beaches.

VOCALIZATION

Snow and McKay's Buntings make warbling, finch-like sounds and will sing in flight or from an exposed perch.

Their song is sometimes confused with that of the Lapland Longspur. Other flight calls include a sweet, mellow "teew" and a rather rough rattle.

BREEDING BEHAVIOR

Male buntings arrive on the breeding grounds in early April when the temperature can still drop well below freezing, three weeks to a month before the females arrive, to establish a territory. The females arrive on the breeding grounds and choose from the singing, displaying males, who coax them and invite them to inspect nest sites. Once a female chooses a mate, the pair bond remains monogamous. Competition is fierce for coveted nest sites scattered among rock fissures and crevices. Placing their nests deep in these nooks and crannies provides security from ever-present predators such as Peregrine Falcons, Gyrfalcons, Long-tailed Jaegers, and Snowy Owls. These nests are cold "closets,"

requiring the male to feed the brooding female so she can spend her time on the nest protecting the eggs and keeping them warm. Typically only one brood is attempted and clutches contain three to six eggs.

Dark-eyed Junco

BREEDING RANGE

McKay's Bunting has the most restricted breeding range, nesting mainly on St. Matthew Island and nearby Hall Island in the Bering Sea. This poorly differentiated species is known to breed (and interbreed with Snow Buntings) on the Pribilofs and St. Lawrence Island. The Snow Bunting is found breeding throughout much of the Arctic in North America, Iceland, Greenland, Scandanavia, and Russia.

MIGRATION

Snow Buntings are strongly migratory and move from their Arctic breeding grounds to open agricultural areas, prairies, and beaches in southern Canada and the northern and northeastern United States. McKay's Buntings withdraw from the islands in the Bering Sea where they breed to coastal Alaska for the winter months.

OBSERVING BUNTINGS

Plectrophenax buntings are tough to observe off the breeding grounds as they will not tolerate a close approach, but after heavy snows or on rural routes where traffic volume is low, Snow Buntings can be found in flocks feeding on roadsides or out in fields where they may allow good scope studies. They can often be seen feeding in the lee of tussocks on barrier islands and coastal dunes. Most often they are detected in flight when giving flight calls, and the contrast of their black-and-white plumage is striking. Flocks may be mixed with Lapland Longspurs.

STATUS AND CONSERVATION

Neither *Plectrophenax* has undergone a noticeable trend in terms of their population, but the remoteness of McKay's Bunting's habitat makes it difficult to study. Introduced rats could threaten this species as their breeding population is limited to only a few islands.

OTHER SPECIES FIELD NOTES

■ **Dark-eyed Junco**
Junco hyemalis
L 6.25"
Extremely variable, white outer tail feathers

■ **Yellow-eyed Junco**
Junco phaeonotus
L 6.25"
Bright yellow eyes, reddish back, bicolored bill

■ **Chestnut-collared Longspur**
Calcarius ornatus
L 6"
Chestnut collar, black belly

■ **McCown's Longspur**
Calcarius mccownii
L 6"
Dark "T" on tail, black bib

■ **Smith's Longspur**
Calcarius pictus |
L 6.25"
Striped head, rich buffy underparts

■ **Lapland Longspur**
Calcarius lapponicus
L 6.25"
Black face and crown, yellow bill

■ **McKay's Bunting**
Plectrophenax hyperboreus
L 6.75"
White plumage with black primaries and tertials

■ **Yellow-breasted Bunting**
Emberiza aureola
L 6"
Rufous-brown upperparts, yellow underparts

■ **Gray Bunting**
Emberiza variabilis
L 6.75"
Large size, heavy bill, no white on tail

■ **Reed Bunting**
Emberiza schoeniclus
L 6"
Breeding male black head and throat

■ **Pallas's Bunting**
Emberiza pallasi
L 5"
Breeding male black head and throat, less rufous overall than Reed Bunting

■ **Little Bunting**
Emberiza pusilla
L 5"
Small size, short legs, creamy eye ring

■ **Rustic Bunting**
Emberiza rustica
L 5.75"
Slight crest, pale nape spot, pale line behind eye

See also

Old World Sparrows, Exotics, page 418

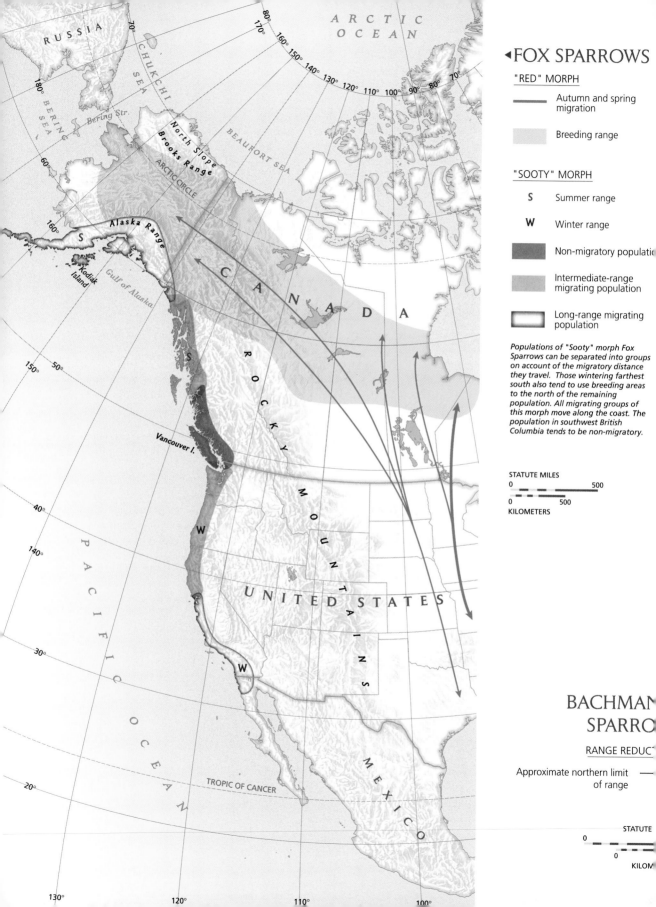

"RED" MORPH

— Autumn and spring migration

[ ] Breeding range

"SOOTY" MORPH

S Summer range

W Winter range

[ ] Non-migratory populatic

[ ] Intermediate-range migrating population

[ ] Long-range migrating population

Populations of "Sooty" morph Fox Sparrows can be separated into groups on account of the migratory distance they travel. Those wintering farthest south also tend to use breeding areas to the north of the remaining population. All migrating groups of this morph move along the coast. The population in southwest British Columbia tends to be non-migratory.

STATUTE MILES
0   500
0   500
KILOMETERS

BACHMAN
SPARRO

RANGE REDUC

Approximate northern limit — of range

STATUTE
0
0
KILOM

70° 160° 150° 140° 130° 120° 110° 100° 90° 80°   70° 60°   50°   40°   70°   30°   60°

ARCTIC CIRCLE   ARCTIC CIRCLE

Banks
Island

Victoria
Island   Baffin Island

C A N A D A

HUDSON
BAY

LABRADOR
SEA

R O C K Y   M O U N T A I N S

G R E A T   P L A I N S

L. Superior

L. Michigan Lake
Huron

L. Ontario

L. Erie

A P P A L A C H I A N   M O U N T A I N S

U N I T E D   S T A T E S

1940s

ATLANTIC
OCEAN.

1960s

2000

P A C I F I C   O C E A N

Baja California

Gulf of California

M E X I C O

2000
1960s
1940s

TROPIC OF CANCER

GULF OF

MEXICO

BAHAMAS

TROPIC OF CANCER

C U B A

W E S T   I N D I E S

Yucatán
Pen.

G R E A T E R   A N T I L L E S

HAITI

JAMAICA

GUATEMALA

BELIZE

HONDURAS

EL SALVADOR   NICARAGUA

COSTA RICA   P A N A M A

COLOMBIA

CARDINALS, GROSBEAKS, BUNTINGS

Edward S. Brinkley

The cardinalids are small to medium-size songbirds famed for their brilliant plumage and rich, ringing songs. There are 43 species of cardinalids worldwide, all in the New World; of these, 13 are known from North America, and three of these are Mexican strays: Crimson-collared and Yellow Grosbeak, and Blue Bunting. Best known of the cardinalids is the Northern Cardinal, a frequent patron of bird feeders in the East and a bird whose range has expanded northward gradually over the last century. The male's plumage resembles the mantle of a Roman Catholic cardinal, hence its name *Cardinalis cardinalis* and the scientific name of the family, Cardinalidae. The Northern Cardinal sometimes withdraws from the northernmost parts of its range in winter, especially during harsh winters, but cardinals, and their close relatives, the Pyrrhuloxia, are essentially nonmigratory, unlike other temperate-zone members of the family. A year-round presence through most of its range has made the colorful cardinal a strong incentive for many people to set up backyard feeders, igniting an interest in the natural world that begins at home. This is one of a few bird species whose entire suite of breeding and nonbreeding behaviors can be observed from home. It is no wonder, then, that five states have made the cardinal their state bird.

The other cardinalids that nest in North America are no less striking, but most avoid attending feeders unless under stress, as in periods of unusual cold weather in springtime. The Black-headed and Rose-breasted Grosbeaks, two differently plumaged but closely related species that often hybridize with one another, do attend feeders in increasing numbers, some even taking sunflower kernels to supplement their diet while feeding the young at the nest. Their distant relative, the Blue Grosbeak, is rarely seen at feeders; it is more closely related to the four smaller-billed North American buntings of the genus *Passerina*, the Lazuli, Indigo, Painted, and Varied Buntings. As their names attest, adult males are decked out in vivid hues of plum, scarlet, pink, orange-peach, purple, neon green—and of course, indigo and lazuli. At those rare sites in North America where all four species might gather around a puddle to drink—at the Sam Nail Ranch in Big Bend National Park, Texas, or at Rattlesnake Springs, New Mexico—a bird-watcher might well claim sensory overload, particularly on days when dozens of warblers and other neotropical migrants are gathered around the same watering hole.

Another cardinalid, the colorful Dickcissel, was traditionally grouped with blackbirds, to which it bears some resemblance, but genetic studies have proved its relation to cardinals and their allies. More recent genetic studies have shown that four more species—Hepatic, Scarlet, Western, and Summer Tanagers—are probably also best considered cardinalids rather than being aligned with other tanagers in Thraupidae, and that the Blue Finch of Brazil and the saltators, tropical species currently classified in the family Cardinalidae, are probably not cardinalids at all. This is one family whose membership is almost certain to change as science continues to investigate relationships among the nine-primaried oscine passerines of the New World.

(Left) Blue Grosbeak

Northern Cardinal: *Cardinalis cardinalis*, L 8.75", prominent crest, pink bill, black face

CARDINALS AND ALLIES

Among the most colorful birds of the striking family Cardinalidae, the Northern Cardinal (above) is seen ever more wide-ranging throughout northeastern North America. The species, which does not store fat and thus lacks fuel to increase its metabolism in cold weather, resided mainly in the Southeast in the early 1800s. It began moving northward in the mid-1800s in response to climatic warming (less snow and easier foraging in winter), and also by finding new edge-habitat in landscaped yards and parks, in addition to feeding stations. The cardinal reached Massachusetts in 1958, Vermont in 1962, and Maine in 1969. In the central states, cardinals followed the Mississippi River and its tributaries north, reaching the Great Lakes by 1895, and southern Ontario, Canada, by 1910. Since then the cardinal's expansion to the West has dwindled, and its populations are concentrated along the Colorado and the Guadalupe Rivers.

Range of Northern Cardinal

CLASSIFICATION

The cardinals and allies, family Cardinalidae, form a group of about 43 species, organized within 12 genera. These groupings are likely to be modified in the near future, as more genetic studies of close relatives are completed. Other families, such as Emberizidae and Fringillidae, also have members known as buntings and grosbeaks, but these are not closely related to the cardinalids, although their body and bill structures appear similar. The nine-primaried oscine passerines, which include the cardinalids, tanagers, blackbirds, orioles, wood-warblers, and sparrows of the New World, appear to be so closely related that many were recently merged into a large family, Emberizidae.

Widespread cardinalids, such as Blue Grosbeak and Northern Cardinal, show enough variation in populations across their ranges that they are classified into many different subspecies, most of which are difficult to identify as such except by an in-hand study, and many subspecies overlap in appearance, songs, and measurements. The breeding range of some of these subspecies, too, are poorly known or defined. Genetic studies of differences in the disjunct breeding populations of both Painted and Varied Buntings, however, may reveal that more than one species is contained within these complexes. Differences in plumage, migration, and body size among these allopatric (geographically separated) populations suggest that these new investigations could produce interesting results.

STRUCTURE

All cardinalids share the trait of a heavy, conical bill, used for hulling or cracking seeds, their primary food source. Smaller species, with smaller bills, eat smaller seeds than the heavy-billed grosbeaks and cardinals, so that it is common to see two or more species with different-size bills inhabiting the same small field. All species have moderately long tails. The two crested species, Pyrrhuloxia and Northern Cardinal, have the longest tail. Cardinalids have short, slender legs and, as passerines, share with all members of this order the arrangement of three toes forward, one posterior. In some species, males are heavier and larger than females.

PLUMAGE

Most field guides to North American birds illustrate the definitive alternate plumage of male cardinalids and the plumage of adult females. The plumages and molts of cardinalids are rather complex, and when one adds the stumbling block of hybrids, as between Indigo and Lazuli Bunting, or Rose-breasted Grosbeak and Black-headed Grosbeak—both species pairs with similar female plumages—the complexity is greater still.

During the breeding season, cardinalids are sexually dimorphic, with adult males showing the striking colors that lend many species their names. Females are countershaded, darker above than below, and colored chiefly in browns, grays, and olives but often still subtly striking in their own right. Males of the grosbeaks, buntings, and Dickcissel undergo a complete molt after the breeding season into duller plumages resembling the females', much as wood-warblers and other relatives do. In late winter and early spring, they have another partial molt to acquire the rich alternate plumage. Adult females also undergo two molts per year.

Younger cardinalids, however, differ from some other nine-primaried oscine passerines in their molt cycles. Whereas young wood-warblers have only one molt from their first (juvenile) plumage to their winter first basic plumage, young buntings have an intermediate or supplemental (pre-basic) molt—which produces a plumage much like the juvenile plumage—before they molt into their first basic plumage. (Grosbeaks and Dickcissels are exceptions, showing only one post-juvenile

Dickcissel

molt.) In their first spring, these birds undergo another molt of body feathers—called a first pre-alternate molt—that produces the first alternate plumage. In this plumage, one-year-old males look very similar to females but can be aged by careful study of their flight feathers. Because young male cardinalids can breed in such plumages, they are said to show delayed plumage maturation.

Interestingly, some cardinalids molt at a specific location in between their nesting and wintering grounds. The Western Painted Buntings, for example, molt their remiges in northwestern Mexico before proceeding to wintering areas farther south (eastern birds, of the nominate race *ciris*, molt before their southward migration). This process is known as molt-migration.

FEEDING BEHAVIOR

During the nesting season, most cardinalids forage by themselves, in pairs, or in small family groups, but in winter, some species such as Indigo Buntings and especially Dickcissels form feeding flocks, which may include thousands of birds. All species feed on seeds and grain, with fruit and insects making up a large portion of the diet during the nesting season for temperate-zone nesters. Cardinalids feed at all heights, from ground to treetop, depending on the food source. In winter, most foraging is done on or near the ground, but when trees are budding and fruiting, the larger species can often be found in the canopy. Some plants appear to be irresistible to the birds at certain times of year. Knowing the location of fruiting mulberry (*Morus*) or similar trees in an area can be a surefire shortcut for finding migrating Rose-breasted Grosbeaks in the East, for instance.

VOCALIZATION

All cardinalid males sing rich, rollicking, or warbling songs that vary from pure-toned in the Northern Cardinal to highly modulated or "burry" in Varied Bunting. These songs are usually delivered from a conspicuous song perch during the nesting season, but the nonmigratory species occasionally sing during the nonbreeding season as well. To a greater degree than in related families, female cardinalids are known to sing male songs. The reason for this behavior is not known, but it could be that song functions in females much as it does in males, to define territory and to establish and strengthen pair bonds. Female Northern Cardinals regularly sing with males after the territory is established and before nesting begins; it is thought that such countersinging (singing antiphonally, or in alternation)

OTHER SPECIES FIELD NOTES

■ **Rose-breasted Grosbeak**
Pheucticus ludovicianus
L 8"
Rose red breast and wing linings

■ **Black-headed Grosbeak**
Pheucticus melanocephalus
L 8.25"
Orange breast and yellow wing linings

■ **Crimson-collared Grosbeak**
Rhodothraupis celaeno
L 8.5"
Black hood, dark wings

■ **Yellow Grosbeak**
Pheucticus chrysopeplus
L 9.25"
Massive bill, yellow plumage

■ **Pyrrhuloxia**
Cardinalis sinuatus
L 8.75"
Prominent red-tipped gray crest, curved yellow bill

■ **Dickcissel**
Spiza americana
L 6.25"
Chestnut wing coverts, black bib above yellow breast

■ **Blue Grosbeak**
Passerina caerulea
L 6.75"
Mostly blue, black face, chestnut wing bars

■ **Indigo Bunting**
Passerina cyanea
L 5.5"
Deep blue overall

■ **Lazuli Bunting**
Passerina amoena
L 5.5"
Turquoise above, cinnamon breast, white wing bars

■ **Painted Bunting**
Passerina ciris
L 5.5"
Distinctive gaudy plumage

■ **Varied Bunting**
Passerina versicolor
L 5.5"
Good light reveals colorful plumage, otherwise looks blackish

■ **Blue Bunting**
Cyanocompsa parellina
L 5.5"
Blue-black overall with bright blue patches

synchronizes their reproductive cycles. Male cardinalids of some species, notably the well-studied Indigo and Lazuli Buntings, appear to learn their songs from neighboring males during their second calendar year, rather than from their male parents. In overlapping territories between these two species, males may sing elements of both Lazuli and Indigo songs.

In addition to songs, cardinalids have a variety of rich chip notes, again more modulated in the buntings, that are relatively distinctive between species, though most ears detect no differences in the "phinc" call notes of Rose-breasted and Black-headed Grosbeaks, or among the similar buzzy chips of the Indigo and Lazuli Buntings. In strongly migratory species, nocturnal flight call notes are also delivered during migration, and these differ from diurnal calls in the case of some species, such as the *Pheucticus* grosbeaks.

BREEDING BEHAVIOR

As with many other closely related New World passerines, almost all cardinalids are territorial and nest largely in well-spaced territories that are defended by the male, who sings a primary song to mark territory through the nesting season. The female may countersing with the male in a few species, most prominently in the Northern Cardinal. In this species, courtship feeding and displays are frequently observed as well, the displays involving a mutual lopsided pose in which male and female tilt toward one another, exposing their bellies. Song flight is also known in this and other species. Painted Buntings and others in the genus spread wings and tail, puff up their body feathers, and perform herky-jerky postures in front of the female. Many cardinalids defend their territories vigorously, with clashes between females hardly uncommon. Male Painted Buntings often draw blood in their fights over territory, and fights to the death have often been reported. Females do most of the nest construction and incubation, attended by the male, and both sexes feed the young in the nest and for several weeks after the young fledge. Nests are cup-shaped and well concealed in shrubs, thickets, and trees.

Breeding strategies among the cardinalids are mostly based on monogamy. The polygynous Dickcissel is the clear exception, as one male may mate with many females, reducing the role of the male in raising the young. As cardinalids are more closely studied using DNA research, however, it is becoming clear that male *Passerina* buntings are likely to break the monogamous mold and mate with females from other pairs. One study of Indigo Buntings found that up to one-third of male buntings mated with females other than their primary partner. Dickcissels often form small colonies, in which multiple males may sing their "dick-dick-ciss-ciss-el" song at close quarters. Pair bonds are seasonal in most species; Northern Cardinals may remain paired throughout the winter, though males can be aggressive toward both sexes at feeding stations.

BREEDING RANGE

Cardinalids range throughout all vegetated habitats of the temperate through the tropical areas in North to South America, with only the *Pheucticus* grosbeaks' and the Lazuli and Indigo Buntings' ranges extending northward to the edge of the boreal forests. The hardy Rose-breasted Grosbeak nests the farthest north, as far as the Northwest Territories of Canada.

PAINTED BUNTING

The male Painted Bunting is often called the most colorful bird in North America, but its bewitching plumage has led to it being one of the most widely trapped and traded species in the illegal traffic in caged birds. Most are caught in Mexico and sold there, but some make their way to the United States and Europe. Not only does this add to conservation concerns surrounding a species that already faces an acute habitat loss, it also creates a problem for those studying the distribution of the species outside its typical range. Fortunately Painted Bunting females and young males with delayed plumage maturation (in a female-like greenish plumage during their first breeding season) are not desirable. Although Painted Buntings do occur as vagrants north of typical range, when one turns up at a feeding station way out of range, there is usually skepticism concerning its arrival, since it could be an escapee.

MIGRATION

Almost all cardinalids that nest in North America are long-distance neotropical migrants; the Pyrrhuloxia and Northern Cardinal are exceptions, as they occupy much of their breeding range during the winter months. Cardinals, however, have been detected in facultative migration, that is, making movements that appear to be prompted by food scarcity and the onset of harsh weather. Such movements are difficult to detect, but research on Block Island, off the coast of Rhode Island, as well as informal observations at other East Coast sites, has confirmed that influxes of cardinals do occur in some years. Interestingly, these movements may be partly diurnal, in contrast to the mostly nocturnal migration of other cardinalids.

On migration, it is possible to find large, loose flocks of buntings, especially Indigo in the East and Lazuli in the West, sometimes in company with other granivores such as Chipping Sparrows. As long-distance migrants, which in some cases cross open water to reach their wintering areas, Indigo Buntings and especially Blue and Rose-breasted Grosbeaks, are susceptible to being displaced by weather systems, sometimes as far away as the British Isles. Birders here count such finds among the most exciting ones of the fall migration. More often, such systems transport the migrants out of range in North America, as when large numbers of cardinalids are swept up to the Canadian Maritime Provinces in mid-April or in October. To what degree some of these birds are disoriented migrants, whose navigational systems are flawed, is not known.

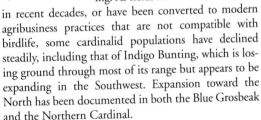

Lazuli Bunting

WINTER RANGE

Most migrant cardinalids winter in Central America and the Caribbean Islands, though the unusual Dickcissel migrates all the way to northern South America, concentrating on agricultural areas in the llanos of Venezuela in particular.

OBSERVING CARDINALIDS

A short morning drive into the country is all that's required to find most of North America's nesting cardinalids, which are largely absent from the suburbs and cities. Locating proper habitat is a straightforward task, and then it's just a matter of listening for the rich, mellifluous songs of the male birds during the nesting season. The most range-restricted species, Pyrrhuloxia and Varied Bunting, require travel to southwestern

haunts and, in the case of the bunting, a little effort to locate a singing male. For those in search of the Blue Bunting, a regular vagrant species to the United States, a trip to Bentsen-Rio Grande State Park in southernmost Texas is in order, as a few show up at feeders in this park annually, among the many Indigo Buntings and other granivores. To see Yellow Grosbeaks or Crimson-collared Grosbeaks requires a trip to Mexico, but both have turned up as strays in North America, chiefly in Arizona, New Mexico, and Texas.

STATUS AND CONSERVATION.

As seed-eating species, the cardinalids' distributions have changed according to many variables over the past several centuries. As eastern forests were cleared during European settlement of North America, millions of acres of habitat for many species were rapidly created, and this was surely a time of great abundance for species such as the Indigo Bunting, which nests and forages largely in early successional habitats and field edges. Dickcissels were abundant nesters in farm fields along most of the Atlantic coast in the 19th century, but they declined and disappeared here in the 20th, for reasons not known. Their numbers increased and their range expanded in the Midwest, probably due to the benefits of expanding agricultural practices there, at the same time that eastern birds were vanishing. As fields have reverted to forest in recent decades, or have been converted to modern agribusiness practices that are not compatible with birdlife, some cardinalid populations have declined steadily, including that of Indigo Bunting, which is losing ground through most of its range but appears to be expanding in the Southwest. Expansion toward the North has been documented in both the Blue Grosbeak and the Northern Cardinal.

The National Audubon Society's WatchList includes two cardinalids, the Painted Bunting and the Dickcissel. The bunting is threatened by habitat loss, brood parasitism by Brown-headed and Shiny Cowbirds, and the cage-bird trade. The Dickcissel, a nomadic species prone to large summer invasions east of its range, also shows decline in its stronghold, the continent's center, and is killed by the thousands on South American wintering grounds every year because of the birds damage the grain fields.

See also

Tanagers, Bananaquits, page 371
Sparrows, Allies, page 379

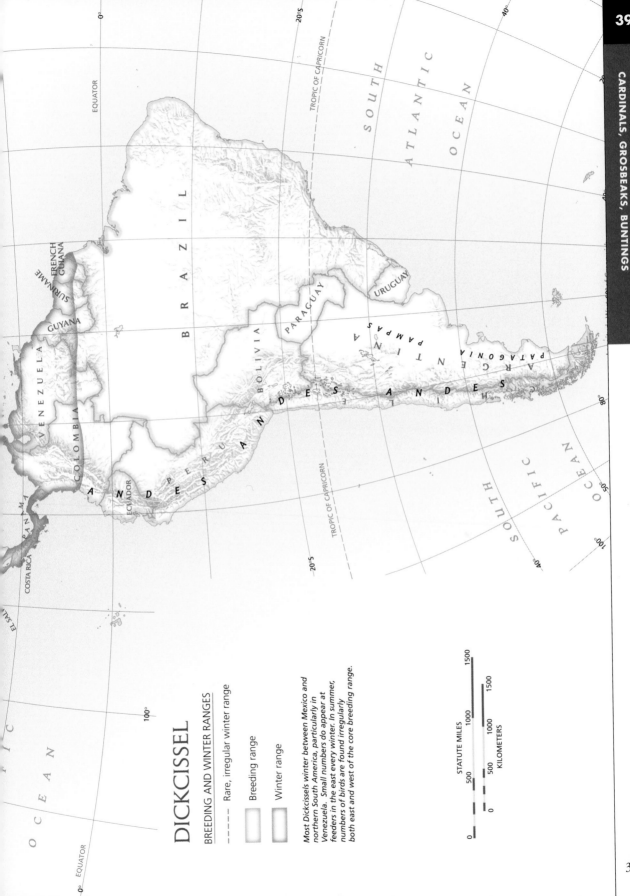

DICKCISSEL

BREEDING AND WINTER RANGES

- - - - - Rare, irregular winter range

Breeding range

Winter range

Most Dickcissels winter between Mexico and northern South America, particularly in Venezuela. Small numbers do appear at feeders in the east every winter. In summer, numbers of birds are found irregularly both east and west of the core breeding range.

STATUTE MILES

0   500   1000   1500

KILOMETERS

0   500   1000   1500

BLACKBIRDS, ORIOLES

Members of the roughly hundred species of the exclusively New World family Icteridae are among some of our best known birds. The family contains the orioles, the meadowlarks, and the Bobolinks, as well as grackles, cowbirds, and blackbirds. Once called the Icterinae and thought to be a subfamily of the family Emberizidae—the wood-warblers, tanagers, buntings, grosbeaks, cardinals, American sparrows, towhees, juncos, and longspurs—the icterids have recently been elevated to separate family status.

Like their erstwhile emberizid counterparts, icterids have nine functional primary feathers rather than the ten common to most other songbirds. They all have strong legs and feet that are well suited for the blackbirds' long walks as they forage on the ground and the orioles' acrobatics in treetops and shrubbery as they search for food.

Unlike most songbirds, blackbirds and orioles share a rather unique jaw musculature—a trait found in starlings as well—that not only allows them to forcefully close their bill, but lets them open their bill with some force. This so-called gaping lets them pry into crevices, soft bark, dirt, leaf litter, and matted grass thatch to expose prey hidden to other birds. In addition, as they gape, their eyes roll forward in their head, increasing their binocular vision to help pinpoint any prey they might uncover. Gaping gives them an advantage that may help explain the success of these species.

In spite of obvious similarities, this is a very diverse family. The species range in color from jet black with purplish iridescence—some with bright touches of color—to bright yellows and brilliant sunset oranges. Most of the blackbirds and grackles have harsh and coarse voices, whereas meadowlarks, Bobolinks, and orioles deliver blissfully melodic songs. Orioles are primarily birds of the treetops and shrubs, whereas meadowlarks and Bobolinks are mainly open grassland species. The blackbirds and grackles are generalists, exploiting a variety of environments.

Philip Brandt George

All icterids are largely insectivorous, but some species consume plenty of fruit, and others add large amounts of grains and seeds to their diet. They practice a variety of breeding patterns that range from basic monogamy to almost total promiscuity. Some nest as single pairs, and others form large nesting colonies. Orioles weave intricate hanging nests, and meadowlarks often line simple ground scrapes. Grackles and other blackbirds build rather coarse cup nests, whereas the cowbirds build no nests at all. Although all are known to form at least small flocks at some times of the year, Red-winged Blackbirds may join other blackbirds, cowbirds, grackles, and starlings to form huge flocks during the winter. Occasionally numbering in the hundreds of thousands, these mixed flocks can be observed as long ribbons or rivers of dark birds, seemingly flying from horizon to horizon.

The icterid family is so diverse that DNA sequencing suggests dividing the North American species into three separate groups. In these pages, the colorful, more arboreal orioles are treated separately, but the other two groups are combined to include the meadowlarks, Bobolinks, and Yellow-headed Blackbirds, as well as all the others—such as cowbirds and grackles—that are often simply called the "blackbirds."

Red-winged Blackbird: *Agelaius phoeniceus*, L 8.75", red shoulder patches

BLACKBIRDS

After the long New England winter, the first sounds of spring are surely the voices of spring peepers mixed with the creaky "cong-a-REEE!" of the male Red-winged Blackbird (above). The birds return as early as February, when snow and ice still lock the landscape for most other passerine species. Perched on a cattail stalk, and flashing epaulets of red and gold, males sing through the day to defend their territory against other males. The females linger in wintering areas; on arrival on the nesting grounds, females select mates based in part on the desirability of the territories they defend. During the winter, the sexes flock together and forage in wooded swamps and farm fields, where waste grain is available. In late autumn males have molted into fresh plumage and show buffy tips to many of the feathers, giving them a scaly appearance. As winter wears on, these paler tips become abraded, then wear off, so that the male attains his breeding plumage through feather wear, rather than a molt, which occurs only once a year.

Range of Red-winged Blackbird

CLASSIFICATION

The family name Icteridae, meaning "jaundiced" or "yellowish," seems to fit only the orioles, but several of the genus names for the other icterids are accurately descriptive. The three North American cowbirds share the genus *Molothrus,* meaning "a parasite or greedy person." The Rusty and Brewer's Blackbirds are of the genus *Euphagus,* "good to eat," and Red-winged and Tricolored Blackbirds belong to the genus *Agelaius,* meaning "flocking." *Xanthocephalus,* "yellow head," well describes the Yellow-headed Blackbird. Only the three grackles bear an inappropriate name, *Quiscalus,* from the Latin word for quail. Given their similarities in behavior, appearance, and song, Western and Eastern Meadowlarks were long considered a single species until it was determined that the two do not interbreed where their ranges overlap. Having been overlooked, the Western Meadowlark was given the species name *neglecta.*

STRUCTURE

The non-oriole icterids range in length from the Great-tailed Grackle at 18 inches to the Bobolink at 7 inches. Most present a solid, almost stocky appearance. The proportionally shorter tail of the meadowlarks enhance this bulky effect while the longer tail of the Boat-tailed and Great-tailed Grackles—accounting for up to one third of their length—make these two appear sleeker than they really are. The tails of all grackles are uniquely "keeled" with the central retrices lower than the other feathers, yielding a deep V-shape in cross section. Viewed from the side, the tails can appear to be held on a vertical, rather the normal passerine horizontal plane.

The bills of most icterids are sharp tipped, fairly straight, and strong. The Brown-headed Cowbird and the Bobolink have shorter, stubbier bills similar to those of finches, whereas orioles and meadowlarks possess thinner and longer bills. Most of the rest fall somewhere in between the two extremes. All can gape, and the proportionally longer bill of the meadowlarks is the extreme enhancement to this icterid ability: By adding leverage, meadowlarks can pry even deeper into soil and matted grasses where they forage.

PLUMAGE

Icterid molts, like those of most other songbirds, take place following the breeding season, but there is no spring molt to bring them into breeding plumage. They molt their tail feathers, beginning with the outer feathers first, then progress to the central ones in a centripetal molt. A few lose all of the retrices almost simultaneously, leaving the birds tailless for up to three weeks. Any seasonal changes in their appearance are due to feather wear. Rusty-toned feather tips on male Rusty Blackbirds wear away over the winter to give that species its basic black spring coloring. Similar changes occur as the Bobolink and Red-winged Blackbird lose the buff tones and mottling of fall to emerge in the spring in more solid blacks, reds, and yellows.

FEEDING BEHAVIOR

Although many species have their preferences, blackbirds, meadowlarks, and Bobolinks are foraging generalists that consume whatever might be available. During the breeding season a variety of insects, worms, mussels, snails, crayfish, frogs, and lizards make up most of their diet. In fall and winter more seeds and fruits are added to the mix. Some species such as Red-winged Blackbirds, Brown-headed Cowbirds, and Bobolinks are believed to eat more vegetable than animal matter and are often viewed as a threat to crops. Large flocks of migrating Bobolinks swarm into southern rice fields, consuming large quantities of grain, earning themselves the name "rice birds." Brewer's Blackbirds have been known to assemble in western parking lots to pick protein-rich

insects from car grilles, and some grackles snatch small fish from the shallows of streams and ponds. Common Grackles sometimes eat smaller birds or their eggs and nestlings. Grackles, cowbirds, meadowlarks, Brewer's and Rusty Blackbirds are primarily ground feeders, walking through marsh edges, lakeshores, fields, meadows, and lawns to glean whatever might be available.

Western Meadowlark

VOCALIZATION

Of the non-orioles in this family, only the meadowlarks and the Bobolinks are truly songbirds. While the song of the Eastern Meadowlark is somewhat less melodic and flutelike than that of its western cousin, they project similar rich, musical, territorial songs that carry far across the open grassland habitats they prefer. Likewise the Bobolink has a sweet, bubbly flight-song that may stir the listener. Henry D. Thoreau claimed that a young boy on Cape Cod, upon hearing a Bobolink, inquired, "What makes he sing so sweet, Mama? Do he eat flowers?" It appears that distinct populations of Bobolinks have varying dialects of song. The greater the distance between colonies, the greater the difference.

The songs of blackbirds, on the other hand, often seem harsh and almost mechanical. Some claim the name Rusty Blackbird derives from their song since it is reminiscent of the noise made by a gate swinging on its rusty hinge. Yellow-headed Blackbirds have a similar song. Grackles may produce sounds like ripping cloth, breaking or cracking twigs, crackling dry leaves, and other squeaks, squawks, clicks, or rattles. Cowbirds often produce some whistle-like notes, usually rather buzzy, and they, too, utter a variety of rattles and "chucks."

BREEDING BEHAVIOR

In addition to song and extensive bowing performances to attract a mate, most of these icterids also engage in a song-spread display in which males splay out their wings and tails while singing. The most well-known version is that of Red-winged Blackbirds: They extend their wings, displaying their bright red-and-yellow epaulettes while uttering their exuberant song. The Common Grackle and Brewer's Blackbirds spread their tails while drooping their wings and giving voice to their raucous calls. Brown-headed Cowbirds fluff their feathers, cock their tail, droop their wings, and sometimes hop about as they sing. Bronzed Cowbirds go a step further and spread their wings, cape-like, as they hop about singing.

OTHER SPECIES FIELD NOTES

■ **Bobolink**
Dolichonyx oryzivorus
L 7"
Buff hindneck, black face and underparts

■ **Eastern Meadowlark**
Sturnella magna
L 9.5"
Black V on breast, mostly white submoustachial

■ **Western Meadowlark**
Sturnella neglecta
L 9.5"
Black V on breast, yellow submoustachial

■ **Yellow-headed Blackbird**
Xanthocephalus xanthocephalus
L 9.5"
Yellow head and breast, white wing patch

■ **Tricolored Blackbird**
Agelaius tricolor
L 8.75"
Red-and-white shoulders

■ **Common Grackle**
Quiscalus quiscula
L 12.5"
Keel-shaped tail, glossy purple or bronze plumage

■ **Boat-tailed Grackle**
Quiscalus major
L 16.5"
Long, keel-shaped tail, rounded crown

■ **Great-tailed Grackle**
Quiscalus mexicanus
L 18"
Keel-shaped tail, flat crown

■ **Rusty Blackbird**
Euphagus carolinus
L 9"
All-black male has rusty tipped feathers in fall and winter

■ **Brewer's Blackbird**
Euphagus cyanocephalus
L 9"
Male glossy black, yellow eyes

■ **Shiny Cowbird**
Molothrus bonariensis
L 7.5"
Glossy purple-black plumage

■ **Brown-headed Cowbird**
Molothrus ater
L 7.5"
Brown head, glossy green-black plumage

■ **Bronzed Cowbird**
Molothrus aeneus
L 8.75"
Red eyes, glossy blue wings

Native to North America, the Brown-headed Cowbird (above) was named for traveling with cattle to feed on insects flushed by the grazing animals. Five species of cowbirds, of the genus *Molothrus*, occur in the Western Hemisphere—three species in North America. The Bronzed Cowbird is restricted to the Southwest, and the Shiny Cowbird arrived from South America to take up residence in Florida in 1985. All are brood parasites, laying their eggs in other birds' nests and leaving the responsibilities of feeding and fledging of the young to the host birds. The Brown-headed flourishe throughout North America adapting to land being cleared and exposing new songbirds—now over 200 species—to its parasitic brooding habit. The female lays up to 40 eggs per season and impacts several endangered species such as Kirtland's Warbler and Black-capped Vireo.

Unlike the orioles and the Rusty Blackbird, which tend toward monogamy and at least semisolitary nesting, many of the icterids tend toward polygyny and more colonial nesting patterns. Although the meadowlarks, Brewer's Blackbird, and Common Grackle are largely monogamous, it is estimated that at least 15 percent of the males practice polygyny. For these birds territoriality is not of great importance, especially in areas where food resources are rich. Among the rest of the icterids, several varying polygamous strategies are employed. Tricolored Blackbirds breed in colonies without territorial boundaries, and several males may mate with the same females.

The eggs in any one nest may be from several different pairs. There is apparently little competition for sexual favors. Yellow-headed and Red-winged Blackbirds, in contrast, defend territories in which they mate with several females, but these females may sneak out of the territory to mate with males in nearby territories. Boat-tailed—and probably Great-tailed—Grackle dominant males gather about them a harem of females with which they mate and will defend,

denying copulations with other, lesser males. The greater the need to defend a territory or harem the greater the sexual size dimorphism among these birds. The more monogamous icterid males are only about 6 percent larger than the females, the more polygynous Yellow-headed Blackbird males are about 19 percent larger than their mates, and alpha male Boat-tailed Grackles are up to 22 percent larger.

Whatever the nesting pattern, females build cup- or bowl-shaped nests. The nests may be bulky and unsightly, as those of the larger grackles, or finer and more intricately woven like those of some of the blackbirds. Marsh-dwelling Red-winged, Tricolored, and Yellow-headed Blackbirds often weave nests of sedges and grass in emergent vegetation over or near water. The Yellow-headed seems to consciously use wet material in the weaving—as it dries, it shrinks, tightening the weave. For the grassland-loving meadowlarks and Bobolinks, coarse grasses are used to form the nest in a natural or scraped depression, often in dense cover. If the natural cover is not deemed sufficient, the female meadowlark constructs a canopy from surrounding grasses to improve the camouflage and perhaps to shade the nest.

Most of these birds lay four to six eggs per clutch, but the two larger grackles produce only two to four eggs. Females alone incubate until the altricial young are hatched, less than two weeks after incubation begins. With the exception of the Boat-tailed and Great-tailed Grackles, among which only females draw the duty, both sexes protect, feed, and care for the young.

The major exception to all of the above comes in the form of the Brown-headed and Bronzed Cowbirds —and presumably the Shiny Cowbird. Both sexes appear utterly promiscuous, mating randomly with any member of the opposite sex. They are brood parasites and make no nests of their own, laying their eggs instead in the nests of a variety of host species. Cowbirds don't develop brood patches, and they neither incubate or care for their young but leave those tasks to the foster parents.

Eclectic in their choice of host nests, Brown-headed Cowbirds have been known to lay eggs in the nests of more than 200 species, primarily those of tyrant flycatchers, wood thrushes, vireos, finches, and wood-warblers. They rarely, if ever, perpetrate this hoax on cavity nesters. The Bronzed Cowbirds parasitize more than 60 species, largely finches and other icterids. Since the Bronzed Cowbirds breed as far south as Panama, some of their more tropical hosts may not yet have been identified.

After establishing a territory in which to parasitize, the female looks for the nesting activity of other birds. When a nest is completed or nearly so, she drops in to lay an egg during the early morning while the host is out foraging. She may even destroy host-bird eggs. Female cowbirds routinely produce 10 to 15 eggs in a season, and one is reported to have laid 25. Rarely does a cowbird female lay more than two eggs in a single host nest, but the nest may be visited by more than one female, and as many as eight cowbird eggs have been found in a single host nest.

About 50 percent of the host pairs accept the eggs and odd nestlings, feeding and caring for them until they fledge. Cowbird incubation is of short duration so the chicks hatch along with or before those of the host. While altricial at hatching, they are usually larger than their adopted siblings and, therefore, demand and get more attention and food from the attending adults. Although they rarely attack those siblings, by consuming more than their share of the food, they may cause the smaller host chicks to succumb to starvation.

Apparently a few species—American Robins and Gray Catbirds, for example—can recognize the foreign eggs and will remove them from the nest. When cowbird eggs are found in their nests, Yellow Warblers are known to build a new nest on top of the parasitized one, thus abandoning their own eggs as well as those of the cowbird.

Brewer's Blackbird

BREEDING RANGE
Red-winged and Brown-headed Blackbirds breed thoughout most of North America. The former prefer freshwater marshes with thick vegetation, the latter breed in edge woodlands associated with farmlands and suburbs. Rusty Blackbirds and Bobolinks nest virtually from coast to coast—the Rusty in wet swamps and woodlands of Canada and the Bobolink in meadows and hayfields in the northern United States. From lower Canada to Mexico, Eastern and Western Meadowlarks split the continent in half as their names imply, overlapping ranges only in some of the central states. The Common Grackle breeds across eastern Canada and the U.S., the Boat-tailed Grackle confines itself to a narrow strip of the Florida coast. The Great-tailed breeds in the Southwest, and deep into Mexico. Brewer's and Yellow-headed Blackbirds are concentrated in the Northwest and Canada. The Tricolored is a permanent resident of a coastal strip of California and Baja California, and the Bronzed Cowbird breeds from the coasts of Mexico to Arizona, New Mexico, and Texas.

MIGRATION
Bobolinks are the premier icterid migrants, evacuating their breeding ranges in North America each year to fly more than 6,000 miles to wintering grounds in the Caribbean and South America and retracing their routes in the spring. Most seem to move to coastal wetlands in the fall to molt before continuing over the Gulf of Mexico. Some fly nonstop from farther north to South America. Some of the nonoriole icterids are at best short-distance migrants, and others remain year-round on their breeding grounds.

WINTER RANGE
In winter many icterids abandon what territorial concerns they may have had to join single- and mixed-species flocks to forage. They can number in the thousands and are often seen as pests. These flocks serve a variety of purposes. Many eyes help locate areas of rich food sources that are then shared. As they forage, some may flush insects or other prey. Individuals can spend less time on the alert for predators since all periodically glance around for danger. If a predator appears, the birds fly off, expanding and contracting the flock to confuse the interloper, or they may harass and mob it.

OBSERVING BLACKBIRDS
Most of these birds are highly social and easy to find on their ranges. Yet they are adept at disappearing into the thickets when danger approaches. Female Red-winged and Tricolored Blackbirds can be mistaken for sparrows, but their bill shape and larger size help with identification. The apparently vertical plane of their keeled tail can help identify grackles even at long distances.

STATUS AND CONSERVATION
Most icterids are expanding in population and none is listed as endangered, although, as with other grassland breeders, they are on the decline nationwide. Bobolink and meadowlark populations have suffered from early mowings for hay harvests that destroy nests and nestlings. Christmas Bird Counts and Breeding Bird Surveys indicate a dramatic decrease in Rusty Blackbird populations, probably due to human encroachment and the impact of acid rain on their wooded pond and swamp habitats. Tricolored Blackbird colonies in California have suffered due to human expansion but overall numbers remain stable and they are apparently expanding their breeding range northward.

See also

Crows, Jays, Magpies, page 277

Baltimore Oriole: *Icterus galbula*, L 8.25", orange with black hood.

ORIOLES

One of the more widespread species, the Baltimore Oriole (above) is named for the orange-and-black family coat of arms of Lord Baltimore. Formerly known as Northern Oriole, which included the western Bullock's Oriole, these two neotropical migrants were temporarily combined into a single species, when evidence arose that

Range of Baltimore Oriole

they hybridize where their ranges overlap. They were split again into two species in the 1980s when it was demonstrated that, though some hybridization takes place, the majority of Bullock's and Baltimore Orioles select members of their own kind as mates. In the Great Plains, hybridization is known between a number of other species. Even when birds formerly considered distinct species are merged into one, birders tend to stick to the old names, and the colorful name of Baltimore Oriole never fell out of fashion. Often, birders use names such as Audubon's Warbler to indicate identification to the level of subspecies, and so Baltimore Oriole in that sense was never technically incorrect.

CLASSIFICATION

Oriole, from the Latin meaning "golden," is the common name for some 50 species of birds worldwide. About half are of the family Icteridae, found only in the Western Hemisphere. They are not related to the Old World Oriolidae with whom they share their name and brilliant coloring. Of icterid orioles, only ten live in or visit North America.

STRUCTURE

Generally orioles appear more slender than their icterid relatives, and, with the exception of the larger grackles, oriole tails are proportionally longer and thinner. To find meals inaccessible to other birds, Orioles gape while inserting their thin, sharply pointed bills into holes and crevices. The Hooded Oriole's longer, thinner, and more decurved bill is probably an adaptation for probing into flowers for nectar. The Altamira Oriole's heavy bill with a hard bony palate can break small branches and twigs to expose hidden prey.

PLUMAGE

Orioles, gorgeously pattered in orange and yellow with black, are by far the most striking icterids. Oriole females are duller than males, but the degree of sexual dimorphism varies from species to species. Female Altamira, Audubon's, Black-vented, and Spot-breasted Orioles appear similar to males, whereas differences among Orchard, Hooded, Bullock's, Streak-backed, and Scott's are easily seen. Some female Baltimore Orioles rival their male counterparts in brilliance. In species with the greatest dimorphism, juvenile males often resemble adult females but usually have more black on the face, head, and back.

Orioles undergo a single molt after the breeding season and do not go through the typical passerine molt into breeding plumage in the spring. As with the other icterids, color changes are caused by feather-tip wear. Oriole tail molts are centrifugal—the central feathers are replaced first, the outer feathers last.

FEEDING BEHAVIOR

Orioles feed on ants, mayflies, grasshoppers, cankerworms, and spiders. Baltimore Orioles prefer caterpillars, even some of the hairier varieties that most insectivores reject. They also consume berries and other fruits. Several species will drink nectar from flowers. The Spot-breasted Oriole is a fruit and nectar specialist, using its bill to snip off hibiscus blooms to get at the nectar. Most orioles forage in trees and shrubs, but those living in more arid areas glean insects, fruit, and nectar from cactuses, aloes, and agaves. Hooded, Bullocks', Scott's, and Baltimore Orioles visit feeding stations for peanut butter and suet mixtures, fruit jams, halved oranges, and drink from hummingbird feeders.

VOCALIZATION

Only the meadowlarks, Bobo-links, and orioles have melodic songs. Some oriole species produce clicks and rattles, but most have clear, whistling, multinote songs, sometimes reminiscent of robin song. The Audubon's Oriole sings in soft, tentative tones, others including the Orchard, Baltimore, Bullock's, and Hooded Orioles can be clear, precise, and loud.

Orchard Orioles

BREEDING BEHAVIOR

Among migrating species, males arrive on the breeding grounds before females and begin to sing to attract a mate. The male may initially chase after the female, and she may respond with wing drooping. Eventually the male perches near her and bows deeply and repeatedly, displaying the brilliance of his plumage. Orioles remain monogamous during a season. Not highly territorial in particularly rich areas, several oriole pairs may nest in the same tree. Although females build the nests, males often supply materials. Renowned for their hanging baskets or pouch-shaped nests, orioles intricately weave structures of grasses and other items to be lined with finer materials such as hair or moss, hung from the tips of branches too fragile to support the weight of many

predators. Laying an average of three to five eggs, females incubate, but both sexes help feed and tend the altricial hatchlings.

BREEDING RANGE

Baltimore and Orchard Orioles breed throughout most of the eastern two-thirds of the United States, Bullock's Orioles are birds of the West. Hooded and Scott's Orioles are primarily of the Southwest and parts of Mexico. The Streak-backed and Black-vented Orioles, common in Mexiso, have strayed occasionally into southern California, Texas, and Arizona.

MIGRATION

Most orioles are either permanent residents or only partially migratory. Only Baltimore, Bullock's, and Orchard Orioles are true neotropical migrants. They begin their nocturnal fall migrations earlier than most passerines, beginning in July. The northernmost populations of Hooded and Scott's Orioles move south to winter and may overlap with permanent southern populations.

WINTER RANGE

A few northern populations move to join southern populations or may leapfrog slightly over them. Bullock's, Baltimore, and Orchard Orioles abandon their summer range to winter south from Mexico to Venezuela.

OBSERVING ORIOLES

Orioles are often hard to spot but can be heard moving or singing. Sitting high on an exposed perch, brightly lit by direct sun, Baltimore, Bullock's, and Hooded Orioles can almost appear to be aflame.

STATUS AND CONSERVATION

None of the orioles appears seriously threatened at this time. Declines in Audubon's and Hooded Orioles in Texas may be due in part to increases in cowbird parasitism, but they seem to be doing well in the rest of their ranges. Altamira Orioles in Texas have not been as heavily parasitized. Although the Orchard Oriole population has decreased slightly in some parts of its range, it seems to be expanding toward the northern Great Plains.

OTHER SPECIES FIELD NOTES

■ **Orchard Oriole**
Icterus spurius
L 7.25"
Black hood, chestnut body

■ **Hooded Oriole**
Icterus cucullatus
L 8"
Orange with black throat and face

■ **Bullock's Oriole**
Icterus bullockii
L 8.25"
Bold white wing patch, black eye line on orange face

■ **Black-vented Oriole**
Icterus wagleri
L 8.5"
Black breast and upperparts, orange belly

■ **Streak-backed Oriole**
Icterus pustulatus
L 8.25"
Orange back with black streaks

■ **Altamira Oriole**
Icterus gularis
L 10"
Orange shoulder patch, thick blackish bill

■ **Audubon's Oriole**
Icterus graduacauda
L 9.5"
Greenish yellow back, black hood

■ **Spot-breasted oriole**
Icterus pectoralis
L 9.5"
Dark spots on breast

■ **Scott's Oriole**
Icterus parisorum
L 9"
Lemon yellow, black hood, white wing bars

See also

Crows, Jays, Magpies, page 277

ARCTIC

OCEAN

★ North Pole

Meridian of Greenwich

90°

80°

70°

60°

20°

40°

60°

80°

120°

140°

160°

180°

160°

140°

RUSSIA

Chukchi
Peninsula

CHUKCHI

SEA

BEAUFORT SEA

ARCTIC CIRCLE

U.S.A.

CANADA

Kodiak
Island

Bristol Bay

Gulf of
Alaska

BERING

SEA

ALEUTIAN ISLANDS

GREENLAND

QUEEN ELIZABETH IS.

PARRY IS.

Banks
Island

Victoria
Island

Great Bear
Lake

Great
Slave Lake

Baffin Island

C A N A D A

Hudson

Bay

L. Winnipeg

L. Superior

L. Huron

L. Erie

L. Ontario

L. Mich.

LABRADOR

SEA

Island of
Newfoundland

ROCKY   MOUNTAINS

U N I T E D   S T A T E S

APPALACHIAN MOUNTAINS

Vancouver I.

Gulf of California

Baja California

M E X I C O

GULF
OF
MEXICO

BAHAMAS

CUBA

Bermuda

N O R T H

A T L A N T I C

O C E A N

TROPIC OF CANCER

20°N

TROPIC OF CANCER

20°N

20°

40°

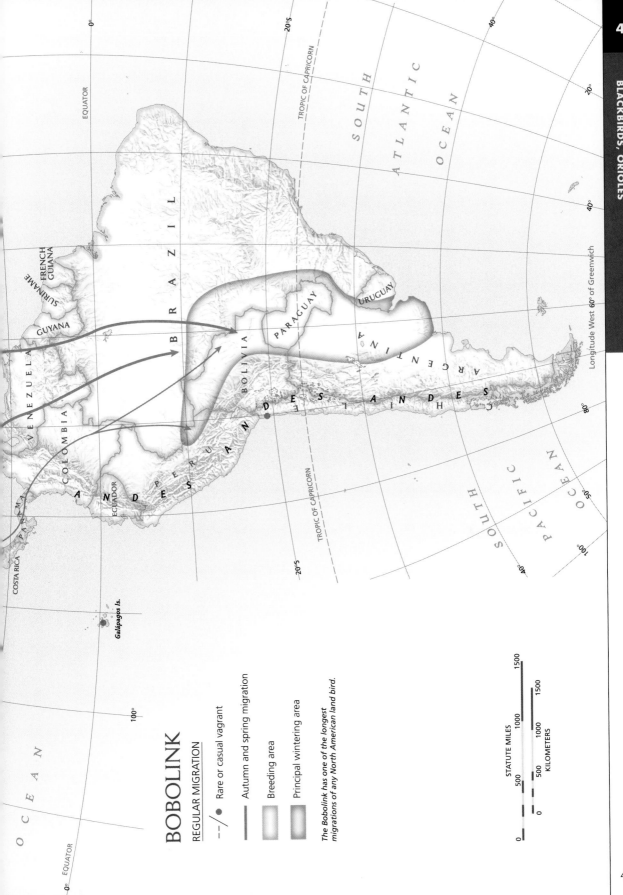

BOBOLINK

REGULAR MIGRATION

- --/ ● Rare or casual vagrant

- —— Autumn and spring migration

- Breeding area

- Principal wintering area

The Bobolink has one of the longest migrations of any North American land bird.

STATUTE MILES

0   500   1000   1500

KILOMETERS

0   500   1000   1500

FINCHES

The finch family (*Fringillidae*) is composed of 134 species worldwide. Twenty-three species have been recorded north of Mexico, 16 of which are regular breeders in the United States and Canada. Finches are favorites for many North American bird-watchers. Several species are familiar backyard birds that visit bird feeders and bird baths. The brightly colored American Goldfinch is the state bird for New Jersey, Iowa, and Washington, attesting to the species' wide distribution across much of North America. Since the introduction of House Finches to Long Island in 1940, these birds have spread so that their range now includes portions of all of the lower 48 states and bordering provinces of Canada. Although House Finches and American Goldfinches are fairly widespread, most species have more limited distributions. Many are found mostly at high-elevations or in Canada and neighboring parts of the United States.

Late-fall and winter irruptions of finches are one of the most anticipated events for bird-watchers. Erratic and irruptive best describes many North American finches, which may be common in one year and completely absent the next. Little data exist to suggest finches move in relation to severe cold; instead, finch movements correspond with a lack of available food (cones, seeds, etc.). Irruptions of several species (i.e. Pine Siskin, redpolls, Purple Finch) typically occur every two years, but occasionally take place in consecutive years or less frequently. Even species such as the American Goldfinches which move south regularly, vary greatly in terms of numbers and distribution. Crossbills are particularly erratic. Red and White-winged Crossbills apparently search for areas with conifer cones. When cones

Christopher Wood

are widely available, crossbills will usually nest—even in the middle of winter.

Studying finches on their breeding grounds can be challenging. While House Finches may nest in hanging baskets or on buildings, most of our species breed in less accessible terrain. Hoary Redpolls are found as far north in the tundra as available patches of scrub are found. Many Rosy-Finches breed in crevices and holes along cliffs and rock faces in alpine mountains; others breed on remote Aleutian Islands. Even the widely distributed Purple Finch is not particularly well studied, perhaps because the species is not abundant enough for easy study nor scarce enough to warrant study because of conservation concerns.

Studying finch vocalizations can provide bird-watchers with endless enjoyment. The songs of Cassin's Finch and Lesser Goldfinch commonly include mimicked vocalizations of other birds. It is fun to figure out what these species are mimicking, since songs may include species encountered only on migration or on the wintering grounds. Finches have distinctive flight notes, and learning these calls is the best way to find and identify them. Vocalizations often differ between subspecies (e.g. Pine Grosbeak, Purple Finch, Evening Grosbeak) and deserve more study. Jeffrey Groth has identified at least seven different types of Red Crossbills, which may represent different species. These differences are based largely on difference in vocalizations and structure. For more details, see the *Crossbills Audiovisual Guide* created by Jeffrey Groth, which includes descriptions of seven types of Red Crossbills, information on their natural history and life history, and recorded vocalizations at: http://research.amnh.org/ornithology/crossbills/contents.html.

(Left) **Common Redpoll**

House Finch: *Carpodacus mexicanus,* L 6", brown cap, red forehead and breast

FINCHES

As its specific name *"mexicanus"* implies, the House Finch is not originally a bird of the eastern United States. In 1940, a small number of House Finches were released in New York State, and by the mid-1980s the species was breeding from eastern Texas through the Midwest and most of the eastern seaboard. Their spread mirrored that of the House Sparrow—another nonnative—almost a century earlier, and some observers who feed birds at backyard stations are convinced that the spread of House Finches has displaced House Sparrows. The eastern populations of House Finches have developed a consistent pattern of autumn migration, when they are seen passing overhead at coastal sites. In their native range in the western U.S. and Mexico, such regular flights are not known. The House Finch is variable in plumage, with some males in southern Mexico sporting a cherry-wine-colored breast and head; others in the desert Southwest have a rather pallid yellowish color. These differences in color are attributable to differences in diet.

Range of House Finch

CLASSIFICATION

Finches are usually considered to be most closely related to other songbirds with nine primaries in the New World (e.g. wood-warblers, tanagers, grosbeaks, sparrows, blackbirds, and orioles). Biochemical studies support this hypothesis and suggest a close relationship with Old World sparrows and pipits, which also have nine primaries. Fringillidae is divided into two subfamilies: Fringillinae, which includes two chaffinches and the Brambling; and Carduelinae, which includes siskins, redpolls, finches, and some grosbeaks. The Hawaiian honeycreepers are sometimes considered to be a subfamily of Fringillidae, but we follow Clements (2000) in treating them as their own family, Drepanididae. Several species with the common name finch or grosbeak are not part of Fringillidae, but are members of other families (e.g. Black-headed, Rose-breasted, and Blue Grosbeaks are part of Cardinalidae).

Species limits within the finches are also controversial. Jeffrey Groth has identified at least seven types of Red Crossbills based mostly on call notes, but also on morphology. He suggests these may represent separate species. Several of these are nomadic and two or more forms can often be found breeding near each other, but only rarely form pairs between different types. Common and Hoary Redpolls are now regarded as separate species; others suggest there are six species of redpolls. Rosy-Finches are currently treated as three species in North America, but some authorities suggest that only one is involved. Differences in vocalizations in Evening Grosbeak and Pine Grosbeak deserve more study.

STRUCTURE

Finches are chunky, small- to medium-size birds. Males are larger than females. Heavily dependent on eating seeds, finches have evolved bills that help them open these seeds. Crossbills are the only species in the world with crossed bills, which allow them to wedge open conifer cones and extract seeds with their tongue. Different types of Red Crossbills have evolved different bill shapes to help them open cones of different species of conifer. Species with larger bills usually feed on larger-coned trees such as pines, whereas those with smaller bills feed on smaller coned spruces, firs, and hemlocks. White-winged Crossbills have a bill that is smaller than all but "type 3" Red Crossbills and, as with the smaller-billed Red Crossbills, feed predominantly on small-coned species such as spruce and tamarack.

PLUMAGE

All finches are sexually dimorphic, with the males exhibiting more yellow, pink, or red than females, depending on the species. Most finch species appear similar in winter and summer. The American Goldfinch is unusual among finches in having a pre-alternate molt that makes each sex much more brightly colored in spring and summer. In several species such as Purple Finch, Cassin's Finch, Pine Grosbeak, and Common Redpoll young males and females look nearly identical because of delayed plumage maturation. That is, males do not attain their definitive reddish-purple plumage until they are over one year old and conduct their second pre-basic molt. This means that it is impossible to say that a "brown" finch seen in winter is necessarily a female. It may be, but it could be a young male that has not yet acquired its definitive plumage.

American Goldfinch

FEEDING BEHAVIOR
Active birds, finches are often seen spiraling overhead as they travel in flocks during the nonbreeding season. Sometimes these flocks contain a hundred or more birds, and often include several species. Finches are acrobatic foragers that can hang upside down to reach seeds or buds, whereas buntings and sparrows usually feed on seeds that have fallen to the ground. Most species of finches will occasionally visit bird feeders, particularly when natural food is scarce. Several species will come to road edges to feed on salt and grit. Driving along roads early in the morning within the habitat of Pine Grosbeaks is one of the best ways to see this colorful species.

Finches have the most vegetarian diet of any North American bird. Unlike other species such as the New World Sparrows that also eat a variety of seeds, finches do not switch to an insect diet during the nesting season. Even in summer, finches eat more seeds and vegetable matter than insects, although they do eat insects and other animal matter when abundant. Rosy-Finches appear to consume more animal matter, particularly in early July, than many other finch species. In studies in the southern Rockies, Brown-capped Rosy-Finches were shown to feed on 85 percent animal matter in early July compared to 5 percent in late June and September. Lawrence's Goldfinches feed mostly on native plants, particularly fiddleneck in the summer and chamise in the winter.

VOCALIZATION
Finches are typically vocal birds at all seasons. Birders often encounter and identify finches by listening for

OTHER SPECIES FIELD NOTES

- **Oriental Greenfinch**
  Carduelis sinica
  L 6"
  Male greenish face and rump, gray nape and crown

- **Brambling**
  Fringilla montifringilla
  L 6.25"
  Black head and back, orange shoulders

- **Common Chaffinch**
  Fringilla coelebs
  L 6"
  Gray crown and nape, pinkish face and underparts

- **Gray-crowned Rosy-Finch**
  Leucosticte tephrocotis
  L 5.75"
  Gray head, black forecrown

- **Brown-capped Rosy-Finch**
  Leucosticte australis
  L 6"
  Dark crown, brown face

- **Black Rosy-Finch**
  Leucosticte atrata
  L 6"
  Blackish overall, gray headband

- **Purple Finch**
  Carpodacus purpureus
  L 6"
  Rose red head and breast

- **Cassin's Finch**
  Carpodacus cassinii
  L 6.25"
  Crimson cap contrasts with nape, pinkish breast

- **Common Rosefinch**
  Carpodacus erythrinus
  L 5.75"
  Male red head, breast, and rump

- **Red Crossbill**
  Loxia curvirostra
  L 6.25"
  Crossed bill, males brick red

- **White-winged Crossbill**
  Loxia leucoptera
  L 6.5"
  Crossed bill, white on wings, males pinkish red

- **Pine Grosbeak**
  Pinicola enucleator
  L 9"
  White wing bars, stubby bill, males red and gray

- **Pine Siskin**
  Carduelis pinus
  L 5"
  Yellow stripe on wings in flight

- **American Goldfinch**
  Carduelis tristis
  L 5"
  Bright yellow, black cap

- **Lesser Goldfinch**
  Carduelis psaltria
  L 4.5"
  Black crown, green or black back

- **Lawrence's Goldfinch**
  Carduelis lawrencei
  L 4.75"
  Extensive yellow wing bars, black face

- **Common Redpoll**
  Carduelis flammea
  L 5.25"
  Red cap, streaked flanks

- **Hoary Redpoll**
  Carduelis hornemanni
  L 5.5"
  Red cap, frosty overall

- **Evening Grosbeak**
  Coccothraustes vespertinus
  L 8"
  Yellow forehead and eyebrow, black-and-white wings

- **Hawfinch**
  Coccothraustes coccothraustes
  L 7"
  Brownish head, heavy blue bill

- **Eurasian Bullfinch**
  Pyrrhula pyrrhula
  L 6.5"
  Rosy cheeks and breast, black cap

the distinctive flight notes given by most species. Flight notes of finches that have been studied in detail differ subtly but consistently between individuals and may allow for individual recognition. The male and female in pairs of Cassin's Finches, Red Crossbills, and American Goldfinches have been recorded to have identical flight calls; it is thought that this may help maintain pair bonds.

Many finch vocalizations appear to be learned. Several finches are known to mimic vocalizations of other species and incorporate them into their songs. These include four North American breeders: Lesser and Lawrence's Goldfinch, Purple and Cassin's Finch. It appears that the Lesser Goldfinch may learn vocalizations into winter and possibly into adulthood, based on observations of the bird's incorporating vocalizations of the Tufted Flycatcher and other species only found on the wintering grounds or in migration.

BREEDING BEHAVIOR

As with many other songbirds, finches appear to be monogamous. Unlike other species that defend a territory around a nest, male finches defend a territory around the female. Several species are loosely colonial nesters, and the paired male only chases another male when that bird approaches the defended female.

Finches vary considerably between species in terms of the onset of breeding. American Goldfinches are one of the latest nesting species in North America, often not nesting until late June or July. Red Crossbills may nest at any time of year, although they tend not to nest while molting in fall. When a large cone crop creates appropriate conditions, even juvenile-plumaged

Red Crossbills who less than four months old may breed. The heavy reliance on seeds even during the breeding season may make it difficult for Brown-headed Cowbirds to parasitize many finches. For instance, American Goldfinches feed on few insects even during the nesting season, and nestlings are fed a regurgitated sticky semi-solid mass mostly composed of seeds. While cowbird eggs in American Goldfinch nests hatch, most young cowbirds die before they can leave the nest, apparently because of their inability to obtain enough protein from the seed diet.

BREEDING RANGE

Finches breed throughout almost all of North America. The family reaches its greatest breeding diversity in the western United States and Canada. Several species range far to the north. Both redpoll species breed in the high Arctic, moving as far south as the Hudson Bay. Hoary Redpolls breed as far north as patches of tundra scrub—which provide suitable nesting habitat—can be found. Brown-capped Rosy-Finches regularly breed at elevations of more than 14,000 feet, where they typically feed near the edges of snowfields. Some subspecies of the Gray-crowned Rosy-Finch are restricted to the Pribilof Islands (*Leucosticte tephrocotis umbrina*) and the Aleutian Islands (*L.t.littoralis*). Lawrence's Goldfinches breed only in dry interior foothills and mountain valleys and along watercourses on the western fringe of deserts in California.

MIGRATION

Perhaps no North American bird family is as irregular in their movements as the finches. Data does not

ROSY-FINCHES

The three species of rosy-finches—the Gray-crowned Rosy-Finch (left), the Brown-capped Rosy-Finch, and the Black Rosy-Finch—are found in some of the most remote locations in North America. During the breeding season, these three species nest in isolated alpine habitats with steep rocky terrain. The birds usually place nests along cliffs, caves, rock slides, and old buildings, in areas near the glaciers and snowfields where they feed. Winter is often the best time to see Rosy-Finches. In parts of Colorado and north central New Mexico it is sometimes possible to see all three species at feeders in the higher elevations. The distinctive Hepburn's subspecies of the Gray-crowned Rosy-Finch can at times be seen at mountain birdfeeders, particularly on days with some light snow.

support the notion that cold weather influences finch movements; rather finch irruptions seem to be in response to a lack of available food. Most finches are thought to be diurnal migrants, but will begin movements well before sunrise. Finches are not known to give flight notes at night, although several species have been heard delivering them while moving before sunrise.

Some species have fairly regular movements. The American Goldfinch leaves the northernmost portions of its range annually and regularly moves into the southern states and northern Mexico. Lesser Goldfinches depart from breeding grounds in Colorado, Utah, northeastern Arizona, and northern New Mexico. Purple Finches and Common and Hoary Redpolls typically stage invasions every two years or so.

Lawrence's Goldfinches are erratic and unpredictable, although the species typically retreats from its northern breeding range. In some years, the birds wander in small numbers as far east as southwestern New Mexico, most likely in response to available water and food. Crossbills are the most irregular of all species; they may be abundant in one year and absent the next, depending on the availability of cone crops.

Evening Grosbeak

WINTER RANGE

Finches are easy to see in winter, but irregular movements of most species means that predicting an occurrence can be challenging. As long as food is available, most finches remain in all but the northernmost breeding areas. In captive studies in Alaska, Hoary Redpolls could survive temperatures of -89°F and Common Redpolls endured temperatures of -65°F. The winter distribution of some species appears to have changed. Evening Grosbeaks that colonized areas east of the Great Lakes in the late 19th century appeared less often in the 1980s and 1990s. Changes in forestry practices in Canada may reduce the hardwoods that Evening Grosbeaks feed upon. Other studies suggest that greater numbers of birdfeeders to the north reduce the number of birds that move south. Rosy-Finches once wintered regularly in large numbers in the low foothills west of Denver, Colorado. In recent years, these three species have become rare in the foothills and are now found mostly at feeders at higher elevations. Many also attribute these changes to more bird feeding at higher elevations.

OBSERVING FINCHES

Within the lower 48 states, several species are found along the border with Canada. Fall trips to places such as Duluth, Minnesota, and Whitefish Point, Michigan, provide observers with opportunities to watch migrating finches. In some years, flights can be spectacular with flocks of hundreds or even thousands of Pine Siskins, Common Redpolls, and crossbills. Flight years for Common Redpolls offer the best chance at seeing the Hoary Redpoll in the U.S. Since irruptions are hard to predict, the best bet is to watch Internet birding lists to see where invasions are occurring. City parks with large conifers often provide a chance to see finches, particularly crossbills, during irruption years.

Several finch species occur as rarities in North America. Of the Eurasian finch species, Brambling is the most regular. It is seen annually in western Alaska, and there are scattered records for Canada and the lower 48 states. Seeing other stray finches requires more luck. The Western Aleutians, St. Paul Island (Pribilof Islands), and Gambell (St. Lawrence Island) are the best bet for casual strays like Common Rosefinch and Hawfinch. Eurasian Bullfinch sightings are scattered in Alaska with no obvious seasonal pattern. Most Oriental Greenfinches have been seen on the western Aleutians. Common Chaffinch and Eurasian Siskin are accidental in North America.

STATUS AND CONSERVATION

The Audubon WatchList includes three species of finch: Lawrence's Goldfinch and Brown-capped Rosy-Finch are thought to be declining rapidly, have small populations or limited ranges, and face major conservation threats; the Black Rosy-Finch is also thought to be declining but at a slower rate. Each of these species has a limited range, which could place them at higher risk than more widely distributed species. Luckily, both rosy-finches breed in remote areas, mostly on federal land. Worldwide, nine finches are classified by Birdlife International as globally threatened (none of which is found in North America). Loss of habitat represents the greatest threat to these species. Some species are at risk by the cagebird trade, none more so than the stunning Red Siskin. By contrast, populations of House Finches, introduced in New York around 1940, have since grown and expanded their range across the continent.

See also

Wood-Warblers, Olive Warblers, page 359
Old World Sparrows, Exotics, page 419

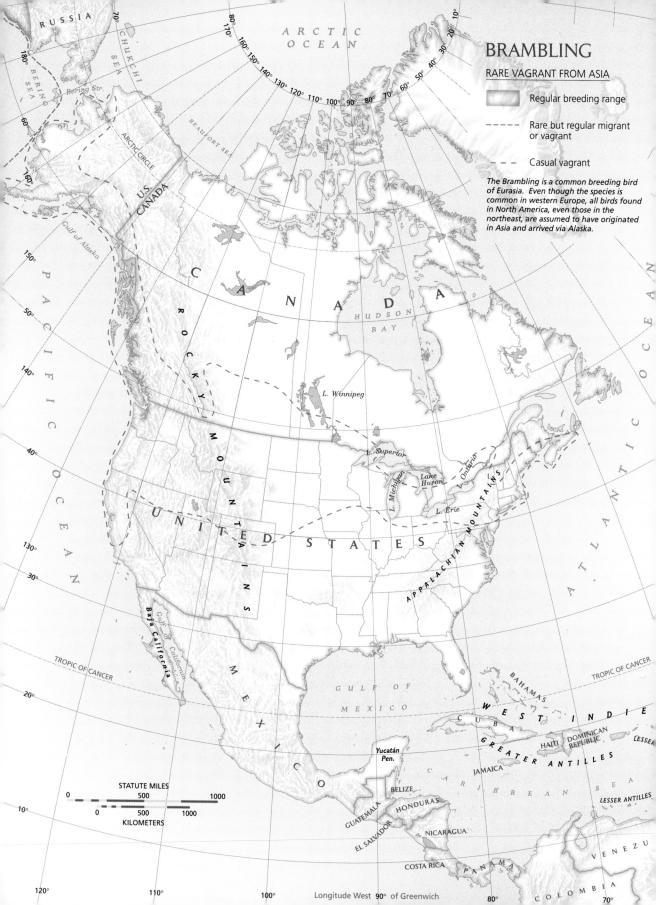

BRAMBLING

RARE VAGRANT FROM ASIA

Regular breeding range

- - - - - Rare but regular migrant
or vagrant

- - - Casual vagrant

The Brambling is a common breeding bird
of Eurasia. Even though the species is
common in western Europe, all birds found
in North America, even those in the
northeast, are assumed to have originated
in Asia and arrived via Alaska.

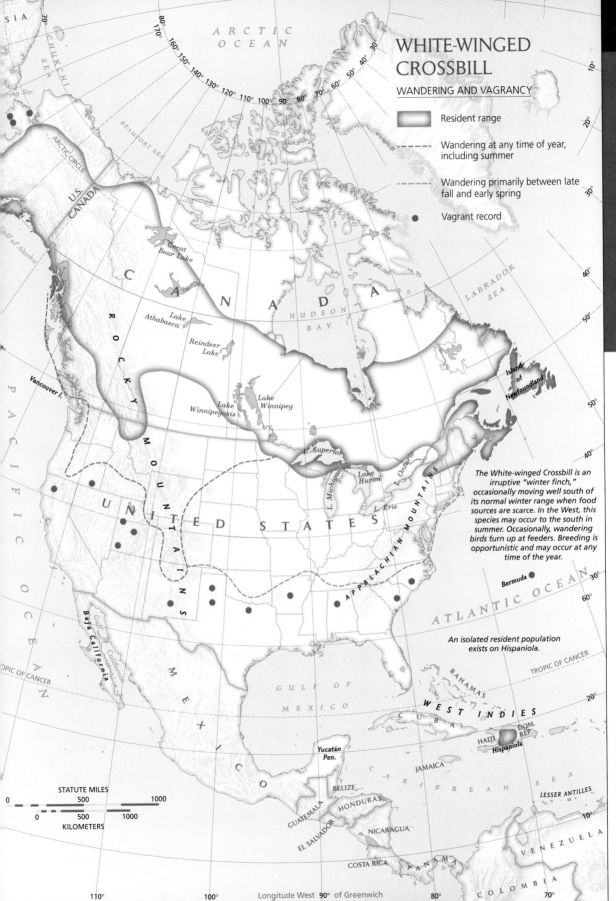

WHITE-WINGED CROSSBILL

WANDERING AND VAGRANCY

Resident range

- - - - - Wandering at any time of year, including summer

– – – – – Wandering primarily between late fall and early spring

● Vagrant record

The White-winged Crossbill is an irruptive "winter finch," occasionally moving well south of its normal winter range when food sources are scarce. In the West, this species may occur to the south in summer. Occasionally, wandering birds turn up at feeders. Breeding is opportunistic and may occur at any time of the year.

An isolated resident population exists on Hispaniola.

STATUTE MILES
0   500   1000

0   500   1000
KILOMETERS

Longitude West 90° of Greenwich

OLD WORLD SPARROWS, EXOTICS

This group of sparrows, often referred to as passerids, consists of two species that are familiar to most people. Both species are usually found in close proximity to humans and are observed in urban and suburban areas and in rural landscapes that are inhabited by humans and livestock. It is this close association to people that has resulted in mixed sentiments about these birds. To many birders, sparrows are a symbol of urban sprawl and the havoc that humans have wrought over the countryside, whereas to others they represent an intriguing and resilient biological unit.

Of the two species, only the Eurasian Tree Sparrow is much sought after by birders, and many make special pilgrimages to the St. Louis, Missouri, area to see this bird in the only place it is regularly found in North America.

The two species in this group are small and pudgy birds with stouter bills and shorter legs than native sparrows, and they exhibit a pleasant collage of browns and grays combined with black. In fact, they are more closely related to the weavers such as the Orange Bishop and estrildid finches such as the Nutmeg Mannikin of Africa and Eurasia than to any American sparrow species.

All Old World Sparrows in North America are either known as part of introduced populations or are thought to be wanderers from them. Mostly though, these birds are sedentary and as far as is known, no passerid has occurred in North America without the aid of humans. Both were introduced to the United States in the mid- to late 1800s.

House Sparrows were first introduced in 1851 to New York City from England, and their spread was

George Armistead

accelerated by the release farther west of birds supposedly from Europe and from other recently established American populations. The House Sparrows expanded their range so that by the early 1900s they had colonized much of the country. They ballooned to an estimated 150 million by 1943. Attempts to control their spread have largely failed, but a decline ensued as horse travel was replaced by automobile traffic and as a shift occurred from small farms to large plantation monoculture. Numbers are still high—over 700,000 were counted on Christmas Counts in 2002.

The Eurasian Tree Sparrows in the Midwest are of German stock and were first known to have been released in St. Louis in 1870. They have spread gradually into nearby Illinois and Iowa.

The two sparrow species nest sometimes in isolated pairs but more often in loose colonies in urban parks, farms, or woodlots. They prefer nest boxes and cavities in trees or buildings, but they may also build nests in the crooks of trees. Both species are found on the American Ornithologists' Union checklist of North American Birds (2000), and they are deemed to have established sustainable populations.

Although neither species is a particularly strong candidate for natural vagrancy, it is conceivable that the House Sparrow could occur as a vagrant. A specimen from Gambell, St. Lawrence Island, Alaska, in June of 1993 seems possibly a natural vagrant from Russia, rather than a wandering, introduced bird. The House Sparrow is becoming even more remote as a candidate for natural vagrancy, however, as it is undergoing an alarming and mysterious decline in parts of its native range (especially in Britain).

(Left) Orange Bishop

House Sparrow: *Passer domesticus,* L 6.25", gray crown, chestnut nape, black bib

OLD WORLD SPARROWS, EXOTICS

For people who live in heavily urbanized areas, the House Sparrow (above), Rock Dove, and European Starling might be the only birds routinely observed close to home. "Exotic" birds are those that are not native to an area but have established breeding populations. The success of the House Sparrow in North American cities and farms is the result of a deliberate introduction around 1850 into New York's Central Park, where bird lovers hoped that "all the birds mentioned in Shakespeare's plays" might flourish in a kind of open-air zoo. Within a few human generations, these birds have spread from coast to coast, and what was at first a local curiosity became the most successful bird species in North America. In England, however, the populations of House Sparrows have been in steep decline in recent decades, almost certainly the result of large-scale changes in modern, monoculture agriculture, with its heavy use of pesticides. As such, the House Sparrow serves as something of a "canary in a coalmine," an early-warning signal of the relative health of the environment.

Range of House Sparrow

CLASSIFICATION

House and Eurasian Tree Sparrows belong to the family Passeridae of which there are 36 species whose ranges are sprinkled over Eurasia and Africa. Their name and appearance might suggest a relationship to the North American sparrows, but in fact they are allied with the weavers and estrildid finches native to Africa and Eurasia. The two species will hybridize on rare occasions, with one such occurrence known in Headlily, Montana, in November of 1986 when a male Eurasian Tree Sparrow paired with two female House Sparrows producing three male and one female young. Eurasian Tree Sparrows established in North America are believed to have originated from the *P. montanus montanus* population in Germany. House Sparrows were introduced from their nominate population in England, and for many years this bird was referred to commonly as the English Sparrow.

STRUCTURE

These small birds are short-winged, squat, and plump with strong, conical bills. They are tough, hearty birds and outcompete many native birds for food and nesting sites. Since their introduction to North America, House Sparrows have evolved according to Bergmann's rule with the more northerly birds out-sizing their southern counterparts. They are largely nonmigratory.

PLUMAGE

Male House Sparrows are boldly patterned and combine black, white, and brown ranging from a pale tan to a rich chestnut with grays that span the spectrum from a pale cloudy white to silver. Females and juveniles exhibit more muted browns and grays offset by more subtle black and white markings. Adult Eurasian Tree Sparrows are similar in plumage, and juveniles appear paler and more muted overall. In their native ranges these birds display much variation in plumage, size, and structure, but within their introduced North American range they show little variation.

FEEDING BEHAVIOR

Passerids may feed on any combination of grains and seeds, or on buds and shoots of germinating plants. Bird feeders offering millet, sunflower, and milo are well attended by these birds. Eurasian Tree Sparrows will take insects and spiders during the breeding season. Food is foraged from the ground, directly from plants or by digging through animal dung, and in urban areas House Sparrows may beg for food from humans and will clean up any crumbs left behind.

VOCALIZATION

Singing males give persistent "cheep" (House Sparrow) or "chirp" (Eurasian Tree Sparrow) songs and these involve single notes repeated with slight variations in pitch, and they may last for many minutes. The songs communicate that a male is on territory or is trying to attract a mate. Neither species has a large repertoire and most calls are only a variation on the "cheep" or "chirp" call. Other vocalizations may be heard when birds are feeding, flocking, or alerting the group to a predator. Females are less vocal than males but call when confronting other females, when flushed, or in contact calls with mates.

BREEDING BEHAVIOR

First breeding occurs in the bird's first year, and pairs mate for life, but an individual may adopt a new mate if one of them dies. Female House Sparrows choose mates based mostly on their song display. The males stiffly profile for the females by fanning their cocked tail, sticking out their chest, drooping their wings slightly, and calling repeatedly as they hop around. Other males will gather when a male is displaying for a female and may compete by chasing her and singing vigorously. If initial attempts do not draw interest from a female, the male may begin calling rapidly and quivering its wings. Generally, the more extensive the black bib is on a male, the more sexually active he is. Pair bonds are formed in the first year and maintained throughout much of the year. Pairs of Eurasian Tree Sparrows practice mutual preening while sitting in front of

Nutmeg Mannikin

their nest. This practice is unique among Passerids. Nestbuilding can occur at anytime but usually begins in early spring and then again in the fall when cavities are often selected. Clutch sizes vary from four to seven eggs, and both males and females incubate them, with an average of 11 days elapsing between the last egg laid and the first egg hatched. First broods occur as early as March with subsequent broods continuing into August. The altricial chicks average 14 days in the nest before fledging and then are capable of moderate, sustained flight. The longest living House Sparrow ever known was 13 years old.

OTHER SPECIES FIELD NOTES	
■ **Eurasian Tree Sparrow** *Passer montanus* L 6" Black ear patch, chestnut cap	■ **Orange Bishop** *Euplectes franciscanus* L 4" Orange-red with black cap, breast, and belly
■ **Nutmeg Mannikin** *Lonchura punctulata* L 4.5" Reddish-brown above	

BREEDING RANGE

Now rather cosmopolitan, House Sparrows breed in loose colonies on every continent except Antarctica, but remain native only to Eurasia and Africa. In North America they breed throughout the lower 48 states north to Canada with their most northerly points in Nunavuk (formerly Northwest Territories) and the Hudson Bay at Churchill, Manitoba. The Eurasian Tree Sparrows' breeding range is confined to St. Louis, Missouri, southern Illinois, and southeastern Iowa.

MIGRATION

Both species are sedentary in North America, but they may wander some distance in fall or winter. In Eurasia, some House Sparrow populations, especially at higher latitudes, move south in winter, whereas others exhibit dispersal that can land birds a long way from where they are born. In summer these wanderers are usually juveniles searching for a place to settle. But in spring some birds—failing to find suitable breeding grounds perhaps because of habitat saturation—may travel far in search of new territory. A specimen from Gambell, St. Lawrence Island, Alaska, may be an example of the latter, and may represent the only naturally occurring House Sparrow known from North America. This is difficult to assess, however, as House Sparrows have some migratory populations in Russia, yet in northeast Siberia they have been introduced. Eurasian Tree Sparrows perform only local migrations. They stray from their core range in and around St. Louis in winter. Records from Oregon and British Columbia are likely escapees or birds from aboard ships from Asia.

WINTER RANGE

Neither species exhibits much movement, but birds in rural areas will retreat to more urban settings in winter to take refuge in buildings and find food more easily.

OBSERVING OLD WORLD SPARROWS

House Sparrows are easy to find. To see a Eurasian Tree Sparrow, a birder will have to travel to the St. Louis area.

STATUS AND CONSERVATION.

House Sparrows have undergone a decline in recent years. Christmas Bird Count data show a peak of 28 per party hour detected in 1963 with a decline to about 6 per party hour in 2002.

See also

Sparrows, Allies, page 379
Finches, page 411

EURASIAN TREE SPARROW

INTRODUCTION AND RANGE EXPANSION

—— Approximate area of expansion

● Vagrant record

Eurasian Tree Sparrows were introduced into the St. Louis area from Germany in 1870. They have since spread slowly northward to southeastern Iowa.

1989

Initial introduction
1870

1909

HOUSE SPARROW

INTRODUCTION AND RANGE EXPANSION

—— Range expansion (by year)

--- Very rare or casual

● Isolated record

ARCTIC OCEAN

CHUKCHI SEA

U.S. CANADA

CANADA

HUDSON BAY

1910

1930

Vancouver I.

1910

1895

1900

L. Superior

Lake Michigan

Lake Huron

L. Erie

Ontario

1886

ROCKY MOUNTAINS

1873

1871

UNITED STATES

1909

1913

Baja California

1900

Initial Introduction
1851

APPALACHIAN MOUNTAINS

ATLANTIC OCEAN

STATUTE MILES

0   500   1000

0   500   1000

KILOMETERS

TROPIC OF CANCER

1886

1886

1930

GULF OF MEXICO

Yucatán Pen.

BAHAMAS

TROPIC OF CANCER

WEST INDIES

1900

CUBA

1978

HAITI   DOMINICAN REPUBLIC

LESSER ANTILLES

1950's

GREATER ANTILLES

JAMAICA

MEXICO

BELIZE

GUATEMALA   HONDURAS

EL SALVADOR   NICARAGUA

COSTA RICA   PANAMA

CARIBBEAN SEA

LESSER ANTILLES

VENEZUELA

COLOMBIA

Since its original introduction from England,
House Sparrows have spread to most parts of
North America. The first birds arrived
through New York City in 1851 and 1852, and
additional transplants occured along the East
Coast during the 1800's. Still more
introductions were made in Salt Lake City
and San Francisco in the 1870's and on
islands in the Caribbean. Since the middle of
the twentieth century, a decline in their
population has been recorded in many areas.

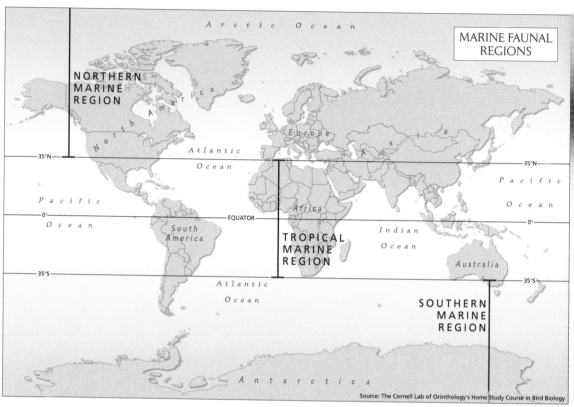

MARINE FAUNAL REGIONS

NORTHERN MARINE REGION

TROPICAL MARINE REGION

SOUTHERN MARINE REGION

Source: The Cornell Lab of Orinthology's Home Study Course in Bird Biology

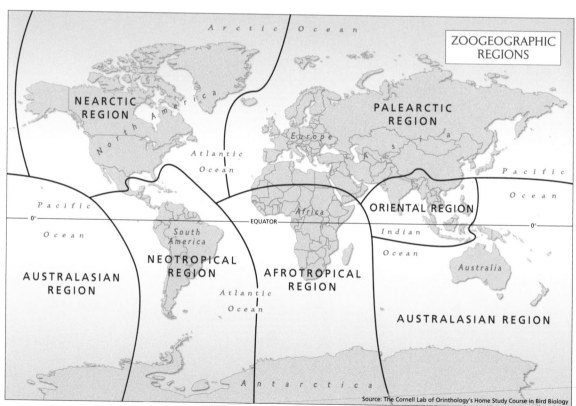

ZOOGEOGRAPHIC REGIONS

NEARCTIC REGION

PALEARCTIC REGION

ORIENTAL REGION

NEOTROPICAL REGION

AFROTROPICAL REGION

AUSTRALASIAN REGION

AUSTRALASIAN REGION

Source: The Cornell Lab of Orinthology's Home Study Course in Bird Biology

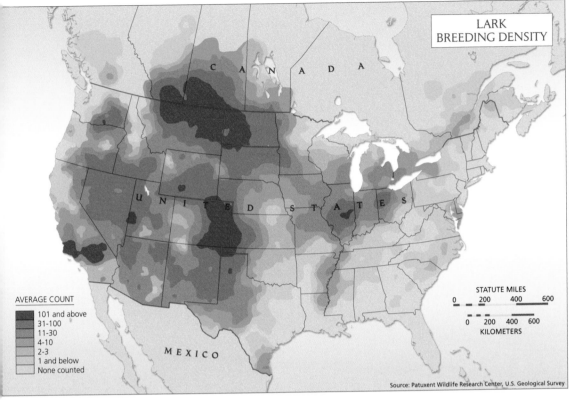

LARK
BREEDING DENSITY

AVERAGE COUNT

- 101 and above
- 31-100
- 11-30
- 4-10
- 2-3
- 1 and below
- None counted

STATUTE MILES
0   200   400   600

0   200   400   600
KILOMETERS

Source: Patuxent Wildlife Research Center, U.S. Geological Survey

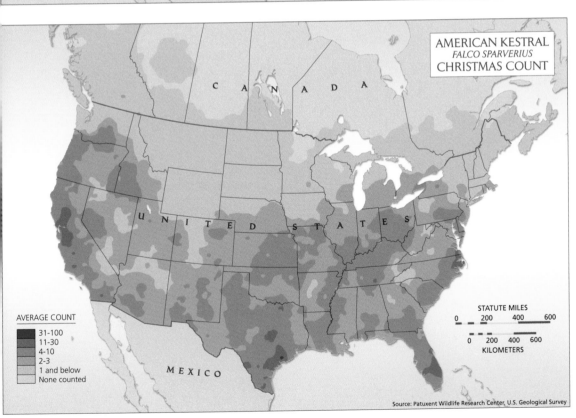

AMERICAN KESTRAL
FALCO SPARVERIUS
CHRISTMAS COUNT

AVERAGE COUNT

- 31-100
- 11-30
- 4-10
- 2-3
- 1 and below
- None counted

STATUTE MILES
0   200   400   600

0   200   400   600
KILOMETERS

Source: Patuxent Wildlife Research Center, U.S. Geological Survey

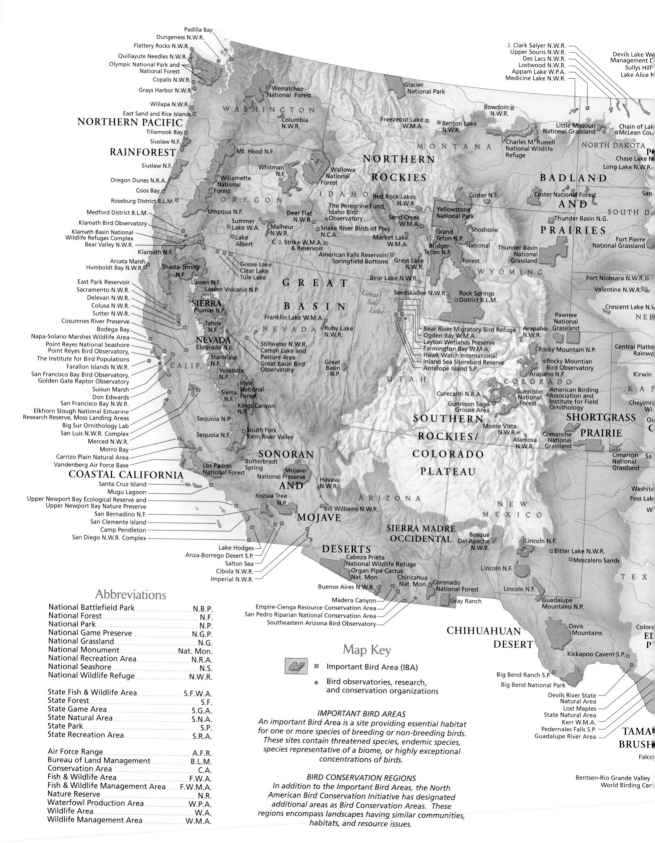

Padilla Bay
Dungeness N.W.R.
Flattery Rocks N.W.R.
Quillayute Needles N.W.R.
Olympic National Park and National Forest
Copalis N.W.R.
Grays Harbor N.W.R.
Willapa N.W.R.
East Sand and Rice Islands

NORTHERN PACIFIC

Tillamook Bay
Siuslaw N.F.

RAINFOREST

Siuslaw N.F.
Oregon Dunes N.R.A.
Coos Bay
Roseburg District B.L.M.
Medford District B.L.M.
Klamath Bird Observatory
Klamath Basin National Wildlife Refuges Complex
Bear Valley N.W.R.
Klamath N.F.
Arcata Marsh
Humboldt Bay N.W.R.
East Park Reservoir
Sacramento N.W.R.
Delevan N.W.R.
Colusa N.W.R.
Sutter N.W.R.
Cosumnes River Preserve
Bodega Bay
Napa-Solano Marshes Wildlife Area
Point Reyes National Seashore
Point Reyes Bird Observatory,
The Institute for Bird Populations
Farallon Islands N.W.R.
San Francisco Bay Bird Observatory,
Golden Gate Raptor Observatory
Suisun Marsh
Don Edwards
San Francisco Bay N.W.R.
Elkhorn Slough National Estuarine
Research Reserve, Moss Landing Areas
Big Sur Ornithology Lab
San Luis N.W.R. Complex
Merced N.W.R.
Morro Bay
Carrizo Plain Natural Area
Vandenberg Air Force Base

COASTAL CALIFORNIA

Santa Cruz Island
Mugu Lagoon
Upper Newport Bay Ecological Reserve and
Upper Newport Bay Nature Preserve
San Bernadino N.F.
San Clemente Island
Camp Pendleton
San Diego N.W.R. Complex

Lake Hodges
Anza-Borrego Desert S.P.
Salton Sea
Cibola N.W.R.
Imperial N.W.R.

WASHINGTON

Wenatchee National Forest
Columbia N.W.R.

Mt. Hood N.F.
Whitman N.F.
Willamette National Forest

OREGON

Umpqua N.F.
Summer Lake W.A.
Lake Albert
Malheur N.W.R.
C. J. Strike W.M.A. & Reservoir

Shasta-Trinity N.F.
Lassen N.F.
Lassen Volcanic N.P.

SIERRA

Plumas N.F.
Goose Lake
Clear Lake
Tule Lake

Tahoe N.F.

NEVADA
Eldorado N.F.

Stanislaus N.F.
Yosemite N.P.

CALIF.

Sierra N.F.

Inyo National Forest

Kings Canyon N.P.

Sequoia N.P.

Sequoia N.F.
South Fork Kern River Valley

SONORAN

Los Padres National Forest
Butterbredt Spring
Mojave National Preserve

AND

Joshua Tree N.P.

MOJAVE

DESERTS

GREAT

BASIN

NEVADA

Franklin Lake W.M.A.
Ruby Lake N.W.R.

Stillwater N.W.R.
Carson Lake and Pasture Area
Great Basin Bird Observatory

Great Basin N.P.

Glacier National Park

MONTANA

Freezeout Lake W.M.A.
Benton Lake N.W.R.

Charles M. Russell National Wildlife Refuge

Bowdoin N.W.R.

NORTHERN

ROCKIES

IDAHO

Red Rock Lakes N.W.R.

The Peregrine Fund, Idaho Bird Observatory
Snake River Birds of Prey N.C.A.
Deer Flat N.W.R.
Sand Creek W.M.A.
Market Lake W.M.A.
American Falls Reservoir/ Springfield Bottoms
Grays Lake N.W.R.
Bear Lake N.W.R.

Yellowstone National Park

Custer N.F.

Shoshone

Grand Teton National Park
Bridger-Teton N.F.

WYOMING

Great Salt Lake
Seedskadee N.W.R.

Rock Springs District B.L.M.

Bear River Migratory Bird Refuge
Ogden Bay W.M.A.
Layton Wetlands Preserve
Farmington Bay W.M.A.
Hawk Watch International
Inland Sea Shorebird Reserve
Antelope Island S.P.

UTAH

Curecanti N.R.A.
Gunnison Sage-Grouse Area

Monte Vista N.W.R.
Alamosa N.W.R.

SOUTHERN

ROCKIES/

COLORADO

PLATEAU

ARIZONA

NEW MEXICO

SIERRA MADRE OCCIDENTAL

Bosque Del Apache N.W.R.

Havasu N.W.R.

Bill Williams N.W.R.

Cabeza Prieta National Wildlife Refuge
Organ Pipe Cactus Nat. Mon.
Chiricahua Nat. Mon.
Buenos Aires N.W.R.
Coronado National Forest

Madera Canyon
Empire-Cienga Resource Conservation Area
San Pedro Riparian National Conservation Area
Southeastern Arizona Bird Observatory

Gray Ranch

Lincoln N.F.
Bitter Lake N.W.R.
Mescalero Sands

Lincoln N.F.
Lincoln N.F.

NORTH DAKOTA

J. Clark Salyer N.W.R.
Upper Souris N.W.R.
Des Lacs N.W.R.
Lostwood N.W.R.
Appam Lake W.P.A.
Medicine Lake N.W.R.

Devils Lake W Management D
Sullys Hill
Lake Alice N

Chain of Lak
McLean Cou

Little Missouri National Grassland

Custer National Forest
Thunder Basin N.G.

BADLAND

AND

PRAIRIES

Chase Lake N
Long Lake N.W.R.

SOUTH DA

Fort Pierre National Grassland

Thunder Basin National Grassland

Fort Niobrara N.W.R.

Valentine N.W.R.

NEB

Crescent Lake N.

Pawnee National Grassland

Arapaho N.W.R.
Rocky Mountain N.P.
Rocky Mountian Bird Observatory

COLORADO

Arapaho N.F.

American Birding Association and Institute for Field Ornithology

Gunnison National Forest

Comanche National Grassland

SHORTGRASS PRAIRIE

Central Platte
Rainwa

Kirwin

KAN

Cheyenne
Qu

Cimarron National Grassland

Washita
Foss Lak

TEX

CHIHUAHUAN

DESERT

Davis Mountains

Kickapoo Cavern S.P.

Colora
El
P

Big Bend Ranch S.P.
Big Bend National Park

Devils River State Natural Area
Lost Maples State Natural Area
Kerr W.M.A.
Pedernales Falls S.P.
Guadalupe River Area

Guadalupe Mountains N.P.

TAMA
BRUSH

Falco

Bentsen-Rio Grande Valley
World Birding Cen

Abbreviations

National Battlefield Park .... N.B.P.
National Forest .... N.F.
National Park .... N.P.
National Game Preserve .... N.G.P.
National Grassland .... N.G.
National Monument .... Nat. Mon.
National Recreation Area .... N.R.A.
National Seashore .... N.S.
National Wildlife Refuge .... N.W.R.

State Fish & Wildlife Area .... S.F.W.A.
State Forest .... S.F.
State Game Area .... S.G.A.
State Natural Area .... S.N.A.
State Park .... S.P.
State Recreation Area .... S.R.A.

Air Force Range .... A.F.R.
Bureau of Land Management .... B.L.M.
Conservation Area .... C.A.
Fish & Wildlife Area .... F.W.A.
Fish & Wildlife Management Area .... F.W.M.A.
Nature Reserve .... N.R.
Waterfowl Production Area .... W.P.A.
Wildlife Area .... W.A.
Wildlife Management Area .... W.M.A.

Map Key

■ Important Bird Area (IBA)

◆ Bird observatories, research, and conservation organizations

IMPORTANT BIRD AREAS

An important Bird Area is a site providing essential habitat for one or more species of breeding or non-breeding birds. These sites contain threatened species, endemic species, species representative of a biome, or highly exceptional concentrations of birds.

BIRD CONSERVATION REGIONS

In addition to the Important Bird Areas, the North American Bird Conservation Initiative has designated additional areas as Bird Conservation Areas. These regions encompass landscapes having similar communities, habitats, and resource issues.

IMPORTANT BIRD AREAS IN THE CONTIGUOUS UNITED STATES

Upper St. John River Project
Baxter S.P.
MAINE
Northeast Coastal Maine
Acadia N.P.
Waters around Machias Seal Island
Merrymeeting Bay

ATLANTIC NORTHERN FOREST

Mount Mansfield
VT.
White Mountain N.F.
Green Mtn. N.F.
N.H.

Parker River N.W.R.
Crane Beach
Manomet Center for Conservation Sciences

MASS.
Cape Cod N.S.
Monomoy N.W.R.
Nantucket Sound
Nantucket
Martha's Vineyard
R.I.
Block Island N.W.R.
Falkner Island
Great Gull Island
Long I. Piping Plover Nesting Beaches
CONN.

Isle Royale N.P.
Lake Superior
Whitefish Point Bird Observatory
Whitefish Point N.W.R.
Hiawatha N.F.
Seney N.W.R.

Superior National Forest
Apostle Islands
Hawk Ridge N.R.
McGregor Marsh Scientific & Natural Area
Lake N.W.R.
Crex Meadows Wildlife Area
Nicolet National Forest

BOREAL HARDWOOD TRANSITION

MINESOTA
WISCONSIN
PRAIRIE HARDWOOD TRANSITION

National Eagle Center
Trempealeau N.W.R.
Upper Mississippi River National Wildlife Refuge & Army Corps of Engineers lands
International Crane Foundation
Horicon Marsh

Lake Huron
Lake Michigan
MICHIGAN
Allegan S.G.A. & Kalamazoo River
Rouge River Bird Observatory
Detroit River/Lake Erie
Maumee Bay
Cedar Point N.W.R.
Ottawa N.W.R.
Black Swamp Bird Observatory
Lake St. Clair
Sandusky Bay

Lake Huron
Saginaw Bay
Kirtland's Warbler Management Area

Derby Hill Bird Observatory
Hamlin Beach S.P.
Braddock Bay Bird Observatory
Niagara River Corridor
NEW YORK
Montezuma N.W.R.
Kestrel Haven Farm Avian Migration Observatory
Cornell Lab of Ornithology
Roger Tory Peterson Institute
L. Ontario

LOWER GREAT LAKES/ ST. LAWRENCE PLAIN

Adirondack Park

IOWA
Upper Mississippi River N.W.R. & U.S. Army Corps of Engineers Lands
Goose L. Prairie
Chicagoland Bird Observatory
LaSalle Lake
Mark Twain N.W.R. & U.S. Army Corps of Engineers Lands
Marshall S.F.W.A.
Jasper-Pulaski F.W.A.

L. Erie
PENN.
Allegheny N.F.
Sandy Hook Bay Complex
Hawk Mt. Sanctuary
Conowingo Dam
N.J.

NEW ENGLAND/ MID-ATLANTIC COAST

Edwin B. Forsythe N.W.R.
Fortescue & Egg Island
Cape May N.W.R.
Cape May Bird Observatory
Cape May & Higbee Beach W.M.A.
Cape Henlopen
Prime Hook N.W.R.
Blackwater N.W.R.

EASTERN TALLGRASS PRAIRIE
Rice Lake S.F.W.A.
Chautauqua N.W.R.
ILLINOIS
Lake Shelbyville F.W.M.A.

OHIO
INDIANA
Chipper Woods Bird Observatory
Morgan-Monroe S.F.
Yellowwood S.F.
Brown County S.F.
Big Oaks N.W.R.
Hoosier N.F.
Wayne N.F.

Mt. Zion-Piney Tract
Bombay Hook N.W.R.
Little Creek W.A.
Ted Harvey W.A.
Eastern Neck N.W.R.
DEL.
MD.

Swan Lake
Clarence Cannon N.W.R.
Pere Marquette S.P.
Mark Twain N.F.
Carlyle Lake
Reclaimed Coal Mine Grasslands
Rend Lake

Prairie Ridge Natural Area
John Redmond Reservoir
Hills Grass Area
MISSOURI
Mark Twain N.F.
Shawnee N.F.
Lower Cache River Complex
KENTUCKY
Daniel Boone N.F.

ABC, The Plains
The Nature Conservancy
Jug Bay
Monongahela N.F.
George Washington N.F.
Shenandoah N.P.
VIRGINIA
W.VA.

Prime Hook N.W.R.
Blackwater N.W.R.
Assateague Island National Seashore
Chincoteague N.W.R.
Smith Island N.W.R.
Virginia Coast Reserve
Coastal Virginia Wildlife Observatory
Kiptopeke S.P.
Fisherman Island N.W.R.
Great Dismal Swamp N.W.R.

CENTRAL HARDWOODS

George M. Sutton Avian Research Center
Mark Twain N.F.
Trail of Tears S.F.
Mingo N.W.R.
Ozark N.F.

CENTRAL HARDWOODS
Reelfoot Lake
Fort Campbell
Cherokee N.F.
Great Smoky Mts. National Park
Pisgah N.F.
Jefferson N.F.
Piney Grove Preserve
Roanoke River Floodplain & Wetlands
Roanoke River N.W.R.
Fort Bragg
NORTH CAROLINA

Pocosin Lakes & Pungo N.W.R.
Alligator River N.W.R.
Nags Head Woods
Pea Island N.W.R.
Dare County Air Force Range
Cape Hatteras National Seashore
Mattamuskeet N.W.R.
Cape Lookout National Seashore
Swanquarter N.W.R.
Croatan N.F.

ARKANSAS
White River N.W.R.
Big Lake N.W.R.
Memphis Earth Complex
Wheeler N.W.R.
William B. Bankhead N.F.
Talladega N.F.
TENNESSEE
Chattahoochee N.F.
Kennesaw Mt.
U.S. Army Corps of Engineers Savannah Spoil Area
Nantahala N.F.
Cherokee N.F.
Sumter N.F.

PIEDMONT
SOUTH CAROLINA
Carolina Sandhills N.W.R.
Congaree Swamp N.W.R.
Francis Beidler Forest
Francis Marion N.F.
Santee Coastal Reserve
Cape Romain N.W.R.
Tom Yawkey Wildlife Center
ACE Basin

Ouachita N.F.
County Wilderness Area
Ouachita N.F.
WEST GULF
COASTAL PLAIN/
OUACHITAS

MISSISSIPPI
Noxubee N.W.R.
Yazoo N.W.R.
Delta N.F.
Bienville N.F.
Tensas River N.W.R.
Felsenthal N.W.R.
Caddo Lake

ALABAMA
GEORGIA
Talladega N.F.
Piedmont N.W.R. &
Hitchiti Experimental Forest
Fort Benning

MISSISSIPPI ALLUVIAL VALLEY
SOUTHEASTERN COASTAL PLAIN

Fort Stewart
Wolf Island N.W.R.
Little Egg Island Bar &
Little St. Simons Island
Cumberland Island National Seashore
Pinhook Swamp

Okefenokee N.W.R.
Osceola National Forest

Angelina N.F.
Kisatchie N.F.
Catahoula N.W.R.
Fort Polk
LOUISIANA
Atchafalaya N.W.R.
Sabine N.W.R.
Lacassine N.W.R.
Delta N.W.R.
L. Pontchartrain
Causeway

Big Thicket National Preserve
Jones S.F.
Sea Rim S.P.
Bolivar Flats Shorebird Sanctuary
Brazoria N.W.R.
San Bernard N.W.R.
Big Boggy N.W.R.
Mad Island Marsh Complex

Blackwater River S.F.
Elgin Air Force Base
Ochlockonee River S.P.
St. Marks N.W.R.
Apalachicola N.F.
Dog I.
Gulf Islands N.S.

Breton N.W.R./
Chandeleur Islands
Gulf Islands National Seashore
Gulf Coast Least Tern Colony
Mississippi Sandhill Crane N.W.R.
Pascagoula River W.M.A.
Dauphin Island
Ft. Morgan Historical Park
Bon Secour N.W.R.

Lower Suwannee N.W.R.
Cedar Key Scrub State Reserve
Cedar Keys N.W.R.
Lake Apopka Restoration Area
Honeymoon Island S.R.A.
Cross Bar Ranch Wellfield &
Al-Bar Ranch
Archbold Biological Station &
Lake Placid Scrub Preserve

Ocala N.F.
FLORIDA
Avon Park A.F.R.
Canaveral National Seashore
Merritt Island N.W.R.
Cape Canaveral Air Force Station
Three Lakes W.M.A.
St. Sebastian River State Buffer Preserve

PENINSULAR FLORIDA
Jonathan Dickinson S.P.
Belle Glade Area
Arthur R. Marshall
Loxahatchee N.W.R.
Lake Okeechobee

GULF COASTAL
PRAIRIE
Matagorda Island W.M.A. & S.P.
Matagorda Island
Aransas N.W.R.
Hazel Bazemore Park
Padre Island National Seashore &
South Padre Island Preserve
Kenedy Ranch
King Ranch
Laguna Atascosa N.W.R.
Sabal Palm Grove Sanctuary
Rio Grande Valley Bird Observatory
Santa Ana and Lower Rio Grande
National Wildlife Refuges

Corkscrew Swamp
Florida Panther N.W.R.
Marco Island
Everglades National Park
Great White Heron N.W.R.
Dry Tortugas N.P.
Key West N.W.R.
Big Cypress National Preserve
Key Largo Hammocks State Botanical Site
Crocodile Lake N.W.R.
John Pennekamp Coral Reef S.P.
National Key Deer Refuge
Torchwood Hammock Preserve
& Terrestris Preserve

STATUTE MILES
0   100   200   300   400

0   100   200   300   400
KILOMETERS

Source: American Bird Conservancy (in partnership with the National Geographic Society)

427

RANGE MAPS

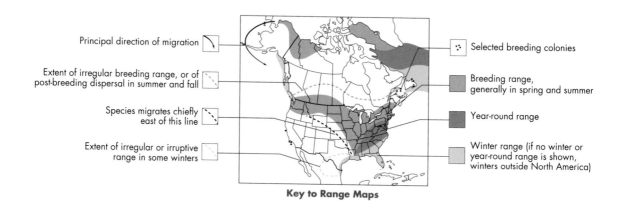

Principal direction of migration

Extent of irregular breeding range, or of post-breeding dispersal in summer and fall

Species migrates chiefly east of this line

Extent of irregular or irruptive range in some winters

Selected breeding colonies

Breeding range, generally in spring and summer

Year-round range

Winter range (if no winter or year-round range is shown, winters outside North America)

Key to Range Maps

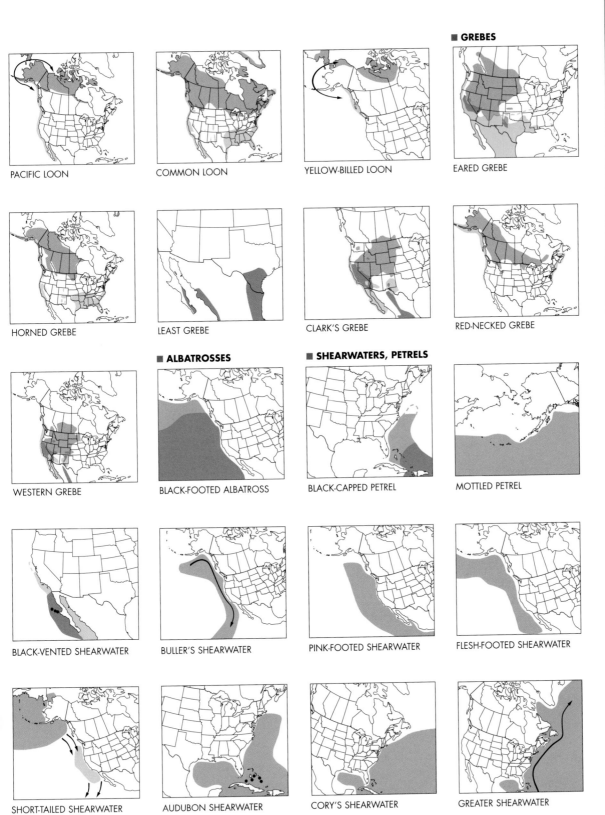

PACIFIC LOON

COMMON LOON

YELLOW-BILLED LOON

■ **GREBES**

EARED GREBE

HORNED GREBE

LEAST GREBE

CLARK'S GREBE

RED-NECKED GREBE

WESTERN GREBE

■ **ALBATROSSES**

BLACK-FOOTED ALBATROSS

■ **SHEARWATERS, PETRELS**

BLACK-CAPPED PETREL

MOTTLED PETREL

BLACK-VENTED SHEARWATER

BULLER'S SHEARWATER

PINK-FOOTED SHEARWATER

FLESH-FOOTED SHEARWATER

SHORT-TAILED SHEARWATER

AUDUBON SHEARWATER

CORY'S SHEARWATER

GREATER SHEARWATER

429

MANX SHEARWATER

LEACH'S STORM-PETREL

ASHY STORM-PETREL

BAND-RUMPED STORM PETREL

■ **BOOBIES**

BLACK STORM-PETREL

FORK-TAILED STORM-PETREL

LEAST STORM-PETREL

BLUE-FOOTED BOOBY

■ **PELICANS**

■ **CORMORANTS**

BROWN BOOBY

MASKED BOOBY

AMERICAN WHITE PELICAN

GREAT CORMORANT

NEOTROPIC CORMORANT

BRANDT'S CORMORANT

PELAGIC CORMORANT

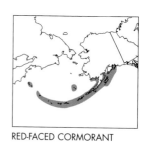

RED-FACED CORMORANT

■ **HERONS, BITTERNS, EGRETS**

AMERICAN BITTERN

BLACK-CROWNED
NIGHT-HERON

LEAST BITTERN

YELLOW-CROWNED
NIGHT-HERON

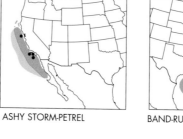

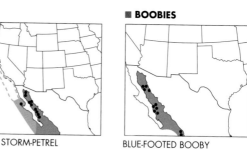

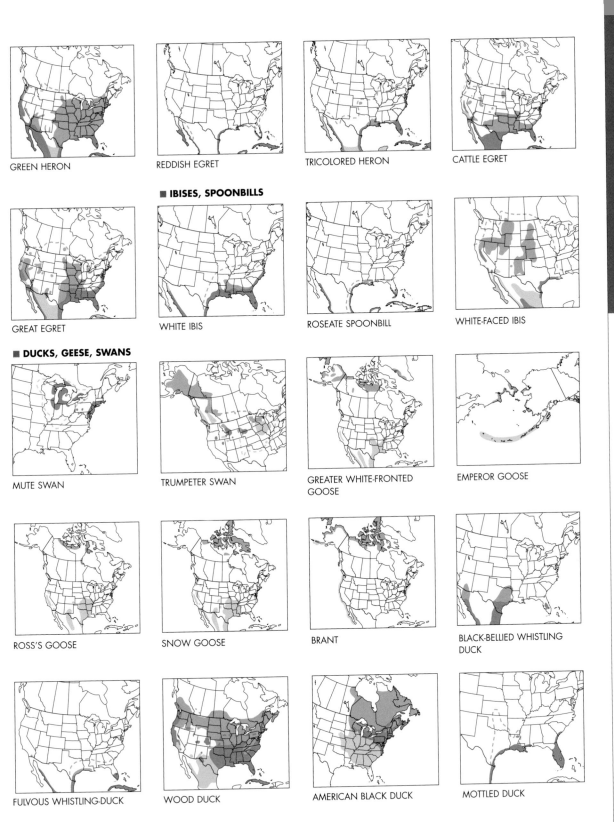

GREEN HERON

REDDISH EGRET

TRICOLORED HERON

CATTLE EGRET

■ IBISES, SPOONBILLS

GREAT EGRET

WHITE IBIS

ROSEATE SPOONBILL

WHITE-FACED IBIS

■ DUCKS, GEESE, SWANS

MUTE SWAN

TRUMPETER SWAN

GREATER WHITE-FRONTED GOOSE

EMPEROR GOOSE

ROSS'S GOOSE

SNOW GOOSE

BRANT

BLACK-BELLIED WHISTLING DUCK

FULVOUS WHISTLING-DUCK

WOOD DUCK

AMERICAN BLACK DUCK

MOTTLED DUCK

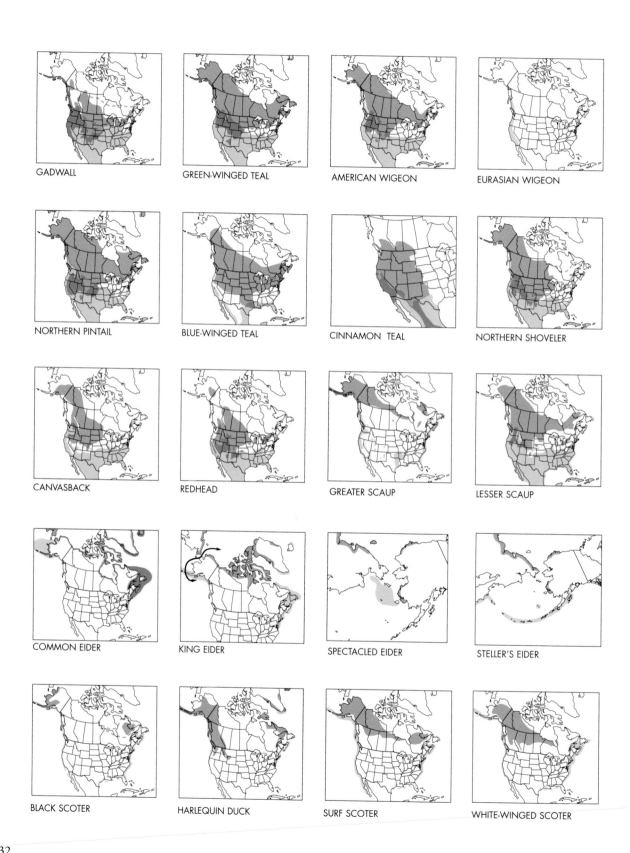

GADWALL

GREEN-WINGED TEAL

AMERICAN WIGEON

EURASIAN WIGEON

NORTHERN PINTAIL

BLUE-WINGED TEAL

CINNAMON TEAL

NORTHERN SHOVELER

CANVASBACK

REDHEAD

GREATER SCAUP

LESSER SCAUP

COMMON EIDER

KING EIDER

SPECTACLED EIDER

STELLER'S EIDER

BLACK SCOTER

HARLEQUIN DUCK

SURF SCOTER

WHITE-WINGED SCOTER

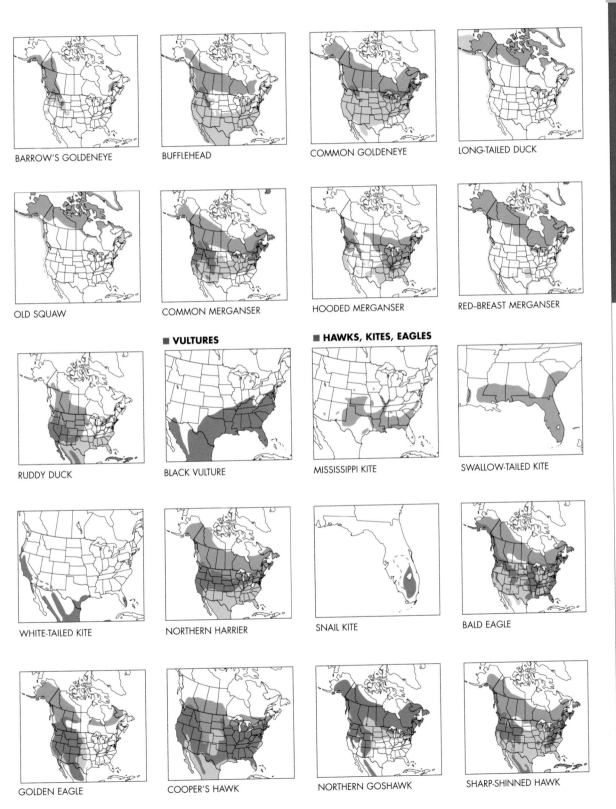

BARROW'S GOLDENEYE

BUFFLEHEAD

COMMON GOLDENEYE

LONG-TAILED DUCK

OLD SQUAW

COMMON MERGANSER

HOODED MERGANSER

RED–BREAST MERGANSER

■ **VULTURES**

■ **HAWKS, KITES, EAGLES**

RUDDY DUCK

BLACK VULTURE

MISSISSIPPI KITE

SWALLOW-TAILED KITE

WHITE-TAILED KITE

NORTHERN HARRIER

SNAIL KITE

BALD EAGLE

GOLDEN EAGLE

COOPER'S HAWK

NORTHERN GOSHAWK

SHARP-SHINNED HAWK

433

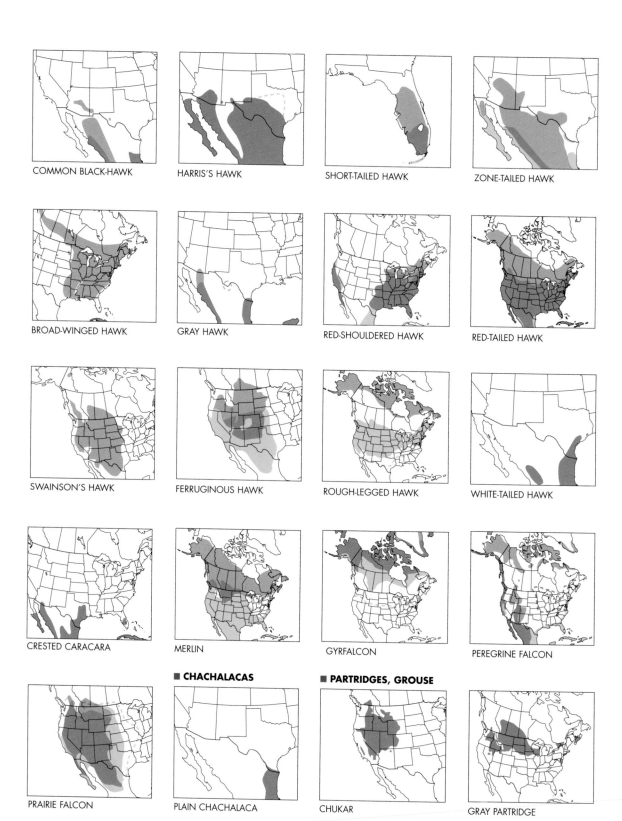

COMMON BLACK-HAWK

HARRIS'S HAWK

SHORT-TAILED HAWK

ZONE-TAILED HAWK

BROAD-WINGED HAWK

GRAY HAWK

RED-SHOULDERED HAWK

RED-TAILED HAWK

SWAINSON'S HAWK

FERRUGINOUS HAWK

ROUGH-LEGGED HAWK

WHITE-TAILED HAWK

CRESTED CARACARA

MERLIN

GYRFALCON

PEREGRINE FALCON

■ **CHACHALACAS**

■ **PARTRIDGES, GROUSE**

PRAIRIE FALCON

PLAIN CHACHALACA

CHUKAR

GRAY PARTRIDGE

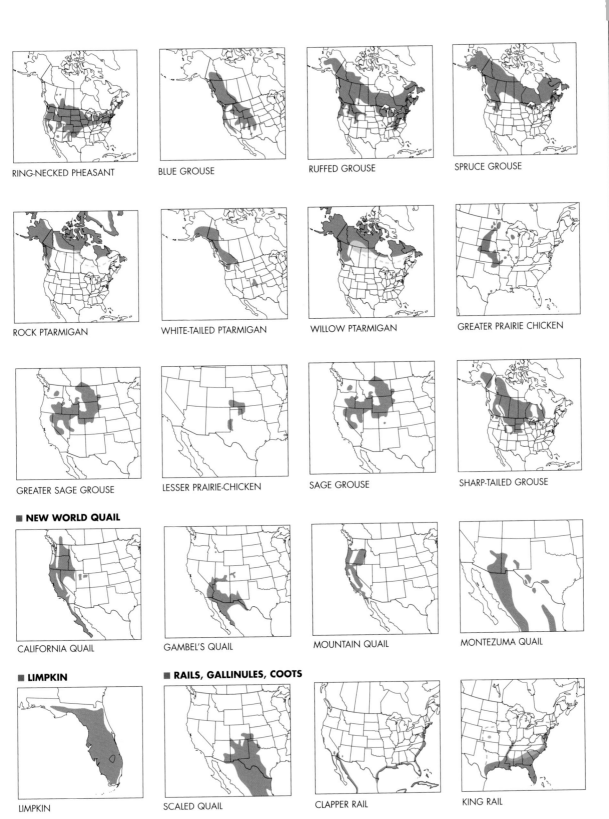

RING-NECKED PHEASANT

BLUE GROUSE

RUFFED GROUSE

SPRUCE GROUSE

ROCK PTARMIGAN

WHITE-TAILED PTARMIGAN

WILLOW PTARMIGAN

GREATER PRAIRIE CHICKEN

GREATER SAGE GROUSE

LESSER PRAIRIE-CHICKEN

SAGE GROUSE

SHARP-TAILED GROUSE

■ **NEW WORLD QUAIL**

CALIFORNIA QUAIL

GAMBEL'S QUAIL

MOUNTAIN QUAIL

MONTEZUMA QUAIL

■ **LIMPKIN**

■ **RAILS, GALLINULES, COOTS**

LIMPKIN

SCALED QUAIL

CLAPPER RAIL

KING RAIL

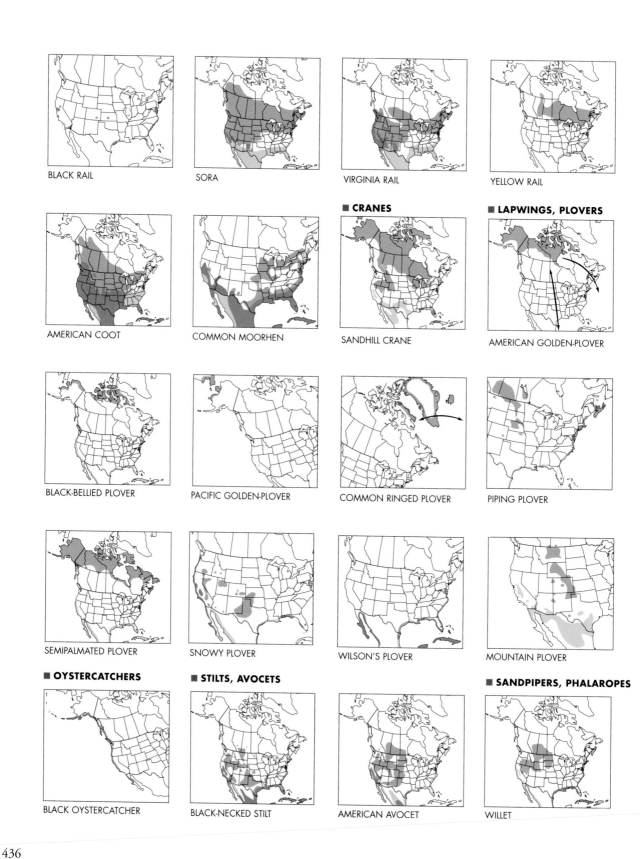

BLACK RAIL

SORA

VIRGINIA RAIL

YELLOW RAIL

AMERICAN COOT

COMMON MOORHEN

■ **CRANES**

SANDHILL CRANE

■ **LAPWINGS, PLOVERS**

AMERICAN GOLDEN-PLOVER

BLACK-BELLIED PLOVER

PACIFIC GOLDEN-PLOVER

COMMON RINGED PLOVER

PIPING PLOVER

SEMIPALMATED PLOVER

SNOWY PLOVER

WILSON'S PLOVER

MOUNTAIN PLOVER

■ **OYSTERCATCHERS**

BLACK OYSTERCATCHER

■ **STILTS, AVOCETS**

BLACK-NECKED STILT

AMERICAN AVOCET

■ **SANDPIPERS, PHALAROPES**

WILLET

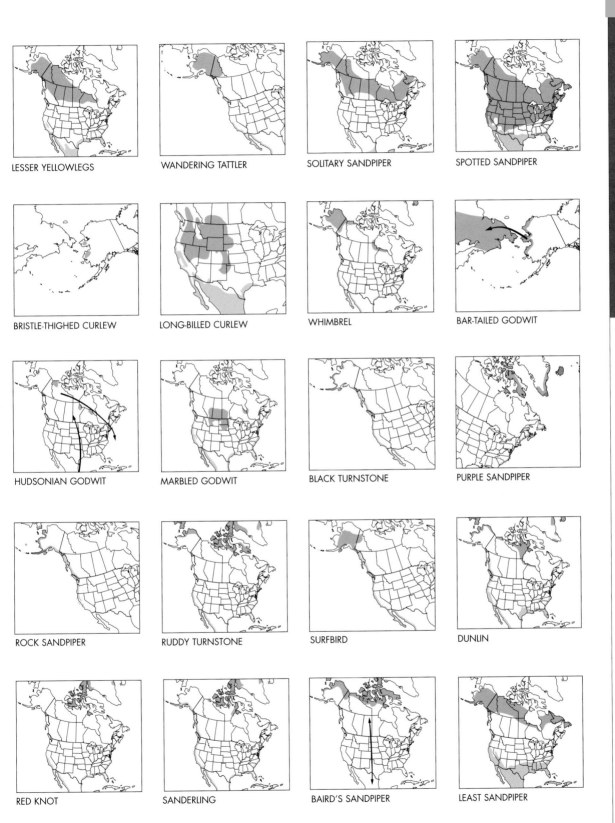

LESSER YELLOWLEGS

WANDERING TATTLER

SOLITARY SANDPIPER

SPOTTED SANDPIPER

BRISTLE-THIGHED CURLEW

LONG-BILLED CURLEW

WHIMBREL

BAR-TAILED GODWIT

HUDSONIAN GODWIT

MARBLED GODWIT

BLACK TURNSTONE

PURPLE SANDPIPER

ROCK SANDPIPER

RUDDY TURNSTONE

SURFBIRD

DUNLIN

RED KNOT

SANDERLING

BAIRD'S SANDPIPER

LEAST SANDPIPER

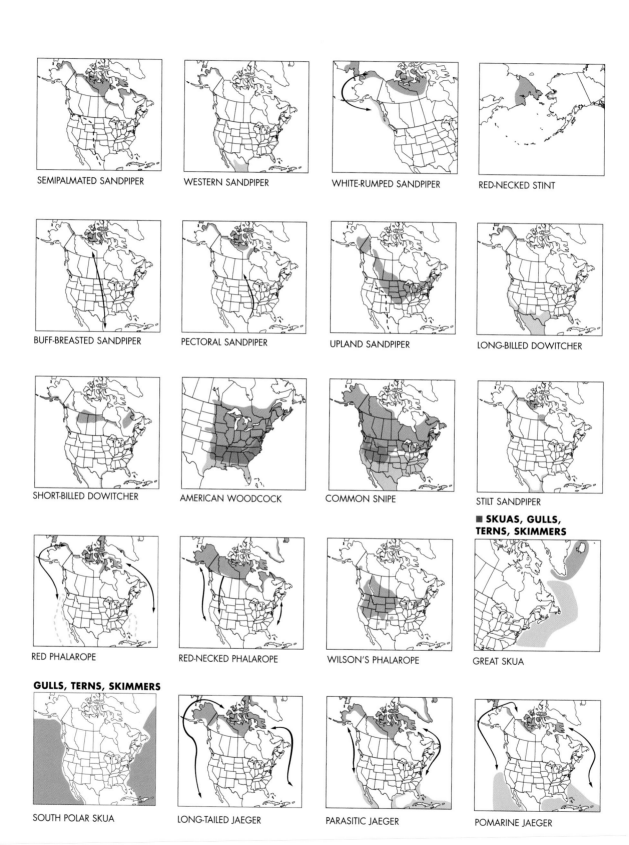

SEMIPALMATED SANDPIPER

WESTERN SANDPIPER

WHITE-RUMPED SANDPIPER

RED-NECKED STINT

BUFF-BREASTED SANDPIPER

PECTORAL SANDPIPER

UPLAND SANDPIPER

LONG-BILLED DOWITCHER

SHORT-BILLED DOWITCHER

AMERICAN WOODCOCK

COMMON SNIPE

STILT SANDPIPER

■ SKUAS, GULLS, TERNS, SKIMMERS

RED PHALAROPE

RED-NECKED PHALAROPE

WILSON'S PHALAROPE

GREAT SKUA

GULLS, TERNS, SKIMMERS

SOUTH POLAR SKUA

LONG-TAILED JAEGER

PARASITIC JAEGER

POMARINE JAEGER

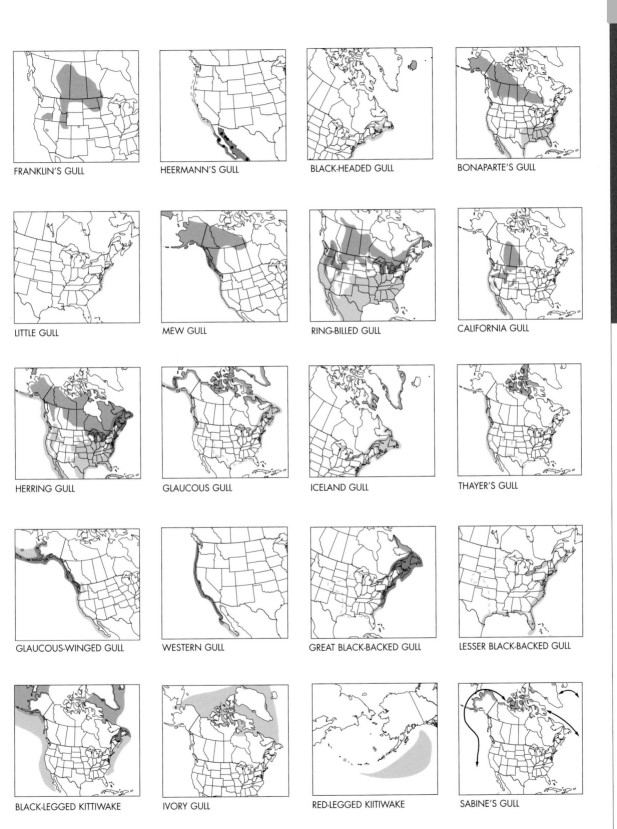

FRANKLIN'S GULL

HEERMANN'S GULL

BLACK-HEADED GULL

BONAPARTE'S GULL

LITTLE GULL

MEW GULL

RING-BILLED GULL

CALIFORNIA GULL

HERRING GULL

GLAUCOUS GULL

ICELAND GULL

THAYER'S GULL

GLAUCOUS-WINGED GULL

WESTERN GULL

GREAT BLACK-BACKED GULL

LESSER BLACK-BACKED GULL

BLACK-LEGGED KITTIWAKE

IVORY GULL

RED-LEGGED KIITIWAKE

SABINE'S GULL

439

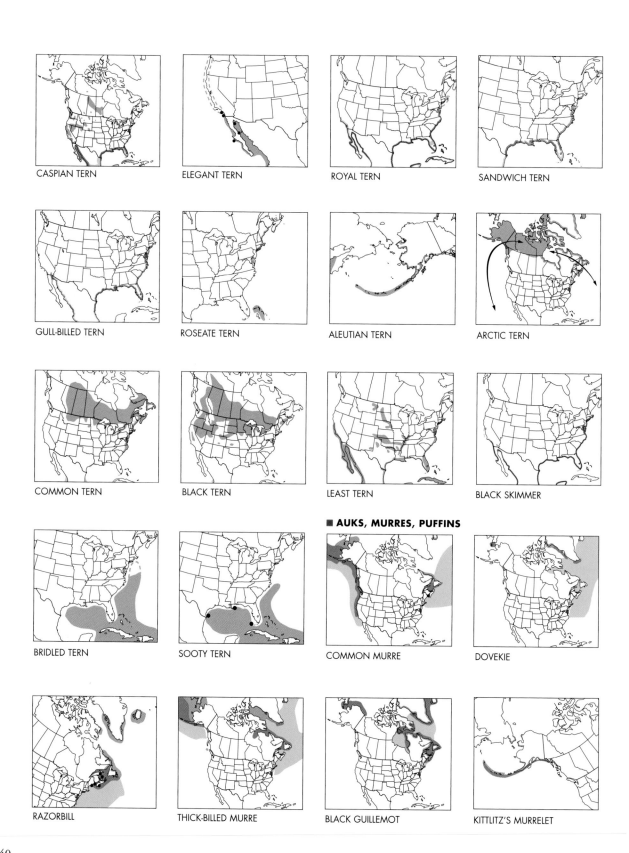

CASPIAN TERN

ELEGANT TERN

ROYAL TERN

SANDWICH TERN

GULL-BILLED TERN

ROSEATE TERN

ALEUTIAN TERN

ARCTIC TERN

COMMON TERN

BLACK TERN

LEAST TERN

BLACK SKIMMER

■ **AUKS, MURRES, PUFFINS**

BRIDLED TERN

SOOTY TERN

COMMON MURRE

DOVEKIE

RAZORBILL

THICK-BILLED MURRE

BLACK GUILLEMOT

KITTLITZ'S MURRELET

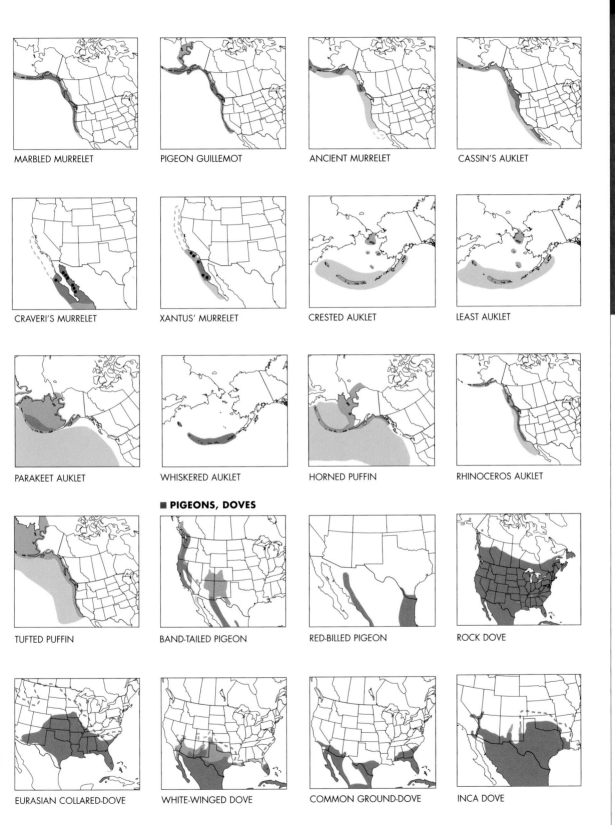

MARBLED MURRELET

PIGEON GUILLEMOT

ANCIENT MURRELET

CASSIN'S AUKLET

CRAVERI'S MURRELET

XANTUS' MURRELET

CRESTED AUKLET

LEAST AUKLET

PARAKEET AUKLET

WHISKERED AUKLET

HORNED PUFFIN

RHINOCEROS AUKLET

■ **PIGEONS, DOVES**

TUFTED PUFFIN

BAND-TAILED PIGEON

RED-BILLED PIGEON

ROCK DOVE

EURASIAN COLLARED-DOVE

WHITE-WINGED DOVE

COMMON GROUND-DOVE

INCA DOVE

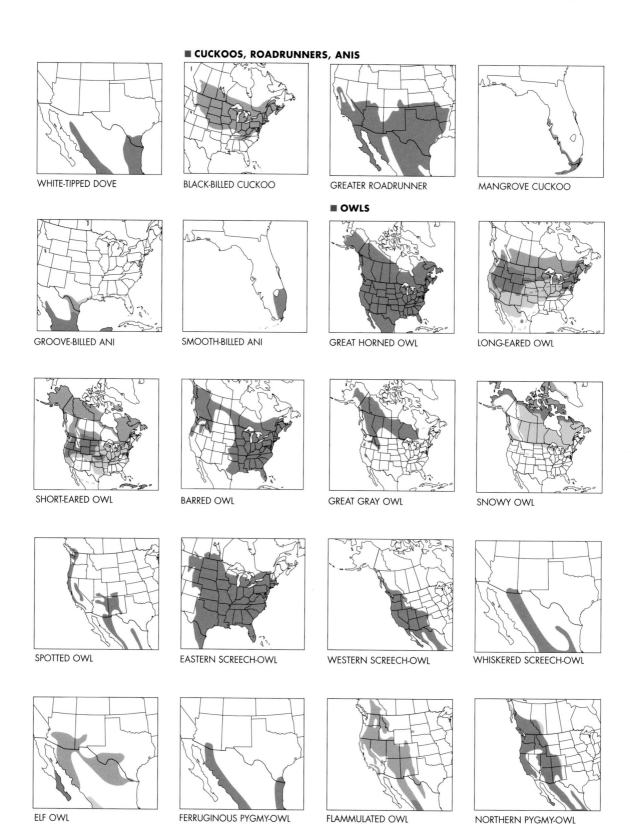

■ **CUCKOOS, ROADRUNNERS, ANIS**

WHITE-TIPPED DOVE

BLACK-BILLED CUCKOO

GREATER ROADRUNNER

MANGROVE CUCKOO

■ **OWLS**

GROOVE-BILLED ANI

SMOOTH-BILLED ANI

GREAT HORNED OWL

LONG-EARED OWL

SHORT-EARED OWL

BARRED OWL

GREAT GRAY OWL

SNOWY OWL

SPOTTED OWL

EASTERN SCREECH-OWL

WESTERN SCREECH-OWL

WHISKERED SCREECH-OWL

ELF OWL

FERRUGINOUS PYGMY-OWL

FLAMMULATED OWL

NORTHERN PYGMY-OWL

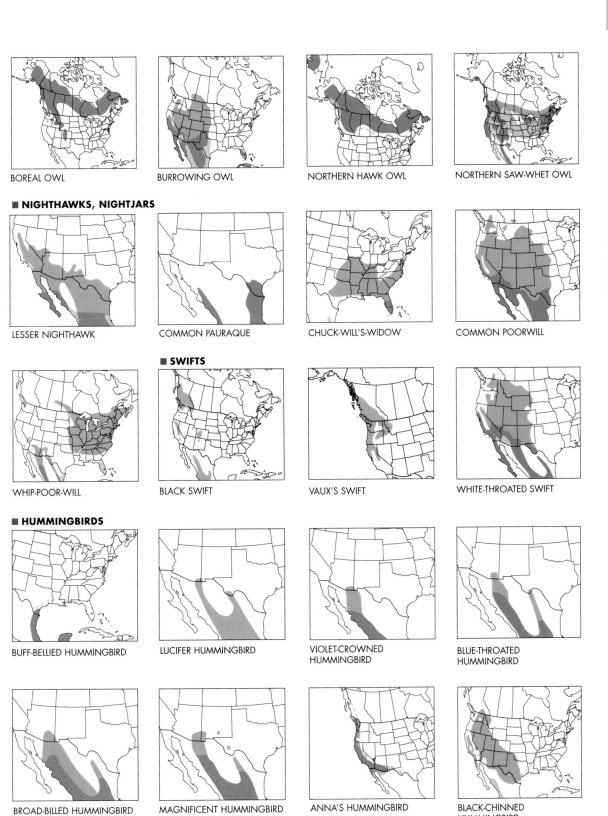

BOREAL OWL

BURROWING OWL

NORTHERN HAWK OWL

NORTHERN SAW-WHET OWL

■ NIGHTHAWKS, NIGHTJARS

LESSER NIGHTHAWK

COMMON PAURAQUE

CHUCK-WILL'S-WIDOW

COMMON POORWILL

■ SWIFTS

WHIP-POOR-WILL

BLACK SWIFT

VAUX'S SWIFT

WHITE-THROATED SWIFT

■ HUMMINGBIRDS

BUFF-BELLIED HUMMINGBIRD

LUCIFER HUMMINGBIRD

VIOLET-CROWNED
HUMMINGBIRD

BLUE-THROATED
HUMMINGBIRD

BROAD-BILLED HUMMINGBIRD

MAGNIFICENT HUMMINGBIRD

ANNA'S HUMMINGBIRD

BLACK-CHINNED
HUMMINGBIRD

443

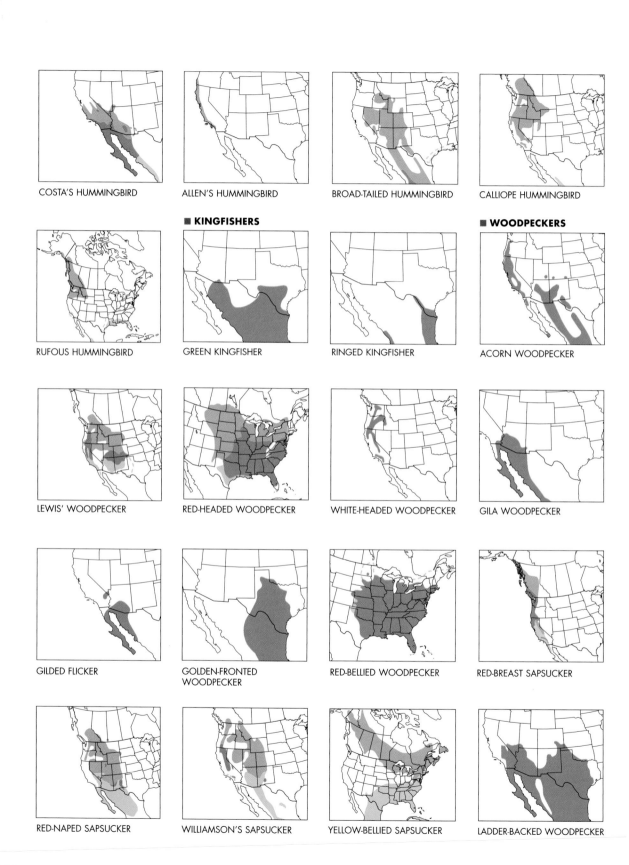

COSTA'S HUMMINGBIRD

ALLEN'S HUMMINGBIRD

BROAD-TAILED HUMMINGBIRD

CALLIOPE HUMMINGBIRD

RUFOUS HUMMINGBIRD

■ **KINGFISHERS**

GREEN KINGFISHER

RINGED KINGFISHER

■ **WOODPECKERS**

ACORN WOODPECKER

LEWIS' WOODPECKER

RED-HEADED WOODPECKER

WHITE-HEADED WOODPECKER

GILA WOODPECKER

GILDED FLICKER

GOLDEN-FRONTED WOODPECKER

RED-BELLIED WOODPECKER

RED-BREAST SAPSUCKER

RED-NAPED SAPSUCKER

WILLIAMSON'S SAPSUCKER

YELLOW-BELLIED SAPSUCKER

LADDER-BACKED WOODPECKER

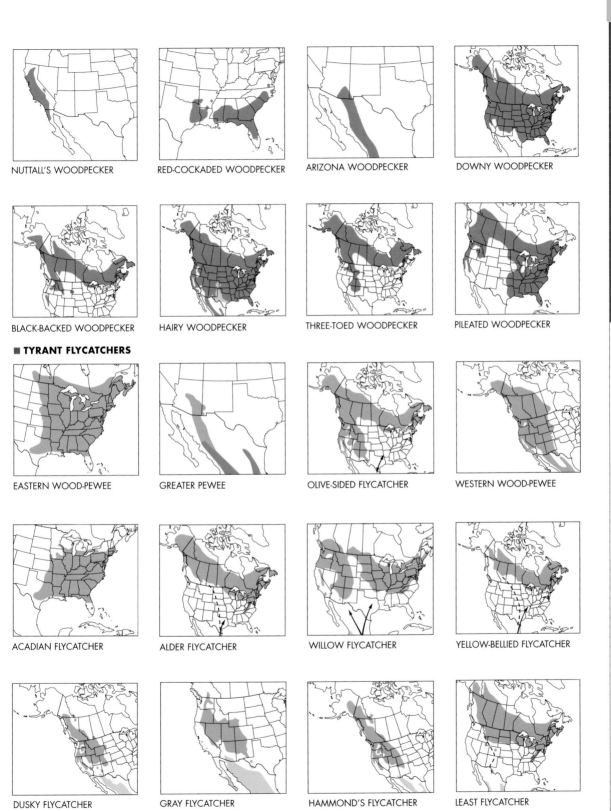

NUTTALL'S WOODPECKER

RED-COCKADED WOODPECKER

ARIZONA WOODPECKER

DOWNY WOODPECKER

BLACK-BACKED WOODPECKER

HAIRY WOODPECKER

THREE-TOED WOODPECKER

PILEATED WOODPECKER

■ **TYRANT FLYCATCHERS**

EASTERN WOOD-PEWEE

GREATER PEWEE

OLIVE-SIDED FLYCATCHER

WESTERN WOOD-PEWEE

ACADIAN FLYCATCHER

ALDER FLYCATCHER

WILLOW FLYCATCHER

YELLOW-BELLIED FLYCATCHER

DUSKY FLYCATCHER

GRAY FLYCATCHER

HAMMOND'S FLYCATCHER

LEAST FLYCATCHER

BUFF-BREASTED FLYCATCHER

CORDILLERAN FLYCATCHER

NORTHERN BEARDLESS-
TYRANNULET

PACIFIC-SLOPE FLYCATCHER

BLACK PHOEBE

EASTERN PHOEBE

SAY'S PHOEBE

VERMILION FLYCATCHER

ASH-THROATED FLYCATCHER

BROWN-CRESTED FLYCATCHER

DUSKY-CAPPED FLYCATCHER

GREAT CRESTED FLYCATCHER

CASSIN'S KINGBIRD

COUCH'S KINGBIRD

TROPICAL KINGBIRD

WESTERN KINGBIRD

GRAY KINGBIRD

THICK-BILLED KINGBIRD

GREAT KISKADEE

ROSE-THROATED BECARD

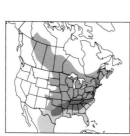

446

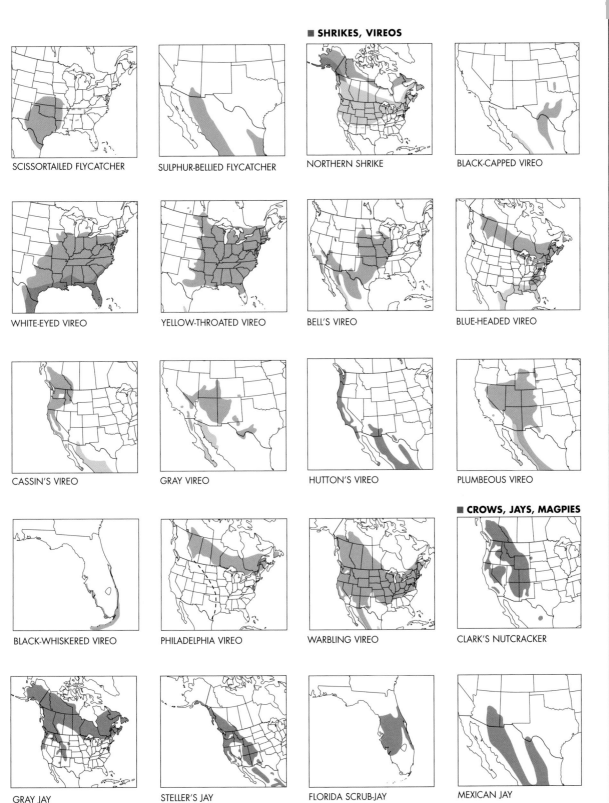

■ SHRIKES, VIREOS

SCISSORTAILED FLYCATCHER

SULPHUR-BELLIED FLYCATCHER

NORTHERN SHRIKE

BLACK-CAPPED VIREO

WHITE-EYED VIREO

YELLOW-THROATED VIREO

BELL'S VIREO

BLUE-HEADED VIREO

CASSIN'S VIREO

GRAY VIREO

HUTTON'S VIREO

PLUMBEOUS VIREO

■ CROWS, JAYS, MAGPIES

BLACK-WHISKERED VIREO

PHILADELPHIA VIREO

WARBLING VIREO

CLARK'S NUTCRACKER

GRAY JAY

STELLER'S JAY

FLORIDA SCRUB-JAY

MEXICAN JAY

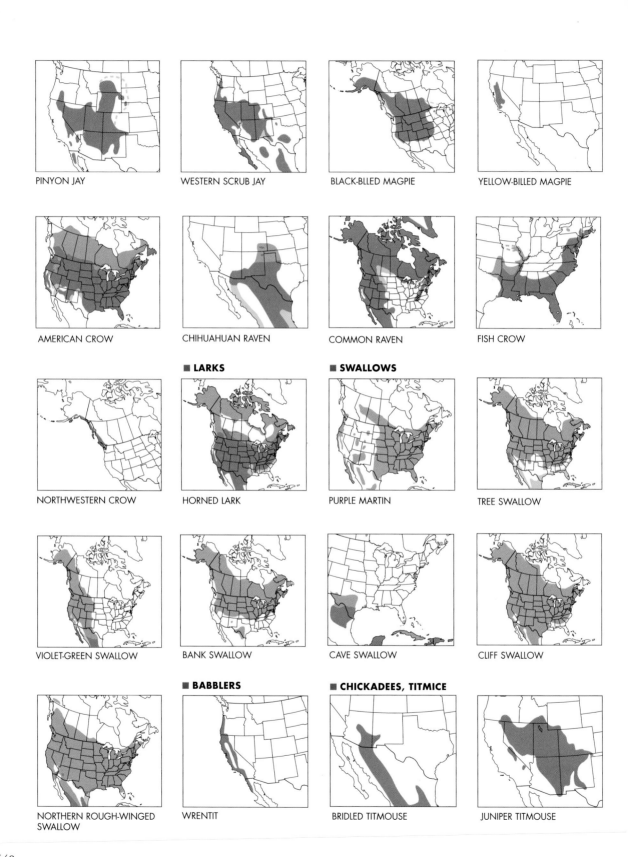

PINYON JAY

WESTERN SCRUB JAY

BLACK-BLLED MAGPIE

YELLOW-BILLED MAGPIE

AMERICAN CROW

CHIHUAHUAN RAVEN

COMMON RAVEN

FISH CROW

■ **LARKS**

■ **SWALLOWS**

NORTHWESTERN CROW

HORNED LARK

PURPLE MARTIN

TREE SWALLOW

VIOLET-GREEN SWALLOW

BANK SWALLOW

CAVE SWALLOW

CLIFF SWALLOW

■ **BABBLERS**

■ **CHICKADEES, TITMICE**

NORTHERN ROUGH-WINGED
SWALLOW

WRENTIT

BRIDLED TITMOUSE

JUNIPER TITMOUSE

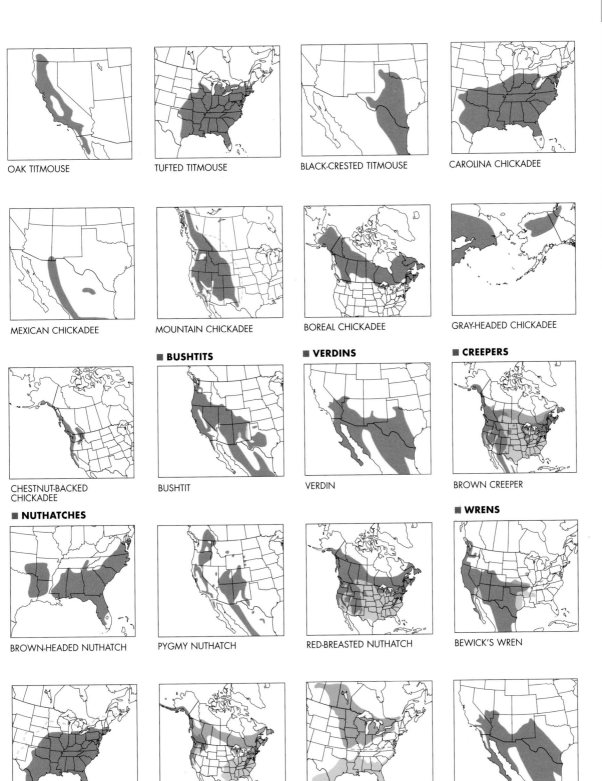

OAK TITMOUSE

TUFTED TITMOUSE

BLACK-CRESTED TITMOUSE

CAROLINA CHICKADEE

MEXICAN CHICKADEE

MOUNTAIN CHICKADEE

BOREAL CHICKADEE

GRAY-HEADED CHICKADEE

■ **BUSHTITS**

■ **VERDINS**

■ **CREEPERS**

CHESTNUT-BACKED
CHICKADEE

BUSHTIT

VERDIN

BROWN CREEPER

■ **NUTHATCHES**

■ **WRENS**

BROWN-HEADED NUTHATCH

PYGMY NUTHATCH

RED-BREASTED NUTHATCH

BEWICK'S WREN

CAROLINA WREN

WINTER WREN

SEDGE WREN

CACTUS WREN

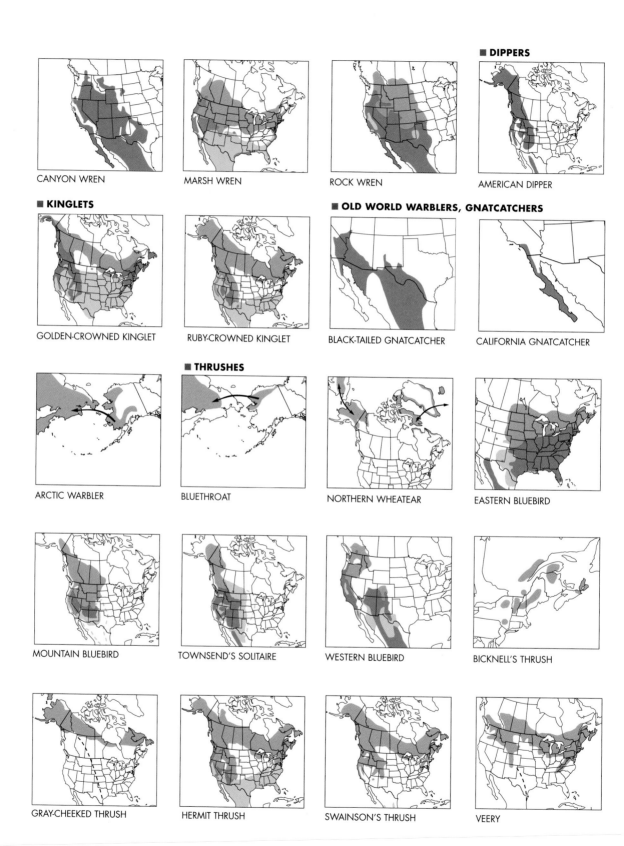

CANYON WREN

MARSH WREN

ROCK WREN

■ **DIPPERS**

AMERICAN DIPPER

■ **KINGLETS**

GOLDEN-CROWNED KINGLET

RUBY-CROWNED KINGLET

■ **OLD WORLD WARBLERS, GNATCATCHERS**

BLACK-TAILED GNATCATCHER

CALIFORNIA GNATCATCHER

■ **THRUSHES**

ARCTIC WARBLER

BLUETHROAT

NORTHERN WHEATEAR

EASTERN BLUEBIRD

MOUNTAIN BLUEBIRD

TOWNSEND'S SOLITAIRE

WESTERN BLUEBIRD

BICKNELL'S THRUSH

GRAY-CHEEKED THRUSH

HERMIT THRUSH

SWAINSON'S THRUSH

VEERY

450

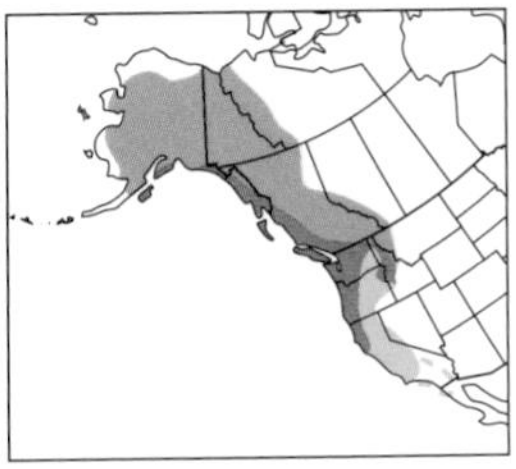

■ **MOCKINGBIRDS, THRASHERS**

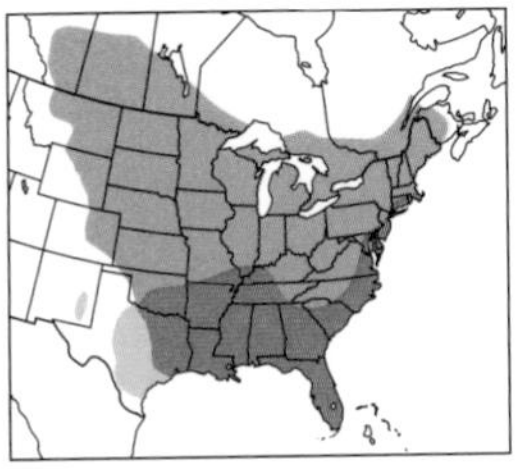

VARIED THRUSH

BROWN THRASHER

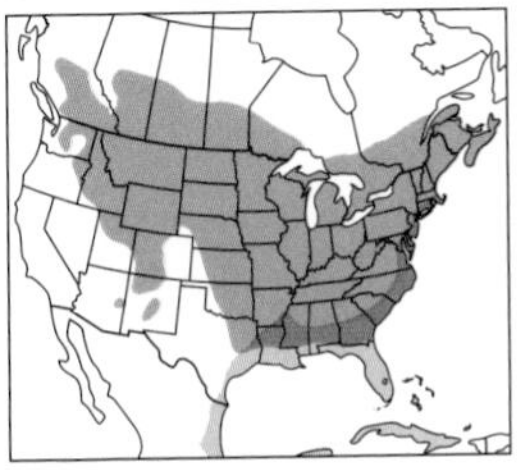

GRAY CATBIRD

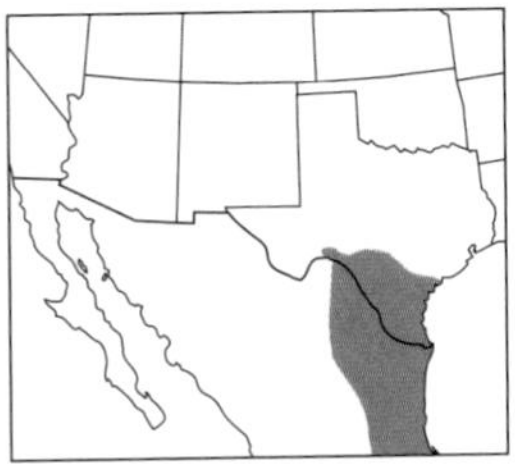

LONG-BILLED THRASHER

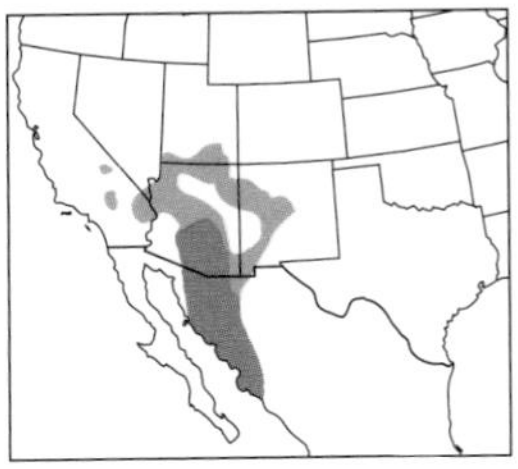

BENDIRE'S THRASHER

CALIFORNIA THRASHER

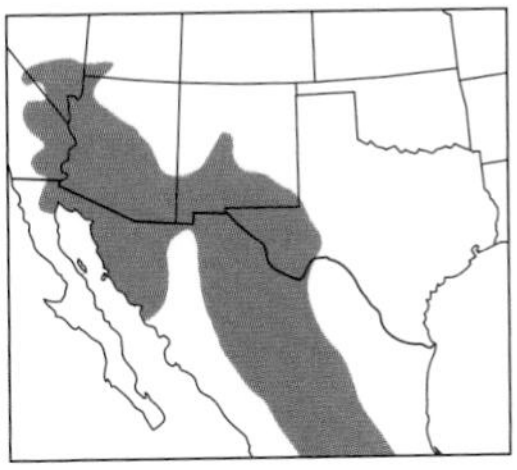

CRISSAL THRASHER

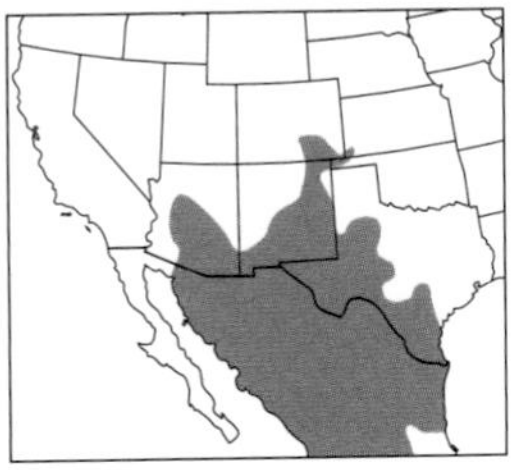

CURVE-BILLED THRASHER

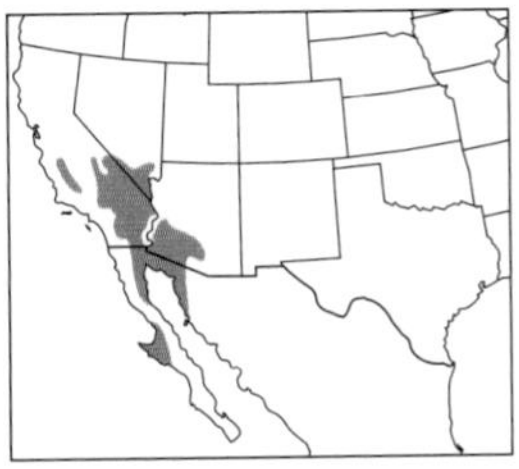

LE CONTE'S THRASHER

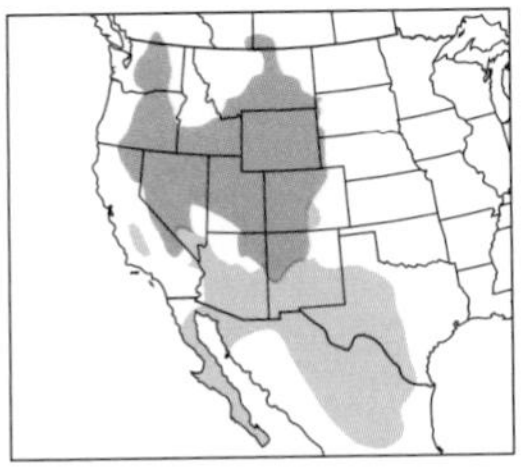

SAGE THRASHER

■ **WAGTAILS, PIPITS**

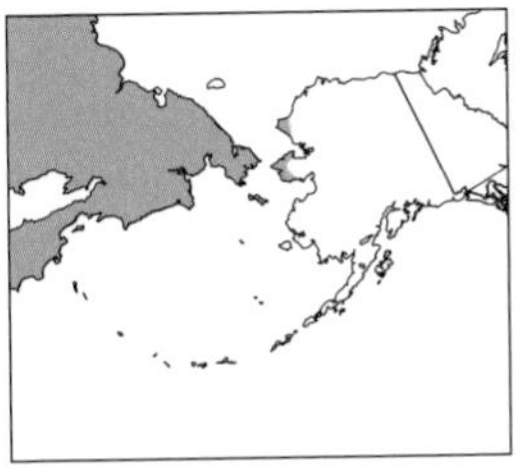

WHITE WAGTAIL

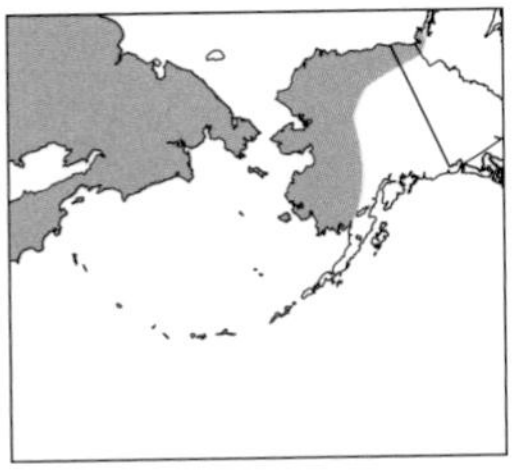

YELLOW WAGTAIL

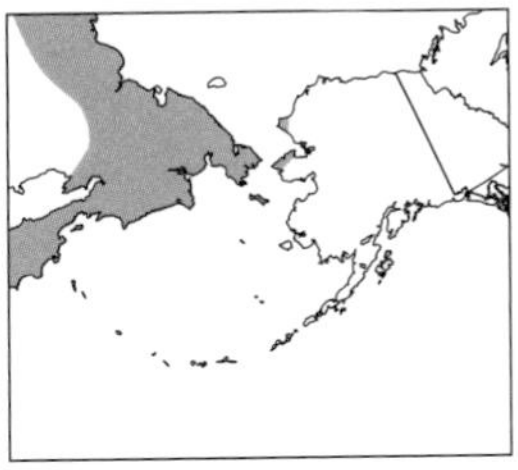

■ **WAXWINGS**

■ **SILKY-FLYCATCHERS**

RED-THROATED PIPIT

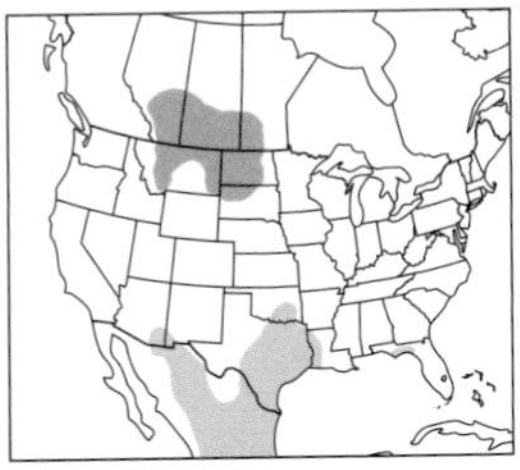

SPRAGUE'S PIPIT

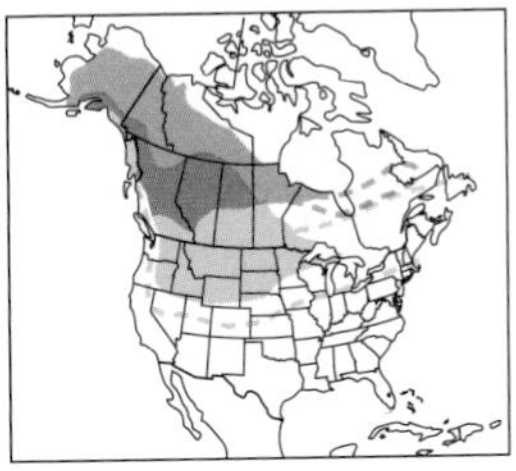

BOHEMIAN WAXWING

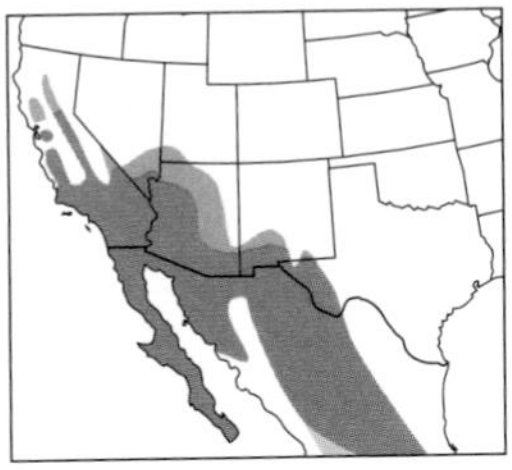

PHAINOPEPLA

■ **WOOD-WARBLERS**

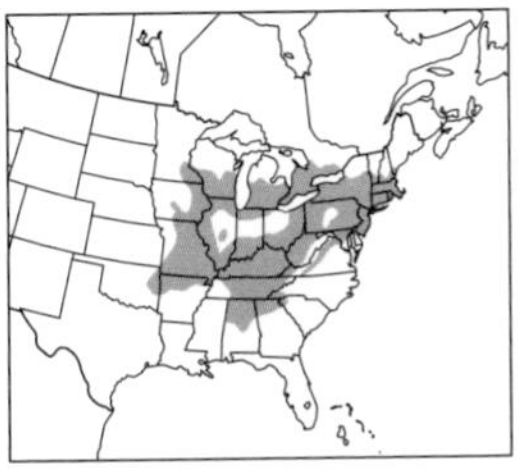

BLUE-WINGED WARBLER

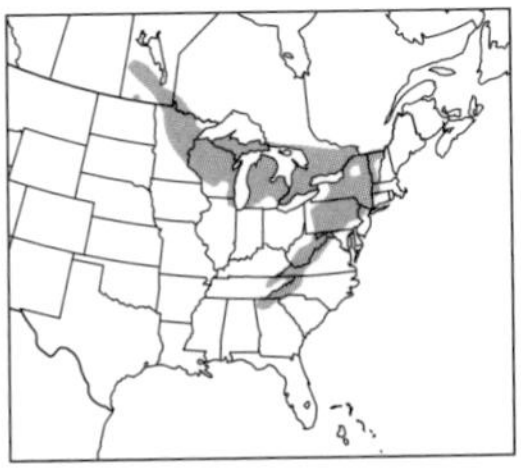

GOLDEN-WINGED WARBLER

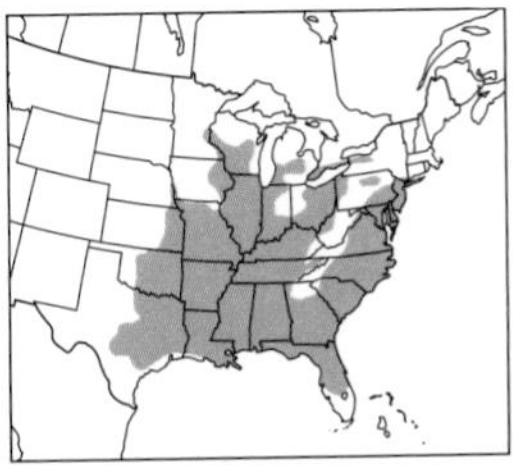

PROTHONOTARY WARBLER

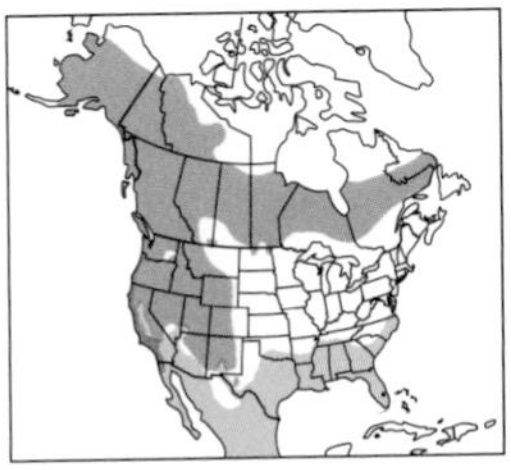

ORANGE-CROWNED WARBLER

451

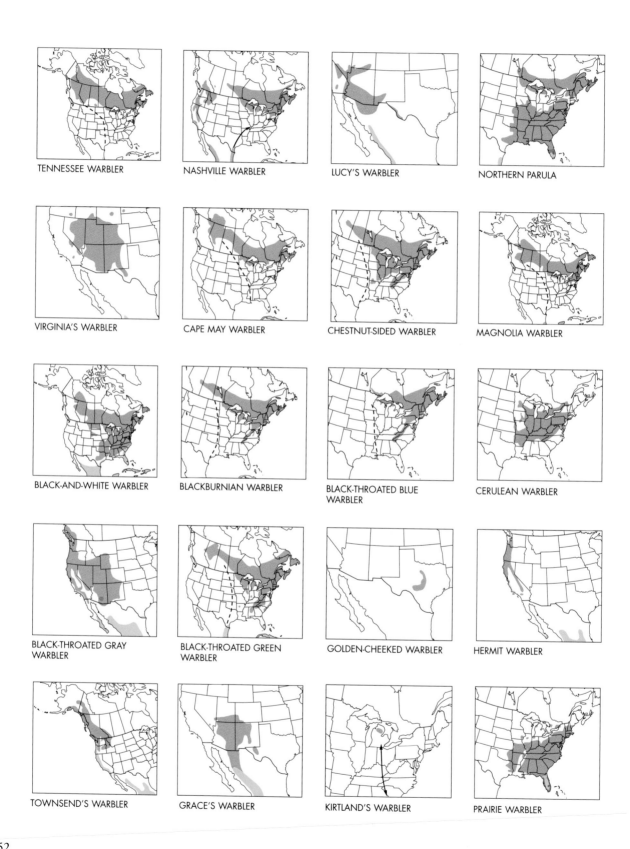

TENNESSEE WARBLER

NASHVILLE WARBLER

LUCY'S WARBLER

NORTHERN PARULA

VIRGINIA'S WARBLER

CAPE MAY WARBLER

CHESTNUT-SIDED WARBLER

MAGNOLIA WARBLER

BLACK-AND-WHITE WARBLER

BLACKBURNIAN WARBLER

BLACK-THROATED BLUE
WARBLER

CERULEAN WARBLER

BLACK-THROATED GRAY
WARBLER

BLACK-THROATED GREEN
WARBLER

GOLDEN-CHEEKED WARBLER

HERMIT WARBLER

TOWNSEND'S WARBLER

GRACE'S WARBLER

KIRTLAND'S WARBLER

PRAIRIE WARBLER

452

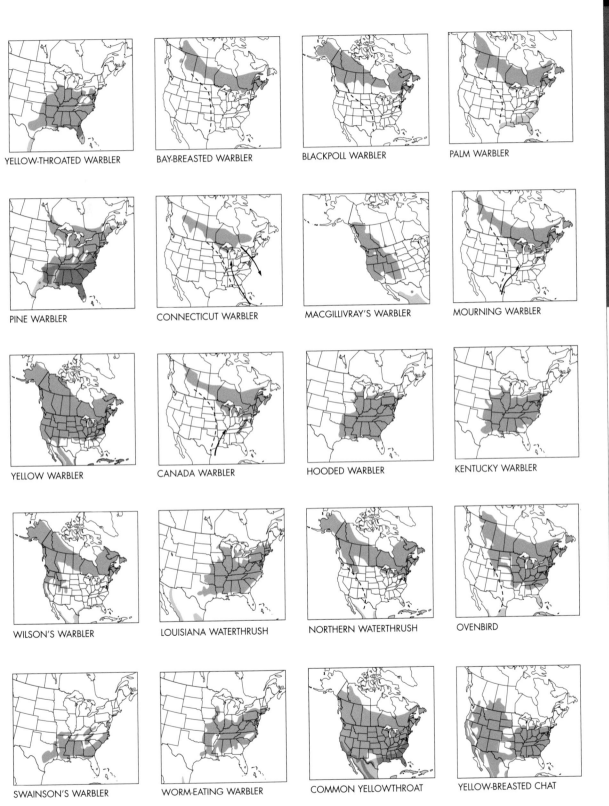

YELLOW-THROATED WARBLER

BAY-BREASTED WARBLER

BLACKPOLL WARBLER

PALM WARBLER

PINE WARBLER

CONNECTICUT WARBLER

MACGILLIVRAY'S WARBLER

MOURNING WARBLER

YELLOW WARBLER

CANADA WARBLER

HOODED WARBLER

KENTUCKY WARBLER

WILSON'S WARBLER

LOUISIANA WATERTHRUSH

NORTHERN WATERTHRUSH

OVENBIRD

SWAINSON'S WARBLER

WORM-EATING WARBLER

COMMON YELLOWTHROAT

YELLOW-BREASTED CHAT

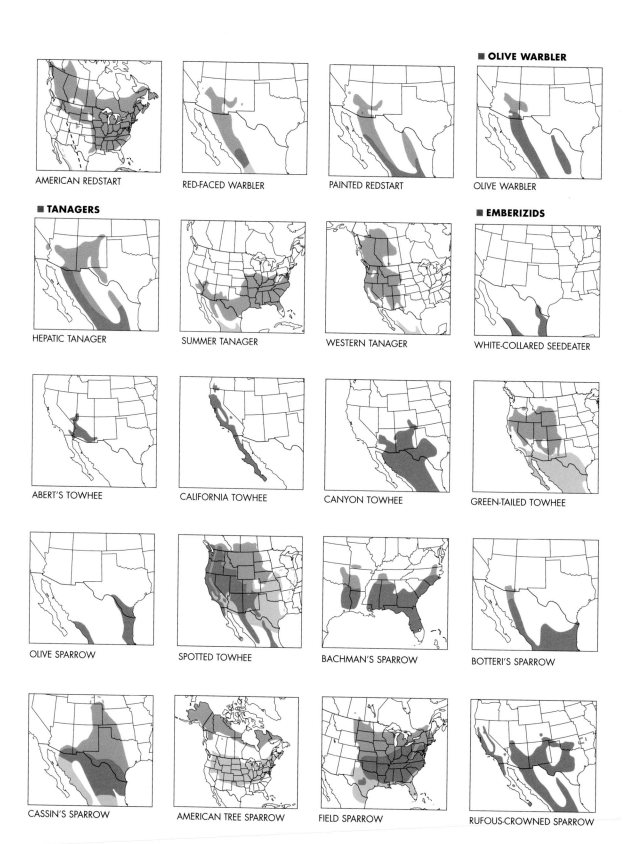

AMERICAN REDSTART

RED-FACED WARBLER

PAINTED REDSTART

■ **OLIVE WARBLER**

OLIVE WARBLER

■ **TANAGERS**

HEPATIC TANAGER

SUMMER TANAGER

WESTERN TANAGER

■ **EMBERIZIDS**

WHITE-COLLARED SEEDEATER

ABERT'S TOWHEE

CALIFORNIA TOWHEE

CANYON TOWHEE

GREEN-TAILED TOWHEE

OLIVE SPARROW

SPOTTED TOWHEE

BACHMAN'S SPARROW

BOTTERI'S SPARROW

CASSIN'S SPARROW

AMERICAN TREE SPARROW

FIELD SPARROW

RUFOUS-CROWNED SPARROW

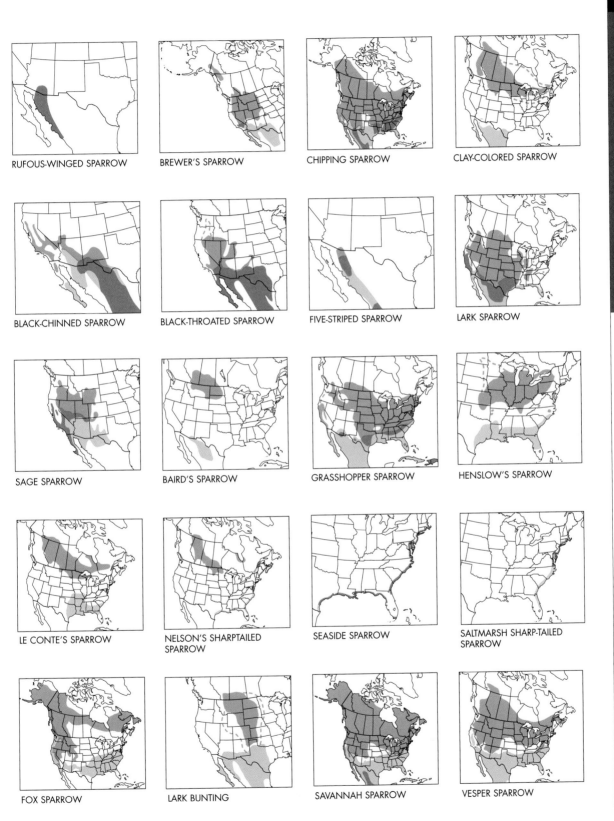

RUFOUS-WINGED SPARROW

BREWER'S SPARROW

CHIPPING SPARROW

CLAY-COLORED SPARROW

BLACK-CHINNED SPARROW

BLACK-THROATED SPARROW

FIVE-STRIPED SPARROW

LARK SPARROW

SAGE SPARROW

BAIRD'S SPARROW

GRASSHOPPER SPARROW

HENSLOW'S SPARROW

LE CONTE'S SPARROW

NELSON'S SHARPTAILED SPARROW

SEASIDE SPARROW

SALTMARSH SHARP-TAILED SPARROW

FOX SPARROW

LARK BUNTING

SAVANNAH SPARROW

VESPER SPARROW

455

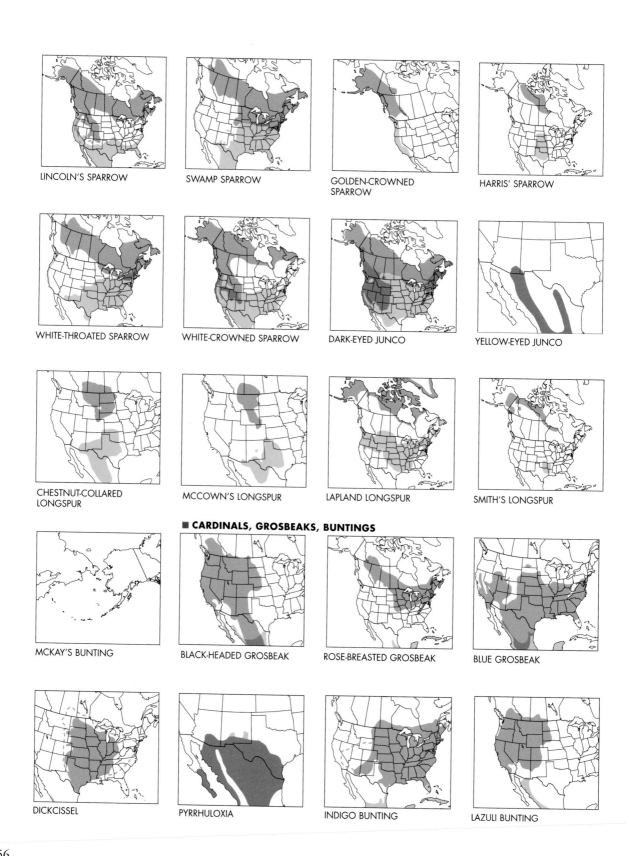

LINCOLN'S SPARROW

SWAMP SPARROW

GOLDEN-CROWNED SPARROW

HARRIS' SPARROW

WHITE-THROATED SPARROW

WHITE-CROWNED SPARROW

DARK-EYED JUNCO

YELLOW-EYED JUNCO

CHESTNUT-COLLARED LONGSPUR

MCCOWN'S LONGSPUR

LAPLAND LONGSPUR

SMITH'S LONGSPUR

■ **CARDINALS, GROSBEAKS, BUNTINGS**

MCKAY'S BUNTING

BLACK-HEADED GROSBEAK

ROSE-BREASTED GROSBEAK

BLUE GROSBEAK

DICKCISSEL

PYRRHULOXIA

INDIGO BUNTING

LAZULI BUNTING

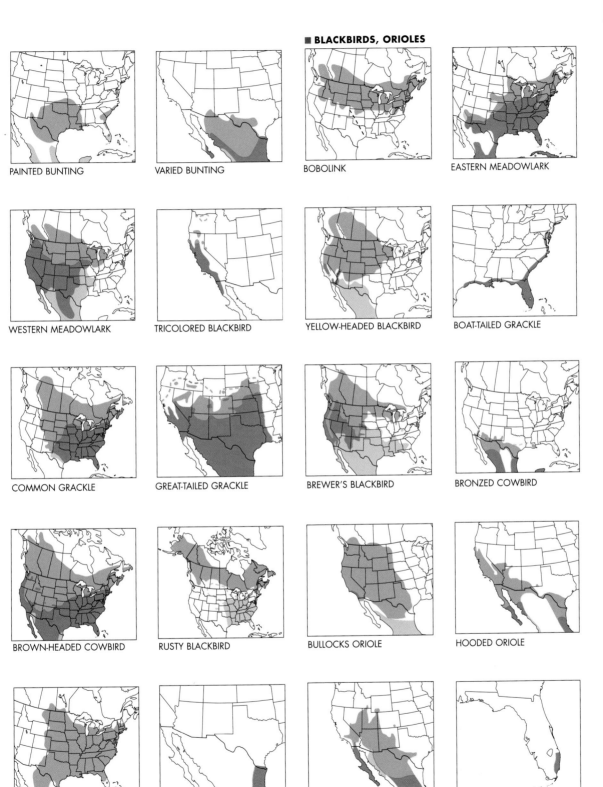

■ **BLACKBIRDS, ORIOLES**

PAINTED BUNTING

VARIED BUNTING

BOBOLINK

EASTERN MEADOWLARK

WESTERN MEADOWLARK

TRICOLORED BLACKBIRD

YELLOW-HEADED BLACKBIRD

BOAT-TAILED GRACKLE

COMMON GRACKLE

GREAT-TAILED GRACKLE

BREWER'S BLACKBIRD

BRONZED COWBIRD

BROWN-HEADED COWBIRD

RUSTY BLACKBIRD

BULLOCKS ORIOLE

HOODED ORIOLE

ORCHARD ORIOLE

ALTAMIRA ORIOLE

SCOTT'S ORIOLE

SPOT-BREASTED ORIOLE

457

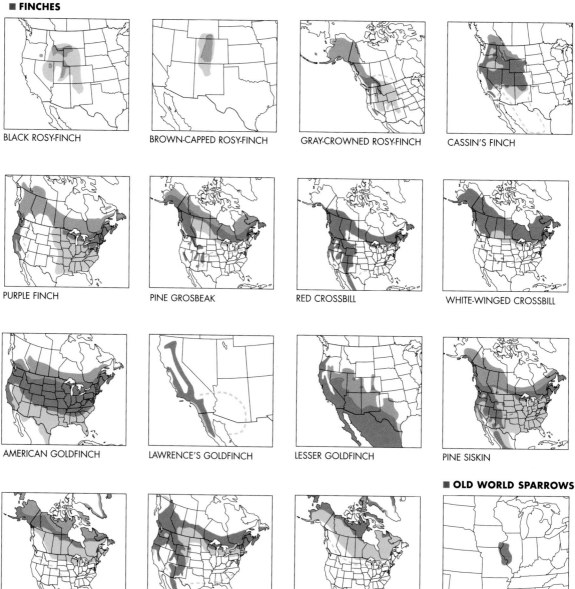

BLACK ROSY-FINCH

BROWN-CAPPED ROSY-FINCH

GRAY-CROWNED ROSY-FINCH

CASSIN'S FINCH

PURPLE FINCH

PINE GROSBEAK

RED CROSSBILL

WHITE-WINGED CROSSBILL

AMERICAN GOLDFINCH

LAWRENCE'S GOLDFINCH

LESSER GOLDFINCH

PINE SISKIN

COMMON REDPOLL

EVENING GROSBEAK

HOARY REDPOLL

■ OLD WORLD SPARROWS

EURASIAN TREE SPARROW

GLOSSARY

allopreening: Mutual preening during which two birds preen each other, usually around the head and neck. In many species allopreening not only keeps the plumage clean and orderly, but also helps to establish social bonds between individuals.

alternate plumage: In the Humphrey-Parkes system of nomenclature, alternate plumage is the plumage worn by an adult bird during the breeding season, if that plumage is produced by a partial molt before breeding. If a bird does not molt before breeding, it continues to wear its basic plumage during breeding. In the traditional system, the alternate plumage was known as the **nuptial plumage** or the **breeding plumage**.

altricial: Describes young birds that hatch undeveloped and in many cases naked or with sparse down; such helpless young require complete parental care.

alula: A group of two to six feathers projecting from the phalanx of the bird's first finger (its thumb) at the bend of the wing. It reduces turbulence by allowing fine control of airflow over the wing.

anisodactyl feet: Foot arrangement in which the hallux points backward and the other three toes point forward. Found in most passerines.

auricular feathers: A patch of feathers covering the external ear opening. Their open texture protects the ear from debris and wind noise, yet helps to channel sounds into the ear.

axillaries: A cluster of feathers in the bird's "armpit"; they are recognizably longer than those lining the wing.

basic plumage: In the Humphrey-Parkes system of nomenclature, the plumage worn by an adult bird for the longest time each year; it usually is produced by a complete molt. In the traditional system, this plumage was known as the **nonbreeding** or **winter plumage**. If a bird does not molt before breeding, it continues to wear its basic plumage during breeding.

bend of the wing: The prominent angle at the wrist, where the bird's wing bends noticeably.

bill: A bird's upper and lower jaws, including the external covering; also called the **beak**.

binomial nomenclature: The currently accepted system of naming organisms, devised by Linnaeus, in which each species is designated by two words: the genus and the species names.

biodiversity: The great wealth of living organisms that occur on earth.

boreal forest: Coniferous forest ecosystem dominated by spruce and fir trees and found around the world, generally in a belt north of temperate zone deciduous forests and south of the arctic tundra. Many birds migrate to the boreal forests to breed, taking advantage of the long daylight hours and abundant insects for feeding their young. Some bird species are year-round residents. Also called **taiga**.

Breeding Bird Survey (BBS): A count of the breeding birds of North America conducted each summer since 1967 and coordinated by the U. S. Fish and Wildlife Service. Observers count birds seen or heard during three-minute periods at half-mile (0.8-km) intervals along a 25-mile (40-km) stretch of road. Because the same routes and stops are sampled each year, BBS data can be used to track population trends, and the results can be correlated with habitat.

call notes: Bird sounds that are generally shorter and simpler than songs. Many seem to convey a specific message, such as begging calls (hunger), alarm calls (danger), and contact calls (the caller's location).

cere: A leathery band of skin covering the base of the bill, into which the nostrils open; presumably the cere protects the nostrils. Present only in certain birds, such as hawks, pigeons, and some parrots.

chaparral: North American ecosystem found on the low hillsides of southwestern California; it consists of dense stands of broad-leaved evergreen shrubs, dominated by chamise and manzanita. This ecosystem is dry, with long hot summers, frequent fires; rain falls only in winter. A moderate number of birds breed in the chaparral.

Christmas Bird Count (CBC): A count of the wintering birds of North America conducted each year since 1900 and coordinated by the National Audubon Society. Observers count as many individual birds as possible within one of the circular count areas 15 miles (24 km) in diameter that are scattered across North America and beyond. Observers record their time spent and distance covered, so the numbers of birds seen can be adjusted for observer effort. The data can be used to track winter bird distribution and abundance, as well as long-term population trends.

conspecifics: Members of the same species.

contour feathers: Feathers that make up the exterior surface of a bird, including the wings and tail; they streamline and shape the bird, and usually have well-developed barbules and hooklets.

countershading: A type of coloration in which an organism is darker on top than below; countershading provides camouflage by reducing the contrast between the top and shadowed underside of an organism so that it appears less three-dimensional.

coverts: The smaller feathers that partly overlie the flight feathers of the wing and tail at their bases, like evenly spaced shingles on a roof. For more information, see specific types.

crepuscular: Active at dawn and dusk.

crop: A dilation of the lower esophagus that stores food; it is found in many birds that eat dry seeds or fruit containing seeds.

crop milk: Milk-like substance produced by pigeons and doves; it is composed of fluid-filled cells sloughed from the lining of the crop and is regurgitated to feed to nestlings. Crop milk is high in lipids and vitamins A and B, and has a greater protein and fat content than human or cow milk. Also called **pigeon's milk**.

dabbling: A foraging technique in which a bird moves the beak rapidly on the surface of shallow water to pick up small aquatic animals and plant materials; it is used by "dabbling ducks" and a few other species.

definitive plumages: Any of the plumages of a fully mature bird; they may change seasonally, but do not change from year to year as the bird ages. Some species, such as gulls, large raptors, and pelagic seabirds, take several years to reach their definitive plumage.

disruptive coloration: A type of cryptic coloration with patches, streaks, or other bold patterns of color that break up the shape of the organism, catching the eye and distracting the observer from recognizing the whole organism.

distal: Away from the center of the body (fingers are distal to the elbow) or from the origin of the structure (the tip of a feather is distal to its base—where it is attached).

diurnal: Active during daylight.

DNA-DNA hybridization: A technique used to determine the degree of similarity (in nucleotide sequence) between two different samples of DNA. It is often used to compare the DNA of two different species, to estimate how closely related they are and to hypothesize their evolutionary relationships.

down feathers: Soft, fluffy feathers, typically lacking a rachis. Because the barbules lack hooks, the barbs do not cling together, so they trap more air and thus provide extra insulation. Some adult birds have **body downs** under their contour feathers, and young birds have **natal down** before molting into their juvenile0 plumage.

dynamic soaring: A type of flight in which birds use the gradient in wind speed that exists over the surface of the ocean to travel for long distances without spending much of their own energy: the bird glides down the gradient at an angle, then turns and abruptly rises into the wind, using its momentum to gain height quickly, then turns and glides down again, crossing the ocean in large zig-zags. Dynamic soaring is used most by albatrosses and other large pelagic birds with high-aspect-ratio wings.

eclipse plumage: The set of dull-colored feathers worn briefly after the breeding season by some adult birds, such as ducks. In eclipse plumage, male ducks look like females, which do not change much in appearance. Eclipse plumage is acquired by a complete molt after the breeding season, and is soon replaced through a partial molt that produces the brighter colors of the breeding plumage.

endemic: Found only in a particular region; describes a species or other taxonomic group. For example, kiwis are *endemic* to New Zealand.

eyeline: A distinctively colored line that passes through the eye.

eye ring: A circle of distinctively colored feathers or skin surrounding the eye.

facial disc: Flat, relatively round, forward-facing part of the head of owls; it probably funnels sounds into the bird's ear openings. Also spelled **facial disk**.

feather tracts: Areas of a bird's skin where feathers are attached; also called **pterylae**.

flight feathers: The remiges of the wings and rectrices of the tail.

frugivorous: Feeding mainly or exclusively on fruits.

gallinaceous birds: Grouse, quails, turkeys, pheasants, and all other birds in the order Galliformes; includes domestic chickens.

generalist: In biology, an organism that is able to use a wide range of some type of resource; for example, animals with generalist diets eat many different types of foods.

genus (plural, **genera**): Level of classification of organisms above "species" and below "family." Genus is always capitalized, and is underlined or printed in italics.

gleaning: A foraging technique in which a bird takes insects and other small invertebrates from the surface of vegetation or other substrates. In **perch gleaning**, practiced by many wood-warblers and other species, a bird grabs prey without flying from its perch. In **sally gleaning**, practiced by birds such as Red-eyed Vireos, chickadees, titmice, and some small flycatchers, the bird sits still and watches the surrounding vegetation until it sees an insect move, then flies out and grabs it from the surface. In **hover gleaning**, practiced by kinglets, phoebes, and Great Crested Flycatchers, among others, the bird hovers while taking food from the surface of vegetation.

greater coverts: The feathers partly overlying each remex on the upper surface of the wing. A **greater primary covert** overlies each primary feather, and a **greater secondary covert** overlies each secondary feather.

gular fluttering: Opening the bill wide and vibrating the thin, expansive gular membranes of the throat, in order to dissipate heat. This cooling method is used by pelicans, cormorants, herons, owls, and nighthawks.

gular region: Upper part of the throat, just below the chin.

habitat specificity: How wide a range of different habitat types in which a given species can live and breed successfully.

hallux: The first toe, composed of two phalanges. In nearly all birds, it points backward. The hallux is well developed in perching birds and is reduced or absent in many running birds.

hawking: A foraging technique in which a bird sits very still on a high or exposed perch, and when it sees an insect, flies out and snatches it in midair, returning to the same or a nearby perch; used by many flycatchers, kingbirds, bee-eaters, waxwings (sometimes), and some woodpeckers, among others.

heterodactyl foot: Foot arrangement in which the third and fourth toes point forward and the hallux and second toe point backward; found in trogons.

high-aspect-ratio wings: Wings that are long, narrow, and unslotted; the length derives primarily from the lengthened inner wing (as compared to high-speed wings, in which the length results primarily from the long outer wing). High-aspect-ratio wings are highly efficient at producing lift at relatively high flight speeds, but they are difficult to maneuver, especially during take-offs. They are found in a few seabirds that are highly specialized for dynamic soaring over the ocean, such as albatrosses, shearwaters, petrels, and some gulls.

inner wing: The portion of the wing from the wrist to the shoulder; the secondary feathers are located on one section of the inner wing.

irruptive migration: Migratory movements that are irregular in time and space, depending upon factors other than a change of seasons, such as food availability. For example, the seeds and buds eaten by finches such as Pine Siskins and redpolls fluctuate in abundance not only seasonally but from year to year and from region to region, so in some years large numbers of the birds move out of northern forests to breed, yet in others they stay put.

jizz: Birding term for a quick impression of a bird's major features. Jizz harkens back to the "general impression of size and shape" (G. I. S. S.) that British observers used during World War II to distinguish between enemy and friendly aircraft.

juvenile: A young bird.

kettle: A large aggregation of birds, usually hawks, that are spiraling upward in a thermal.

lek: A traditional courtship area where many males of the same species gather to attract females for mating; each male spends a large amount of time defending a small site at which he displays to compete with other males and, in particular, to earn copulations with sexually receptive females who visit the lek to choose among the males. In most species, the top few males secure most of the matings. The lek contains no nest sites, food, or other resources useful to nesting females

lesser coverts: The feathers on the upper surface of the wing that partly overlie the median coverts and extend to the marginal coverts.

lore: Small area between the eye and the base of the upper beak.

malar region: Small area caudal to the base of the lower beak; also called the **cheek**.

malar stripe: A distinctively colored stripe in the malar region of birds; also called a **mustache stripe** or **whisker stripe**.

manus: The portion of the forelimb distal to the wrist; also called the **hand**. The primary feathers attach to the manus.

median coverts: The covert feathers lying between the lesser and greater coverts on the upper surface of the wing.

melanin: Pigment, usually present as tiny granules, that produces a range of earthy colors from dark black, brown, and red-brown to gray, yellow-brown and pale yellow. Birds can synthesize their own melanin by oxidizing the amino acid tyrosine.

migration: The regular movement of all or part of a population to and from an area; usually refers to seasonal journeys to and from breeding grounds or feeding areas.

mobbing: Behavior in which a number of birds (often different species) swoop and dash at a potential predator; they usually give broad-band, raspy calls (**mobbing calls**) that are easy to locate and thus attract additional birds.

molting: The process of shedding all or part of the feather coat and replacing it with new growth.

morph: A set of individuals within a species that are similar to one another in some genetically determined morphological characteristic, but are distinctly different from other sets of individuals within that species. Morphs may differ in characteristics such as color, body size, or bill length or shape, but not in characteristics that are related to sex, age, locality, or season.

nape: The back of the neck.

natal down: The soft down feathers covering young birds before they molt into juvenile plumage.

Neotropical migrants: Birds that winter in the Neotropics but migrate to the Nearctic region to breed. Examples include many wood-warblers, tanagers, and orioles.

nomadic: Pattern of movement in which individuals are constantly on the move, showing no tendency to return to previously occupied places. Crossbills and perhaps Budgerigars may be considered nomadic.

oil gland: A gland, located at the base of the tail on the dorsal side of the bird's body, that secretes oils that birds spread over their feathers during preening. The oils keep the skin supple and the feathers and scales from becoming brittle, but they do not appear to waterproof the feathers. Also called the **uropygial gland** or **preen gland**.

order: Level of classification of organisms above "family" and below "class"; similar families are placed in the same order. The scientific names of bird orders end in "iformes" (for example, Passeriformes).

outer vane: The vane located on the side of a wing or tail feather that is away from the midline of the bird. On a wing feather, the outer vane is on the edge of the wing that leads in flight. In flying birds, the outer vane is narrower than the inner vane, producing an asymmetry that aids in flight.

outer wing: The portion of the wing from the wrist to the wing tip; the primary feathers are located on the outer wing.

parasitic: Describes a relationship between two species or individuals in which one benefits as a result of some cost to the other.

partial migration: Migratory pattern in which some individuals in a population migrate while others remain as year-round

461

residents. When the specific individuals that migrate are determined genetically, a situation that occurs in environments where the resources always are sufficient to enable some, but not all, individuals to overwinter, the migrating birds are called **obligate partial migrants**; examples include the European Robin and populations of the Blackcap in southern Europe. When the number of birds the environment can support varies from year to year, **facultative partial migration** evolves, in which the number and identity of the individuals migrating change from year to year in response to the availability of resources, usually food. In this case, the individuals that migrate are not determined genetically. Facultative partial migration occurs in the Blue Tit and some North American chickadees.

passerines: All birds in the Order Passeriformes; also called **perching birds**. The order contains approximately 4,600 species, nearly one-half the world's bird species, all of which have a foot adapted for perching on branches or stems.

pelagic: Of the ocean; pelagic birds spend most of their life on the open sea, feeding at the surface or just below it and coming to land only to nest. Pelagic birds include species in the order Procellariiformes, as well as tropicbirds, some penguins, the boobies and gannets, most alcids, the skuas and jaegers, the noddies, kittiwakes, Sabine's Gull, and some terns.

pellet: A compact ball of indigestible food, such as bones, fur, feathers, and insect exoskeletons, that is formed by the gizzard of birds that eat meat or fish—such as owls, hawks, and kingfishers—and is regurgitated through the mouth; also called a **cast**.

plumage: 1. A bird's entire feather coat. 2. The set of feathers produced by a particular molt. With this usage, a bird wears parts of two different plumages after a partial molt.

plunge diving: A foraging technique in which an airborne bird dives under water to pursue aquatic prey; performed by birds such as Brown Pelicans, auks, gannets, Osprey, and kingfishers.

polyandry: Mating system in which one female mates with several males within the same breeding season.

polygamy: General term for a mating system in which individuals of one sex (either the males or females) mate with more than one partner during the same breeding season. Both polygyny and polyandry are forms of polygamy.

polygyny: Mating system in which one male mates with several females within the same breeding season. Polyandrous species include Spotted Sandpipers, most jacanas, and certain phalaropes.

polymorphism: A situation in which one species contains two or more distinct morphological types (**morphs**) of individuals, which are determined genetically. Morphs may differ in physical characteristics such as color, body size, or bill length or shape, but not in characteristics that are related to sex, age, locality, or season.

precocial: Describes young birds that hatch in a relatively developed state—downy and with their eyes open. Many are soon able to walk or swim and even eat on their own.

preening: Feather maintenance behavior in which a bird grasps a feather near its base, then nibbles along the shaft toward the tip with a quivering motion; this cleans and smooths the feather. Many birds gather on their bill oily secretions from the oil gland, and then spread them on their feathers as they preen.

primary feathers: The flight feathers of the outer wing; they are attached to the manus.

race: A population of a species, usually in a particular geographic area, that is morphologically distinct from other populations of the same species, but whose members remain capable of interbreeding with members of those other populations. Also called a **subspecies**.

range: The geographic area within which a species or population generally remains at a particular time of the year; a species may have different breeding and nonbreeding ranges. Also called the **geographic range**.

raptors: Members of the orders Falconiformes and Strigiformes, which contain all the diurnal and nocturnal birds of prey.

rectrices (singular, **rectrix**): The long, stiff flight feathers of the tail.

remiges (singular, **remex**): The longest wing feathers, also called the **flight feathers of the wings**; they include the primary and secondary feathers.

rictal bristles: Stiff, hairlike feathers projecting from the base of the beak in birds that catch insects. They may protect the face and eyes of some birds that capture large, scaly insects; they also may help birds detect movements of prey held in the beak.

scapulars: A group of feathers in the shoulder region.

siblicide: The killing of one's sibling; in birds whose offspring practice siblicide, usually the stronger, older nestlings kill the younger, weaker nestlings, either by direct attack or by pushing them out of the nest.

site fidelity: Loyalty shown by birds or other organisms to places they previously occupied; the places may be breeding locations, nonbreeding locations, or stopover points between the two. Also called **site tenacity**.

slope soaring: A type of static soaring in which a bird derives lift from air deflected upward when wind strikes a hill, ridge, or cliff; or from rising eddies created when wind spills over a cliff. Slope soaring is particularly common along seacoasts among gulls, terns, fulmars, and gannets; it also is common along mountain ridges, where ravens, crows, and migrating hawks may soar.

soaring: In a bird or other animal, flying without flapping the wings or limbs, while gaining altitude or remaining horizontal (as compared to gliding, in which the animal loses altitude).

songbirds: Members of Suborder Passeri, which is one of the two large suborders of Order Passeriformes (perching birds); songbirds also are known as **oscines** or **true songbirds**. Songbirds have particularly complex voice boxes, which allow them to sing more complex songs than other birds.

songs: Loud vocalizations, often delivered from an exposed perch, that are presumed to attract mates or repel territorial intruders. Strictly speaking, songs are given only by songbirds—passerines in the suborder Passeri (oscines). In practice, however, similar vocalizations made by nonsongbirds (and even other animals) often are called songs.

species: Level of classification below "genus"; similar species are placed within the same genus. A species usually is defined as a group of potentially interbreeding individuals that share distinctive characteristics and are unlikely to breed with other such groups of individuals. Distinguishing which groups of organisms constitute species is not always easy, however, and slightly different criteria may be used by different scientists.

spread-wing posture: A stance in which a bird stands motionless with the wings extended to the side, either to dry the wings or to absorb sunlight. Adopted by many large birds, such as cormorants, anhingas, pelicans, storks, and New World vultures.

stooping: A foraging technique used by falcons in which a bird drops through the air at great speed in pursuit of a flying bird or insect.

subadult: A bird that has not yet reached maturity; immature.

subspecies: A subset of a species, usually in a particular geographic area, that contains individuals that are morphologically distinct from other individuals of the same species, but are still capable of interbreeding with those other individuals. Also called a **race**.

synchronous hatching: Pattern of hatching in which all the eggs of a single clutch hatch at about the same time (on the same day), resulting in a brood of young all the same size and age. This hatching pattern occurs when incubation is delayed until the last egg is laid. Because development of laid eggs does not begin until they are warmed, all the embryos begin to develop at the same time and are ready to hatch at the same time.

syndactyl feet: Foot arrangement in which the hallux points backward and toes two, three, and four point forward, with toes two and three (the inner and middle toes) fused for much of their length. Found in many kingfishers and hornbills.

tarsus: The upper section of the avian foot, between the heel and the toes.

taxonomy: The classification of organisms—assigning names and relationships.

thermal soaring: A type of **static soaring** in which birds use the rising air in thermals (rising columns of warm air) to propel themselves upward, circling higher and higher with little energy expenditure of their own. Once high in the air, they can glide out of the thermal and across the countryside in whatever direction they wish to travel.

torpor: A profound state of sleep in which the body temperature drops and consequently all metabolic processes and stimulus-reaction processes slow down. Used by swifts, hummingbirds, nighthawks, and some other birds to conserve energy when food resources are unavailable. Birds may enter torpor on a nightly basis, or for extended periods up to an entire season of cold weather. Also called **hibernation**.

tubenoses: Birds in the order Procellariiformes, including albatrosses, shearwaters, fulmars, petrels, and storm-petrels, all of which have **tubular nares.**

undertail coverts: The short contour feathers that cover the bases of the rectrices on the ventral side of the tail.

uppertail coverts: The short contour feathers that cover the bases of the rectrices on the dorsal side of the tail.

vocal repertoire: All the different types of vocalizations that are produced by an individual bird, including both songs and calls.

waterfowl: Ducks, geese, and swans; family Anatidae.

wing-flashing: A foraging technique used by some herons, egrets, and storks in which a bird wading through the water quickly raises or brings forward one or both wings, apparently to frighten prey out of hiding or to provide a shady place where unsuspecting prey may try to hide, thus bringing the prey within the bird's reach.

wing loading: The ratio of body weight to wing area; wing loading is a measure of how much "load" each unit area of wing must carry.

winnowing: Part of a twilight territorial and courtship display given by both male and female Common Snipe. The birds circle high in the air and produce a series of rapid, pulsating, whistle-hums (called **winnows**) by spreading the tail and diving at high speeds—causing the stiff outer tail feathers to vibrate. European Snipe also winnow.

zygodactyl feet: Foot arrangement in which toes two and three point forward, and the hallux and toe four point backward. Found in woodpeckers, cuckoos, toucans, owls, Osprey, turacos, most parrots, and some other birds.

Glossary excerpted from The Cornell Lab of Ornighology's Home Study Course in Bird Biology, Second Edition.

BIBLIOGRAPHY

American Bird Conservancy, 1977. *All the Birds of North America,* Harper Perennial.

Burns, Kevin J., 1998. *Society Encyclopedia of North American Birds.*

Chantler, Phil. 2000. *Swifts: A Guide to the Swifts and Treeswifts of the World,* 2nd edition. Yale Univ. Press.

Chapman, Frank. 1966. *Handbook of Birds of Eastern North America,* Dover Publications.

Collar, N. J., 1997. *Family Psittacidae (Parrots).*

Elliott, A., and J. Del Hoyo, J., Sargatal, J, and A. Elliot, 2002. *Handbook of Birds of the World,* v. 4. Sandgrouse to cuckoos. Lynx Edicions.

Farrand, John, Jr., 1988. *Aububon Handbook of Western Birds,* McGraw-Hill Book Company.

Forshaw, J. 1989. *Parrots of the World,* 3rd Edition. Lansdowne Editions.

Gill, Frank and Poole, Alan. Editors, 2000. *The Birds of North America,* Birds of North America Inc.

Harrison, George H., "Cedar Waxwing," Birder's World, Oct. 2000 .

Isler, Morton L. and Phyllis R. Isler, 1999. *The Tanager: Natural History, Distribution, and Identification,* Smithsonian Institution Press.

Jackson, Jerome A., "Galloping gourmands, Eastern Red-Cedars." Birder's World, 1997.

Johnsgard, Paul A. 1975. *North American Game Birds,* University of Nebraska Press.

Juniper, T. and M. Parr, 1998. *Parrots: a guide to parrots of the world.* Yale University Press.

Marin, Manuel. "Breeding Biology of the Black Swift," The Wilson Bulletin, Vol. 109. No. 2. June 1997

Marin, Manuel. "Swifts: A Guide to the Swifts and Treeswifts of the World." The Wilson Bulletin, 1999. Vol. 111, No.1

National Geographic Society, 2002. *National Geographic Field Guide to the Birds of North America,* 4th edition.

Netherton, John. 1998. *North American Wading Birds,* Great Outdoors Publishing Company.

Niemeyer, Lucien, and Mark Riegner, 1993. *Long-Legged Wading Birds of the North American Wetlands,* Stackpole Books.

Peterson, Roger Tory. 1980. *Peterson Field Guide to Eastern and Western Birds,* Houghton Mifflin Co.

Pranty, B. and K. L. Garrett, 2003. *The parrot fauna of the ABA Area: a current look.*

Roberts, Christopher, and Norment, Christopher "Effects of Plot Size and Habitat Characteristics on Breeding Success of Scarlet Tanagers,"

Rosenberg, Kenneth, 1999. "Effects of Forest Fragmentation on Breeding Tanagers: A Continental Perspective." Conservation Biology, Volume 13, No. 3.

Rosenberg, Gary H. and Witzeman, Janet L., 1974-1996. ARIZONA BIRD COMMITTEE REPORT,: PART 2 (PASSERINES)<[http://mywebpages. comcast.net/ ghrosenberg /CommitteeReports/CommitteeReport-1996b.html>

Sibley, David, 2001. *The Sibley Guide to Bird Life & Behavior,* Alfred A. Knopf.

Stiles, F.G. and A.F. Skutch, 1989. *A Guide to the Birds of Costa Rica.* Cornell University Press. <http://www.cloudforestal-ive.org/tour/hcam/field_guide/bnqt.htm>

Stokes, Don & Lillian 1996. *Stokes Field Guides to Birds,* Little Brown and Company.

Terres, 1996. *Audubon Society Encyclopedia of North American Birds.*

OTHER RESOURCES

Biota Information System, 2002. <http://www.cmiweb.org/states/nmex_main/species/042010 .htm>

Butler, Luke K., Michael G. Donahue, and Sievert Rohwer. Migratory Birds/Research/Symposia/ Birds_of_Two_Worlds /posterabstracts.pdf "Age class differences in molt-migration in the Western tanager Piranga ludoviciana)" Department of Zoology and Burke Museum of Natural History, University of Washington.

Cornell Laboratory of Ornithology, 2000. <http://birds.cornell.edu/BOW/CHISWI/>

Ehrlich, Paul R. David S. Dobkin, and Darryl Wheye, 1988. Feet. <http://www.stanfordalumni.org/birdsite/text/essays/Feet. html>Tobago Home for Birds. <http://www.tobago.hm/folk/bm001bird.htm#bana>

McGraw, K.J., G.E.Hill, R.Stradi, R.S.Parker, 2002. Department of Neurobiology and Behavior, Cornell University. <http://www.aces.edu/ dept/hilllab/82.pdf>

Rosenberg, K.V., R.W. Rohrbaugh, Jr., S.E. Barker, J.D. Lowe, R.S. Hames, Dhondt, 1999. *A land managers guide to improving habitat for scarlet tanagers and other forest-interior birds.* Cornell Lab of Ornithology.

University of Michigan, 2003. Bananquit. <http://animal diversity.ummz.umich.edu/accounts/ coereba/c._flaveola$narrative.html>

USGS Patuxent Wildlife Research Center. <http://www.npwrc.usgs.gov/resource/1998/forest/species/ phainite.htm>

ABOUT THE CONTRIBUTORS

Jonathan Alderfer is a well-known field guide illustrator and author. His artwork is featured in the *National Geographic Field Guide to the Birds of North America* and the American Bird Conservancy's *All The Birds of North America*. He is the Associate Editor of *Birding* magazine and serves on the Maryland/District of Columbia Bird Records Committee. He is illustrating a new book, *Ocean Birds of North America*, for Princeton University Press.

George L. Armistead has been birding the mid-Atlantic coast between Cape May, NJ, and Cape Hatteras, NC, for two decades. He obtained an M.A. in environmental studies from the University of Pennsylvania and also worked at the Academy of Natural Sciences of Philadelphia in the ornithology department for seven years. Currently George leads bird tours domestically and abroad for Field Guides, Inc.

Philadelphia librarian, **Henry T. Armistead**, has birded since 1949. Bird bander for 25 years, a regional editor of *American Birds* (1979-1993), and book review editor of *Birding* magazine (1973-1986), he is compiler of the Cape Charles, VA, Christmas Bird Count (1968) and the Dorchester County, MD, spring and fall bird counts (1966).

Edward S. (Ned) Brinkley is currently Editor for *North American Birds Journal*. He has published over 50 articles in the field of ornithology and birding, as well as several books, including a children's book on birds in *Readers' Digest's "Pathfinders"* series. He also guides international birding tours for Field Guides, Inc. and runs a bed-and-breakfast inn for birders at Cape Charles, Virginia.

Kimball L. Garrett is the Ornithology Collections Manager at the Natural History Museum of Los Angeles County and writes frequently about birds and bird identification. He is a long-time member of the California Bird Records Committee and currently serves on the American Birding Association Checklist Committee. He has studied naturalized parrots in California for over ten years.

Philip Brandt George has been watching and studying birds since seeing his first Black Skimmers and White Ibises at Pea Island National Wildlife Refuge on North Carolina's Outer Banks in 1997. Currently Associate Editor of *American History* magazine, he is a 22-year veteran of Time-Life Books and has contributed articles and photographs to various publications.

Paul Lehman is the primary range-map consultant for a number of North American field guides, including The *National Geographic Field Guide to Birds of North America* (3rd and 4th editions), The Sibley Field Guides to *Birds of Eastern And Western North America,* and the *Peterson Field Guide to the Birds of Eastern and Central North America* (5th edition). He has written many articles on the distribution and identification of North American birds, has traveled extensively throughout the United States and Canada, was a former university instructor of physical geography and environmental studies, was a past editor of *Birding* magazine, and leads bird tours for WINGS, Inc.

George Reiger is conservation editor of *Field & Stream*, co-founder of the Wachapreague, Virginia, Christmas Bird Count, co-author of *The Birder's Journal and Illustrated Lifelist*, and has written or contributed to 35 other books on natural history and outdoor recreational subjects.

Howard Robinson formerly directed the books and special publications division of the National Wildlife Federation. He has served as managing editor of *American BirdWatcher*, the newsletter of the American Bird Watchers Society, and as a researcher and writer for *BirdWatcher*, a birders' newsletter published by the National Geographic Society.

Brian Sullivan is currently a Field Coordinator for Point Reyes Bird Observatory Conservation Science, working with several organizations in the recovery effort for the endangered San Clemente Loggerhead Shrike. Birding travels have taken him to Central and South America, as well as North America. He has published work on North American bird life in both popular and scientific literature.

Clay and Pat Sutton live near Cape May, New Jersey, a world renowned migratory crossroads. They have keenly studied the natural world for nearly 30 years. Pat and Clay Sutton co-authored *How to Spot Butterflies, How to Spot an Owl,* and *How to Spot Hawks & Eagles* (Houghton Mifflin Company). Clay is a freelance writer and naturalist and co-author of *Hawks in Flight* and *Birds of Prey of North America*. Pat works for New Jersey Audubon Society as the Cape May Bird Observatory's Program Director and is a founding Board Member of the North American Butterfly Association.

Jerry Uhlman is a Richmond, Virginia, based nature writer who is both an avid birder and inveterate traveler. His travel and conservation writing has appeared in numerous birding and outdoor magazines and he authored two Virginia birdfinding guides. He currently writes a nature column for the *Richmond Times-Dispatch*.

Sheri Williamson and Tom Wood are co-founders and directors of the Southeastern Arizona Bird Observatory based in Bisbee, Arizona. Native Texans, they moved to Arizona in 1988 and became immersed in hummingbirds. Ms. Williamson is the author of *A Field Guide to Hummingbirds of North America* published in 2001.

Chris Wood is a research associate for Rocky Mountain Bird Observatory and a field leader for WINGS Inc. His interests include bird identification, distribution, vocalizations, and conservation. He is co-editor for the Mountain West region for North American Birds, and is a member of the Colorado Bird Records Committee. He lives in Niwot, Colorado.

Julie Zickefoose is a widely published natural history writer and artist. Educated at Harvard University in biology and art, she worked for six years as a field biologist for The Nature Conservancy before turning to a freelance career. Her observations on the natural history and behavior of birds stem from more than three decades of experience in the field.

CREDITS

H. Douglas Pratt; 278 Marie Read; 279 H. Douglas Pratt; 280 Peter LaTourrette/VIREO; 281 H. Douglas Pratt; 284 Tom Vezo/Danita Delimont.com; 285 John P. O'Neill; 286 Ray Tipper/VIREO; 287 John P. O'Neill; 290 Tom Vezo/Danita Delimont.com; 291 H. Douglas Pratt; 292 Bates Littlehales; 293 H. Douglas Pratt; 294 James R. Hill III; 295 H. Douglas Pratt; 298 Marie Read; 299 John P. O'Neill; 300 Tom Vezo/Danita Delimont.com; 301 John P. O'Neill; 302 (top) Arthur Morris/VIREO; (bottom) John Hoffman/VIREO; 303 John P. O'Neill; 304 Marie Read; 305 H. Douglas Pratt; 308 Marie Read; 309 H. Douglas Pratt; 310 Bates Littlehales; 311 H. Douglas Pratt; 312 H. Douglas Pratt; 313 Rick & Nora Bowers/VIREO; 316 Tom Vezo/Danita Delimont.com; 317 H. Douglas Pratt; 318 Greg Lasley/VIREO; 319 H. Douglas Pratt; 320 Brian E. Small; 321 H. Douglas Pratt; 324 Marie Read; 325 David Quinn; 326 Bates Littlehales; 327 H. Douglas Pratt; 328 H. Douglas Pratt; 329 (both) John P. O'Neill; 330 Nathan Barnes/VIREO; 331 Thomas R. Schultz; 334 Marie Read; 335 H. Douglas Pratt; 336 Wendy Shattil/Bob Rozinski; 337 H. Douglas Pratt; 338 Crawford H. Greenewalt/VIREO; 339 H. Douglas Pratt; 340 Arthur Morris/VIREO; 341 H. Douglas Pratt; 344 Tom Vezo/Danita Delimont.com; 345 H. Douglas Pratt; 346 Wendy Shattil/Bob Rozinski; 347 H. Douglas Pratt; 348 H. Douglas Pratt; 349 Brian E. Small; 352 Tom Vezo/Danita Delimont.com; 353 H. Douglas Pratt; 354 Marie Read; 355 H. Douglas Pratt; 358 Bates Littlehales; 359 H. Douglas Pratt; 360 Bates Littlehales; 362 Roger Eriksson; 363 H. Douglas Pratt; 364 H. Douglas Pratt; 365 Brian E. Small; 366 John Hoffman/VIREO; 367 Thomas R. Schultz; 370 Arthur Morris/VIREO; 371 Peter Burke; 372 Bates Littlehales; 373 Thomas R. Schultz; 374 Barry Miller/VIREO; 375 Peter Burke; 378 Marie Read; 379 Diane Pierce; 380 Doug Wechsler/VIREO; 381 Peter Burke; 382 Bates Littlehales; 383 Diane Pierce; 384 Tom Vezo/Danita Delimont.com; 386 Rob Curtis/VIREO; 387 Diane Pierce; 388 Tom Vezo/Danita Delimont.com/VIREO; 389 Diane Pierce; 392 Tom Vezo/Danita Delimont.com; 393 Diane Pierce; 394 Tom Vezo/Danita Delimont.com; 395 Diane Pierce; 396 Tom Vezo/Danita Delimont.com; 397 Diane Pierce; 400 Tom Vezo/Danita Delimont.com; 401 H. Douglas Pratt; 402 Bates Littlehales; 403 Thomas R. Schultz; 404 Brian E. Small; 405 H. Douglas Pratt; 406 Richard Day/Daybreak Imagery; 407 Peter Burke; 410 Marie Read; 411 Diane Pierce; 412 Marie Read; 413 Diane Pierce; 414 Brian E. Small; 415 Diane Pierce; 418 Johann Schumacher/VIREO; 419 N. John Schmitt; 420 Tom Vezo/Danita Delimont.com; 421 N. John Schmitt

We wish to thank the following individuals for their invaluable assistance in revising the 100 bird range maps as well as providing background material for the migration maps: Wendell Argabrite, Giff Beaton, Louis Bevier, Bob Bond, Edward Brinkley, Chuck Carlson, Chris Charlesworth, Brian Dalzell, Ricky Davis, Cameron Eckert, Scott Edwards, Doug Faulkner, Gary Felton, Bob Fisher, Ted Floyd, Glenn Giroir, Tony Hertzel, Roy Jones, Joel Jorgensen, Tom Kent, Rudolf Koes, Paul Lehman, Tony Leukering, Rich Levad, Mark Lockwood, Ron Lockwood, Derek Lovitch, Ron Martin, Ian McLaren, Dave Muth, Arvind Panjabi, Max Parker, Tom Parsons, Stacy Peterson, Bill Pranty, Larry Rosche, Will Russell, Tom Schultz, Larry Semo, Chris Siddle, Ross Silcock, Mark Stackhouse, Steve Stedman, David Swanson, Lu Ann Tracy, Chuck Trost, Bill Tweit, Jeff Wilson, Chris Wood.

National Geographic Reference Atlas to the Birds of North America

Published by the National Geographic Society

John M. Fahey, Jr., *President and Chief Executive Officer*
Gilbert M. Grosvenor, *Chairman of the Board*
Nina D. Hoffman, *Executive Vice President*

Prepared by the Book Division

Kevin Mulroy, *Vice President and Editor-in-Chief*
Charles Kogod, *Illustrations Director*
Marianne R. Koszorus, *Design Director*
Barbara Brownell Grogan, *Executive Editor*

Staff for this Book

Mel Baughman, *Editor*
Melissa L. Hunsiker, *Project Manager*
Karin Kinney, *Text Editor*
Mark Godfrey, *Illustrations Editor*
Alexandra Littlehales, *Art Director*
Carl Mehler, *Director of Maps*
Matt Chwastyk, *Map Production Manager*
James Huckenpahler, Nicholas P. Rosenbach,
Gregory Ugainsky, Martin S. Walz, The M Factory and
XNR Productions, *Map Research, Edit, and Production*
Jonathan Alderfer, *Text Consultant*
Carol Norton, David Evans, *Design Consultants*
Paul E. Lehman, *Chief Map Consultant*
Ric Wain, *Production Project Manager*
Sharon Berry, *Illustrations Assistant*
Lise Sajeweski, Melanie Patt-Corner, *Copy Readers*
Connie Binder, *Indexer*

Manufacturing and Quality Control

Christopher A. Liedel, *Chief Financial Officer*
Phillip L. Schlosser, *Managing Director*
John T. Dunn, *Technical Director*
Alan Kerr, *Manager*

One of the world's largest nonprofit scientific and educational organizations, the National Geographic Society was founded in 1888 "for the increase and diffusion of geographic knowledge." Fulfilling this mission, the Society educates and inspires millions every day through its magazines, books, television programs, videos, maps and atlases, research grants, the National Geographic Bee, teacher workshops, and innovative classroom materials. The Society is supported through membership dues, charitable gifts, and income from the sale of its educational products. This support is vital to National Geographic's mission to increase global understanding and promote conservation of our planet through exploration, research, and education.

For more information, please call 1-800-NGS LINE (647-5463) or write to the following address:

National Geographic Society
1145 17th Street N.W.
Washington, D.C. 20036-4688 U.S.A.

Visit the Society's Web site at
www.nationalgeographic.com.

Library of Congress Cataloging-in-Publication Data
Reference atlas to the birds of North America / edited by Mel M. Baughman.
 p. cm.
 Includes bibliographical references and index.
 ISBN 0-7922-3373-5
 1. Birds--North America. 2. Birds--North America--Geographical distribution. 3. Birds--North America--Maps. I. Title: Birds of North America. II. Baughman, Mel M. III. National Geographic Society (U.S.)

QL681.R44 2003
598'.097--dc21